2ND EDITION

GREAT AMERICAN LEARNING VACATIONS

Fodor's Travel Publications, Inc.
New York • Toronto • London • Sydney • Auckland
http://www.fodors.com/

Second Edition

ISBN 0–679–03224–X

Fodor's Great American Learning Vacations

Project Editor: Caroline Haberfeld
Editors: Glen Berger, Matthew Lore, Amy McConnell, Rebecca Miller, Stephen Wolf
Editorial Contributors: Stacy Abramson, Christine Begley, Bernard Burt, Amy Calabrese, Sean Elder, Maria Kourebanas, Laura M. Kidder, Andrea Lehman, Natasha Lesser, David Low, Melissa Rivers, Heidi Sarna, Melanie Sponholz, Celestine Ware
Creative Director: Fabrizio La Rocca

Cover Photographs: background, Mark J. Ferrari/Center for Whale Studies; left spot, Kay Chernush/Image Bank; middle spot, Julie Graber/Santa Fe Photographic Workshops; right spot, Dann Coffey/Image Bank
Cover Design: Tigist Getachew

Special Sales

PRINTED IN THE UNITED STATES OF AMERICA

10 9 8 7 6 5 4 3 2 1

CONTENTS

INTRODUCTION *iv*

Archaeological Digs *1*

Arts and Crafts Workshops *12*

Birding *40*

Campus Vacations *53*

Cooking Schools *62*

Cultural and Natural History Cruises *73*

Cultural Tours *93*

Foreign-Language Immersion
 Programs *108*

Garden Tours *121*

Holistic Centers *139*

Music Programs *156*

Nature Camps *170*

Painting Workshops *188*

Photography Workshops and Tours *203*

Spas and Wellness Centers *221*

Volunteer Research Vacations *250*

Volunteer Vacations in Public and
 Community Service *266*

Whale-Watching Cruises *279*

Writing Conferences and Workshops *289*

APPENDIX: WHERE THE
 PROGRAMS ARE *315*

Why not spend your vacation making a quilt, weaving a rug, building a log cabin or an adobe hut, or lapstraking a wooden sailboat? How about setting out to photograph bald eagles in Alaska's Chilkat River valley, to listen for Antillean nighthawks at dusk around Key West, or to find the path to a perfect puff pastry?

An increasing number of people are realizing that a vacation can be so much more than a trip to the beach. They're taking advantage of the many programs that enable them to learn things that they had previously only fantasized about. This guide will help you to join them by turning you on to hundreds of ways to return from your vacation with more than a suntan.

You might clear brush from the Appalachian Trail, build houses in south-central Los Angeles, star-watch at ancient observatories with an astrophysics professor, or help scientists study the Great Lakes' declining loon population or survey bottlenosed dolphins in Monterey Bay. Instead of visiting the same old tourist haunts, you could opt to learn Czech or Arabic; study

mountain dulcimer, fusion jazz, watercolor painting, or Zen meditation; or explore the riddles of creation at Dartmouth or underwater photography with Nikon.

Whether you're young or old, alone or traveling with family or friends, this book will give you a lifetime of ideas for great 5- to 14-day vacations, courses, and group trips in the United States. In addition to the programs described here, there are shorter ones, longer ones, and many to other destinations inside and outside North America. Each chapter contains a comprehensive checklist of questions to help you choose the right program—from among those described here as well as those you discover on your own.

If you have special needs, don't forget to query the program directors before you sign up. If you're traveling with your family, for instance, be sure to ask whether youngsters may participate or if there's something else for them to do in the area.

If you're traveling solo, inquire about the single-occupancy policy. Although some programs have separate prices for tuition, lodging, and meals, others have one price that includes tuition, room, and board. Such all-inclusive prices are per person based on double occupancy, so you will probably be paired with another single or asked to pay extra for a room of your own.

If you observe a special diet, ask whether the program can accommodate you. If it is unable to do so, but it is convenient to restaurants or accommodations with cooking facilities, find out whether a deduction can be made from the cost of the package. If you use a wheelchair or need any other assistance, check that the program can give you what you require.

Finally, once you've made your decision, be sure to ask:

How much of a deposit is required, and when is the balance due? To reserve a spot, most schools and operators require you to put down a deposit by a particular day and then pay the rest sometime before the starting date.

What is the cancellation policy? If you cancel your reservation, you may get a refund— then again, you may not. Policies vary from full refunds offered up to 30 days before the program begins, to partial refunds offered up to seven days before, to no refunds offered ever. Find out how far in advance you must cancel to get a full refund, and ask whether any allowances are made for cancellations due to medical emergencies. If cancellation insurance is available, take it. You'll receive a full refund regardless of why you don't show up as planned.

Are taxes included in the cost? Generally taxes are not included, and they can add substantially to the cost of your trip. Depending on the program, you should also ask about tipping—specifically, who customarily gets tipped and how much that tip should be.

Every care has been taken to ensure the accuracy of the information in this guide, and all prices and dates quoted here are based on information supplied to us at press time. Still, trips and workshops that run one year often aren't available the next. In fact, cancellations can occur right up to the departure date. Stay flexible and you are sure to find something that appeals to you at the time you want to travel. The publisher cannot accept responsibility for errors that may have occurred.

We at Fodor's would love to hear about your travel experiences. When a program fails to live up to its billing, please let us know—we'll investigate your complaint and revise our entries as the facts warrant. If a program proves better than our descriptions suggest, tell us that, too. Send your letters to the editors of Fodor's Travel Publications, 201 East 50th Street, New York, NY 10022. We'll look forward to hearing from you. And have a wonderful trip.

Karen Cure

Karen Cure
Editorial Director

Archaeological Digs

Updated by Celestine Ware

magine standing on a bluff in the desert Southwest, holding a sandal woven from a yucca plant, knowing that sandal was worn by a person over 900 years ago. Imagine digging in a Maine potato field, looking for the tools used by the first European farmer who tried to break the rocky soil in 1677. Imagine looking through a pile of garbage for a piece of evidence—not for some sensational 20th-century news story but for a story that unfolded hundreds or even thousands of years ago.

All of these experiences are part of the rituals and rewards of archaeological digs—as everyday as bones and bowls and as exciting as Indiana Jones, minus the chase scenes and special effects. Archaeology is not just about collecting artifacts; it's about understanding people from times past. However, it's by examining artifacts, most often ordinary objects used in daily life, that archaeologists learn about how people lived. The programs profiled below allow you to work alongside professionals at archaeological sites, helping to excavate some of the same types of objects you see on display in museums—pottery, stone tools, and religious artifacts.

Most of these programs do not require any previous dig experience or knowledge of archaeological techniques. In fact, most have as part of their mission teaching the public about archaeology and its methods,

along with conducting research and documenting, preserving, and protecting sites threatened by weather, construction, pot-hunters, or vandals. The only prerequisites are a willingness to learn and to perform some basic physical activities. Although not overly strenuous, some of these vacations may require hiking, shoveling, lifting, carrying, or pushing a wheelbarrow.

A typical day at an excavation begins early, especially if you're staying at the site. (Some sites are so remote that you must hike in and camp there, while others are so accessible you can drive right to the dig.) Once on location, you are briefed on what you're looking for and what you hope to accomplish that day. Each site varies, so different excavation techniques are used and different tasks performed: surveying a location to determine possible excavation sites, laying out a grid over a site you want to explore, carefully removing topsoil without disturbing artifacts, sifting to find small items, logging and recording the position of artifacts in the grid, removing pieces, and, finally, cleaning and storing them. Good programs rotate people through the tasks so you can experience them all. The whole process is slow and methodical: You watch, you listen, you ask questions, and you dig carefully, so as not to damage anything. It may seem to take forever, but at the end of the day there's always plenty of satisfied conversation about what was found and its relationship to the people you are studying.

Celestine Ware is a freelance travel writer who has visited many archaeological sites in Southeast Asia.

1

Participants range in age from teens to senior citizens, though most programs have a minimum age of 17 or 18 and do not provide day care. To allow for enough attention from the professional archaeologists, groups are usually small (5 to 25), creating an atmosphere of camaraderie. You can expect to be in the field (and sometimes lab) for eight hours a day. Projects that run throughout "the season" start in the spring, as early as the weather permits, and run into the fall; others last only the short sessions that faculty, trip leaders, or volunteers are available. Some programs do offer off-season work, especially in the lab, but openings are very limited.

The biggest difference between programs is the peoples they study; digs cover all types of cultures, in all types of places, and at all points in time. The representative ones listed in this chapter are just that; if you're interested in a particular aspect of history (or prehistory), there's a good chance you'll find a program out there for you. Other significant differences between programs include the weather, the physical demands, and the "comfort factor." Only you can decide what you want; what's challenging and fun for one person could be daunting and uncomfortable for another. Ask for suggestions regarding appropriate dress for the time of year you will be on site; it could make a big difference.

So, is a dig for you? If you don't mind getting down and dirty, literally, and slowing your pace a bit, working on an excavation can be a rewarding and educational experience. Once you've found your first artifact and held it in your hand, you'll be hooked.

CHOOSING THE RIGHT DIG

Though it might at first seem that a dig is a dig is a dig, if you dig a little deeper you'll find that programs vary by as much as 3,000 miles and 10,000 years. Be sure to ask the questions that concern you.

What is the subject of the excavation, and what is the site? Archaeological digs are as different as the sites at which they're located and the cultures they're attempting to uncover. Not surprisingly, in this country, and especially in western states, many excavations focus on prehistoric or historic-period Native Americans. You might learn about the Anasazi, Apache, or Nez Percé and dig at pueblos, cliff dwellings, or plains settlements. For those interested in more recent American history, other, typically eastern, excavations take place at such locations as Colonial villages and Civil War–era plantations with slave quarters.

What types of activities are offered? Chances are if you're looking for an archaeological dig, you're interested in, well, digging. But most programs also offer activities that put excavating in a broader context— lectures, tours of other historic sites, and trips to museums being the most common— as well as those that teach other archaeological skills, such as cleaning, analyzing, and cataloging the artifacts you discover. Decide whether you want to be out in the sun, trowel in hand, as much as possible, or if you want to sample different facets of the field. Many programs, especially those of at least a week, are designed to expose you to different activities and then allow you to tailor your day to suit your interests.

Where is the dig and what are the conditions (including weather) like? If, when you hear the phrase *archaeological excavation,* visions of hot, dry, dusty digs pop into your mind, you're probably not far off. Many programs are in the South, Southwest, Midwest, and West, and most are offered in summer, the prime research time. You're outside much of the day, far from the comforts of soda machines and swimming pools. (Isn't that what it's all about, after all?) You'll probably look forward to sunshades and ice water, afternoon lab breaks and afternoon thundershowers. For many, hot weather is no big deal, but if you can't stand the heat, stay out of the Sun Belt or opt for spring or fall sessions.

What kind of experience or skills are necessary? In almost all cases, the answer is none: no previous dig experience, no knowledge of archaeology, and not even any particular physical skills. The only requirement is the desire to learn, but it's best to check on this anyway. If the work is strenuous and you're out of shape, or if most of the other participants will have a level of knowledge you don't, you might want to reconsider.

How long has the program been in operation? Older doesn't necessarily mean better, but it can mean more organized. A few years of working with volunteers can help staff fine-tune how to train them.

What's the cost and what's included? Roughly speaking, archaeological digs come in two varieties: full-service and self-service. The majority of the programs listed here, most sponsored by government agencies, universities, museums, and archaeological societies, are the latter. Open to volunteers, they generally charge nothing, save the occasional small fee for supplies or association membership, but then nothing is included either. For self-service digs, you are responsible for your own meals, lodging, and transportation unless otherwise noted. Ask about transportation from the nearest airport to the site; sometimes it's supplied. Also ask whether there are camping fees.

Full-service digs, on the other hand, charge a fee for participation ($500 to $1,500 for several days to several weeks); unless otherwise stated, those listed in this chapter include accommodations, meals, and transportation to the site from a nearby airport or other rendezvous point. Part of the fee covers the cost of the research project itself. These programs are usually operated by national organizations, most nonprofit, that are in the learning vacations business, offering a variety of projects beyond digs. In either full- or self-service digs, the program generally supplies the equipment and materials needed in the research.

This explanation oversimplifies the distinction between these two types a bit, and many programs fall somewhere in between.

It's always best to check exactly what is and what isn't included, especially if particular items, such as tents and sleeping bags, are an issue for you.

What are the accommodations like? Most volunteer programs encourage or at least make arrangements for you to camp out. It's part of the whole experience: Just pitch a tent and pitch in. As a rule, you're closer to the site if you camp, so you can participate in evening activities and stay part of a group. However, for those who prefer not to rough it, programs almost always provide lists of reasonably priced local motels or even bed-and-breakfasts and nice hotels, especially at sites near cities or popular tourist attractions. Many bigger and more established programs have arrangements with nearby colleges to provide low-cost accommodations. Ongoing research sites often provide lodgings near the excavation, though they tend to be rustic—cabins, bunkhouses, and the like.

What's the food like? If you camp, your food is likely to be what you cook yourself; if you stay in a motel, you'll probably be eating in restaurants. Programs that offer lodging usually provide meals in a common dining hall. If meals are provided and you have any special dietary needs or restrictions, be sure to ask whether they can be accommodated.

How long can I stay? If you have never done anything like this before and want to try archaeology on to see how it fits, perhaps as part of a longer vacation, a program that enables you to stop in for a day or so is ideal. For more than a taste, you need a good week or longer. Programs that are designed in one- or two-week sessions have a learning curve and some flexibility built in. You not only have more time to perfect excavation techniques, but you also can learn more in the lab and at lectures and possibly develop your own small projects based on special interests. Some projects allow you to work a month or all season, staying over a number of sessions (where formal sessions are offered). Of course, to become truly knowledgeable takes more than a handful of weeks.

How far in advance do I need to book? Check the literature you receive for application deadlines. Most programs don't have them and take applicants as long as space is available, so try to sign up two to six months in advance. For programs with fees, check for cancellation deadlines and policies; changing your mind too close to dig time can cost you.

Do you have references from past participants? You may not choose to check references if you're only going for a few days, but if you're going for several weeks or more, a talk with someone who has gotten his or her hands dirty is invaluable. Ask not only whether a given program is well run but also what a day at the dig feels like; it'll help you decide if the dig is right for you.

MAJOR PLAYERS

EARTHWATCH Since 1972, Earthwatch has been providing scientists with the resources they need—funding and volunteers—to conduct significant research in varied fields, all of it with the aim of protecting the planet. Nearly 40,000 volunteers, known as the EarthCorps, have shared in the experience and the cost of mounting this research. Though many projects deal with the physical and biological sciences, a number each year fall in the human-impacts categories, which include archaeological excavations in the United States and abroad. (Some are listed under Favorite Digs, *see below.*)

Anyone 16 or over can take part, regardless of education, cultural background, or experience. You must be a member ($35 individual; $55 two people), and it helps to have a sense of adventure and a sense of humor. Participation is on a cost-shared basis, which means your fee helps fund the research in addition to covering your lodging and food, and is 100% tax-deductible. Typically, accommodations are rustic—permanent tents, bunkhouses, dormitories,

or camping under the stars—and meals are usually prepared by a cook, though you might be asked to help. Costs are based on the total project cost; sessions in recent years have run about two or three weeks and from $1,000 to $1,800. *680 Mt. Auburn St., Box 403, Watertown, MA 02272-9924, tel. 617/926–8200, program coordinator Alison MacRae, ext. 180, or 800/776–0188, fax 617/926–8532.*

FOUR CORNERS SCHOOL Referring to itself as "the premier outdoor ed-venture classroom in the Southwest," Four Corners School has been conducting educational adventure programs all over the Colorado Plateau for more than a decade. Though many of its programs have an archaeology component, only some involve actual excavation. Specific programs are devoted to other archaeological activities—mapping and surveying sites or drawing and photographing features and artifacts—or they may simply be exhilarating quests to see rock art or ruins. None offer lab-work opportunities.

Programs generally run between May and October, from 4 to 10 days and cost about $500 to $1,000, which covers supplies, food, lodging, and transportation during the program. The programs range from those that make few physical demands (no camping or hiking) to those with sites that require being on your feet for lengthy periods to those that entail strenuous climbing in extreme temperatures. Excavations tend to cluster at the lower elevations of the plateau. Some might require camping at a primitive base camp and day hikes of 4 to 6 miles. Groups, which usually include two experts plus an occasional intern, range in size from 8 to 25, and participants are generally 35 to 65, though students under 18 are welcome if supervised by an adult. *Box 1029, Monticello, UT 84535, tel. 801/587–2156, fax 801/587–2193.*

PASSPORT IN TIME Through this volunteer program of the U.S. Forest Service, individuals and families, young and old alike, work with professional archaeologists and historians on exciting heritage projects in national forests nationwide. Projects have been as varied as they are far-flung: stabilizing ancient cliff dwellings in New Mexico, excavating a 10,000-year-old village site in Minnesota, restoring an historic lookout tower in Oregon, cleaning vandalized rock art in Colorado, surveying for sites in a rugged Montana wilderness, and excavating a 19th-century Chinese mining site in Hell's Canyon in Idaho. They run from a weekend to a month, some even longer, and there's no registration fee. Facilities vary according to the activity and location. Many of the 87 projects involve backcountry camping for which volunteers are responsible for their own food and gear. Others offer meals prepared by a camp cook, often for a small fee. Still others provide hookups for RVs, or volunteers may stay at local hotels and travel to the site each day.

The "Passport in Time Traveler" is a free catalog published twice annually. The September issue covers projects from November through May, while the March catalog announces June through November projects. Look through it and apply for some that interest you. Don't be disappointed if you're not accepted to your first choice; though PIT tries to accommodate everyone, sometimes interest exceeds the number of available spaces. *Passport in Time Clearinghouse, Box 31315, Tucson, AZ 85751-1315, tel. 800/281–9176 or 520/722–2716, fax 520/298–7044.*

SCRAP The New Hampshire State Conservation and Rescue Archaeology Program, better known as SCRAP, is an adult participation program (minimum age 17) administered by the state's Division of Historical Resources. Its goal is to educate the public about archaeology and in so doing increase site discovery, reduce site destruction, recover information from sites about to be destroyed, and conduct original research. Part of SCRAP's mission is to debunk the image of the elitist archaeologist; toward that end, the staff tries not only to train participants but also to raise them to the level

of colleagues. (In fact, New Hampshire was the first state in the country to legislate the training and certification of avocational archaeologists.) An example of the program's populist philosophy is its name: The acronym SCRAP was inspired by the Persian word for archaeologist, *bastanshanas*, whose literal translation is "one who collects garbage."

Though SCRAP also sponsors workshops, lab work, and independent research projects, the centerpiece of the program is the Summer Prehistoric Archaeology Field School, which offers formal course work through Plymouth State College (credits are transferable) as well as welcoming volunteers. The prehistoric Native American sites change from year to year, but students will learn basic site excavation methods and field laboratory procedures through direct participation and a hands-on method of instruction. The ratio of professionals to participants is about six to one. And while each project has a formal research design, there is room to tailor your work to your interests.

The field school holds three two-week sessions from the last week of June to the first week of August, with a fee of $110 for Monday through Friday meals and housing (usually in private schools and summer camps). Participants may find their own housing, or they may use program facilities. The program generally requests a $25 donation to help defray the cost of supplies. Transportation to sites is included. Flyers come out in late January or early February, and enrollment is filled by early May. *Summer Archaeology Field School, New Hampshire Division of Historical Resources, 19 Pillsbury St., Box 2043, Concord, NH 03302-2043, tel. 603/271–3483, fax 603/271–3433.*

UNIVERSITY RESEARCH EXPEDITIONS PROGRAM The aim of UREP is to encourage public participation in University of California field research projects worldwide. UREP puts together teams of volunteers and scientists (with a typical ratio of professionals to participants of one to five) to conduct research about life on Earth. As a member of a University of California research expedition (usually age 16 and older), you participate in fieldwork, share in the cost of the project, gain new skills, make new friends, and experience the excitement of discovery.

UREP's emphasis is on other cultures in other lands, but it has some archaeological programs in the United States. Recently it has offered such program subjects as Hawaii after Captain Cook, a pre-Inca site at Lake Titicacca in Peru, and pueblo dwellers of the Southwest. Projects last two to three weeks, and accommodations and costs (actually a tax-deductible contribution to the university) vary with the destination (they typically range from $900–$1,400). The contribution covers meals and shared lodging, ground transportation, nonpersonal camping and field gear, and research equipment and supplies. *2223 Fulton St., University of California, Berkeley, CA 94720-7050, tel. 510/642–6586, fax 510/642–6791.*

FAVORITE DIGS

THE MID-ATLANTIC

VIRGINIA **Colonial Williamsburg.** In the same quaint reconstructed Colonial village where tourists visit originals or replicas of houses, forges, and taverns, an innovative program, Learning Weeks in Archaeology (for ages 16 and up), gives you a chance to dig up the real thing. Working under the guidance of Williamsburg archaeologists (one professional to three or four participants), you may unearth postholes or privies, buttons or bones; while you do, you'll be learning how to take field notes, map finds, identify artifacts, and analyze site remains. Tours and lectures supplement the hands-on work, enabling you to understand how scholars use what is found to recreate 18th-century life in Virginia's Colonial capital.

Four two-week sessions are held each year, with weekends free for you to explore Jamestown, Yorktown, the James River plantations, or, if you've had enough American history, Virginia Beach or Busch Gardens. (If you'd like to stay just one week, it's better to attend the first week of a session.) Sessions are held from spring to fall, and weather varies accordingly. May and late September have cooler temperatures (typically in the 70s), while summer brings the high 80s or warmer. Rain comes more often in the early session; by summer it's drier, with the exception of some late-afternoon thunderstorms. Since sites, which change from year to year, are in the Historic Area, you won't be roughing it: Terrain is flat and not rocky, there's no wildlife to worry about (not even ticks and mosquitoes), and rest rooms and vending machines are only a walk away.

You have to arrange your own accommodations and dining, with the exception of a farewell dinner at one of Colonial Williamsburg's taverns. Lists of lodgings and restaurants are provided; though some are within walking distance of the Historic Area, a car is recommended so that you can fully enjoy local attractions. Generally, small groups of participants tend to eat and spend evenings together, and many are returnees. *Department of Archaeological Research, Colonial Williamsburg Foundation, Box 1776, Williamsburg, VA 23187-1776, tel. 804/220–7330, fax 804/220–7990. May–early Oct.: 1–2 wks (1 wk, $350; 2 wks, $550). Price does not include lodging or most meals, but does allow entry to all exhibits and the night programs, discounts, and tours.*

WEST VIRGINIA **St. Albans.** On the banks of the Kanawha River at St. Albans, archaeological evidence points to almost continuous occupation of the site for the past 10,000 years, making this perhaps the oldest continuously occupied site in North America. Archaeologists sponsored by Marshall University are exploring the site's deep, stratified deposits, looking for evidence of the Adela tribe. The first excavations here, conducted between 1964 and 1968, exposed important early Archaic period levels. Subsequently, woodland levels were found, with finds such as hearths and tools. More recent findings have turned up strong evidence of religious activity, including 118 burial mounds, fire pits, 28 petroglyph sites in the vicinity, and traces of red ocher, which were likely used for ritual face painting.

Volunteers are welcome for any length of time, and dates change from year to year. You must be at least 18 and must join the State Archaeological Society ($12). Conditions are generally warm (in the 80s) and humid. Dining and lodging arrangements are your responsibility. Within a mile or so are many fine hotels and motels, starting at $22 a night, as well as restaurants that are varied in both cuisine and price. Camping facilities are within 10 miles. With some of the more dramatic recent findings, future plans for the site are up in the air, so call to verify that the public is still being admitted. *Dean Braley, 301 4th Ave., St. Albans, WV 25177, tel. 304/722-1704, fax 304/722-1709 or Jim Recknagel, 103 Riverview Dr., St. Albans, WV 25177, tel. 304/727-0418. June–July: no limit on stay, no charge, but donation accepted.*

THE SOUTH

ARKANSAS **Parkin Archeological Research Station.** In a flat, mostly agricultural area in northeast Arkansas, part of the Mississippi River floodplain, lies the Parkin site. Here a 17-acre Native American town on the St. Francis River, surrounded by a moat and a log palisade for protection, was occupied between 1200 and 1550. An ongoing archaeological research project conducted by the Arkansas Archeological Survey is gathering information on the original residents and searching for additional evidence that the site was indeed the town of Casqui, visited by the expedition of Hernando de Soto in 1541. Evidence to support the theory is found not just in expedition accounts, which describe a town resembling the Parkin village, but also in the discovery at the site of Spanish artifacts of the type carried by the expedition: a brass bell, which was placed on a child at burial, and a glass chevron bead, used by the Spanish for trading.

The specific purposes of excavations change each field season, but general research topics include learning about the architecture of Native American houses, investigating plants and animals grown for food, searching for more evidence of contact with the de Soto expedition, investigating the moat and palisade, and determining how long the site was occupied. Current research focuses on recovering information about domestic structures and subsistence. The remains of house floors are abundant in the village area, as an estimated 2,000 people lived within the moat, and both botanical and animal remains are well preserved. Deposits are over 6 feet deep in some areas.

Volunteers (usually 17 and older; 12–16 if accompanied by an adult) are invited to help excavate, working mainly with trowels and small hand tools. Excavated soil is then water-screened on site. If it's raining or too hot—and it gets extremely hot in the summer (temperatures in the 90s are common, readings over 100°F are occasional), with rain more frequent in early fall—work is done in the lab instead. You receive sunshades and ice water at the site.

You are on your own for dining and lodging. If you'd like to camp, you may do so for free, courtesy of the project, at a nearby state park. Otherwise, there are motels and restaurants about 15 miles away in Wynne and a small café and a grocery store in Parkin. *Dr. Jeffrey M. Mitchem, Parkin Archeological State Park, Box 241, Parkin, AR 72373, tel. 501/755-2119, fax 501/755-2168. July–Oct.: no limit on stay, no charge.*

SOUTH CAROLINA **Stono Plantation.** Founded by the English in 1670, Charleston was the center of a flourishing plantation economy, and by the early 18th century, Stono Plantation—about 6 miles away and now within the Dill Wildlife Sanctuary on James Island—was home to the Hamiltons, a wealthy and politically active family who enjoyed an elegant lifestyle. It was Paul Hamilton, Sr., a loyalist, who named this 350-acre tract Stono and who ultimately lost it due to his allegiance to the Crown.

Here, in an area of fallow fields and secondary forest, the Charleston Museum, which owns and administers Stono, is working with the College of Charleston to conduct investigations on all aspects of southern plantation life. Since excavations started in 1989, the site has revealed a planter's house, occupied from about 1790 to 1830, and adjacent yard areas, while the search continues for an 18th-century slave settlement. The site is also yielding data on prehistoric and historic-period Native American occupation.

Volunteers (minimum age 18) are invited to join the excavation alongside students from the College of Charleston, for whom the project is a formal archaeological field-study course. You can take part for a day or several weeks. After the digging in the heat (90°F) and humidity is over in July, work returns to the lab, where excavated materials are washed and sorted. Volunteers are also welcome in the lab, where they will learn to analyze artifacts.

You are responsible for your own room and board, though college dorms are often available for a modest fee. Accommodations and restaurants in the Charleston area are plentiful and diverse, and the city has a wealth of museums, historic sites, beaches, and forests to enjoy. *Ron Anthony, Charleston Museum, 360 Meeting St., Charleston, SC 29403-6297, tel. 803/722–2996, fax 803/722–1784. June 1–end of July: no limit on stay, no charge.*

TENNESSEE Andrew Jackson's Hermitage. The focus of this Earthwatch plantation archaeology project is slavery, as excava-

tions around the Greek Revival mansion belonging to the seventh president of the United States yield information on the lives of those who labored here. In 1994 EarthCorps teams focused on areas occupied by those assigned to the mansion, kitchen, and stable. Work includes surveying and screening, washing, labeling, and sorting artifacts.

Volunteers (age 16 or over) stay in a 1930s-era house east of Nashville and share cooking duties. *Earthwatch, 680 Mt. Auburn St., Box 403, Watertown, MA 02272-9924, tel. 617/926–8200 or 800/776–0188, fax 617/926–8532. Mid-June–mid-Aug.: 13 days, $995.*

THE MIDWEST

KANSAS Kansas Archeology Training Program. Established in 1974 under the joint sponsorship of the Kansas State Historical Society and the Kansas Anthropological Association, the Kansas Archeology Training Program (KATP) runs a 16-day field school the first two weeks in June. Whether you attend for as little as a day or for the full session, you can take part in original research and further your knowledge of archaeological methods and theory. Among the activities you're encouraged to experience are block excavation, site surveying, artifact processing in the lab, and soil flotation. Classes can be taken for college credit or just for fun.

Over the years, investigations have been conducted at a wide range of prehistoric and historic-period sites across the state, and attendance has grown from 50 to nearly 300. To take part, you must be at least 14, become a member of the Kansas Anthropological Association ($22 individual; $25 family), and pay a daily dig site fee ($25); other expenses, including food, lodging, and transportation, are your responsibility. *Virginia A. Wulfkuhl, Kansas State Historical Society, Kansas History Center, 6425 S.W. 6th Ave., Topeka, KS 66612-*

1291, tel. 913/272–8681, fax 913/272–8682. *June: 16 days maximum.*

SOUTH DAKOTA **Earth-Lodge Villages.** Every year since 1983, the U.S. Army Corps of Engineers has selected archaeological sites for excavation by volunteers. The sites, which change yearly, are generally chosen because they are threatened by erosion at reservoirs managed by the corps. The Omaha District volunteer's project, which is not always at a prehistoric site, usually occurs between the end of July and mid-August, to avoid conflicts with harvesting and the county fair.

The Smithsonian Institution's Missouri River Basin Survey first identified and partially excavated the sites in the 1950s, and the corps's volunteer archaeological program began working here again in 1992.

If you're willing to commit at least eight hours total (it can be either two mornings or a variation) to the dig, you can volunteer. Children under 17 must be accompanied by a parent or guardian who's also volunteering. When work hours are over, there are free evening activities, e.g., slide shows, etc., and you may visit local museums and other archaeological sites. One word of warning: Summers are generally hot and humid next to the lake, and thunderstorms are to be expected.

There is no housing, but the corps offers free camping for volunteers, or you can find creature comforts in any of the many hotels and restaurants in Chamberlain or across the Missouri River in Oacoma. Volunteers need to arrange their own transportation to sites. *Justin Runestad, U.S. Army Corps of Engineers, Omaha District, Planning Division, 215 N. 17th St., Omaha, NE 68102-4978, tel. 605/224–5862, ext. 3269, fax 605/224–5945. Late July–mid-Aug.: 10 days, no charge.*

THE SOUTHWEST

ARIZONA **Grand Canyon Anasazi Project.** Since 1989 the Upper Basin Archaeological Research Project has been excavating for traces of 11th- and 12th-century Anasazi people in the Kaibab National Forest on the South Rim of the Grand Canyon. The work is geared to understanding how they survived in this harsh landscape. The project, intended to be long-term and under the leadership of Dr. Allan Sullivan of the University of Cincinnati, includes studies of artifacts, soil, and botanical and palynological (pollen and spore) fossils.

EarthCorps teams of five to six people are excavating a pueblo ruin and two nearby areas that show signs of Anasazi activity. Volunteers learn to identify sites using topographical maps and aerial photos. Excavations involve shoveling, screening earth, and identifying and labeling artifacts. Team members are also intensively surveying sites using Global Positioning System satellite technology. Teams will occasionally encounter Navajo families harvesting firewood and piñon nuts. Volunteers should be fit enough to be on their feet all day and walk some miles at a stretch.

Volunteers may stay in the Albright Training Center, at Grand Canyon National Park, or at one of the many hotels and lodges within the park. Cooking and cleaning duties are shared. The cost is $1,695 for 14 days occurring between the end of June and mid-August. *680 Mt. Auburn St., Box 403, Watertown, MA 02272-9924, tel. 617/926–8200. Earthwatch program coordinator Alison Macrae is at ext. 180, or 800/776–0188, fax 617/926–8532.*

ARIZONA **Raven Site Ruin.** Classic southwestern desert archaeology is at its best at the White Mountain Archaeological Center and its adjacent Raven Site Ruin excavation, named for the abundance of bird symbols found on ceramics and petroglyphs in the area. Here on a 5-acre knoll in east-central Arizona is an 800-room pueblo, occupied between AD 1000 and AD 1500. Despite damage by pothunters, the site is still rich in cultural material; it has more than 80 ceramic types, including White Mountain redwares, vitreous Zuni glazed wares, and many other kinds used for trading. Excavations continue on more than 200 rooms at surface level and two ceremonial rooms known as kivas.

Flanked on all sides by mountain ranges, the high-desert landscape, some 6,500 feet in elevation, is covered with over 200 extinct volcanoes that are now surreal, grass-covered domes. Summer days tend to be hot (85°F to 90°F) and dry except for brief afternoon thunderstorms, but nights are cool (50°F to 55°F). Fabulous sunsets darken to a night sky so clear that the Milky Way looks like smoke.

Working alongside professional archaeologists (the participant-to-archaeologist ratio is about 6:1), you spend your day learning all three facets of archaeology: surveying, excavation, and analysis. The daylong program starts with an artifact orientation, followed by hands-on excavation at the ruin. After lunch, you might try a guided hike or horseback ride through the surrounding area, seeing and discovering prehistoric rock art panels. By midafternoon, it's off to the lab to clean and sort artifacts, reconstruct ceramic vessels, or catalog materials; the day ends with a lecture. If you elect to stay more than a day, there's dinner and, usually, an after-dinner campfire—the silence of the night broken by a coyote chorus in the nearby hills. Since only meals and lectures are at set times, your activities can be adapted to your interests, even in a day visit. If you stay longer, however, you can really focus on a particular area of research.

If you do opt to stay, you can lodge in the bunkhouse (private rooms are available for an extra fee). Although linen is provided, you need your own sleeping bag in May, September, and October. You can also camp with a tent or RV; however, only the state park 6 miles away has hookups. Reasonably priced motels can be found in Springerville and St. Johns. Meals are served in the chow hall. Children from 9 to 17 accompanied by an adult are welcome

and are often very able and enthusiastic participants. *White Mountain Archaeological Center, Western Office, HC 30, Box 30, St. Johns, AZ 85936, tel. 520/333–5857, fax 520/333–5567. Early May–mid-Oct.: 1 day, $59 adults, $37 children 9–17; overnight, $83 adults, $61 children; 6 days, $498 adults, $366 children. Price includes lunch for day program, lodging and meals for overnight program.*

SOURCES

ORGANIZATIONS At Boston University, the **Archaeological Institute of America** (656 Beacon St., Boston, MA 02215-1401, tel. 617/353–9361), also known as AIA, has served both the public and the scholarly community for more than 100 years. It encourages and supports archaeological research, informs the public about archaeology, and protects the world's cultural heritage. **State archaeologists** and **state historic preservation offices,** often under the jurisdiction of a department of cultural resources and historic preservation, are excellent sources of information.

PERIODICALS The AIA has recently replaced its magazine with six publication programs that issue two newsletters, two catalogs, and two magazines per year. The magazines do features on such field research topics as the biologically diverse ecosystems of the Togan Islands of Indonesia, mating habits of the manakin (a small, songless passerine) of Costa Rica, or endangered species studies. Among many publications listing upcoming excavations are Earthwatch's eponymously titled magazine, which you may write to at 680 Mt. Auburn St., Box 910, Watertown, MA 02272-9924, tel. 617/926–8200. *Earthwatch* is available gratis to members. Also free is "Passport in Time Traveler" (U.S. Forest Service, Box 18364, Washington, DC 20036, tel. 800/281–9176), the newsletter published every spring and fall by Passport in Time, a volunteer program described earlier in this chapter.

BOOKS The *Guide to Academic Travel* (Shaw Guides, tel. orders 800/247–6553) contains extensive information about worldwide academic learning vacations sponsored by schools, colleges, museums, educational and cultural organizations, and travel companies. Information updates are available at the publisher's Web site address: http://www.Shawguides.com. AIA's *Fieldwork Opportunities Bulletin,* issued annually in January, provides a comprehensive directory of education opportunities in the field for students and amateur archaeologists.

ALSO SEE For more information, see the Volunteer Research Vacations and Volunteer Vacations in Public and Community Service chapters.

Arts and Crafts Workshops

Updated by Andrea E. Lehman

 aybe you want to make a quilt, build a log cabin, weave a rug? Do you harbor a hankering to bind a book or throw a pot? How about lapstraking a wooden sailboat or applying paper-thin mahogany veneer to a dining room table you've just made by hand? Or maybe you want to learn historic crafts such as adobe building or blacksmithing.

There are literally hundreds of arts and crafts workshops nationwide that offer every specialty imaginable. Some are at large crafts centers that attract students interested in a broad range of disciplines; other workshops are offered by individual craftspeople in their specialty. Some advertise extensively in glossy magazines; others rely on simple word of mouth. Many courses, like most of those described here, last between five and seven days. However, some courses last as long as a month, and weekend programs are widely available. (If that's all the time you have to spend, just contact any of the schools we describe to see whether they have weekend courses.)

Your companions are an equally mixed bag, an interesting mélange of thirtysomething professional singles, vigorous senior citizens, and baby boomers traveling with their teenage children. Generally, there are more women than men—except in the workshops that concentrate on hefty subjects like boat building and log home construction.

Days start early at most crafts workshops, and lectures, critiques, and studio time fill most of the day. At night, you might still be hard at work on a project or listening to a lecture or slide presentation. In the course of the program, you not only acquire a whole new vocabulary and information about a range of techniques in the field covered by the workshop—you usually complete at least one piece. The souvenirs you take home from an arts and crafts vacation won't sit around gathering dust. Long after you've unpacked your bags, washed your socks, and gone back to the nine-to-five, you'll have precious handmade memories of your week in the woods, beside the ocean, or perched high in the mountains. Every time you toss a salad in that hand-turned walnut bowl, wear that hand-knit sweater, or sleep under that colorful patchwork quilt, you'll remember. And the memory will bring you pleasure.

One caution. Since arts and crafts schools are often run by artistic, independent, free-spirited and, sometimes, eccentric people, it's best to verify schedules. In other words, make certain the master glassblower with whom you've always dreamed of studying hasn't dashed off to Venice to participate in an international competition or to Budapest to accept a design award.

Freelance writer and editor Andrea Lehman is an exuberant crafter, having knit, crocheted, molded, stitched, beaded, or hewn something for every friend and family member willing to accept it.

This seldom happens, but it doesn't hurt to check.

CHOOSING THE RIGHT WORKSHOP

For this chapter, we reviewed a large number of crafts schools and determined our favorites based on quality, reliability, and that intangible thing called "just plain fun."

When choosing a school, first decide what you want to learn and what level of skill you want to attain in the time your vacation allows. Then decide how far you want to travel. Some crafts are very regional. For example, if you want to learn how to carve a santo or embroider a *colcha* (coverlet), you'd best head for New Mexico. You can only learn how to carve totem poles in the Pacific Northwest or Alaska. Wyoming is the best place to learn how to make that rugged cowboy furniture that's so popular. For Adirondack chairs, it's upstate New York.

Courses in some crafts, like glassblowing or ceramics, are conducted all over the country and, indeed, all over the world. In these cases, you need to be more specific about your needs. Do you want to create art glass—the kind you see in museums or galleries—or are you more interested in making a dramatic statement with your dinnerware? Your choice of school and instructor necessarily will depend on what you want out of the class.

Once you've narrowed your search for a program, be sure to ask a few questions to help you compare similar programs and find the one that's right for you.

Is it a large school with many topics or a single-subject program? The biggest advantage of larger schools is the exciting flow of ideas—between instructors and students and among students of different disciplines—that naturally seems to occur outside of class. At night, it's more likely that other things will be going on—from campfires to lectures to musical entertainment—

and sometimes there's even a theme, such as Appalachian life, that permeates and unites the whole experience. The primary advantage of smaller, single-subject workshops is the more intense, focused nature of both the programs and the instructors, who often are the workshops' founders. Classes are frequently taught in the craftsperson's studio.

How big are the classes? Do you want individual instruction or the camaraderie of working with others in a classroom situation? Some crafts centers accept as few as one or two students; others are geared more to classes of 20 or more.

What's the cost and what's included? Costs vary widely, depending on length of workshop, subject covered, location, accommodations, and what's included. For example, of the five- and six-day programs below that charge one price for tuition, room, and board—listed in profiles as "complete package"—costs range from $350 to over $900. Other workshops have separate tuition and room and board fees, usually enabling you to live and eat elsewhere if you so choose. The smallest programs generally charge just for tuition, as they don't have on-site lodging. However, all schools are glad to recommend attractive, reasonably priced places to stay.

When it comes to comparing costs, don't just look at the sticker price. Materials may or may not entail an additional fee (and that fee, when levied, varies wildly depending on whether it's for raffia to make a basket or 14-karat gold to use in a ring). Tools are usually included, but not always, so it's a good idea to ask about that, too. When it comes to on-site lodging, you often have a choice. Most accommodations are doubles or dorm-style rooms with shared baths; if singles and private baths are available, they undoubtedly cost a little more. Camping is a good way to keep expenses down, as is cooking at least some of your own meals. You might want to look for housing with kitchen facilities. Also factor in any extras or any missing items. For example, a small workshop without room and board might nevertheless include catered lunches, whereas a larger school that covers room and board might leave you on your own for a dinner or two.

What are the accommodations like? You might stay in a B&B, a dorm, a cabin or lodge, a room in someone's home, or even a great 19th-century resort; lodging styles range from no-frills or rustic to quaint to downright posh. Sharing your room is common, and campsites are often available.

What is the food like? Most schools that include meals do so in communal dining rooms or cafeterias, where students gather and talk about the day's discoveries. In general the cuisine is pretty basic, but there are exceptions. Freshly grown produce is an added treat at some rural schools. In other situations you have the option of lodging in a place with a small kitchenette, so that you can cook what you want.

Is this a school or camp for singles or are families welcome? Are other activities available nearby for your family if they are not as enchanted as you are by, let's say, building the perfect Adirondack chair?

How long has the workshop been in business? New schools can be good, but longevity is a sign that students over the years have given it a thumbs-up. In addition, a program that has been around for a while will have worked out the kinks and handled any challenges that you're apt to throw its way.

Do you have references from past guests? Willingness to provide names is another green light. Follow up with a telephone call by all means; speaking with someone who has actually been there may help you resolve any questions you may have when you're ready to decide between two equally appealing programs.

Is laundry service available? The answer to this question, while not a deciding factor in where you go, will probably help you determine what to pack.

How far in advance do I need to book? Plan as far ahead as you can so that you get the dates, course, housing, and instructors you want. This is especially true when the course you have your heart set on taking is taught by a visiting instructor who puts in limited appearances on the crafts-workshop circuit. It's not uncommon for some workshops to start filling up a year in advance, but generally three to six months should be enough time. Workshop reservations are generally taken on a first-come, first-serve basis, so be sure to ask about the popularity of a specific topic that interests you. Quite often, when a school offers a variety of crafts, a certain course such as ceramics or glassblowing will fill up especially quickly.

THE NORTHEAST

MAINE **Haystack Mountain School of Crafts.** World-renowned as an artists' colony, Haystack Mountain fits in perfectly on Deer Isle. The campus, designed by Edward Larrabee Barnes and built in 1962, was modeled on the weathered gray-shingled buildings typical of the Maine coast. A short drive across the high bridge over Eggemoggin Reach takes you to the campus, which has panoramic views of Jericho Bay and the islands beyond.

The Haystack community is made up of approximately 80 participants, comprising staff, students, and an internationally respected faculty. Classes in clay, wood, glass, quilts, fiber, baskets, metals, jewelry making, and book arts are open to crafts workers at all levels from beginning to advanced. The two- and three-week classes, which run from early June until the beginning of September, are conducted by artists who are well-established, award-winning professionals—a different group each summer. Classes average 14 students with one instructor.

Days start early with a hearty breakfast served cafeteria-style in the airy, wood-beamed dining room. Classes, scheduled Monday through Friday, last until noon, when there's a casual lunch. Afternoons are divided between lectures, classes, critiques, and hands-on studio time. Studios are open around the clock daily. Shorter workshops are available in the spring and in the colorful fall foliage season.

In the area, you can stroll the rocky coastline, pick wild blueberries, drive to Blue Hill (where E. B. White lived after retiring from the *New Yorker*), explore the picturesque villages on the island, or, weather permitting, take a small boat to a neighbor island. Some local lobstermen may take you out to help pull their traps—of course that means waking up at 4 AM.

Accommodations vary from an open bunkhouse to a single room with bath. Bring warm clothing—Maine can be chilly at night—but if you do get cold, electric blankets are available (for a small fee) to warm you right up. *Haystack Mountain School of Crafts, P.O. Box 518-F, Deer Isle, ME 04627, tel. 207/348–2306, fax 207/ 348–2307. Topics: basketry, blacksmithing, book arts, ceramics/pottery, drawing, fiber arts, furniture making, glassblowing, jewelry, painting, printmaking, quilting, weaving, woodworking. Early June–early Sept.: 14 days, tuition $480; 21 days, tuition $630; 14–21 days, room and board $260–$1,490.*

MAINE **The Woodenboat School.** Imagine pulling your oar through the water to carry yourself away from shore in a boat that you built yourself. Looking up to see the wind billowing the sail that you designed and sewed. Running your hand down the side of your carefully constructed canoe's perfectly bowed cedar rib. With its more than 50 different classes covering boatbuilding, woodworking, and related crafts, the Woodenboat School can help you learn all you need to know to make these musings reality, whether you're a novice or a skilled woodworker and sailor. You can learn any-

thing from basic boat design to sail making to black-and-white seascape photography; you can even work on your sailing techniques in courses on both small and large crafts.

The school, in operation since 1980, occupies 64 acres on Penobscot Bay, about five hours north of Boston and an hour's drive southeast of Bangor and Acadia National Park. Courses take place on the waterfront and in a converted 1916 brick barn known as the Shop, which houses three boatbuilding spaces stocked with power tools and building materials. Each year, about 600 to 700 people of all ages attend the school's one- and two-week courses, which operate from June to September; the school also takes its courses on the road to California, Maryland, Virginia, and Canada.

Most students stay on the school's grounds, either in one of two old New England inns with simple double rooms and shared baths or at a campground nearby, which is basic, with toilet and shower facilities, but no electrical outlets or tent platforms. Everyone eats together in the dining hall in one of the inns. The school can also provide a list of local B&Bs and house rentals. The cost of materials, which can run to $1,000 or more, is not included. *The Woodenboat School, Box 78, Naskeag Rd., Brooklin, ME 04616-0078, tel. 207/359–4651, fax 207/359–8920. Topics: boatbuilding, sail making, seamanship, woodworking, marine photography. June–Sept.: 6–14 days, tuition $500–$900, room and board $300 per wk, campsites $65 per wk (campers can take meals for $100).*

MASSACHUSETTS **Heartwood Homebuilding School.** Heartwood, established in 1978 to teach the skills necessary to build an energy-efficient house, offers five-day and three-week workshops. Your day begins with lectures and discussion in the design studio. After lunch, the class rides off to a construction site for some hands-on experience. Some of the students are skilled builders, some have never held a hammer, but all attend with a serious purpose in mind—they want help in designing and building their dream home. A list of tools is provided when you register, but all tools are available at the Heartwood Tool Store. The program equips you to act as your own contractor; knowing the basics helps you speak a common language with the plumbers and carpenters you hire.

Typical five-day workshops, most offered twice each summer, include timber framing, cabinetmaking, renovation, carpentry for women, drywall, and masonry. The four-member resident faculty are all licensed building contractors and architects with years of experience.

You're on your own for breakfast and dinner, and you make your own arrangements for accommodations at the hotels, bed-and-breakfasts, and campgrounds in the area, which offer special rates for people in the program.

Once you've graduated and started building your dream home, Heartwood offers a free design consultation service. You can call them to discuss and solve any problems you encounter during construction. It's almost as if you never left. *Heartwood Homebuilding School, Johnson Hill Rd., Washington, MA 01235, tel. 413/623–6677, fax 413/623–0277. Topics: carpentry, furniture making, house building, masonry. May–Sept.: 5 days, tuition $450. Price includes lunch.*

MASSACHUSETTS **Horizons: The New England Craft Program.** You probably won't find a better student-teacher ratio at any of the colleges that surround Horizons, among them Smith and Amherst. Founded in 1983 by Jane Sinauer, whose large porcelain pieces have been exhibited in museums and galleries around the world, each class is limited to three students per instructor, and there are no more than 12 students and four instructors per class. The small class size offers the opportunity to explore new techniques through instruction and practice. Intensive three-, four-, or six-day studios, as courses are called, are offered once a month from April through October; they are open to students of all levels and conducted by prominent artists and craftspeople, assisted by graduate students. Since workshops are always open, some students work late into the night.

The intensives take an unusual approach to crafts by covering such topics as Japanese and African Dye Techniques: Painting and Illustrating on Fabric; Tableware, Function and Decoration: Terra-Cotta and Majolica; and Out of the Woods: Furniture and Beyond.

Horizons comprises a complex of 12 buildings on a 50-acre farm surrounded by pastures and apple orchards in the foothills of the Berkshire Mountains. Located in the five-college area around Amherst and Northampton, it's two hours from Boston, three hours from New York.

The farmhouse was built in 1780 and is the oldest house in the valley, whereas the students' quarters and most of the studios, designed by a local architect, are contemporary. Built with high ceilings, they are very bright and full of sunshine.

At meals, everyone socializes and discusses their projects over home-baked breads, fresh vegetables, and other delicious fare. *Horizons, 108 N. Main St., Sunderland, MA 01375, tel. 413/665–0300, fax 413/665–4141. Topics: boatbuilding, book arts, ceramics, fiber arts, furniture making, glassblowing, jewelry, painting, photography, quilting, sculpture, surface design (various techniques for painting, dyeing, and designing textiles). Late Apr.–late Oct.: 3–6 days, complete package $300–$590.*

NEW YORK **Sagamore Historic Adirondack Great Camp.** The Adirondacks have long been the playground of the discreetly rich. There was a time in the late 19th century when roughing it for the fortunate few simply meant traveling from a sumptuous 5th Avenue setting to an equally sumptuous bucolic setting—one of the great timbered lodges called the Adirondack Great Camps. Sagamore, dating from this Gilded Age, sits among the birches and fir trees beside Sagamore Lake and is maintained much as it was at the turn of the century— no television, no locks on the doors, bathrooms in the halls, and few phones. Guest rooms, most of them doubles with twin beds, have many of the original turn-of-the-century furnishings.

Meals are served buffet-style and eaten family-style at large tables in a dining room overlooking the lake. A typical dinner tends to be chicken, turkey, or fish; lunch is soup, salad, and a sandwich; breakfast always features a hot entrée. On clear evenings, dinners are often served on picnic tables at the lake's edge. Smoking is too much of a fire hazard to these old wood structures to be permitted in any of the buildings.

From May 1 to November 1, Sagamore offers classes for all ages in traditional Adirondack crafts, such as wood carving (e.g., timber wolf, miniature loon, Adirondack St. Nick), ash-splint basketry, rustic furniture, Adirondack guide boats, birch bark baskets, handmade twig paper, and so on. There are also classes in storytelling (the "tall tales" made famous by Natty Bumppo around the campfire), exploration of other historic camps (including J. P. Morgan's Camp Uncas), and a unique grandparents' and grandchildren's summer camp (traditional crafts, canoeing, storytelling). Several weekends are also reserved for Elderhostel participants. Some classes are two days, others last five days, and, unlike most programs, materials *are* included in the cost.

When you're not in a class or workshop, you can hike on the numerous well-marked trails through the surrounding state forest preserve or bowl on the refinished, semi-outdoor bowling alley that dates from 1914. A word about the weather: Spring comes late to the Adirondacks and winter early, so you might want to take something warm

and weatherproof to zip into. *Sagamore, Box 146, Raquette Lake, NY 13436-0146, tel. 315/354–5311, fax 315/354–5851. Topics: basketry, blacksmithing, boatbuilding, drawing, furniture making, photography, rug braiding, wood carving. Early May– early Nov.: 2–5 days, complete package $235–$500. Price includes materials.*

NEW YORK **Thousand Islands Craft School and Textile Museum.** This school in Clayton, New York, on the shores of the St. Lawrence and just 7 miles from the International Bridge to Canada, is housed in a large 19th-century Victorian home in which nearly 50 workshops in the traditional arts and crafts are held. Specialties are weaving, basketry, and especially pottery (a pottery studio has electric and gas-fired brick kilns), but classes are also offered in early American decorative arts, jewelry, folk art, and bird-decoy carving. A popular class is theorem painting, which teaches the techniques of painting on unlikely surfaces such as pillows, plates, and pitchers.

The school encourages a hands-on approach. You and your class of no more than 12 students work from 9 to 5, and the instructor, who might demonstrate a technique in the morning, spends the day helping and advising you as you work on your own project. Lunch is scheduled for 12 to 1, but enthusiasm for a braided rug or a bird decoy often means that you'll work right through until the end of the day. Some workshops, such as the songbird carving class, require some intensive research: in this case, you research a bird of your choice to determine the correct body shape, pose, and feather detail. At the end of the workshop you'll have learned feather burning, acrylic painting, and how to use power carving tools with accuracy.

When you're not working, you can visit the school's textile museum, which specializes in 20th-century North American handwoven fabrics, or explore Clayton's Antique Boat Museum, Opera House, and the Thousand Islands Museum.

The school does not provide accommodations, but a list of options, including lodging in a Victorian home in town, is provided upon request. The only dining facilities on campus are a small kitchen with a microwave, coffeemaker, refrigerator, and sink, which all students are welcome to use. There are, however, plenty of restaurants, burger joints, and diners in town, and the school has a picnic area should you feel like packing a lunch. An arts and crafts program for children ages 6 to 12 is held every summer and includes a Children's Craft Day that concentrates on pottery, weaving, and other kids' activities. *Thousand Islands Craft School, 314 John St., Clayton, NY 13624, tel. 315/686–4123. Topics: basketry, fiber arts, folk art, jewelry, painting, pottery, quilting, surface design, weaving, wood carving. Mid-Mar.–Dec.: 2– 10 days, tuition $65–$275. Price does not include some equipment.*

VERMONT **Camp Terra-Cotta.** Sculptor Steffi Friedman has been teaching sculpture in her studio in Westport, Connecticut, for over 25 years. For one week each summer, she picks up shop and moves to a quaint country inn in Vermont ski country. The Landgrove Inn in Landgrove, east of Manchester and close by the Bromley and Stratton ski areas, is the perfect backdrop for the classes, held outdoors (there's a large indoor space available if it rains). Only 17 students can take the course, which allows Friedman to individualize the eight-hour-a-day instruction; she also has an assistant.

The media used are terra-cotta, stone, wax, and winter stone, and both figurative and abstract concepts are taught. Covered topics include the standing figure, portraiture, and the maquette, while bronze casting, mold making, and patina are discussed.

You share cozy, attractive rooms in the inn, originally built as a farmstead in the early 1800s (singles are available but cost more), and get to enjoy the cooking of the Snyder family at meals taken in the inn's dining room. The food includes blueberry pancakes for breakfast and delicious home-baked breads, rolls, cakes, and pies. The attractively landscaped grounds have two tennis courts, a swimming pool, and a stocked fishing pond. One evening the group goes to the nearby Weston Playhouse. *9 Yankee Hill Rd., Westport, CT 06880, tel. 203/227–9650. Topic: sculpture. July or Aug.: 7 days, complete package $775–$975.*

VERMONT **The Carving Studio and Sculpture Center.** In a 400-acre stone yard consisting of nine nonworking quarries 6 miles west of Rutland, this unique facility, founded by Bernadette D'Amore in 1986, is dedicated to the art of stone carving. It's housed in what was once a company store, where workers exchanged scrip for food, clothing, and other necessities. Modeled after similar schools in Carrara, Italy's marble center, the Carving Studio provides space and instruction for beginners as well as experienced sculptors, with two-day to three-week programs that include figure carving, bronze casting, and wood carving and laminating, all of which run from April to November. During the winter there are artists' residencies.

Classes kick off on Monday at 9 with the first of five daily half-hour demonstrations by the instructors. Here you learn about the range of tools, their uses, and the various techniques of sculpting marble, including traditional hand stonework and the latest in abrasive technology as well as how to avoid flying chips. Tools are provided, but students supply their own media; you can pick out your own piece of marble for purchase right at the site. Prices vary depending on the size and quality of the stone. The instructor to student ratio is three to five, so there's plenty of individual instruction. Classes run until 5, with a break for lunch at 12. You have the choice of three restaurants a stone's throw from the studio—a pizzeria, a greasy spoon–style diner, and a restaurant that serves soups and salads—or you can make your own lunch in the studio kitchen.

Dinner is served at the studio; a typical menu might include vegetarian lasagna and a Caesar salad, followed by strawberry shortcake, all prepared by the center's cook. After dinner, you have the option of sitting in on a slide show or a discussion by instructors, visiting artists, or even the students themselves, who are encouraged to show and discuss their own work. The studios are open until 2 AM, should your creative juices continue flowing through the evening, and they open every morning at 8.

Lodging is not included in the price, but the center provides a list of 15 area bed-and-breakfasts, inns, and hotels when you first apply. *The Carving Studio and Sculpture Center, Box 495, West Rutland, VT 05777, tel. and fax 802/438–2097. Topic: stone carving. Apr.–Oct.: 5 days, tuition $425. Price includes dinner.*

VERMONT **Fletcher Farm School.** In 1947, the descendants of Revolutionary War soldier Jesse Fletcher invited the Society of Vermont Craftsmen to establish an arts and crafts school on this secluded 600-acre farm on land first settled by Fletcher in 1793. The school gives classes in July and August—many of the 50 faculty members hold teaching jobs at nearby colleges—that cover a wide variety of fine, decorative, and folk arts for adults of all ages and skill levels. There are also numerous classes organized especially for children.

With more than 100 workshops to choose from, you're sure to find something that sparks your interest. If you're keen on decorative arts, you can take theorem painting, primitive portraiture, Ukrainian egg decorating, Norwegian rosemaling, wood graining, or marbleizing. Needlework aficionados will delight in subjects like bobbin lace, and quilting. Other craft classes include rug hooking, doll making, book arts, wood carving, tinsmithing, bonsai, basket making, and even lamp-shade construction.

Workshops with two, three, or five class days begin with a casual gathering that allows you to mingle with the instructors, get acquainted, and discuss the upcoming week's activities. An orientation acquaints you with the physical layout of the school so that you can take full advantage of its many acres of natural woodlands, criss-crossed by miles of pine-needle-carpeted hiking trails. The Green Mountain National Forest is less than a 10-minute drive, and the nearby villages of Proctorville and Ludlow have wonderful historic houses. Ludlow's landmark-designated historical museum is well worth a visit.

The two dormitories, known as the Roost and the Nest, give you a choice of single or double rooms (with twin beds), all of which share bathrooms. Meals, in the new dining hall, are included in the daily rates.

The 200-year-old barn vibrates with classroom activity. A typical day begins with an early breakfast, followed by hands-on workshops from 9 to 5. During the lunch breaks, you can take a picnic into the woods or stop in at the charming crafts shop to admire or buy the handcrafts made by instructors and other members of the Society of Vermont Craftsmen. In the shop, you might find a floral hooked rug, a log-cabin quilt, or numerous other objects that, after a week at the Fletcher Farm School, could have your signature one day. *Fletcher Farm School, 611 Rte. 103 S, Ludlow, VT 05149, tel. 802/228–8770. Topics: basketry, bobbin lace, book arts, braiding, calligraphy, decorative painting, doll making, glasswork, painting, photography, quilting, rug making, weaving, wood carving. Late June–late Aug.: 3–6 days, tuition $85–$170, room and board $45–$50 per night.*

VERMONT **Yestermorrow.** Planning to restore an old house? Gathering stamina to design and build one from scratch? If either is true, this is a great place to start. Yestermorrow, founded by John Connell, a licensed architect, is one of the only schools that integrates home design with building skills. Here, the way in which you want to live plays an integral role in what course will be right for you. Students of all levels, from ground zero on up (so to speak), range from 18 to 80 years old; 70% are men. They come to help solidify not just how they're going to build their house, but also the reasons why they want it that way. The faculty comprises licensed architects, registered builders, designers, and woodworkers. Many have graduate degrees, but all are interested in helping your dream house come true.

The curriculum offered is divided into two general categories: layperson and professional—although the nonprofessional is encouraged to cross the line into more advanced work and the professional to pick up a new skill. Classes are intimate, with 5 to 10 people per course. The one- and two-week courses offer a remarkable array of subjects covering almost every aspect of design and building: interior design, nontoxic construction, cabinetry, electrical wiring, power and hand tools, architectural crafts, and historic restoration, to name a few. At the end of some of the courses, you and four other students design and complete a group project. Most courses are held during the summer months. (Weekend workshops are also offered.)

If you choose a course in the Layperson's Curriculum, you stay at the White Horse Inn in Fayston, about 8 miles from the school. The inn provides a substantial breakfast, a bag lunch to take to school with you, and dinner. Students in the Professional Curriculum stay at condominiums in Warren and prepare their own meals.

The school, which includes an old inn on its site, spreads out over 37 acres. Though offices, the woodworking shop, student campsite, and some studio space are on campus, other studios and classrooms are at other facilities in the area. Warren is a typical example of the small New England towns that pepper Vermont's Mad River Valley. A church, the inn, a few imposing houses, and the courthouse square off across the village green. Though the area is best known for its skiing—Mad River Glen, Sugarbush, and Stowe—there are also possibilities to hike, swim, bicycle, and horseback ride. *Yestermorrow Design/Build School, R.R. 1, Box 97-5, Warren, VT 05674, tel. 802/496–5545, fax 802/496–5540. Topics: architectural crafts, cabinetry, faux marbling, furniture building and design, landscaping, straw-bale construction, timber framing. Mar.–Oct.: 6 days, tuition $675–$825, room and board $275; 13 days, tuition $1,200–$1,425, room and board $580.*

THE MID-ATLANTIC

NEW JERSEY **Peters Valley Craft Center.** In northwest New Jersey's Delaware Water Gap, bordering the Delaware River, stands Peters Valley Craft Center, surrounded by waterfalls, ponds, and well-maintained hiking trails (including a segment of the Appalachian Trail). Seventy different summer workshops are offered in blacksmithing, ceramics, surface design, weaving, photography, woodworking, and fine metals. Subjects run the gamut from toolmaking and metal sculpture (large and small scale) to silk painting, silk-screening, and pottery, while skill levels range from beginner to advanced.

One accomplished professional craftsperson in each discipline is selected for a year-round residency program (lasting one to four years) to manage the studio, plan programs, and earn a living at his or her craft, while paying a nominal fee for a house and studio space. Each resident artist chooses an assistant to help run the summer program. The assistant has the opportunity to learn new techniques, sell and show work, and live in a supportive setting for a summer. A store and a gallery with ongoing exhibitions are open April–December.

Each summer up to 10 well-known professional artists in each discipline are invited to Peters Valley to teach. Classes run from 9 to 5 every day. Following a demonstration of a new skill by the instructor, you begin work on your project, and throughout the day the instructor moves from student to student, answering questions and offering advice on technique. The courses are largely run in a classroom setting, but as the class never exceeds 12 students, personal attention and a spirit of familiarity make it feel more like a workshop than a class.

Accommodations for a maximum of 20 students, based on double occupancy, are available in one of the center's houses, some of which are on the National Register of Historic Places. Other options, including B&Bs, inns, hotels, motels, hostels, and even campgrounds, are on an alternative housing list provided by the center. Meals are served in a communal dining hall. If you are staying at Peters Valley, all meals are included in the accommodations price; otherwise, you can buy a meal plan for about $20 a day.

Special programs include an 11-day workshop in November for firing an *anagama* (wood-fueled) kiln as well as May children's weekends, whose topics include ceramics, jewelry, photography, silk-screening, basketry, woodworking, and weaving. *Peters Valley Craft Center, 19 Kuhn Rd., Layton, NJ 07851, tel. 201/948–5200, fax 201/948–0011. Topics: basketry, blacksmithing, ceramics, jewelry, fine metals, furniture design, photography, surface design, weaving, and woodworking. June–Aug.: 2–8 days, tuition $190–$365, room and board $110–$360.*

PENNSYLVANIA **Sawmill Center for the Arts.** Founded in 1975, this rural arts center is in the middle of the 6,000-acre Cook Forest State Park. From May to October, more than 160 workshops are offered, covering a wide variety of the traditional arts, such as wood carving, basketry, quilting, spinning, and calligraphy.

Most workshops meet from 9 to 4 daily with a generous lunch break and are open to those with all levels of experience.

Enrollment is usually limited to 12–15 students per instructor. Especially popular is wood carving, which includes such typical workshops as Wood Carving in the Round, Realistic Bird Carving, Caricature Carving, and Chip Carving.

The center has no accommodations or dining facilities, but due to its location in the state park, there are an abundance of B&Bs, inns, hotels, motels, and campgrounds in the vicinity. A directory of housing options is available upon request. For weeklong classes, you have the option of ordering specially catered meals daily; menus are posted every morning in the workshop.

Bordered by the Clarion River, the park has 30 miles of hiking trails and a virgin forest that's a Registered National Natural Landmark. The center also sponsors the Nuthole Children's Craft Program, Elderhostel weeks, and a variety of other activities, including crafts markets and live theater performances at the Verna Leith Sawmill Theater. *Sawmill Center for the Arts, Box 180, Cooksburg, PA 16217, tel. 814/927–6655 (May–Sept.) or 814/744–9670 (Oct.–Apr.), fax 814/744–8660. Topics: basketry, block printing, calligraphy, dulcimer building, embroidery, painting, papermaking, quilting, rug braiding, spinning, teddy bear making, and wood carving. Late May–late Oct.: 5 days, tuition $175–$210.*

PENNSYLVANIA **Touchstone Center for Crafts.** This 147-acre mountain retreat, 10 miles east of Uniontown and 60 miles southeast of Pittsburgh, offers more than 70 intensive (weekend and weekday) workshops from June to September for all levels, from preschoolers on up. A wide choice of regional, national, and international crafts is emphasized—anything from how to forge a Damascus steel knife to making Japanese *momigami* paper for bookbinding.

Those who take the weeklong courses arrive on Sunday and may stay over to Saturday. A typical day begins with a hearty breakfast, followed by classes from 9 to 4 with a 1½-hour break for lunch that allows plenty of time for exploring the woodland trails on Touchstone's grounds. The workshops combine lectures, demonstrations, and hands-on experience. You work on and complete a project that you can take home after the session.

Accommodations are in rustic cabins or in stream-side campsites on the grounds. Though neither has showers or bath, there is a bathhouse on the property. Still, if you want a little more in the way of creature comforts, you can choose from several affordable hotels nearby, many of which offer discounts to Touchstone students. A list is available. Meals, served cafeteria-style in the dining hall, can be bought as a weekly package or on a meal-to-meal basis. The menu might include roasted chicken, broiled fish, and hamburgers for the kids. Since cooking is forbidden at campsites, the meal plan remains one of your few options. On Thursday evenings, there is a student art auction; students donate pieces, and the proceeds are used for studio improvements. After dinner on Fridays, there's always a musical or theatrical performance by guest artists.

Nearby attractions include Frank Lloyd Wright's masterpiece "Fallingwater," Fort Necessity National Battlefield (a French and Indian War–era fortification), several state forest preserves with excellent hiking trails, and local glass factories that host tours. *Touchstone Center for Crafts, R.D. 1, Box 60, Farmington, PA 15437, tel. 412/329–1370, fax 412/329–1371. Topics: basketry, blacksmithing, ceramics, drawing, fiber arts, metalwork, painting, papermaking, woodworking. June–Sept.: 7 days, tuition $150–$280, housing $60–$75, camping $30, board $85. Meal plan price does not include Sun. dinner.*

WEST VIRGINIA **Augusta Heritage Center.** Part of Davis & Elkins College, this center is on 170 wooded acres at the edge of the Monongahela National Forest in the mountains of central West Virginia. Summer workshops offer intensive classes in the folk arts, including in-depth "theme weeks"—for example Irish and blues weeks—which focus on a specific cultural theme while spanning several art forms, including music and dance.

Most workshops are a week long and open to all levels, but a few are geared to more advanced levels. For example, several classes are given on musical instrument construction, open to students familiar with woodworking tools. These classes complete a guitar, banjo, or an Appalachian dulcimer. Daily schedules vary from class to class; most meet mornings and afternoons for four to six hours daily and work in intensive small-group sessions with 10–15 students and one instructor. The final week includes the Augusta Festival, a non-instructional weekend with an excellent crafts fair.

In addition to regular classes, each week there are separate workshops on folk arts for kids ages 8–12. One workshop features mountain games, songs, square dancing, storytelling, and crafts. Elderhostel weeks are also offered.

Housing for Augusta students is available in the Davis & Elkins College residence halls. There are semiprivate rooms, common bathrooms, furnished lounges, and laundry rooms. Housing is coed, but the bathroom on each floor is designated either male or female. Wholesome meals are served cafeteria-style in the dining hall; they are an opportunity for the students and master folk artists to mingle informally.

The surrounding countryside offers white-water rafting, canoeing, caving, rock climbing, and hiking. The campus has recreational facilities that include tennis courts, swimming pool, fitness trail, and Nautilus center. *Augusta Heritage Center, David & Elkins College, Elkins, WV 26241-3996, tel. 304/637–1209, fax 304/637–1317. Topics: basketry, blacksmithing, bookbinding, fiddle and bow repair, musical instrument construction, pottery, quilting, stained glass, treenware (handmade functional wooden utensils), stone* carving, stonemasonry, timber framing, weaving, wood carving. *July–mid-Aug.: 5 days, tuition $280–$290, room and board $220–$240.*

WEST VIRGINIA **The Basketry School.** Connie and Tom McColley make functional and art baskets from the abundance of natural basketry materials surrounding the school, including white oak, hickory, and honeysuckle. Weeklong and two-week classes are taught in the couple's spacious home and studio in the Appalachian foothills 52 miles east of Charleston.

Classes are run in a large, well-lighted studio with plenty of space for you to work in. A friendly, concentrated atmosphere is created by the relatively small class size of 10 students. During the course of the week, you will learn everything about white oak basketry—how to select and gather the right tree; then how to trim, split, shave, and shape it. Along the way, you'll also learn the history of traditional and contemporary basketry through discussions, demonstrations, and slide presentations.

Two- and three-person cabins, each with bath, are available, or the meadow around the school can be used for camping. Electricity, water, and shower facilities are available for campers. The school also has a dining hall, which serves three meals a day. *The Basketry School, Rte. 3, Box 325, Chloe, WV 25235, tel. 304/655–7429. Topic: basketry. May–Aug.: 5 days, tuition $250, room and board $200.*

THE SOUTH

FLORIDA **Priscilla's Studio by the Sea.** The founder of the National Society of Tole and Decorative Painters, Priscilla Hauser is part teacher, part performer, and all business. In addition to putting out countless books and videos, she teaches her painting method in intensive 5½-day seminars at her Studio by the Sea in Panama City, right on the Gulf of Mexico in the Florida panhandle. The range of seminars, offered throughout the

year, begins with Basic I, which covers the fundamentals of her techniques. You paint a variety of fruits, flowers, and leaves in acrylics or oils on surfaces such as wood and metal, glass and fabric. More advanced seminars include faux finishes, painting on lace, Christmas items from poinsettias to gingerbread people, and roses, Priscilla's specialty.

Seminars usually begin with orientation on Sunday from 4 to 9 PM. On weekdays, the studio opens at 7:30 AM, so you can come in early to practice before class starts at 9. Coffee and a hot lunch (casserole, salad, and dessert, for example) are provided. Priscilla's instruction ends at 5 (4 on Friday, the last day), but her assistant stays on, so you can continue to practice or work on a project until 8, when the studio closes.

You may either bring your own supplies, such as brushes and paints, or purchase them at the studio. A fee is assessed for each seminar's set of project materials. You are responsible for your own lodging, though Priscilla sends recommendations of nearby inns, beach houses, and RV parks, some of which give discounts to her students. Classes, filled on a first-come, first-served basis, are limited to 20 students but are open to all levels and all ages. Workshops are frequently offered in other locations around the country and in Canada. *Priscilla's Studio by the Sea, Box 521013, Tulsa, OK 74152-1013, tel. 918/743–6072, fax 918/743–5075. Topic: decorative painting. Year-round: 5½ days, tuition $350. Price includes lunch.*

GEORGIA **Callaway School of Needle Arts.** Since 1972, the annual Callaway School of Needle Arts has been held at Callaway Gardens, a 14,000-acre resort in the foothills of the Appalachians southwest of Atlanta. The school gives four-, two-, and one-day classes within a framework of two consecutive five-day sessions in January. Courses are primarily for the intermediate or advanced stitcher and are open to no more than one or two dozen. Just look through the catalog and pick a project that interests you—perhaps an Oriental fan in Japanese embroidery, a drawn-thread sampler, or a butterfly made with traditional needlepoint stitches.

Though you are in class much of the day, generally 8:30 to 4:30, there's plenty to occupy your off hours. You can go to a home room to visit and share ideas with other participants, see the needlework exhibit, or attend merchandise night, held once each session. If you've had enough of tiny stitches, you can indulge in any of Callaway Gardens' many recreational activities: golf on three championship courses, tennis, biking, swimming, boating, fishing, or walking around its lush gardens and wildlife-filled woodlands and lakes. In fact, this is a great vacation getaway for the whole family; guest and golf packages are available specifically for the noncrafter.

Classrooms and accommodations are in the four-star, full-service Callaway Gardens Inn, and meals are buffet-style in the hotel's Plantation Room. The comprehensive fee not only covers tuition, room (single or double occupancy), and board (including a reception, banquet, and coffee breaks), but also use of the fitness center and entrance to the gardens. A list of the basic equipment and supplies needed is sent to you ahead of time, so you can bring them from home or buy them at the school's boutique. A kit fee covers the materials used in class. *Callaway School of Needle Arts, Box 2000, Pine Mountain, GA 31822-2000, tel. 706/663-5060 or 800/763-3353, fax 706/663-5068. Topic: embroidery. Mid-Jan.: 5 days, complete package $717-$913.*

GEORGIA **Timber Framing in Southern Appalachia.** When you see a barn raising, such as the one in the movie *Witness*, what you're seeing is timber framing—the method used centuries ago to build houses and barns. Large timbers, used sparingly and placed symmetrically, are bound together by mortise and tenon joints and secured by wooden pegs to construct the frame. During the 20th century, the need for

quick and economical housing production caused sturdy, but labor-intensive, timber-frame construction to fall out of favor; today, however, it's enjoying a bit of a resurgence, and people who want a more craftsmanlike approach to home building are rediscovering the skill.

Near the northeast Georgia town of Clayton, John Koenig, a second-generation timber framer, founded Upper Loft Designs. Since 1987, it has offered intensive, hands-on, product-oriented timber-framing workshops in addition to its home-building services, and previous students have ranged from building tradespeople and architects to people who have gone on to construct their own home or have one built for them.

Courses range from the Timberframe Design & Planning Seminar to the hands-on Basic Timberframe Joinery Workshop. New this year is a one-day seminar called General Contracting by the Owner/Builder, a response to the growing number of owners who want a great deal of input in the building process. Typically seminars and workshops are held on weekends. Break periods, lunchtimes, and evenings are often filled with discussion, sharing, minilectures, and even an occasional party. Spouses may watch or take part in any of the courses at no extra charge.

Koenig provides a list of accommodations available in the area, which includes the newly opened Inn at Lofty Branch, a bed-and-breakfast nestled within Upper Loft's timber-framed Art & Craft Village. All you need are a notebook and pencil (for seminars), the willingness to expend some energy (for hands-on workshops), and a desire to learn and build. *Upper Loft Design, Inc., Rte. 1, Box 2901, Lakemont, GA 30552, tel. 706/782-5246, fax 706/782-6840. Topic: home building. Year-round: 1 day, tuition $75; 2 days, tuition $125.*

LOUISIANA **Needlework Seminars.** Each fall, the Embroiderers' Guild of America, founded in 1958, offers its members an annual weeklong seminar series. More than 50 one-, two-, and four-day classes for all ability levels are offered, covering all sorts of techniques: canvas, pulled thread, surface embroidery, silk and metal on silk, crewel, and quilting, to name a few. Seminars are in a different city each year. In 1997 it's New Orleans; in 1998, the guild's 40th anniversary, it's in Louisville, the guild's headquarters.

Classes take place on Monday, Tuesday, Thursday, and Friday, so, for example, you can opt to take two two-day courses, with a day off between, or a four-day course that brackets the week. You are in class from about 9 to 4, with an hour and a half for lunch. Otherwise, your time is your own; peruse the seminar's education exhibit, fiber forum, bookstore, and boutique or enjoy the diversions of your surroundings. On Wednesday, you can take a planned tour or an extra one-day workshop, both for additional fees, or just leave the day free to do what you want, which for many participants means spending time with their spouse or family. Seminars generally include banquets, which may be included in the price.

Membership in the guild includes its magazine, and it's in the March edition that you find details on that year's seminars. List several choices when you apply, as classes frequently fill early. When you receive your class assignment, you also get a list of supplies to bring, usually hoops and other standard needlework equipment. The magazine also gives information on the host hotel, and though you make lodging arrangements on your own, a group rate is offered. Meals, too, are your responsibility. Details of the seminars change from year to year, so it's wise to confirm them in advance. *Embroiderers' Guild of America, 335 W. Broadway, Suite 100, Louisville, KY 40202-4122, tel. 502/589-6956, fax 502/ 584-7900. Topics: embroidery, quilting. Sept. or Oct.: 4 days, tuition $280.*

NORTH CAROLINA Faux Finishing. Fe Fi Faux is the warehouselike shop of hus-

band-and-wife faux finishers Kevin and Cheryl Rutan, but about once a month it serves as the setting for four-day workshops in their craft. During eight-hour days, you learn all about faux finishes, from base coat to finish coat. After an introduction, which covers glaze formulas and choosing background colors, you spend the rest of the first and second days learning marble and stone finishes. Day three is dedicated to wood grains. Kevin teaches these classes and provides demonstrations of some more difficult methods, such as strié (a striped design), silk moiré, and linen look, while you practice basic techniques on high-gloss paper. On the fourth day, Kevin and Cheryl take you to a local home to put your newly acquired wall-glazing skills to the test. The group of 10 to 15 students works in two groups, applying a mottled, simulated suede finish and the cloudy, less-dense French brush.

The only thing you have to bring is clothes you don't mind getting dirty. Materials, handouts, and a box lunch with sandwich and salad are included. You are responsible for your accommodations, though many participants stay at two local hotels that offer special rates to Fe Fi Faux students. A camaraderie tends to develop, and chances are you and the rest of the group might spend some of your off hours together. Workshops have been attended by designers, house painters, homemakers, and retirees, from curious beginners to more advanced decorative painters who wish to improve their technique. *Fe Fi Faux, 337 S. Davie St., Greensboro, NC 27401, tel. 910/272-3289. Topic: decorative painting. Year-round: 4 days, tuition $400. Price includes lunch.*

NORTH CAROLINA John C. Campbell Folk School. Founded in 1925, the folk school is tucked away on 365 acres in a scenic valley in the southwestern tip of the state. The campus consists of 27 historic buildings, some built in a romantic European stone-and-wood style, others more typical of Appalachian farmhouses. Instructors are nationally recognized folk artists from all over the country. Many are from the local area, and some maintain their own studios nearby.

The list of workshops is voluminous. For example, there are 46 different basketry classes, which can teach you how to make baskets of native vine or white oak or a Shaker cat-head or traditional Cherokee basket. Similar variety is offered in fields from blacksmithing and book arts to weaving and woodworking, and there are even classes in broom making, felting, and kaleidoscopes, as well as noncrafts courses in dance, folklore, writing, gardening, music, and nature studies. Most of the workshops are a week long (from supper and orientation on Sunday to Saturday breakfast), but some span a weekend, a short week (ending at Friday lunch), or two weeks.

A typical day begins with Morningsong, an informal session of singing and discussions of local folklore and history. Then comes breakfast, followed by classes until lunch. Afternoon classes end at 4:30, when you can take part in an optional planned activity, such as a historical tour or a visit to a neighbor's home and workshop. Reflecting the regional cooking of southern Appalachia, the family-style dinner comes complete with memorable home-baked wheat bread. Afterward, you can continue to work on your project or, perhaps, visit a nearby artist's studio, attend a concert of Appalachian music, or drive to the Cherokee reservation (35 miles away). Whitewater kayaking and rafting are also popular diversions.

You can stay in a dorm room, which sleeps up to eight people and has a bathroom, or in a double room, with either private or shared bath. There's also a small 12-site campground with bathroom facilities, but board isn't included for campers. Meals can be purchased separately, however. Instructors keep track of the materials you use during your workshop, and you are billed for them on the last day of class. Many folk school courses are also available through Elderhostel, so if you're over 55, you may be able to register through that organization at a substantial savings. *John C. Campbell Folk School, Rte. 1, Box 14A, Brasstown, NC 28902-9603, tel. 704/837-2775 or 800/365-5724, fax 704/837-8637. Topics: basketry, beadwork, blacksmithing, book and paper arts, broom making, calligraphy, caning, ceramics/pottery, design/printing, doll making, dyeing, embroidery, enameling, felting, furniture making, glasswork, jewelry, knitting and crocheting, lace, metalwork, painting, photography, quilting, rug making, spinning, weaving, wood carving, wood turning. Year-round: 5–6 days, tuition $210–$232, room and board $178–$266, camping $40–$72. Camping price does not include meals.*

NORTH CAROLINA **Penland School of Crafts.** This artists' community, founded in 1929, is set on 450 wooded acres and nestled right up against the Blue Ridge Mountains of western North Carolina. Gifted visiting artists and resident teachers offer classes for all levels of experience (most classes are open to beginners) in all kinds of mediums: clay, fiber, glass, iron and other metals, paper, and wood. A sampling of recent courses includes Glass and Mixed Media, Hollow Construction in Metal, and Toolsmithing (ironwork). Most summer classes run two weeks, though a one- and a 2½-week session are held as well; fall and spring workshops are eight weeks. Because of the energy demands, glasswork classes are more expensive than the others.

The intensive program emphasizes hands-on learning, so most of your day is spent in the well-equipped studios in classes of 10–15. (Instructors may request that you bring certain items from home, such as old photos or collage materials, but most supplies are covered by a studio fee.) Should the muse strike, you can continue work into the evening, as studios are open and in use 24 hours a day. Or you can attend slide shows or dances, visit nearby studios, or take a walk in the beautiful countryside. An occasional volleyball game or, on a hot day, a refreshing dip in the North Toe River are just the ticket. Asheville, world-renowned for its late-19th-century mega-mansion Biltmore House, is only a few miles away along the scenic Blue Ridge Parkway.

On-campus housing—dorms, semiprivate rooms, and private rooms with bath—is modest and rustic, but this only adds to Penland's considerable charm. The dining room buffet features a wide variety of good food, including numerous vegetarian dishes, and the leisurely meals are a springboard to conversations that extend the learning experience. You can also choose to live and eat off campus at any of a number of B&Bs and hotels. *Penland School of Crafts, Penland, NC 28765-0037, tel. 704/765-2359, fax 704/765-7389. Topics: book and paper arts, ceramics, drawing, fiber arts, glasswork, metalwork, photography, printmaking, woodworking. Late May–early Sept.: 7–18 days, tuition $240–$740, room and board $200–$1,120.*

NORTH CAROLINA **Woodworking in the Appalachians.** On Drew and Louise Langsner's secluded mountain farmstead, not far from the Appalachian Trail and the Tennessee border, the expert craftspeople of Country Workshops have been teaching traditional woodworking with hand tools since 1978. Much of the work is done with a wood lathe, carving knives, drawknives, hewing axes, and hollowing adzes. Summer workshops focus on such varying techniques as spindle turning and 17th-century joinery and on such varying projects as end tables and boats. The best-known courses are in chair making (ladderbacks, Windsors, and Welsh stick Windsors) and carved Swedish woodenware (spoons and bowls), but there are also more exotic classes—lapstrake boat building, Japanese woodworking, and Swiss cooperage, practically a lost art. Workshop director Drew Langsner apprenticed to a master cooper (barrel maker) in Switzerland.

Instruction is given over either five days (Monday–Friday) or seven days (Sun-day–Saturday), and you arrive the afternoon before your workshop starts. Classes run from 9 to 6:30, though they end earlier on the last day. In most workshops, several evenings are devoted to slide shows and lecture-discussions. Bring work clothes and basic tools; specialized tools are provided, and an extra fee covers materials used. You can camp on the farm for free or stay in the dorm or guest cabin at an additional cost. (Bedding is provided in the guest cabin but not the dorm.) Louise loves to garden and cook and incorporates freshly harvested fruits and vegetables into three delicious meals daily. You can even arrange to stay for dinner after your workshop is over or through breakfast the following morning. Spouses and other guests are welcome for an extra charge.

Summer classes are composed of eight to 12 students, primarily men ages 25 to 70. All skill levels can be accommodated. Together you are practically sequestered, with nowhere nearby to go and nothing to see save the inspiring mountain views. Besides, after all that hewing and chopping, you don't have much energy for sightseeing.

In the winter, Drew offers five-day tutorials limited to two people. The subject matter is similar to that of summer workshops but is more customized. The comprehensive fee includes heated lodging and meals at the family table. There's also an annual volunteer week in May, during which friends of Country Workshop help make improvements to the shop and dorm facilities; there is no charge for the week. *Country Workshops, 90 Mill Creek Rd., Marshall, NC 28753-9321, tel. and fax 704/656-2280. Topics: basketry, boatbuilding, furniture making, wood carving, wood turning. Jan.–Apr.: 5 days, complete package $750. June–Aug.: 6–8 days, tuition and board $375–$525, housing $12–$20 per night, camping free.*

TENNESSEE **Appalachian Center for Crafts.** Five-day workshops in five areas—clay, fibers, glass, metals, and wood—are held at this middle Tennessee crafts center, which is part of Tennessee Tech. The variety within those areas is enormous. Clay includes hand building, wheel throwing, and raku; fiber courses range from papermaking and bookbinding to painting on silk. Glass comprises both hot (glassblowing and casting) and cold (stained glass and kaleidoscopes), and metal classes might find you in a blacksmith's forge or a jewelry studio. Within wood are furniture making and carving, but the emphasis is on wood turning.

Though weekend classes are available all year, the more in-depth, weekday workshops wait for summer, when the college is not in session. One set of courses is offered through Elderhostel (for information on them, see Sources in the Campus Vacations chapter). The other workshops are for teens on up to senior citizens. For these, you arrive on Sunday, and from 9 to 4 Monday through Friday you attend classes, which have 10 or 12 students and are taught predominantly by visiting craftspeople, some nationally and internationally known. The incredibly well-equipped studios stay open until 11, in case you want to work late, which is not uncommon. Most participants want to make at least one finished piece during their stay; in some fields, such as basketry and bookbinding, you can complete several.

If you want to do something other than work, you don't have to look far. Evenings frequently have slide lectures. The countryside around the beautiful 180-acre hillside center is full of waterfalls and caves, and tree tours, revealing such local species as papaw and ginseng, are conducted in the woods. The July 4th weekend brings the Smithville Jamboree, a celebration of bluegrass. On your way to the center, you may want to visit Knoxville, 140 miles to the east, or Nashville, 70 miles west and site of the nearest major airport.

While at the center, you stay in chalet-style cabins, which have clusters of double-occupancy bedrooms and shared baths. The air-conditioned lodgings come with linens. Meals are served cafeteria-style in a dining hall. Also on campus are a library and a supply store, where you can buy materials if you didn't bring them from home; only occasionally are supplies included in tuition. *Appalachian Center for Crafts, 1560 Craft Center Dr., Smithville, TN 37166, tel. 615/597–6801, fax 615/597–6803. Topics: basketry, beadwork, blacksmithing, book and paper arts, ceramics/pottery, dried floral arrangement, dyeing, fiber arts, furniture making, glasswork, jewelry, metalwork, quilting, weaving, wood carving, wood turning. May–July: 6 days, tuition $175–$200, room and board $180–$200.*

TENNESSEE **Arrowmont School of Arts and Crafts.** On 70 acres of wooded hillside just 3 miles from the entrance to Great Smoky Mountains National Park, Arrowmont sponsors more than 70 one- and two-week courses each summer, covering the gamut of arts and crafts disciplines. Typical workshop titles are Watercolor: An Approach to Creative Realism, Basics of Lost Wax Casting, Landscape Drawing in Pastels, Beading, Expressive Hand Embroidery on Painted Fabric, Woodturning–Carved Vessels, and the Pot Beyond the Wheel. The 75-member faculty comprises prominent visual artists and craftspeople. You can audit a class or, in some fields, receive undergraduate or graduate credit.

You and other adults of all ages and abilities are in class Monday through Friday from 9 to 11:30 and 1 to 4. Should you wish to work late, studios, as well as the resource center and gallery, remain open until midnight. Slide lectures and demonstrations, along with the recreational opportunities of the national park and the town of Gatlinburg, provide respite from the intensity of course work.

Living arrangements range from dorm-style cottages that accommodate 10 to 12 students to an air-conditioned building whose rooms have private baths. Prices vary accordingly, but all come with home-style cooking in a common dining area from Monday through Saturday breakfast. Lab fees are charged for expendable materials used in the studio, but you are encouraged to bring other supplies and tools from home. *Arrowmont School of Arts and Crafts, Box 567, Gatlinburg, TN 37738, tel. 423/436–5860, fax 423/430–4101. Topics: basketry, beadwork, ceramics/pottery, doll making, drawing, embroidery, enameling, fabrics, fiber arts, glasswork, jewelry, metal-work, painting, papermaking, photography, quilting, sculpture, stained glass, weaving, wood turning. Early June–mid-Aug.: 6–13 days, tuition $200 per wk, room and board $180–$410 per wk. 2-wk room and board price does not include all meals on the weekend.*

THE MIDWEST

OHIO **The Loom Shed School of Weaving.** If you're an absolute beginner looking to come to grips with the principles of basic weaving, an expert who wishes to brush up on Moorman technique, or just an amateur who weaves for fun, master weaver Charles Lermond will create a curriculum tailored to your needs. Founded by Lermond in 1980, the school, housed in what was once a slaughterhouse, is on the edge of Oberlin, a town 35 miles southwest of Cleveland that contains a liberal arts college and con-servatory of music.

There are no schedules here other than the ones set by Lermond and the students. Classes usually run from 9 to 5, but you are free to organize your day to suit your needs and habits. Beginners start on Monday morning in front of a pre-warped loom and then learn to warp a loom for their proj-ect—part of Lermond's belief in the need for getting people weaving before they learn the intricacies of the art. For the more advanced student, the course is designed to focus on a particular technique, such as warping and drafting, block switching, summer/winter, double weave, overshot, and computer-assisted draft analysis. The

instruction is project-oriented, so the goal is for you to leave at the end of the week with a finished piece.

Room and board are available for a maxi-mum of three nonsmoking students at the Lermond home, a couple of miles from the school. Other accommodations options, which the school can arrange for, include area B&Bs and motels. If you're staying in the Lermond house, meals are included in the price. *The Loom Shed School of Weav-ing, 14301 State Rte. 58, Oberlin, OH 44074, tel. 216/774–3500. Topic: weaving. Year-round: 5 days, tuition $200, room and board at Lermond home $125.*

WISCONSIN **The Clearing.** The Clearing, a series of rustic log and stone cabins, was built in the woods of Wisconsin's Door County in 1935 by Jens Jensen, a distin-guished landscape architect and contempo-rary of Frank Lloyd Wright. Today it plays host to sessions in music and drama; nature studies; philosophy, literature, and writing; and rest and relaxation in addition to arts and crafts. One-week courses are offered for all levels, ages 18 and over. In addition, there are a handful of three- and five-day minisessions as well as a four-day mini–folk art school, offered twice in October, which has a choice of courses, such as Carve and Paint a Songbird, Create a Crazy Quilt, and Whittle a Whirligig.

The group usually meets on Sunday evening for a get-acquainted supper. A 7:30 AM bell on Monday calls you to breakfast, after which classes begin for a full-day's work with a break for lunch at noon. Classes never have more than 20 students, and many have as few as five. The amount of instruction varies, depending on the class; some instructors offer lectures and demonstrations followed by full-time supervised instruction, while others pro-vide a morning demonstration and then allow the class to develop their projects individually, offering advice and critique. Of course, you are not confined to working during class hours alone; the studios are open until late evening. There are no art stores in the area, so you need to bring all of your own materials and equipment.

Use the evenings to relax. After dinner, served in the main lodge, you can read or play the piano. If it is warm enough, there's a marshmallow roast around a campfire, accompanied by the inevitable ghost stories. Accommodations are in stone and log cabins at the center, where you have a choice of a bed in a three- or six-bed dormitory, or a hotel-style room in which you must share with one other person.

Door County, a spit of land that sticks out from Green Bay into Lake Michigan, is Wisconsin's premier vacation spot if you like to sail, fish, camp, hike, or cycle. There's swimming, too, if you can stand cold water. It's a rustic area composed of small colonies of gray-shingled and white-clapboard summer houses in picturesque towns, with names like Fish Creek and Egg Harbor. The Clearing is within a brisk walk of the Door County Maritime Museum and a short drive from Chief Oshkosh Indian Museum, the Pioneer School Museum, and the ferry to Washington Island and Rock Island State Park. *The Clearing, Box 65, Ellison Bay, WI 54210, tel. 414/854–4088, fax 414/854–9751. Topics: embroidery, jewelry, painting, photography, quilting, rug making, stained glass, weaving, wood carving. May–Oct.: 7 days, complete package $506–$549. Price does not include 1 dinner.*

WISCONSIN **Dillman's Sand Lake Lodge.** On a 250-acre peninsula on White Sand Lake in northern Wisconsin, Dillman's Lodge, built in 1935, is a family-owned and -run, family-oriented resort complex of rustic lakefront lodges and cabins. More than 30 one- to six-day visual arts workshops are offered from May to October each year. Most run for five days and are open to all levels, with a few geared to the intermediate or advanced student. Instructors are all well-known professional artists and craftspeople.

All classes run from 9 to 5, with a one-hour break for lunch. Mornings usually include a demonstration or a lecture, depending on the individual instructor. Some teachers give an afternoon lecture or a critique; others prefer to let the participants pursue their individual projects with relatively little interference. The average class size is 15, with one instructor per class.

The studios are open 24 hours a day, so you can work into the night if you want to, but there's plenty to do each day: tennis, trout fishing, waterskiing, horseshoes, or hiking on hunting trails used by the Lac du Flambeau Indians hundreds of years ago. There are also several golf courses within a short drive. In the mornings, children meet in the Round House for games and activities, leaving parents free to attend workshops or participate in sporting activities. In the evenings there are classic movies in the Round House or a Native American pow-wow in nearby Lac du Flambeau. Most classes reserve one night for a slide show of artists' work—including your own.

Dillman's has three lodging options: You can stay in the family-oriented log cabin, the motel-style annex, or the North Shore condo units, added to the grounds in 1992. A breakfast plan can be purchased, and you can sign up each morning for a box lunch of sandwiches, salad, and fruit.

A series of miniworkshops on Wednesday mornings focuses on local lore and craft. Students of all ages—sometimes including parents, grandparents, and grandchildren—gather for two hours to create (and finish) a project like cattail mats, masks, and twisted baskets, using grasses and twigs. *Dillman's Sand Lake Lodge, Box 98, Lac du Flambeau, WI 54538, tel. 715/588–3143 or 715/588–3110. Topics: birch bark crafts, calligraphy, intaglio carving on gems and glass, painting, quilting, wood carving, woven boxes. May–Oct.: 5 days, tuition and housing $515–$725. Price does not include meals.*

WISCONSIN **Sievers School of Fiber Arts.** Sievers School of Fiber Arts occupies the refurbished Jackson Harbor School on remote Washington Island in Lake Michigan. Established in 1979 as a natural outgrowth of a successful mail-order loom design and kit business, the school now offers more than 60 classes each year in fiber-related subjects: weaving, spinning, dyeing, quilting, papermaking, and basketry. Many classes are geared toward beginners, although every year several are designed for more advanced students. Two-, five-, and seven-day classes, of between 8 and 10 students and one instructor, are held from May through October. The 30-member faculty is made up of fiber artists who teach at crafts schools or are in a related business.

After a day of workshops, students retire to a 90-year-old landmark building, with hand-hewn beams and exposed lumber construction, that serves as Sievers School's dormitory. The sleeping area has bunk beds and portable, curtained room dividers. There are complete kitchen facilities with all cooking and eating equipment and utensils needed for meals. The dormitory is for women only; male students have to take lodgings in one of the nearby resorts, B&Bs, motels, or campgrounds (a list of area accommodations is provided when you register).

Washington Island (population 650) is reached by a 30-minute car ferry over a narrow strait originally called "Door to Death" by the Indians because of its treacherous currents. The island has a riding stable, tennis courts, three historical museums, and several beautiful beaches. On Sunday in the summer, you can attend a baseball game with teams from Door County, and the centrally located Red Barn hosts evening music and theater productions. There is also a yarn and book shop with handmade items by instructors and students. *Sievers School of Fiber Arts, Jackson Harbor Rd., Washington Island, WI 54246, tel. 414/847–2264, fax 414/847–2676. Topics: basketry, beadwork, dyeing, felting, knitting, papermaking, quilting, rug making, sewing, spinning, surface design,* *weaving, wood carving. Mid-May–late Oct.: 2 days, tuition $125, housing $45; 5 days, tuition $225, housing $105; 7 days, tuition $330, housing $148.*

THE SOUTHWEST

ARIZONA **Book Arts in Bisbee.** Near the Mexican border, 1½ hours from Tucson, and just down the road from Tombstone, is Bisbee, a colorful cross-cultural town where you can read the history of the old West in the ornate facades of turn-of-the-century buildings or hear it firsthand from veterans of copper-mining days. Bisbee is jammed with antiques, boutiques, quaint inns, galleries, and live theater. It is here in this southeastern Arizona community that Pat Baldwin, owner of Waterleaf Mill & Bindery and Pequeño Press, gives private workshops in the book arts to adults, regardless of experience. Materials are provided.

Pat works with you one-on-one in four-hour afternoons—four days in bookbinding or five (weekdays) in hand papermaking or book production. Two intensive days of marbling instruction are also offered. During mornings and evenings, you can explore the area's many attractions, and Pat is happy to advise you on sightseeing and transportation. She can even make arrangements with one of the charming and reasonably priced lodgings nearby. *Waterleaf Mill & Bindery, Box 1711, Bisbee, AZ 85603, tel. 520/432–5924, fax 520/432–3065. Topics: bookbinding, papermaking. Year-round: 4–5 days, tuition $100–$185.*

ARIZONA **Fiber Arts in Bisbee.** In the southeast corner of Arizona, the southwest corner of the United States, Joan Ruane runs the appropriately named Southwest Corner, a retreat center that offers customized workshops in fiber arts. Most of what Joan teaches is spinning and weaving, but you can also study beading, basketry, quilting, papermaking, and related arts given by other local instructors.

This quaint, historical, mile-high mining town is a perfect setting for the retreats. Bisbee is noted for its many fine artists, and its climate is exceptional year-round. Delightful B&Bs and well-equipped art studios foster relaxed learning experiences.

Joan has been teaching spinning and weaving for over 20 and 14 years, respectively, and she's offered fiber arts classes in Bisbee for six. Her staff is made up of local and regional professional artists with expertise in their field. Classes are geared for all levels. Since equipment and supplies are made available, all you need is enthusiasm and a desire to learn.

Workshops are tailored to suit, based on medium, skill level, and number attending. Place and time are worked out for students' convenience but range from one hour of instruction ($20 an hour or $75 per day) to a five-day package that includes instruction, lodging, meals, and sightseeing, including a mine tour.

Bisbee is 90 miles southeast of the Tucson International Airport and 45 miles from Benson, where there's an Amtrak station. Bus service is available to and from Bisbee daily. *Southwest Corner, Box 418, Bisbee, AZ 85603, tel. 520/432–3603 or 800/879–8412. Topics: basketry, beadwork, bookbinding, knitting, papermaking, quilting, spinning, weaving. Year-round: 5 days, complete package $850 (25% discount for each additional person taking same workshop).*

ARIZONA **Spin 'N Weave.** In a classroom attached to a shop that sells wool, spinning wheels, and looms, a whole variety of fiber workshops are given, but the emphasis is on weaving. One- to five-day classes, taught by instructors from Tucson and beyond, range from clothing design to rug weaving. Weekend courses might cover silk painting, dyeing, tapestry, or marbling, while other topics—knitting, crocheting, and spinning, to name a few—are taught a day each week for several weeks. If you want to immerse yourself in fiber arts, you can stay a few weeks and take a number of these classes. A special murder mystery weekend combines a mystery dinner and movie with classes, including the appropriately titled "Dying for Color." In April a needle arts festival is held. For even shorter forays, there are workshops that last for just a few hours or a half-day.

Though courses are scheduled year-round, the most pleasant time to come is from fall to spring, when Tucson is not scorchingly hot. Classes are given from 9 to 4 with a break for lunch. You can continue to work after hours as long as the shop is open or the instructor stays. If you haven't finished your project when the workshop is over, you can use the facilities until it's completed. Some materials are furnished, but others you must purchase. You may use Spin 'N Weave's looms or bring your own. For accommodations, there are local B&Bs and motels; recommendations are provided. *Spin 'N Weave, 2801 W. Ina Rd., Tucson, AZ 85741, tel. and fax 520/797–6535 or 800/579–0059. Topics: basketry, beadwork, calligraphy, clay sculpture, decorative painting, dyeing, embroidery, floral arrangement, knitting and crocheting, papermaking, quilting, sewing, spinning, surface design, weaving. Year-round: 1–5 days, tuition $10–$500.*

NEVADA **Tuscarora School of Pottery.** Dennis Parks, a well-known and widely exhibited potter, chose this nearly deserted old mining town (population 20) as the site of his pottery school in 1966 because of its quiet and isolation. At 6,400 feet, it sits under clear skies, perched on the side of Mount Blitzen in the high desert of northern Nevada. Summer workshops, geared to adults from advanced beginners to professionals, are taught by Dennis along with his son Ben and other distinguished visiting artists. Different aspects of earthenware, stoneware, and porcelain, both wheel-thrown and hand-built, are covered. Work is glazed raw and single fired in kilns fueled by diesel and used crankcase oil. If you're interested, you can experiment with local materials, such as native rocks, exotic earths, and sagebrush ash. Kick wheels are provided, but you are welcome to bring an electric wheel if you wish.

The summer program consists of four two-week sessions, and you may attend from one to all four. Due to its popularity, however, there are often waiting lists, and priority is given to students staying four weeks or more. Arrive the day before your session. You can arrange to be picked up in Elko (50 miles away), the nearest town with air and bus service and site of the original Cowboy Poetry Gathering.

The workshops at Tuscarora are a little less structured than at many other pottery schools. Classes consist of dialogue and demonstration rather than lecture, and instructors are always ready to provide individualized attention. The well-equipped studios are open 24 hours a day. In your spare time, you can have fun fishing, cycling, backpacking, or hiking in the surrounding countryside—sagebrush-covered hillsides, grassy valleys, and canyons with cottonwood and aspen. The area is dotted with lupine, sego lily, and Indian paintbrush and inhabited by fauna from chipmunks to coyote, orioles to eagles.

An easy camaraderie comes from working and living together in relative isolation. You are housed in "the Hotel," a rustic 19th-century building that once served as a boardinghouse for gold-panning miners. You and the other students help with chores, and Dennis's wife, Julie, cooks hearty meals that are made with vegetables from the garden and served in the lace-curtained dining room. The fee covers room and board, instruction, glazing, and firing; the only thing you pay extra for is clay. *Tuscarora Pottery School, Box 7, Tuscarora, NV 89834, tel. and fax 702/756–6598. Topic: ceramics/pottery. Mid-June–mid-Aug.: 14 days, complete package $790; 28 days, complete package $1,420.*

NEW MEXICO **Fabrile Workshops.** About three times annually, the artists of Fabrile

Studio offer five-day workshops for six to eight students, and though the dates and sites may change from year to year, the subject matter remains the same: hand papermaking. Coralie Silvey Jones is an artist who uses handmade paper in most of her work, in addition to owning and operating Sage Papers and Printers along with her husband. Her courses explore different papermaking processes as well as a brief history of the craft.

Workshops run Monday through Friday from 9 to 5 with a break for lunch. Lectures, like the work itself, are interwoven into the fabric of the day. Most equipment and materials are provided, but part of your time might be spent building your own mould and deckle.

What to do after hours is up to you, and Taos certainly offers many options. Though room and board are not furnished, a list of suggested local lodgings is. *Fabrile Studio, Box 1551, Taos, NM 87571, tel. 505/751–0306, fax 505/758–3086. Topic: papermaking. May–Oct.: 5 days, tuition $300–$350.*

NEW MEXICO **Taos Institute of Art.** The 60 courses the institute offers each year cover topics from gold- and silversmithing to writing pearly prose, but the focus of each is the uniqueness of northern New Mexico, especially its multicultural diversity as reflected in Native American and Hispanic arts. Favorites include Navajo weaving and pueblo pottery. Nationally recognized, professional artists provide multilevel teaching, accommodating the beginner on up to the advanced. You and 5 to 11 others spend 40 hours, Monday through Friday, not in classrooms but in the artist's own studio or in the field. Most courses can be taken for advanced undergraduate or graduate credit.

Tuition includes most materials, though occasional fees are added to cover expensive items like precious metals. You are responsible for making your own housing and dining arrangements; however, the institute distributes a 10-page guide to local lodgings that would do a chamber of commerce proud. Though most courses run a week, a few two- and three-day classes are held. Plans are under way to offer some courses in late fall, winter, and spring. *Taos Institute of Art, Box 5280 NDCBU, Taos, NM 87571, tel. and fax 505/758–2793. Topics: basketry, beadwork, ceramics/pottery, jewelry, painting, photography, weaving. Late June–early Oct.: 5 days, tuition $300–$400.*

▬▬▬ NEW MEXICO ▬▬▬ **Turley Forge Blacksmithing School.** Founded in 1970, Turley Forge is the granddaddy of blacksmithing schools. Master blacksmith Frank Turley came to blacksmithing through the back door—as a farrier. After shoeing horses full-time for several years, he became more interested in architectural ironwork, builders' hardware, and tool-smithing. Now five times a year he teaches three-week courses—with instruction five days per week—in traditional blacksmithing techniques, but not horse-shoeing.

Enrollment is limited to six students, who work at their own forge and anvil. Essential smithing techniques developed are drawing, upsetting, twisting, bending, forge welding, forge brazing, striking with sledge, and power hammer use. Early on you make a fire rake and shovel, which you use during the course, and move on to steel tools, hinges, and scrollwork. About half your time is spent in lab and half in demonstration and lecture. Tools and materials are furnished.

The forge is approximately 5 miles west of the center of Santa Fe, which, at 7,000 feet, is cool in spring and fall and bright and cold in winter, when it snows intermittently. Most students stay in local apartments or motels with kitchenettes. Though you make arrangements for your own housing, a list of reasonably priced lodgings as well as campgrounds in the nearby mountain ranges is furnished. *Turley Forge Blacksmithing School, Rte. 10, Box 88C, Santa Fe, NM 87501, tel. 505/471–8608.*

Topic: blacksmithing. Early Feb.–late May and early Sept.–early Nov.: 15 days, tuition $1,800.

▬▬▬ TEXAS ▬▬▬ **Southwest Craft Center.** The Southwest Craft Center is located on the grounds of the old Ursuline Academy and Convent, built as a girls' school in 1848. The secluded parklike grounds are situated on the scenic River Walk, nestled in among the skyscrapers of downtown San Antonio.

In addition to ongoing courses, the center offers one- to four-day workshops, Thursday through Sunday, in its autumn and spring sessions. Almost all the workshops, which have maximums of 6 to 15 students, are hands-on, and each usually has a corresponding slide lecture, which is free and open to the public. You work in the studio from 10 to 4. Well-known visiting artists from around the country teach approximately a dozen workshops each session in the center's six media studios: ceramics, fibers, metals, papermaking, photography, and surface design.

Also on campus are an exhibition gallery and contemporary crafts gallery, open Monday through Saturday. A delicious lunch is served weekdays at the center's Copper Kitchen, amid an exhibition of handmade quilts by the San Antonio Quilt Guild. Hospitality, information, and refreshments are dispensed weekdays at the Garden Room, from which volunteers lead tours of the center's historic buildings and grounds.

You can also take advantage of the pleasures of the River Walk and surrounding San Antonio. The center readily gives suggestions of places to stay within walking distance, many of which offer discounted group rates, as well as places to dine. A varying lab fee covers facility use and some materials. *Southwest Craft Center, 300 Augusta St., San Antonio, TX 78205-1296, tel. 210/224–1848, fax 210/224–9337. Topics: beadwork, bookbinding, ceramics/pottery, drawing, fiber arts, jewelry, metalwork, papermaking, photography, surface design. Sept.–Apr.: 1–4 days, tuition $125–$150.*

THE ROCKIES

COLORADO **Anderson Ranch.** In 1966, the developers of Snowmass Village invited ceramist Paul Soldner to choose one of seven ranches in the valley for an art center. He chose the Anderson family's sheep ranch for the wonderful view it commands from the head of the valley and for its rustic old log barns and ranch house. On the present-day ranch, renovated log cabins and barns have been joined by new buildings that were designed in keeping with the historical setting.

More than 100 summer workshops are taught annually by respected professional artists from all around the country. Typical courses include basic woodworking, faux and painted finishes, classic European carving, clay construction, Japanese woodblocks, and mixed mediums. Numerous classes and even field expeditions are offered in painting, drawing, and photography as well. Workshop size ranges from 12 to 18 participants, and the skill level required varies from beginner to advanced. Many classes are open to all. Usually there's an equal number of men and women. Scholarships are available.

Sessions run one or two weeks, from Sunday to Saturday, and classes themselves are Monday through Friday from 9 to 5. On evenings and weekends, you can continue to work (studios are open 24 hours), or you can attend demonstrations or slide lectures by visiting faculty. Snowmass Village is just west of Aspen, which hosts the Aspen Music Festival, Dance Aspen, and the International Design Conference. World-class restaurants, art galleries, and repertory theater companies abound. There is also hiking, cycling, mountain biking, and fishing.

Accommodations at the ranch are in a dormitory, and the room-and-board fee includes meals in the cafeteria-style communal dining hall. If you wish, you can make arrangements, through the ranch or on your own, to stay at other nearby lodgings, including condominiums with kitchen facilities. If you do live elsewhere but would like to eat at the ranch, you can purchase a weekly meal ticket.

In addition to the regular workshops, open to adults 18 and over, there's an extensive children's program for two age groups, 6 to 8 and 9 to 12. Limited to 14 kids per class, these one- and two-week courses are held mornings or afternoons and range from weaving and mask making to a study of Native American crafts. Unlike the adult workshops, they include materials. *Anderson Ranch Arts Center, Box 5598, Snowmass Village, CO 81615, tel. 970/923–3181, fax 970/923–3871. Topics: book arts, ceramics/pottery, creative studies, digital imaging, drawing, furniture design, painting, photography, printmaking, sculpture, woodworking, writing. June–Aug.: 7–14 days, tuition $400–$650, room and board $325 per wk.*

UTAH **Rocky Mountain USA Faux Finishing Workshops.** Chuck James, who does faux finishing professionally when he isn't teaching, holds a five-day, 40-hour workshop in a different city each month. Chicago, Detroit, Los Angeles, Miami, New York, Philadelphia, and Washington, D.C., are typical locations, and once a year, the site is Salt Lake City, Rocky Mountain USA's home base. Call for a schedule to see if a workshop is being given in a place you'd like to visit.

Designed to teach all aspects of faux finishing—graining, gilding, marbling, wall glazing, and stencil work—workshops are set up for people with a basic understanding of color theory and painting but are open to everyone. Class size, which averages 15, is limited to 24, and the student-to-instructor ratio is eight to one. Each day is filled with instruction and hands-on practice, and by the time the workshop is over, you will have completed 20 to 24 sample boards, each an example of a faux-finishing technique. All materials are included in tuition.

A catered lunch is served, but other than that you're on your own to eat and enjoy the sights of the city however you wish. A list of accommodations close to the workshop site is provided. The cost of tuition is lower for more than one participant signing up together. *Rocky Mountain USA, 5390 S. Cottonwood La., Salt Lake City, UT 84117, tel. 801/277–8097 or 800/527–9284, fax 801/272–0685. Topic: decorative painting. Year-round: 5 days, tuition $795. Price includes lunch.*

THE WEST COAST

CALIFORNIA **American School of Japanese Arts.** The San Francisco Zen Center at Green Gulch Farm in Muir Beach is the serene setting of the unique, 10-day Japanese Arts Seminar and has been every summer since 1987. Modeled after the Oomoto School of Traditional Japanese Arts in Kyoto, the seminar gives 20 to 25 students the unique opportunity to learn traditional tea ceremony, calligraphy, *kyogen* (comic theater), and *shintaido* (sword movement). Each is covered for one-and-a-half hours daily, complemented by demonstrations in flower arrangement and tea-bowl pottery—you make the tea bowls used in the final tea ceremony. The four instructors are all well versed in the history and teachings of Japan, but their Western backgrounds smoothly bridge the gap between the two cultures. Evening lectures given by the instructors on such topics as Japanese clothing, printmaking, and woodblock prints provide you with a well-rounded look at the traditions of Japan. To get you in the mood for a Zenful experience, you wear traditional Japanese clothing—so leave the suit at home.

The 100-acre Green Gulch Farm is in a valley 25 minutes outside of San Francisco. The full-time monastery is a practicing Zen community, but it opens its doors as a community center year-round. There's a traditional Japanese-style teahouse on the grounds, along with a facility, built using traditional Japanese joinery (no nails), where you sleep in either single or double rooms. Vegetarian meals are prepared using homegrown produce. In your free time, which isn't too often, a five-minute walk gets you onto the beach, and you can hike in the hills around the center. *The American School of Japanese Arts, 2000 Los Olivos Rd., Santa Rosa, CA 95404, tel. 707/578–8014, fax 707/537–9508. Topic: Japanese arts. Late July–early Aug.: 10 days, complete package $1,250. Price includes supplies, equipment, and traditional Japanese clothes.*

CALIFORNIA **The Fabric Carr Sewing Camp.** In 1981, Roberta Carr, realizing that 40% of all stitchers live in California, established the Fabric Carr Couture Sewing Camp in her private studio in the hills of San Jose. To guarantee personal attention and an informal atmosphere, Ms. Carr, producer of nine videos on couture techniques, has limited the weeklong classes to five students, all of whom must at least know how to read a pattern and run a sewing machine.

There are 12 sessions per year, each highlighting a different theme, among them tailoring, casual couture, drafting patterns, and perfection of couture. In addition, there is a week called "Art to Wear," where you learn how sewing can be useful as an art form, as well as a professional week, limited to those in the business of making or repairing clothes. In the morning, you attend a three-hour lecture that presents the techniques you work with in the afternoon's four-hour master class. The week's work emphasizes technique, and you may leave with 50 new ones under your belt. Rather than having you work to finish one specific project, Ms. Carr wants you to master the different techniques demonstrated by working with you on a number of projects. The evenings are unstructured and you are free to continue your work or to relax your hands and minds in any way you choose.

Ms. Carr not only takes care of your sewing for the week, she also takes care of you. You are made to feel at home from day one, which begins with cocktails and dinner. From then on in it's three gourmet meals a day, with the exception of a night out at the San Jose Country Club. There's maid service at Ms. Carr's New Orleans–style home, where wrought-iron balconies and decks overlook the Santa Clara valley. You sleep two to a room and have full run of the house, which you may not want to leave when the week is up. *The Fabric Carr Sewing Camp, Box 32120, San Jose, CA 95152, tel. 408/929–1651, fax 408/259–8012. Topic: sewing. Year-round: 7 days, complete package $1,450. Price includes materials and equipment.*

CALIFORNIA Quilt Camp Shaver Lake. Don't let the name fool you—it's not all quilting at the Quilt Camp, established in 1977. In fact, the emphasis here is on surface design and new techniques for fabric design. There are three six-day seminars covering a wide range of topics such as silk-screen painting, photo emulsion silk screen, and printing through copy machines and faxes. Each year, two additional classes are offered, such as Polaroid transfer, discharge dyeing, or cyanotype (blue printing).

Quilt maker and author Jean Ray Laury is director, assisted by Susan Macy, an instructor at CSU–Fresno. Their hands-on workshops are offered to no more than 30 students of all levels each week. Open studio time enables students to pursue their own direction in fabric design, clothing, or quilts. Evenings are set aside for slide shows, lectures, viewing one another's work, working, and socializing. You're asked to bring your own fabrics for any specific projects you may have in mind.

The camp is held in a large, well-lit studio at the community center of Shaver Lake, a resort town 5,000 feet above sea level in the High Sierra range one hour outside Fresno. As this is a ski area, the town isn't crowded

during the summer, so you have a variety of housing options. The camp will rent a room or bed for you in a chalet that sleeps two to four or a cabin that sleeps five to eight and tack it onto the price for the week, or you can fend for yourself and either camp or rent on your own—good if you want to bring your family along to enjoy the scenery. Healthy buffet-style meals are cooked by the house chef, except for the two nights that dinner isn't served; filling the gap are a number of small restaurants scattered around the town. Basic supplies and equipment are included.

The High Sierras provide the perfect place for backpacking. Just make sure you bring along your needle and thread in case you get inspired by the view. *The Quilt Camp, c/o Jean Ray Laury, 19425 Tollhouse Rd., Clovis, CA 93611, tel. and fax 209/297–0228. Topics: fabric design, quilting, sewing, silk-screening, surface design. July–Aug.: 6 days, complete package $350–$550. Price does not include 2 meals and fabric.*

OREGON The Creative Arts at Menucha. Every August since 1966, the Creative Arts Community has held two weeks of residential workshops, inviting students and artists of all skill levels to learn about such subjects as furniture, sculpture, ceramics, the art of jewelry, paper sculpture, and printmaking. There are 14 workshops to choose from in all, seven each week. Since instructors change each week, you can choose to study the same subject from two different angles by enrolling for two sessions.

Workshops run from 9 to 4, Monday through Friday, but studios are open 24 hours a day. The instructors are mostly local artists and professors, and with classes kept small—only 8 to 10 students— they are able to give you a lot of attention. At night the instructors present their works in slide shows or give lecture demonstrations, and on Friday night they guide you on a studio tour through the many different art forms covered here. A gallery of works is also on site.

Menucha is the former estate of the Meiers, a prominent local family, and its heritage still shows even though it was converted into a conference center in 1950. Just 20 minutes east of Portland, the setting is rural, and facilities include jogging trails, tennis courts, an outdoor swimming pool, and meditative gardens, as well as a fantastic view of the Columbia River Gorge. Both students and instructors sleep in the dormitory rooms, but there are a few private rooms for couples and families. The home-style fare is heavy on homemade breads and fresh vegetables, and lean on meat. Upon applying, you will be given a list of supplies you will need to bring with you for your particular course; some additional supply fees may be charged. *The Creative Arts Community, Box 4958, Portland, OR 97208, tel. 503/760–5837 or 503/236–4109. Topics: ceramics, drawing, jewelry, painting, sculpture, writing. Aug.: 6 days, complete package $475; 13 days, complete package $875.*

WASHINGTON **Pilchuck Glass School.** The well-respected Pilchuck Glass School has conducted rigorous glassblowing programs every summer since 1971, in which both novice and advanced glassblowers come together to learn design techniques from the very best. In the five intensive 18-day sessions each summer, leading art-world figures and European master craftsmen explain in detail hot glass sculpture, fusing, casting, flame working, neon, mosaic, engraving, cutting, and enameling, to name a few. You pick one of the five different classes offered in each session. Some classes are juried, requiring you to submit slide samples for admittance, but the majority can be taken by anyone with a serious curiosity, with or without glass-working experience.

Studios have state-of-the-art equipment, and all forms of hand tools are provided; the school store sells the books, special tools,

glass, and other supplies. Sessions are limited to 50 students, and there's plenty of one-on-one instruction from the 50 faculty members, resident artists, and staff. You attend lectures and demonstrations throughout the day and evening according to your instructor's schedule, and nightly programs, such as slide shows, panels, critiques, and readings are presented by a faculty or staff member. As this is a highly intensive program, it is not uncommon to be working well into the night on various projects. Class is not held on Sunday, but the studios and library are open for students who wish to work independently.

In the middle of a 15,000-acre tree farm one hour north of Seattle, students sleep two to a room in cottages and dormitories that sit on the hillside meadows overlooking Puget Sound. The homey three-story Pilchuck Lodge houses an extensive reference library, a gallery where student and faculty works are displayed, and a gathering place where you dine on three buffet meals prepared daily by the kitchen staff. Every studio on campus comes equipped with a beer-filled refrigerator for those long, late hours you spend blowing glass and making glass sculpture. Though there is little free time to explore the surrounding wilderness or drive into Seattle for some alternative fun, you might not want to stray from the campus and all of its charm anyway. *Pilchuck Glass School, 1201 316th St. NW, Stanwood, WA 98292, tel. 206/445–3111 (mid-May–early Sept.), fax 360/445–5515; 315 2nd Ave. S, Suite 200, Seattle, WA 98104, tel. 206/621–8422 (mid-Sept.–early May), fax 206/621–0713. Topic: glasswork. May–early Sept.: 18 days, complete package $1,900–$2,825.*

SOURCES

ORGANIZATIONS Every state and many cities have arts councils that can lead you in the direction of arts and crafts workshops.

BOOKS The *Guide to Arts & Crafts Workshops,* published by Shaw Guides, covers arts and crafts workshops, travel programs, residencies, and retreats throughout the United States, giving program descriptions and other helpful information.

ALSO SEE If taking a workshop or just reading about one has sparked your interest, and you'd like to try your creative hand at other crafts, *see* the Painting Workshops and Photography Workshops and Tours chapters. For a different angle on folk arts, *see* the Music Programs chapter.

Birding

Written by Paul M. Konrad

Updated by Andrea E. Lehman

atching a profusion of migrants alight for a stop on one of their immense biannual journeys. Rising before the horizon even hints that the sun is on its way to see birds that go into hiding after dawn. Listening for birdsong as night settles on branches around you. Hiking through spectacular mountain, coastal, forest, desert, or wetland scenery (choose one or more) in search of that rare and elusive species or some dramatic avian spectacle. These are the wonders attracting people of all ages and all walks of life to birding tours. The common bond is an interest in birds and a broader love of nature.

You can set off bird-watching on your own just about anywhere, but a guided group tour provides an opportunity to benefit from the experience of group leaders and other birders, explore an area you are not familiar with, and let someone else take care of the nonbirding aspects of the trip. There are three major U.S. bird tour operators described below, and some nature-tour packagers also cater to birders. Tours cover every region of the country, but most flock to renowned birding hot spots in such states as Alaska and Texas. Outfitters plan the itinerary, arrange lodging and usually meals, provide the transportation, and employ one or more professional guides who know local bird life.

There are three points to consider when planning a birding trip: when to go, what to see, and where to see it. Not surprisingly, these issues are all connected, because certain species tend to be in certain parts of the country at certain times of the year.

On some tours you concentrate on a given area and stay fairly close to it, perhaps even lodging in the same hotel the entire time. More commonly, however, tours move to different locations every few days or even daily, sometimes traveling great distances, covering vastly different terrain, changing hotels along the way. Travel time is usually arranged so that it does not interfere with prime birding hours, and occasionally you'll spend much of a day in transit.

Though daily activities may vary—some trips take time for mammals, other natural wonders, or sites of cultural or historic interest—most concentrate on hard-core birding. You may pass much or all of a day visiting every inch of a wildlife refuge or bird sanctuary at a leisurely pace, or you may pop in and out of the van for short stints at a number of birding spots. Nearly every tour has some predawn or after-dark birding, but often these excursions are optional, unless the group does not plan to return to the hotel for breakfast before going back into the field. Since tours usually stay far from commercial development, the only nightlife you're likely to encounter is owls.

Professional ornithologist and editor of WildBird *magazine, Paul M. Konrad lives, works, and birds in southern California. New Jersey resident Andrea Lehman spent much of her childhood following her brother around on birding expeditions; 20 years later, the mating call of the sage grouse still echoes in her ears.*

Tours generally run from 5 to 14 days, with most going to readily accessible areas. Though terrain varies, the walking and hiking involved is usually comfortable for young and old alike, as long as you're in relatively sound physical shape. Since noise levels in the field need to be kept low, tours tend to exclude children under 14.

Costs range from $100 to almost $300 per day, but none of these tours is luxurious. You spend most nights at moderately priced hotels and motels, eating in modest restaurants for breakfast and dinner (many with intriguing local fare), and often helping to prepare your own picnic lunch. Yet the rewards of these trips go far beyond creature comforts or even new additions to your life list. If your interest is genuine, there are beautiful and bountiful experiences to be had.

CHOOSING THE RIGHT TOUR

Because there are so many birding tours to choose from, when you are trying to pick one, it is best to ask plenty of questions. Start with these.

What birds do you aim to see on this trip? Tours are often planned around particular species, although on most tours, the leader will happily stop for a look at any interesting birds that you come across. Very few tours focus on one bird and exclude all others, and very few have you indiscriminately chasing after any bird you see. Ideally you want a tour that is focused but flexible.

How long has the company been in business? As a general rule, stick with an outfit that has been around for several years. Not to insult newcomers, but companies with a few years behind them have already addressed the questions and challenges that you are likely to present to it.

How long has the company conducted this tour? If the company has not done this tour before, scrutinize the credentials of the designated tour leader all the more carefully.

What are the guide's qualifications? A birding guide might be a professional ornithologist or a very knowledgeable local birder, but whatever his or her professional training, the guide should be well-informed about the ecology of the area you are visiting and the birds you are seeking out. It also helps if the guide is personable and knows enough about the area to lead you to the best places to eat.

What's the cost and what's included? Most operators include lodging and meals in the price of tours, but some exclude food. Unless otherwise noted, prices listed in this chapter are per person and include double-occupancy lodging and meals. You must room with another birder or pay a single supplement for a private room. Transportation between birding destinations once the tour is under way and other en-route expenses, such as park entrance fees, are included in the price.

What are the accommodations like? Because what most birders want from a lodging are clean sheets, a comfortable bed, and plenty of hot water, most tours use reliable national chain hotels and motels or comparable local establishments that are clean and comfortable but not fancy. Sometimes, however, tours go to areas where there are more interesting inns and bed-and-breakfasts. In national parks, often the only accommodations are in somewhat nicer lodges and cabins with charm and character.

Will laundry service be available? If your trip of choice is in a hot, humid climate or involves slogging through mud, the availability of laundry service will help you cut down on what you pack.

What is the food like? No tour operator provides gourmet dining, but most try to find local restaurants that serve good food, including regional dishes that you will not find at home. Many operators arrange for picnics, sometimes quite tasty, so that you do not have to leave your birding spot at midday.

What kind of transportation is used? Most companies use 15-passenger vans, which tend to carry about 10 birders plus their luggage and the driver in relative comfort. Since you spend quite a bit of time in the van, make sure you do not have to share it with too many people. Some small buses are also used.

How long are the days and how difficult is the hiking? The amount of daily walking varies from tour to tour just as the definitions of easy and strenuous vary from individual to individual. Generally, however, the pace is moderate enough to be comfortable for those in good health. On trips with more than one leader, you might be split up into faster and slower groups. On some trips, walks will last up to four hours, whereas others might require nothing longer than a stroll. Uneven or wet terrain and high altitudes are not unusual, which might be stressful for some birders. Count on occasional early risings—and corresponding early turn-ins. Some tours allow for midday breaks, especially in heat, while others plow right through.

How far in advance do I need to book? Most outfitters ask that people reserve several months in advance at least; you may, however, want to book earlier to make sure you are not left out of popular tours. Signing up early for less popular trips can help ensure that they actually run; it can happen that tours that are under enrolled about two months prior to departure get canceled.

Do you have references from past guests? It is often helpful to talk with someone who has already taken a trip with the outfitter you are considering. That person can supply an unbiased view.

MAJOR PLAYERS

The following big three tour companies are similar in most respects. If there are good birds to be seen, more than one might run trips to the same place at roughly the same time of year, so you might want to comparison shop to find the tour that interests you most. All three companies hire dedicated, knowledgeable, and personable guides and provide participants with excellent birding opportunities. Tours are limited to about 13 to 18 participants; if numbers warrant, a second leader is sent. Affiliated travel agents can take care of your pre- and post-trip transportation needs.

FIELD GUIDES Founded in 1985, Field Guides offers more than a dozen birding tours in the United States and about 70 more worldwide. Most tour leaders are full-time employees (a rarity in the birding world), and many are part owners of the company. Field Guides limits its trips to 16 people. Transportation is usually by 15-passenger van, and meals are included in the price. *Box 160723, Austin, TX 78716-0723, tel. 512/327–4953 or 800/728–4953, fax 512/327–9231.*

VICTOR EMANUEL NATURE TOURS In business since 1976, VENT offers over 50 natural history and birding tours in the United States, out of about 140 worldwide. Groups consist of up to 18 birders, who are transported from site to site in 15-passenger vans, as well as planes, ferries, boats, and trains when necessary. Meals are included. *Box 33008, Austin, TX 78764, tel. 512/328–5221 or 800/328–8368, fax 512/328–2919.*

WINGS This tour operator was founded in 1973 as Northeast Birding and conducts over 100 tours in the United States and 60 other countries on seven continents. Groups range from 6 to 18 participants, with one leader for every 8 to 10 birders. Wings uses 15-passenger vans and larger coaches for transportation. Lodging is included with all tours, but—unlike the other companies—in North America, meals are not, enabling participants to keep costs lower. Time is allowed for grocery shopping for those who want to make their own lunch or dinner rather than paying for restaurant meals. *1643 N. Alvernon Way, Suite 105, Tucson, AZ 85712, tel. 520/320–9868, fax 520/320–9373.*

FAVORITE TOURS

THE NORTHEAST

MAINE **Monhegan Island.** This trip, offered by Wings since its beginning, is one of only a handful of tours in this part of the country. Genteel, relaxed Monhegan, a 2½-square-mile island 10 miles offshore, provides some very pleasant birding, especially in the tranquil postseason when lobster traps are stacked and land-bird migrants and off-course vagrants are frequent visitors.

The group ferries over to the island from Port Clyde (15 miles south of Rockland, near Camden) and spends days visiting and revisiting Monhegan's traditional bird-watching haunts, from spruce forests to rocky headlands to the village itself. Some favorite spots are as simple as certain hedges, clotheslines, and bird feeders. Typical sightings include warblers, merlins, and peregrine falcons hanging in the updrafts, and annual totals are about 100 species.

Atypical of Wings tours, meals are included, and dinners are had at the Trailing Yew, the only eatery on the island open this time of year. *Wings, 1643 N. Alvernon Way, Suite 105, Tucson, AZ 85712, tel. 520/320–9868, fax 520/320–9373. Late Sept.: 7 days, $930. Sign up 6 months in advance.*

THE MID-ATLANTIC

NEW JERSEY AND PENNSYLVANIA **Fall Raptor Migration Around Cape May and Hawk Mountain.** Focusing on the migration of hawks, this eight-day tour alights at the two best places to see this spectacle: Cape May, at the south end of the New Jersey coastline, and Hawk Mountain, near the Delaware River in southeastern Pennsylvania. You might see up to 15 species of birds of prey flying above the vivid autumn colors of the region, including *Accipiter* and *Buteo* hawks, falcons, bald eagles, and ospreys. Some days you may see more than 1,000 birds as they fly along the avian equivalent of the New Jersey Turnpike.

Many other species migrate along the Appalachian Mountains and Atlantic Coast at this time of year, and your skills are tested trying to identify fall warblers, thrushes, orioles, tanagers, and shorebirds. In addition, you might visit the wetlands of Forsythe National Wildlife Refuge, north of Cape May, where there are a variety of waterbirds and waterfowl ranging from terns and shorebirds to ducks and geese.

Fairly easy walking typifies this tour, but the rocky trails through Hawk Mountain Sanctuary require good balance. The tour leaves from Philadelphia, where you gather for a welcome dinner and do some local birding early the next morning before driving to Cape May. You spend three days at Cape May, then take a day to drive to Nottingham, the base for two days at Hawk Mountain and its environs. On the morning of the last day, you can take an optional excursion at no additional cost to Conowingo Dam on the Susquehanna River, where bald eagles can sometimes be seen feeding on the fish that pass through the dam's power turbines.

You stay at Cape May's Montreal Inn, amid the gingerbread Victorian architecture of the old-fashioned seaside resort town. Expect to eat at least one blue-claw crab dish, a local favorite. Near Hawk Mountain, you spend three nights at the Nottingham Inn, in the heart of Pennsylvania's mushroom-growing region. Be sure to try one of the many dishes made with fresh mushrooms. *Victor Emanuel Nature Tours, Box 33008, Austin, TX 78764, tel. 512/328–5221 or 800/328–8368, fax 512/328–2919. Mid-Oct.: 8 days, $1,295. Sign up 6 months in advance.*

VIRGINIA AND WEST VIRGINIA **Warblers in Breeding Season.** From Virginia's rolling Piedmont and Blue Ridge Mountains across the spacious Shenandoah Valley to her western sister's Allegheny and Cheat mountains, this trip is a showcase of breeding bird biology. Considerable attention is given to nesting ecology and bird vocalization and its discrimination, and you can easily see 25 types of wood warblers in a few days, among which the territorial males are more visible than are the nesting females and their nestlings.

The tour starts in Charlottesville, Virginia. You can choose to come early for a tour of Monticello, led by your guide, before embarking on the ornithological portion of the program, which starts at the James River bottoms, home to prothonotary and yellow-throated warblers. From there, the trip heads to the oak-forested Blue Ridge, where you might see cerulean, Kentucky, hooded, worm-eating, and black-throated blue warblers. Farther west, in the George Washington and Monongahela national forests' Allegheny Mountains, at close to 4,500 feet, wood warblers (as well as other tuneful species) abound in spruce bogs, rhododendron thickets, and forests. In the bird-rich Durbin area, more than 20 wood warbler species and four types of brown-backed thrushes nest within earshot.

Days start early so you can be in the field by dawn, when the avian chorus is at its boldest. But don't worry; you won't go hungry. You'll either return for breakfast or take a picnic along. At day's end, you'll be back out to hear the subdued, beautiful songs of dusk. Accommodations are in good, standard motels. *Field Guides, Box 160723, Austin, TX 78716, tel. 512/327–4953, fax 512/327–9231. Early June: 5 days, $695. Sign up 3–6 months in advance.*

THE SOUTH

FLORIDA **Tropical Birdlife of South Florida and the Dry Tortugas.** Spring is an exciting time for birding in south Florida. On a good day, you can spot reddish egrets, roseate spoonbills, yellow-crowned night herons, snail kites, limpkins, Florida sandhill cranes, and short-tailed hawks—along with plenty of gators. During this tour, many resident birds are nesting and migrants are arriving daily.

The 12-day tour starts in Miami, then heads for the area's wealth of birding hot spots, including Loxahatchee National Wildlife Refuge, with its mottled ducks, smooth-billed anis, and purple gallinules; and Corkscrew Swamp, a mysterious-looking wetland landscape of bald cypress trees covered with Spanish moss that attracts swallow-tailed kites and wood storks among resident and migrant raptors and wading birds.

A visit to the Everglades is followed by a trip through the Keys. Around Key West, you listen for Antillean nighthawks at dusk after watching wading birds and shorebirds in area ponds and "the world's cutest" burrowing owls near Marathon.

From Key West, you set sail on a 100-foot motorized vessel for the seabird nesting colonies of the Dry Tortugas, about 70 miles west. On Bush Key, the activity of thousands of sooty terns and brown noddies is an overwhelming sight, but watch for rarer species like black noddies, masked boobies, and brown boobies. Magnificent frigate birds soar above Ft. Jefferson, a spectacular, long deserted 19th-century fortress that is now a national park. In addition to the fort, you explore Loggerhead Key, Middle Key, and smaller keys for migrant warblers and other songbirds making their way across the Caribbean Sea. On the way to and from the Dry Tortugas, you are kept busy watching for seabirds such as bridled terns, Audubon's shearwaters, and roseate terns. While in the Dry Tortugas, you stay aboard the ship for a couple of nights. This can get a bit cramped, but sighting masked boobies and migrating warblers and thrushes makes it worthwhile.

Returning to the lower Keys, you search for rare mangrove cuckoos, along with more common white-crowned pigeons, black-whiskered vireos, and gray kingbirds. Finally, back in Miami, time is spent on introduced species: red-whiskered bulbuls, common mynahs, spot-breasted orioles, and an unbelievable variety of parrots.

Expect 10- to 12-hour days, with the earliest reveille at 5 AM. Aside from the boat and one night in the Clewiston Inn, an antebellum-style hotel built in the 1920s, lodging is in comfortable if unremarkable hotels. The garlic poppyseed rolls at Donzanti's Italian restaurant in Homestead are considered one of the culinary high points of this tour. Those interested in just the Keys and Dry Tortugas can join the tour on the evening of day six. Wings also has three-day shuttles to the Dry Tortugas with itineraries similar to that portion of this tour. *Wings, 1643 N. Alvernon Way, Suite 105, Tucson, AZ 85712, tel. 520/320–9868, fax 520/320–9373. Mid-Apr.: 12 days, $1,950; 7 days, $1,230. Price does not include meals; sign up 6 months in advance.*

THE MIDWEST

MINNESOTA AND NORTH DAKOTA **From Duluth in Search of Nesting Birds.** This late-spring tour wends its way from the dense pine forests, marshes, and bogs of Minnesota to the North Dakota prairie, providing chances to see both familiar and sought-after birds nesting and in full song and full breeding plumage. At this time of year, the forest and lake country blooms with ruffed and spruce grouse, northern saw-whet owls, black-backed woodpeckers, and boreal chickadees.

The 10-day tour begins (and ends) in Duluth, Minnesota, on the southwest shore of Lake Superior. You spend a full day in the field, but it is fairly easy going; you hike only 1 to 2 miles at a slow pace in level forested areas (bring insect repellent). More than 20 species of warblers can be seen in these remote northern forests, along with least, alder, and yellow-bellied flycatchers and other passerine birds. You spend time in such prime birding spots as Sax-Zim Bog, McGregor Marsh, Solon Springs, Grand Marais, and Superior National Forest, and on the Gunflint Trail. There is also a 100-mile drive along Lake Superior, with stops for a look at common loons and peregrine falcons, as well as an optional night excursion into a wetland in search of yellow rails (bring your own flashlight).

The rolling grasslands and alkaline potholes of the area around Jamestown, North Dakota, provide a refreshing change of habitat. The highest-priority species here are Baird's sparrow, Sprague's pipit, and chestnut-collared longspur.

Accommodations are in modest motels. Although this tour is not renowned for its gourmet dining, trip leaders say a good bet is always the fresh fish, especially walleyed pike, which will appear on many restaurants' menus. *Victor Emanuel Nature Tours, Box 33008, Austin, TX 78764, tel. 512/328–5221 or 800/328–8368, fax 512/328–2919. Late June: 10 days, $1,535. Sign up 6 months in advance.*

NEBRASKA **Spring Migration of Cranes.** The great wingspreads and guttural sounds of thousands of sandhill cranes rising in the spring sky along the Platte River in Nebraska make for an awesome experience. Estimates put the number that visit these staging grounds at some half million, about 80% of the world's population. They are joined in migration by countless waterfowl: Canada geese, white-fronted geese, snow geese, and a variety of ducks that are most abundant in the wetlands south of the river.

Other harbingers of spring in the area include western meadowlarks, ferruginous hawks, and northern harriers. Wintering birds may also linger, including bald eagles, rough-legged hawks, northern shrikes, and American tree and Harris' sparrows. A dawn outing to see displaying greater prairie-chickens is another major sight.

This five-day tour starts and ends in Omaha, and you spend a couple of nights in Grand Island. Short March days make rising before dawn routine, and among this trip's highlights is the cacophony of bird-calls that breaks the morning silence. You spend all six or seven hours of daylight out in the field. Accommodations are in Ramada and Holiday inns. The weather at this time of year is wildly unpredictable, so be prepared for anything from a balmy 70°F to snow. *Victor Emanuel Nature Tours, Box 33008, Austin, TX 78764, tel. 512/328–*

5221 or 800/328–8368, fax 512/328–2919. Mid-Mar.: 5 days, $695. Sign up 6 months in advance.

THE SOUTHWEST

ARIZONA **Hummingbirds from Tucson to the Mexican Border.** Southeast Arizona offers the chance to see as many as 15 species of hummingbirds—more than in any other single area of the United States. On this midsummer tour, you see varieties more commonly encountered in Mexico and Central America, including blue-throated and magnificent hummingbirds, as well as migrating species—such as Anna's and Allen's hummingbirds—that nest along the West Coast. You also see many indigenous southwestern species and get the area's astonishing scenery in the bargain.

Before venturing into the field, the tour heads to a desert museum in Tucson for a quick lesson in local flora and fauna. You visit Madera Canyon, where, along with hummingbirds, there are painted redstarts, black-throated gray warblers, and varied buntings. Also on the itinerary is Nogales, at the Mexican border, for a couple of days birding in and around the nearby Huachuca Mountains, and Cave Creek Canyon, in the Chiricahua Mountains, where you see some rarer birds, such as the elegant trogon.

Accommodations are in modest motels. At Cave Creek Ranch (where you stay for two nights), near Portal, Arizona, you can watch hummingbirds at feeders just outside the cabins. More memorable meals, which are included in the cost of the trip, come at the Portal Cafe, a favorite haunt of locals for its burgers and Mexican dishes. *Victor Emanuel Nature Tours, Box 33008, Austin, TX 78764, tel. 512/328–5221 or 800/328–8368, fax 512/328–2919. Late July: 7 days, $895. Sign up 6 months in advance.*

ARIZONA AND UTAH **Canyonlands in September.** Birds almost take a backseat to the dramatic southwestern landscapes of this 13-day trip. A partial list of destinations reads like a What's What of regional natural wonders: Zion, Bryce Canyon, Petrified Forest, and Grand Canyon national parks; Monument Valley; the Painted Desert; Pipe Springs, Cedar Breaks, Navajo, and Canyon de Chelly national monuments; and the White Mountains. And the birding in these parts is outstanding, too. You can expect to spot black-headed grosbeaks, Clark's nutcrackers, pinyon and Steller's jays, prairie falcons, and Lewis's woodpeckers, along with many migrating species that pass through the region in fall.

Even though you spend some 10 hours each day on the go and in the field, the pace is easygoing, sometimes slow. The longest walk is only about half a mile. Days can be very hot in September—summer comes early and stays late in the Southwest—but elevations of 5,000 to 8,000 feet on most of the tour make conditions relatively comfortable.

Lodging is in standard motels, and transportation is by van. In addition to the local wonders of nature, you visit historic sites in the heart of Navajo country and have a chance to sample at least one authentic Native American meal—if you like it, there are more where that came from. *Wings, 1643 N. Alvernon Way, Suite 105, Tucson, AZ 85712, tel. 520/320–9868, fax 520/320–9373. Early Sept.: 13 days, $1,475. Price does not include meals; sign up 6 months in advance.*

TEXAS **Big Bend, the Davis Mountains, and the Hill Country.** The 800,000-acre Big Bend National Park is twisted with limestone canyons and igneous mountains and running with hidden springs and waterfalls. In this desert canyon land, nearly 450 species of birds have been documented, including such regulars as Lucifer hummingbirds, gray vireos, hepatic tanagers, and elf owls, as well as migrants and Mexican vagrants "trapped" by the Chisos Mountains and desert oases. An optional, long, and fairly strenuous hike to Boot Spring—other hikes cover easy to moderate terrain—should yield several singing colima warblers, an essentially Mexican species that makes its only U.S. breeding locale in the wooded upper canyons of the Chisos.

After four days in Big Bend, the tour moves to the volcanic Davis Mountains to see common black-hawk and Montezuma quail. The last two nights are spent at Utopia, in the west Texas hill country of the Edwards Plateau, where you see golden-cheeked warblers, black-capped vireos, and the dramatic evening flights of Mexican free-tailed bats as they emerge by the tens of thousands from their hillside cave entrances.

The weather varies; although daytime on the desert floor can be hot, part of the time you are at an elevation of some 6,500 feet. Come prepared for hot days and cool nights.

The tour starts and ends in San Antonio. While in Big Bend, you stay at the Chisos Mountain Lodge and eat in its restaurant, which serves basics like chicken-fried steak and burgers. Lunches are usually picnics in the field, sometimes with elaborate fixings—pasta, shrimp—prepared by the tour leaders, and delicious baked goods from Field Guides headquarters. *Field Guides, Box 160723, Austin, TX 78716-0723, tel. 512/327–4953 or 800/728–4953, fax 512/327–9231. Late Apr.–early May: 10 days, $1,545. Sign up by mid-Feb.*

TEXAS Coastal Migration Spectacle. Every evening in late April and early May, huge numbers of warblers, vireos, buntings, grosbeaks, and orioles set out from the southern rim of the Gulf of Mexico on a 650-mile overnight flight to Texas. If the weather is good, many continue inland before landing, but if wind or rain saps their strength, huge numbers will land in the first vegetation they encounter. When this happens, as it does occasionally, two migration sanctuaries around the small community of High Island become the scene of spectacular "fall outs," as thousands, or even hundreds of thousands, of birds drop out of the sky.

Even when this doesn't come to pass, this area is still a prime vantage point for seeing migratory birds. In addition to High Island, a low, live-oak studded rise surrounded by marsh ¼ mile from the coast, you visit flooded rice fields, inland forests, brackish and freshwater marshes, and the Bolivar tidal flats, a protected shorebird preserve. Species range from spoonbills and bitterns to a host of warblers and woodpeckers. Daily activities are based on weather conditions and projections of the best birding. All major habitats are covered, however, to ensure that you manage to see the greatest variety of species—probably around 200.

After spending nights in Houston and Silsbee, the trip moves to High Island, where accommodations are in a small, simple, and clean motel only two blocks from the sanctuaries. Since it's hard to get great meals in this part of Texas, guides supplement with some fairly extravagant lunches. *Field Guides, Box 160723, Austin, TX 78716-0723, tel. 512/327–4953 or 800/728–4953, fax 512/327–9231. Late Apr.–early May: 7 days, $895. Sign up 2 months in advance.*

THE ROCKIES

COLORADO Breeding Prairie Grouse in Spring. The main attractions of this nine-day tour from Pueblo to Denver are the fascinating breeding displays of grouse seen at this time of year. The wild dancing and strutting behaviors of each of the four plains species—sharp-tailed and sage grouse along with greater and lesser prairie chickens—are highlighted by the bizarre sounds that emanate from each of the rival males' inflated neck sacs. Be prepared for *very* early risings to get to the display grounds at dawn.

In the cactus-studded foothills near Pueblo are species more common to the Southwest; you may even spot a greater roadrunner, the real-life version of Wile E. Coyote's nemesis (beep beep). Halfway through the trip you bird the Pawnee National Grasslands, which is almost sure to add something to your life list: mountain plovers, McCown's and chestnut-collared longspurs, prairie falcons, ferruginous hawks, and burrowing owls, among others. In the Rocky Mountains near Steamboat Springs, you should see blue grouse, along with mountain bluebirds, Williamson's sapsuckers, and, perhaps, a golden eagle or two.

You move around a lot on this tour, with a good deal of daytime driving, broken up by frequent stops. You also travel from prairie grasslands to fairly high elevations in the Rockies, so prepare for cool evening temperatures. Lodging is in Holiday Inns, Days Inns, and comparable local hotels, and meals are adequate if unremarkable. *Victor Emanuel Nature Tours, Box 33008, Austin, TX 78764, tel. 512/328-5221 or 800/328-8368, fax 512/328-2919. Late Apr.: 9 days, $1,385. Sign up 6 months in advance.*

WYOMING **Birds of Summer in Yellowstone and the Grand Tetons.** The sight of birds does not prompt the same sense of awe as Old Faithful or a herd of bison, and they certainly are not the reason that most people visit Yellowstone and Grand Teton national parks. Birds are, however, a part of the richness of these dramatic showplaces of the western landscape, and a wide variety of western mountain species can be seen here.

In the pine-dominated forest, you might see three-toed and black-backed woodpeckers, Steller's jays, Clark's nutcrackers, and Williamson's sapsuckers. Meadows of wildflowers attract calliope and broad-tailed hummingbirds, and mountain bluebirds are common as well. American dippers, common mergansers, and harlequin ducks visit waterways. At lakes, watch for cinnamon teal and trumpeter swans. Other waterbirds in the area include western and Clark's grebes, American white pelicans, common loons, and sandhill cranes. A few surprises are always in store for Yellowstone birders; keep an eye out for a blue grouse, an immature bald eagle, sage grouse, or even a great gray owl hunting along a forest edge.

Even with one 10-hour day, this nine-day tour is not particularly strenuous; you travel by van to sighting locales within each of the parks, and the longest walk is 2 miles. As part and parcel of your birding, you take a ride on an aerial tram, a raft trip on the Snake River, and strolls to Yellowstone's famous geysers, mudpots, and fumaroles, looking for large mammals, as well as birds.

You spend four nights in the town of Jackson, just south of Grand Teton National Park, a couple of nights in two-person cabins in Grand Teton's Colter Bay, and another two nights in Yellowstone's Grand Canyon Village. For dining, a perennial favorite is Dornan's, a restaurant on the Snake River that has a moderately priced all-you-can-eat menu and stunning views of the Tetons. *Wings, 1643 N. Alvernon Way, Suite 105, Tucson, AZ 85712, tel. 520/320-9868, fax 520/320-9373. Mid-June: 9 days, $1,285. Price does not include meals; sign up 6 months in advance.*

THE WEST COAST

CALIFORNIA AND ARIZONA **Desert Birds in Winter.** When cold weather blankets most of the country, many birders join this Wings tour to the balmy environs of the deserts of southern California and southeastern Arizona, traveling from San Diego to Tucson.

In and around San Diego, you can hope to see California gnatcatchers, wrentits, Clark's grebes, and a wide variety of coastal waterbirds, among the abundance of birds that regularly winter here. As you move east, you may encounter sage and LeConte's thrashers, Scott's orioles, lesser and (maybe) Lawrence's goldfinches, and verdins. Inland, around the Salton Sea, a huge saltwater lake in the California desert, are literally hundreds of thousands of birds—wintering flocks of snow and Ross's geese, a variety of wintering ducks, sandhill cranes, mountain plovers, white-faced ibis, long-billed curlews, and burrowing owls.

In the deserts of Arizona south of Phoenix, you see Harris's hawks, phainopeplas, cactus wrens, and Gila woodpeckers. The area southwest of Tucson—Madera Canyon, Patagonia, and Nogales—is one of the finest birding locales in the nation, and where you might see vermilion flycatchers, Mexican jays, bridled titmice, Sprague's pipits, McCown's and chestnut-collared longspurs, and yellow-eyed juncos. You could easily spot more than 200 species on this 10-day tour.

You rise at about dawn and press on for most of the day. Most viewing is done from within sight of the vans, so only a few short walks are called for. Among the variety of cuisines available on this trip, there is a plenitude of high-quality Mexican food. *Wings, 1643 N. Alvernon Way, Suite 105, Tucson, AZ 85712, tel. 520/320–9868, fax 520/320–9373. Late Jan.: 10 days, $1,250. Price does not include meals; sign up 6 months in advance.*

OREGON **Land, Shore, and Pelagic Birds from Coast to Mountains.** Over the course of nearly two weeks, you'll see about 200 species as this trip traverses varied landscapes and habitats, from Oregon's rocky shore through broken woodlands, farming areas, wetlands, coastal forests, eastern deserts, and high mountains. Starting on the coast, where there is a boat trip 20 miles out into the Pacific in search of seabirds, the tour next heads inland, passing through the humid Coast Range and the majestic Cascades and on to the Malheur National Wildlife Refuge, on the high plateau of the southeastern Oregon desert. The grand finale of this trip, the refuge is a great spot for viewing the migration along the Pacific flyway.

Despite the amount of ground covered (you change locales and hotels every couple of days), the pace is relaxed. You can expect to rise before sunup on a couple of mornings only, and generally days in the field are not overly long—about eight hours is average, although energetic birders will have the chance for owling some nights. Sandhill cranes, trumpeter swans, a variety

of ducks, American white pelicans, four species of grebes, Wilson's phalaropes, and a range of birds of prey typically make appearances on this tour.

You start and finish in Portland, staying in local hotels and motels en route. Each is clean, comfortable, and characteristic of its surroundings (seaside motel, mountain lodge). Meals are often eaten in a given hotel's restaurant—for example, the elegant Inn at Face Rock, in Bandon, offers a selection from pepper steak to fresh chinook salmon to homemade soups—or at local restaurants that trip leaders know are interesting and good. *Field Guides, Box 160723, Austin, TX 78716-0723, tel. 512/327–4953 or 800/728–4953, fax 512/327–9231. Mid-Sept.: 13 days, $1,825. Sign up 6 months in advance.*

WASHINGTON AND BRITISH COLUMBIA **Birds of the Pacific Northwest.** Picture images of misty coastlines and lush fern- and moss-cloaked forests, and you're only partway there. There are indeed shores and woodlands on tap on this tour, but there are also grasslands and lakes, a pocket desert and picturesque cities, and even a waste disposal site famous for its shorebirds and frequent rarities this time of year.

Starting in Seattle, the tour heads northeast across the Cascades and along the Grand Coulee to some high basalt cliffs favored by white-throated swifts. You'll spend time in both the U.S. and Canadian portions of the Okanagan Valley, parts of which are in the rain shadow of the Coast and Cascade ranges. Species of interest here include the red-necked grebe, the calliope hummingbird, and Lewis' and black-backed woodpeckers.

In British Columbia's Manning Provincial Park, the glacial landscape and extensive forests, streams, and meadows are home to barred owls, red-naped sapsuckers, and spruce and blue grouse. As a change from the more standard lodging, you stay in comfortable, rustic park-style accommodations. From here it's on to the lovely city of Vancouver and a ferry ride to Vancouver

Island and Victoria. This is waterbird country: Brandt's and pelagic cormorants, marbled murrelet, and gulls.

Upon returning to Washington, the tour concludes with visits to Olympic National Park and Port Townsend. More ferry rides around Puget Sound and the Straits of Juan de Fuca increase the opportunity for pelagic species. You finish back in Seattle, where, if you choose, you can have one last seafood dinner before heading home. *Wings, 1643 N. Alvernon Way, Suite 105, Tucson, AZ 85712, tel. 520/320–9868, fax 520/320–9373. Late June–early July: 12 days, $1,580. Price does not include meals; sign up 6 months in advance.*

ALASKA

STATEWIDE **Alaska's Special Species in the Early Arctic Summer.** Alaska is known for its snowcapped peaks, icy blue fjords, and bountiful wildlife, including moose, caribou, Dall sheep, wolves, and grizzly bears. But on this tour the emphasis is squarely on birds, many of which you simply cannot see in the lower 48. There are actually two trips: Part I (10 days) includes visits to Denali National Park and the Pribilof Islands, whereas Part II (11 days) covers Nome, Barrow, Seward, and the Anchorage area. They can be combined into a comprehensive, 21-day survey of this ultimate birding frontier.

In the first trip, you'll visit the coastlines of the Pribilof Islands, which teem with nearly 3 million nesting seabirds, including tufted and horned puffins, murres, kittiwakes, and auklets. You stay at the King Eider Inn on St. Paul Island, which has no rooms with private bath. Although the inn's restaurant is pretty good, this area is not exactly renowned for its fine dining, so organizers supplement what is available locally with baked goods from Austin and provide simple meals of granola, yogurt, and fruit in the field.

At Denali, sightings of gyrfalcons, northern hawk owls, willow ptarmigan, and arctic terns compete with the continent's tallest peak, Mt. Denali (McKinley), for birders' attention. Accommodations are at the Kantishna Lodge, which has 50 rooms and 24 cabins and is 92 miles from the park entrance. Despite the ruggedness of the terrain, this trip does not require difficult walking, and people at all fitness levels should be comfortable with the pace.

The second trip offers chances to see a variety of nesting waterfowl, including emperor, brant, and white-fronted geese; king, common, and spectacled eiders; willow and rock ptarmigan; red and red-necked phalaropes; and a variety of forest birds. You may even spot Asian strays, such as bluethroats, northern wheatears, white wagtails, and Arctic warblers, which often fly off course and land around Nome. A boat trip to Kenai Fjords National Park reveals nesting seabirds along the rocky cliffs of the rugged coastline.

Not surprisingly, the climate is cool to cold, and Alaskan summer days are long. Birders make the most of it, spending 8 to 10 hours in the field, with some optional night birding. *Field Guides, Box 160723, Austin, TX 78716-0723, tel. 512/327–4953 or 800/728–4953, fax 512/327–9231. June: 10 days, $2,995; 11 days, $2,995; 21 days, $5,795. Sign up 3–4 months in advance.*

SOUTHWEST **Photographing Seabirds in the Pribilof Islands.** Though other Alaskan bird tours identify more birds, this one to St. George in the Pribilof Archipelago has an additional, well, focus: photography. Led by photographers with strong natural history backgrounds, Josef Van Os Photo Safaris teach you how to take high-quality photographs rather than merely document on film the birds you encounter.

Staying at the island's charmingly rustic hotel, participants have three full days to photograph the millions of seabirds that perch on the precipitous cliffs. St. George is said to have the largest seabird colony in the northern hemisphere: 1.1 million thick-billed murres, 98% of the global population of red-legged kittiwakes, and the world's largest breeding colony of parakeet auklets, as well as tufted and horned puffins. Arctic foxes may make themselves available for photo ops, and inland carpets of verdant moss, lichen, and arctic wild-flowers complete the scene.

The trip begins and ends in Anchorage, from which the group (limited to 13) flies out to the little island in the Bering Sea. *Joseph Van Os Photo Safaris, Box 655, Vashon Island, WA 98070, tel. 206/463–5383, fax 206/463–5484. Early July: 7 days, $2,495. Sign up 6 months in advance.*

HAWAII

OAHU, MAUI, THE BIG ISLAND, AND KAUAI

Island-Hopping Extravaganza of Native and Introduced Species. Gaining access to areas that are often difficult or impossible for individual birders to visit, this American Birding Association tour is designed to turn up indigenous species (about 100), while observing introduced ones as well. Avoiding tourist traps while still fitting in some sightseeing during dawn-to-dusk for-ays, you work your way from island to island, ecosystem to ecosystem, moving your base every two to four days.

The tour starts in Honolulu, on Oahu, with visits to Kapiolani Park and the James Campbell National Wildlife Refuge (for most of the native waterbirds) and a short hike on the Kuliouou Trail to search for the Oahu Elepaio. An eight-hour pelagic excursion is scheduled as well.

A trip to the summit of Haleakala is in store on Maui, where you may see the reintroduced nene as well as chukars. The Nature Conservancy's Waikamoi Preserve brings the first of the relatively difficult hikes (in general, the hikes are not overly strenuous, though you may encounter some rocky, muddy, log-strewn, slippery, and steep terrain), but the setting of nearly pristine rain forest and the chance to see iiwi and crested honeycreeper more than compensate.

In six days on the island of Hawaii, you'll practically circle the island. Highlights include Hawaii Volcanoes National Park, where you might spot white-tailed trop-icbirds, nene, or black noddy, and the McCandless Ranch Ecotour, where you'll search for the last wild flock of alala and visit the "hacking" facility, where captive-hatched birds are habituated before release. Then it's on to the garden isle of Kauai before returning to Honolulu.

A full group consists of 12 participants with two leaders. Most transportation is by van or minivan, but some four-wheel-drive vehi-cles are used. Accommodations are chosen for their location. On Maui, for example, you'll stay at the Kula Lodge, whose nice chalets require sharing by more than two people and whose restaurant provides both delicious food and a fantastic view. *Voyagers International, Box 915, Ithaca, NY 14851, tel. 607/257–3091, fax 607/257–3699. Late Oct.–early Nov.: 16 days, $2,995 (if trip is not fully enrolled, there will be a surcharge). Price does not include meals except for breakfasts in Kona and 1 lunch; sign up 4–6 months in advance.*

SOURCES

ORGANIZATIONS The **American Birding Association** (Box 6599, Colorado Springs, CO 80934-6599, tel. 800/634–7736) is the major national organization for serious birders; it has about 17,000 members and acts as a clearinghouse for information on a variety of topics of interest to birders.

In addition, many states have ornithologi-cal societies and bird clubs that have regu-lar meetings, publish newsletters and journals with information of local interest, and schedule field trips and weekends. Don't be too intimidated to join, they're just made up of birders. Local Audubon chap-ters also run field trips and other bird-related functions.

PERIODICALS *Birder's World* (44 E. 8th St., #410, Holland, MI 49423, tel. 800/753–

4873) is a bimonthly magazine featuring articles of general interest to birders. *Birding*, published bimonthly, is the magazine of the American Birding Association (*see* Organizations, *above*). It's geared for active (intermediate to experienced) field birders and emphasizes identification, bird-finding, taxonomy, and reviews. Members of ABA also receive the monthly newsletter *Winging It*. *Birdwatcher's Digest* (Box 110, Marietta, OH 45750-9977, tel. 800/879–2473) is a small format, general-interest birding magazine published six times a year; it's designed for beginner to intermediate and backyard birders. The National Audubon Society publishes *Field Notes* (700 Broadway, New York, NY 10003, tel. 212/979–3000), seasonal summaries of bird sightings region by region. *Living Bird* (159 Sapsucker Woods Rd., Ithaca, NY 14850, tel. 607/254–2425) is the quarterly publication of the Cornell Lab of Ornithology. The monthly *WildBird* magazine (Box 5060, Mission Viejo, CA 92690, tel. 714/855–8822), also for the beginning to intermediate birder, prints regular columns and feature articles about topics from natural history and travel to photography techniques and equipment descriptions.

BOOKS There are many reliable field guides; among the best known are *Field Guide to Eastern Birds* and *Field Guide to Western Birds,* by the late Roger Tory Peterson, published by Houghton Mifflin. The Peterson's series is the granddaddy of all birding field guides, and its use of arrows and in-flight drawings are particularly useful for identifying birds. The edition covering the western United States was most recently updated in 1990; another updating of the eastern edition is under way. *Field Guide to the Birds of North America,* published by the National Geographic Society, is overall the most up-to-date guide. Its design makes this book easy to use, with a range map on the same page as the picture of each bird and pertinent information about it. *A Guide to Field Identification— Birds of North America* (Golden Press), a.k.a. the Golden Guide, is an old standard, recently expanded, that has a range map and sonogram for each bird. For beginning birders in the East, the recently released *Eastern Birds: A Guide to Field Identification of North American Species,* by James Coe (Golden Press), contains superb artwork and leaves out most of the rarer species. *The Audubon Society Master Guide to Birding* (Alfred A. Knopf) is a three-volume set with photos (other field guides depict the birds in paintings) that is really more of an at-home reference work than a portable field guide. However, the Audubon Society also produces two paperbacks, *An Audubon Handbook: Eastern Birds* and *An Audubon Handbook: Western Birds,* by John Farrand, Jr. These both feature photographs, too.

Campus Vacations

Written by Carole Martin

Updated by Natasha Lesser

hether you frequently wax nostalgic for your carefree college days or are simply in need of some personal enrichment, a campus vacation may be just the restorative you need this summer. Want to know more about Victorian England? The history of jazz? Capitalism in China? Film noir? The Information Superhighway? All you need to do is head for your favorite campus and choose a subject. Continuing education divisions and alumni offices at colleges and universities across the country have developed scores of special programs that allow inquisitive nonstudents to spend their vacations exploring new intellectual horizons in an academic setting, in the spirit of Chautauqua—the granddaddy of all such programs, founded in 1874 in western New York State and still offering a rich schedule of classes, lectures, and other educational programs. The number of people going to campus for personal enrichment rather than a degree grows from year to year.

The beauty of one of these campus vacations, whether at a bucolic little college or amid the hallowed halls of a great university, is that there are no tests or grades, and you rarely have homework. Instead, you listen to experts lecture on a topic, read as much or as little as you want to supplement the lecture, and then discuss the pros, the cons, and the nuances with your peers beneath leafy boughs beside the quad or at

spur-of-the-moment pizza parties in the dorm. There are no admission requirements beyond a desire to expand your mind in a collegial atmosphere and an ability to pay the fees, which range from under $300 for five days at the Big Ten's Indiana University to around $900 for five days at Cornell University in upstate New York. These prices include not only tuition but also a single room in a dorm, usually with shared bath, and two or three basic institutional meals a day.

The idea that intellectual growth needn't stop with graduation has become more than conventional wisdom in the second half of the 20th century. In 1956, the first Great Books group was formed in Chicago by University of Chicago president Robert Hutchkins, and others soon followed; people liked the idea of spending two hours in the hands of a leader trained to ask questions to spark discussions examining an author's words, meaning, and lessons. After World War II, night-school courses flourished to serve the needs of returning veterans; they attracted substantial numbers of students well into the 1960s and 1970s.

In the mid-1960s, Brown and Dartmouth adapted the idea of continuing education to vacation-length programs; they were a novel way to allow graduates to revisit and reacquaint themselves with their alma

---

Carole Martin's lifelong passion for learning has taken her from a career as a journalist, travel writer, and editor to her current job as a teacher in the New York City public school system. Natasha Lesser is an editor at Fodor's and a perennial student.

maters while strengthening the schools' ties with alumni—and encouraging alums to provide increased financial support. Cornell University soon joined Brown and Dartmouth. The mid-1970s saw a host of schools across the country opening their doors to lifelong learners, people who thought immersing themselves in the classics or exploring the latest scientific breakthroughs with leading academicians might be the best of all possible vacations. Other institutions, both public and private, jumped on the bandwagon, sometimes as part of their outreach efforts to their communities. Surprised by the extent of interest they found, these colleges and universities responded by offering even broader arrays of self-contained courses, running from several days to several weeks.

Although today's learning vacations vary from campus to campus, all share a few basic characteristics. They tend to attract people who have been away from campus for years, not only alumni but also other people who love learning, ranging in age from 30 to 65 (with some as young as 18 and as old as 80). Unlike programs for regularly matriculated students, they last just a week or two. They use the same campus facilities, however: dorms, dining rooms, classrooms, auditoriums, and other venues. They also use existing faculty: Professors who teach regular summer school classes have a lighter load than usual, and those who have the summer off are often delighted to teach short-term courses in their areas of expertise.

All campus vacations offer the chance to exercise your mind and spend time with other people who are energized by discovering new interests and new ideas. Whether you participate in a program at a huge university like Indiana or at a tiny school like Maine's Colby College, the campus can seem like an oasis, far removed from the concerns of day-to-day life. Which is just what a vacation should be.

CHOOSING THE RIGHT PROGRAM

Beyond subject matter, a number of things will affect whether your campus vacation turns out to be the kind of experience you expect. You need to ask some key questions before deciding whether a particular program is right for you.

Who's teaching? Most colleges and universities showcase their own faculty at their campus vacation programs. However, depending on the theme or topic, prominent guest lecturers or visiting professors from nearby colleges and universities may supplement the home-campus staff.

What are the accommodations like? What's available can range from rather spartan dormitories, with two twin beds to a room and communal bathrooms that serve an entire floor, to on-campus inns, conference centers, or even hotels—where all rooms have private baths, television sets, telephones, and other amenities. Somewhere in the middle are the dormitory situations sometimes called suites, where two to four rooms share a bathroom. Not all dorms have air-conditioning, and in certain parts of the country, you need it. In hot, humid areas, window fans may be provided—or you may be asked to bring your own.

You may or may not need to bring soap, towels, sheets, and television sets, and other things that hotels commonly provide. Ask what's supplied and pack accordingly.

There are usually a few commercial motels right on the periphery of college campuses, and some institutions block off rooms in them for summer program participants who wouldn't call it a vacation without 24-hour room service.

Can you earn academic credit? Although most of the summer programs are designed for edification, not certification, a few can award academic credit—a consideration if you are a teacher or are working part-time toward a degree.

How much of the day do you spend in the classroom? The more academic the program, the more hours you are likely to spend in the classroom. Generally, classes are scheduled for only part of the day to allow free time for physical activity, visits to nearby cultural centers, and informal discussions among students.

How large are the classes? Class size can range from as few as half a dozen for hands-on classes in the arts or computer technology to 75 for lectures. The norm is 15 to 25.

How much work is required outside the classroom? A few programs send enrollees reading lists before arrival, with the expectation that they'll complete some or all of the books. During the course, some require at least minimal homework. However, most are designed to allow students to complete their study within the classroom, and reading lists are handed out at the end of the program by way of suggestion to those who wish to pursue a subject off campus.

What other campus facilities can you use? As a student in residence, you usually have free run of the college, including the library and athletic facilities—tennis courts, golf courses, swimming pools, weight rooms. Some colleges have more to offer than others. Make sure that the campus provides what matters to you.

How big is the campus, and how easy is it to get around? Strolling through the bucolic grounds of a big university can be exhilarating. It also can be tiring if the campus is hilly and the places you need to go are at opposite ends of the grounds. Really big universities often have some type of van or bus system; some have bicycles for rent (or you might want to bring your own).

What's the cost and what's included? As a rule, there is a single all-inclusive price for college and university vacation learning programs, covering tuition, housing, and all meals. This is the case for the programs described here, unless otherwise noted. However, a number of colleges and universities either include only two meals a day or charge separately for tuition, rooms, and meals—an appealing price structure if you prefer to live off campus and eat in restaurants, or if you live nearby.

What is the food like? Almost everyone who has been out of school for a while remembers institutional cafeteria food with something less than enthusiasm. But things have improved a great deal on most college campuses. In addition to mystery meat and other blue plate specials, you'll frequently find salad bars and campus grills. If you have specific food preferences, make sure they can be accommodated.

What programs are available for nonparticipating family members? A number of campuses coordinate programs for children and teenagers who accompany their parents. Find out if an accompanying but nonparticipating traveling companion will also be able to take advantage of the university athletic facilities.

How long has the college been running these programs? For the most part, a young program can be as well designed and energizing as some of the more established ones. But chances are that a program that has been around a few years has ironed out all the kinks and has already answered the questions and met the challenges that you throw their way.

How far in advance do I need to register? Brochures describing the programs are typically available around January. Often, priority is given to alumni and parents of current students. Because these programs sell out fast, don't wait to sign up once you have decided what you want.

FAVORITE PROGRAMS

THE NORTHEAST

MAINE **Colby College Summer Institute.** In August, about 250 people from across the country head for this pretty little Waterville, Maine, campus to immerse themselves in great works of literature at a summer institute run by Wachs Great Books Forum, Inc.—a New York–based nonprofit corporation. Each year the program focuses on a different theme, and you read and talk about an eclectic group of six or seven books relating to the topic. In past years, themes have included solitude, truth, destiny, and female writers (one year, the institute was devoted entirely to Plato). When you register and mail your deposit, Wachs sends you paperbacks of the books to be discussed so that you can read them before arrival. On campus, you're assigned to a group of 15 to 18 for two-hour conversations led by instructors trained to lead discussions of books using Great Books methods: The instructors ask specific questions in order to encourage participants to talk about the meaning and implications of an author's words. Afternoons are free, and institute participants can take advantage of the college tennis courts, pool, and other facilities. In the evenings there are films, dancing, and concerts. Colby is all classic Georgian buildings and well-kept lawns; its relative isolation makes it an ideal spot for getting away from it all. Lodging is in dorms, which have window fans but lack air-conditioning (a feature you don't usually need anyway). And although the food served in the campus dining hall is modest, there is one feast, the celebratory outdoor lobster bake that ends each session. A program for children aged 4 through 15 is available. Brochures about the coming summer's program are prepared by January. *Colby College Summer Institute, 680 Elton St., Riverhead, NY 11901, tel. 516/727–8600, fax 516/727–7592. Early Aug.: 6 days, $420. Sign up 3–4 months in advance.*

NEW HAMPSHIRE **Dartmouth Alumni College.** Since the mid-1960s, around 250 students have gathered every August in Dartmouth's copper-top Colonial frame buildings, which surround a classic New England green, for this popular campus vacation program. The six-day session is an in-depth, interdisciplinary course on a given theme, such as the riddles of creation, ethnic conflict and world security, or the reinterpretation of great literature. Taught primarily by Dartmouth faculty with occasional guest lecturers, sessions usually involve a two-hour talk in the morning and another at 4 PM. Afterwards, the audience breaks up into groups of about 15 for an hour's discussion, facilitated by faculty.

Students can continue the debate after class, since the faculty often eat breakfast and dinner in the campus cafeterias. Afternoons are free for hiking or biking in the White Mountains or for exploring New England villages and area back roads, and in the evening there are lectures, films, concerts, and plays to attend. Each year's program opens with a Sunday banquet and a guest speaker and closes with a picnic. The program is limited to 250 students. Books and a collection of readings for the course are sent months in advance.

Dorms offer simple singles, doubles, and suites. Although some accommodations have air-conditioning, others have only fans; the college-owned, air-conditioned Hanover Inn is the place to stay if you like your comforts. Brochures for each summer's Alumni College usually are mailed out by March, and alumni, financial supporters, students' parents, past participants, and other friends of the college have priority; registration is not open to the general public until mid-April. Children over 15 often participate with their parents. *Dartmouth Alumni College, 6068 Blunt Alumni Center, Room 309, Hanover, NH 03755, tel. 603/646–2454, fax 603/646–1600. Aug.: 6 days, $500. Price does not include lodging ($175–$225 per person double occupancy) or meals ($66–$90). Sign up 3–4 months in advance.*

NEW YORK **Cornell's Adult University.** Begun in 1968, this is one of the oldest campus vacation programs in the country; it's also one of the most extensive. Each July, four five-day sessions are held on the sprawling, hilly upstate New York campus. The array of courses is eclectic, covering a range of topics from DNA in the modern world, Islamic art and society, and Tolstoy's *Anna Karenina,* to how to create digital images and how to determine what makes a great painting great.

Some courses are lectures for 40 people or more, but there are also workshops and hands-on classes limited to 12 to 14 people. Some 100 to 150 people sign up weekly, and Cornell faculty members teach all the courses, which meet mornings, afternoons, and sometimes in the evening as well. If you're dedicated, you can log up to 35 hours of classroom time during the week, and you can even come for more than one week. Reading materials to be discussed are sent to you before classes start; no further homework is assigned.

Away from class, there are squash and tennis courts, a state-of-the-art fitness room, a Robert Trent Jones–designed golf course, and two swimming pools. You can also go horseback riding, hike the hills of a 3,000-acre nature reserve or the stream-crossed Cornell Plantation, or look for the waterfalls and ravines high above Ithaca and Cayuga Lake.

Cornell, which has a strong academic program for hotel and restaurant management, has a reputation for serving some of the best college food in the country. Menus have everything from eggs to order to Healthy Heart selections to ice cream made at the Cornell Dairy. Housing options range from dormitories with communal bathrooms (not air-conditioned but equipped with fans) to air-conditioned dorm rooms with private baths to quarters in a full-service hotel off campus; the fancier your accommodations, the greater your program fee. A well-developed youth program for children aged three to 16 runs concurrently with the Adult University. The brochure is available in February. *Cornell's Adult University, 626 Thurston Ave., Ithaca, NY 14850, tel. 607/255–6260, fax 607/254–4482. July: 4 5-day sessions, $765–$1000.*

Price does not include 1 dinner; sign up 3–4 months in advance.

NEW YORK **Summer Six at Skidmore.** Saratoga Springs, where Skidmore College is located, is the summer home of the New York City Ballet and the Philadelphia Orchestra. So it's appropriate that the arts are the focal point of virtually all the summer programs at this college in the foothills of the Adirondacks. Skidmore's highly regarded Summer Six art program draws 150 to 250 people who want to try something new or sharpen rusty skills and sensibilities. A number of workshops lasting two days to five weeks are available in figure modeling in clay, jewelry making, watercolor painting, and graphic design. Workshops meet between 9 and 4 daily. There are usually about 10 students in each course.

In addition to the cultural activities in Saratoga Springs, students have access to the school's swimming pool, racquetball and squash courts, weight rooms, and 850 acres of attractively landscaped grounds. Summer students can stay on campus in modern, air-conditioned dormitories and take meals in a dining hall, the spa, or a snack bar. Although accommodations near campus are heavily booked in summer because of Saratoga Springs's popularity as a resort area, you can also stay off campus. The Summer Six brochure is available in late February. *Summer Six, Skidmore College, Saratoga Springs, NY 12866, tel. 518/584–5000, ext. 2372, fax 518/581–8386. Late May–June and July–early Aug.: 2 days–5 wks, $130–$2,000. Price does not include lodging ($150 per wk, $270 with meals) or meals ($150 per week); sign-up begins 3–4 months in advance.*

RHODE ISLAND **Brown University Summer College.** Brown was one of the pioneers in campus learning vacations, and this program, started in the 1960s, is a more intense intellectual experience than most. It involves a series of lectures and sophisticated discussion groups that focus on and develop a single topic—in recent years,

America in the Gilded Age, the breakup of Eastern Europe, and education and high school reform. Although the idea of the summer college is to showcase Brown's own faculty, outside experts from business, government, and academe, such as Arthur Schlesinger, Jr., have participated.

The format usually calls for between five and seven hour-long lectures each day, which are attended by all participants; each is followed by a discussion in groups of about a dozen people. At one point, Brown officials considered making the program less rigorous, but the message from previous participants was "Don't baby us." In addition to the academic program, Brown schedules evening performances of theater, music, film, and dance that relate in some way to the theme or topic under study.

Because the number of participants is limited to between 100 and 130, registration is offered first to alumni and parents of current students, then to the general public. Housing is in campus dormitory suites, which share bathroom facilities; some are air-conditioned, some are not. A more expensive option is the hotel-style room with air-conditioning, private bath, television, and daily maid service. The program brochure is usually available in early January. *Summer College, c/o Brown's Continuing College, Box 1920, Brown University, Providence, RI 02912, tel. 401/863–2474, fax 401/863–2785. June: 4 days, $750–$875 ($495 without lodging and dinner). Sign up 3–4 months in advance.*

THE MID-ATLANTIC

PENNSYLVANIA **Penn State University Alumni College.** The five-day program held every July at this 540-acre campus in the shade of Mt. Nittany, in a scenic Appalachian valley, ordinarily shows off two of the university's colleges or schools: One year may highlight subjects typical of those studied in Penn State's School of Liberal Arts and its College of Engineering, for

instance. Classes may range from earthquakes and faults to biomedical engineering to the art of writing personal essays. Nine or so courses are offered in a summer and you can generally sign up for as many as you like. All classes are held in the morning; each lasts one to two hours per day, with a short break during longer classes. Afternoons are reserved for computer workshops; organized recreational activities, which can be as accessible as rollerblading or as challenging as spelunking; or field trips and lab tours of campus facilities such as the Learning Factory, a rapid prototyping facility. The size of classes varies: While lectures may have 30 to 40 students, courses involving hands-on instruction and individualized attention are much smaller. The program draws between 70 and 100 adults each year. Although there are no assigned books or homework, professors provide optional pre-course reading, class handouts, and bibliographies of related material so that you can pursue a subject further after the program has ended.

As students in residence, participants have access to all campus facilities, including two 18-hole golf courses, an Olympic-size swimming pool, and tennis courts. During the Alumni College, Penn State also operates a day camp for children aged 6 to 13; teenagers may choose to attend a sports camp or the adult program. Lodging is in the Nittany Residence Hall, the university's only air-conditioned dorm, although you can opt to stay at a nearby hotel. Food is wholesome and adequate, except for the ice cream, made on the campus, which is top-notch. Breakfast and lunch are included with the tuition; dinners are always on your own. The program brochure is usually available in mid-April. *Penn State University Alumni College, 105 Old Main, University Park, PA 16802-1559, tel. 814/865–5466, fax 814/865–3589. July: 5 days, $330, includes tuition, breakfast, and lunch. Price does not include lodging ($32 a night in dorm, $65 a night in hotel); sign up 2–3 months in advance.*

THE SOUTH

GEORGIA **Emory Alumni University.**
Every June for five days, Alumni University convenes at Emory's Italian Renaissance–style campus, in the suburbs of Atlanta. The program has only been around since 1993, but it has already become very popular, with about 150 participants yearly. Courses, taught by Emory professors, cover an array of topics from "Joan of Arc: A Study of Film" and "Writing the New South's History" to "Moral Responsibility in the Twenty-First Century" and "Cyberspace and the InternetEmory." Students take two 1½-hour classes in the morning; in the afternoon they attend faculty round-table discussions on contemporary issues such as "The Forces of Disease: Fighting a Global War" and the "Universality and Relativity of Human Rights." The emphasis is on encouraging students to think about big questions in society, history, literature, and other topics. About 12 to 24 students take each class and 70 to 100 attend the afternoon seminars. Homework is rare, though it varies with the course: Some professors assign readings, and assignments are always given in writing classes.

In the evening, the university organizes social and cultural events, including readings, receptions, films, concerts, and even trips to Braves games. Participants can also take advantage of Emory's art museum, gym, libraries, and computer labs, where Internet-surfing sessions are held. Downtown Atlanta is only 25 minutes away, but most participants find they have enough to do on campus. For children of participants, the university offers child care and camp programs.

Housing is in suites with shared bathrooms in the modern, air-conditioned Woodruff Residential Center. Hotel-like accommodations with private bathrooms, air-conditioning, television, and maid service are available in the Emory Conference Center. Discounts are given for early registration, double occupancy, and parties of four or

more. Lodging is included in the tuition, as are six Continental breakfasts, the opening dinner party, the closing party, and evening social events. Occasional lunches and afternoon teas with the college president or a dean are organized, but more often students head to the fast-food court, the campus café, or the coffeehouse for lunch. For dinner, there are plenty of restaurants in the university area. *Emory Alumni University, Atlanta, GA 30322-1740, tel. 404/727–6405, fax 404/727–2557. June: 5 days, $545–$800 including lodging and limited meals, $300 tuition only. Sign up 3–5 months in advance.*

NORTH CAROLINA **University of North Carolina Vacation College.** This is one of the nation's oldest universities, and its 730-acre campus is lovely in summer with its lush lawns, ancient trees, shaded walkways, and spacious quadrangles. Redbrick Federal buildings dating from the early 19th century predominate, but the architecture ranges from Palladian to postmodern; the nationally famous Morehead Planetarium is among the campus focal points.

Vacation College, sponsored by UNC's Program in the Humanities and Human Values since 1980 and held from mid-June through early August, consists of six or so 2½- to 4-day courses on literary, cultural, societal, and moral topics, which can range from Jane Austen to Chinese history and culture to current scientific and theological speculation about the origins of the universe. About 250 to 300 people sign up each summer, and classes vary in size from 30 to 95.

Courses here tend to be fairly academically focused, but the most intensive of all are the courses that last just 2½ days; these include two hour-long lectures in the morning, one in the afternoon, and one in the evening, each followed by a half-hour discussion period. In the four-day courses, there are usually two lecture and discussion periods in the morning and one in the afternoon. Most instructors are UNC professors, but the faculty occasionally includes guests from nearby Duke University and North Carolina State. You are sent course materials before classes start, as well as bibliographies for follow-up reading. On the schedule of evening activities are lectures, films, and special dinners.

Vacation College students have access to a limited number of campus facilities, such as the track and the library. Accommodations are in Carmichael Hall, which has clusters of four air-conditioned rooms that share a bathroom; you can also stay at a university-owned hotel next to the campus, the Carolina Inn. There's no meal plan, but accommodations are near a campus cafeteria, which offers three meals daily, including burgers, pizza, salads, yogurt, and fruit; in the Carolina Inn, there's a table-service restaurant that serves three meals a day. In addition, you can find a number of good eating spots nearby along Chapel Hill's main street. Brochures for each summer's Vacation College are generally available by March. Registration is open right up until the start of class, but some courses fill up early. *Vacation College, Humanities Program, CB#3425, 3 Bolin Heights, University of North Carolina, Chapel Hill, NC 27599, tel. 919/962–1544, fax 919/962–4318. Mid-June–early Aug.: 2½–4 days $180–$250. Price does not include lodging ($30 a night in dorms, $75–$125 in hotel) or meals; sign up 3–4 months in advance.*

THE MIDWEST

INDIANA **Indiana University Mini University.** For five days every June, some 350 students attend the annual Mini University at this Big Ten school in the rolling southern part of the state. The program, which got its start in 1971, is a smorgasbord of lectures, with IU faculty members talking on as many as 100 individual topics clustered in eight categories: the arts, business, domestic issues, humanities, health and fitness, international affairs, science, and technology.

Many classes, particularly those on current events, vary from year to year, but some favorites are repeated, such as the one about big band musician Hoagy Carmichael—IU is renowned for its music school—and the one that probes the nuances of body language. Morning classes last two hours, afternoon and evening classes about an hour; you can sign up for one each morning, two each afternoon, and one in the evening. Classroom discussion is encouraged, and while there are no tests or homework, you get reading lists of books and articles for future reference.

In the afternoon, instead of lectures, you can participate in tours of university facilities such as the famous Kinsey Institute; or you can take advantage of the two 18-hole golf courses, tennis courts, weight rooms, and several swimming pools, one of which is Olympic-size—IU is also known for its swimming program. The library is one of the largest in the country, and you can visit the I. M. Pei–designed art museum. The campus itself sprawls with high-rise labs and dorms surrounded by parking lots but also has beautiful lawns anchored by huge old trees and late-19th-century buildings. Evening activities range from theater trips and movies to faculty receptions and recitals.

Most people stay either in the air-conditioned campus hotel, which is in the same building as the lecture rooms and has private baths, or in an air-conditioned student residence hall with shared baths, three shuttle-served blocks away. Staying on campus is not mandatory; however, if you stay in the residence hall, the fee includes three meals a day as well as accommodations. For children (age 4–16), there is a day camp with age-graded programs; teenagers can opt to attend classes with you. Brochures for the Mini University's annual offerings are available in March. *Mini University, Indiana University Alumni Association, Box 4822, Bloomington, IN 47402-4822, tel. 812/855–0291 or 800/824–3044, fax 812/855–4228. June: 5 days, $120. Price does not include lodging (at varying prices depending on the quarters) or meals; the* *residence hall package, including accommodations and meals, is $195–$230; sign up 2–3 months in advance.*

OHIO **The College of Wooster Summer of . . .** Begun in the 1970s, this alumni college is rooted in the strong liberal arts foundation of the College of Wooster, the very picture of a small, traditional college with its English Collegiate Gothic-style buildings and 320 green acres of ash, elm, maple, oak, and sycamore trees. Every year for seven days in June, some 40 to 60 students come to the school for its summer program, which involves five courses; past topics have included Eastern Europe after Communism; International Migration to the United States; From Main Street to the Information Superhighway; Marriages, Family, and Community in the Middle Ages; and Understanding Earth Hazards. College of Wooster faculty members do the teaching and may assign readings in advance and provide bibliographies for those who want to continue their studies after the program concludes. The name of the session changes every year to incorporate the current year—for example, Summer of '97 or Summer of '98.

Each course involves three hour-long lectures, scheduled so that you can attend all five courses. Time is also built into the schedule for organized off-campus excursions to nearby attractions such as the Cleveland Museum of Art and Amish Country; these complement the academic program. You also have use of the college pool, golf course, tennis courts, running track, game room, and personal conditioning room. After dark, there are frequently performances by the Ohio Light Opera Company, in residence at the college in summer, as well as films and other activities.

Lodging options are an air-conditioned residence hall with shared baths, or the Wooster Inn, which has private baths as well as air-conditioning. Food at the campus cafeteria is simple but good institutional fare; it's served buffet-style in a

private dining room for participants. The program brochure is ready in late March. *Summer of '97, Office of Alumni Relations, Gault Alumni Center, The College of Wooster, Wooster, OH 44691, tel. 330/263–2324. June: 7 days, $385. Price does not include lodging ($160 in residence hall, $375 in inn without breakfast); sign up 3–4 months in advance.*

SOURCES

ORGANIZATIONS There is no central registry of campus vacation programs, and even colleges with long-standing programs do little to publicize them outside of alumni publications and local media.

To find out about other campus learning vacations, a good first step is to make a list of colleges or universities that you wish you could attend (don't forget your own alma mater!), or of institutions in regions you'd like to visit. Then contact their alumni offices or extension program offices and ask if they offer a summer learning program that's open to the general public. If they don't, they may be able to refer you to schools that do.

Elderhostel (75 Federal St., Boston, MA 02110, tel. 617/426–8056), a nonprofit educational organization founded in 1975, offers a vast array of inexpensive, short-term academic programs at educational institutions around the world. The hitch: You must be at least 55 years old to participate, and your spouse or companion, if you bring one, must be no younger than 50.

ALSO SEE If enriching your mind in a traditional educational setting appeals to you, check out the chapters on Foreign-Language Immersion Programs, Painting Workshops, and Writing Conferences and Workshops. Want to associate with professorial types? Look into Archaeological Digs, Cultural Tours, and Garden Tours, led by experts in their fields.

Cooking Schools

Written by Sean Elder

Updated by Maria Kourebanas

or many of us, the desire to cook comes late in life and is the result of a lifetime of bad food. Unless you hail from one of those fortunate families that takes cooking seriously—that knows the importance of fresh basil, say, or the virtues of blackened tuna (as opposed to Charlie Tuna)—you probably grew up thinking of cooking as a necessity rather than an enjoyable hobby. I came from the latter type of home, and when I set out on my own I attempted to avoid the kitchen completely. The problem with this approach was that eating in restaurants required money, which I had even less of than I had cooking skills. I was left with no choice but to don an apron and learn to feed myself, and so I did. Not very imaginatively, at first, and not very well, but I persevered. I was lucky to be living in San Francisco, where on those rare occasions when I could afford to eat out, the food was so varied and international that it intrigued my awakening abilities and challenged my culinary limitations. Repeated visits to the Hunan Restaurant finally convinced me to buy a wok and Henry Chung's cookbook. In lieu of frequent repasts at Chez Panisse, I bought Alice Waters's collected pasta recipes and learned the difference between arugula and endive.

Years have passed, and I no longer cook because I'm broke; I cook because I enjoy it. Most of my days are spent in front of a computer, writing myself into corners, and cooking provides me with a simple form of relaxation that is almost pre-lingual in its logic: "Chop garlic. Heat oil. Put garlic in oil. Brown. Chop anchovies. Add. Don't burn." And so on. Once you know the basics, from sautéing to baking, you can do anything. The benefits of my culinary efforts are quite tangible, for my family as well as myself, and cooking is one of those harmless hobbies you can pursue while savoring a glass of wine.

For those who cook all the time, a cooking vacation might sound like a busman's holiday, but cooking schools can go beyond the techniques they teach and provide a culinary window to a new world. Explore New York through the produce of Chinatown or the fish market on Fulton Street, or discover the Southwest through its Native American–Mexican cooking heritage. The schools also give you the chance to meet like-minded chefs of all abilities; all classes listed below are open to everyone, from the rank amateur to the seasoned pro.

Going to a cooking school can also make cooking more fun by freeing you from dependence on recipes. Once you know the basic cooking techniques—knife skills, sauces, roasting, sautéing, puff pastry, baking, and so on—you can use cookbooks only for ideas, with the confidence that your meal will not only be good, but origi-

Sean Elder lives in Brooklyn with his wife and two children. His writing has appeared in many publications, but his cooking appears only in his own kitchen. Maria Kourebanas is an associate editor at Gourmet *magazine.*

nal as well. And once you thoroughly understand your kitchen and the local market, you can improvise with what you have and what's in season—not at all like the painstaking process of following instructions that might as well be in Greek and hoping everything turns out all right. You may learn to savor the whole production, from picking out produce to choosing wines, and do all of this while seeing a new part of the country and eating some tasty homework.

CHOOSING THE RIGHT SCHOOL

Most courses do not include accommodations and involve a lot of free time, so be sure there are other things you want to do in the area. Also, be sure to double-check all course information: A good school will vary its programs just to keep things interesting.

Here are some questions you should ask when selecting a school:

What is the cost and what's included? The prices given here are for courses of at least four days and include the cost of all cooking ingredients and equipment, unless otherwise specified. Most courses include at least one meal a day (often lunch), which is prepared during class. For the classes in this chapter, we have noted any meals not provided. Prices do not include accommodations, transportation to and from the school, or other entertainment, unless otherwise noted.

What are the instructors' qualifications? Many of the instructors in the schools listed here are professional chefs and authors of cookbooks. Find out how long an instructor has been teaching, and take a look at any books he or she has written. The International Association of Culinary Professionals (IACP) certifies cooking professionals and teachers, but there are many qualified chefs and teachers who are not members, so ask about experience, education, and philosophy.

How long has the school been in business? The more experience a school has, the more likely it is that your course will run smoothly.

What are the accommodations like? Many schools offer only suggestions on accommodations in the area. If accommodations are included in the price of your course, find out if rooms and bathrooms are private or shared.

What is the food like? If, as at the majority of cooking schools, you prepare some of your meals in class, the course description should give you a good idea of what you'll be eating. You're probably on your own for at least one meal a day, so find out what the dining options are in the area.

What is the teacher-student ratio? The size of the class and the number of instructors is important to the quality of the course. Make sure your instructor will have time to observe you individually.

Is the class participation oriented or demonstration oriented? If you really want to get up to your elbows in flour, make sure you'll have the opportunity. In some courses you simply watch and take notes. If it is a demonstration class, make sure you get printed recipes and ample time to take notes and ask questions.

How is the kitchen designed? A good teaching kitchen will feature an overhead mirror, so everyone can see what the instructor is doing, and a work station for each participant. This means counter space and preferably somewhere to stash your knives and cooking utensils. In a smaller class, and a smaller kitchen, these things are less essential.

What do I need to know to participate? Most schools will answer "nothing," but make sure that's what they mean. If you don't know the difference between sautéing and broiling, it might make for some communication problems.

THE NORTHEAST

MASSACHUSETTS **Macrobiotics in Massachusetts.** For advocates of macrobiotic cooking, the books of Michio Kushi are something close to religious texts. In titles such as the *Macrobiotic Way* and the *Cancer Prevention Diet*, Kushi and his wife, Aveline, give the guidelines for a diet that's low in saturated fat and high in fiber, natural vitamins, and minerals. At the Kushi Institute in Becket, Massachusetts, in the heart of the Berkshire Mountains, you learn not only how to change your diet, but also how to use exercise to lead a more healthful lifestyle. You are encouraged to attend seminars here with someone who can help you stick with the changes you make when you go home. You can take a weeklong cooking seminar or opt for the Way to Health seminar, which includes exercise classes as well as cooking instruction.

Fifteen students—usually of all ages and from diverse backgrounds—attend each cooking seminar. The rigorous daily schedule begins at 7 AM with some light morning exercise, followed by breakfast. There is a daily cooking class, from 9:30 AM to 12:30 PM, in which you learn how to select and prepare a variety of fish, how to use tofu and tempeh, how to make hearty soups and stews, and how to prepare healthful snacks and desserts. The evening, from 7 to 9, is filled with lectures and discussions, chaired by Kushi Institute graduates such as Charles Millman, Ed Esko, and John Kozinski. In these sessions you study the relationship between diet and health and get practical tips on how to use what you've learned, including how to eat healthfully on the road and how to prepare macrobiotic meals quickly.

All you have to take to the seminar is a notebook and pencil; everything else you need is provided. Accommodations are in a turn-of-the-century hunting lodge and a dormitory, set amid 600 acres of secluded meadows, woodlands, and streams. You share a simply furnished room with one other student, and there are shared bathrooms. Private rooms are available at an extra cost. All meals are included in the price of tuition, are prepared on the premises, and are, of course, macrobiotic. *Kushi Institute, Box 7, Leland Rd., Becket, MA 01223, tel. 413/623–2102, fax 413/623–8827. Year-round: 6 days, $1,250. Discounts for early registration; sign up anytime.*

NEW YORK **Chinese Fusion.** They call it Chinois, this meeting of French and Chinese cuisine, and Wolfgang Puck and others in California were some of the original practitioners. New York–based Chinese chef and caterer Karen Lee has been making her own inroads in this cuisine. After studying for five years with Madame Chu, the woman who brought Chinese haute cuisine to the West, Lee wrote her popular cookbook, *Chinese Cooking for the American Kitchen.* It was the editor of this book who suggested that Lee do something a little more nontraditional—say, stuff wonton with goat cheese—and a fusion-chef was born. The style she has developed has strong Oriental influences with French and Italian overtones. If the idea of a Szechuan steak au poivre or Chinese risotto appeals to you, come spend five days in her Manhattan apartment's kitchen developing a fusion style of your own.

Classes are 2½-hour learning lunches, each a combination of demonstration and participation. You eat dishes as they are completed, and sample wines selected to accompany your meal. You and the other seven or eight students in the group spend a lot of time around a 6-foot-by-3-foot butcher block table, because, as is the tradition in Chinese cooking, about two thirds of the work is preparation. You begin by learning the importance of choosing good ingredients and may even take a field trip to Chinatown for some firsthand experience. Equally important is learning techniques, such as stir-frying, dry cooking, steaming, and deep-fat frying. Dishes prepared range from wild-mushroom spring rolls to parchment salmon in ginger-saffron sauce.

No previous cooking experience is required. In fact, this cuisine is so original that even the most advanced cook is unlikely to be bored. Although Lee's apartment is near 59th Street and Central Park, the land of top-dollar hotels, she's happy to help you find more reasonably priced accommodations. *Karen Lee, 142 West End Ave., Apt. 30V, New York, NY 10023, 212/787–2227, fax 212/496–8178. Oct. and May: 5 days, $650. Price does not include breakfast or dinner; sign up at least 2 months in advance.*

NEW YORK **Fundamentals of Healthy Cooking.** This 10-day class is designed for those committed to learning the fundamentals of healthy cooking and learning them *now*—very New York. It's offered by the Natural Gourmet Institute of Food and Health, which has been running courses on cooking and food theory since it was established in 1977. You are taught by a team of teachers, each with at least 10 years of professional cooking experience, and each with a different area of expertise.

Each day you have two three-hour classes, separated by lunch. While the Natural Gourmet is not exclusively macrobiotic, you do learn about such macro staples as tofu, *seitan* (wheat gluten that has been cooked and rinsed of starch, so you're left with chewy high protein, "a little bizarre" admits one convert), and tempeh (made from whole soy beans, it is called "the Roquefort cheese of soy beans"). These foodstuffs provide the basic structure for countless healthy meals. Other class topics include knife skills, herbs and spices, grain identification and cooking techniques, soups, salads and dressings, whole-grain bread making, and sea vegetables.

Classes are a combination of demonstration and participation. Although shopping trips aren't part of the course, you do learn what to look for when you're on your own. Groups are limited to 25 students, with one teacher and several apprentices circulating

to observe and give individual help. Lunch is a kind of daily review session: On a day when fish is being discussed, you might make a salad from the previous day's vegetable class, and so on. Your day ends at 5 PM, leaving you with plenty of time to explore downtown Manhattan and the many largely nonorganic pleasures the city has to offer in the summer.

Classes are held in the institute's two teaching kitchens. All you need to provide is a knife, preferably a Japanese cutting knife, which can be bought or rented at the school. Although the school has no accommodations of its own, there are many hotels in midtown Manhattan. *The Natural Gourmet Institute for Food and Health, 48 W. 21st St., 2nd Floor, New York, NY 10010, tel. 212/645–5170, fax 212/989–1493. July or Aug.: 2 wks, $1,190. Price does not include breakfast or dinner; sign up at least 1 month in advance. Discounts for early registration.*

NEW YORK **Spa Style in a Week.** What is spa-style cuisine? It's low in fat, cholesterol, and salt, yet high in flavor, and it has become more popular as more and more studies link fatty diets to heart disease. This five-day course, offered three times a year by the New School for Social Research, teaches you how to prepare foods that meet these healthy standards. It's taught by Mr. Arlyn Hacket, a former chef at the Pritikin Longevity Center in Santa Monica, California; author of *Can You Trust a Slim Chef?*; and host of the PBS series "Health Smart Gourmet Cooking."

The course is limited to 12 students. You meet for three hours a day in kitchens in the New School's main building, a 150-year-old town house that's part of the Greenwich Village Historic District. Before you start cooking, you spend an afternoon learning to shop for everything from fruits and vegetables to packaged foods. Other classes teach you how to replace oil-based cooking methods, such as deep-frying and sautéing, with water-based methods such as poaching and steaming, and other low-fat alternatives, such as broiling. Juices, wines, and herbs are used as flavoring substitutes for sugars, salts, and fats. Each class includes demonstrations and participation, and you always finish by eating what you've made. Dishes vary seasonally, and may include strawberry-rhubarb crisp and twice-cooked salmon with apricot glaze in the spring and summer, and potato-and-bean soup and chili in the winter. *New School for Social Research, Registration Office, 66 W. 12th St., New York, NY 10011, tel. 212/229–5690, fax 212/229–5648. Jan., May, and Aug.: 5 days, $405. Sign up at least 1 month in advance.*

NEW YORK **A Week of Fine Cooking.** Peter Kump's School of Culinary Arts has an international reputation for excellence. When you read that another school has an instructor that studied at Kump's, you know you're in good hands. Kump himself studied in Europe and New York under such renowned chefs as James Beard, Diana Kennedy, and Marcella Hazan, before he began giving classes in his New York apartment in 1974. Today, the school has two Manhattan locations, one on the Upper East Side and the other on 23rd Street in Chelsea. A staff of 30 instructors and 30 assistants teaches a variety of courses for professionals and amateurs. The student-teacher ratio is never greater than 12 to 1, so you get a lot of personal attention.

For the nonprofessional, Kump's offers five-day, no-prerequisite courses on the techniques of fine cooking, pastry and baking, bread, cake decorating, spa cuisine, and Italian cooking. The classes meet Monday through Friday, usually from 10 AM to 3 PM, and have curriculums designed to teach you the basic techniques of your chosen subject. The course Techniques of Fine Cooking I (formerly called French Cooking) is the most popular, and for good reason. Within minutes you're up and cooking, learning everything from soufflés to sauces. You walk out knowing it all (or at least enough to impress your friends).

The daily itinerary varies according to the instructor (all Kump graduates), but each lesson is a combination of demonstration and participation. You start small, with a lesson on knife skills, and progress to braising, roasting, sautéing, and other techniques. By the end of the week you're preparing roast tarragon chicken, sautéed rib lamb chops, butter-braised leeks, and salade Niçoise. Practice recipes are handed out in class for those who are going home each day to a kitchen.

You must bring two knives (10-inch chef's knife and 3-inch paring knife), an apron, and a dish towel to class each day. The uptown school is not far from Central Park and the museums (including the Metropolitan Museum of Art and the Guggenheim) that dot upper 5th Avenue. And the 23rd Street school is nearby all the new big-name shops that have revitalized the Chelsea area. An information sheet with restaurant and hotel recommendations is provided to visiting students. *Peter Kump's School of Culinary Arts, 307 E. 92nd St., New York, NY 10128, tel. 212/410–4601 or 800/522–4610, fax 212/348–6360. Year-round: 5 days, $295, plus $180 material fee. Price does not include knives, apron, dish towel, breakfast, or dinner; sign up 1 month in advance.*

VERMONT **Fundamentals at a Farmhouse.** Teacher, chef, and restaurateur Tom Chiffriller offers custom-tailored cooking lessons at his rustic Vermont bed-and-breakfast. You and up to five other students spend five days learning to cook just about any type of cuisine: Mexican is the only one Chiffriller doesn't teach. You start with a basic curriculum—learning how to make a meal from what's in your kitchen (as long as it's not one beer and some peanut butter!), how to streamline recipes to save time, and basic techniques, such as making a cream sauce without lumps. From there Chiffriller adapts the course to the interests of the group, showing you how basic techniques can be adapted to many different cuisines.

Tom gleaned his own knowledge while studying restaurant management at the University of Vermont, working as a teacher at the Culinary Institute of America and the New England Culinary Institute, managing the food services for Bryn Mawr College, and establishing the Butternut Tree Restaurant in Woodstock, Vermont. The Farmhouse 'Round the Bend bed-and-breakfast is his latest venture, and he's been offering classes there since 1991.

Each morning, you gather in the kitchen, where Tom whips up breakfasts of scones, muffins, and apple Betty. Next it's four hours of demonstration and participation. Preparing such dishes as Szechuan shredded cabbage and pork and Portuguese paella with seafood and chicken, you learn not just how to cut vegetables and make sauces, but also the skill of menu-planning. Self-sufficiency and improvisation are emphasized. Lunch each day is a sampling of the dishes prepared. Afternoon field trips include visits to a local winery, a wholesale produce company, and a local vegetable farm.

Chiffriller restored the 1844 Greek Revival farmhouse himself, and your tuition includes lodging (private or shared) in one of the three guest rooms, decorated with early 19th-century antiques. The house is a five-minute walk from the historic village of Grafton, settled in 1780. There are also miles of trails for biking, walking, and skiing; a few local shops such as the Grafton Village Cheese Company; antiques and art shops; and sheep, lots of sheep. *Farmhouse 'Round the Bend, Box 57, Grafton, VT 05146, tel. 802/843–2515. Year-round: 5 days, $650–$750. Price does not include dinner; sign up at least 1 month in advance.*

THE MID-ATLANTIC

MARYLAND **Primary Skills of Cooking.** What sauce goes with what? What technique should be used to cook this as

opposed to that? Who knows? François Dionot does, and he should. A native of Reims, France, Dionot studied at the College Techniques de Barbezieux in Charentes, and L'Ecole Hôtelière de la Société Suisse des Hôteliers in Lausanne, Switzerland. Decrying the lack of a European-style culinary arts school in the United States, Dionot founded L'Academie de Cuisine in Bethesda in 1976. What began with one simple course in French cooking is now a celebrated school educating countless chefs in the fine art of fine food, from purchasing to preparation, with a little philosophy thrown in for flavor. Past students include the chefs at Red Sage and Palladines in Washington, DC, and the pastry chef at the White House.

For the amateur enthusiast, L'Academie offers the four-day Primary Skills of Cooking course. Three-hour classes start at 9:30 AM, 2 PM, or 6:30 PM, depending on which of four summer sessions you attend. The first day covers meats, the second poultry, and the third and fourth fish and shellfish. You learn to make stocks and sauces to go with each meat or fish and get lessons on handling, preparation, boning, and stuffing. Roasting, braising, sautéing, poaching, and searing are also covered. The philosophy at L'Academie is that once you know the proper techniques for cooking each type of food, you can work without a recipe.

The course is limited to 21 pupils. Kristin Dunn, a graduate of the Culinary Institute of America and a veteran teacher, is the primary instructor and has four assistants. The class is held in a working kitchen, set up with five rows of countertop-covered individual work spaces. Around the perimeters of the room are stoves, a convection oven, and a large broiler. In the front is a demonstration counter. The school has a discount package with a local Holiday Inn, and your free time can be spent exploring the nation's capital, or nearby Bethesda. *L'Academie de Cuisine, 5021 Wilson La., Bethesda, MD 20814, tel. 301/986–9490, fax 301/652–*

7970. July–Aug.: 4 days, $265. Price does not include meals; sign up 2 months in advance.

WEST VIRGINIA **French Cooking in Luxury.** This is the Cadillac of cooking schools. Anne Willan, founder and president of the highly acclaimed La Varenne cooking school in Paris, offers five-day programs at the posh Greenbrier Hotel, where spa treatments and afternoon tea are part of the package. You and the other 60 or so students are welcomed with a champagne reception, and it only gets better from there. This class is demonstration only, but what demonstration: Teaching with Willan have been guest chefs such as Julia Child, Barbara Tropp of China Moon, and Jamie Shannon and Dickie Brennan of Commander's Palace in New Orleans.

La Varenne at Greenbrier, which began in 1991, has a ritualized schedule, which begins upon your arrival, when you receive a notebook with a roster of the week's activities and events. Classes begin each morning at 9:30 AM and are taught by Anne Willan or a guest presenter. You always have a printed recipe to follow along with, and questions are freely asked and answered.

The first morning Willan teaches a class, "Foods with Friends," which features favorite recipes from Chateau du Sey, her cooking school in Burgundy; the results make a lovely buffet lunch. In fact, each day's demonstration is followed by a tasting of the foods that have been prepared. Willan spends another class on current cooking trends. On other mornings, various visiting chefs and authors use their own signature dishes to teach such techniques as sautéing, steaming, and puff pastry.

The second daily class is from 1:00 to 2:30 each afternoon. One day this is a show-and-tell by Greenbrier executive chef Robert Wang, followed by a tour of the hotel kitchen. Mark Liebendorfer, Director of Dining Services, and Werner Stoessel, Wine Sommelier, conduct a tasting session pairing white wines with five different menus. Several members of the Greenbrier staff also pick one afternoon to team teach a lesson on food presentation.

You have free time in the afternoon to golf (there are three championship golf courses), play tennis on one of the 20 courts, shoot trap and skeet, go horseback riding, or visit the health spa. Dinner each night is in the Main Dining Room, except Tuesday, when the visiting chef hosts a special three-course meal. And Thursday's Gold Service dinner is a black-tie optional, seven-course grand finale to the course. Friday morning you have one last class with Willan on entertaining and receive your La Varenne at The Greenbrier certificate as a memento of your stay.

The course is offered during eight separate weeks, from early March through early May. The stiff price, $1,850 per person, includes accommodations, breakfast and dinner daily in the Main Dining Room (lunch in class), and the plethora of hotel amenities. Amtrak stops right at the front gate. *La Varenne at Greenbrier, White Sulphur Springs, WV 24986, tel. 304/536–1110 or 800/624–6070, fax 304/536–7834. Early Mar.–early May: 5 days, $1,850. Sign up at least 3 months in advance.*

THE SOUTH

GEORGIA **Paris Trained, Georgia Bound.** Diane Wilkinson studied French cuisine at the Cordon Bleu and La Varenne in Paris and Italian cuisine with Marcella Hazan in Bologna. Since 1974 she's been teaching five-day courses in her native Georgia. Wilkinson believes that knowing the basic French techniques equips you to prepare almost any other cuisine, so here you'll learn the French approach to making stocks, pastries, breads, pastas, and poultry.

Classes are held from 10 AM to 5 PM each day in Wilkinson's kitchen and are a combination of demonstration and participation. Lunch and dinner preparation provide the structure for the lessons. One day you may prepare crispy skinned salmon with capers for lunch, learning how to sauté. For dinner you may make lamb shank with confit of Vidalia onions and sweet garlic, which teaches you how to braise. The kitchen opens up into a large room with plenty of counter space. There is a six-burner gas stove, a four-burner electric cooktop, a baking oven, and a wood-burning fireplace, specially designed for grilling.

Each course is limited to eight students, and groups are often friends who have planned their trip together. The school is near downtown Atlanta, just west of the fashionable Buckhead district. There are several shopping malls nearby, but after all the eating you do, the walking trails along the nearby Chattahoochee River may be a wiser choice for free-time activities. Diane can recommend hotels in the area. *Diane Wilkinson's Cooking School, 4365 Harris Trail, Atlanta, GA 30327, tel. 404/233–0366, fax 404/233–0051. Year-round: 5 days, $650. Price does not include breakfast; sign up 2 months in advance.*

THE MIDWEST

ILLINOIS **The Art of the Cake.** If you've longed to do more than write "Happy Birthday" on a double-layer angel food cake, take the Wilton School of Cake Decorating's five-day, 40-hour course for the total decorator. Here you learn the Lambeth Method of making piping, shells, scrolls, and scallops—that layer upon layer look that you've marveled at before, wondering, "How *do* they do that?" This is a hands-on, up-to-your-elbows course, and although it's not just for professionals, a fundamental background and some knowledge of cake decorating is required.

The school was founded in 1929 by Dewey McKinley Wilton, who had learned the craft of cake decorating in Europe and wanted to bring the art to the United States. His first-things-first philosophy has remained the school's: You learn the fundamentals, then build on (or break) the rules

of traditional cake-decorating in order to achieve greater self-expression. (If you think self-expression and cake decorating have nothing to do with each other, check out the Wilton School.)

The Lambeth Method course, offered twice a year, is the mother of all cake-decorating courses. Sue Matusiak, a Wilton graduate and a veteran cakemeister, guides your 15-student class through the paces of decorating two killer cakes. The 6-inch cushion cake will be used to teach you how to create a puffy "cushion" effect by layering icing. The 12-inch sampler cake is divided into quarters that will each have a different design: violet, forget-me-not, pansy, and orange blossom. Classes are a combination of demonstration and participation. Your instructor demonstrates a skill—for instance, making an intricate piping border—then you practice on your cake until you get it right. There's a lot of scraping and starting over!

All work is done in the school's teaching kitchen, where you are given plenty of room to work and a drawer to store your supplies. All class materials are provided and included in the cost of the course, as is the *Wilton Way of Cake Decorating, Vol. II,* the Big Book of the Lambeth Method. There is also a Wilton retail store here, where you can buy everything you need to work your new magic at home. There are several hotels and bed-and-breakfasts near the school; ask secretary Laura Lane for suggestions. *Wilton School of Cake Decorating and Confectionery Art, 2240 W. 75th St., Woodridge, IL 60517, tel. 630/963–7100, ext. 211, fax 630/963–7299. Twice a year: 5 days, $320 plus $50 application fee (refunded if you are not accepted). Sign up 3 months in advance.*

THE SOUTHWEST

NEW MEXICO **Spring Thing in Santa Fe.** This five-day course goes beyond cooking lessons to give you an education on the rich culinary culture and history of the Santa Fe area. Susan Curtis, who founded the Santa

Fe School of Cooking in 1989, schedules field trips to wineries, museums, microbreweries, tortilla factories, and farms. She also invites such experts as Deborah Madison, author of *The Greens Cookbook,* Cheryl and Bill Jamison, authors of *Smoke and Spices,* and Kathi Long, author of *Mexican Light Cooking,* to join the school's staff of six chefs in giving cooking demonstrations. These busy days are generally followed by free evenings for you to explore Santa Fe.

Your week begins on Sunday at 6:30 PM when you join the staff for a tapas reception. You can mingle with the other 15 to 25 students, while listening to a strolling guitarist. On Monday morning at 9 AM, it's off to El Rancho de Los Golondrinas living history museum, where you see reenactments of the daily lives of the Spanish colonists of the 18th and 19th centuries, including their farming and baking techniques. After eating the results, it's on to a tour, lunch, and beer sampling at the Santa Fe Brewing Company. The evening is spent at the home of cookbook authors Cheryl and Bill Jamison. Local brew master Laura Pomianmowski leads a tasting of microbrews, and there's a seminar given by the Jamisons on barbecuing, followed by dinner in the garden.

Tuesday's schedule is relatively light. Deborah Madison, an authority on vegetarian cuisine, usually leads a tour of the city's farmers market, selecting fresh ingredients for lunch. She then gives a demonstration on using regional produce, and lunch follows. At 3 PM you regroup at the school for a seminar on chilies by Dave DeWitt, founder and editor of Chile Pepper magazine. The evening is free.

Wednesday starts with a visit to Rancho Casados, where you witness the traditional preparation of corn *pozole* (a thick, hearty soup) and *chicos* (partially shucked corn roasted on the cob and dried). After a tour of La Chirapada Winery, it's on to Embudo Station, a former stop on the Chile Line (a railroad line that carried crops south to Taos). The Station, on the banks of the Rio Grande, is now a smokehouse and microbrewery. The proprietors give you a lecture on smoking meat and feed you a lunch of samples that you wash down with some of their other products, hearty ales and lagers. Your journey continues (don't worry, the bus driver hasn't been sampling the same beverages you have), perhaps to Leona's Tortilla Factory in Chimayo.

Thursday morning the School's staff members give a demonstration on contemporary Southwestern cuisine. Traditional techniques and dishes are combined with non-indigenous ingredients to create such dishes as polenta with smoked jalapeño, pork tenderloin with chili and black peppercorn, and grilled salmon marinated with chili. After eating the results, you can join in a tour from 2 to 4 PM of Native American pottery, baskets, and weavings at the School of American Research in Santa Fe. Finally you return to school and rest up, before attending a reception at the school and a grand finale dinner at one of the city's famed restaurants, such as Coyote Cafe or Santacafe.

There are no prerequisites for the course, and noncooking traveling companions can accompany you to everything but the demonstrations and lunches for a reduced price. Curtis usually works out a deal with a local hotel to give participants a discounted rate on accommodations. *Santa Fe School of Cooking, 116 W. San Francisco St., Santa Fe, NM 87501, tel. 505/983–4511, fax 505/983–7540. Once a year: 5 days, $849. Price includes transportation to all field trips, but does not include breakfast or dinners (except for Mon. and Thurs. night); sign up at least 2 months in advance.*

THE ROCKIES

COLORADO **Basic French in Boulder.** Offered four times a year, this beginning French cooking course at the Cooking School of the Rockies emphasizes organizational skills along with cooking techniques.

You learn how to strategically plan your meal preparation so everything is ready at the proper time. You also learn the art of *mise en place,* setting up all your ingredients and equipment before you begin cooking. Each day you prepare a four-course meal, which lets you practice these skills while learning the basics of sauces, omelets, soups and stocks, poaching, roasting, grilling, sautéing, and braising.

Poached pears in spiced red-wine sauce, salade Niçoise, grilled tuna with orange-basil beurre blanc sauce, bananas flambé, roasted tarragon chicken, and lemon mousse with red currant sauce, are a few of the dishes you may prepare. The techniques you learn while making them can be adapted for use in day-to-day cooking. Each day's menu also provides a lesson on mixing and matching dishes and sauces and making wine and cheese selections. You get a notebook with recipes and detailed instructions and spend ample time taking notes before the hands-on portion of class. At the end of each session, you and the other 10 students sit down and enjoy the meal you've created. The bonus here is that after this less-than-diet-conscious French feast, you can hike off the extra calories in the beautiful surrounding mountains.

The teaching staff here is well trained. Joan Brett trained at Peter Kump's New York Cooking School, studied with Julia Child, and is a member of the International Association of Culinary Professionals; Sue Dubach is a career teacher, food writer, and caterer; Diana Hoguet is also a teacher, food writer, and former caterer; and James Moore taught at the California Culinary Academy. Each instructor has two assistants to aid with preparation and cleanup. Classes are held in a full professional kitchen, with 10 burners, three ovens, personal work stations, and a cook island and mirror so that no matter where you are you can see what's going on. You need to bring an 8- or 10-inch chef's knife, a 3-inch paring knife, and an apron. The School provides a list of accommodation recommendations. *Cooking School of*

the Rockies, 637 S. Broadway, Suite H, Boulder, CO 80303, tel. 303/494–7988, fax 303/494–7999. 4 times a year: 5 days, $395. Price does not include knives and apron or breakfast and dinner; sign up at least 1 month in advance.

THE WEST COAST

CALIFORNIA **Culinary California.** Hugh Carpenter's five-day Napa Valley Food and Wine Adventure is a grand excursion to some of the region's best wineries and restaurants, with cooking courses along the way. Carpenter has taught over 2,000 courses throughout the United States and Canada since 1975. He specializes in fusion cooking that combines elements of Asian, southwestern, New Orleans, and Caribbean cuisines with indigenous American ingredients, and is the author of several cookbooks, including the *Fusion Food Cookbook, Chopstix,* and a new cookbook series, the latest of which is *Hot Pastas.*

Your adventure begins on Sunday evening, with a reception held at Carpenter's home in Oakville, California. You mix and mingle with the other 15 students in your group, while munching on Asian-Californian appetizers—gravlax with spicy Thai sauce, panfried shrimp dumplings in chipotle chili sauce. Then it's on to dinner at Cafe Pinot, the recently opened restaurant by famed chef Joachim Splichal, of Patina Restaurant in Los Angeles.

In the morning, you convene in the kitchen of the Cakebread Cellars winery, where Carpenter guides you through the preparation of such dishes as papaya and avocado salad, Caribbean prawns with cinnamon and pineapple, and Santa Fe cornbread sticks. You eat the lunch you've created, with the accompaniment of Cakebread wines. The early evening finds you at the Meadow Resort for a croquet tournament. Dressed in whites, you ply yourself with wine and appetizers to sustain you through a grueling croquet match.

If you've recovered by morning, you attend another class at Cakebread, taught by Carpenter and Cakebread's chef, Brian Streeter. The class breaks up into teams to prepare appetizers, salad, two entrées, and dessert. Then you're free until the class gathers at Chappellet Winery, in the evening. This prestigious small winery, which is never open to the public, is famous for its cabernet sauvignon. The tour, which includes tasting some of their older wines and hors d'oeuvres, fills the evening.

Class convenes the next morning for a cooking class and lunch at Cajun chef Jan Birnbaum's Catahoula Restaurant. In the late afternoon you meet at the Culinary Institute of America's Greystone campus for a tour of the facility. A tapas appetizer party and wine tasting on the terrace overlooking the valley follows.

On day five your morning is free and at noon you meet at Schramsberg Vineyards, one of California's most famous small wineries, for a picnic, sparkling wine tasting, and tour of caves dug by 19th-century Chinese laborers. Later that afternoon, you attend a tasting hosted by wine maker, Mark Aubert, at the Peter Michael Winery. The evening is free.

The last day starts a tour of Opus One Winery, then you're free or you can join in for lunch at Bistro Don Giovanni (this is a no-host, you-pay meal), and then visit the French barrel-making facility of Seguin Moreau to see artisans using century-old techniques. At 4 PM, you take your final class at Cakebread. You may prepare a dinner of freshly smoked quail, chilled prawns, and homemade chocolate truffles or dishes such as grilled Sonoma lamb,

fresh San Francisco Dungeness crab, and Asian dishes from Carpenter's cookbook, and enjoy the repast in the winery's idyllic garden.

The course is limited to 16, and no previous cooking knowledge or experience is required. Carpenter is happy to recommend hotels, though the Vintage Inn in Yountville is his first choice. *Hugh Carpenter/Camp Napa Culinary, Box 114, Oakville, CA 94562, tel. 707/944–9112, fax 707/944–2221. June–Oct.: 6 days, $860. Sign up 3 months in advance.*

SOURCES

ORGANIZATIONS The **American Institute of Wine & Food** (1550 Bryant St., Suite 700, San Francisco, CA 94103, tel. 415/255–3000 or 800/274–2493), a nonprofit educational organization, was founded in 1981 to help food and wine enthusiasts exchange information and to foster food and wine research and education opportunities. The tax-deductible membership fee includes subscriptions to the *Journal of Gastronomy* and the *American Wine & Food* newsletter.

International Association of Culinary Professionals (IACP, 304 W. Liberty St., Louisville, KY 40202, tel. 502/581–9786) endorses cooking schools and professional instructors and can give you a list of amateur, short-term courses.

BOOKS The *Guide to Cooking Schools* (ShawGuides, Inc., 8th edition, 1996, $19.95) is a comprehensive resource to culinary education with detailed descriptions of programs in the United States and other countries.

Cultural and Natural History Cruises

Written and updated by Melissa Rivers

ature cruises are wilderness expeditions for travelers who want to heed the call of the wild but don't cherish the thought of bug bites, pitching tents, cooking out, lugging gear, and taking cold showers or none at all. The cruise ship is a more civilized means of exploring nature: All the comforts of home (and then some) float into areas untouched by modern development.

You can have a relaxing vacation on a nature cruise and come away with a lot more than a good tan. You get the chance to see the stuff of *National Geographic* specials, firsthand. Picture the ship cutting through the water, the wind ruffling your hair as you keep a lookout for wildlife. Suddenly a black-footed albatross soars overhead, a whale spouts in the distance, or a shoal of dolphins dances in the water so close that you can hear them breathe. Then, before you can say "Ah!" you're racing across the deck to see the action on the opposite side of the ship.

There are hundreds of cruises to choose from—and the options are multiplying as more and more cruise lines, seeing trips sell out between 6 and 12 months in advance, recognize the demand and add additional departures. Such factors as the focus of the cruise, the size of the ship, and the itinerary mean that no two nature cruises are alike.

Some present an overview of the biological, geologic, and historical makeup of the region visited; others concentrate on the wildlife there. Depending on the program, you may spend most of your time on the ship watching the passing scenery or you may make frequent excursions to explore onshore or collect specimens. Motorized inflatable rafts, often Zodiacs, may be used to convey you and your fellow passengers to dry land or to move you closer to whales and other marine life.

Some cruises explore several areas—for instance, cruises that travel throughout the Pacific Northwest. Others stick to just one, such as Alaska. If you want to study wildlife and animal habitats in depth, choose one of the latter. Cruises on the northeastern seaboard and in Alaska and the Pacific Northwest are good examples of this type; they usually include frequent sightings of cetaceans (whales, dolphins, and porpoises), pinnipeds (seals, sea lions), fish life (including flying fish, a popular sight), and various pelagic birds (those whose habitat is the open ocean). On cruises that travel inland—for instance, up the Columbia River in Washington and Oregon or along New York's Erie Canal—you can expect to learn about the history and geology of the shore area, as well as the plants, mammals, and birds that spend their lives there.

Perhaps the greatest difference among nature cruises is the intensity of the focus on the natural world. True, all such cruises

---

Writer Melissa Rivers has cruised the world over in ships of all sizes and particularly enjoys the up-close views of wildlife and the environment as seen from small ships.

sail with a naturalist aboard (and most of these experts have postgraduate degrees and are affiliated with a professional research or educational institution). But the naturalist lectures and other activities are the main events on some cruises, while they're just one of many activities on others. When you're deciding upon a nature cruise, the first thing to ask yourself is whether you could get bored sighting the umpteenth bald eagle or whale. If you want to learn about the tiniest facets of an orca's breeding habits, go for it. If not, you'd better pick a cruise that gives you plenty of other things to think about.

To a great extent, your options in this area depend on the size of the ship you sail on. Most nature cruises use small, yacht-size, motor-driven ships that accommodate between 75 and 100 passengers; they feel intimate, the lifestyle aboard is decidedly casual, and the wildlife focus is pervasive. Announcements of wildlife sightings and lectures on passing flora and fauna are often made over ship-wide public-address systems, so you can hear them wherever you go. Hours of observation may be broken only by morning and afternoon lectures on area flora and fauna or daily field trips for shore observation and the gathering of plant specimens. The ships themselves have features that make it possible to get breathtakingly close to wildlife: A shallow draft lets them sail very close to shore, and powerful bow thrusters help them maneuver in bays, fjords, inlets, and other tight areas that larger ships can't manage safely. Because they are small, you are physically fairly close to the water, so you see marine life at closer range than you can from a large cruise ship. Shore excursions and the use of binoculars while on board are usually included in the cost of your trip on these small ships. Moreover, an open-door policy often prevails regarding visits to the bridge—fascinating if you're interested in navigation.

Other aspects of these small ships may or may not appeal to you. Schedules are tight and group-oriented, with set meal and activity times. Cabins tend to be compact, with a shower in a tiny head (bathroom, in shipboard parlance), which is sometimes shared. Finally, meals are generally served family style at open seatings and consist of basic steak, pasta, chicken, and fish dishes. After dark, there are informal lectures on upcoming sites and the occasional dance, film, or night of casino games.

Large cruise liners accommodating from 1,000 to 1,500 passengers, which also make nature cruises, offer an entirely different experience. Because of their size, large ships can't give you the close encounters with nature that are possible aboard more maneuverable vessels; what you see is usually very far away—some of these ships are as high as a 14-story building. Yes, there is generally a naturalist on board. But, other than a slide show on whales, you'll probably be on your own to learn more about wildlife. Other kinds of classes—perhaps aerobics, cooking, or finance—are generally available though.

The PA systems on large ships are used only for occasional park ranger talks and whale sightings. You have to select those shore excursions that highlight the natural environment, and sometimes you may have to explore on your own. The naturalist activities are only one of a huge range of diversions: several restaurants serving a variety of cuisines, lounges, snack bars, courts for various sports (paddle tennis, basketball, volleyball, and such, depending upon the ship), swimming pools and hot tubs, spas, casinos, theaters, and discos. Most of these large ships also offer a supervised children's program. Shore excursions usually cost extra. The creature comfort quotient is greater than on small ships. Staterooms have such amenities as a bathtub, minibar, and TV. The passenger-to-crew ratio is lower than on small ships, so the service is more personalized. Only you can say whether the buzz of a thousand other cruisers and the wealth of comforts and activities on board will enhance your experience of nature or diminish it.

For any given destination, you usually have a variety of options. Most lines that cruise in North America reposition their ships seasonally, spending winter in the Caribbean, summer in Alaska, and spring and fall on inland waterways or on the Panama Canal and along the Atlantic or the Pacific seaboards.

The greatest number of options in North America, however, are available for cruises to Alaska, particularly the Inside Passage, the 1,000-mile waterway stretching between Seattle, Washington, and Skagway, Alaska. Alaska is the single most popular destination among the growing ranks of nature cruises. Some Alaska cruises start in the south and head north; these are the hottest tickets because the beauty of the sights seems to grow exponentially along the way. Others head south, taking in the same sights but in a different sequence; reservations for these trips used to be easier to come by, as were discount fares, but Alaska is now so popular that this may no longer be the case. Typical stops include the colorful gold rush boomtowns of Wrangell and Skagway; Juneau, the capital city; the small seaport of Seward; Switzerland-like Valdez; Russian-influenced Sitka; and Alaska's wettest town, Ketchikan. A few Alaska cruises also typically stop in Victoria, known for its gardens.

Regardless of the destination, the average cruise lasts about eight days and costs $2,000 per person based on double occupancy—and up. Prices on any given ship will vary by cabin category and sometimes by sailing date. In Alaska, for instance, early- and late-season departures are less expensive than mid-season sailings.

If you find that a particular trip is sold out, be sure to check with other lines for a comparable itinerary; there's a great deal of overlap in territories covered by nature cruises, and if one cruise line does well with a particular itinerary, it's a safe bet that other lines offer it as well.

CHOOSING THE RIGHT CRUISE

While some smaller operators allow you to book a cruise directly, most major cruise lines only accept reservations from travel agents. No matter who you are dealing with when you are choosing your cruise, be sure to ask the following questions:

How large is the ship? The size of the ship determines whether your cruise is a luxury vacation with an environmental motif or an intense nature experience with a few of the comforts of home. The smaller the ship, the more maneuvering the crew can do to get you closer to the wildlife. Small ships tend to foster closer friendships among passengers who become chummy due to tighter quarters. Fewer passengers also means that the ship is easier and far faster to board and disembark.

On the other hand, large ships are a better bet for many cruisers. You'll prefer a large ship if the environmental aspects of the trip are only one of your vacation interests. The same is true if you have any hearing impairment, because the sound quality of loudspeaker systems aboard small ships tends to be poor and announcements can be difficult to understand. Large ships are better, too, if you have a mobility problem: Small ships typically lack the ramps, handrails, and elevators commonly found on large ships. Unless the cruise you are contemplating is on rivers and other protected waterways, you may also want to stick with large ships if you suffer from motion sickness. (To further reduce the chance you'll be afflicted, book a cabin at the true center of the ship—on a midlevel deck halfway between the bow and the stern, and avoid alcoholic beverages, which further irritate upset stomachs and magnify feelings of imbalance.)

What are the qualifications of the naturalists leading the cruise? The experience and ability of your guide or guides greatly affect your learning experience. Make sure that they have the background to provide the kind of information you expect to get when you sign up for a nature cruise.

What will the naturalist contribute? Find out exactly what the naturalists will do. They might simply point out and identify the wildlife along the shore. Or, at the time of sightings, they might lecture informally on the animals' habits and habitats. They might lecture on area flora and fauna by day or after dark. Sometimes naturalists are constantly available to answer your questions; sometimes they have a few set hours. On larger ships, you are much less likely to receive the personal attention of a naturalist, who may have to answer questions from 1,000 or more people.

What is the focus of the trip? Find out if you'll primarily be observing wildlife, studying the geographic features of the area, or learning about the region's history.

How much time is spent observing and learning about nature? Especially on larger ships, you may spend most of your time enjoying sports and other activities not related to the environment. On small ships, the environment is the star of the show, and virtually all activities aboard ship and ashore revolve around observing and exploring it.

Are Zodiacs or other landing craft available so you can get off the ship and explore frequently? If getting up close and personal with the wildlife and environment around you matters, make sure that Zodiac excursions are an integral part of the program.

What is the itinerary? Ports of call vary, as does the amount of time in each port—typically between three or four hours and a full day. Boston and Montreal are frequent stops on itineraries through the Northeast, and San Francisco, Portland, Seattle, and Vancouver, British Columbia, on cruises along the West Coast. Virtually all Alaska itineraries include stops in Juneau, Sitka, and Ketchikan.

What's the cost and what's included? It's typical for cruise fares to be per person, based on double occupancy, and to include (like all prices quoted in the following cruise reviews unless otherwise noted) all meals, lectures, and evening entertainment but not airfare to the port of embarkation or from the port of disembarkation, port taxes, optional shore trips, gratuities to the crew, and baggage or trip insurance. Be sure to ask whether your fare covers alcoholic beverages, carbonated beverages, snacks, and shore excursions. It varies from one cruise to the next.

A simple way to compare costs of different cruises is to look at the per diem—the price of a cruise on a daily basis per passenger, based on double occupancy. Also, look at what you get for the per diem, since this varies from ship to ship. As a rule, cruises on small ships are more expensive than those on large ships; small ships must charge more to meet the expenses that the big lines make up in volume.

If you plan to arrive a day or two early at the port of embarkation, or to linger a few days for sightseeing after debarkation, estimate the cost of your hotel, meals, car rental, sightseeing, and other expenditures. Cruise lines often sell packages for such pre- and post-cruise stays. These may or may not cost less than arrangements you make independently, so shop around.

What are accommodations like? Make sure you know what you're getting into. Will you be sleeping in a tiny cabin or a luxury stateroom? If you care about the size of your bathroom or whether it's down the hall, ask. If you don't relish cold showers, make sure that hot ones are available. If you don't mind taking cold showers, make sure that the water is at least fresh; some of the simpler ships let you rinse off in seawater. If you must have a lower bunk, a double bed, or a window, make sure that the ship can provide it.

What are meals like? A smaller ship has a smaller galley, a smaller staff, and, therefore, a more limited menu. On large ships, you have a selection of restaurants and snack bars serving a variety of foods. The quality of food varies from ship to ship; in general, the better the ship, the better the food, and the more you'll spend for the cruise.

Find out if there are table assignments and whether there are one or two seatings; ask when these are arranged. You may be able to do it when you book, or you may have to wait until you board.

Many small ships have open seating for all meals, which means you may switch tables and dining partners as often as you wish. However, on many larger ships dining rooms are not big enough to accommodate all passengers at once, so mealtimes are divided into two seatings, usually from 1½ to 2½ hours apart. Dinner, for example, is often between 6 and 6:30 for early seating, between 8 and 8:30 for the late seating. On some ships, these seating times are strictly observed, and the dining room doors close 10 to 15 minutes after the scheduled mealtime; on other ships, you may enter the dining room at your leisure, but must leave by the end of the seating.

Make sure you know what the policies are on the ships you are considering, since meals play such a big part in the cruise experience.

If it matters to you, ask about the ship's policies on serving liquor. A few of the smaller ships don't serve liquor at all or serve only wine; and even then, you're expected to bring your own.

To what degree is shipboard life scheduled? As a general rule, the larger the ship, the more choice you'll have in how you spend your time.

What other onboard activities are offered? If you don't want to spend all your time nature-watching, make sure you pick a ship that gives you something else to do. Even smaller ships offer a few diversions, but they may be limited to a library for reading or a small exercise room.

What is the typical makeup of passengers? Each cruise attracts a specific audience. Find out what it is before you book, and make sure you'll be comfortable in that company. (This is especially important on small ships, where the group is smaller.) The number of cruising families is on the rise, accounting for 25% of cruise passengers. Alaska itineraries tend to have a majority of passengers who are older than 55, while on California, New England, and Caribbean cruises, the average age is lower and couples mix with families. Single travelers are usually in the minority.

What programs and facilities are available for families traveling with children? You must shop especially carefully for a nature cruise if you plan to sail with children. Some ships don't allow younger children (usually those under eight); the material covered by the naturalists is too advanced. However, some cruises do provide special children's programs and activities. If these are available, question the cruise line closely to find out what they're like. Ask the same questions about activities, schedules, facilities, and supervision that you would of any day care provider. But also find out what ages of children are accepted (some require that participants be out of diapers or at least three); what hours the program runs (it may cover you for only parts of days, and it may or may not be available after dark); and whether babysitting is available (and from whom).

How formal is the cruise? Some cruises require fancier attire than others. On some, you will never need anything dressier than chinos and sweaters; on others, there may be one dressy evening, or several. On a select few, men tend to wear jackets and ties to dinner every evening. In general, small ship cruising is casual, while larger ships call for a dressier wardrobe.

Will laundry service be available? You may be able to pack lighter when traveling on a large ship with laundry service or a laundromat. Most smaller ships don't offer laundry facilities, but these ships' more casual atmosphere doesn't require an extensive wardrobe.

How long has the company been in business? Try to stick with an operator who has been in business for several years. Experience is some insurance, though not a guarantee, that the trip will run smoothly.

Do you have references from past guests? If you have doubts about whether or not you'll enjoy a given cruise, there's no substitute for a conversation with another traveler. Ask the travel agent for names of previous clients. It's a good way of judging the agent's expertise and advice, as well as the merits of a particular cruise line or ship.

How far in advance do I need to book? As nature and adventure cruises attract more and more people, ships are sailing near or at capacity. In Alaska, cruise lines begin selling their next year's sailings as soon as the current season is underway. Departures on the most popular itineraries and sailing dates begin selling out between 6 and 12 months in advance. To make sure that you get the accommodations you want on the sailing of your choice, it's imperative to reserve well ahead of the sailing date. Early booking discounts are often available as well.

MAJOR PLAYERS

ALASKA SIGHTSEEING/CRUISE WEST This operator, founded in 1973, has the largest fleet of small ships in North America and the highest number of annual cruises in the Pacific Northwest. Five vessels—the 101-passenger *Spirit of '98*, the 54-passenger *Spirit of Discovery*, the 80-passenger *Spirit of Columbia*, the 82-passenger *Spirit of Alaska*, and the line's new 107-passenger *Spirit of Endeavour*—will make a variety of 4- to 10-night trips. Because of the size of these ships, you can reach areas that you can't get to in larger ships. Cruises travel between Seattle and Juneau in spring, summer, and fall. The spring and fall shoulder seasons have added itineraries in the San Juan and Gulf Islands and in California's Wine Country. One ship, the *Spirit of Columbia*, cruises up and down the Columbia and Snake rivers in Washington, Oregon, and Idaho throughout the spring, summer, and fall.

The cruise coordinator on each trip is trained to teach you about the flora, fauna,

and geologic features that you encounter en route. Over the public address system, he or she alerts you to sights that range from a bald eagle soaring overhead to unusual plants growing in the semi–rain forest climate of Columbia Gorge. When you're following the path of the Lewis and Clark expedition, you get some history lessons, too.

Life aboard ship is fairly unstructured: Arrivals and departures, meals, and occasional evening entertainment are the only firmly scheduled events. The close quarters create a sense of camaraderie among the passengers, but you won't get the luxury and service you do on larger ships. Cabins are small and simply decorated, and most have windows and doors that open to fresh breezes. Meals are basic but well-prepared; the small galley and prep staff limit the selection. Two entrées are offered for dinner, and you must make your choice in advance. Local foods, including salmon and fresh fruit and berries, are often served. Beyond evening cocktail parties, entertainment is limited—perhaps a movie and casino night. Trips are designed for adult participants; bringing children is not encouraged. American owned and operated, this outfitter has young and energetic American crews. Prices range from $649 to $4,249. *2401 4th Ave., Suite 700, Seattle, WA 98121, tel. 206/441–8687 or 800/426– 7702, fax 206/441–4757.*

AMERICAN CANADIAN CARIBBEAN LINE This was one of the first lines to offer cruises on small ships. In 1964, Captain Luther H. Blount of Blount Marine Shipbuilders predicted the growth in demand for smaller ships and started designing yachtlike ships with shallow drafts and bow ramps to provide direct access to the shore. Thus was born the small fleet of American Canadian Caribbean Line: the *Caribbean Prince*, the *Mayan Prince*, and the *Niagara Prince*, the last being 1994's addition to the line. These ships, almost identical, cruise along the eastern seaboard and the Florida coast, through the Erie Canal and the bayou country of the Gulf Coast, and around the U.S.

Virgin Islands. Trips focus on both the cultural and natural history in these areas.

Cabins are simple and small, measuring just 8 by 10 feet, but they're air-conditioned, with built-in berths and private bathrooms with toilet and handheld shower. Rates tend to be low, and as a result, ACCL offers few traditional services and facilities—sheets and towels are changed every *other* day, for instance, and it's even suggested that you pack your own beach towel. Hearty homemade fare, such as sandwiches on fresh-baked bread, and classic pastas are interspersed with such gourmet treats as chilled peach soup and crab-stuffed pastry. Generally speaking, cuisine is basic American, and many offerings use fresh seafood and produce picked up in ports along the way. Meals are served family style at a single open seating (dinner at 6); breakfast is a buffet. No alcohol is sold on board, although you are free to bring your own. Mixers and other nonalcoholic drinks are available free from the bar at all hours. Cruises are narrated by a naturalist or historian who points out the flora, fauna, and sites of interest along the route; and authorities on local history and wildlife are frequently brought on board in port to share their insights and expertise. A cruise director arranges evening entertainment; he or she may play the piano or bring in a steel drum band or guest lecturer. The minimum age on ACCL cruises is 14, but the average guest is over 55. These no-frills cruises are an excellent value, with the cost of a 12-day cruise ranging from $1,622 to $2,599 per person. *461 Water St., Box 368, Warren, RI 02885, tel. 401/247–0955 or 800/556–7450, fax 401/245–8303.*

BLUEWATER ADVENTURES This Canadian adventure tour operator has been running wildlife and natural history cruises since 1974. Their trips are chartered several times each year by organizations such as the Oceanic Society and the Los Angeles Country Natural History Museum, testament to the quality of their natural history focus. In addition to years of practical field experience, most crew members have backgrounds in anthropology, marine biology, ecology, or ornithology, so they are fully capable of teaching passengers about wildlife encountered on the trip. Informal lessons in sailing, ocean navigation, knot tying, and seamanship can also be a part of the learning experience aboard Bluewater's vessels.

Facilities on their 68-foot ketch *Island Roamer* include eight double cabins and three heads with hot showers. The 65-foot motorized yacht *Snow Goose* sleeps 12 in six double cabins that share three heads (only two showers). Both are equipped with a salon, a well-stocked natural history library, and a snug galley where a cook prepares meals using local produce and seafood. Wine is served with dinner, otherwise it's BYOB. Most guests are between 20 and 60 years old, active, highly educated, and well traveled; there are often more women than men. Because quarters are tight, longer trips are not particularly suited to families (though Bluewater will take up to two older children on some trips).

In addition to the San Juan and Gulf Islands itineraries run each spring and fall and Southeast Alaska cruises run throughout the summer, Bluewater offers an array of Pacific Northwest trips that focus on natural history adventures. Orcas and Totems, an eight-day voyage along Vancouver Island, is offered in the fall; spring and late summer bring eight- and nine-day trips to the remote Queen Charlotte Islands. *Bluewater Adventures, Suite #3, 252 E. 1st St., North Vancouver, British Columbia, V7L 1B3, Canada, tel. 604/980–3800, fax 604/ 980–1800.*

CLIPPER CRUISE LINE This company offers professional naturalist–led cruises in more areas of North America than any other, including Alaska, the eastern and western seaboards, Chesapeake Bay, the Great Lakes, the Intercoastal Waterway of the South, the wine region of Northern California, the island-dotted straits of the Pacific Northwest, and the warm crystal-clear waters of the U.S. Virgin Islands. Motorized landing craft, carried aboard each ship, ferry passengers to remote beaches, pristine forests, small villages, and wildlife refuges; Ph.D.-level naturalists and/or historians and other experts give lectures on board and walking tours ashore. Clipper is more sophisticated and service-oriented than most other small ship lines, and its passengers, who tend to be over 55, are wealthy, educated, and keenly interested in discovering the world around them.

Clipper operates two shallow-draft vessels: the 138-passenger *Yorktown Clipper* and the 100-passenger *Nantucket Clipper.* The *Clippers* look more like yachts than cruise ships. The trademark design, dominated by a large bridge and big picture windows that ensure bright interior public spaces, is sleek and attractive. Public areas, from the glass-walled observation lounge to the decks, are larger and more inviting than most ships of comparable size, but remain cozy enough to either create camaraderie or claustrophobia. Generally, passengers are made to feel like invited guests. Staterooms are modern and pleasantly decorated, with lower beds (no bunks, except for a third fold-down bed in the largest cabin category), individual thermostats, and private bathrooms.

Food served on Clipper vessels is far above the average fare served on other small-ship cruise lines. Meals are cooked by chefs trained at the Culinary Institute of America and are served in a single open seating. Fresh salmon, Alaska king crab, Chesapeake soft-shell and blue crabs, gumbo, fresh tropical fruits, and other regional specialties are highlighted. Guests usually choose from among four to five entrées that are prepared to order, and two salads, and three or more desserts. Fresh chocolate chip cookies (affectionately referred to as Clipper Chippers) are available every afternoon and disappear amazingly fast. There are two dressier evenings on each cruise, but they don't require formal attire (about half the passengers dress up).

Shipboard life on the vessels is unregimented, with no crowds and a more casual pace than found on many larger ships. Crews are young, cheerful, highly motivated, and as quick to please as the naturalists and historians are to answer questions.

Clipper's cruises are designed for those with an interest in exploring new places, rather than on shipboard entertainment. There are no special facilities or activities for children. Prices range from $1,200 to $5,700 per person, double occupancy, on itineraries that range from 6 to 15 days. *7711 Bonhomme Ave., St. Louis, MO 63105, tel. 314/727–2929 or 800/325–0010.*

HOLLAND AMERICA LINE This line, founded in 1873, is one of the few in the luxury class that has highly trained naturalists aboard to lecture on the fabulous flora and fauna of the Inside Passage. Each summer you can choose from more than 100 Alaskan cruises on six modern Holland America liners, which depart from Vancouver, British Columbia. The MS *Nieuw Amsterdam,* the MS *Veendam,* and the MS *Statendam* cruise the Inside Passage, making calls at Ketchikan, Juneau, Skagway, and Glacier Bay; while the SS *Rotterdam,* the MS *Ryndam,* and the MS *Noordam* cruise the Glacier Route, which includes stops at points farther north, including Hubbard Glacier, Valdez, and Seward. Although these are typical luxury cruises, there is always a naturalist on hand, showing films, lecturing, and standing watch on deck at regular intervals to help you spot wildlife and to answer questions.

Each ship is a floating city. Nautical antiques and memorabilia, from historic artifacts to nostalgic soap boxes, reflect the line's 100-year-plus seafaring heritage. Cruises are conservative affairs, renowned for their grace and gentility. No money changes hands (you sign for everything), and loudspeaker announcements are kept to a minimum. Accommodations are luxurious: On the line's newest ships (MS *Statendam,* MS *Veendam,* and MS *Ryndam*), even standard cabins come with a small sitting area with a sofa; outside cabins have tubs in the bath, inside cabins just showers. On all the Holland America ships, breakfast and lunch are open seating; dinner is served at two assigned seatings (5:45 and 8:00). Food is good by cruise-ship standards and is served on Rosenthal china. The emphasis is on American cuisine, with an occasional Dutch or Indonesian dish for variety. Dinner menus often include fish fresh from the market in that day's port of call, and every menu has a "healthy choice" selection. Once during each cruise there's an Indonesian lunch and an outdoor barbecue dinner, and each day there's a lunch of barbecued sausages and hamburgers, pasta, stir-fry, or make-your-own tacos on the Lido deck, which is also home to a self-serve ice cream and frozen yogurt parlor. Youth counselors accompany each ship to supervise school-age children. The movies, scavenger hunts, and games of the children's program are not nature-related, but Holland America's new line of "Just For Kids" shore excursions are often naturalist-led adventures. There are two formal evenings each week and loads of entertainment: big-band sounds, comedy, magic and dance acts, revues, dance orchestras, a piano bar, string trios, and jazz quartets. The Filipino, Indonesian, and Dutch crew members are extremely attentive and adept at pampering passengers, who number as many as 1,100 to 1,500 on each ship. Despite all this, prices are affordable, starting at $1,198 ($899 with early booking discount) and $2,590 ($1,943 with early booking discount) per person, double occupancy for 7- and 14-day cruises, respectively. *300 Elliott Ave. W, Seattle, WA 98819, tel. 206/281–3535 or 800/426–0327, fax 206/281–7110.*

OCEANIC SOCIETY EXPEDITIONS This nonprofit organization affiliated with Friends of the Earth, a global environmental advocacy group, has specialized in educational ecotravel since it was established in 1972. All proceeds exceeding expenses go directly toward environmental causes, from research projects to conservation efforts. The expert naturalists who lead the trips follow a strict code of ecotourism ethics—conducting tours that do not disturb wildlife or harm sensitive habitats, properly disposing of all wastes, and minimizing impact on the cultures that are visited. The leaders, trained in interpreting wildlife reaction to tour groups, can avoid triggering animal escape behaviors, thus allowing closer observation.

Destinations include New England, Alaska, the Pacific Northwest, and California (with excursions to Baja), as well as numerous foreign countries. In each area, ships are chartered for one or two journeys a year; sailing vessels are chosen for their minimal impact on the environment. Although each is different, you can usually count on compact cabins, simple meals served family style, and shared heads with freshwater showers—some cold ones, however. Schedules are quite flexible; activities are organized according to the presence of wildlife and to the whims of the weather. Although one program for teens is offered each year, most Oceanic Society cruises are for adults only. Trips range in length from 7 to 19 days and cost between $800 and $3,900. *Ft. Mason Center, Bldg. E, 2nd Floor, San Francisco, CA 94123, tel. 415/441–1106 or 800/326–7491, fax 415/474–3395.*

SPECIAL EXPEDITIONS The fact that such top institutions as the Smithsonian, the Audubon Society, the World Wildlife Fund, the American Museum of Natural History, the Museum for Comparative Zoology, and the California Academy of Sciences hire Special Expeditions to run their natural history cruises is persuasive evidence that it's the best in the industry. Special Expeditions has grown steadily since it was founded in 1979 by Sven-Olof Lindblad, son of adventure travel pioneer Lars-Eric Lindblad.

Special Expeditions operates a collection of shallow-draft vessels designed to explore nature and visit remote ports. The yachtlike, 70-passenger *Sea Bird* and *Sea Lion* are tiny, and even the 84-passenger *Polaris* is among the smallest of expedition ships. While all carry Zodiacs for landings almost anywhere, none of these vessels—not even the *Polaris*—has an ice-hardened hull. Very different is the meticulously restored, four-masted, 70-passenger *Sea Cloud,* perhaps the most beautiful barque afloat, built as the *Hussar V* for heiress Marjorie Merriweather Post and financier E. F. Hutton and for a time the world's largest privately owned yacht. It's truly a sight to watch crew members scamper up the 20-story masts to unfurl the ship's 29 billowing sails (which cover 34,000 square feet).

Cruises aboard Special Expeditions ships have a friendly atmosphere and tend to draw an easygoing 50-something crowd. The company employs about 150 natural-ists and historians, in most cases experts in the historical, natural, and geographic makeup of the areas that the ships visit. Between four and eight naturalists accom-pany each cruise to lead shore excursions during the day and present lectures and slide shows in the evening; no other line provides so many experts per cruise. Unlike guest experts on some ships, who are treated either as employees or celebri-ties, specialists on Special Expeditions cruises eat and socialize with passengers. You'll feel less like a paying spectator and more like part of a grand adventure.

Cruises have flexible schedules. Some-times the captain makes the decision about where to go next; at other times, passengers vote—say, to decide whether the ship should follow a pod of whales or head for a nearby fishing village. Shipboard activities consist mainly of lectures by the naturalists and historians on the wildlife and cultural history of the ports of call.

Individual cabins are functional and extremely compact. Public areas aboard the ships, though still small, give a little relief. For instance, the *Polaris*'s main public room is more like an oversize living room than a cruise-ship lounge, and a smaller lounge in the stern doubles as the library, which is well stocked with reference books, best-sellers, and atlases. The dining rooms of the *Sea Lion* and *Sea Bird* com-mand a magnificent view of the sea. Hearty meals draw on ingredients available in ports along the way and are heavily influ-enced by Northern European cooking tradi-tions. They're served in single, unassigned seatings, so guests can mingle during the voyage. There are no special facilities for children but also no restrictions about who can cruise. Note that the lilliputian *Sea Bird, Sea Lion,* and *Sea Cloud,* while very friendly and homey, rock so noticeably in rough waters that packets of Dramamine are kept in a bowl outside the purser's office. However, most itineraries are on protected inland waterways, where you won't have a problem. The outfitter's trips range in length from 4 to 28 days and start at $860 per person. *720 5th Ave., New York, NY 10019, tel. 212/765–7740 or 800/762–0003, fax 212/265–3770.*

FAVORITE CRUISES

THE NORTHEAST

RHODE ISLAND **Cruising the Erie Canal and Saguenay Fjord.** Because there are so many historical sites to see in the North-east, very few cruises here concentrate exclusively on nature; this one from the American Canadian Caribbean Line is no exception. The captain—who does double duty as the naturalist on these trips—talks not only about the flora, fauna, geography, and ecology of the places you visit but also about the events that took place there.

For almost 30 years, ACCL ships have cruised the winding route from Warren, Rhode Island, through Long Island Sound, past the Statue of Liberty and New York City, up the Hudson River, through the Erie Canal, across Lake Ontario, and into the St. Lawrence Seaway past Montreal, into the magnificent Saguenay Fjord and its scenic Baie Eternité. Because of the retractable pilothouse aboard the *Niagara Prince,* the

ACCL is the only cruise line able to negotiate the narrow, bridge-covered waterways along this route.

The Erie Canal follows the Mohawk, Seneca, and Oswego rivers, hemmed in by steep cliffs and gentle foothills covered with hardwood trees. You often see large beaver mounds near the water's edge. The Mohawk River Valley is a prime habitat for otter, mink, great blue heron, egret, and ibis; while coho salmon make their way up fish ladders in the Oswego River to spawn. As you sail through the canal, the captain talks about the ecology of the region and how it has changed since the canal opened. Along the St. Lawrence River, an onboard historian discusses the numerous historical sites relating to the early French and native settlers. Guest speakers occasionally come on board—a diamond miner, for instance, joins you in Little Falls, New York, to discuss geology. You make frequent trips ashore, visiting villages along the canal and spending two days each sightseeing in Montreal and Quebec.

If you have an interest in whales, plan your trip for summer, when humpback and minke whales congregate at the confluence of the Saguenay and St. Lawrence to feed on the rich supply of fish. If you are more interested in the bold changing colors of the oak and maple trees that line the route, book one of the fall sailings, which adds West Point and Clayton, New York, in place of Saguenay ports of call. A bus trip through the scenic White Mountains back to your starting point ends each journey. If these cruises are sold out or the dates don't work for you, ask ACCL about the Gaspé Peninsula/Nova Scotia/New England trips, which are similar. *American Canadian Caribbean Line, 461 Water St., Box 368, Warren, RI 02885, tel. 401/247–0955 or 800/556–7450, fax 401/245–8303. Late June–early July and late Sept.–early Oct.: 12 days, $1,560–$2,299. Sign up 3 months in advance.*

THE SOUTH

LOUISIANA TO TENNESSEE **New Orleans to Nashville.** Music, history, southern rivers, fall foliage, and great birding opportunities are the focus of this new ACCL itinerary aboard the *Niagara Prince*. The 12-day trip begins in New Orleans with a full day of sightseeing and plenty of toe-tapping Dixieland jazz and ends with a full day of sightseeing in Nashville, including the unforgettable twang of country music at the Grand Old Opry. The course of the trip takes you through many lakes and rivers of the South, each with its own particular brand of river music and all lined with trees in their full fall glory. In the gulf you're likely to see porpoise, while blue heron, ibis, osprey, muskrat, deer, and beaver are typically spotted along the Mississippi, Mobile, Tombigbee, Tennessee, and Cumberland rivers or the shores of Lake Pickwick, Kentucky Lake, and Lake Barkley.

The region is also rich in history, as seen from the southern perspective, of course, so you'll have the chance to learn from the onboard historian about the "War of Northern Aggression" and other bits of American history seen in a new light. Ports of call include Mobile, Coffeeville, and Demopolis, Louisiana; visits to Waverly Plantation, Shiloh National Park, and Ft. Donaldson are part of the package. *American Canadian Caribbean Line, 461 Water St., Box 368, Warren, RI 02885, tel. 401/247–0955 or 800/556–7450, fax 401/245–8303. Late Oct.–Nov.: 12 days, $1,465–$2,499. Sign up 3 months in advance.*

SOUTH CAROLINA TO FLORIDA **The Antebellum South Along the Intercoastal Waterway.** The graceful antebellum architecture, gracious and colorful southern history, colonial port towns with lush gardens, and a calm ribbon of interconnected water known as the Intercoastal Waterway are highlights of this weeklong cruise between Charleston and Jacksonville aboard the *Nantucket Clipper*. You'll spend days on deck observing the passing scenery—an array of wildlife and waterfowl (from gators and turtles to ibis, heron, egret, and osprey) that inhabit these saltwater marshes; moss-draped tree-lined shores; stately Victorian, Georgian, or Greek Revival homes; small fishing villages—as you cruise between ports of call that include St. Mary's, St. Simons Island, and Savannah, Georgia, and Hilton Head, Beaufort, and Charleston, South Carolina.

Informative talks given by regional speakers in different ports of call are an integral part of the voyage, bringing history and the wit and wisdom of the South to life. Dr. William Moore, chairman of the Political Science Department of the College at Charleston comes aboard to talk about the "New South"; Martha Rudd or Lib Richardson of the Historic Savannah Foundation drop by for an irreverent discussion of "High Life in the Low Country." An optional excursion in St. Mary's takes in the phenomenal Okefenokee Swamp; this day trip is led by naturalists from the National Wildlife Refuge who lecture on the ecology of this vast peat bog and the various wildlife encountered. Other optional excursions are generally city tours with either a historic or cultural bent. *Clipper Cruise Line, 7711 Bonhomme Ave., St. Louis, MO 63105, tel. 314/727–2929 or 800/325–0010. Early Mar.–mid-Apr. and Nov.: 8 days, $1,850–$2,900. Sign up 6 months in advance.*

THE MIDWEST

OHIO **Exploring the Great Lakes.** Plenty of pleasure craft sail the waters of Erie, Huron, Michigan, and Superior, but the best ship to turn to for extended exploration of the Great Lakes is the intimate, 100-passenger *Yorktown Clipper*. This modern, yachtlike vessel departs from Toledo, Ohio, to cruise the Great Lakes twice each summer. Each of these trips is escorted by a naturalist and a historian, along to help passengers learn more about the vivid Native American and European history and rich natural environment that have shaped this part of North America.

Birding fanatics find themselves deckside during much of the voyage, watching for osprey, heron, cranes, loons, geese, ducks, cormorants, finches, sparrows, swifts, and swallows. Chipmunks, rabbits, bats, squirrels, and other small mammals account for other wildlife typically spotted in the region. The natural highlight for most passengers is the afternoon spent cruising through Georgian Bay and the scenic 30,000 Islands.

There are loads of educational opportunities to choose from on the 11-day trip; guided nature walks on shore through hardwood forests focus on the habitat of the wildlife and summer wildflowers, while back on board, informative presentations cover topics such as French-American relations, the effect of Ford's invention of the automobile on modern history, and the whales, beavers, birds, and the transitional forest of the region. Ports of call, including the small picturesque communities of Windsor, Goderich, Midland, and Parry Sound, Ontario, and Presque Isle, Leland, Mackinac Island, and Sault Sainte Marie, Michigan, offer an array of optional shore excursions, from city tours that focus on local history and Victorian architecture to shopping and museum tours. *Clipper Cruise Line, 7711 Bonhomme Ave., St. Louis, MO 63105, tel. 314/727–2929 or 800/325–0010. Late June–mid-July: 11 days, $2,800–$4,200. Sign up 6 months in advance.*

THE WEST COAST

CALIFORNIA **Wine Country Cruising.** These four- and five-day itineraries out of San Francisco are a fine introduction to Northern California because they cover both the cultural and natural heritage of the region. Wine, of course, is the primary focus of the voyage through the Napa Valley by way of the San Joaquin, Napa, and Sacramento rivers. The trip gets underway by cruising around Tiburon and Angel islands in search of wildlife before heading inland through the Delta to Old Sacramento to see the riverboats, stage coaches, and steam railroad engines, and continue on to wine tastings, vineyard tours, and private luncheons at top vineyards in the Napa Valley.

With only 39 outside staterooms and a very shallow draft, the intimate *Spirit of Discovery* is small enough to cruise up the scenic, narrow rivers into the heart of California's wine country. These spring and fall cruises start out near the Golden Gate Bridge and cross the San Pablo Bay before winding up the San Joaquin to Sacramento. Crisp, sunny days are perfect for sitting out on the teakwood deck to watch the passing shoreline rife with wildlife; in the bay you'll find harbor seals and sea lions, in the delta an enormous variety of waterfowl, and in the sloughs perhaps playful river otters. The cruise director is always on hand to answer questions, help spot and identify wildlife, and give informal evening lectures on the geological and historical makeup of Northern California.

A great deal of time is spent ashore on escorted trips (included in the package) to Sonoma Mission and the homestead of General Mariano Vallejo for a look at California's pre–Gold Rush history, to several top vineyards, the champagne bottle–filled caverns at Schramsberg, to noted museums such as the California Railroad Museum, and to quaint shopping districts. Optional excursions include hot air ballooning over vineyards or a rejuvenating spa day in Sonoma. *Alaska Sightseeing/Cruise West, 4th & Battery Bldg., 2401 4th Ave., Suite 700, Seattle, WA 98121, tel. 206/441–8687 or 800/426–7702, fax 206/441–4757. Late Sept.–Nov.: 4 and 5 days, $449–$1,399. Sign up 3–6 months in advance.*

CALIFORNIA AND BAJA **West Coast, Baja, and the Sea of Cortez.** Oceanic Society Expeditions runs several natural history cruises from San Diego into Baja California. Some focus primarily on the whales, while others, like this one, include lessons on the rich geology, habitats, and wildlife of Baja

and the Sea of Cortez. Discussions are led by expert Oceanic Society naturalists who hold degrees in environmental sciences and have extensive experience in field research and travel.

The leisurely 12-day voyage begins with an orientation and a night birding cruise through San Diego Harbor, then heads south following the migration path of gray whales. Island stops at Todos Santos and San Benitos are opportunities for birdwatching for brown pelicans, egrets, herons, ibis, cormorants, ospreys, and other migratory species. These stops along the way also allow time for viewing giant seal breeding colonies and exploring tidal pools. Perhaps the highlight of the trip is the days spent farther south in San Ignacio Lagoon, the winter breeding grounds and nursery for gray whales. Here, 22-foot Mexican *panga* boats, piloted by local fishermen, provide close encounters with these inquisitive creatures, which sometimes come close enough to touch. The trip also takes in the Sea of Cortez, breeding ground for humpback whales. These rich, warm waters provide a habitat for giant blue whales, Byrde's whales, fin whales, minke whales, sperm whales, and orcas. Opportunities for beachcombing, nature walks, and skiff excursions round out the voyage, which concludes in Cabo San Lucas.

The ship is the 88-foot *Spirit of Adventure,* a long-range motor cruising vessel with 14 small, air-conditioned cabins that can accommodate up to 28 passengers in doubles and triples. It has four heads, three hot showers, and an air-conditioned salon. Meals, prepared by a professional cook, feature American cuisine with a few spicy Mexican touches. *Oceanic Society Expeditions, Ft. Mason Center, Bldg. E, 2nd Floor, San Francisco, CA 94123, tel. 415/441–1106 or 800/326–7491, fax 415/474–3395. Mid-Feb.–Mar.: 12 days, $2,250. Sign up 4–6 months in advance.*

PACIFIC NORTHWEST **Canada's Inside Passage.** The annual eight-day foray into the

Pacific Northwest takes in much of the route followed by intrepid Capt. George Vancouver during his explorations of the late 1700s. The 82-passenger *Spirit of Alaska* covers more of the Pacific Northwest than most regional cruises and provides a fine view of its many facets.

The cruise departs from Seattle and makes its way among the islands in the salmon-rich waters off the coasts of Washington and British Columbia, where you watch bald eagles, sea lions, harbor seals, and porpoises feeding. Highlights along the way include Desolation Sound and Princess Louisa Inlet, two incredibly beautiful wilderness areas that few get the chance to see. The ship pulls in close to protected sanctuaries while weaving through the San Juan and Gulf islands to give passengers a closer look at grebes, ducks, murrelets, and great blue heron. Because several pods of killer whales live in the region, chances are very good that you'll see them at some point before you leave the straits of Georgia and Juan de Fuca.

The itinerary also includes stops at sites of historical and cultural interest, such as Victoria, British Columbia's capital city; Vancouver, the seat of culture and business of British Columbia; Chemainus, an old mill town revitalized by a series of artistic outdoor murals; Washington's Port Townsend, a national historic district notable for its Victorian architecture; La Conner, a cozy community of artists nestled beside the sea, the charming community of Friday Harbor on San Juan Island, and Rosario Resort, once the private home of a shipping magnate on Orcas Island. *Alaska Sightseeing/Cruise West, 4th & Battery Bldg., 2401 4th Ave., Suite 700, Seattle, WA 98121, tel. 206/441-8687 or 800/426-7702, fax 206/441-4757. Late Mar.–Apr. and late Sept.–Oct.: 7 nights, $1,195–$3,065. Sign up 3–6 months in advance.*

PACIFIC NORTHWEST Coastal Waterways. Most of the hundreds of cedar- and fir-clad islands that dot Puget Sound, the Strait of Juan de Fuca, and Georgia Strait are acces-

sible only by private boat and remain unspoiled. Special Expeditions's six-day fall cruises aboard the MV *Sea Bird* and MV *Sea Lion* out of Vancouver, British Columbia, visit Tongass National Forest, Alaska State Park lands, and rustic port towns throughout the region, en route to Seattle. Naturalists and historians lead the trip, giving talks on the ecology of Princess Louisa Inlet (a seldom-visited fjord) and about Johnstone Strait, the San Juans, and the historical background of ports of call including San Juan, Victoria, Vancouver, and Seattle.

The sheer abundance of wildlife typically seen on this trip makes it stand out. Here, you observe harbor seals and sea lions stretched out in the sun on rock outcroppings; there, you catch sight of black-and-white Dall porpoises, often mistaken for baby killer whales, cavorting in the sea, or bald eagles diving from the sky to snatch fish from the water. Sightings of killer whales are not unusual, since several pods live in the deep channels between the islands. Twice a day you can take Zodiacs out to remote, protected islands for hikes through thick forests of Douglas fir to waterfowl habitats with ducks, puffins, cormorants, herons, and marbled murrelets. *Special Expeditions, 720 5th Ave., New York, NY 10019, tel. 212/765-7740 or 800/762-0003, fax 212/265-3770. Sept.: 6 days, $1,990–$2,960. Sign up 6 months in advance.*

PACIFIC NORTHWEST In the Wake of Lewis and Clark. Special Expeditions' weeklong spring and fall cruises aboard the MV *Sea Bird* and MV *Sea Lion* follow the westernmost leg of the historic expedition of Meriwether Lewis and William Clark, who set out in 1804 on a two-year journey to map the newly purchased Louisiana Territory and the Oregon Territory for President Jefferson. The cruise is accompanied by three regional specialists—a historian, a naturalist, and a botanist—who teach you about the Pacific Northwest of today, and that seen by the expedition almost 200 years ago.

Your cruise begins in Portland, Oregon. Cruising up the Columbia River, on the way to your first stop at the Umatilla Wildlife Refuge in eastern Oregon, you pass through the Blalock Islands Wildlife Refuge, where you see meadowlarks, western tanagers, Canadian geese, great blue heron, grebe, and cormorants. At Umatilla, you can choose to take a bus into a nearby Washington vineyard for a tour, or go on a naturalist-led hike through the refuge.

You continue up the Columbia River to the Snake River, where you stop in Clarkstown, Washington, and move to several twin-engine jet boats for an all-day excursion through the rapid waters of Hell's Canyon. There you see Rocky Mountain bighorn sheep, mule deer, raptors, and maybe even a rattlesnake. Next you follow the Snake to its confluence with the Palouse River. You stop for a day in Palouse Canyon, where you can take a leisurely hike, or follow the more strenuous route along the rim of the Canyon to Palouse Falls.

Cruising back into the Columbia River Gorge, you make a stop in the town of Hood River and take a ride on the Mount Hood Scenic Railroad through coniferous forests and pastureland. Then it's back on the river for a trip to the Bonneville Dam, where you observe the salmon migration on the fish ladders. Cruising on to the mouth of the Columbia, at the Pacific Ocean, you stop at the city of Astoria. The Columbia River Maritime Museum here is a good place to learn about the historical significance of the waters you've cruised, including their role in the Lewis and Clark expedition. The exploring party spent a winter at nearby Fort Clatsop, where another guided nature walk introduces you to the animals and medicinal and edible plants that sustained the expedition team. After your visit here, it's back to Portland and the end of the journey.

This is the most popular Special Expeditions itinerary, in part because of the in-depth look it gives at the history, geology, flora, and fauna of this richly diverse region, and in part because the route passes through eight fascinating dam locks on the Columbia and Snake rivers, rising to 725 feet above sea level. *Special Expeditions, 720 5th Ave., New York, NY, 10019, tel. 212/765–7740 or 800/762–0003, fax 212/265–3770. Late Apr.–May and early Sept.–Oct.: 6 days, $1,900–$2,960. Sign up at least 6 months in advance.*

PACIFIC NORTHWEST **Sailing the San Juan and Gulf Islands.** Small sailing yachts provide one of the best ways to explore the Pacific Northwest, and the *Island Roamer* is a good example of why this is true. This 68-foot ketch carries 16 passengers on six-day expeditions out of Victoria, British Columbia, through the San Juan and Gulf islands. The itinerary is generally flexible: You go where the wildlife is. The captain, naturalist, and passengers make itinerary decisions together; most trips visit Brethour, Mandarte, Jones, Sucia, San Juan, and the Orcas islands off the coasts of British Columbia and Washington. You spend your days sailing from island to island, dropping anchor in a new area each night. Along the way, you observe wildlife, study sailing, and get experience in steering the boat, navigating, and rigging sails.

Years of practical field experience, as well as their backgrounds in marine biology, ecology, ornithology, and anthropology, qualify the crew to tell you about the region's natural history, and there's lots to talk about. Moreover, because the yacht moves so quietly, it doesn't frighten wildlife away. As you cruise through protected waterways, it's common to see tawny-hued Steller's sea lions, speckled harbor seals, killer and minke whales, Dall porpoises, bald eagles, and great blue herons.

Kayaks are available for paddling along the islands' quiet shorelines, and large Zodiacs are used regularly to go ashore to visit area villages and hike through the forests and along the shore to look at plants, birds, and intertidal life. After dark, there are slide shows and lectures by the naturalist about local wildlife and their habitats.

This trip is chartered once a year (in late September) by Oceanic Society Expeditions, when one of their own expert naturalists leads the journey. *Bluewater Adventures, Suite #3, 252 E. 1st St., North Vancouver, British Columbia, V7L 1B3, Canada, tel. 604/980–3800, fax 604/980–1800. Late Sept.–Oct.: 5 days, $750. Sign up 3–6 months in advance.*

ALASKA

SOUTHEAST **Alaska Yacht Cruise.** Morning, noon, and night, the focus of this trip is observing nature—they'll even send someone to wake you at first light if whales are near. The 101-passenger *Spirit of '98,* flagship of the Alaska Sightseeing/Cruise West fleet, can slip into constricted areas such as Desolation Sound, Le Conte Bay, and Tracy Arm Fjord, a wilderness area in Tongass National Forest. It can nose up close to spectacular waterfalls and inch close to glaciers and shorelines. In protected areas such as Misty Fjords National Monument, park rangers join the group for briefings and question-and-answer sessions.

In tiny Petersburg, a fishing village with a strong Norwegian heritage, educator-turned-fisherman Syd Wright comes aboard. From his duffel bag, he pulls out a native rattle, shaking it fiercely as he relates native folklore. He passes around fishing nets, describing Alaska's highly regulated fishing industry. He reads poetry relating to the state, explains how it came to join the Union, and relates the origin of Alaska's gold-on-blue state flag, singing a song in its honor that resounds with the pride and determination of the state's settlers.

The *Spirit of '98* is named for the famous gold fever that swept Alaska in 1898, and the ship's turn-of-the-century decor and distinctive lines recall those of coastal steamers of the day. Redecorated in 1995, the ship now features a video library, and guest cabins with upgraded furniture and with coordinating carpets, curtains, and comforters, and TVs with VCRs. The staff members are friendly and quick to respond—they fetch fresh-from-the-oven cookies and steaming cocoa when you get chilly on the outside decks. After all, most guests spend the entire week perched at the railing, listening to the cruise director's commentary (over the ship-wide public address system) on dolphins swimming in the bow wake or a humpback whale feeding just yards away. Aside from a few nature lectures, occasional guest speakers, evening socials, and shore excursions in Ketchikan, Juneau, Petersburg, and Sitka, there are few activities to draw your attention from the scenery. *Alaska Sightseeing/Cruise West, 2401 4th Ave., Suite 700, Seattle, WA 98121, tel. 206/441–8687 or 800/426–7702, fax 206/441–4757. Mid-May–Sept.: 7–10 nights, $2,095–$3,795. Sign up 6–12 months in advance.*

SOUTHEAST **Exploring Alaska's Coastal Wilderness.** Four to six top naturalists lead this 10-day Alaska cruise from Special Expeditions, and each is an authority on a different area: ornithology, marine biology, glaciology, botany, history, and the like. Two ships make the trip, the MV *Sea Lion* and the MV *Sea Bird,* one northbound and the other southbound. Each carries four Zodiacs, and there are one or two shore excursions a day, each led by a different naturalist and focusing on that leader's specialty: An ornithologist may lead hikes to look for land and sea birds, a biologist may take you beachcombing, or a geologist may motor out for a discourse on icebergs.

Another unique feature of trips with Special Expeditions is their flexibility. Rather than follow rigid schedules, itineraries hinge on what presents itself along the way. Time is spent in the areas that are most compelling. You may visit a tribal house in Haines, a community with a strong Tlingit native heritage; cruise the glassy waterways of Misty Fjords National Monument looking for mountain goats, black-tailed deer, and black bears; or drift through the iceberg-choked waters of Le Conte and Glacier bays, Tracy Arm, and Frederick

Sound, prime feeding grounds of humpback whales, dolphins, sea lions, and sea otters. If there is an unusual amount of wildlife to see in a specific area or if guests are more interested in one area than another, the captain and expedition leader keep the ship there longer.

The price is on the high side for this cruise, because of all the special service and expert guidance and because each ship can accommodate only 70 passengers. The fare also includes overnight accommodations in Seattle at the beginning of the trip. *Special Expeditions, 720 5th Ave., New York, NY 10019, tel. 212/765–7740 or 800/762–0003, fax 212/265–3770. June–Aug.: 7 days, $2,990–$4,290. Sign up 6 months in advance.*

SOUTHEAST **Inside Passage Cruise.** Holland America is the choice to make if you are looking for a traditional ocean voyage through the Inside Passage with a good dose of natural history; this seven-day cruise aboard the elegant, newly commissioned MS *Veendam* is accompanied by a naturalist who is well qualified to teach passengers about the flora and fauna seen en route. He or she gives several slide presentations during the cruise and is available during the day to answer your questions. Stops along the way include Ketchikan, Juneau, and Skagway. The high point of the trip for most people is remote Glacier Bay National Park, where you will have a good chance of observing puffins, bald eagles, humpback whales, and brown bears. During the rest of the trip, you'll watch for marine mammals along the distant shoreline with binoculars (don't leave home without them).

The ship's strong suit is the traditional cruise experience, with all the luxury, entertainment, shopping, and dining that experience entails. Staterooms are plush, the international staff courteous and extremely attentive, and the cuisine decidedly gourmet, with more selections than anyone could possibly try—it sometimes seems that there's something being served

around the clock. All kinds of facilities and activities draw passengers away from nature observation: a casino, a spa, sports courts, swimming pools, and whirlpools; and, after dark, dances, shows, and karaoke. Plus there's a challenging fitness program, with awards for participation at the end of the trip, and a children's program and exclusive "Just for Kids" shore excursions. *Holland America Line Westours Inc., 300 Elliott Ave. W, Seattle, WA 98819, tel. 206/281–3535, fax 206/281–7110. Mid-May–Sept.: 7 days, $1,295–$3,945. Sign up 6–12 months in advance.*

SOUTHEAST **Sailing the Panhandle.** Once a year, Oceanic Society Expeditions charters the 68-foot *Island Roamer* for an 11-day sailing expedition out of Prince Rupert, British Columbia, through Alaska's Inside Passage. The region is famous for its glaciers, fjords, mountain ranges, forested islands, humpback whales, and other wildlife. This expedition, which sails with a dozen passengers, is devoted to whale watching and exploration, from poking around in native villages (some of them abandoned) to looking for brown bears, bald eagles, waterfowl, mountain goats, and porpoises. An Oceanic Society naturalist is along to share his or her enthusiasm and expertise.

After an orientation meeting in Prince Rupert, you are transported by floatplane to the ship's dock in Petersburg, where the journey begins. From that point the itinerary is flexible—you make schedule decisions with the naturalist, according to where the most interesting wildlife is. You spend several days in Frederick Sound, the summer home of up to 100 humpback whales, and stop to view the glaciers in Le Conte Bay and the totem poles at Ketchikan's Totem Heritage Center. You also visit Misty Fjords National Monument, Wrangell Narrows, Prince of Wales Island, and, possibly, the U.S. Forest Service bear observatory in Anan Bay, to see brown and black bears fishing for salmon. To hike on the various islands en route and explore the intertidal zone, you make frequent shore excursions in kayaks and inflatable rafts.

Back on board, you can get involved in sailing the yacht and learn navigation, knot tying, and seamanship from the crew, most of them old salts with 20 years of sailing experience. Facilities include eight double cabins, three heads with hot showers, a library, and a well-equipped galley, where a cook prepares meals using local produce and seafood. Wine is served with dinner, otherwise it's BYOB. Most guests are between 20 and 60 years old, active, highly educated, and well traveled; there are often more women than men. Because presentations and excursions are designed for adult learning capacities and attention spans and the quarters are tight, the trip is not particularly suited to families. If this particular cruise is full or the date is inconvenient, don't give up hope: Bluewater Adventures (tel. 604/980–3800) offers several similar 8- to 11-day Alaska itineraries throughout the summer on their *Island Roamer* and MV *Snow Goose. Oceanic Society Expeditions, Ft. Mason Center, Bldg. E, 2nd Floor, San Francisco, CA 94123, tel. 415/441–1106 or 800/326–7491, fax 415/474–3395. Late July: 12 days, $2,895. Sign up 6 months in advance.*

SOUTHEAST **World Explorer Cruises.** During the academic year, the 550-passenger SS *Universe Explorer* cruises the globe as college at sea, sponsored by the Institute for Shipboard Education in cooperation with the University of Pittsburgh. Since 1978, this midsize ship has spent her summers in Alaskan waters, carrying vacationers on educational cruises along the state's south-central and southeastern coasts. So comprehensive is the program on this 14-day cruise that you can earn college credit in history, geology, and anthropology for taking it. A faculty of professors and other Ph.D.'s from universities all over North America leads seminars covering the region's culture, arts, history, botany, geology, and anthropology. In addition, the *Universe Explorer* stops in more ports of call than any other Alaska cruise—nine, including Wrangell, Skagway, Juneau, Seward, Valdez, Sitka, Ketchikan, and Victoria, as well as Vancouver, the ship's home port. There are over 40 optional shore excursions to these cities and villages. In Wrangell and Seward, park rangers lead botanical walks; you gather specimens and learn to identify area flora.

No Alaska cruise would be complete without glaciers. On this trip, you can see the water turn from deep ocean blue to the milky brown caused by the presence of glacial silt, as you approach Hubbard Glacier, near Valdez, and inch close enough to Glacier Bay's Margerie Glacier to hear the deep boom and see the splash when huge chunks of icebergs shear off into the sea. Presentations in glaciology teach passengers the difference between tidewater, alpine, galloping, and valley glaciers in the shadow of these white giants.

Despite the educational content of this trip, there are also many opportunities for play: You can tour the wheelhouse, sign up for art workshops (and put your youngsters in the special Junior Cruisers program), play bingo and bridge, watch recent-release movies, work out in aerobics classes, and, after dark, enjoy groups performing everything from South American folk music to opera. Facilities include a theater, four lounges, two bars, a fitness center, a beauty salon, a barbershop, a massage facility, a gift shop, a launderette, and a 15,000-volume library, larger than that in any other ship at sea, with a librarian to help you find what you want. Meals include well-prepared American, Continental, and Asian offerings, and are served at two assigned seatings. The cabins are comfortable and functional rather than luxuriously appointed. Considering the length of time you spend at sea on this cruise and the caliber of the instruction, entertainment, and service, the price is exceptionally reasonable. *World Explorer Cruises, 555 Montgomery St., San Francisco, CA 94111-2544, tel. 415/393–1565 or 800/854–3835, fax 415/391–1145. Late May–early Sept.: 14 days, $1,195–$3,395. Sign up 3–6 months in advance.*

VIRGIN ISLANDS

ALL ISLANDS Caribbean Nature Cruise. This eight-day cruise through the U.S. and British Virgin Islands immerses you in the Caribbean's wildlife. From Crown Bay Marina, St. Thomas, the 100-passenger *Nantucket Clipper* cruises in and out of secluded bays beyond the main shipping lanes to cover Tortola, Salt Island, Norman Island, Virgin Gorda, Jost van Dyke, St. John, and St. Thomas. The captain drops anchor frequently in shallow coves and near protected reefs to let you swim, snorkel, and view the abundant marine life. You can also take Zodiacs to shore to hike and explore the tropical flora and fauna. A marine biologist and other naturalists are along to provide information about the wildlife of the region. They even teach you to snorkel, so that you can view the colonies of corals and sponges, stingrays, moray eels, silver barracuda, and other fish that tend to dominate the talk at drinks and dinner.

The ship ties up at several marinas along the way, so you can also enjoy the islands' powdery, white sand beaches, their lively bars, and their small boutiques. Optional excursions include a shopping trip and a submarine tour in St. Thomas and an island tour of St. John that takes in its many scenic vistas and the ruins of Annaberg Sugar Plantation. *Clipper Cruise Line, 7711 Bonhomme Ave., St. Louis, MO 63105, tel. 314/727–2929 or 800/325–0010. Mid-Dec.–mid-Feb.: 8 days, $1,950–$3,050. Sign up 6 months in advance.*

ALL ISLANDS Tall Ship Nature Expedition. If you want to leave motorized craft behind and see the U.S. Virgin Islands under sail, turn to Dirago Cruises. This line offers a series of annual nature expeditions on board the schooner *Harvey Gamage,* led by a naturalist who, in addition to presenting lectures, acts as a guide for birding expeditions ashore. Sights in store for birders include the colorful plumage of the Antillean crested hummingbird, loggerhead kingbird, brown-throated parakeet, man-grove cuckoo, green-throated carib, banana quit, and other colorful species.

Also on the program is snorkeling along the underwater trail at Trunk Bay, St. John, and around the reef of Buck Island, St. Croix. Brain and antler corals, sea fans, sea urchins, and sea stars are just a few of the creatures that populate the protected reef waters.

The itinerary is generally flexible, although you begin and end in St. Thomas and make island stops each day. All nature excursions, snorkeling, shopping trips, and sailing lessons are included in the package price; an optional scuba trip costs $50. This is not a luxury cruise—facilities include 14 compact cabins with upper and lower berths and a washbasin, shared heads with cold water showers, a small library, and a salon where meals are served family style—but the simplicity of the quarters means that costs are low. There is no bar; you must bring not only your own wine and hard liquor but even your own soda. However, lemonade, snacks, and fruit are available around the clock. *Dirigo Cruises, 39 Waterside La., Clinton, CT 06413, tel. and fax 860/669–7068. Nov.–Dec.: 7 days, $695. Sign up 4 months in advance.*

SOURCES

ORGANIZATIONS The **Cruise Line International Association** (500 5th Ave., Suite 1407, New York, NY 10110, tel. 212/921–0066) can answer most questions on cruising and provide general information on cruise lines and comparison charts of itineraries, but it doesn't handle bookings. The **Department of Health and Human Services** (1015 N. American Way, Room 107, Miami, FL 33132) can supply a free sanitation inspection report on any cruise ship sailing in American waters.

PERIODICALS *Cruise Travel Magazine* (Box 342, Mt. Morris, IL 61054, tel. 815/734–4151 or 800/877–5893), published every two months, has photos and features on cruise ships and ports of call. "Ocean &

Cruise News" (World & Ocean Cruise Liners Society, Box 92, Stamford, CT 06901, tel. 203/329–2787) profiles a different ship each month. The quarterly *Specialty Travel Index* (Alpine Hansen Publishers, 305 San Anselmo Ave., San Anselmo, CA 94960, tel. 415/459–4900) lists tour operators and outfitters that offer special interest, learning, and adventure vacations around the globe.

BOOKS *Fodor's Worldwide Cruises and Ports of Call* gives general advice on cruising and specific descriptions of lines, ships, itineraries, and ports of call; the Alaska chapter describes several nature cruise options. *Traveling on Your Own,* by Eleanor Berman, gives advice to singles on choosing the right cruise and what to expect in the way of singles activities and pricing.

ALSO SEE If you enjoy relaxing breezes off the water and close encounters of the wildlife kind, turn to the Whale-Watching Cruises chapter.

Cultural Tours

Written by M. T. Schwartzman

Updated by Heidi Sarna

ave you ever stood before a famous landmark, contemplating its architecture, wondering about its story, imagining who had been there before you, and wishing that you had an expert at your side who could fill you in on the details? On a cultural tour, that expert would be your guide. Cultural tours focus on the many expressions of civilization: the visual and performing arts, architecture, literature, folk traditions, and historic sites. Many focus on aspects of Native American culture, but in general, topics range from railroads and petroglyphs to burial mounds and textiles. In some cases, you may even have the chance to live the way people would have during the period you are studying by spending the night in a tepee or eating meals prepared as they would have been in that bygone time.

Your guides may be writers, archivists, researchers, scholars, curators, or historians. One Smithsonian Institution tour, a two-week trip across the United States on famed Route 66, is led by Michael Wallis, author of the definitive book on the historic interstate, *Route 66: The Mother Road*. Typically, expert leaders share a wealth of knowledge collected throughout a lifetime of work. On a popular James Henry River Journeys trip to Alaska, a wilderness literature forum examines Tlingit oral histories, which leaders Nora and Dick Dauenhauer have been collecting and translating for 20 years.

On cultural tours, your learning takes place not in a classroom environment, as in other study programs, but in the world at large while moving from place to place. On a typical motor-coach trip, the most common kind of cultural tour, you get up early each morning, breakfast in your hotel, then head for a day of sightseeing that ends at the next site on the itinerary, where you stay the night.

Depending on how much ground your tour covers, you may use one or two hotels or camps as a base and make day trips from there, or you may change hotels daily, as on traditional escorted tours. Private behind-the-scenes tours of museums and historical districts and visits to sites not normally open to the public are a hallmark of cultural tours. Occasionally, special receptions are organized exclusively for your group, as are lectures and slide shows, depending upon the facilities at the sites you visit.

Cultural tours are essentially run by two types of groups: commercial tour companies that specialize in educational travel, and not-for-profit organizations such as museums, trusts, societies, research centers, and alumni organizations. Often, a

M. T. Schwartzman began his writing career at the American Museum of Natural History in New York, one of the country's oldest operators of educational tours. Heidi Sarna, a contributor to many Fodor's guides, attributes her insatiable curiosity about the past to growing up immersed in the history of 18th-century south-central Pennsylvania.

nonprofit group sells a trip but does not run it: In an arrangement known in the travel industry as private labeling, the institution develops the itinerary, selects the expert leaders, then leaves the actual travel arrangements to an outside operator. It's especially common for cultural institutions to charter small ships with an itinerary matching that of cruises sold to the general public and the institution's own experts on board. In other cases, a cultural organization books space on a larger vessel, in which case you sail with other passengers who may be individual travelers or members of cultural tours from other institutions.

Often, the opportunity to join cultural tours run by a nonprofit group is considered a benefit of membership, limited to members who contribute between $250 and $500 or more annually. However, an institution usually makes its tours available to anyone willing to join at a cost of $20 to $40. This money helps to support the organization's work and may be tax-deductible.

Whether sponsored by a nonprofit group or a commercial operator, cultural tours are not inexpensive: Groups tend to be small and destinations out-of-the-way and therefore costly to get to, and lodging, often in historic properties, can come at a premium, as can meals, when they're included. Which is not to say that you must be rich to join a cultural tour. While the price of some packages reaches $3,000 per person per week, there are worthwhile programs for less than $1,000 per person.

Before giving your money to anyone, shop around. Don't book the first trip that suits your fancy. There are many players in the field, and often their programs visit a few of the same sites. Call or write for brochures and look for what best suits your interests. Remember that the expertise of the operator is just as important as the qualifications of the expert who travels with you. Some institutions, particularly larger ones, are generalists in the field of cultural tours. Because they have a broadly stated mission

and a large membership to satisfy, they must produce trips that cover many fields. The advantage is that you will have the greatest choice of programs, and many trips may be interdisciplinary. If you have a specific interest, look into tours from smaller institutions and commercial operators, which tend to have a more limited focus. Many are mom-and-pop operations. You are likely to get more personalized service and may even be accompanied on your trip by the organization's founder or director.

CHOOSING THE RIGHT TOUR

Cultural tours share certain characteristics with other group tours. They also have qualities that are unique to educational travel. Among the questions you should ask are:

What's the cost and what's included? Like all group tour packages, those for cultural tours vary. Generally speaking, cultural tours include all accommodations, activities, transportation during the tour, and breakfast, unless otherwise noted. Be sure to ask whether transportation between your home and the trip's starting and ending points is included; usually it isn't.

How many experts accompany the group? The number of lecturers and guides, especially as compared with the number of travelers, determines how much personal attention you can expect. A single expert usually accompanies most cultural tours, but some have two full-time experts plus guest speakers, who join the group for special presentations throughout the trip.

Do the experts mingle and dine with the group? Perhaps the most fulfilling aspect of a cultural tour is the chance for informal conversation at special receptions, over dinner, or afterward. The more you are on your own for meals, especially dinner, the fewer the chances for this informal social interaction.

Are there escorts other than the expert guides? It can be helpful to be accompanied by a professional tour director whose sole responsibility is seeing to your group's needs during the trip; he or she handles the logistics and confirms hotel and restaurant reservations, coach timetables, and site visits—and solves problems on the spot should they arise. Sometimes this role is filled by a representative of the sponsoring organization or the tour operator.

What are the qualifications of the tour leaders? Experts with impressive academic and professional credentials lead the most serious and in-depth cultural tours. They have earned advanced degrees, written books, and otherwise established themselves as recognized authorities. However, sometimes a nonacademic representative of the sponsoring organization is the tour's only escort. Know what you're getting before you make a commitment. Experts should be more than museum administrators or volunteers.

How long has the institution been running cultural tours? How long has the operator been in business? Choose a trip from an organizer that has significant experience in planning and operating the type of tour that interests you. Ask both when the institution or operator was founded and how long it has been running cultural tours. A museum may be a century old but could have gotten into the tour business only recently; fledgling operations do not have a track record by which you can judge their performance. If the museum uses a commercial venture for the travel arrangements, find out the name and history of that operator. As a general rule, book with an outfit that has been in business for at least five years. If an organization or operator is new on the scene or if you're unsure of its expertise, make a special point of asking for references from past travelers.

Do you have references from past participants? To clarify your ideas about what the trip will be like, there's no substitute for a talk with someone who has followed the itinerary, slept in the beds, and eaten the meals.

What lectures and enrichment programs are planned? An important distinction between a cultural tour and a typical escorted program is the depth of the learning experience. Ask how many educational presentations will be held daily or during the trip as a whole. Find out how they will be tied in to the program—will there be lectures and slide shows in your hotel or informal talks at the sites to be visited?

How many people are in the group? Although all groups tend to be small—usually no more than 20—the exact number will shape your experience and affect your opportunity to meet experts one-on-one.

How will the group travel? A cultural tour may get around by land or by sea. Most move from place to place by motor coach, but minivans may be used when the group is small; some tours involve long and perhaps strenuous hikes.

What are the accommodations like? You will stay in modern chain hotels or historic inns. You may pitch tents in campgrounds. Or you may live and sleep in nontraditional surroundings as part of the living-history experience. Don't let yourself be surprised.

If you're staying in hotels, inns, or motels, find out exactly what the rooms are like. Will there be double beds or twins? Antique furnishings or standard Formica pieces? Private baths or shared? Be sure to ask about anything that matters to you—fitness center, swimming pool, phones or cable TV in the rooms, or the like.

If you will be sleeping in the open air, find out who supplies the camping equipment. If the operator provides it, make sure it's of a quality you'll be happy with; you don't want a sleeping bag that isn't warm enough or a tent that you have to wrestle with to set up. Also ask about the campground facilities—what are shower and latrine arrangements?

What is the food like? Meals may be served outdoors or in fine restaurants. Sometimes, restaurants are selected to reflect the tour's theme. The National Trust for Historic Preservation, for example, often schedules meals in historic taverns, inns, or houses. Cuisine can be as varied as cultural tours themselves: On an itinerary that explores Native American history or lifestyles, you may eat dishes representative of the tribes you are studying. On a tour of New England, seafood and shellfish may be more likely to appear on your menu. The lively restaurant scene in Santa Fe is a highlight of the Smithsonian Institution's annual trip there.

Be sure to find out how many meals are included and how they are served. For meals that are included, ask whether they're sit-down or buffet and whether you can order anything on the menu or have a more limited selection. If you have special dietary needs or culinary preferences, make sure that they can be taken care of.

How much free time will there be? Most cultural tours schedule time for you to explore on your own, especially in the evenings. However, some tours keep to a very demanding schedule, limiting time for independent activity.

How far in advance do I need to book? You must ordinarily sign up at least three to four months in advance, although some organizers recommend booking as much as a year ahead if you want to be sure of a space. Tours that are new for an institution with a loyal following, such as the Smithsonian, tend to fill up the most quickly. Once you find out about a trip and make up your mind to go, don't dawdle about signing up—you may never again have the opportunity to travel with this particular leader and this particular group.

MAJOR PLAYERS

Virtually every major museum and college or university runs a travel program of some kind: There are more than 1,000 members of the Network for Educational Travel (*see* Sources, *below*), an association of travel sponsors and suppliers. The following operators were selected for their stature, the extent of their domestic programs, and the unusual nature of the niche they fill. The list below includes some of the cultural world's most famous institutions— but not all. Some run few or no domestic tours and their programs fall outside the scope of this book. Others do offer domestic cultural programs, but in activities covered elsewhere in this book, such as birding and whale-watching, whose focus is predominantly on natural history.

GENERALISTS

DENVER MUSEUM OF NATURAL HISTORY

Sponsoring study tours since 1972, the Denver Museum of Natural History runs an average of 15 domestic and eight international tours per year. A museum curator or educator leads tours of 3 to 14 days. Past trips have included a prehistoric journey into the northern Rockies with a paleontologist, family canoe trips on rivers winding through the wilds of the Southwest, and a hiking and camping expedition into Mancos Canyon in southern Colorado under the guidance of a natural historian and educator. Many trips are family-oriented and include hands-on activities, camping, cookouts, and even goodies for the kids like a Dinosaur Discovery Kit (part of the Jurassic Journey tour into Utah's Dinosaur National Monument park). If you're not camping, accommodations are in small hotels or lodges. Three hearty meals a day, served family-style, are included in the price of most trips. The museum rates the physical exertion level of each tour: 1 means very little walking and no camping, 9 signifies intense activity, such as white-water rafting or an 8-mile hike, in a remote location. Joining the museum is not required to take trips, but tour participants are asked to support the institution with voluntary donations ranging from $25 to $100 per person. *Denver Museum of Natural History, 2001 Colorado Blvd., Denver, CO*

80205-5798, tel. 303/370-6304, fax 331-6492.

JAMES HENRY RIVER JOURNEYS This outdoor specialist, founded in 1973, schedules several culturally oriented tours annually. Wine, fine cuisine, music, and literature are the focus of these river rafting trips, which travel through California, Oregon, Idaho, Arizona, and Alaska. Vintners, chefs, musicians, and poets host the groups. Destinations and itineraries remain the same each year, but themes may change according to the experts signed up to accompany the trips. You might discuss literature about the wilderness in southeast Alaska or taste wine during the stops on a trip down Idaho's Salmon River. Tours last from 3 to 13 days; participants are a mix of singles, couples, and older and younger travelers. At night, the operators set up camp along the rivers and, around the campfire, discuss literature or hold recitals or readings. Although meals are cooked over the open fire, the menus are surprisingly sophisticated: At dinner, there might be chicken flavored with orange juice, ginger, and soy sauce; barbecued lamb marinated for six days in olive oil, lemon and orange juice, garlic, and honey; or barbecued salmon, with brownies for dessert. Most prices include all meals. *Box 807, Bolinas, CA 94924, tel. 415/868-1836 or 800/786-1830, fax 415/868-9033.*

NATIONAL TRUST FOR HISTORIC PRESERVATION Art and architecture of cultural and historic significance are the emphasis of tours from the nation's premier preservation society. Chartered in 1949 by an act of Congress, the trust began its travel program in 1970 and now takes members to New England, the South, and the West by land and by sea. Itineraries vary from year to year, but half of the two dozen–odd annual trips may be repeated in a subsequent year. Most last 8 to 10 days; leaders include writers, educators, architects, and society directors past and present. In addition to these expert guides, a representative of the National Trust for Historic Preservation accompanies each tour, along with a special escort who handles travel arrangements. Groups number 20 on average but never include more than 30 participants—largely, it seems, women aged 65 to 70. Accommodations are often selected from among participants in the National Trust's Historic Hotels of America program, which means that they're of architectural and historical significance; many are designated national historic landmarks, and lunch stops are often made at sites of historical importance, including Colonial inns and even historic homes, where the kitchen prepares a meal for the occasion. To participate, you must join the National Trust ($20). *1785 Massachusetts Ave. NW, Washington, DC 20036, tel. 202/673-4000 or 800/944-6847, fax 202/673-4246.*

THE SMITHSONIAN INSTITUTION Founded in 1846, the Smithsonian has been running its study tours since 1970 and now has more trips than almost any other cultural organization. Like the great museum's collections, its tours cover virtually every topic, and locations range all over the United States. In the Smithsonian's semiannual catalog, you're sure to find something that piques your interest. Cruises along inland waterways and overland tours to sites and regions of historic importance are among the wide range of choices. Native American art, American painting, urban architecture, and western folklore and settlement are just some of the topics explored. Itineraries change yearly, but perennial favorites are repeated just as new trips are introduced. Tours last six days to two weeks. A representative of the Smithsonian accompanies each group to act as escort, organizer, and all-round arranger, and there's also at least one expert on hand and sometimes two—here known as study guides—who are often joined by guest speakers. Leaders and lecturers include writers, historians, and professors. Trips rarely include more than 30 participants, most of whom are around 55, with a mix of couples and single women. Accommodations and restaurants are often chosen to tie in with the theme of the particular tour. Menus are often preselected with a limited number of choices; lunches may be served buffet style. A reading list is provided before the start of each trip. You must join the institution to take part ($24). *Smithsonian Study Tours and Seminars, Smithsonian Institution, 1100 Jefferson Dr. SW, MRC 702, Washington, DC 20560, tel. 202/357–4700, fax 202/633–9250.*

NATIVE AMERICA SPECIALISTS

Native American culture is a popular theme of cultural tours, and a number of operators schedule such trips. Among them are the following.

THE ARCHAEOLOGICAL CONSERVANCY Of the archaeological foundations that run cultural tours, the nonprofit conservancy's program is perhaps the most wide-ranging. The conservancy was founded in 1980 and began its tour program in 1986. Every year about four to six domestic trips are sponsored. Most concentrate on Native American and Spanish colonial historic sites in the Southwest, but there are also river raft trips to Utah that explore prehistoric cliff dwellings and other ruins. Basic itineraries rotate every couple of years. Various anthropologists and archaeologists lead the tours—different experts may join the group en route, and several may participate in a given trip. One conservancy staffer is also in attendance. Groups are limited to 20 to 25 people; most average in their mid-50s, although the conservancy attracts everyone from kids to senior citizens, singles and couples. Lodging is in first-class hotels and motels on land-based trips, or the best available; you camp out on river trips. Lunches are always included; on bus tours, you often have box lunches, and on raft trips meals are cookouts. You automatically join the conservancy when you book one of its trips; the cost is included in the price ($100). *5301 Central Ave. NE, #1218, Albuquerque, NM 87108-1517, tel. 505/266–1540.*

CROW CANYON ARCHAEOLOGICAL CENTER Best known for its classroom-style seminars and archaeological digs open to vaca-

tioners, this Colorado desert center, founded in 1984 for research and education, also offers a series of what it calls cultural explorations: four- to eight-night, academically oriented tours, led by native guides and nonnative scholars, that examine the prehistory of the ancient inhabitants of the Four Corners region. The first of these trips ran in 1988, and new explorations are added each year; some favorites are repeated annually, while others may retain the same theme or topic but follow a different or expanded itinerary. Because some 35% to 40% of tour participants are repeaters, the center tries not to run any particular program more than two or three years in a row. Groups set out with between 10 and 20 participants, most in their mid-40s to early 50s (people from their 20s through their 80s have also participated). There are usually singles as well as couples, and more men than women. The center's 70-acre, mountain-ringed campus full of adobe buildings is the base camp, from which you journey into the desert each day and return to the center each night. Although some programs have you overnighting at campsites in the desert, lodging is usually in Navajo-style hogans—small cabins that accommodate up to four (although on tours, only two or three individuals are housed in each unit). If you come alone, they assign you a roommate. On-campus meals, served cafeteria style, include both basic American fare such as baked chicken and pasta and such southwestern specialties as burritos and enchiladas; there are always fresh fruits, vegetables, and salads. Off-site meals may be brought in from the cafeteria or prepared in the open air. Membership is required to participate, from which proceeds help support the center's efforts to educate the public about archaeology and Native American culture ($40). *23390 County Road K, Cortez, CO 81321, tel. 970/565–8975 or 800/ 422–8975, fax 970/565–4859.*

FOUR CORNERS SCHOOL Another educational center well-known for its on-site workshops, the nonprofit Four Corners

School sponsors 5- to 10-day cultural tours every year in both its cultural studies and archaeology series. Sometimes cosponsored by such institutions as the Denver Museum of Natural History, New Mexico Museum of Natural History, San Diego Museum of Natural History, and the Heard Museum, tours in both series explore the folk traditions of native Navajo, Pueblo, Hopi, and Ute peoples, and are led by anthropologists. You take in museums, cultural centers, historic cities, and dance performances. Destinations and basic itineraries in the Southwest remain constant from year to year. Eight to 15 individuals are in each group; typical participants are between 35 and 55, and there's an equal mix of men and women. You overnight in hotels and motels en route and eat in restaurants, except for the occasional picnic, box lunch, or traditional native meal. Founded in 1984, the school is more advocacy-oriented than most other cultural tour operators—for instance, it's deeply involved in studying and preserving the flora and fauna of the Colorado Plateau—and the school encourages you to get involved. Membership is not required for any Four Corners tour. *Box 1029, Monticello, UT 84535, tel. 801/587–2156, fax 801/587–2193; also see Archaeological Digs chapter.*

JOURNEYS INTO AMERICAN INDIAN TERRITORY
Tours of this organization, founded in 1988 with the goal of furthering communication between Indian and nonnative peoples, focus exclusively on the heritage of Native America. Some itineraries examine the history and prehistory of America's native peoples, while others concentrate on their folk music, crafts, and dances, or the spiritual life of the continent's original inhabitants. Programs are designed for those who want not just to view Native American ways of life but also to experience them: You live in a tepee for the duration of the tour and the menu includes Native American as well as institutional fare. On some itineraries you return to the same encampment each night after making day trips to tribal settlements in the surrounding area, while on others you move from one encampment to another. These eight-day trips visit significant native sites in Oklahoma, Arizona, New England, Wisconsin, and South Dakota; specific itineraries often vary from year to year. Robert Vetter, the nonnative anthropologist who founded the organization, leads the tours, assisted by a Native American staff. There are usually no more than 20 participants in each group, mostly women, and primarily in their late 30s through their 50s, although there are many students as well as children and senior citizens. *Box 929, Westhampton Beach, NY 11978, tel. 516/878–8655 or 800/458–2632, fax 516/878–4518.*

SACRED SITES The cultural tours from this nonprofit group reflect the organization's unusual mission: to preserve sacred places and the practices of the cultures that created them. Their way of living in harmony with the environment constitutes part of the subject matter of the tours. While the foundation's travel program extends from Alaska in the north to Peru in the south, many of its domestic programs concentrate on the desert Southwest—this is the only destination that consistently appears on the foundation's annual list of programs. Other offerings vary from year to year, with the most popular itineraries repeated and new ones added. Groups include between 12 and 20 participants, and they are led by anthropologists and other scientists—an ethnobotanist, perhaps—and accompanied by a tour escort and sometimes a representative of Sacred Sites and, on occasion, members of the native tribes being studied. Most participants are professional women in their 40s or retirees, but there are couples as well as single travelers. You overnight in basic motels—sometimes B&B's—and generally dine in restaurants; there are box lunches or picnics in the field at noontime. Founded in 1990, Sacred Sites began offering tours a year later. Prices include a contribution to the foundation. *1442A Walnut St., #330, Berkeley, CA 94709, tel. 510/540–0671, fax 510/540–1057.*

FAVORITE TRIPS

Most nonprofit operators change their programs annually: Since they draw participants from a limited pool—namely, their members—they must vary their offerings to keep members coming back. Commercial tour operators tend to repeat itineraries year after year. Both nonprofit and commercial operators tend to repeat their most popular tours. When the same program runs in consecutive years, the exact itinerary and leaders may vary. The following tours are representative. If the one that interests you is not available when you call, ask about similar or equally intriguing programs.

THE NORTHEAST

MAINE **Painterly Landscapes.** This eight-day trip from the National Trust for Historic Preservation focuses on art and architecture of the rugged Maine coastline. In Prouts Neck, you visit the studio of Winslow Homer, who painted many of his most important works in Maine. You also visit Rockland, one of Andrew Wyeth's haunts. The work of Maine artists of the past is on view at the Farnsworth Art Museum and Homestead, in Rockland. After a short ferry ride to the 10-mile-long island of Islesboro, a local resident guides you through the area's late-19th-century grand summer cottages built by the wealthy from Boston and New York. Once back on the mainland, the tour pays a visit to the Penobscot Marine Museum, home to portraits of 284 sea captains as well as whaling artifacts and other seafaring treasures. Camden, home to a fleet of two- and three-masted schooners, is another stop. Lunches, dinners, teas, and receptions are sometimes held at the private homes of art dealers or other local families, and other meals include a clambake and a lobster dinner at a local lobster shack. You spend two nights in Prouts Neck (15 minutes from Portland) in a shingle-style resort-inn overlooking the ocean, and another two at the historic landmark Camden Harbour

Inn, decorated with period antiques and Victorian pieces. Accommodations for the remaining nights are in the historic Bar Harbor Inn. Leaders change from year to year. In 1996, they included a preservationist, an architectural historian, and a curator, and the group was joined by the director of the Maine Historic Preservation Commission and other local experts, including a representative from Greater Portland Landmarks, as part of a tour of historic neighborhoods there. *National Trust for Historic Preservation, 1785 Massachusetts Ave. NW, Washington, DC 20036, tel. 202/673–4000 or 800/944–6847, fax 202/673–4038. Late Sept.: 8 days, $1,775; price includes 3 lunches and 5 dinners; sign up 9–12 months in advance.*

MASSACHUSETTS AND RHODE ISLAND **Mansions and Music.** The anchors of this 10-day study tour sponsored by the National Trust for Historic Preservation are Newport, Rhode Island, known for its grand seafront mansions, and Massachusetts's Berkshire Mountains, abuzz with cultural activities all summer long. The tour is scheduled to coincide with the area's annual summer festivals. En route, the director of the Newport Historical Society and a resident Berkshires expert join the group. In Newport, where you spend four nights, seven historic homes open their doors to you for tours, and three mansions are the venue for classical music recitals. In the Berkshires, you attend five performances by symphony orchestras and dance and theater groups, and visit the re-created rural New England town of Old Sturbridge Village, the completely restored Hancock Shaker Village, the Norman Rockwell museum and studio, Edith Wharton's summer mansion, and the studio where Daniel Chester French created the statue of Abraham Lincoln for the Lincoln Memorial in Washington, D.C. Some lunches and dinners are at historic sites or private clubs. Lunch might consist of lobster and mango salad and zabaglione with Grand Marnier and fresh berries, and dinner might start with vichyssoise and a green salad then move on to swordfish grilled with lime and pepper or an aged sirloin in a brandy-pepper cream sauce. Accommodations are in a harborfront Newport hotel with private bath, and in Victorian bed-and-breakfasts in the Berkshires, also with private bath. *National Trust for Historic Preservation, 1785 Massachusetts Ave. NW, Washington, DC 20036, tel. 202/673–4000 or 800/944– 6847, fax 202/673–4038. Mid-July: 10 days, $3,245. (You can also choose to take just the 4-day Newport trip, $1,450, or the 6-day Berkshires tour, $1,795.) 10-day trip price includes 6 lunches, 2 brunches and 5 dinners; sign up 9–12 months in advance.*

NEW YORK **Gilded Age Adirondacks.** Scheduled to show off the landscape during foliage season, this eight-day tour sponsored by the National Trust surveys the natural beauty and rich cultural history of the Adirondacks. An architectural historian leads the way to the villages and scenic camp retreats that inspired 19th-century writers and painters, such as Ralph Waldo Emerson, Robert Louis Stevenson, Mark Twain, and Winslow Homer. After the Civil War, America's wealthy industrialist tycoons flocked to the wilds of the Adirondacks and built rustic summer camps, which were virtually self-sufficient villages. The tour explores the camps built in what became known as the "Adirondacks style," using native red spruce, northern white cedar, and granite, which inspired the design for many of our National Park buildings. You will also visit the Adirondack Museum, which has extensive displays on area history. The tour begins and ends in Albany. The first three nights are spent at the Adirondacks-style Lake Placid Lodge, and for the next four nights you stay in the Minnowbrook Lodge on the shores of Blue Mountain Lake. Gourmet meals are often provided at the lodges, and you lunch at the grand estates and camps visited throughout the tour. Savor delicacies like cherry rhubarb bread pudding and iced papaya souffle. This trip is planned for 1997. *National Trust for Historic Preservation, 1785 Massachusetts Ave. NW, Wash-*

ington, DC 20036, tel. 202/673–4000 or 800/944–6847, fax 202/673–4038. Late Sept.: 7 days, $2,795. Price includes all meals; sign up 5–7 months in advance.

THE MID-ATLANTIC

VIRGINIA **Grand Houses and Plantations.** Famous homes of America's founding fathers are linked together on this seven-day tour of the first of Britain's American colonies. Sponsored by the National Trust for Historic Preservation, it is led by architectural historian William Kloss and takes in such architectural treasures as Mount Vernon, George Washington's ancestral estate, Montpelier, home of president James Madison, and Monticello, Thomas Jefferson's masterpiece. Other sites include Westover Plantation, built in 1730 and considered by some to be the finest example of Georgian architecture in America, and the ornate 33-room neo-Romanesque Maymont estate, built by the Dooley family in the late 1800s. On many of these visits, you see buildings or rooms not normally open to the public. A Colonial cooking demonstration shows how and what our forebears ate. To bring the 1700s to life, an actor dressed as an 18th-century gentleman joins you for dinner by candlelight at the Mount Vernon Inn. Other dining experiences include lunch at the Willow Grove Inn, which dates from 1778, and dinner at the private Commonwealth Club, founded in 1890. Overnights are in the 70-year-old Renaissance Mayflower hotel in Washington, D.C., an icon of the city's importance whose guests include presidents, senators, and foreign heads of state, and in Richmond's Jefferson Hotel, a National Historic Landmark with a grand lobby and a staircase straight out of *Gone with the Wind.* All accommodations have private bath. *National Trust for Historic Preservation, 1785 Massachusetts Ave. NW, Washington, DC 20036, tel. 202/ 673–4000 or 800/944–6847, fax 202/673– 4038. Mid-Apr. and mid-Oct.: 7 days, $1,495. Price includes 5 lunches and 2 dinners; sign up 9–12 months in advance.*

THE SOUTH

OKLAHOMA **People of the Red Earth.** Explore the native culture and art of northeast Oklahoma on a 10-day tour from the Smithsonian with study leader Dr. Lydia Wyckoff, curator of Native American art and director of the Native American Outreach program at the Philbrook Museum in Tulsa. Learn from the Cherokee and the Muscogee (or Creek) about the "Trail of Tears" across the southeastern United States. Visit the Osage reservation near Tulsa to meet Native American artisans demonstrating finger weaving, silver work and ribbon work. The tour visits museums including Tulsa's Gilcrease Museum, housing the world's most comprehensive collection of art of the American West, and the Philbrook Museum with its Native American exhibits. Spend a day at the Red Earth Festival in Oklahoma City, enjoying its music and dance performances, art, storytelling, and film presentations. Meals include a dinner at the Osage reservation with guest artists in a restored 1880s home, and a traditional Cherokee meal in Tahlequah, capital of the Cherokee nation since 1839. Speakers and escorts throughout the week include author Michael Wallis, who shares colorful stories of famous outlaws, oilmen, and Indians of the Oklahoma territory, and Kevin Smith, a Cherokee artist and museum curator. Accommodations are in hotels in Tulsa, Bartlesville, and Oklahoma City. *Smithsonian Study Tours and Seminars, Smithsonian Institution, 1100 Jefferson Dr. SW, MRC 702, Washington, DC 20560, tel. 202/357–4700, fax 202/633–9250. Mid-June: 10 days, $1,895. Price includes 3 lunches and 6 dinners; sign up 5–7 months in advance.*

THE MIDWEST

KENTUCKY, INDIANA, AND ILLINOIS **In the Footsteps of Lincoln.** Last run in 1996, this seven-day Smithsonian study tour follows the life of Abraham Lincoln, from his birthplace in Lexington, Kentucky, to Illinois where he first dabbled in politics. Study leader Edwin Bearss is an independent scholar and historian, the author of numerous books, and a noted Civil War expert. He guides you through this doorway into American history, visiting important sites in the life of Lincoln, his family and his peers. Visit the birthplace of Mary Todd Lincoln, and the home of Cassius Marcellus Clay, an abolitionist and Lincoln ally. See the famous log cabin where Abraham Lincoln was born and lived for the first two years of his life, and the Knob Creek Farm, where Lincoln spent his boyhood. Go to the Vandalia State House, where Lincoln first sat in the state legislature. Accommodations are in hotel chains such as Comfort Inn and Renaissance Hotel. *Smithsonian Study Tours and Seminars, Smithsonian Institution, 1100 Jefferson Dr. SW, MRC 702, Washington, DC 20560, tel. 202/357–4700, fax 202/633–9250. Mid-Sept.: 7 days, $1,125. Price includes most meals; sign up 3–4 months in advance.*

MISSOURI TO CALIFORNIA **Route 66.** This 2,400-mile odyssey, a Smithsonian-sponsored trip last offered in 1995, follows one of America's most celebrated roads, crossing six states in 14 days and taking in its many curiosities, taste treats, panoramas, drive-ins, and tourist attractions old and new. Traveling with you are writer-photographer Suzanne Wallis, and Michael Wallis, author of *Route 66: The Mother Road*, considered the definitive book on this historic road, one of the first interstate highways. Numerous guest speakers join the group en route. In Oklahoma City, you visit the National Cowboy Hall of Fame. On the way to Santa Fe, you see Amarillo's pop art monument, Cadillac Ranch, a row of 10 vintage cars buried nose down in the desert. And in Albuquerque you can photograph examples of Route 66's renowned neon signs. Many participants take along copies of the book to have them autographed en route by the various local characters profiled in its pages. Lodging is in simple mom-and-pop motels with names like the Big Texan; meals include barbecue feasts, a steak cookout at a ranch, and a dinner in a fancy restaurant. *Smithsonian Study Tours and Seminars, Smithsonian Institution, 1100 Jefferson Dr. SW, MRC 702, Washington, DC 20560, tel. 202/357–4700, fax 202/633–9250. Mid-Oct.: 14 days, $1,895. Price includes 9 lunches and 7 dinners; sign up 5–7 months in advance.*

OHIO TO KENTUCKY **Steamboatin'.** On this eight-day Smithsonian trip you join other cruisers rolling down the Ohio River from Cincinnati to Louisville aboard the *Delta Queen.* One of the last steam-powered paddle wheelers still in service, it is a National Registered Historic Landmark that serves as a floating hotel and classroom. The river journey focuses on the horse breeding heritage in America, with three days spent in Lexington, Kentucky, and special seats at the Kentucky Derby. The length, itinerary, and theme of the cruise vary each year: In 1996, the trip followed the Arkansas and Mississippi Rivers from Memphis to Tulsa, taking in the flavor of Memphis blues and exploring historical towns and sites along the way. Experts present lectures on board and accompany guests ashore during excursions. The *Delta Queen* provides the perfect way to travel through the antebellum South. Between stops, you can relax in a rocking chair on deck, like a country gentleman, or settle back into a plush leather wing chair in one of the boat's parlors. Accommodations are in small but homey wood-paneled cabins for two, and prices vary according to the cabin's size and facilities. Meals are served in two seatings; cuisine is Continental with some Cajun seasonings. *Delta Queen* trips are also usually available from the National Trust for Historic Preservation (*see* Major Players, *above*). *Smithsonian Study Tours and Seminars, Smithsonian Institution, 1100 Jefferson Dr. SW, MRC 702, Washington, DC 20560, tel. 202/357–4700, fax 202/633–9250. Late Apr.–early May: 8 days, $2,725–$4,975. Price includes all lunches and dinners; sign up 5–7 months in advance.*

OKLAHOMA **Indian Spirituality and Social Relations.** From Journeys into American Indian Territory, this seven-day trip takes a look at two levels of the Indian experience—spirituality and social relations—and how the two worlds meet. Meet with a Cheyenne Sun Dance priest, and visit the home of Doc Tate Nevaquaya, a Comanche master painter and flute player. The group explores the Wichita Mountains, spiritual center of many of the Plains Indian tribes and home to herds of wild buffalo. The week's activities include visiting a Cheyenne family home and a visit with an Apache family. You stay in tepees (in sleeping bags) that accommodate about 10 people each. Meals often feature traditional native dishes. Nonnative anthropologist and organization director and founder, Robert Vetter, leads the group, accompanied by three Native American staffers, each from a different tribe. *Journeys into American Indian Territory, Box 929, Westhampton Beach, NY 11978, tel. 516/878–8655 or 800/458–2632, fax 516/878–4518. Early–mid-June: 7 days, $795. Price includes 2 meals per day; sign up 4–8 months in advance.*

THE SOUTHWEST

ARIZONA AND NEW MEXICO **Native Art Past and Present.** The focus of this 10-day study tour from the Smithsonian Institution is how present-day Native American artists are using traditional skills with new materials to express traditional ideas. The unique opportunity to visit private homes, studios, and meetings of Navajo, Hopi, Zuni, and other Pueblo artists comes along with stopping at archaeological ruins such as those in Chaco Canyon National Historic Park. The tour takes in some of the most dramatic mesas in North America. A study leader accompanies the group; in addition, you will meet innovative Native American artists who are using traditional skills to create artifacts out of nontraditional materials, and on some tours, an anthropologist or other expert will lecture on aspects of Native American culture. Accommodations are in hotels in Flagstaff, Albuquerque, Scottsdale, and other towns in the region. One meal is a traditional Hopi dinner, and another is in the home of a local art collector. *Smithsonian Study Tours and Seminars, Smithsonian Institution, 1100 Jefferson Dr. SW, MRC 702, Washington, DC 20560, tel. 202/357–4700, fax 202/633–9250. Mid-Oct.: 10 days, $1,935. Price includes 5 lunches and 4 dinners; sign up 5–7 months in advance.*

ARIZONA, NEW MEXICO, AND UTAH Rock Art. Many of the petroglyphs you see in remote desert locations on archaeologist-led Jeep excursions during this 11-day Archaeological Conservancy tour are not open to the public. That's one feature of the program, which was last offered in 1996 and is planned to run again in 1998; you also visit ancient cliff dwellings and Spanish colonial missions, as well as a few national monuments. Lodging along the way is in Best Westerns and similar places in cities such as Albuquerque and Santa Fe. Other lodgings include a night at the Inn on the Mountain Gods on the Mescalero Apache reservation, and two nights at the Thunderbird Lodge at Canyon de Chelly. Box lunches are provided in the field; breakfast and dinner are up to you. *The Archaeological Conservancy, 5301 Central Ave. NE, #1218, Albuquerque, NM 87108-1517, tel. 505/266–1540. Early–mid-June: 11 days, $1,795. Price includes lunches; sign up 6 months in advance.*

NEW MEXICO Santa Fe Music and Gardens. Typical of Smithsonian tours, this weeklong extravaganza, a perennial favorite, is not strictly horticultural. Instead, it takes in not only gardens but also galleries, concerts, and opera. Leading the group is Charles Mann, a professional photographer specializing in garden imagery and horticultural subjects. He is joined by several guest speakers, including garden designers and expert gardeners. You start the tour with lunch at the home of a local artist and have time to tour the Museum of International Folk Art, which houses the world's largest collection of its kind, with some 100,000 objects ranging from rugs to dolls. Turning your atten-

tion to plants and flowers, you then visit several private gardens: Elizabeth Berry's vegetable ranch grows more than 100 varieties of vegetables, sought after by restaurants all over the country; Elizabeth cultivates antique plants for their seed. A former home of Georgia O'Keeffe high in the desert near Santa Fe, Sol y Sombra is a private botanical garden known for its collection of native plant species. Evenings, you attend performances at the Santa Fe Opera, at the Santa Fe Chamber Music Festival, and by the Santa Fe Desert Chorale. The 1997 tour is scheduled to coincide with Spanish Market, a festival featuring Hispanic art by over 150 artisans as well as music, food, and craft demonstrations. You also explore the city's celebrated restaurant scene, where Pueblo, Spanish colonial, and Mexican and American frontier culinary flavors commingle. Accommodations throughout the tour are at the Inn on the Alameda, within walking distance of galleries and museums. *Smithsonian Study Tours and Seminars, Smithsonian Institution, 1100 Jefferson Dr. SW, MRC 702, Washington, DC 20560, tel. 202/357–4700, fax 202/633–9250. Late July: 7 days, $1,785. Price includes 3 lunches and 2 dinners; sign up 5–7 months in advance.*

THE ROCKIES

COLORADO Ancient Astronomers. This eight-day tour through the southwest Colorado desert near the Utah, Arizona, and New Mexico state lines takes you from the Crow Canyon Archaeological Center to ancient observatories and other sites of cosmic significance to native stargazers. Under the direction of a University of Colorado professor of astrophysics, the program has been so popular that there have been waiting lists in the past. One night is spent camping near Chimney Rock and another in Chaco Canyon; the other evenings are spent at the center's Cortez, Colorado, campus. *Crow Canyon Archaeological Center, 23390 Country Road K, Cortez, CO 81321, tel. 970/565–8975 or 800/422–8975, fax 303/565–4859. Mid-June: 8 days, $995.*

Price includes all meals; sign up 6–8 months in advance.

COLORADO **Hands-On Weaving and Pottery.** The Four Corners School sponsors this seven-day survey of Native American weaving and pottery traditions, led by a Navajo potter and a Navajo weaver. An anthropologist also joins the weeklong program, lecturing about Navajo culture, the history of weaving and pottery, its importance as a metaphor for life, specifically a woman's life, and the historical significance of collections visited throughout the tour. Last run in 1996, the program takes place in Durango, Colorado, beginning with a visit to a private collection of historical weavings. Days are spent learning either pottery or weaving (participants are asked to sign up for one or the other prior to the trip). Weather permitting, instruction takes place outside. There is one pottery instructor for the group, and one weaving instructor for every five students. The cost of the trip includes all supplies. Four nights are spent at a guest ranch in private rooms with shared bath, and for two nights you lodge at a local hotel. Meals are either in restaurants, where you have a choice of American, Mexican, New Mexican, or California cuisine, or you have picnic lunches or meals prepared by ranch staff. *Four Corners School, Box 1029, Monticello, UT 84535, tel. 801/587–2156, fax 801/587–2193. Late Sept: 7 days, $1,495. Price includes all meals; sign up 2–3 months in advance.*

IDAHO **Fine Wine in the Wilderness.** During a six-day paddle trip down the Main Salmon River through rugged central Idaho, sumptuous California-style meals cooked at river campsites headline each evening. Dinners include pleasures like caviar pie, peppers Provençal, grilled Alaska king salmon with pineapple-mango salsa, barbecued marinated lamb, and fresh summer fruit compote with biscotti, prepared by a professional chef or one of the experienced crew members. Owner-winemaker Joel Peterson, named one of the world's 15 outstanding vintners by the prestigious *Wine Advocate,* pours the zinfandels, chardonnays, and cabernet sauvignons from Sonoma, California's, Ravenswood Winery. Vintner Michael Havens, who is known for his merlot rated by *Wine Advocate* as among those few that consistently "will satisfy even the most demanding palate," likewise pours his creation. The morning after the feasts, you and your four to five fellow rafters, working under a professional guide, take the raft through 10- to 15-foot, roller-coaster early summer waves, or the less spectacular but still challenging waters that characterize the stream in late August. *James Henry River Journeys, Box 807, Bolinas, CA 94924, tel. 415/868–1836 or 800/786–1830, fax 415/868–9033. June–late Aug.: 6 days, $950. Price includes all meals; sign up 4–6 months in advance.*

IDAHO AND OREGON **In the Wake of Lewis and Clark.** Small-ship cruises that many institutions offer generally focus on the environment (*see* the Cultural and Natural History Cruises chapter). Those from the National Trust for Historic Preservation concentrate on history. This cruise down the Columbia and Snake rivers follows the entire route of explorers Meriwether Lewis and William Clark, who forged a pathway to the West during a three-year expedition across uncharted wilderness to the Pacific and back. Unlike Lewis and Clark, who traveled over this terrain in wagons and rafts, you will have the benefit of Zodiacs—motorized rubber landing craft—to explore the river's side canyons and rugged shoreline. In the company of a historic preservationist and a local historian native to Oregon, you make excursions to such early settlements as Astoria and the Whitman Mission. Your vessel is Special Expeditions' 70-passenger *Sea Bird,* a favorite among educational tour groups. Accommodations are in small cabins for two, designed for little more than sleeping. Meals, served family style in a single seating, include both typical American fare and the traditional northern European dishes favored by the crew. *National Trust for Historic Preservation, 1785 Massachusetts*

Ave. NW, Washington, DC 20036, tel. 202/673–4000 or 800/944–6847, fax 202/ 673–4038. Early May: 9 days, $2,530– $3,560. Price includes all meals; sign up 9– 12 months in advance.

MONTANA **Rockies by Rail.** This nine-day Smithsonian trip travels through the riches of the Montana Rockies by private rail. Spend a day touring Glacier National Park's wildlife in vintage "jammer" touring cars (open-air train cars built in the 1920s). Visit one of the largest 19th-century cattle ranches in the country. Take a private boat tour of the part of the Missouri River Lewis and Clark dubbed the "gates to the mountains." Travel via motor coach through scenic Yellowstone National Park, climbing to a dramatic elevation of nearly 11,000 feet via Beartooth Highway. From Billings, visit the Little Bighorn Battlefield National Monument, where Sioux and Cheyenne warriors defeated General Custer in 1876. Guests spend three nights on board the vintage passenger cars of the Northern Park Limited. Built between 1942 and 1955, the cars have been refurbished in mahogany and oak furnishings and period detailing to reflect rail travel at the turn of the century, lending a casually elegant atmosphere to the tour. All cabins have a private toilet and sink and the two highest cabin categories have private showers. All drinks and alcoholic beverages are included on the train; an onboard gourmet chef whips up regional specialties. The remaining nights are spent in rustic lodges and in resorts such as the Northern Radisson Hotel in Billings. Meals are served aboard the train or at local haunts like the Izaak Walton Inn, a restored rustic inn built in 1937 to house railroad workers. *Smithsonian Study Tours and Seminars, Smithsonian Institution, 1100 Jefferson Dr. SW, MRC 702, Washington, DC 20560, tel. 202/357–4700, fax 202/673–4038. Early Sept.: 9 days, $2,990–$5,290, depending on cabin category. Price includes 3 meals a day, except 1 dinner in Billings when guests are on their own; sign up 4–6 months in advance.*

ALASKA

SOUTHEAST **Tlingit Tales.** The Tlingit, the original inhabitants of this part of the state, created Alaska's famous totem poles, yet they have no written language. Their oral history is the focus of this two-week river trip along the region's forest-bordered Tatshenshini and Alsek rivers. Billed as a wilderness literature forum, it is one of James Henry River Journeys' most popular tours and is repeated yearly, always with an anthropologist and a poet as leaders. You camp along the river banks and dine on salmon, halibut, and other local specialties; the food has a certain California flair in its unfussy presentation and the freshness of the ingredients. In summer, temperatures range from 50°F to 75°F by day down to the 40s at night; rain is common. *James Henry River Journeys, Box 807, Bolinas, CA 94924, tel. 415/868–1836 or 800/786– 1830, fax 415/868–9033. Late June–early Aug.: 13 days, $2,375. Price includes all meals; sign up 4–6 months in advance.*

HAWAII

MAUI AND LANAI **Ancient Hawaiian Culture.** This eight-day trip journeys to sacred sites of natural and historical significance throughout Maui and Lanai. Led by native Hawaiian Akoni Akana, your exploration of Maui takes you to a cliff face where petroglyphs have been carved, and to Iao Valley, a sacred site where 26 native Hawaiian kings are buried. This is also the site of a bloody battle that marked the end of the reign of the King of Maui when his forces were defeated by King Kamehameha I in 1790. One morning you travel to the top of Haleakala mountain, over 10,000 feet above sea level, for the spectacular sunrise. Visit a school of healing arts that combines traditional practices with Western healing arts, and meet with its director, Kalua Kaiahua, to learn about native Hawaiian healing plants and the role of the mind in healing the body. A full-day excursion takes you to a botanical park to see the largest temple in the state of Hawaii, built by Piilani chiefs in the 15th century. Accommodation for the week is at the Ka'anapali Beach Hotel in Maui. *Sacred Sites International, 1442A Walnut St., #330, Berkeley, CA 94709, tel. 510/540–0671, fax 510/540–1057. Early May: 8 days, $2,195. Price includes 4 lunches and 5 dinners; sign up 4–6 months in advance.*

SOURCES

ORGANIZATIONS The **Network for Educational Travel** (329 Main St. SW, Ronan, MT 59864, tel. 406/676–2255), a group of 1,000 museums, universities, historical societies, and other nonprofit and commercial tour operators, maintains a database on educational travel. If you're interested in booking a cultural tour, you can request information by destination, date, interest, or sponsoring institution. The network will provide you with an up-to-date list of what's available and the tours' durations and prices.

A few other organizations include some domestic cultural tours on their roster of mainly international trips: The **Art Institute of Chicago** (111 S. Michigan Ave., Chicago 60603, tel. 312/443–3600), offers around a dozen domestic trips annually; and the **National Geographic Society** (Box 96090, Washington, DC 20090-6097, tel. 202/857–7500) has cultural cruises as well as trips to the southwestern United States.

University- and college-sponsored tours allow you to learn as you travel in the company of fellow alumni. To find out more about school-sponsored trips, contact your alma mater's alumni relations office.

ALSO SEE Culture, as in horticulture, is another option (*see* Garden Tours). For a look at life in ancient times, look through Archaeological Digs. Also see Cultural and Natural History Cruises, Photography Workshops and Tours, Volunteer Research Vacations, and, if you don't mind staying in one place, Campus Vacations.

Foreign-Language Immersion Programs

Written by Mary King Nash

Updated by Stacy Abramson

onjour, hola, konnichiwa, guten Tag, god dag, ciao, zdravstvuyte, ni hao ma, bom dia. Hello, in other words. Although this greeting is a good way to start a conversation in any country, it doesn't exactly constitute a dialogue. Reaching back to high school French, Spanish, or Italian, you may come up with *c'est un livre, qué hora es?* or *mia gatta è bianca,* but comments on books, the time, or your white cat won't get you very far.

Many travelers find that learning another language makes a vacation or business trip much more enjoyable: It gives them the opportunity to make friends and do business with the locals, order food not on the tourist menu, and venture off the beaten path. At the same time, even people who don't plan to step foot outside an English-speaking country anytime soon can benefit from language courses. Schoolteachers might learn to communicate with Spanish-speaking parents; food lovers might learn to order from a fancy French menu.

There are various ways to get a better handle on a foreign language: You can take a refresher course through a high school or college continuing education department, meeting at least once a week for an entire semester with as many as 20 students; or choose one at a language school, such as Berlitz, Alliance Française, or the Goethe Institute, where classes are smaller and you meet once or twice weekly for six or more weeks. You could also hire a private tutor for 10 hours a day at $30 an hour through one of the InLingua schools or the International Center for Language Studies in Washington, DC, or Houston. Or you could really immerse yourself by signing up for, what else?—a language immersion program, either in the United States or abroad.

We cover language immersion programs in the United States only. These provide a sort of college-cum-summer-camp experience and are fun and relatively inexpensive. During the one to nine weeks that you are enrolled in such a program, you spend every waking moment practicing the language—even when you're playing Ping-Pong or volleyball—because speaking English is generally forbidden.

The programs are often based on college campuses, where you sleep and eat along with your instructors and classmates. Every day, you attend at least four hours of classroom sessions—in the morning and sometimes in the afternoon. You're grouped according to fluency level in small classes (usually fewer than eight students) that allow for a lot of personal attention, and your entertainment also revolves around the language. There are foreign films, lectures, evenings of folk dancing and singing, and games of foreign-language Scrabble.

Mary King Nash, a freelance writer and editor who lives in New York City, has a fascination with foreign cultures. Stacy Abramson is a freelance journalist who travels extensively (yet never quite enough).

Depending on your fluency level when you start, you can walk away from an immersion program with various skills. Beginners usually master basic travel survival tactics; they should be able to ask questions, order from menus, tell a little about themselves, and, in general, explore on their own in a country where the language is spoken. Intermediate students often enter the realm of writing and reading, in addition to speaking. Advanced students work on writing skills and are given the opportunity to discuss current foreign affairs with other fluent speakers; they also read great literature in the original language. Everyone in an immersion program should at least find a few new language-loving friends.

Most programs also try to meet your specific language needs. They may offer a drill of medical terms if you're planning to study medicine abroad, or business phrases if you're an entrepreneur who wants to make foreign investments. Just tell the program director what your needs are before classes begin. Remember, however, that you can't expect a roomful of potential travelers to spend hours reviewing medical terms or negotiating business contracts.

Immersion programs use many learning tools, including cassette tapes and instructional videos. Foreign-language newspapers, books, magazines, and films all contribute to bringing a foreign culture to life. Some programs have satellite hookups that transmit television programs from other countries and computer networks that link you to students overseas. Instructional foreign-language software programs are starting to appear at some schools, but right now these are designed only for advanced students. Be sure to pack a foreign-language dictionary and thesaurus as well as a portable cassette player and several blank tapes. You can use these to record class sessions. Using a cassette player, you can also listen to yourself speak, which is a good way to improve your accent.

Although the first few days of a language program can be strenuous, especially for beginners, you're likely to gain enthusiasm thanks to patient and encouraging teachers, the camaraderie of your classmates, and the fact that you will, eventually, learn. Language immersion programs work: If you hear and speak foreign words for hours on end, in a variety of settings and with everyone you meet, it won't be long before you're discussing books, forgetting about the time, and carrying on in a foreign tongue.

CHOOSING THE RIGHT PROGRAM

Here are some questions to help you determine if a foreign-language program will suit your needs.

What languages are taught? Some programs teach only a few languages, while others teach up to 20. Make sure the language you want to learn is part of the curriculum.

How long has the program been running? Like any business, programs with a few years behind them are more likely to run smoothly and efficiently than new programs.

Is English spoken in the program? The general rule with immersion programs is that students are asked to leave their English at the door and speak only in a foreign tongue for the remainder of the program. If this makes you uncomfortable, try to find a program in which some English is used.

What is the methodology of the program? Some programs tend to be more academic and straightforward. These tend to require more homework and many hours in the language lab. Other programs encourage learning a language with emphasis on culture: performing in skits, paying attention to gestures, or producing radio shows in your target language. The type of program you choose should depend largely on how you like to learn—be sure you know what you're getting into.

How many fluency levels are there? Most programs have beginning, intermediate, and advanced courses, but those with lots of students may divide these levels further, separating beginning intermediates from more advanced intermediates, for example. This makes it easier for you to find an appropriate class with students of comparable ability.

How are students placed? Can students switch classes if their original placement doesn't work out? Novices and fluent conversationalists are easier to place than those who fall somewhere in between. Language immersion programs usually have someone on staff to help you select the right class, and they often use written and oral tests to place students. If you still end up in a class that is either too easy or too difficult, you should be able to switch to a more appropriate class; make sure the program allows this.

What are the teacher's qualifications? Is he or she a native speaker? Teaching a language is very different from merely speaking it. Find out if the instructor is trained to teach and how many years of teaching experience he or she has. In addition, make sure the instructor is native-fluent, that is, has a command over the language equivalent to that of a native speaker (someone who was raised with the language).

This gets tricky when you're learning a language that's spoken in many parts of the world. For example, the Castilian Spanish of Madrid is quite different from Mexican Spanish, so if you're going to Mexico you want a teacher who is aware of those differences.

If you take a course to prepare for a trip, make sure the teacher can discuss the country's history, customs, cultural nuances, and current events. Find out how much time he or she has lived and traveled in that country; someone who has spent a few years in a place will have more insights than someone who has only traveled there, no matter how many times.

How many teachers and teaching assistants (if any) are there, and how many students? What is the student-to-teacher ratio? A program with five or six hours of daily language instruction per class may have three or four teachers and teaching assistants who rotate from class to class throughout the day. It is often easier to keep plugging away at a language if a new face—a teacher with a fresh supply of enthusiasm—periodically pops up. It also helps if classes are kept small, with no more than 10 students. The student-to-teacher ratio should be no higher than five to one.

How many hours are devoted to formal instruction and how long are the breaks? If you haven't attended school lately, you may not realize how *long* a classroom hour can seem, and some programs schedule six hours of formal instruction a day. It is up to you to decide how much you can take. Learning a language shouldn't be a punishment, so don't sign up for the most intensive class unless you're sure you can sit still. Beginners are strongly discouraged, often barred, from participating in these classes, because it is simply no fun for them to spend hours upon hours going over grammar and vocabulary drills.

Can the classes be altered to address my special needs? So you want to go to Germany to sell automobiles, and you need to learn some German car-talk. Make sure the teacher will spend some time going over the special terminology you need to learn.

Is there a language lab, and what hours is it available to students? Every worthwhile language immersion program should have a language lab where you have access to foreign-language books, newspapers, magazines, and instructional videos and cassette tapes. Some programs also provide satellite broadcasts of foreign telecasts and instructional foreign-language software.

What's the cost and what's included? Language programs range in cost from $495 to more than $6,000, although most are under $2,000, including meals and lodging. Unless otherwise noted, prices here are per person and cover instruction, double-occupancy lodging, three meals a day, a textbook, and cultural programs, such as foreign films and lectures. When a program charges different prices for single and double rooms, the two prices are given.

What are the accommodations like? Most programs are held on university campuses, and you sleep in a sparsely furnished dormitory room with a shared bath. You are usually assigned a roommate, but you can often get a single if you are willing to pay more for it. Some programs provide linens and towels; others don't, so be sure to ask. A few programs make use of pleasant hotels, and a few expect you to make your own arrangements.

Will laundry service be available? Most campuses have laundry facilities. This could save you a suitcase—if you have time to do the wash.

What is the food like? Again, because these programs are on college campuses, the food is mostly standard college fare: sandwiches, fresh fruit, a salad bar, and a choice of unexciting entrées at dinner. Be sure to ask if there are restaurants in the area and if you can opt out of the meal plan.

How much free time is there? Don't be surprised if the answer is none. Language immersion programs take it for granted that you want to practice the language every minute, in a variety of settings, both formal and informal.

What additional planned activities are there? You may not have free time, but you should certainly have fun time. Most programs schedule sing-alongs, acting skits, and walks off campus to help you develop an informal vocabulary. Lectures, music performances, and foreign films usually dominate the evenings.

What recreational facilities are available? A college campus usually has tennis courts, a gym with a swimming pool, a weight room, a running track, and basketball courts. Finding time to use them is another matter.

Do you have references from past students? To clarify your perception of

instruction, lodging, and food, there's no substitute for a talk with someone who has done the drills, slept in the beds, and tasted the meals.

How far in advance do I need to register? Most programs expect you to sign up one to three months in advance, but often a program's less popular classes have openings until the last minute, and there's always a chance of a last-minute cancellation for even the most sought-after class. Also, be sure to find out the minimum number needed to enroll in your class, and how many are enrolled at the time you register. This way you'll know if you should keep another language program on the back burner in case of cancellation.

FAVORITE PROGRAMS

THE NORTHEAST

NEW HAMPSHIRE **Accelerated Language Programs.** Expect the unexpected when you tackle the highly intensive Accelerated Language Programs (ALPs) at Dartmouth College. These programs bear the stamp of their creator, Dartmouth French professor Dr. John A. Rassias: The instructors are active, enthusiastic, and determined to teach. You may find yourself shouting, crying, laughing, frowning, smiling, whispering, jumping, crouching, or using whatever theatrical gesture it takes to communicate foreign words and concepts without using English. Expect to leave the outside world, as you immerse yourself here in another culture.

Under the direction of Dr. Rassias, this immersion program follows the Rassias Method, a holistic language-learning approach he developed based on his work teaching languages at Dartmouth and his experiences with the Peace Corps in the 1960s. The program, referred to by staff members as the "Club Med for Masochists" or the "Lingual Outward Bound," is thought to be rigorous but never boring. Held each summer since 1982, the fast-pace classes cover beginning, intermediate, and advanced French, Spanish, German, and Italian, as well as beginning Japanese, Mandarin Chinese, English as a Second Language (ESL), and Portuguese. (Greek, Swedish, and Russian have been offered in the past, but weren't in 1996, as a minimum of 10 people must sign up for the language.) The goal here is to learn a language through immersion in a simulation of its culture in just 10 days.

The Rassias Method—at times referred to as the Rassias Madness—is described as "an all-out assault on the emotions and the senses, as well as the intellect" in the "Rassias Connection," a newsletter that provides the latest news on Rassias-related developments. The method seeks to eliminate your inhibitions by creating an atmosphere of free expression through both drama and repetition.

Your 10- to 15-hour days begin with a 7:15 breakfast and continue well into the night, following a regimented schedule that allows for only three 20-minute breaks. You experience the core of the program—the Master-class and breakout-group combination—twice a day. During these sessions, the Master instructor (one per fluency level) teaches a lesson to the group as a whole (maximum 15 students) for 50 minutes. Then, groups of four or five students gather with a teaching assistant (three or four assistants rotate among the groups each day) for 50 minutes of fast-pace oral drills, during which students are called on every minute. While the norm in most courses for the number of student responses is 5 times an hour, these 50 minute drills elicit an average of 65 responses. These exercises, which you will enjoy five times a day, reinforce material from the Master instructor's lesson. Repetition, positive rewards, rhythmic pacing, and role-playing help keep students actively involved in language learning without *thinking* too much about the process.

You may find the first days to be strenuous and stressful, but the energy of the one-on-one interaction is contagious and gets the adrenaline flowing. You will enjoy 30-minute feedback sessions every day and can also turn to the assistants for tutoring at any time. Eventually your mind will click on the language and your tongue will follow; you'll begin responding automatically, knowing a correct word, phrase, or idiom without knowing exactly how you picked it up. A textbook provided by the program reiterates the lessons. Songs, skits, gesture lessons, and poems also teach you the language, as do cultural activities, such as a Japanese tea ceremony and a French cooking class.

Although ALPs accept day students, most students reside on campus, where the accommodations are spartan. You get a private dorm room equipped with a single bed, a desk and chair, a lamp, and a phone. Linens are provided, and there are laundry facilities in each dorm. Meals become extensions of the classroom, as teachers, teaching assistants, and students dine together in Hanover Inn, a short walk from campus. Students from different fluency groups mingle at tables determined by language. Three meals a day are included (with lunch only for day students). Salads, sandwiches, or a choice of entrées are standard fare, but a few dishes with a foreign flavor are available at some meals.

In the evening, cultural films are shown. At the end of the program, you are expected to perform in a skit made up by your drill group. On the last day, you'll participate in a three-hour graduation ceremony, enjoy a final luncheon, march in the parade, and receive a special graduation certificate. If you're lucky, you may be chosen to be your group's valedictorian. Your schedule here is packed, so you don't have much time to take advantage of the language resource center with its cassette tapes, language videos, and foreign books, magazines, and newspapers. Although it will cost you $30 extra, you may want to check out some of Dartmouth's facilities: tennis courts, golf course, gym with running track, swimming pool, and basketball courts. Realistically, you'll probably find yourself too busy learning to indulge in such luxuries. *The Rassias Foundation, ALPs, Dartmouth College, 6071 Wentworth Hall, Hanover, NH 03755-3526, tel. 603/646–2922 or 603/646–3155, fax 603/646–3838. June and July: 10-day sessions, $1,500 for day students and $2,000 for on-campus students. Price includes single room; sign up at least 2 wks in advance. Minimum age is 17. The Rassias Foundation offers similar satellite programs at college campuses in New York, Maryland, Connecticut, and Chicago.*

NEW YORK **Language Immersion Institute.** For a no-frills language-learning bargain, sign up for a summer workshop at the Language Immersion Institute of the State University of New York, College at New Paltz. These are some of the cheapest classes available, and you still get 50 hours of instruction—five hours a day, Monday to Friday for two weeks—the equivalent of a one-semester three-credit undergraduate course.

You can choose from classes in 20 languages—American Sign Language, Arabic, Chinese, Czech, Dutch, ESL, French, German, Greek, Hebrew, Hungarian, Italian, Japanese, Polish, Portuguese, Russian, Spanish, Swedish, Ukrainian, and Yiddish. Courses have a minimum of six students, a maximum of 15, and one instructor per class.

The native-fluent teachers create a supportive and nonthreatening class atmosphere that is conducive to learning. They are trained language professionals who teach at various schools and universities in the New York metropolitan area. Conversational skills are stressed at all levels. You buy your own textbook, usually priced under $60. Cassette tapes complementing the text can be checked out of the language laboratory or purchased.

The program begins with an orientation meeting. You attend weekday classes from 8 until 1, when you break for lunch. Students generally eat lunch with their instructor in town, which is about a 10 minute walk from campus. After lunch, you are free to explore New Paltz and surrounding areas, do homework, or work in the language lab. Since meals are on your own, you may pick a restaurant off campus, but if you don't mind cafeteria-style food, the campus snack bar serves hot and cold dishes, including vegetarian fare. Weekly meal plans at the college dining hall can be purchased through the institute. At the end of the day, entertaining foreign films with English subtitles are shown on a big screen in the lecture center.

Students sleep in dormitory double or single rooms, where linens are supplied but fans are not—bring one, it's hot. Bathrooms are shared. You receive a temporary ID card that lets you use college facilities: library, tennis courts, running track, gym with swimming pool, racquetball courts, and exercise equipment. In your free time, you can take a tour of New Paltz, settled by French Huguenots in the 17th century; the Huguenot Historical Society (tel. 914/255–1660) has summer tours in the area.

Dr. Henry Urbanski, director of the institute, developed this program in 1981 and has honed the teaching methods to ensure rapid language acquisition. Fluent in seven languages, he is also professor of Russian Studies at SUNY New Paltz, and he organizes a one-week session at the historic Mohonk Mountain House (*see below*). *Language Immersion Institute, 75 South Manheim Blvd., SUNY, College at New Paltz, New Paltz, NY 12561, tel. 914/257–3500, fax 914/257–3569. July: 12 days, $625. Price does not include lodging ($325 single, $275 double for 12 days), meals, or textbook; sign up 1 month in advance. 15-hour weekend immersion courses are offered throughout the year in Westchester ($295), at the New Paltz campus ($250), and in Manhattan at a hotel ($295); the cost is for instruction, you're on your own for lodging.*

NEW YORK **Tower of Babble.** If you seek a language program in a resort-type setting, look no farther than the one held at Mohonk Mountain House, a towering, turreted stately 273-room hotel with a Victorian feel. Each January, Mohonk invites the Language Immersion Institute from the SUNY, College at New Paltz (*see above*) to host a week of classes in American Sign Language, Arabic, Chinese, French, German, Hebrew, Italian, Japanese, Russian, Spanish, and Yiddish.

You can choose from classes at four levels of proficiency (Elementary I, Elementary II, Intermediate, and Advanced); sometimes, however, to meet the minimum of six students, classes of different levels are combined when two small groups of students are fairly close in terms of proficiency. The maximum class size is 12, with one instructor per class and no teaching assistants; instructors are native-fluent speakers and trained language professionals who teach at colleges and universities.

You arrive at the hotel in New Paltz at 4 PM on a Sunday, and you meet your instructor and classmates that night at dinner. Classes are conducted throughout each day, beginning with breakfast and ending after dinner with evening entertainment; a few hours every afternoon are left open for you to rest and recharge.

You might take an afternoon walk with your instructor on the grounds, learning the language in a beautiful setting. Evening entertainment includes foreign-language films with English subtitles. After hours and hours of listening to and speaking a foreign tongue, you begin to "live" that language—and sing it, act in it, and play games using it. As part of your final exam, you will perform in a five-minute skit during the Bon Voyage luncheon for other "Babblers."

Your home for the week is a stone-and-wood Victorian extravaganza, built between 1869 and 1910 and now listed on the National Trust for Historic Preservation's honor roll of Historic Hotels of America. Victorian and Adirondack-style furnishings fill the hotel's nooks and crannies. You pay separately for your room and board at the resort. There are both single and double rooms within a range of prices that corresponds to escalating levels of luxury; the most elegant guest rooms contain working fireplaces, balconies with lake or mountain views, and claw-foot bathtubs.

All meals, included in the cost of your room, are taken in one of the resort's dining rooms: buffet-style breakfast and lunch, afternoon tea at 4, and dinner with a choice of several well-prepared entrées and decadent desserts. The food here is much closer to gourmet cuisine than what you find at language programs held on college campuses. Since you share a dinner table with your classmates and instructor all week, you continue to learn throughout the evening.

The hotel has views of Lake Mohonk (a glacial lake), the Hudson River Valley, and the Catskill and Shawangunk mountains. The sprawling grounds take in 2,200 acres of lawns, 85 miles of winding trails, formal and informal gardens, and 127 gazebos. In your free time, from 2 to 4 daily, you can take advantage of the resort's sports facilities; there's tennis, golf, swimming, ice-skating, horse-drawn carriage rides, and cross-country skiing and snowshoeing on 35 miles of groomed trails. *Mohonk Mountain House, Lake Mohonk, New Paltz, NY 12561, tel. 914/255–1000 or 800/772–6646, fax 914/256–2161 (register at: Language Immersion Institute, Faculty Tower 916, SUNY, College at New Paltz, New Paltz, NY 12561, tel. 914/257–3500 or 914/257–3501, fax 914/257–3569). Jan.: 6 days, $475. Price does not include meals and lodging (singles: $175–$291; doubles: $228–$316). Lodging rates are per night and include 3 meals per person. The instruction rate includes use of textbook during program; sign up as much in advance as possible. For hotel reservations call 800/772–6646. Weekend immersion programs: April and November: $250, not including meals and lodging.*

RHODE ISLAND **Deutsche Sommerschule am Atlantik.** If German is the language you want to study, you might choose the German Summer School of the Atlantic at the University of Rhode Island (URI), which offers a three- or six-week summer immersion program in conjunction with the Goethe Institute, a German cultural organization. In its 16th year, this language program has enough social and recreational activities to make it resemble a summer camp, but its classes are rigorous and you must speak German at all times.

An encouraging camaraderie quickly develops among the program's 60 students, the native-fluent professors, and the teaching assistants and tutors, who share meals and meet for social events. Professors and assistants are from URI and from the Goethe Institute; some tutors are students from German universities.

Students are divided according to fluency level (beginning, intermediate, advanced intermediate, and advanced) for small (8–15 persons), intensive classes held from 8 to noon Monday through Wednesday and Friday and Saturday. All classes stress speaking and listening skills. Novices concentrate on basic vocabulary, intermediates practice speaking and writing, and advanced students discuss German news and current events after reading German newspapers and watching satellite broadcasts of German television programs. If you're at the intermediate or advanced level, you can sign up for supplementary classes held in the afternoon three times a week at no extra charge. These include a business class, which covers vocabulary and terminology needed to conduct business in Germany; a theater workshop; conversation classes; German studies classes; and a language-learning technique class. Master's degrees can also be earned over a three-summer period.

All students have access to the language lab, where a computer network links URI to the Universität Bochum in Germany 24 hours a day. Students in Germany who are learning how to teach German and English serve as long-distance tutors. You can transmit your essays, letters, or even sim-

ple sentences, which the German tutors correct and return. This service has paired many pen pals, who continue communicating after the summer program ends.

Campus housing and a meal plan are mandatory and are included in the cost of the program. You stay in a sorority house in shared double rooms with shared baths or in single rooms at an extra cost. Rooms are equipped with basic dorm furniture—beds, desks, lamps, dressers. You eat in the house dining room, where breakfast and lunch are served buffet style and dinner is family style. Fresh fruits and vegetables are always available, and you can try a few German entrées offered at some meals. The meal plan does not include Saturday dinner or Sunday meals. For those meals many students go to the coast for fresh seafood, though there are restaurants closer to campus.

Afternoon recreational activities—picnics, volleyball, and soccer games—help alleviate the morning brain drain of classes. The campus is only 5 miles from the Atlantic Ocean, and beach trips are popular on Thursdays. But don't forget that you are learning an entire semester's worth of material, so although you have less class time here than most programs, you make up for it in homework. German feature films and lectures about German cultural and political events fill evening hours, as do sing-alongs and German Scrabble games. *German Summer School of the Atlantic, University of Rhode Island, Department of Languages, Bldg. 129 Independence Hall, Kingston, RI 02881-0812, tel. 401/874–5911, fax 401/874–4694. Late June–early Aug.: 3 wks, $1,050 double; 6 wks, $2,100 double. Single rooms available for an additional cost. All meals included in the price; textbook not included. Sign up by June 1.*

VERMONT **Middlebury College Languages Schools.** If you're looking for a time intensive, cost intensive, and learning intensive program—this is it. Middlebury College in peaceful Vermont near the New York border is sandwiched between the Green Mountains and the Adirondacks, and is a neighbor to Lake Champlain. Don't be fooled though: this is *not* a restful vacation in the mountains. Behind the sloping hills and majestic mountains, you'll discover very intense language enclaves with a strong focus on learning.

Since the summer of 1915, people have been journeying to Vermont to study languages at Middlebury College. Today many people, from medical teams to clergy, come here to enhance their careers by learning a language. Last year two married journalists from the *Washington Post,* who were to be posted in China, chose to attend the immersion course at Middlebury in preparation for their trip. Although children are not usually allowed, an exception was made in their case to permit their newborn baby to accompany them. However, they were required to hire a Chinese nanny so that they wouldn't interact with their child in a way that would be breaking their commitment to total immersion.

Over 1,000 students and 200 faculty flock to Middlebury to study in one of the school's highly rigorous immersion programs. Seven-week courses in French, German, Italian, and Spanish are offered at all levels; nine-week courses are available for those languages that require learning a new alphabet, such as Arabic, Chinese, Japanese, or Russian. Middlebury also offers six-week graduate programs in French, German, Italian, Spanish, and Russian. An integral part of the Opening Ceremonies, and of the program, is when you are asked to make the Language Pledge, a formal commitment to speak only the language—whether you're on campus or making a phone call home— you are choosing to study.

Classes meet weekdays in the early mornings and afternoons. The rest of the time— late afternoons and weekends—is your own. You can attend lectures or concerts, enjoy plays, or watch films. You can also visit the recording studio where students are encouraged to produce their own radio programs. (Each language operates with its particular school and each school runs its own radio show.) You might broadcast a news show in your language, play music from that country, or explore a topic relevant to that culture. Be sure to check out the multimedia work stations in the Interactive Learning Center. This is where you'll do some "cyber-learning" (and really get your money's worth). You can watch satellite broadcasts of news and other programs from all over the world. Here you'll also learn to integrate text, video, sound, still images, and even the Internet in all sorts of ways that facilitate learning. For example, you can record your responses to exercises and then play them back alongside of those of a native speaker's. You can also explicate text by highlighting words, which then triggers a large glossary or larger explanations. Or you can just buckle down the old-fashioned way and sit under a big tree and begin your homework. You should expect a minimum of five hours of work a night.

All students and faculty are required to live in the campus dorms. The rooms are typically spartan with only a bed, desk, wastebasket, and bureau. Pillows and blankets are provided but you'll need to bring your own linens and fan. Lest there be any confusion, there is no air-conditioning. All meals are served in the cafeteria, where you sit with the others in your language school. *Middlebury College Languages Schools, Sunderland Language Center, Middlebury College, Middlebury, VT 05753, tel. 802/443–5510, fax 802/443–2075. June–Aug.: 6 wks (graduate program), $4,170; 7 wks, $4,260; 9 wks, $3,710. Cost includes 3 meals a day. Assume you will be in a double room—they don't offer a rate for single accommodation. Financial aid and loans may be available if you apply early. Classes tend to fill up by early April; May 1 is the deadline for graduate classes.*

VERMONT **The Russian School at Norwich University.** There isn't a single Tom, Dick, or Harry at the Russian School; instead, you'll find Ivan, Gregor, Olga, and Katrina. From the moment you exchange your name for a Russian or Czech one and pledge to speak only Russian or Czech, you know you're part of something exceptional. An extension of Norwich University, the Russian School has two- and three-week crash courses at the beginning and advanced levels, in addition to eight-week undergraduate and graduate classes scheduled each summer. The Russian School has a master's program during the seven weeks and they also now offer a Czech program for beginners.

Classes here are small, with four to six students, allowing for a lot of one-on-one coaching from the instructors. You're in class six hours a day, every day, with no weekend breaks, so three or four instructors rotate daily among classes to keep the teaching varied. Because conversational skills are emphasized, by the end of the program even a beginner should be able to communicate comfortably with a native speaker.

Each day is divided into lessons that cover the following: A grammar session introduces vocabulary words and phrases that are repeated throughout the day; exercises in role-playing help develop conversational skills; and another session teaches you how to phrase questions. In reading sessions, you learn word formations and sentence structure as well as words you might encounter while traveling; and by watching videos of Russian advertisements, cartoons, and television programs, you strengthen your listening and comprehension skills. During the free conversation session, students talk with one another under the observation of an instructor who keeps the dialogue ball rolling when necessary.

The school's language lab contains instructional videos and cassette tapes and has a satellite hookup that brings in Russian television news programs, and the university library has an extensive collection of Slavic newspapers, journals, books, and magazines. A Russian ensemble, made up of several members of the Russian School's staff, teaches folk singing and dancing, and the Russian School choir gives performances of Russian Orthodox choir singing. There is

also a theater group led by Serge Kokovkin, the resident playwright and actor. Everyone is encouraged to participate.

Language students stay in two handsome brick dormitories with both single and double rooms. Each room is sparsely furnished with twin beds (linens are not provided), wardrobes, desks, and desk chairs, and you share hall bathrooms. You dine with fellow students and instructors in the campus dining room or Food Court supplied by Marriott. The menu in the dining room sometimes includes entrées with a foreign flair, such as British fish-and-chips, Russian beef Stroganoff, borscht, and chicken Kiev. A fresh-fruit and salad bar is standard.

From 7 PM to midnight, students gather at the on-campus Russian Café for coffee and Russian cookies, even more Russian conversation, and, while it's still light, a picture-window view of the Green Mountains. The university's rural Vermont setting (15 miles from Montpelier and 50 miles from Burlington) makes hiking a favorite activity, and all wanna-be Russians learn to ask directions to the floating bridge in nearby Brookfield, where they can go swimming. The campus has tennis courts, a gym with an indoor swimming pool, a racquetball court, a basketball court, and a weight room. *The Russian School, Norwich University, Northfield, VT 05663, tel. 802/485–2000 or 800/468–6679, ext. 2165, fax 802/485–2580. June-July: 2 wks, $695; 3 wks, $995; 7 wks, $3,500; 8 wks, $3,800. Singles are $200 extra. Board is included. Price does not include textbook; sign up 3 months in advance. Financial aid is available if you apply by late February.*

THE WEST COAST

CALIFORNIA **Custom Language Services.** Just one of the programs offered by the renowned Monterey Institute of International Studies, Custom Language Services (CLS) allows you to tailor a class to your needs and schedule. Private tutorial sessions work best, but up to four people at the same level can sign up together, reducing the cost substantially.

The basic CLS program is six hours of instruction each weekday for six weeks; it can be compressed to four weeks by adding three class hours each Saturday, or you can lengthen or shorten the hours and days to fit your timetable. A class of two weeks or less is recommended only as a refresher for those who already know the language or as a way to learn basic travel survival skills.

The Monterey Institute, a world leader in the field of foreign-language studies, attracts students from around the globe to its undergraduate and graduate programs as well as its eight- and nine-week summer language courses. Although the institute was established in 1955, the CLS program started in 1972 as a way to prepare corporate personnel and their families for relocation to foreign countries; it is currently used by people with both business and personal reasons for learning a foreign language.

Given at least three weeks' notice, CLS's program director and instructors plan a class based on how you intend to use the language. They use a questionnaire and phone interview prior to your arrival to help determine the current level of your language proficiency. Your input regarding goals and interests helps chart the course. In summer 1996, group classes were offered in Arabic, Chinese, ESL (English as a Second Language), Japanese, French, German, Korean, Russian, and Spanish. Depending on student interest and faculty availability, a class in practically any language is possible.

The course coordinator chooses instructors for each program, depending on goals and circumstances. Taken into consideration are the home country of the instructors, students' current level of ability, and specialty areas for specific jargon and terminology. If the program is set for six hours of class daily, the common arrangement is a team of three instructors, each for two hours daily. The coordinator ensures communication among the team members and divides areas of responsibility.

When you're not in class, you can use the wealth of multimedia language-learning resources at the CLS center; you can even get a key to use the facility after hours. Textbooks, audiocassettes, and video programs, such as the popular "French in Action," Russian "Let's Get Acquainted," and Spanish "Destinos" programs are in the CLS library. Satellite news broadcasts from 35 countries are of interest to intermediate and advanced students. Broadcasts can be viewed in the student center, and videotapes can be checked out from the Audiovisual Center. A Macintosh computer is housed on the CLS floor, which can be used for drilling with language software. Programs are currently available in Chinese, Japanese, Russian, Spanish, and ESL. There's also a computer system used solely for pronunciation practice.

Authentic materials, such as magazines, maps, menus, brochures, and train timetables, of a foreign region that you are planning to visit are also used in the language programs. If you're a medical student planning to study in a foreign country, you are taught medical terms in the language you'll be using. CLS also tracks down foreign medical journals and articles that deal with the country's hospital system and medical customs.

The institute's campus, always abuzz with foreign and foreign-minded students, makes it easy for you to find a new pal who speaks the language you're studying. During the regular school year, language clubs invite CLS students to join their social and cultural activities, such as picnics, yoga classes (taught in French), concerts, and visits to museums and the local aquarium. Off-campus trips are often part of your instruction. Russian-language students, for instance, enjoy playing chess with opponents at the Defense Language Institute, also in Monterey, which teaches languages to military personnel. Even a simple trip to the farmer's market becomes educational when your instructor teaches you the names of fruits and vegetables in a foreign tongue.

Accommodations are not available through CLS, but among the places to stay are nearby hotels that offer rooms to CLS students at a good weekly rate. You're also on your own for meals. The institute snack bar is open for breakfast and lunch, and the campus is only three blocks from Fisherman's Wharf and downtown, where there are many good restaurants. *Custom Language Service, Monterey Institute of International Studies, 425 Van Buren St., Monterey, CA 93940, tel. 408/647–4115 or 800/995–8403, fax 408/647–3534. Year-round: 2 wks, $3,300; 4 wks, $6,600; 6 wks, $9,000. Price does not include meals and lodging; sign up at least 3 wks in advance.*

CALIFORNIA **Residential Language Institutes.** There aren't too many places where you can soak in a rock-lined hot sulfur spring pool while practicing verb conjugation, but Napa Valley is one of them. If you have at least 10 college credits of French, you can sign up for a language immersion program at the 330-acre White Sulphur Springs Resort and Spa, about an hour's drive from San Francisco. Sponsored by the University of California Berkeley Extension, this Residential Language Institute—La Maison Française—takes over the resort for one week every August.

English is verboten during all programs, which start with a get-acquainted meeting Sunday afternoon and end after lunch on Friday. You are separated into groups of 10 to 12 students based on your level of fluency, and two or three professors from well-respected colleges and universities—including the University of California, Berkeley, and the San Francisco Conservatory of Music—rotate among these groups. Classes concentrate on vocabulary and comprehension, and since beginners are not admitted to the programs, instructors can focus on improving your conversational skills by working on the nuances of intonation, idiom, and accent.

In general, your mornings are devoted to formal class work, with grammar review, oral presentations, skits, and discussion, while your afternoons are set aside for cultural and literary lectures, guest lecturers, oral presentations by teachers, and other structured activities, such as singing and reading plays.

Textbooks are used as reference material but are generally eschewed in favor of handouts with stories, songs, and poems. You don't use many instructional videos or tapes, but you do see films in the language you're studying. Students are encouraged to bring their favorite books, musical cassettes, and periodicals to share with classmates. Guest speakers lecture on such subjects as 17th-century French theater and painting. There are also evening music and dance performances: You can take tours conducted in French of nearby wineries, including Domaine Chandon, which specializes in sparkling wines.

White Sulphur Springs Resort was the first mineral spring resort in California, built in 1852. Your accommodations are either in the white wooden inn or the carriage house, each of which has 14 single rooms. Rooms at the inn have full baths and the carriage-house quarters share hall bathrooms. All students have private rooms with quilt-covered queen-size beds but without televisions or telephones. You're provided with linens and towels.

You eat in a dining room with your professors and fellow classmates. Your meals are prepared by a chef hired by the school to cook only French foods, such as crepes, ratatouille, and escargots. Naturally, the dinner wines are from France, as well.

Outside the classroom, you continue speaking in your new language during games of volleyball, badminton, horseshoes, and croquet, or while walking on trails that pass by redwood, fir, and madrone trees. Those who spend too much time poring over foreign-language books, magazines, and newspapers may find relief in a massage, mud bath, or herbal wrap, which the resort will schedule for an additional charge. And, of course, there is always the hot spring. *Residential Language Institutes,*

University of California Berkeley Extension, 1995 University Ave., Berkeley, CA 94720-7002, tel. 510/642–6362, fax 510/643–0599. Aug.: 6 days, $1,075. Price includes single room and meals; sign up 3 months in advance.

SOURCES

ORGANIZATIONS It is not easy to find information on foreign-language programs in the United States that teach more than ESL classes for foreign students; the **American Council on the Teaching of Foreign Languages** (ACTFL: 6 Executive Plaza, Yonkers, NY 10701-6601, tel. 914/963–8830, fax 914/963–1275) is very helpful. They suggest contacting individual National Teacher Associations for more information. The **Modern Language Association of America** (10 Astor Pl., New York, NY 10003, tel. 212/475–9500) can also be helpful, although the information they have is not always current.

PERIODICALS "Rassias Connection" (6071 Wentworth Hall, Dartmouth College, Hanover, NH 03755-3526, tel. 603/646–2922, fax 603/646–3838), a free newsletter published by the Rassias Foundation, a nonprofit organization at Dartmouth College, follows developments in language learning using the Rassias Method. The Rassias Foundation also publishes the *Ram's Horn* (same address and phone number as the "Rassias Connection"), an annual periodical with articles and commentary on language teaching and the Rassias Method by professors from American, European, and Asian colleges and universities.

BOOKS Opportunities in Foreign Language Careers (VGM Career Books), by Wilga Rivers, gives advice on language education and how to get jobs in foreign-language fields. It also discusses some of those fields, such as world trade, travel and tourism, and civil service. Appendixes include lists of language associations and travel, study, and exchange programs.

Garden Tours

Written by Mary Myers

Updated by Amy Calabrese

lose your eyes, take a deep breath, and imagine this: The sweetness of roses fills the air, mixed with the sharper scent of lavender and catmint. The clean aroma of fresh-cut grass is unmistakable. The sun feels warm on your skin and your ears pick up the lazy drone of a bumblebee. When you open your eyes, you are in a sea of color—the brilliant reds of Oriental poppies, lush pinks of peonies and roses, deep purples of salvia, soft blue of catmint, and clear yellow of coreopsis. In the distance, tall trees cast dappled shade over a smooth green lawn. Have you fallen into an impressionist painting? No. These are the sights and smells of a well-tended garden. And you don't have to travel to Europe to experience them.

There are dozens of magnificently designed gardens all over the United States. And because of the mushrooming public interest in gardening, a number of organizations offer special tours to these preserves. Some programs are offered by tour packagers, others by botanical organizations and horticultural societies (you sometimes have to join these institutions in order to take their tours). A few operations custom design garden tours for individuals or groups. Group tours typically last about a week and cost between $135 and $275 a day per person based on double occupancy, depending on the quality of the accommodations and

meals. A number of short one-of-a-kind tours are also available, usually sponsored by large cities' major botanical gardens. If you plan to travel in the vicinity of one of them, call ahead to see if anything is scheduled at the time of your visit.

No matter which tour you choose, you are likely to be surrounded by sympathetic and knowledgeable people. Gardeners love to exchange information (and plants), and the touring milieu stimulates conversation. Personal experiences with growing and propagating plants, and questions about layout, relentless weeds, and the latest hybrids are likely to be discussed on buses or during free time. You are certain to learn something from your fellow travelers as well as from the tour guides.

Occasionally a tour focuses on a specific period of garden making. However, most tours focus on a specific region or locale and cover a gamut of garden styles there.

In a Colonial garden you might tread the soft gravel walkways of a *physick* garden—a collection of medicinal plants like mint, tansy, plantain, and others. The plants are laid out in an orderly fashion, the paths usually straight and edged with a crisply sheared low hedge. The strict symmetrical layout of many early American gardens illustrates the close connection between Europe and the colonies. For example, the gardens at the Governor's Palace in Colo-

Mary Myers is coordinator of the Landscape Design Certificate program at the New York Botanical Garden and is also principal of a landscape architecture firm in Hastings-on-Hudson, New York. Amy Calabrese works at Garden Design *in New York City.*

nial Williamsburg, Virginia, are a series of hedged parterres (from a French term meaning "on the earth"), composed of low-growing plants arranged with inert materials, such as gravel or coal, in elaborate carpetlike patterns.

Several of these very pleasant Colonial gardens (both domestic and grand) are in the re-created towns of Colonial Williamsburg, in Virginia, and Old Sturbridge Village, in Massachusetts. On your own, you will be able to wander down the back streets for a look at kitchen gardens, as there is usually ample free time.

Garden tours also take in preserves designed during the Country Place Era, a prolific period for American landscape architecture that ran from the mid-19th century until the onset of the Depression, when bankers, industrialists, and others who had suddenly amassed great fortunes commissioned grand houses and gardens. Often these estates were conceived as a single entity, the landscaping interlocked with the design of a mansion and its outbuildings. Some of these estates were planned by Frederick Law Olmsted, the father of American landscape architecture, and by his son and stepson, who worked as the Olmsted Brothers, as well as by such notable designers as Marian Coffin, Ellen Shipman, and Warren Manning. Their works are often huge and might contain terrace gardens, rose gardens, rhododendron or conifer collections, fountains, pools and other water features, and acres of pasture or cropland.

Many of the properties that you visit on garden tours are open to the public; the advantage of seeing them on a garden tour is that you're in the company of like-minded travelers and knowledgeable guides, who can enrich your experience immeasurably. Some garden tours (and these tend to sell out early) also allow you to visit private contemporary gardens—gardens not open to the general public. These were usually designed within the past 50 years, although some are the culmination of several generations of one family's loving care; they tend

to display the most current approaches to garden design, as well as state-of-the-art maintenance techniques. The owner is often available to discuss garden-related problems and solutions, and to provide a personal touch. Occasionally the tour includes a meal or cocktails among the plantings.

Reflecting the trend toward incorporating ecologically sound garden design—that which is self-sustaining and does not require human intervention in the form of chemicals, pesticides, herbicides, and the like—botanical gardens and tour agencies regularly offer regional landscape tours. On walking tours of the Rockies, for example, you can hike through scenic meadows and inspect alpine environments. You might visit large public preserves such as the national parks of the western United States and Canada in the company of accomplished naturalists, horticulturists, or ecologists.

CHOOSING THE RIGHT TOUR

To help you choose a company whose trips will please you, ask a lot of questions. Then put on your sturdy walking shoes and prepare to stroll down the proverbial garden path.

What is the focus of the tour—plants, landscape design, a specific design period, or regional landscape and scenery? Any trip can be interesting, but some may be more relevant than others to your own gardening interests. However, on all tours, a passion for gardening unites participants, and both novices and experts mingle freely.

What are the qualifications of your guides? Professional geologists, naturalists, historians, landscape architects, or horticulturists sometimes accompany trips or give lectures at pertinent stops. Resident experts often meet groups to speak on their own areas of knowledge.

What lectures and enrichment programs are planned? Sometimes there is running commentary en route; sometimes the talks and other programs are restricted to your stops. Slide shows are often on the schedule.

How many people are in the group? Groups are quite small, usually ranging from 15 to 30 participants.

How will the group travel? By van, car, or bus? Most groups use a deluxe coach, equipped with air-conditioning, rest rooms, and sometimes a VCR. As the name suggests, Rail Travel Center tours go by train but use coaches for certain transfers. To move the group from one trailhead to the next, companies that deal in walking tours occasionally use shuttle buses or water taxis.

What sorts of accommodations and meals are provided? Most garden tours use lodgings that are at least comfortable; some operators stick to more luxurious digs with a greater range of facilities. As for meals, they can be adventures in new American cuisine—or simply solid regional fare. In general, the more you pay, the fancier and more sophisticated the food and lodgings.

Is the trip fully escorted or locally hosted? On a fully escorted trip, a guide travels with you every step of the way and can help you unsnarl such problems as lost room reservations. On a locally hosted tour, you're met by a guide at each stop—and you're more or less on your own to work out any problems that may come up en route.

How much free time will there be? A little advance research into the area you're headed for will usually turn up other attractions that can enormously enhance the trip, even for those who love to tramp all day through herbaceous borders. Find out whether the free time is scheduled so that you can use it to pursue the other area offerings that interest you.

What's the cost and what's included? Be sure that this is spelled out in detail. Find out how many nights of lodging the trip price includes, and how many meals. Most tour prices—and all of those quoted for the trips described below, unless otherwise noted—include all meals (lunch on single-day trips), lodging (on multi-day trips), transportation during the tour from the point of origination, and the services of guides and experts, but not gratuities to the guides, or beverages. Sometimes you must join the sponsoring organization or make a donation, as well.

Are garden tours only a sideline with the tour company, or are they a well-developed specialty? Although specialty companies are more likely to offer a trip to a specific garden you'd like to visit and to have a supply of knowledgeable guides to tap, other tour companies often market very appealing trips, too.

How long has the company running the tour been in business? In general, it's best to stick with experienced operators. The company with a few years of garden touring behind it will have worked out the kinks in its programs. At the very least, make sure that those in charge have the experience it takes to orchestrate group trips and keep things moving smoothly.

Do you have references from past guests? If you have doubts or questions about a specific operator or trip, a fellow garden buff may be able to resolve them in ways that the operator cannot. If a company refuses to give you some names, you may well wonder why.

How far in advance do I need to book? Many of the specialized garden tours run just once, so if the program is one that excites you, don't wait to sign up. Although you can always try at the last minute in hopes of snagging a cancellation, you simply can't count on being successful.

MAJOR PLAYERS

BACKROADS This operator, established in 1979, is well-known nowadays for its bike tours; however, it also offers a range of walking tours through the mountains, wildflower meadows, canyonlands, and deserts of eight American states and three Canadian provinces. Although tours don't deal specifically with gardens and don't attract garden buffs exclusively (your companions represent a mix of professions and intellectual interests), guides are knowledgeable about local flora and fauna and there are local experts on hand as well—naturalists, geologists, historians, and artists—so these trips can be wonderful if you're interested in regional flora and ecosystems. Moreover, unlike many operators that focus more exclusively on garden tours, Backroads may have more than one departure for each trip and usually repeats successful trips in successive years.

Routes typically cover between 6 and 10 miles per day, but you may opt to walk only 3 to 6 miles—or tackle up to 15 miles. A sag wagon is on hand to give you a lift whenever you want to ride (and to transport your luggage and pick up purchases made along the way; you carry only a day pack with rain gear, a snack, and water). Group size ranges from 14 to 20, with a balance of singles and couples. Most six-day trips are at the high end of the scale but do include all meals, with fairly sophisticated cuisine, as well as accommodation at inns or rustic lodges with private bath. Camping trips are also available; participants are put up in four-person tents, but with a maximum of two people per tent. Amenities are basic but comfortable—Backroads can rent you a sleeping bag and pad unless you've brought one along, and most campsites have showers. Lunches are usually on the road, and are either prepared by the rolling kitchen that is the company's trademark, or by the leaders themselves, who serve up a lavish picnic of sandwiches made on the spot. Dinners on inn-based trips are in a variety of restaurants and inns, but in each case the emphasis is on regional fare prepared with the freshest ingredients. Destinations include California's northern coast, the rain forests of Washington's Olympic Peninsula, and the black sand beaches and fern groves of the emerald highlands of Hawaii's Big Island; prices range from $200 to $250 a

day depending on the program. *801 Cedar St., Berkeley, CA 94710, tel. 510/527–1555 or 800/462–2848, fax 510/527–1444.*

EXPO GARDEN TOURS This operation's tours, which range throughout North America, from the gardens of the antebellum South to the prairies of the Midwest, take in not only public parks and gardens but also private estates and commercial growing and breeding operations. The company also arranges symposia with well-known garden designers and writers, sometimes as part of a tour, and sometimes there are dinner receptions at historic plantations or other properties. Specific itineraries vary from year to year, but each is researched by a horticulturist or landscape architect and each group is accompanied by such an expert. Michael Italiaander, who founded the business in 1988, sets aside 1% of its net profits for the maintenance and preservation of the sites visited. Tours are first-class, not deluxe; the cost runs around $200 a day. The lodgings are good, clean, comfortable hotels, but it's the gardens that make the trips. The welcome and farewell dinners are special; other meals consist simply of tasty regional fare: fish gumbo in New Orleans, salmon in the Pacific Northwest, scrod in Massachusetts, barbecue in the South. Destinations have included gardens and rhododendron and bonsai collections in the Pacific Northwest, homes and gardens of the Brandywine Valley in Pennsylvania, and Louisiana in spring. *70 Great Oak, Redding, CT 06896, tel. 203/938–0410 or 800/ 448–2685, fax 203/938–0427.*

LEARNED JOURNEYS This company runs tours for botanic gardens around the country. Specific offerings vary from year to year, and there may be only one or two departures for each trip, because they are timed to coincide with the most colorful blooming periods, which are short. Learned Journeys carefully researches its tours, and itineraries are reviewed by top professionals in such fields as horticulture, history, architecture, and geology; small groups and expert backup—authorities in the field, who accompany the group—are hallmarks. Since the company arranges trips for many organizations, its price levels vary widely. Learned Journeys tailors its tours to each group, planning carefully so that every hotel and restaurant stop complements the theme of the tour. Accommodations are in charming, luxurious inns and lodges; all have private baths and many have a garden. Not all meals are included in the tour price, but those that are included are in restaurants and inns with strong regional character. Expect to have your fill of scrod and lobster around Boston, grilled trout in the Rockies, and pralines, jambalaya, and chicken with creole sauce in New Orleans. Destinations have included gardens in Hawaii, the Pacific Northwest, New England in autumn, and the South in spring; the schedule has also included Mississippi River cruises aboard the *Delta Queen,* a restored circa-1926 steam-powered paddle wheeler. *3412 Calle Noguera, Box 30626, Santa Barbara, CA 93130-0626, tel. 805/682–6191 or 800/682–6191, fax 805/682–4154.*

MAUPINTOUR This travel industry giant, known for its deluxe fully escorted tours, offers a broad spectrum of programs that include gardens while concentrating on the history, local color, and scenery of the regions visited. Although the tours do not include lectures by garden specialists, many of them do take in noteworthy public gardens. They also offer more than one departure annually, and the successful trips tend to run for several years. Because Maupintour is generalist in approach, its trips are good even if your traveling companion doesn't share your green thumb. All are $250 to $350 per person per day, and average group size is about 30, with a maximum of 44. Itineraries include gardens in northern New England; Lake Placid, New York; Old Sturbridge Village, Massachusetts; Longwood Gardens and the Amish Country, in Pennsylvania; and North and South Carolina. Accommodations are in either first-class chain hotels, such as the Hyatt and Hilton, or in deluxe local inns and rustic lodges with pronounced regional personality. Although dining options vary from group to group, à la carte menus are often available, but not always; when they're not, Maupintour tries to offer regional specialties with some culinary interest. *1515 St. Andrews Dr., Lawrence, KS 66047, tel. 913/843–1211 or 800/255–4266, fax 913/843–8351.*

TOURS A LA CARTE Because Tours à la Carte does not reveal names in its brochures, the company has gained entrée to private gardens that you could probably never visit on your own. Garden buffs like that. They also appreciate the organization's attention to detail and the fact that it makes a dry run of each trip ahead of time. The company was founded in 1973 to provide custom-planned itineraries. Its trip to Savannah, Charleston, and nearby plantations was typical: Arranged for the Pennsylvania Horticultural Society, it traveled under the guidance of a local horticulturist, visiting several private gardens. Groups are usually limited to 30, and lodgings are usually first-class hotels and inns with a local flavor, such as the Beekman Arms in Rhinebeck, New York; the Lodge Alley Inn in Charleston, South Carolina; and the White Hart Inn in Salisbury, Connecticut. Although the company usually includes only breakfast and one other meal per day, meals included are always interesting: In South Carolina, a picnic—salad, sandwiches, and southern fried chicken—was served in straw baskets lined with flowered napkins; in the Hudson River valley, meals were at the Culinary Institute of America and at the Beekman Arms, whose chef is C.I.A.-trained. Occasionally, there are lunches in private homes large enough to cater to a group. Group trips usually cost around $200 per day. An additional donation is requested for the organization for which the journey was designed. *Spread Eagle Village, 503 W. Lancaster Ave., Wayne, PA 19087, tel. 610/687–4185, fax 610/688–2421.*

REPRESENTATIVE TOURS

Although organizations such as Backroads and Maupintour do repeat tours to destinations of interest to gardeners, specialized garden tour companies and botanical institutions do not run the same tours year after year. Instead, they offer a different menu of tours annually. Only group size, accommodations quality, and price levels remain similar from one year to the next. The following tours are representative. Most last about a week, but a few are only a day long—included, although they're beyond the usual scope of this book, simply because they're interesting enough to warrant planning an entire vacation around. If the one we describe isn't offered when you want to travel, it's entirely possible that the sponsoring organization will have something similar and equally intriguing to offer you. By all means, call.

THE NORTHEAST

CONNECTICUT **Private Gardens in Litchfield.** This is the perfect day for gardeners and history enthusiasts alike. Nancy McCabe, garden designer and expert in historic garden restoration, will be your guide as you spend the day in the scenic Connecticut hills. You will visit McCabe's own garden, which features unusual border plants, a collection of antique pots and garden implements, and a fascinating greenhouse. Continue to South Kent to a private garden designed by McCabe, with formal plantings and a stonework terrace, as well as a cutting garden and a Chinese Chippendale twig fence. *New York Botanical Garden, Education Department, Bronx, NY 10458-5126, tel. 718/817–8747, fax 718/ 220–6504. Mar.: 1 day, $95. Price does not include NYBG membership ($35–$45); sign up 1 month in advance.*

MASSACHUSETTS TO MAINE **Autumn in New England's Forests and Gardens.** This nine-day trip from Learned Journeys—put together in 1993 for a consortium of organi-zations, including the California Arboretum Foundation and the Friends of San Luis Obispo Botanical Garden—explored the landscape and botanic gardens of New England in early October, when the woods are ablaze with color. The group traveled in the company of a horticulturist and was met by local historians and naturalists at key points. The itinerary ranged from Harvard University's Arnold Arboretum, with its collection of 7,000 varieties of plants, to such period plantings as Sedgwick Gardens in Long Hill, Massachusetts, and the Colonial gardens in Old Sturbridge Village, Massachusetts, and at the Moffatt-Ladd House in Portsmouth, New Hampshire. Other stops: Stowe, Vermont, and L. L. Bean in Freeport, Maine. Daily afternoon tea added a pleasant British touch. *Learned Journeys, Box 30626, Santa Barbara, CA 93130, tel. 805/682–6191 or 800/682– 6191, fax 805/682–4154. Oct.: 9 days, $1,443, not including some meals; sign up 3 months in advance.*

MASSACHUSETTS TO MAINE VIA NEW YORK
New England Fall Foliage. Although you can visit period gardens at historic Fort Ticonderoga in upstate New York and at central Massachusetts's Old Sturbridge Village, this nine-day journey from Maupintour, an annual favorite, is really designed to show off the region's spectacular landscapes in their autumnal best. You explore the Maine coastline in Acadia National Park; admire the Old Man of the Mountains and the forests of Franconia Notch, New Hampshire; and pass through New York's Adirondack Mountains, where you take a ferry ride on Lake Champlain and make a stop in Lake Placid, host of the 1932 and 1980 Olympics. As is usual with this operator, you are not accompanied by a garden specialist. *Maupintour, 1515 St. Andrews Dr., Lawrence, KS 66047, tel. 913/843–1211 or 800/255–4266, fax 913/843–8351. Mid-Sept.–mid-Oct.: 9 days, $1,508–$2,053. Price does not include some meals; sign up 4 months in advance.*

NEW YORK **Spring Bulbs in the Hamptons.** Landscape designer Tish Rehill will guide you as you tour spring bulb gardens in East Hampton and Southampton. Learn the fine points of designing bulb gardens, both formal and naturalized. You will see three private gardens where designers have taken widely varying creative approaches using bulbs. The highlight of the tour is Long House, the property of renowned designer, Jack Lenor Larsen. His spectacular Daffodil Walk has more than 100,000 daffodils from 200 cultivars (plants bred for specific qualities). The views from the terrace are equally spectacular. *New York Botanical Garden, Education Department, Bronx, NY 10458-5126, tel. 718/817–8747, fax 718/220–6504. Apr.: 1 day, $98. Price does not include NYBG membership ($35–$45); sign up 1 month in advance.*

THE MID-ATLANTIC

PENNSYLVANIA **Bucks County.** Under the guidance of Joe Kerwin, Manager of the Enid A. Haupt Conservatory, you will visit Cedaridge farm, the home of well-known photographer and garden writer Derek Fell. The Fells give a personal tour through some of the farm's 10 major theme gardens, whose old-fashioned plant varieties complement the 1790 stone farmhouse. The tour continues on to Renny, the Perennial Farm in Wrightstown, where the renowned floral and party designer Renny Reynolds has transformed 72 acres of distinct and diverse gardens. Renny will be there to show you his vision of the 18th-century farmstead—complete with exotic silver and golden pheasants and a boxwood garden, centered by a replica of the Eiffel Tower. *New York Botanical Garden, Education Department, Bronx, NY 10458-5126, tel. 718/817–8747, fax 718/220–6504. Apr.: 1 day, $90. Price does not include NYBG membership ($35–$45); sign up 1 month in advance.*

PENNSYLVANIA **The Dutch Country.** Rural scenery and Amish farms and markets are constants on this eight-day Maupintour trip, offered in spring and fall out of Philadelphia. But for garden buffs, the highlight may be Longwood Gardens, one of the country's great public gardens (*see* Gardens Worth Visiting, *below*), where you stop early in the trip. The contrast between its formality and the gently rolling fields and farms around it is particularly striking. Stops include an Amish homestead, Lancaster's farm market, Philadelphia, Valley Forge, and Gettysburg. *Maupintour, 1515 St. Andrews Dr., Lawrence, KS 66047, tel. 913/843–1211 or 800/255–4266, fax 913/843–8351. Mid-Apr.–mid-May and mid-Sept.–mid-Oct.: 12 days, $2,778. Price does not include some meals; sign up 4 months in advance.*

PENNSYLVANIA **Philadelphia Flower Show.** Every year the New York Botanical Garden assembles a group for a day trip by bus down to America's largest indoor flower show, one of the premier horticultural events in the country. The event's former floor manager hosts the tour there, and there's a private lunch with some of the notable floral exhibitors, privately catered in a convention center meeting room, with your choice of chicken Véronique or vegetarian lasagna, plus green salad and white chocolate mousse. Breathtaking exhibits by nurseries and horticultural organizations as well as floral designs by 700 individual exhibitors highlight the show. *New York Botanical Garden, Education Department, Bronx, NY 10458-5126, tel. 718/817–8747, fax 718/220–6504. Mar.: 1 day, $95. Price does not include NYBG membership ($35–$45); sign up 1 month in advance.*

THE SOUTH

GEORGIA AND SOUTH CAROLINA **Gardens and Plantations of the Colonial South.** This eight-day Learned Journeys trip, sponsored by the Elizabeth Gamble Garden Center, coincides with the time that the area's dogwoods, magnolias, jasmines, azaleas, and other flowering plants are in bloom——and with the annual festivals of homes and gardens in Savannah and Charleston, when you can see many private gardens. You also visit the formal landscapes of Middleton Place plantation, which has one of the most beautiful gardens in the South, with gentle terraces rising up out of the nearby river; it is one of the oldest still functioning in the United States. Other highlights include Magnolia Plantation just outside Charleston. An old-fashioned garden party is included in the trip. *Learned Journeys, Box 30626, Santa Barbara, CA 93130, tel. 805/682–6191 or 800/682–6191, fax 805/682–4154. Early April: 8 days, price not available; sign up 6 months in advance.*

LOUISIANA **Landscape Lagniappe.** This Expo Garden Tours program was especially designed for amateur and professional gardeners. The first stop: Live Oak Gardens on Jefferson Island. Its Georgian house is embellished by elements of the Moorish and Victorian steamboat styles. Formal gardens are overshadowed by 200-year-old live oaks draped with Spanish moss; a profusion of boxwood hedges, seasonal flower beds, and grass lawns; and a gazebo overlooking the Bayou Teche. Other highlights of the tour include Greenwood Plantation and the famous Rosedown; a boat tour of plantation tours along the Mississippi; a walking tour through New Orleans's French Quarter to the Vieux Carré; and a lesson in horticulture and architecture in the Garden District. *Expo Garden Tours, 70 Great Oak, Redding, CT 06896, tel. 203/938–0410 or 800/448–2685, fax 203/938–0427. Mar.: 7 days, $1,099, not including some meals; sign up 45 days in advance.*

NORTH AND SOUTH CAROLINA **Plantation Gardens and the Blue Ridge.** The grounds of Biltmore, in Asheville, North Carolina, the home of George Vanderbilt, were designed by Frederick Law Olmsted, and they represent one of the country's best examples of the landscape design of the Country Place Era. Here, the father of American landscape architecture created acres of luxuriant gardens with beautiful views of the surrounding mountains. But there are other notable stops on this trip. You also visit Boone Hall Plantation, redolent of the flavor of South Carolina's Low Country; Middleton Place; and the Grand Strand in South Carolina, one of the longest

sand beaches along the Atlantic Coast. The route takes you along a portion of the famed Blue Ridge Parkway, with splendid mountain views. *Maupintour, 1515 St. Andrews Dr., Lawrence, KS 66047, tel. 913/843–1211 or 800/255–4266, fax 913/843–8351. Mid-Apr.–early May and Oct.: 8 days, $1,438–$1,469. Price does not include some meals; sign up 2–3 months in advance.*

THE ROCKIES

MONTANA **Majestic Glacier National Park.** On this six-day walking trip from Backroads, you can look for 18 species of orchids among the ferns and pines and explore a stunning ice field. Glacier National Park, the focus of the trip, hugs the U.S.–Canadian border and has more than a million acres of mountain ranges, wildflower meadows, and dense forests. The trip sets off down the trail in summer, when wildflowers are in bloom and the weather is usually warm and bright by day and cool at night. On this trip, paths skirt turquoise lakes and penetrate groves of western red cedar, Douglas fir, and western hemlock. Although there are some short steep sections, ascents and descents are mostly moderate, and vans take you to the highest elevations, such as 6,680-foot Logan Pass on the Going-to-the-Sun Road, which winds upward through forests and past lakes to the Continental Divide. Depending on which departure you choose, accommodations are in rustic lodges or comfortable Glacier National Park campgrounds with hot running water and showers; on camping trips, Backroads provides four-person tents that sleep two; they also can rent sleeping bags and pads. Groups number between 14 and 20. *Backroads, 801 Cedar St., Berkeley, CA 94710, tel. 510/527–1555 or 800/462–2848, fax 510/527–1444. June–Sept.: 6 days, $749 (camping) or $1,398 (with inn lodging); sign up 12 months in advance.*

THE WEST COAST

CALIFORNIA **The Classic North Coast.** On this six-day Backroads trip, you can breathe in the pungent scent of bay trees as you hike along the San Andreas Fault zone, explore wildflower meadows, and stroll through stands of native oak and fir and clusters of stately iris, not to mention the famous Muir Woods, 485 acres of virgin redwood forest. You also tread the cliffs of the Coast Trail of Point Reyes National Seashore, just north of San Francisco, where meadows filled with wild oats alternate with dense groves of conifers and madronas. Ascents and descents are mostly moderate, although there are some short steep sections. Lodging is in rustic lodges and inns, including the Mountain Home Inn, where all rooms have private terraces with a view of Mt. Tamalpais and the surrounding range. Meals are either in the hotel or in restaurants; the cuisine is usually California style. Groups range in size from 14 to 20 people. *Backroads, 801 Cedar St., Berkeley, CA 94710, tel. 510/527–1555 or 800/462–2848, fax 510/527–1444. May, July, Sept., Oct.: 6 days, $749 camping, $1345 inn; sign up 12 months in advance.*

HAWAII

THE BIG ISLAND **A Natural Side of Paradise.** This six-day Backroads walking tour for nature lovers explores the island's stunning black sand beaches, cascading waterfalls, emerald highlands, and stark volcanoes. You walk through the rich green pastureland of the isolated Waipio Valley, once a center of ancient Hawaiian civilization; through lush jungle past the remains of ancient villages and groves of richly scented fruit trees; and to the ruins of ancient temples, ranged along an interpretive trail, where you can picnic among the palms. Other highlights include hikes around the summit of the active volcano Kilauea, with extraordinary views of the molten lava, and in Hawaii Volcanoes National Park, where you smell the sulfur, see bubbling pools of molten rock, and hear steam hiss through rock fissures. Fern groves and beautiful beaches are also among the trip's pleasures. Hikes are mostly moderate, with only a few short steep sections, although some hiking is at 4,000 feet. Group size is between 14 and 20, and accommodations are in comfortable inns. Meals are in restaurants where the menus are long on fresh seafood and locally grown fruits and vegetables. *Backroads, 801 Cedar St., Berkeley, CA 94710, tel. 510/527–1555 or 800/462–2848, fax 510/527–1444. Oct.–Apr.: 6 days, $1,395; sign up 6–12 months in advance.*

GARDENS WORTH VISITING

Certain notable American gardens frequently put in an appearance on the itineraries of garden tour specialists. Here are some destinations that no aspiring Gertrude Jekyll should miss.

THE NORTHEAST

MASSACHUSETTS **Naumkeag.** This Stockbridge garden highlights two eras' approaches to garden design: the formalism of the Country Place Era and the experimental modernism of the 1930s and 1940s. Nathaniel Barrett designed the older parts of the garden—the Linden Allée and the Evergreen Walk. Fletcher Steele, one of America's best-known landscape architects, began working here in 1926 and continued to reshape the place over the next 30 years. Two of his most successful designs are the Afternoon Garden, patterned after an Italian terrace, and the famous Blue Steps, a compositional masterpiece. The steps themselves are made of concrete block, with risers and treads of varying dimensions. The balustrades are curved pipe rails painted white; the landings are interplanted with specimen birch trees; and the fountains below the stairs are painted blue. The overall effect is that of an Art Deco painting come to life. The Afternoon Garden also illustrates Steele's flair for modern materials and composition. It contains an oval pool lined with black glass and parterres with patterns of pink stones and black coal. The garden is surrounded by gaily painted "gondola posts" carved out of old pilings dredged up from Boston Harbor, and there are beautiful views out over the distant Berkshire Hills and nearby fields. Stockbridge was once known as the inland Newport because of its number of affluent summering families. Edith Wharton's place, The Mount, is nearby, as is Chesterwood, home and garden of sculptor Daniel Chester French. *Naumkeag, Box 792, Stockbridge, MA 01262, tel. 413/298–3239, fax 413/ 298–5239. Open daily Memorial Day– Columbus Day. Admission: $6.50.*

NEW YORK **Brooklyn Botanic Garden.** This showcase garden at the edge of the borough of Brooklyn's graceful Prospect Park (itself worthy of a visit) educates the public in 14 specialty gardens and a new conservatory. Labeling is excellent, and a 2-acre Local Flora Section showcases nine native ecological zones, careful re-creations of natural habitats at various times in the past. The BBG is at the height of its beauty in early spring, when, on the famous Cherry Esplanade, hardy old Kwanzan cherries bloom near narcissus, hyacinth, and other bulbs. The Japanese Hill and Pond Garden, built in 1914, is a perennial favorite with visitors. Its flowering cherries, quinces, Japanese maples, azaleas, and tree peonies are laid out around a pond in traditional asymmetrical Japanese style with stone pathways and places to stop and meditate. Under soaring domes, a new conservatory houses the largest bonsai collection in the country, along with palms, ferns, and cacti. Other noteworthy plant collections include shrubs, magnolias, roses, and hedge plants. *Brooklyn Botanic Garden, 1000 Washington Ave., Brooklyn, NY 11225, tel. 718/622– 4433, fax 718/857–2430. Open year-round, Tues.–Sun. Admission free.*

NEW YORK **The Gardens at Mohonk Mountain House.** A pristine setting in the Shawangunk Mountains, on the edge of the Catskills, is only one of the distinctions of the old-fashioned gardens at the celebrated 19th-century Mohonk Mountain House resort. Mohonk's 2,500 acres are contiguous to another 5,000 acres of preserved land, where mountain laurel, native rhododendron, columbine, hemlock, oak, and maple line a number of varied and interesting hiking trails. Go in early June to see the mountain laurel in bloom. Or visit in May to admire the old-fashioned favorites in the cultivated gardens near the hotel. The honeysuckle, wisteria, spirea, and lovely old white and purple lilacs bloom in mid- to late spring. The Victorian flower beds, with masses of such annuals as salvia, marigolds, pansies, and impatiens, look best in late summer or early fall; and in autumn, the maple, beech, oak, and sumac are a chorus of riotous color. Some of the trails are ideal for cross-country skiing in winter, when vistas of the surrounding mountains are spectacular.

At the time Mohonk was built by two Quaker brothers, Albert and Alfred Smiley, in the late 1800s, all the earth for the gardens had to be trucked in to cover the mountains' bare bones. The place still retains the ambience of a 19th-century family resort, and the focus is on outdoor activities: hiking on the mountain trails, swimming and boating on the clear mountain lake, croquet, tennis, strolling in the gardens, and lolling on the rustic cedar benches in the arbors and gazebos around the grounds. The hotel rooms are pleasant but not luxurious (although some have fireplaces that are kept stocked with wood), and the food is tasty and bountiful but not fancy. You do not need to stay overnight; day passes allow entrance to the gardens and grounds (pack a picnic), but not the hotel. Reservations are required for overnight stays and for meals; if you come for lunch, the cost of the meal includes a day pass. There are regularly scheduled garden walks and lectures, a well-stocked flower shop, and a greenhouse. *Mohonk Mountain House, Lake Mohonk, New Paltz, NY 12561, tel. 914/255–1000 or 800/772–6646, fax 914/256–2161. Gardens open year-round,*

Tues.–Sun. Admission: $6 weekdays, $9 weekends and holidays.

NEW YORK **New York Botanical Garden.** At this world leader in botanical research and horticultural education, more than 20 beautiful plant collections create a parklike environment on 250 acres in the New York City borough of the Bronx. The magnolias are laid out in a grove and backed by statuesque oaks. The daffodil, rose, viburnum, azalea, rhododendron, and other collections make it an enchanting place in spring. Go to see Daffodil Hill in April or the extensive tulip display in early May. Among the well-maintained specialty gardens are a beautiful perennial garden, a nicely designed herb garden, and a rock garden begun in the 1930s. The Peggy Rockefeller Rose Garden, designed by landscape architect Beatrix Jones Ferrand in 1915 but not built until 1988, is informative as well as beautiful; its 2700 roses and plants are laid out in parterres, radiating from a picturesque gazebo, and handouts and labels rate all the roses for fragrance, color, bloom time, and the like. In the Native Plant Garden, the wet meadow is at its best in August and September, when hibiscus, butterfly weed, goldenrod, and asters are in bloom; in autumn, the pine barren habitat is one of the highlights. Five demonstration gardens are particularly interesting for home gardeners: There's one for shade, another designed to attract birds and butterflies, and yet another created around unusually fragrant plants, as well as an ornamental vegetable garden. The 40-acre NYBG Forest is one of the last remnants of the natural forest that once covered the New York City area. Also on the grounds are the most extensive horticultural library under one roof in the United States, and the NYBG Herbarium, housing the largest collection of preserved plant specimens in the western hemisphere. In addition, the elegant turn-of-the-century Enid Haupt Conservatory has been completely restored and features magnificent desert and rain-forest biomes, aquatic plants, and seasonal displays. *New York Botanical Garden, 200th St. and Southern Blvd., Bronx, NY 10458-5126, tel. 718/817–8700, fax 718/220–6504. Open year-round, Tues.–Sun. Admission: $3 donation suggested, $4 parking.*

NEW YORK **Old Westbury Gardens.** From 1900 to 1925, some 300 estates, complete with opulent houses and gardens of every description, went up along the stretch of Long Island's North Shore, which came to be known as the Gold Coast. This 100-acre estate, built in 1904 by the Phipps family, is the one that started the frenzy of building, and it is one of a handful of the dozen that survive to remain open to the public. The Phippses lived at Old Westbury for 55 years, and the garden continues to have much of the feel of private grounds. In the house, fresh flowers decorate rooms where fine English furniture and paintings by Reynolds and Gainsborough depict the gracious, unhurried life of a bygone era. The well-cared-for gardens, with their flowers and peaceful woodland, do the same. The beech-lined entrance drive, dark and mysterious, opens up into a spacious, brilliantly sunny hillside lawn. Then the openness gives way to a geometric, architectural series of "garden rooms": the Lilac Walk, Rose Garden, Boxwood Garden, Primrose Path, and Autumn Walk, as well as a Ghost Walk of feathery hemlock trees and a spectacular Walled Garden. The walled garden contains a wisteria-covered pergola of intricate chinoiserie design, whose striking image is mirrored in the lotus pond below. Old Westbury is smashing in spring, with its beds of various bulbs in formal parterres. Look for bluebells and tulips, lilies and forget-me-nots. Later on, you will find irises, peonies, phlox, and roses. There is rarely a week without color during the growing season. *Old Westbury Gardens, Box 430, Old Westbury, NY 11568, tel. 516/333–0048, fax 516/333–6807. Open May–Nov., Mon. and Wed.–Sun. Admission: $6.*

NEW YORK **Wave Hill.** So skillfully has Marco Polo Stufano managed the 18-acre garden and 10-acre woodland for the last

29 years in the affluent Riverdale section of the Bronx that, though technically a public park, it still has the character of a private estate. His interest is in residential gardening, and he experiments tirelessly with different techniques that amateurs can use at home—for instance, transforming concrete cinder blocks into planters. The original Greek Revival mansion, built in 1843 for William Morris on a ridge overlooking the Hudson, has been much enlarged and modified. Mark Twain rented the estate, and Teddy Roosevelt summered here, as did the Perkins-Freeman family until they gave the property to the City of New York. The setting remains serene and pastoral. Grand specimen beech and oak trees adorn the wide lawns; the rugged cliffs known as the Palisades loom across the Hudson, by turns framed by elegant pergolas and hidden along curving pathways. Spring in the hilly Wild Garden is particularly beautiful, as the early blooms of narcissus give way to cranesbill geranium and iris. In the ever-changing Perennial Garden you might discover such old-fashioned favorites as larkspur, heliotrope, and dahlias. Take a break and sit down in the rustic arbor, entwined with clematis and roses, or relax on the comfortable, movable seats you'll find throughout the grounds (a rarity in public parks in New York, where most seating is fixed). Wave Hill holds seminars and symposia on landscape design. In addition, ask about free outdoor dance performances in summer on the lawn, indoor music concerts in the Wave Hill House fall through spring, and changing art exhibits in Glyndor Gallery. *Wave Hill, 675 W. 252nd St., Bronx, NY 10471, tel. 718/549–3200, fax 718/884–8952. Open mid-May–mid-Oct., Tues.–Sun. Admission: $4, free Sat. 9–12 and Tues.*

THE MID-ATLANTIC

DELAWARE **Winterthur.** This is a garden made for spring! Its creator, Henry Francis du Pont, used azaleas, flowering dogwoods, quinces, rhododendrons, and lilacs with masses of daffodils, bluebells, and other bulbs to great effect. Du Pont studied horticulture at Harvard at the turn of the century, and his gardens, apparently a work of nature, were laid out with care and precision; bloom sequence and color were carefully considered. Pastel colors dominate, and bright color is used as an accent—a valuable lesson for the suburban gardener: Too much color kills the scene. Plant collections with names like Winter Hazel Area, Pinetum, Azalea Walk, and Magnolia Bend, laid out on 60 of Winterthur's 1,000 acres, are equipped with instructional labels and contain many hybrids and cultivars. Marian Coffin, a well-known landscape architect of the Country Place Era, created the Reflecting Pool Garden, a quiet glade designed in the manner of the Italian Renaissance, and the Sundial Garden, which is bounded by very tall evergreens now over 100 years old. Don't miss either one on your tour. In addition to the gardens, you'll want to visit the Winterthur Museum & Galleries, known around the world for their American decorative arts; the collection of furniture, lamps, textiles, and pictures is without peer. Guided garden tours are available (phone ahead), as are tours of various period rooms in the museum. *Winterthur Museum, Winterthur, DE 19735, tel. 302/888–4600 or 800/448–3883. Open daily year-round. Admission: $8.*

PENNSYLVANIA **Longwood Gardens.** Each year, 800,000 visitors make their way to these 1,050 acres in the rolling hills of the Brandywine River valley, near Philadelphia and not far from Wilmington, Delaware: Longwood is one of the premier public gardens of the United States. The sheer scale of the place, its very high level of maintenance, and its diversity keep you from noticing that it lacks a comprehensive, unified design: Each garden is a world unto itself. Only at Longwood would you find such enormities as the immense old-fashioned Flower Garden Walk, over 600 feet long. There are also 11,000 different kinds of plants and 20 indoor gardens under glass. The use of water is one of the most striking aspects here: The acres of water gardens are full of moats, canals, fountains, woodland streams, and formal Italianate pools. Water shows are held every afternoon in summer, dramatic displays of thundering jets, crossing arcs, spouts, and massive sheets of water. There's a Festival of Fountains, a computerized display of water, light, and music staged on summer evenings. The curtain in an open-air theater is made of water. In addition, there are formal gardens starring roses, peonies, wisteria, heather, and topiary, and 3½ acres of conservatories, whose spectacular displays are a pleasure to visit anytime, but never more than during the Christmas season, when thousands of poinsettias, lights, and fragrant flowers are on display. Children will love the indoor children's garden with a plant-filled maze. Longwood Gardens sponsors 300 horticultural and 400 performing arts events each year. *Longwood Gardens, Box 501, Kennett Sq., PA 19348-0501, tel. 610/388–1000, fax 610/388–2294. Open daily year-round. Admission: $10.*

VIRGINIA **Colonial Williamsburg.** More than 100 gardens flourish in Colonial Williamsburg, the reconstructed 18th-century Colonial capital in the Virginia Tidewater region. The restoration of the town, funded by John D. Rockefeller beginning in 1926, has taken decades to accomplish. It comprises not only 500 buildings spread over 173 acres, including 88 original houses, taverns, shops, and public buildings, but also 90 acres of well-kept gardens and greens. Planted with species known to the Colonial inhabitants, the gardens duplicate those of the 18th century as accurately as possible. Best documented were those of the Governor's Palace, where remains of walls and walks were unearthed, and an early engraver's plate found in England provided details of the plantings. According to English custom, many of Williamsburg's gardens are green gardens, created using evergreen plants, which require minimum maintenance and look attractive year-

round. Yaupon, American holly, live oak, southern magnolia, and boxwood are widely seen, along with evergreen ground covers such as periwinkle. In early April, such small ornamental trees as flowering dogwood and eastern redbud bloom together, and at about the same time, masses of tulips, anemones, and daffodils are studded among the formal evergreen plantings. Later in the spring, you will see catalpa, horse chestnut, and magnolia trees in bloom; in summer, look for crape myrtle (its vibrant pinks are difficult to miss!). Autumn's palette of gold, tan, and russet with some touches of scarlet is more subdued here than that in New England, because oak dominates rather than sugar maple. Herb and vegetable gardens have been planted throughout the town, and corn, tobacco, cotton, flax, and sorghum, mainstays of the Colonial economy, are grown as field crops. Colonial Williamsburg has nearly 40 exhibitions and activities; costumed interpreters relate stories of 18th-century Virginia society and culture, and you can watch many trades being practiced with the tools and methods of the time. *Colonial Williamsburg, Box 1776, Williamsburg, VA 23187-1776, tel. 757/220–7645. Open daily year-round. 1-day admission to trades and historical buildings and museums: $29 adults, $17 children.*

THE SOUTH

MISSISSIPPI **Crosby Arboretum.** This arboretum on the Pearl River, a major stream emptying into the Gulf of Mexico, comprises seven associated natural areas on more than 1,000 acres. The Crosby gives you the opportunity to study the native plants of the coastal plain of the Pearl River watershed in their original habitats—more than 700 species of indigenous trees, shrubs, wildflowers, and grasses. Natural areas include beech-magnolia forests, a white cedar swamp, evergreen hammocks, a cypress swamp, pine savannas, and hardwood-forested bottomlands. The arboretum protects many rare and endangered plants and animals, and the several lovely pitcher plant bogs also contain many orchids. Around the lake are water tupelo and bald cypress trees, along with turtles, great egrets, and kingbirds. Most activities are at Pinecote, the 64-acre native plant and interpretive center; the wonderful pavilion there, designed by architects Fay Jones and Maurice Jennings, seems to float above the lake. *Crosby Arboretum, Box 190, Picayune, MS 39466, tel. 601/799–2311, fax 601/799–2372. Open year-round, Wed.– Sun. Admission: $3.*

THE MIDWEST

ILLINOIS **Chicago Botanic Garden.** There are 20 garden areas in this 385-acre living museum in Glencoe, 25 miles north of downtown Chicago. In the Aquatic Garden, you can see water lilies and other water-loving plants from a boardwalk over a lagoon. The English Walled Garden contains six garden rooms, examples of English gardening style. The Heritage Garden is modeled after Europe's first botanic garden in Padua, Italy. The Prairie peaks in August. The Rose Garden contains more than 5,000 rosebushes, and the Japanese Garden, called Sansho-En, "the garden of three islands," displays carefully styled plants and judiciously placed stones. Native Illinois plants fill the Naturalistic Garden, where woodland, prairie, and bird gardens show off the special beauty of the local flora. The Dwarf Conifer Garden, very popular among homeowners, demonstrates the ways small evergreens can be used in domestic plantings. And three greenhouse areas display a Temperate Collection, Desert Collection, and Rain Forest Collection. Gardening enthusiasts can easily spend most of a day. *Chicago Botanic Garden, Box 400, Glencoe, IL 60022, tel. 847/835–5440, fax 847/835–4484. Open daily year-round except Dec. 25. Admission free; parking $4.*

ILLINOIS **Morton Arboretum.** The hardiest, most attractive trees, shrubs, and vines of the Midwest are displayed in this garden, established in 1922 by Morton Salt Company founder Joy Morton on his 1,700-acre estate 25 miles west of Chicago. An expression of his lifelong interest in trees (his father, J. Sterling Morton, originated Arbor Day), it displays more than 3,000 types of plants from around the world. This is one of the few public gardens that you may tour in your car; it takes about an hour to drive the 12-mile-long route. There are also 13 miles of walking trails, most between 1 and 3 miles long. The Illinois Trees Nature Trail features meadows, woodlands, and spring wildflowers in the best surviving oak-maple forest near Chicago, and the Prairie Trail winds through a reconstructed pre-pioneer grassland. Among the plant collections are a pinetum, a hedge garden with more than 100 formal hedges, a dwarf shrub garden, a "sand beds" garden of plants for sandy soil, a fragrance garden, and a low-maintenance perennial garden. Wildlife watching and bird observation are also rewarding here: More than 160 bird species have been sighted, and you might see deer, raccoons, and foxes. *Morton Arboretum, Lisle, IL 60532, tel. 630/968–0074, fax 630/719– 2433. Open daily year-round. Admission: $6 a car.*

MISSOURI **Missouri Botanical Garden.** This venerable institution, which opened to the public in 1859, stands out for its excellent displays, botanical research, and striking modern buildings, including the Shoenberg Temperate House and its famous Climatron, a half-acre, geodesic-domed greenhouse. As you enter it, you are immediately transported to the tropics: You see a small native hut, sparkling waterfalls, rocky cliffs, and the dense green foliage of tropical rain forest plants. (The garden's tropical botany research program is notably active, primarily in Central and South America, where many of its 50 botanists race against time to seek out, document, and classify the world's unknown tropical plants before they become extinct.) The Climatron displays some 1,200 tropical species, including banana, coffee, and cacao plants, and an orchid collection with more than 10,000 specimens. An imaginative electronic exhibit called the Talking Orchid not only speaks to visitors but sips water from their hands. The Shoenberg Temperate House exhibits temperate-zone species from the southeastern United States, China, Japan, and Korea; most plants in this area are thematically displayed in a Moorish Walled Garden, a Biblical and Economic Collection, a Wildflower, Rock and Vine Collection, and a collection of riparian plants (adapted to the edge of rivers and streams).

Elsewhere in the Missouri Botanical Garden are flowering cherries, azaleas, chrysanthemums, peonies, lotus, and other Asian plantings arranged around a 4-acre lake. You can tour the display gardens by tram: the Azalea-Rhododendron Garden, which peaks in late April; the Bulb Garden, which shows off thousands of tulips, hyacinths, narcissus, and giant flowering onions, as well as summer- and fall-blooming bulbs; the Scented Garden, whose raised beds let you easily smell and touch the plants, with signage in Braille; the Hardy Succulent Garden, full of such plants as sedum, yucca, hardy prickly pear, and cobweb live-forevers, a kind of sedum, that survives outdoors in Missouri with minimal protection; and the 14-acre Japanese garden, Seiwa-En ("garden of pure, clear harmony and peace"), the largest of its type in the Western Hemisphere. Additional display gardens include the Rose Garden, Rock Garden, Desert House, Herb Garden, and Woodland Garden. Other displays focus on home gardening, and two dozen residential-scale gardens will open in 1996. Here you can also arrange a guided tour of the Missouri's Shaw Arboretum, a 2,500-acre nature preserve and wildlife center southwest of St. Louis. *Missouri Botanical Garden, 4344 Shaw Blvd., St. Louis, MO 63166, tel. 314/577–5100, fax 314/577–9598. Open daily year-round. Admission: $3.*

THE SOUTHWEST

ARIZONA **Arizona-Sonora Desert Museum.** This marvelous exhibit of the flora and fauna of the desert region, 14 miles west of Tucson, concentrates entirely on local ecology and attempts to explain the complex relationships between the area's plants, animals, climate, and terrain. More than 1,300 kinds of plants and more than 300 living animals are on display in naturalistic settings. There's a Riparian Habitat, where river otters cavort, and a Mountain Habitat, with Mexican wolves and black bears. The unusual reptiles and invertebrates of the Sonoran Desert, from centipedes, tarantulas, and scorpions to Gila monsters, snakes, and lizards, are also on exhibit. A Cave Walk reveals an underground limestone cavern where you can inspect the beautiful mineral specimens of the region, and trained volunteers give demonstrations and talks throughout the grounds every day and are on hand to answer your questions. Try to visit the museum early in the day, when it is cooler and the animals are more active. Also do not miss the nearby Saguaro National Monument, which preserves a magnificent forest of this distinctive cactus. There you'll see tall, ancient specimens, their great age shown by the number and size of their arms, or branches, which can take up to a century to develop. Walking on one of the trails through the forest, you'll begin to get a sense of the timeless quiet of the desert; it is an experience you will never forget. *Arizona-Sonora Desert Museum, 2021 N. Kinney Rd., Tucson, AZ 85743, tel. 602/883–1380, fax 602/883–2500. Open daily year-round. Admission: $8.95.*

THE WEST COAST

CALIFORNIA **Filoli.** Formality contrasts with the natural vistas and surroundings of northern California at this meticulously maintained estate, 25 miles from San Francisco. Originally built between 1915 and 1917, the house and its gardens are a fine example of the Country Place Era and express the elegant style of the period; they were deeded to the National Trust for Historic Preservation in 1975. The 16 landscaped acres, originally laid out by Bruce Porter and augmented in 1936 by Isabella Worn, were designed to enhance the natural beauty of the site. The Sunken Garden is an example of Worn's hallmark use of color. It contains crisply sheared goblets of silvery olives; beyond them rise the inky, dark columns of tall yews. The lemon yellow of a Sunburst honey locust terminates the formal garden view but draws the eye past it to the gray-green of the native hillside. The Sunken Garden is just one in Filoli's succession of garden rooms, which also includes a Woodland Garden, with rhododendrons set among native oaks; a Yew Allée, with espaliered apple and pear trees; and a Walled Garden, containing the delicate Chartres Cathedral Garden, depicting a stained-glass window, with boxwood borders representing the lead outlines, an English holly hedge standing in for the masonry between the windows, and colorful annuals and standard roses supplying the myriad hues. Look for the climbing hydrangea on top of the south wall of the Bowling Green—a rarity in western gardens. Note the stately trees throughout Filoli's grounds: the magnificent magnolias along the front drive, the very old coast live oaks to the north of the house, and the specimen trees outside the Walled Garden—among them copper beech, American hornbeam, and dawn redwood. And don't miss the canopy of Camperdown elms to the south of the pool pavilion; they provide welcome shade. Filoli has splendid floral displays throughout the year, and you can make advance reservations for a docent-led tour that takes in the mansion, too. On Fridays and Saturdays the public can take self-guided tours of the house and gardens at their leisure. *Filoli, Canada Rd., Woodside, CA 94062, tel. 415/364–2880, fax 415/366–7836. Open mid-Feb.–early Nov., Tues.–Sat. Admission free.*

CALIFORNIA **Huntington Botanical Gardens.** Railroad and real estate magnate Henry Huntington founded this garden in San Marino, 12 miles northeast of downtown Los Angeles, in 1919. The estate is well-known as the home of one of the finest research libraries in the world and a splendid collection of British, French, and American art. The gardens are famous for their 12-acre Desert Garden, which displays 5,000 species of xerophytes (plants that have adapted to a limited supply of water). But there are also 14 other gardens, where 14,000 different types of plants are arranged in a parklike setting of rolling lawns. The Camellia Collection, in two gardens, is one of the largest in the country, and the Japanese Garden has a bridge, a furnished Japanese house, and a tranquil, sand-and-rock Zen Garden. Many of the plants and colorful flowers in the Shakespeare Garden were cultivated during the writer's time; they bloom year-round. You can trace plant development in the Rose Garden, where nearly 2,000 cultivars are arranged historically. A cursory tour of the gardens takes about an hour. *Huntington Botanical Gardens, 1151 Oxford Rd., San Marino, CA 91108, tel. 818/405–2100, fax 818/405–0225. Open year-round, Tues.–Sun. Admission: $7.50.*

OREGON **Hoyt Arboretum.** Here in the hills west of Portland, one of the largest conifer collections in the United States includes many trees grown from seed. Visitors marvel at the collection's 65-year-old coast redwoods and giant sequoias, both from California. There are also dawn redwoods, a species once thought extinct, reintroduced from China during the 1940s; it was a Hoyt Arboretum specimen that produced the first cones in the Western Hemisphere in 50 million years. Ten miles of gentle trails wind through the 175-acre arboretum. Dispersed among the towering native trees are such exotics as the Chilean monkey puzzle tree, the North African cork oak, and the Australian eucalyptus. You'll pass through the interesting Weeping Tree

Collection, where groves of Himalayan weeping spruce grow, along with weeping cedar, European weeping beech, and the rare Brewer's weeping spruce from Oregon's Siskiyou Mountains. Although the magnolias, crab apples, cherries, and dogwoods are spectacular in springtime, many visitors think peak time at the Hoyt is fall, when maples, tupelos, poplars, larches, and witch hazels burst into color. There are free guided tours every Saturday and Sunday from April through October. Maps and self-guiding tour booklets are available at the visitor center. *Hoyt Arboretum, 4000 S.W. Fairview Blvd., Portland, OR 97221, tel. 503/228–8733, fax 503/823–4213. Open daily year-round. Admission free.*

WASHINGTON **Bloedel Reserve.** Designed by landscape architect Richard Haag, the Reflection Garden at this 160-acre expanse of forests and gardens on Puget Sound's Bainbridge Island is one of the most striking and elegant garden spaces in the country. The Reflection Garden, with its elegant 200-foot-long reflecting pool surrounded by formal yew hedge and informal forest, ranks as one of the most striking garden spaces in the country. Nearby, red osier dogwoods, western azaleas, and a small forest of shadblow trees attract trumpeter swans and native waterfowl to islands of the Bird Refuge. Under the tall evergreens of the Glen, rhododendrons and companion plants bloom in late spring and early summer. At other times of the year, thousands of perennials, bulbs, and wildflowers succeed one another in bloom. The Bloedel's enormous swath of more than 15,000 fluttering cyclamens is one of the largest plantings of them in the world. And there are two Japanese gardens: One is enclosed and composed of wood, stone, and sand, and invites introspection and meditation; the other draws you to think of the world outside yourself with its many beautiful views. The centerpiece of this garden is a French chateau–style Visitors Center, with sweeping lawns and formal boxwood hedges. You need a reservation to visit; call one week in advance. The reserve

is accessible by ferry from Seattle and by car from the Olympic Peninsula (use the Agate Pass Bridge). Allow at least two hours at the reserve. *Bloedel Reserve, 7571 N.E. Dolphin Dr., Bainbridge Island, WA 98110-1097, tel. 206/842–7631, fax 206/842–8970. Open year-round, Wed.–Sun. Admission: $6.*

SOURCES

ORGANIZATIONS Many garden tours are sponsored by horticultural societies and botanical institutions. Of these, a few stand out for the breadth and depth of their activity nationwide. The **American Horticultural Society** (7931 E. Boulevard Dr., Alexandria, VA 22308-1300, tel. 703/768–5700 or 800/777–7931) focuses on the exchange of information through its bimonthly magazine, *The American Gardener.* Its reciprocal admission program means that members can visit gardens throughout the country for free or at a discount. The **Botanical Society of America** (New York Botanical Garden, Bronx, NY 10458, tel. 718/817–8700) fosters education by means of publications and a plant information hot line. The **Garden Club of America** (598 Madison Ave., New York, NY 10022, tel. 212/753–8287) has many local chapters that sponsor various educational programs in the gardening field. The **Garden Conservancy** (Albany Post Rd., Box 219, Cold Spring, NY 10516, tel. 914/265–2029) aims to preserve exceptional American gardens by helping them change from private to nonprofit ownership, by fundraising, and through legal research. Members receive a newsletter and can join day tours of worthy private gardens.

PERIODICALS Listings of garden tours as well as of courses and other programs can typically be found in the publication of your local botanical institution. Also consult *Fine Gardening* (Taunton Press, Inc., Box 355, Newtown, CT 06470, tel. 203/426–8171), a good general bimonthly by and for home gardeners; *Horticulture* (98 N. Washington St., Boston, MA 02114, tel. 617/742–5600), which publishes articles and ads of general interest to gardeners 10 times a year; and *Garden Design* (100 Avenue of the Americas, New York, NY 10013, tel. 212/334–1200), a bimonthly magazine written for amateur and professional gardeners. Many other publications and books are available at the stores and bookshops of botanical institutions and public gardens.

BOOKS For excellent descriptions of public gardens, often with color illustrations, see the *American Garden Guidebook: East* and the *American Garden Guidebook: West,* by Everitt L. Miller and Jay S. Cohen;

American Gardens: A Traveler's Guide, edited by Claire E. Sawyers (Brooklyn Botanic Garden, Brooklyn, NY 11225); *Glorious Gardens to Visit,* by Priscilla Dunhill and Sue Freedman; *Public and Private Gardens of the Northwest,* by Myrna Oakley; and the *Traveler's Guide to American Gardens,* edited by Mary Helen Ray and Robert P. Nicholls.

ALSO SEE If it's the idea of traveling in the company of an expert that appeals, look into Cultural Tours. If it's natural ecosystems that fascinate you, turn to the Cultural and Natural History Cruises and Nature Camps chapters.

Holistic Centers

Written by Melissa Rivers

Updated by Natasha Lesser

o be healthy and happy, you must attend both to your spiritual and to your physical needs: That's the underlying philosophy of the country's many holistic centers, institutions that show you how to make permanent changes in the way you live—changes the centers vow will improve your health, give you a sense of fulfillment, and renew your spirituality.

To do this, they draw on philosophies of living espoused by the holistic and New Age movements, which incorporate Eastern and Native American spiritual practices, holism, and concern for nature. Holistic centers often use modern techniques like biofeedback and psychotherapy along with ancient practices such as meditation, yoga, tai chi, wilderness quests (a rite of passage involving seclusion and fasting in the wild), and the use of sweat lodges (for a purification ritual). Their locations, often in beautiful countryside, are chosen to help you reconnect with the natural environment; and their menus, usually vegetarian and macrobiotic fare, aim to benefit your health and provide another way to commune with nature.

Some of these holistic centers concentrate on spiritual awareness and emphasize meditation; others focus on holistic health and pay more attention to healthy cooking and exercise. But no matter what their spe-

cialty, all these centers emphasize the need for balance between mind and body. So you eat vegetarian meals while you meditate, and you take time out to meditate between organic gardening and macrobiotic cooking classes. Many centers have a specialty—fitness, spiritual development, weight loss, bodywork training, health rejuvenation, recovery, or stress management—and some centers offer a variety of programs.

At most centers, you follow a daily schedule that incorporates yoga, aerobics, day hikes, meditation sessions, and classes on nutrition, self-awareness, stress management, Native American spirituality, natural medicine, and other topics. There's also bodywork—physical treatments such as Swedish and shiatsu massage, aromatherapy, herbal body wraps, reflexology, and rolfing. The amount of free time differs from center to center; some have you up before dawn and scheduled throughout the day, while others allow you to decide how much you want to participate. At many centers, too, you can set up a personal retreat; you decide how long you want to stay, which scheduled activities you want to join, and how much time you want to relax, read, meditate, sunbathe, or explore your surroundings. The centers listed here also have various rules for guest conduct: Some stress celibacy; some allow nudity; several call for volunteer work; and many do not allow smoking or drinking. Most centers discour-

Writer Melissa Rivers began her holistic journey a decade ago in Japan, with the study of Zen Buddhism. Natasha Lesser, an editor at Fodor's, is a big believer in the power of holistic healing and the mind-body connection.

age taking children along, because they disrupt the peaceful environment and can't participate in most activities.

Accommodations run the gamut from tents to posh hotels. Simple, shared accommodations in dormitories are the most common option. Meals are often served buffet style; regimens may be lacto-vegetarian, ovo-lacto vegetarian, vegan vegetarian, or either macrobiotic or organic. Centers that focus on fitness or weight loss may also offer spa cuisine, which is low in calories, and supervised juice regimens and fasts, meant to cleanse your body of impurities.

The cost of a stay at the different centers in this chapter varies widely, usually based on accommodations and the time of year you visit. A holistic health or spiritual awareness vacation can be quite a bargain, if you don't mind sleeping in a dorm room with nine other people or sharing a bathhouse with 50 other campers. Of course there are centers that offer accommodations in luxury resorts, but the price, up to $450 per night, versus the $25 a night you can pay to camp out, certainly reflects the additional comforts.

Staffs include everything from doctors to Buddhist monks. In general, they are supportive, understanding, and willing to go out of their way to help you make what are sometimes difficult lifestyle changes. Staffs at centers that emphasize the physical aspects of holistic health tend to include a higher percentage of health care professionals: doctors, nurses, nutritionists. Participants come from all professions and religious persuasions. Usually college-educated people from the ages of 20 to 70, they come to get fit, lose weight, explore their spiritual beliefs, recover physical and mental health, learn to manage stress, or find more meaning in life; or simply to rest and relax, get some exercise, or be pampered. They also come away with their spirits uplifted, and with a better understanding of themselves and a deeper appreciation of nature. Changes like these may last until your next vacation—or far beyond.

GLOSSARY Many terms used in this chapter, from types of bodywork to elements of Zen meditation, may be unfamiliar. The following is a list of the terms that appear most frequently:

Aromatherapy: Inhalation of or massage with oils from essences of plants and flowers intended to relax the skin's connective tissues and stimulate the natural flow of lymph.

Asana: The physical postures that constitute one of the three principal yogic practices.

Biofeedback: Monitoring and control of physical functions such as blood pressure, pulse rate, digestion, and muscle tension with an electronic sensing device.

Bodywork: Umbrella term covering massages, facials, hydrotherapy, and other similar physical spa treatments.

Hatha yoga: One of the four chief Hindu disciplines; a system of physical exercises for the control and perfection of the body.

Holistic health: A nonmedical approach to the healing and health of the whole person that seeks to integrate physical and mental well-being with lifestyle factors.

Hydrotherapy: Underwater massage; alternating hot and cold showers; and other water-oriented treatments.

Kinhin: Walking meditation.

Lacto-vegetarian diet: Vegetarian diet that includes dairy products.

Macrobiotics: Vegetarian diet low in fat and high in antioxidant vitamins; the ultimate goal is to prolong life.

Organic diet: Diet composed of food grown or produced without the use of pesticides, herbicides, or chemical fertilizers.

Ovo-lacto vegetarian diet: Vegetarian diet that includes eggs and dairy products.

Pranayama: The breathing techniques that constitute one of the three principal yogic practices.

Reflexology: Massage of the pressure points on the feet, hands, and ears; intended to relax and stimulate healing in specific parts of the body.

Reiki: An ancient healing method that teaches about universal life energy through the laying on of hands and mental and spiritual balancing. It is intended to relieve acute emotional and physical conditions.

Rolfing: A bodywork system developed by Ida Rolf that improves balance and flexibility through manipulation of rigid muscles, bones, and joints. It is intended to improve energy flow and relieve stress.

Satsanga: "In the company of truth." A gathering for chanting, meditation, and inspiration.

Shiatsu: Massage technique developed by Tokujiro Namikoshi that uses finger (*shi*) pressure (*atsu*) to stimulate the body's inner powers of balance and healing.

Sweat lodge: Native American ritual of purification through time in a steam-filled hut or tepee. The ceremonies vary slightly, depending on the leader's tribal affiliation and individual presentation style.

Vegan vegetarian: Strict vegetarian diet that uses no animal products.

Vegetarian diet: A diet of raw or cooked vegetables, fruit, seeds, and nuts.

Wilderness quest: Rite of passage involving seclusion and fasting in the wild. When following Native American tradition, it is also referred to as a vision quest.

Zazen: Seated meditation.

CHOOSING THE RIGHT CENTER

Every holistic center is different. To understand exactly what a stay at each one involves, it helps to probe beyond the brochures, which tend to be general, and ask many specific questions, such as the ones that follow.

What is the center's philosophy, and how will it affect my experience there? Although the goal is usually to help you attain a balance between your mind and body, centers have their own philosophies about how to do this, resulting in very different programs. One center may promote the use of meditation and vision quests to achieve holistic health, while another may advocate spa cuisine and yoga classes. Programs may be very physical, either fitness- or weight-loss oriented; or very spiritual, involving much meditation and various rituals; or very pampering, providing a great deal of bodywork. Some programs combine several of these approaches. Know exactly what you're getting into.

How large is the facility, and how many guests can it accommodate? If personal attention matters to you, choose a center that offers a small-group experience. If you want to meet more new people, pick a center where you can interact with larger groups.

How structured is the program? Programs range from workshops with full schedules of required activities and little free time to personal retreats in which you determine how you spend your time. Find out whether you must participate in all scheduled events.

What personal services are offered? Most centers offer various types of bodywork, and many centers offer nutritional, psychological, spiritual, or lifestyle counseling. Make sure the center you choose offers the services you want, and find out what they cost.

What's the cost and what's included? The cost of a stay at one of these centers can vary greatly according to where you stay, when you visit, and what program you choose. Costs listed here are by day or by program, depending on the center's offerings, and are for one person in accommodations that range from shared tents and dormitory-style rooms to private rooms in luxury resorts. Unless otherwise noted, the cost also covers meals, use of a center's facilities, and participation in regularly scheduled classes. Special seminars or workshops generally cost more. Be sure to find out what transportation is included; although fees for programs described here never include transportation to the center, a transfer from the nearest airport may be available at no extra charge. Some centers, where accommodations are more basic, ask that you bring bedding and towels. If you want to camp, you may have to furnish your own camping gear.

Are there any hidden costs? There may be additional fees for individual bodywork, beauty treatments, counseling, and child care.

What is the setting of the center? Although locations are usually peaceful, surroundings range from isolated countryside to luxurious resort areas.

What are the accommodations like? Accommodations can be anything from a shared tent and bathhouse to a private room and bath in a resort hotel. Most centers have few private rooms and baths. Know all of your options.

What type of food is served? If the diet is vegetarian, as is common among these centers, you may want to ask about non-vegetarian options or special weight-loss diets.

Will laundry facilities be available? Probably not, but if they are, they could save you a suitcase.

How long has the center been in business? Although there are no guarantees, an experienced staff is more likely to be well-prepared for any questions or problems you may have.

Do you have references from past guests? Speaking to a few former participants about a center's overall philosophic approach or daily activities can be extremely helpful. Keep in mind that personal needs and preferences for holistic centers can vary greatly.

How far in advance do I need to book? How far in advance you must book to attend a particular center may vary according to which of its programs you choose.

FAVORITE CENTERS

THE NORTHEAST

MAINE **Northern Pines Health Resort.** Marlee Turner became a believer in holistic health care when it helped her through a bout with thyroid cancer. In 1980, she opened the Northern Pines Health Resort, focusing on lifestyle management. The Northern Pines regimen of meditation, yoga, Reiki, transformational breathing, iridology, tai chi, and tarot is designed to promote general good health and to teach you to manage stress. With this program—along with a diet of fresh fruits, vegetables, and whole grains—you nourish your mind and spirit as well as your body.

How long you stay is up to you; once there, you can pick and choose your activities from the resort's full daily schedule, which includes early morning meditation, followed by stretch class, walks and hikes (or cross-country skiing), yoga, Reiki, and other activities. You may also attend a class, a discussion session, and an evening presentation on nutrition, cooking, vitamins, herbs, meditation, or other holistic health–related topics. In your free time, you may go canoeing or swimming, take advantage of the sauna or hot tub, or spend a little extra for a Swedish massage, reflexology session, beauty treatment, or time in the flotation tank.

The cabins that dot the wooded, 68-acre lakefront property can accommodate up to 30, but there are usually no more than 15 guests on hand each week—mostly well-traveled, educated women who are often doctors, nurses, teachers, or therapists. Vegetarian dishes of natural foods are served at the communal meals; you can also opt for a supervised juice fast. Children are welcome to participate with parents, and child care can be arranged. *Northern Pines Health Resort, 559 Rte. 85, Raymond, ME 04071, tel. 207/655–7624, fax 207/655–3321. Year-round: daily, $95–$240. Price does not include personal services; sign up at least 1 wk in advance.*

MASSACHUSETTS **Kripalu Center for Yoga and Health.** Some 14,000 visitors a year come to this nonprofit educational and spiritual center in the Berkshires. Built as a Jesuit monastery in 1957, the center is on 300 acres of verdant woodlands and scenic meadows overlooking Lake Mahkeenac. Here you can find a variety of programs aimed at increasing your peace of mind, your health, and your well-being.

The one-day to one-month programs include Kripalu yoga, meditation, self-discovery and holistic health workshops, low-impact aerobic dance movements known as DansKinetics, and massage and other bodywork; month-long training programs certify you to teach Kripalu yoga and holistic lifestyles and practice Kripalu bodywork. In any of the center's programs, the daily schedule consists of morning yoga and a workshop, on topics such as "Discovering the Spirit in Relationship" and "Transformation through Transition"; afternoon DansKinetics, yoga, and another workshop; and an evening, group meditation. You also have free time to practice yoga and meditation, explore the grounds, and have a massage or a facial, or a session of shiatsu, reflexology, or energy-balancing. An evening satsanga brings residents and guests together for chanting, music, and poetry.

Personal retreats you design yourself, known here as Retreat and Renewal, include daily yoga, DansKinetics classes, personal growth workshops, and satsanga in the evening. On selected days you may also choose from such activities as a guided walk, a meditation workshop, or a yoga clinic. You must stay at least two nights for these (except off-season).

The Kripalu Center accommodates up to 300 guests in an array of modest dormitories and private rooms; all but a few more spacious deluxe rooms have shared baths. The vegetarian cuisine is high in protein and fiber, and low in fats and sweeteners. Breakfast is eaten in meditative silence in the dining chapel; a separate, silent dining room is available for lunch and dinner. Children are welcome, and there are special programs in summer and on holiday weekends to keep them occupied. *Kripalu Center for Yoga and Health, Box 793, Lenox, MA 01240, tel. 413/448–3400 or 800/741–7353, fax 413/448–3196. Year-round: daily, $40-$195; 1–28 days, $40–$4,900. Sign up anytime.*

MASSACHUSETTS **Kushi Institute.** Since 1978, the Kushi Institute has been in the forefront of research and education in the field of macrobiotics. Weekend and week-long seminars offer you the opportunity to learn the macrobiotic way of life by living it. Three macrobiotic meals are served each day, using fresh, all-natural ingredients, including whole grains, beans, vegetables, sea vegetables, nuts, and fruit. Classes cover the relationship between diet and health and macrobiotic cooking; personal macrobiotic counseling and shiatsu massage are also available.

The institute offers a number of different programs: The Wellness Weekend provides a quick introduction to macrobiotics; Essentials of Macrobiotic Cooking and Naturally Gourmet focus on cooking skills; the Women's Health Weekend explores lifestyle and diet for women. The week-long Way to Health seminar includes introductory classes in shiatsu massage, visual diagnosis, and natural home remedies, as well as cooking classes and lectures on healthy living. The monthlong Dynamics of Macrobiotics Program provides comprehensive, foundational training in the macrobiotic field. Each year, founder Michio Kushi offers workshops that put you on the road to holistic health through classes on macrobiotic eating, fitness, massage therapy, and healing spiritualities from Christianity to Tao Te Ching. In most programs, days begin at 7 AM with gentle stretching exercises, and continue until 9 PM with classes, lectures, and free time for walks in the woods or a massage.

The center is in the Berkshires on 600 acres of woodlands and meadows. Accommodations are in a former Franciscan lodge or in a dormitory with shared rooms and bath; a limited number of private rooms is available. *The Kushi Institute, Leland Rd., Box 7, Becket, MA 01223, tel. 413/623–5741, fax 413/623–8827. Year-round: 2–7 days, $150–$1,250. Sign up anytime.*

MASSACHUSETTS **Rowe Camp and Conference Center.** The roster of programs here includes summer camps for all ages and weekend workshops on topics such as psychology, Native American spirituality, women's issues, religion, politics, natural medicine, environmental issues, relationships, and how to live from the heart. Although the camp is affiliated with the Unitarian Universalist Association, programs and staff don't proselytize; the goal is merely to provide an environment for personal exploration, spiritual growth, and mental healing. To make the programs accessible to the widest possible audience, fees are pegged to participants' incomes.

Each workshop draws well-known authors, lecturers, and specialists in a given field, who lead five sessions during the weekend, beginning on Friday night and ending on Sunday afternoon. Sessions are a combination of lectures, discussions, and experiential exercises that demonstrate the themes of the retreat. In your free time, you can hike, ski, or relax in the cedar sauna, or take in the art museums in nearby Williamstown.

The vegetarian meals, served family style, are delicious, and the conversation then is one of the nicest parts of a stay here; beer and wine are available at an extra charge. Accommodations in the center's 200-year-old farmhouse and two newer buildings have private rooms with shared baths; some rooms are accessible to people in wheelchairs. You can also bunk in one of several truly summer-camp-style cabins, which share a communal bathhouse; here

you must bring your own linens and a flashlight.

In addition to the summer camps for men, women, children, teenagers, and families, Rowe hosts recovery camps for AA and ACOA members and others with special concerns. Weekend programs are only available between September and mid-June. *Rowe Camp and Conference Center, Kings Highway Rd., Rowe, MA 01367, tel. 413/339–4954, fax 413/339–5708. Year-round: Mid-June–Sept.: 7 days, $195–$425. Sept.–mid-June: 3 days, $180–$320. Sign up anytime.*

NEW YORK **Omega Institute for Holistic Studies.** This center, 100 miles north of New York City, is a kind of New Age mecca, where you can strive to achieve balanced physical and mental health with help from people on the leading edge of preventive medicine and holistic health. Staff counselors are specialists in nutrition, stress management, and holistic medicine. Guest lecturers and faculty who lead the 250 two-to seven-day workshops here—on such topics as Native American studies, wellness and stress management, holistic health, bodywork, recovery, intuitive development, relationships, art, sports and fitness, and spirituality—make up a veritable *Who's Who* of the human potential movement.

Several times each year, in addition to the workshops, there's a Wellness Week program, where you learn the importance of diet, nutrition, exercise, and a positive attitude in developing and maintaining good health. In this program, days start before breakfast, when small groups form to practice yoga or tai chi; lectures, massage sessions, yoga, group support meetings, movement and meditation classes, and more tai chi fill the rest of the time. After dark there are concerts, dances, and films.

On the campus, you'll find hiking, canoeing, basketball, tennis, volleyball, a theater, a café, a bookstore, and the Wellness Center, which has a sauna, massage rooms, flotation tanks, and consultation rooms. There are simple dormitories, cabins, and campsites, accommodating up to 350. Meals, served buffet style, are primarily vegetarian, with some fish and dairy options. Omega offers one family week each summer and provides an optional child care program throughout the season. In addition to what's available at the New York campus, which is in full swing in summer and early fall, in winter there are programs in New Mexico, California, Virginia, and at Maho Bay, on St. John in the U.S. Virgin Islands. *Omega Institute for Holistic Studies, 260 Lake Dr., Rhinebeck, NY 12572, tel. 914/266–4444 or 800/944–1001, fax 914/266–4828. May–mid-Sept.: 2–7 days, $80–$500. Sign up 2–4 wks in advance.*

NEW YORK **Zen Mountain Monastery.** This Zen monastery, in a state forest preserve in the Catskill Mountains, is the only such place in the country that offers programs for visitors year-round. Founded in 1980 as a residential artist center with a spiritual basis in Buddhism, the monastery became a year-round retreat for monastics and laypeople training in Zen in 1983. Traditional arts are still practiced here, but they are integrated with traditional Zen training in self-realization, morality, and social responsibility.

At three- and six-day programs, repeated several times a year, you can attend classes on poetry, calligraphy and brush painting, cooking, music, and *aikido* (a Japanese martial art). You might be treated to a cup of green tea in a Zen tea ceremony, explore the subtleties of *ikebana* (flower arranging), or enjoy a concert of the music of the *shakuhachi* (Japanese flute).

Another option here is *sesshin,* an intense, weeklong silent meditation retreat; the monastery's Introduction to Zen training weekend is a prerequisite. The sesshin schedule is highly regimented. Days begin well before sunrise, are spent in silence, except for Buddhist chanting services, and include lecture sessions with monastery abbot Daido Loori and senior students, walking meditation, short periods of community work, *and* 8 to 10 hours of zazen meditation.

A four-story stone-and-wood structure built earlier in the century by Norwegian craftspeople and Catholic monks houses the dormitory, library, dining hall, classrooms, and *zendo* (meditation hall). Men and women lodge in bunks in sex-segregated rooms that sleep 10; bathrooms are shared. The three meals served daily, buffet style, are vegetarian, with occasional dairy, egg, and fish dishes (and a meat alternative always available); the venue is the main dining hall except during sesshin retreats, when you eat in meditative silence in the zendo. *Zen Mountain Monastery, S. Plank Rd., Box 197PC, Mt. Tremper, NY 12457, tel. 914/688–2228, fax 914/688–2415. Year-round: 3–6 days, $175–$325. Sign up at least 2 wks in advance.*

THE MID-ATLANTIC

PENNSYLVANIA **The Himalayan International Institute of Yoga Science and Philosophy.** Indian yogi Sri Swami Rama, author of numerous books on yoga and meditation, founded this nonprofit institute in 1971 to teach his holistic approach to living, which combines biofeedback, aerobic exercise, breathing, meditation, diet, fasting, and yoga. According to Sri Swami Rama, meditation and relaxation enable you to gain control of your body and mind.

Each year, hundreds of weekend seminars on topics such as homeopathy, vegetarianism, meditation, creative learning processes, movement and energy, pranayama, and spiritual awakening are conducted by members of the Institute's excellent international faculty, many of whom hold M.D. or Ph.D. degrees. You can create a 10-day work-and-study retreat by combining two weekend seminars with a five-day program of personal meditation, community service, and relaxation. There are also health transformation programs that include medical consultations with holistic doctors, biofeedback sessions, exercise and stretch classes, cooking, and self-awareness classes.

Days begin at 6:30 AM with hatha yoga and finish after dinner with a lecture. Schedules and class topics vary from seminar to seminar, but each day includes time for exercise, hatha yoga, and meditation. In your free time, you can hike, socialize in the tea lounge, help with community work, play tennis, or swim in the pond (or skate on it); bring your own sports equipment. You are asked to observe silence from 10 PM until 8 AM and to avoid distractions during your stay.

Accommodations are in the main building, set on 400 acres of woods and meadows in northeastern Pennsylvania's Pocono Mountains. You have a choice of dorm rooms with bunk beds or austere double or single rooms with sinks and shared bathrooms and showers. Low-fat, sugar-free vegetarian meals, with lots of grains, legumes, vegetables, and fruit are served buffet style in the dining hall; all baked goods, tofu, and yogurt are made on the premises. *Himalayan International Institute, R.R. 1, Box 400, Honesdale, PA 18431, tel. 717/253–5551 or 800/822–4547, fax 717/253–9078. Year-round: 2–14 days, $200–$3,400. Sign up 2–4 wks in advance.*

VIRGINIA Yogaville. This ashram of 200 residents was founded by the Reverend Sri Swami Satchidananda to teach the philosophy and practice of Integral Yoga, which combines the three principal yogic practices—meditation, asana, and pranayama—to strengthen the connection between mind and body. During weekend workshops and on personal retreats here, you join the ashram's daily schedule of yoga classes, meditation, service, and lectures on topics such as meditation, stress management, deep relaxation, psychotherapy, naturopathy and yoga, and inner exploration and transformation. Days begin at 5 AM. On Saturday evenings everyone gathers for satsanga, which is led by Reverend Sri Swami Satchidananda when he is in residence.

Yogaville is in the James River valley near Charlottesville. The Lotus Inn, a wood lodge, contains a health food café and

guest rooms with private baths; another two-story building contains classrooms, dormitories, and shared bath and laundry facilities. Motor homes can be parked on the grounds of the 750-acre retreat, and there is plenty of space for tent camping. You take your meals, lacto-vegetarian but with vegan alternatives, in the communal dining hall; the main meal of the day is lunch, which may include steamed organic vegetables from the community garden, whole grains, and legume or tofu dishes. The other meals are usually light buffets: Cereals, yogurt, fresh fruit, and herbal teas are served at breakfast; homemade soups, whole grains, a salad bar, yogurt, and fruit are offered at dinner. There are special rates for children and discounts for those who make a commitment in advance to work in the garden, kitchen, or other areas of the ashram. *Yogaville, Rte. 604, Buckingham, VA 23921, tel. 804/969–3121 or 800/858–9642, fax 804/969–1303. Year-round: daily, $22–$80; 3-day workshops, $145–$175. Sign up at least 10 days in advance.*

THE MIDWEST

IOWA The Raj. The luxurious Raj health center, which opened in 1992 in the heart of Iowa's rolling meadows and woodlands, is devoted to the ancient system of preventive natural medicine known as Ayurvedic therapy. Three-, five-, and seven-day programs are available. After an assessment of your physiological makeup, a physician concerned both with your physical and your spiritual health prescribes deeply relaxing rejuvenation therapies known as *panchakarma*, once reserved for India's royal families, to restore balance in your body: massages with warm herbal oils, herb-perfumed steam baths, and gentle internal cleansings. In addition, staff experts train you in yogic positions and breathing techniques. An optional course in transcendental meditation teaches you how to increase your self-awareness and manage stress in your life.

The pace of daily activities is unhurried, the staff comforting. Concerts of classical Indian music and lectures on natural medicine, meditation techniques, self-massage, optimizing digestion, the role of intellect and the senses in maintaining health, and other health-related topics fill evenings. You can spend your free time hiking on the 100-acre grounds, working out in the exercise room, and visiting the adjacent Vedic Observatory, where ancient instruments allow you to track planetary and astral movements across Iowa's clear night sky.

Even though the daily vegetarian meals are delicious and filling, most participants lose weight on the program without counting calories. For dinner, you might typically have Indian rice or dal (spiced, puréed legumes), vegetables, cooked fruit, and herbal tea. Accommodations in private villas and the hotel are deluxe; the spacious, air-conditioned rooms and suites have French country furniture with Battenburg lace bedcovers, telephones, and large bathrooms. Families with children are encouraged to stay in the villas to preserve the quiet of the hotel. *The Raj, 24th St. NW, Fairfield, IA 52556, tel. 515/472–9580 or 800/248–9050, fax 515/472–2496. Yearround: 3–7 days, $1,350–$2,850. Sign up at least 2–3 wks in advance.*

THE SOUTHWEST

ARIZONA **Global Fitness Adventures in Sedona.** This trip in the Sedona area is the most spiritually oriented program offered by Global Fitness Adventures, an outfitter specializing in fitness and well-being vacations. In an effort to gain deeper spiritual awareness and power, you visit four primary vortexes—energy sources in the Sedona area said to emit positive and negative charges that affect human physiology. You also explore Native American spirituality by participating in a drum and dance workshop, a traditional sweat lodge, and 8- to 15-mile hikes to prehistoric Native

American settlements, Anasazi cliff dwellings, and stone medicine wheels.

Days begin with a power drink of puréed fruit, soy protein, and wheat germ, followed by sessions of yoga or tai chi and a long hike. After lunch there are muscletoning classes, massages (three per week), and a meditation period on a secluded flat rock with panoramic views. Motivational talks on personal power, nutrition, and holistic health follow candlelight suppers in the main lodge. A sunset horseback ride and excursions to Sedona's historic sites and art galleries are also on the schedule.

Accommodations are in spacious, attractively decorated cabins near Juniper Oak Creek. Each has two double bedrooms, two baths, a living room with fireplace, and a large deck overlooking a canyon. The chef's gourmet, organic, primarily vegetarian spa cuisine is geared toward cleansing and detoxification. *Global Fitness Adventures, Box 1390, Aspen, CO 81612, tel. 970/927–9593 or 800/488–8747, fax 970/927–4793. Apr.–early May and mid-Oct.–mid-Nov.: 7 days, $2,175. Price includes 3 massages; sign up at least 2–4 wks in advance.*

THE ROCKIES

COLORADO **Global Fitness Adventures in Aspen.** Fitness with flair best describes the well-being program put together by director Kristina Hurrel and her husband, author and holistic health authority Dr. Rob Krakovitz. Their seven-day program mixes pampering, physical challenges, and classes on holistic health, nutrition, and fitness skills to help you tune up your body and permanently improve your lifestyle.

Only a dozen guests participate each week, so the level of attention you receive is high. You are given a personal fitness evaluation and an individualized, tension-busting daily exercise routine; activities include hikes, white-water raft trips, stress-management classes, massages, horseback rides, and sessions of yoga, tai chi, and muscle toning.

Days begin at 6:15 AM and follow a set schedule; an afternoon siesta gives you two hours to swim, fish, mountain bike, or loll in the Jacuzzi. You spend evenings listening to motivational talks on personal power, relationships, aging and wisdom, nutrition, holistic health, and detoxification. Available for an additional cost are a Native American sweat lodge purification ceremony, a dance and drum workshop, personal holistic health consultations with Dr. Krakovitz, and facials.

Accommodations are in a comfortable and luxurious home on a 1500-acre ranch in the Rocky Mountains, in double rooms with Western-style furnishings and Native American artifacts. Meals are organic vegetarian, with lots of salads, vegetables, legumes, and fruit. *Global Fitness Adventures, Box 1390, Aspen, CO 81612, tel. 970/ 927–9593 or 800/488–8747, fax 970/927– 4793. Mid-June–Sept.: 7 days, $2,175. Price includes 3 massages; sign up at least 2–4 wks in advance.*

MONTANA **Feathered Pipe Ranch.** This 110-acre ranch, nestled in the Rocky Mountains near the Continental Divide, was willed to current director India Supera in 1976 with the stipulation that she operate it as a healing center. Accordingly, she presents a series of weeklong summer workshops conducted by nationally and internationally known instructors such as Lilias Folan, Jean Shinoda Bolen, Andrew Weil, and other masters of yoga, mythology, holistic medicine, nutrition, shamanism, Native American spirituality, astrology, classical Indian music, or bodywork. The center's offerings are purposely diverse: The goal is to help participants find exactly what they need to realize their wholeness and connection to all of life.

Two- to three-hour morning and afternoon classes are separated by long lunch and dinner breaks that give you plenty of time to be outdoors. There are rolling lawns for sunning, miles of trails for hiking, caves to explore, and a 3-acre pond for swimming. Evening entertainment ranges from skits

and storytelling to presentations by naturalists. Optional activities (for an additional cost) include an array of massages and a daylong river float trip.

Vegetarian meals are served buffet style in the main lodge; you can also have fish and organic chicken. Accommodations, for up to 40, are in log and stone chalets, tents, tepees, and Mongolian yurts in the forest; there are a few private rooms (some with private baths) as well as dormitory rooms that sleep four to six. The cedar bathhouse contains a hot tub, a sauna, massage rooms, and bathing facilities. *Feathered Pipe Ranch, Box 1682, Helena, MT 59624, tel. 406/442–8196, fax 406/442–8110. May– early Sept.: 7–11 days, $1,175–$1,695. Sign up 2–4 wks in advance.*

WYOMING **Antelope Retreat and Education Center.** The center's setting—500 acres of highland valley, in the foothills of the Rockies between Medicine Bow National Forest and Red Desert—is a key element in its programs, which focus on expanding your self-awareness as you reconnect with the natural environment. John Boyer grew up on this ranch and opened the place in 1988 because he wanted to share his love of nature and the inner peace he had found through the spiritual practices of his Native American neighbors. Rituals of Lakota and Dakota Sioux and other Native Americans, among them sweat lodge ceremonies and wilderness quests, are a part of many of the center's programs.

You can choose three- or seven-day summer workshops on survival and nature awareness, wilderness quests, sacred Native American rituals, or crafts and skills; other weeklong quests aim to help women reconnect with nature and celebrate themselves, other women, and the environment. The daily schedules of each workshop vary with the topic and the group; the staff responds to the needs and interests of each group of participants. Unstructured personal retreats may be arranged year-round; on these you are free to pitch in with ranch chores, gardening, and cooking, or to fill your time with meditation and hiking or skiing. Steamboat Springs, Colorado, is nearby.

You stay in comfortable if not luxurious quarters in the 100-year-old ranch house, in five double rooms that share a bath, or in two yurts outside, each accommodating four. Meals are generally vegetarian, with occasional fish or fowl options. *Antelope Retreat and Education Center, Box 156, Savery, WY 82332, tel. 307/383–2625. Year-round: daily, $36–$58. Late May–early Sept.: 3–7 days, $235–$650. Sign up 2–4 wks in advance for workshops, anytime for personal retreats.*

THE WEST COAST

CALIFORNIA **Esalen Institute.** Founded in 1962, and widely considered the birthplace of the human potential movement in the United States, the Esalen Institute in Big Sur still offers the country's broadest curriculum focused on the areas of spiritual awareness and holistic health. In workshops, you can study biofeedback, contemplative practices, cooking, cultural arts, dreams, Gestalt therapy, hypnosis, intuitive development, martial arts, massage and bodywork, men's and women's studies, psychological processes, relationships, shamanism, social responsibility, sports, and wilderness and ecology; cost and duration of these workshops vary. When workshop participants do not fill all rooms, you can also stay at Esalen for an unstructured personal retreat.

A workshop's daily schedule depends on the rhythm your leader wants to establish. There is always free time for you to experience all that Esalen offers on a daily basis: tai chi and exercise classes, nature hikes, clothing-optional swimming in the pool and hot springs, massages, rolfing, and other bodywork. Evenings bring lectures, concerts, films, dances, and other relaxing entertainment.

Esalen is situated on a particularly stunning section of the California coast, and some of the guest accommodations are in rustic lodges that overlook the pounding surf. Most bedrooms and baths are shared. Rooms with bunk beds are slightly cheaper, and children get discounted rates when accompanied by both parents. There are special activities and a dining plan just for kids; Esalen's Gazebo Park School, for youngsters aged one to six, runs year-round and can serve as child care (at additional cost). Meals are family style and incorporate meat, fish, dairy products, and fresh produce grown on the property; vegetarian options are always available. *Esalen Institute, Big Sur, CA 93920, tel. 408/667–3000 or 408/667–3005, fax 408/667–2724. Year-round: daily, $80–$125; 2–7 days, $325–$1,220. Sign up 1 month in advance for seminars, and at least 1 wk in advance for personal retreats.*

CALIFORNIA **Global Fitness Adventures in Santa Barbara.** Picturesque Santa Barbara is yet another beautiful location for the physically and mentally challenging week-long vacations put together by Global Fitness Adventures. Under the guidance of director Kristina Hurrel and her staff, you and 5 to 11 other participants will tune up physically through 6- to 16-mile hikes, runs along the beach, and yoga, aquatic aerobics, and muscle-toning classes. You explore the immense volcanic cliffs in the Santa Ynez Mountains, then spend the afternoon cooling off in the ocean while watching for dolphins. Revitalizing massages and hydrotherapy are also part of the program, along with motivational lectures on weight control, stress management, personal empowerment, detoxification, and other holistic health and wellness issues. In addition, trips to the Mountain Vedanta Temple grounds and Wheelers Hot Springs in Ojai are part of all stays.

A chef prepares organic meals of pastas, legumes, fruit, soups, salads, and freshly caught fish of the day. Accommodations are double rooms in the historic El Encanto Hotel, tucked into the foothills of the Santa Ynez mountains on 10 acres of semi-tropical garden overlooking the ocean. *Global*

Fitness Adventures, Box 1390, Aspen, CO 81612, tel. 970/927–9593 or 800/488–8747, fax 303/927–4793. Late Feb–mid-Mar., late Apr.–early May, and late Nov.–mid Dec.: 7 days, $2,175. Price includes 2 massages, meals, and outings; sign up at least 1 wk in advance.

CALIFORNIA **Green Gulch Farm Zen Center.** Although it's only 20 miles from San Francisco, this work-study retreat on 100 acres of pines and open fields stretching to the Pacific seems far removed from the rest of the world; it is a peaceful spot to experience Zen Buddhist traditions. You can come here for free-form personal retreats or for more structured practice retreats.

Personal retreats can be as long or as short as you like, and you are free to come and go as you please. You can join in communal life and work on the organic farm, or quietly meditate on long walks through the nearby woods to Muir Beach. If you are a newcomer or just want to come for one day, you may want to join a "sitting" that introduces the forms, spirit, and detail of the Soto Zen way of life; this includes instruction on zazen and kinhin, a discussion and silent meditation period with some of the community's full-time residents, tea, and lunch.

Weekend to weeklong practice retreats mix free time with participation in some community work and Zen practices. The morning schedule includes meditation, work, and group discussions; afternoons include work, free time, and meditation; and evenings are free. More flexible programs are available as well. There are also scheduled workshops on such topics as flower arranging, organic gardening, *shakuhachi* (Japanese flute), watercolor and zazen, censory awareness, and Buddhism in relation to Christianity and Judaism. In addition, you can sign up for sesshins, intensive meditation sittings, with occasional women-only sessions.

There may be anywhere from 6 to 12 guests at the center at one time. Accommodations are in the Lindisfarne Guest House, con-

structed by hand in the Japanese temple style. It has a suite and 12 double rooms surrounding an atrium that rises to a traditional sloped roof; rates vary with room size and length of stay. Vegetarian meals, cooked using produce from the farm, cost an extra $5 each if you are not taking part in a scheduled workshop or a practice retreat. Miles of hiking trails lead to Muir Beach, Mt. Tamalpais, and the Mill Valley. *Green Gulch Farm Zen Center, 1601 Shoreline Ave., Sausalito, CA 94965, tel. 415/383–3134, fax 415/383–3128. Year-round: 1–7 days, $20–$350. Price does not include meals on personal retreats; sign up anytime.*

CALIFORNIA **Heartwood Institute.** This rustic community on 240 acres of rolling meadows and fir-covered hills seeks to heal the earth by healing and nurturing its people. The Institute provides career training in all types of bodywork, as well as wellness workshops and retreats open to all. It's a place to unwind and treat yourself to some pampering, inexpensive bodywork sessions.

Weeklong workshops are one option; topics include hatha yoga, dietary healing, shiatsu, and other forms of bodywork, self-help, and holistic healing. In spring and summer, you can take a seven-day rejuvenation retreat designed to cleanse your body, mind, and spirit through fasting, massage, meditation, exercise, relaxation, and emotional release. In summer and fall, there is a nine-day polarity cleansing retreat, which involves a simple alkaline diet, eating support group meetings, and daily lessons in polarity balancing bodywork—balancing your body's energy using a combination of massage, meditation, exercise, and diet. The staff can also help you develop two- to 22-day personalized retreats.

Ongoing classes in yoga, tai chi, and meditation are part of every stay, as are dips in the pool and hot tub and visits to the wood-fired sauna. In your free time, you can go hiking or mountain biking through the hills or observe the wild deer, turkeys, bobtail cats, and raccoons that live on the grounds. Unless you're fasting, you have three organic vegetarian meals a day; fish is served occasionally, and dishes containing common allergens such as wheat and milk are clearly labeled and alternatives provided. Accommodations are very simple, with private and shared rooms and communal baths and numerous campsites tucked among the trees around the grounds. *Heartwood Institute, 220 Harmony La., Garberville, CA 95542, tel. 707/923–5004, fax 707/923–5010. Year-round: daily, $80–$120. May–mid-Oct.: 2–14 days, $200–$1,400. Sign up 1 month in advance for workshops, anytime for personal retreats.*

CALIFORNIA **Ojai Foundation.** This center for cross-cultural and spiritual education, personal renewal, and reconnection with the land opened in 1979 on 40 acres of wilderness in the Upper Ojai Valley, north of Los Angeles. Programs here focus on social and spiritual themes, and many, including solstice and equinox ceremonies, are strongly linked to the four seasons and the land. Stays are designed to help you explore and deepen your relationships with others and achieve greater harmony with the earth. A specialty is improving your communications skills through the use of council meetings. You sit in a circle with a group and engage in dialogues, during which you strive to be a better listener and to effectively express your own thoughts.

Workshops last between two and four days and are usually held over a weekend. They may cover meditation, natural healing, permaculture (sustainable patterns in human habitation), relationships, and such Native American practices as wilderness rights of passage and sweat lodge ceremonies. Daily schedules vary with each workshop, but group meditation, classes on the featured topic, and council meetings are part of most days.

You can also arrange a personal retreat. This can be a time of seclusion or another program that meets your needs, which the staff can help you create. You can fill your days with meditation sessions, stretching and toning exercises, long hikes, visits to the ocean or hot springs nearby, or sessions in the ceramic studio.

Accommodations are in your own tent or in one of the foundation's wilderness hermitages—geodesic domes, tepees, or yurts furnished with a futon, table, and lamp. You supply the bedding in the hermitages. During workshops, vegetarian meals are served buffet style in the dining room or on a sunny deck, and everyone helps out with preparation and cleanup. Food is not included in the cost of personal retreats, but you have access to cooking facilities. Families are encouraged to visit, and children are welcome. *Ojai Foundation, 9739 Ojai-Santa Paula Rd., Ojai, CA 93023, tel. 805/646–8343, fax 805/646–2456. Year-round: daily, $20–$35. Mar.–June and Sept.–Dec.: 2–4 days, $150–$325. Price does not include meals on personal retreats; sign up anytime.*

CALIFORNIA **St. Helena Health Center.** What began in 1878 as a rural summer health retreat is now a fully accredited hospital and health care complex. Its programs combine holistic and Western medical practices to help you recover your health and learn to live a lifestyle that preserves it. Personal attention is a feature; the large staff, which includes a dietician, lifestyle counselor, respiratory therapist, clinical psychologist, and exercise physiologist, as well as physicians and nurses, cares for just 10 to 20 guests a week.

The center offers a variety of programs from weekend seminars to 12-day workshops. The five-day Choose to Lose weight-loss program, offered four times each year, includes fitness and nutrition education. The seven-day Nicotine Addiction program, offered each month, relies on group support as well as education to help you stop smoking. Once a month the center also offers the renowned McDougall program, a 12-day workshop that assesses disease risk factors and focuses on prevention through nutrition, exercise, and stress-management techniques. In addition, the weekend seminar, Brainworks Unlimited, focuses on exploring personal potential and relationships using the Benziger Thinking Styles Assessment (BTSA). Group discussions, individual counseling, biofeedback, relaxation and fitness training, and classes on how to shop for and prepare nutritious, low-fat, high-carbohydrate meals are all part of the center's programs, along with massage and time in the sauna, steam room, and whirlpool.

The daily routine at the center changes with the program, but most days start with a walk before breakfast and include a health education seminar and exercise sessions in the gym, followed in the afternoon by stress-management training and perhaps aquatic aerobics sessions in the pool. Evenings bring more educational seminars, free time, and group winery tours, picnics, and shopping trips. The center is on a wooded hillside overlooking acres of vineyards. Although it has hiking and cycling trails, tennis courts, a pool, and a golf course, St. Helena remains very much a health retreat rather than a spa or resort.

Meals, served in the dining room, are lacto-ovo and vegan vegetarian; you may have low-fat desserts but no caffeinated beverages or alcohol. The double rooms in the guest lodge have motel-modern furnishings, private bathrooms, and balconies with views of the valley. *St. Helena Health Center, Deer Park, CA 94576, tel. 707/963–6207 or 800/358–9195, fax 707/963–6461. Year-round: 2–12 days, $450–$4,750. Sign up at least 1 wk in advance.*

CALIFORNIA **Shenoa Retreat and Learning Center.** Shenoa, which means the peace and serenity found in nature, was founded in 1987 by American alumni of the Findhorn Foundation in Scotland—perhaps the most famous holistic learning center in the world. The focus here is on personal and planetary transformation through education and increased self-awareness. One- to 14-day workshops cover topics such as inner focusing, religious studies, organic gardening, ecology, and sustainable agriculture; many of these courses are taught by guest lecturers who rent the space but are affiliated with Shenoa. The center's cornerstone seminar is the Shenoa Sustainability Series, which teaches practical skills for living in harmony with the land; classes are on sustainable structures, nontoxic building materials and techniques, and permaculture, the growing of food for use, not for profit. A variety of three- and four-day family retreats, with workshops for parents, special activities for children, and optional short-term child care, are offered throughout the year, usually over holiday weekends. Unstructured personal retreats are another option. Up to 100 people may be on hand at any given time.

When classes are not meeting, you can take part in meditation sessions, indulge in a massage, tour the nearby vineyards, or take advantage of a list of outdoor activities that includes hiking, biking, swimming, tennis, badminton, and volleyball. The center has a beautiful setting on 160 acres of sunny meadows and cool forests bordered by the Navarro River and the Hendy Wood State Park redwood groves.

Meals are vegetarian, with fresh fruits and vegetables from the center's garden, served buffet style in the dining lodge or outside under the oak trees. The 17 rustic cabins are decorated with handmade quilts and fresh wildflowers and have a private bath and at least two beds; the six cottages have a kitchen and a private bath; there is a nominal fee for towels and bedding. When you stay in the cottages you can choose to pay for meals separately or to cook on your own. Single travelers may be asked to share a cabin if it's busy. There is also a large, forested grove with campsites and a communal bathhouse with private stalls for showering. *Shenoa Retreat and Learning Center, Box 43, Philo, CA 95466, tel. 707/895–3156, fax 707/895–3236. May–Nov.: daily, $30–$70; 1–14 days, $50–$900. Sign up at least 2 wks in advance.*

CALIFORNIA Sivananda Ashram Yoga Farm. This ashram north of Sacramento in peaceful Grass Valley is the place to come for serious learning of classical yoga. Founded by Swami Vishnu-Devananda, the ashram is now led by his disciple, Swami Sita Ramananda. Under her guidance, you and up to 30 other guests join the ashram's 15 full-time residents in a strict schedule of meditation, chanting, and yoga to increase your awareness of the mind-body connection. Yoga classes concentrate on asana, pranayama, *dhyana* (positive thinking and meditation), and *savasana* (relaxation). Guest lecturers conduct special weekend and weeklong retreats on meditation, Native American wisdom, vegetarianism, Ayurvedic healing, classical Indian dance and music, stress management, and Vedantic, Vedic, and yogic teachings. For additional relaxation, there is a sauna, a pond where you can swim, and three classical Indian temples.

Guests here must observe numerous rules. Participation in morning and evening meditation, chanting, and yoga classes is mandatory, and smoking and consumption of alcohol, drugs, and certain foods (including meat, fish, and eggs) are forbidden. You may be asked to help out with communal chores and share a room; accommodations include a few double rooms and several dorm-style rooms in a simple farmhouse, as well as a few private rooms. There's also plenty of camping space on the property. Showers and toilets are shared. Two lacto-vegetarian meals are served buffet style each day: Brunch consists of cereals, yogurt, fruit, rice, vegetables, and salad; dinner may include stir-fried or steamed vegetables, rice, tofu dishes, salad, and homemade soups and bread. Work-study is available in exchange for reduced fees. *Sivananda Ashram Yoga Farm, 14651 Ballantree La., Grass Valley, CA 95949, tel. 916/272–9322 or 800/469–YOGA, fax 916/477–6054. Year-round: daily, $25–$55; additional fees of $5–$10 per day during workshops. Price does not include camping gear; sign up anytime.*

OREGON Aesculapia Wilderness Healing Retreat. Named for Asclepius, the Greek god of healing, the retreat is on 80 verdant acres on the edge of the Siskiyou Mountains in southern Oregon. The focus of this center, founded in 1984, is healing using the Creative Consciousness Process developed by Fred Graywolf Swinney, noted author, philosopher, physicist, and psychologist.

Swinney bases his practice on the idea that chaos is the basis for creativity and that out of chaos there are infinite possibilities for personal transformation, self-healing, and spiritual renewal. Through dreamwork, imagination, storytelling, multisensory imagery, visualization, and psychotherapy, he helps you cure physical and mental illness by getting to the root of fundamental disease structures. Once these fundamental structures have been discovered, you can begin the process of creating new states of consciousness.

There are usually one to four guests here at a time. Your retreat is a completely customized personal exploration. If you have two weeks, you may choose to do the River of Dreams trip, which involves whitewater rafting and camping in the wilderness along the nearby Rogue River. Free time may be spent hiking, meditating, or using the sauna. Lodging options range from rustic cabins and simply furnished lodge rooms to wooded campsites; you supply linens and bedding. During your stay you help prepare the meals, which are vegetarian, and you can do volunteer work around the center in exchange for a discount. *Aesculapia Wilderness Healing Retreat, Box 301, Wilderville, OR 97543, tel. 541/476–0492. Year-round: daily, $100; 1 wk, $550. Sign up at least 2 wks in advance.*

OREGON Breitenbush Hot Springs Retreat and Conference Center. This holistic retreat, nestled in the Willamette National Forest, is named for the natural hot springs and artesian wells that are its major attraction. Although there are many options for soaking—clothing-optional pools in an open meadow, and tubs of varying temperatures in a medicine wheel configuration—guests don't spend all their time here in the water. A 1930s lodge contains gathering rooms where classes address issues relating to self-help, holistic healing, and spiritual growth. Other offerings include yoga, tai chi, meditation, guided hikes, and yogalike spinal maintenance exercises known as EDGU. Certain other treatments cost extra: herbal wraps, massage, aromatherapy, and Reiki. Poetry readings, drumming circles, storytelling, dances, and concerts are held frequently, and a traditional sweat lodge ceremony, presented by a Native American leader, is held every month.

You may choose to take advantage of these activities on a completely unregimented personal retreat; or you may opt to sign up for one of the weekend to weeklong workshops, which cover such topics as permaculture, tarot, nutrition, shamanism, aromatherapy, art, and writing. These workshops include a full schedule of classes on these subjects, in addition to the center's daily activities.

The community is self-sustaining and very environmentally conscious; hydroelectricity and geothermal heat provide power and warmth to all the buildings, among them the natural steam sauna, the forest meditation sanctuary, and a greenhouse. The center is cooperatively owned and managed by 50 full-time residents, each highly trained in yoga instruction, massage, counseling, or other fields. Up to 120 guests stay in a lodge, 41 simply furnished cabins (some with sinks and toilets), and 10 raised-platform tents near a communal bathhouse; you supply bedding and linens. Children are welcome. *Breitenbush Hot Springs Retreat and Conference Center, Box 578, Detroit, OR 97342, tel. 503/854–3314, fax 503/854–3819. Year-round: daily, $35–$70; 3–7 day workshops, $120–$1,000. Sign up 2 months in advance for workshops, 3–4 wks in advance for personal retreats.*

HAWAII

KAUAI **Hawaiian Wellness Holiday and Metaphysical Vacation.** The objective here is to detoxify your body through rigorous exercise, massage, reflexology, chiropractic treatments, Reiki, aura balancing, and other natural therapies, as well as through a cleansing regimen involving diet and the possible use of organic laxatives and colonics. Director Dr. Grady Deal—a psychologist, massage therapist, nutritional counselor, health columnist, and practicing chiropractor—and his wife, Roberleigh—a massage therapist, yoga and aerobics instructor, numerologist, and astrologer—tailor weeklong programs for groups of 10 participants. The Metaphysical Vacation is particularly oriented towards seeking insight through sacred sites, energy vortexes, astrology, numerology, and meditation. The typical guest is between 30 and 65 and female (the ratio is three women to each man), and most want to start an exercise program in this motivational setting or are seeking major life changes because of health problems.

Here you learn to self-diagnose and treat underlying metabolic causes of health and weight problems. Instruction in yoga, aerobics, meditation, and healthy cooking fill a good portion of your day. Three weekly massage or chiropractic treatments and excursions to view Kauai's colorful flowers, inviting beaches, sparkling waterfalls, and lush valleys are also on the schedule. Housing during the program is in a hotel or condominium in the Poipu Beach area. Meals are primarily vegetarian, but fish, chicken, and eggs are served upon request. You can take advantage of the many sports available in the resort area, including tennis, golf, scuba diving, and surfing. Children are welcome and can participate in the various activities with their parents. *Hawaiian Wellness Holiday, Box 279, Koloa, Kauai, HI 96756, tel. 808/332–9244 or 800/338–6977. Year-round: 7 days, $1,995. Sign up 3–6 months in advance for winter stays, anytime for other dates.*

SOURCES

ORGANIZATIONS The **International Spa and Fitness Association** (113 Southwest St., 4th Floor, Alexandria, VA 22314, 703/838–2930) can answer most questions on spa programs and therapies.

PERIODICALS *Body, Mind, and Spirit* (Island Publishing Company, Inc., 255 Hope St., Providence, RI 02906, tel. 401/351–4320 or 800/422–2681), published bimonthly, is filled with articles on spiritual growth and natural healing; it lists conferences and gatherings around the country. *Kindred Spirit Quarterly* (Kindred Spirit Publishing, Foxhole, Dartington, Totnes, Devon TQ9 6EB, England) is a guide to personal and planetary healing. *Natural Health* (Natural Health Limited Partnership, 17 Station St., Brookline Village, MA 02147, tel. 617/232–1000) is a bimonthly publication on holistic health issues. The *New Age Journal* (42 Pleasant St., Watertown, MA 02172, tel. 617/926–0200) also bimonthly, covers a broad base, touching on holistic health, spirituality, self-awareness, and the environment; the New Age Journal's *Holistic Health Directory,* published every other year, defines healing methods, energy and movement techniques, and forms of counseling, and includes an index of resources.

BOOKS *Fodor's Healthy Escapes,* by Bernard Burt, gives thorough reviews of spas and retreats throughout the country.

ALSO SEE If spa treatments appeal to you, take a look at the Spas and Wellness Centers chapter.

Music Programs

Written by Ben Sandmel

Updated by Celestine Ware

aybe you've bought a dulcimer and need a good teacher. Or you play the saxophone and want to team up with a jazz band. Or you have studied classical guitar and want to try your hand at the blues or a musical style that simply isn't taught in your region, such as Appalachian folk music. Or you're a violinist in need of a group with which to practice your chamber music repertoire.

Then perhaps this year you should spend your vacation in one of the many music programs nationwide. They are held at prestigious music schools as well as at college campuses, conference centers, and even state parks. Some programs emphasize technical training on one instrument, such as piano, guitar, or dulcimer. Other programs address a particular musical style or tradition—the Baroque period, Celtic music, blues, or opera, for example. When the program focuses on a specific ethnic heritage or culture, there may also be classes in such associated arts as folk dancing or basketry. The cost ranges from $120 for three days up to as much as $1,500 for three weeks.

You don't have to be a professional musician, although rudimentary knowledge of an instrument is usually assumed. Most programs accept musicians of all ability levels and even have classes for beginners;

the aim is simply to provide as much playing and performance experience as possible. Usually you are placed with other players of similar experience and ability upon arrival or after an audition. Although many programs are geared to adults, several also welcome students from junior and senior high schools. Programs designed for professional musicians and aspiring professionals expect students to have a serious commitment to their studies and require an audition tape, a list of repertoire, and letters of recommendation. The atmosphere tends to be competitive.

Faculty at music camps customarily consists of professional musicians, music educators, or both. West Virginia's Augusta Heritage Center and North Carolina's Swannanoa Gathering attract master folk artists—experts on the musical traditions of certain parts of the country. Most schools give you a choice of instructors so you can learn a variety of playing styles.

Daily routines vary from program to program. Typically you spend about four hours a day in classes; these are small and focus on technique, playing styles, or learning new works. Some schools also offer master classes, group lessons led by instructors of greater than usual renown. The rest of the day may be filled with ensemble rehearsals, performance critiques, private lessons, practice, or lectures on music theory and history.

Ben Sandmel is a New Orleans–based drummer, journalist, and folklore researcher whose articles have appeared in such publications as the Atlantic Monthly, Esquire, *and* Rolling Stone. *Celestine Ware has written about music for several national magazines.*

Some programs impose a rigid daily schedule while others let you plan your own time. After dark there may be jam sessions or faculty concerts. Many programs culminate in student performances.

Consider what you want out of your vacation when selecting a program. You may not want an intensive one with classes all day and concerts at night if relaxation is what you have in mind; you might be happier being in class for only part of each day. If you're not accustomed to spending time with teens, stick to programs that accept only adults. If you want to improve your performance ability, make sure that there are performance critiques. Perhaps you've always wanted to learn about Cajun music: Try a program that not only has instrumental instruction but explores Cajun culture as well. If you want interaction with other musicians, find out if you'll have a chance to attend classes other than those in your own discipline. Some programs expect you to play with ensembles; make sure you want that kind of experience before you sign up.

No matter which you pick, you should be able to immerse yourself in practice and lessons without the distractions of friends, family, or work. Not only will you be surrounded by fellow students who are as enthusiastic about music as you, you're bound to learn new skills and repertoire that you can take back home.

CHOOSING THE RIGHT PROGRAM

The specific focus of the program is the first decision to make. If you want to study dulcimer, some programs will have immediate appeal. If jazz is your interest, you'll go for others. Beyond that, the answer to certain key questions will help you differentiate among your options.

What's the cost and what's included? Most programs have one fee for tuition and another for on-campus room and board, which is usually quite economical. For these programs, we give separate prices for tuition, which covers instruction and other program-related activities, and housing, which includes three meals a day as well as lodging based on double occupancy, unless specified differently. (When singles are available at another price, that figure is also given.) Some programs charge an all-inclusive fee (designated as "complete package") for tuition, room, and board, and unless otherwise noted, they don't offer discounts for staying or eating elsewhere. All prices are per person.

What levels of ability are accepted? Most programs accommodate beginners to advanced students. A few do not accept beginners and expect you to submit an audition tape or résumé with your application.

How are programs structured, what is the daily schedule, and how much free time is there? The answers to these questions help you determine how intense the program is. Find out how many hours are devoted to formal instruction and rehearsal and ask about the length of breaks between classes. Some programs keep you very busy for as many as 15 hours a day, with only short breaks for meals; others occupy you merely most of the morning and afternoon and leave plenty of time for relaxation. Programs that accept teenagers as well as adults plan many activities to keep students amused. The important thing is to know in advance how strict a daily schedule you're expected to follow.

What is the relative importance of performance vis-à-vis technique in the program? Some programs put a lot of weight on technique; others emphasize performance; and still others fall somewhere in between. Make sure that the program's emphasis is right for you.

What are the teachers' qualifications? Make sure that they are credible and that the instructors have the background to teach you what you want to learn. Remember too that personal style is often as important as virtuosity or even teaching experience. Regardless of the teacher's credentials, if you don't like the way you're taught, you won't enjoy learning. If possible, try to talk to the instructor ahead of time to make sure your questions are answered and you are comfortable.

How large are the classes and what is the student-to-teacher ratio? The actual "classes" you'll be in can range from private lessons to orchestra rehearsals, with most workshops falling in the 10- to 20-student range. What's important is to find out how much personal attention you're likely to get. Sometimes larger classes have several instructors, so the number of students per teacher is still relatively small. Look for a program with a low student-to-faculty ratio—between 5:1 and 12:1 is typical.

Are private lessons available? Is the cost included in the program fee or must you pay extra? Several programs offer individual instruction, and it may or may not be included in the fee. If it is, you may get only a specified number of lessons or be left to your own devices to make the arrangements—to get private time with an instructor, it may be up to you to persuade someone. When private lessons cost extra, the fee may be under $10 an hour—or it may be more like what you're used to at home, perhaps $45 or $50 an hour.

How much interaction is there between students and teachers? Associating with professionals in the field is part of the learning experience. Yours will be much richer if you spend time with instructors at meals and in casual jam sessions as well as in class.

What are the accommodations like? Most programs provide sparsely furnished double dormitory rooms with shared baths; a few have singles, which may or may not cost extra. (If you stay in a double room, you are generally paired with a roommate if you don't bring your own.) Ask about air-conditioning. If it's not available or if you want more privacy or more comfort than a dorm affords, you may want to consider lodging in a nearby hotel or B&B. In fact, many programs can help you find suitable

off-campus quarters. In dorms, linens are usually provided, but not always; you may have to bring your own pillows, sheets, blankets, towels, and a fan.

What is the food like? Most programs offer typical cafeteria fare: sandwiches, fresh fruit, a salad bar, and a choice of hot entrées at dinner. If this doesn't sound good to you, make sure that there are appealing restaurants nearby.

Do I need to bring an instrument or is one provided? Most programs expect you to bring your own instrument, at least the portable ones. Pianos, harpsichords, and organs are usually provided, as are some of the more exotic instruments you might want to try out. If, on the other hand, you'd like to study a small and conventional instrument and you don't have one, you have to consider renting one on your own. Many programs do have a few instruments of every type on hand, however, and lend them on a first-come, first-served basis.

How far in advance do I need to book? Most programs expect you to sign up one to four months in advance. But if you make your plans late, there's always a chance of a last-minute cancellation.

How long has the program been in operation? If the program is new, ask about the qualifications and experience of the people in charge. Make sure that the program seems well conceived and well organized.

Does the program provide references from past students? To clarify your impressions about instruction, food, and lodging, it always helps to talk with someone who has studied with the teachers, slept in the beds, and eaten the meals.

What facilities and activities are available for your nonmusical traveling companions? Because the intensive nature of music programs leaves very little free time, students don't usually bring their families along. If you'd like to, however, it's certainly possible, though some programs are better than others. Those held at resorts or vacation areas with a lot of recreational opportunities are your best bet. Ask what housing arrangements can be made or whether recreational facilities are available to your companions.

FAVORITE PROGRAMS

THE MID-ATLANTIC

WEST VIRGINIA **Augusta Heritage Center.** Elkins, a small mountain town (pop. 8,000) near the Monongahela National Forest in east-central West Virginia, is the site of the United States' largest and most comprehensive folk music education program, which was established in 1972. The theme-week offerings are probably the most popular part of this program. They are offered for one week around mid-April, then for five weeks from early July to mid-August, and a week occurring between mid- and late October. At those times, you can take your pick of several five- to seven-day theme sessions, devoted to bluegrass, blues, swing music, singing, or dulcimer, Appalachian Mountain, Cajun/Creole, and Irish music.

Sessions focusing on a particular theme provide you with a wide selection of courses. Bluegrass week offers eight instrument courses, for instance. Every morning, you meet in small groups of 12 to 15 for instrumental instruction; afternoons, you work with students in other classes as part of a bluegrass band. All students enrolled for the week convene periodically for meetings with master artists and workshops in harmony and bluegrass history. In addition, you can sign up for one of the 90-minute miniclasses that meet four times during the week; miniclasses mostly cover the same topics available in the morning but explore them more intensively. In July and August, there are also five-day classes concentrating on specific instruments, including Autoharp, banjo, fiddle, guitar, hammered and mountain dulcimer, piano, and piano accordion; in addition, there are five-day workshops in Celtic band, contra dance piano, group playing, and old-time string band. You must bring your own instrument.

For the five-day instrument sessions, you register for one course per week, which usually meets Monday through Friday for four to seven hours daily. Classes are available for beginning, intermediate, and advanced students and are kept small, averaging 12 students per teacher. In most cases, you spend your days with one instructor in intensive group sessions that usually concentrate on technique, playing styles, and repertoire, but some classes spend less time in group sessions to allow for practice.

Second only to the theme weeks in popularity is Old Time Week, held in October. This is a week devoted to the musical traditions of West Virginia: Appalachian, fiddle, banjo, guitar, Appalachian singing, and mandolin are among its sessions. Most Augusta Heritage Center students come in summer, and each week there are about 400 participants representing a range of backgrounds, ages, and interests. All instructors are accomplished musicians, and some are designated by the program as master folk artists, experts in traditional folk music who have devoted most of their lives to preserving the music from a particular culture. Some instructors are outstanding artists who are little known outside their own communities.

Classes are held on the wooded, 170-acre campus of Davis & Elkins College, a small private liberal arts institution. In summer, you stay in double dormitory rooms with no private baths or air-conditioning; housing for the spring and fall weeks is in a nearby motel. Typical cafeteria fare is provided in the college dining hall. Alternatively, you may choose to eat at one of the many restaurants in town or to stay nearby in an inexpensive bed-and-breakfast or motel.

After dark, you're surrounded by musical activities—impromptu recitals by students and instructors, concerts by master folk artists, and continuous jam sessions. There are also storytelling evenings, slide shows on crafts, and dance performances. Or you can simply join classmates for conversation at the pub or at the no-smoking, no-alcohol coffeehouse. You're free to use the college tennis courts, swimming pool, fitness trail, and Nautilus weight machines, and there is canoeing, white-water rafting, and hiking in the surrounding forests. In summer, simultaneously with its music offerings, the center also sponsors Elderhostel programs, folk arts classes for youngsters ages 8 to 12, and classes in dance, folklore, and arts and crafts. *Augusta Heritage Center, Davis & Elkins College, 100 Campus Dr., Elkins, WV 26241, tel. 304/637–1209, fax 304/637–1317. Mid-Apr.–late Aug. and early Oct.: 5 days, tuition $220–$240, housing $140 in spring and fall, $160 in summer. Spring and fall housing price does not include meals ($50–$85 for cafeteria meal ticket); sign up 6 wks in advance. Free catalogs are available on request. See also chapter on Arts and Crafts Workshops.*

THE SOUTH

NORTH CAROLINA **The Swannanoa Gathering.** This organization, founded in 1992, focuses on traditional folk music during five separate seven-day programs. Sessions are held in July and August on the campus of Warren Wilson College, which borders 600 acres of forested mountains, 15 minutes from the town of Asheville. Most courses incorporate instrumental and vocal instruction at beginning to advanced levels and deal with a particular musical heritage or style. Instructors come from around the world and are experts in their fields; many of them teach, perform, and record regularly. Classes are limited to 20 students per teacher, and no more than 100 students are enrolled each week.

Celtic Week brings together traditional Scottish and Irish music and folklore with classes in such instruments as fiddle, *bodhrán* (a large, tambourine-like drum), bouzouki, tin whistle, *uilleann* pipes (an Irish bagpipe, in which air is pumped with the arm rather than blown), accordion, concertina, harp, guitar, and hammered dulcimer. You can also study traditional Irish songwriting, Scottish folklore and folk song, and Scottish folk dancing.

The gathering's most popular program, the Old-Time Music and Dance Week, investigates the music, singing, dance, and storytelling of the southern Appalachians via more than two dozen courses. Singers can study southern Appalachian singing, unaccompanied singing, and shaped-note spirituals, for example. Instrumentalists can sign up for everything from beginning, intermediate, and advanced old-time fiddle, guitar, banjo, and string band to Appalachian longbow fiddle, mandolin, Autoharp, hammered and mountain dulcimer, string bass, and more. Clogging, buck dancing, and square and contra dancing are also on the schedule. A children's program, which runs concurrently and is open to youngsters ages 6 to 12, includes classes in storytelling, music, and dance ($65 per child).

Mountain Dulcimer Week gives you the chance to learn from some of the top players from around the country. To expose you to several playing styles, each day's afternoon session has a different teacher.

During Contemporary Folk Week, a series of workshops aimed at folk performers, there are classes in songwriting, performance, singing, and sound reinforcement and recording. The faculty critiques your work, coaches you on how to become a more confident performer, stages panel discussions on business matters, shares their knowledge of the recording industry, and provides tips on getting your music published.

Most students sign up for one or two courses in the program they're attending. Things get going on Sunday with supper, an orientation session, and socializing. From Monday through Friday, you spend most of your mornings and afternoons in classes, which last 45 to 90 minutes each. You may also meet with your instructor in the evening for performance critiques, rehearsals, or jam sessions. Other evenings bring concerts by instructors, dances, and open mike nights, followed by jam sessions. You're expected to bring your own instrument, although some are available to rent.

To foster a sense of community, the program's directors encourage students to lodge on campus in the dorms' double rooms. (The nearest alternative accommodations are 15 minutes away in Asheville.) Meals are served buffet-style in the college student center.

During free time, you can use the campus gym, aquatic center, tennis courts, and nature trails; explore its working farm; and make a kayak run on Swannanoa River. Off campus, you may visit the Biltmore Estate (*see* Plantation Gardens and the Blue Ridge in the Garden Tours chapter), Pisgah National Forest, Great Smoky Mountains National Park, and other area attractions. *The Swannanoa Gathering, Warren Wilson College, Box 9000, Asheville, NC 28815-9000, tel. 704/298–3325, ext. 426, fax 704/299–3326. Early July–early Aug.: 7 days, tuition $275, room and board $195. No age restrictions. Sign up 4 months in advance. Swannanoa's newsletter comes out in autumn, its catalog, in early spring.*

THE MIDWEST

INDIANA **Indiana University School of Music.** The 1,860-acre campus of Indiana University is located in lively, sprawling Bloomington (pop. 80,000), in the hilly southern half of the state. Its School of Music has long been considered one of the country's best and is especially famous for its opera and vocal program. From June through August, it opens its doors to students, teachers, advanced amateurs, and professionals for intensive 4- to 12-day workshops devoted to such topics as solo piano literature, chamber music, early music and opera performance, natural horn, fortepiano, recorder, and violin. The early music performance, natural horn, and fortepiano workshops run simultaneously

to allow students in all three classes to work together. Three three-day opera master classes are held consecutively, so you can elect to stay for more than one of them to expose yourself to different teaching styles. If you play regularly with an ensemble, you can apply together for certain workshops.

Instructors include some of the most distinguished and most widely respected musicians and professors of music in the United States. In past years, pianist Menahem Pressler, cellist Janos Starker, pianist Evlyne Brancart, violist and string director Mimi Zweig, conductor and vocals director Joan Dornemann, master class and opera teacher Sherrill Milnes, singer and diction coach Nico Castel, vocals teacher Virginia Zeani, and natural horn and early music instructor Richard Seraphinoff joined the school's summer faculty.

Each day, you have about eight hours of master classes, lectures on music theory and technique, sessions to demonstrate and build on your repertoire, ensemble rehearsals, and/or private lessons (for no additional charge). Most classes meet all day, and there may be mandatory performances to attend at night. Each class contains approximately 20 performing students as well as auditors, who may attend for a reduced fee. Some courses require prospective students to submit audition tapes or a list of repertoire they expect to perform. The university has a few instruments to lend.

Indiana University's School of Music complex encompasses four buildings with more than 110 offices and studios; 260 practice rooms, including 80 soundproofed rooms in a separate practice building; three recital halls; two libraries, the new state-of-the-art Simon Center for Music, all of whose sound recordings are digitized and computerized so that any of the Simon Center's recordings may be heard at a given outlet. Their other library has more than 380,000 books, scores, and periodicals as well as some 160,000 recordings. The 1,500-seat

Musical Arts Center offers musical performances, many of them part of the university summer concert series, in which faculty members perform.

Although you may want to lodge in a hotel—a good option for couples and families—individuals find it most convenient to stay in one of the university dorms, which cost about $28 a night for a single. (For families, a space might be made in family housing on campus by arrangement.) You can sign up for the meal plan, which allows you to eat breakfast, lunch, and dinner in the dorm's cafeteria. Or you can eat in off-campus restaurants—everything from fast-food chains to one-of-a-kind vegetarian spots.

During free time, depending on your mood, you can visit the university art museum or sharpen your game at the campus billiards room. Also available are bowling lanes, running tracks, indoor and outdoor pools, golf course, or tennis, squash, racquetball, and basketball courts. *Indiana University School of Music, Office of Special Programs, Merrill Hall 121, Bloomington, IN 47405-2200, tel. 812/855–6025, fax 812/855–4936. June 10– mid-Aug.: 4–12 days, tuition $200–$600, housing $108–$324. Housing price does not include meals ($16 a day for cafeteria meal ticket); sign up 6 wks in advance.*

KANSAS **Great Plains Jazz Camp.** This five-day June program is an ideal place to get improvisational experience as well as take master classes in your instrument. You're surrounded by jazz in many different styles, ranging from bebop to fusion, and most of your time is spent playing and interacting with others with a passion for jazz. The teachers are leaders in their field, several of them professional musicians who have performed with premier jazz bands.

On Sunday night after an audition, you're assigned both to a jazz combo of between five and eight musicians, based on your improvisational skills, and to one of four or five big bands of about 20 players each. From Monday through Thursday, you practice with your combo for two-and-a-half

hours and with your big band for two hours, both times under the guidance of an instructor. Then, between 2 and 3:30, there are master classes dealing with each instrument's basics, complexities, and techniques, and information about its past and present masters. Class size varies, depending on the number of participants with a particular instrument when you attend. All of this occupies you between 8:30 AM and 3:30 in the afternoon. After that, your time is free to practice, jam, and work in the camp's computerized MIDI (musical instrument digital interface) system, which allows you to compose a piece, score it to as many instruments as you want, and play it back right away—without having to round up six or seven other players to perform it. This is also the time that students rendezvous for private time with instructors who are willing to share their expertise with students who go to the trouble to seek it out. In the evening there are faculty concerts. Although most of the 78 to 85 campers who sign up every year are high school and college students, participants range in age from 12 to 67, and the program is open to students of all levels.

The site is 200-acre Emporia State University, located in the town of Emporia (pop. 25,000), surrounded by prairie and historic ranches in the Flint Hills, 50 miles east of Topeka and 100 miles west of Kansas City. You stay in modern, air-conditioned dorms in standard single or double rooms; there are chain motels and bed-and-breakfasts in town. All meals are served cafeteria-style in the student union cafeteria, which overlooks the campus lake, and the fare is strictly institutional. Alternative choices include the comfortable faculty restaurant and various local eateries. You have access to the campus athletic facilities, including a pool, weight room, and racquetball courts. *Great Plains Jazz Camp, c/o Dr. Alan Kinsey, Emporia State University, Division of Music, Box 4029, Emporia State University, 1200 Commercial, Emporia, KS 66801-5087, tel. 316/341–5431, fax 316/341–5681. Mid-June: 5 days, tuition $133;*

tuition, room, and board, double occupancy, $225; tuition, room, and board, single occupancy, $245. Registration deadline, May 17. There are 10 $50 talent-based scholarship awards available. Scholarship registration must be accompanied by audition tape: deadline April 19.

MISSOURI **The Heartland Dulcimer Camp.** Instructors at this six-day July program, which was established by internationally known dulcimer expert Esther Kreek in 1993, have a high profile in the dulcimer world: Texan Linda Lowe Thompson and Virginian Madeline MacNeil contribute regularly to *Dulcimer Player News,* Janita Baker builds dulcimers and guitars, and all have taught at various workshops and universities around the country. To give students the greatest possible contact with teachers, Ms. Kreek abides by the philosophy that less is more and restricts admission to 75—five classes of 15 each. You can study hammered and mountain dulcimer, Autoharp, and accompanying vocals. Although the program is open to players of all levels of ability, you do need your own instrument.

Most of each day is devoted to instruction. Morning sessions last two and a half hours. Beginners learn tuning, left- and right-hand techniques, chord and harmony positions, and how to play simple tunes. Intermediate and advanced classes cover such topics as group playing, solo improvisation, tuning variations, embellishing, and arranging and adapting. Subjects that aren't covered in the morning are considered during 90-minute afternoon classes, which are taught by other teachers to expose you to alternative playing styles. Afterward, you can practice or relax.

The small size of the program allows time for private, 15- to 30-minute afternoon help sessions for those who need it. The cost of these is included in your tuition. In the evening, concerts showcase the talents of students or instructors; there's also a get-acquainted dance.

The program takes place at a large Presbyterian conference and retreat center, built in 1989 on 316 rolling acres near the Missouri River, 20 miles from Kansas City. A youth camp is held concurrently on a portion of the grounds. Accommodations are in two home-style lodges, which are air-conditioned—welcome, since summer temperatures soar into the 90s—or, when those fill up, in a dorm-style building with fans. Usually two people share a room with bath, but a very limited number of singles are available on a first-come, first-served basis at no extra cost. Lasagna, baked ham, and other hearty fare are served on the premises. For still other culinary options, you can make the easy drive to Kansas City. You can also ride horses ($9 per hour), go swimming in a pool ($2.50 per 90 minutes), hike, or play volleyball or basketball. *Heartland Dulcimer Camp, c/o Esther Kreek, 1156 W. 103rd St., Kansas City, MO 64114, tel. 816/942–6233, fax 816/941–9068. Late July: 6 days, tuition $135 up to mid-June, $150 afterward; room, board, and tuition $305 up to June 15, $325 afterward. Age 16 and over. Sign up 3 months in advance.*

NORTH DAKOTA **International Music Camp.** This June and July camp began in 1956 as an educational summer retreat for high school band and choir students. Today it is open to adults, too, and its two dozen classes cover art and dance as well as music at all levels. You can choose from seven separate seven-day music sessions that focus on piano, guitar, piping and drumming, band, jazz and stage band, orchestra, vibes and marimba, handbells, or choir and show choir. All programs follow a rigorous schedule with about 11 hours out of each day in ensemble rehearsals, classes in music theory and technique, repertoire reviews, private lessons (at an extra $7.50 per lesson), and master classes set up to improve your performance and instrumental techniques. The faculty, recruited mainly from area universities, is made up of experienced musicians and teachers; there are only about 12 students per class. All instruction culminates in student performances at the end of the week.

You're housed in double rooms in modern dormitories, one for young men and another for young women; another dorm is reserved for adults. No singles are available, and bathrooms are communal. Married couples are not allowed to stay together. A few cabins for four, furnished with bunk beds or cots to sleep two to a room, are an option during some weeks. Built in the 1940s, these cabins lack the modern amenities of the dorms, but they do have private baths and are quieter, since they're a mile away from the classrooms. You can also camp nearby, though there's no reduction in price for campers. Three cafeteria-style meals of typical institutional fare—meat and potatoes, burgers, pizza—are served daily.

The camp convenes at the 2,300-acre International Peace Garden, on the border of North Dakota and Manitoba, roughly the geographical center of North America. There's hiking, volleyball, soccer, and swimming in the area, but your schedule doesn't leave much time for it. Taps is played at 10:30 PM (and the younger students do tend to retire then); reveille is at 7 AM for all. *International Music Camp, winter address, 1725 11th St. SW, Minot, ND 58701, tel. and fax 701/838–8472; during June and July, RR 1, Box 116A, Dunseith, ND 58329, tel. 701/263–4211, fax 701/ 263–4212. June–July: 7 days, room, board, and tuition, $185–$205. Private lessons cost an additional fee. Sign up 4 months in advance. Free catalog available upon request.*

OHIO **Baroque Performance Institute (BPI).** From mid-June to early July, as part of its year-round schedule of high-quality classical music training, the prestigious Oberlin Conservatory of Music sponsors an intensive two-week event concentrating on Baroque music for voice, flauto traverso, recorder, oboe, bassoon, harpsichord, organ, fortepiano, violin, viola, cello, and treble, tenor, and bass viol. Students of all ages and skill levels may enroll; about 110 sign up annually. In addition to daily master classes, the program includes sessions that help refine performance skills, provide coaching for chamber music ensembles, and give the opportunity to play in a baroque orchestra. The program fills your time for about eight hours a day, and there are optional lectures and concerts at night.

The faculty consists of 18 distinguished Baroque specialists from around the country and the world. The four-member Oberlin Baroque Ensemble is also in residence during the program. Each summer, BPI also invites a guest artist; in 1994, Christopher Hogwood, director of the Academy of Ancient Music, conducted BPI students in a performance of Purcell's *Dido and Aeneas.*

In addition to classes, which are limited to 10 to 15 students, BPI schedules faculty concerts, student recitals, lectures, and other events. Private lessons are available ($40 per 45 minutes). You have access to the resources of the Oberlin Conservatory of Music, including its extensive library and its 25 studios for private lessons, 10 classrooms, 150 practice rooms, and two performance halls. Several baroque instruments are available for loan, and there is a large collection of harpsichords, organs, and fortepianos for student use.

The Oberlin Conservatory of Music is in the northeast part of the state 30 minutes from Cleveland's Hopkins International Airport and 40 minutes from downtown Cleveland. You can lodge in standard single or double rooms in a newly restored Victorian dorm across from the conservatory or in local houses off campus (BPI can provide a list of landlords). Most students choose to cook on their own, either in their off-campus home or the dorm's cooking facilities, or to eat at any of the varied restaurants in the surrounding blocks, from fast-food places and diners to fancy bistros. However, you may also purchase rather average meals at the campus cafeteria. Rural Oberlin is easy to get around on foot or on a bicycle. Other conservatory summer programs, which run for one to two weeks each, are in flute, piano, vocal performance and pedagogy, electronic and computer music, and stringed instrument restoration.

Baroque Performance Institute, Conservatory of Music, Oberlin College, 77 W. College Street, Oberlin, OH 44074-1588, tel. 216/775–8044, fax 216/775–8942. Mid-June–early July: tuition $350 for 7 days, $660 for 15, housing $95 a week ($130 for a single). Housing prices do not include meals ($19 a day for cafeteria meal ticket); sign up 1–2 months in advance, May 15 deadline.

THE ROCKIES

COLORADO **Mile High Jazz Camp.** Many of the 25 instructors at this six-day July program at the University of Colorado at Boulder are regulars in America's leading jazz ensembles. About 100 professional musicians, music teachers, and students from junior high school to college come from all over the world to study with them every year. If you want more experience playing with jazz combos and big bands, this is the place for you. It was founded in 1985 and is still under the direction of two noted jazz educators with considerable bandstand experience, Bob Montgomery and Dr. Willie L. Hill.

You can take classes, which are all small, in trumpet, trombone, guitar, piano, drums, bass, and alto, tenor, and baritone saxophone. (Bring your own instrument.) At the beginning of the week you audition, so your skill level can be determined. Then from Tuesday through Friday, you spend about five hours a day in jazz improvisation sessions, jazz combo and band rehearsals, and master classes. From late afternoon until dinner, you're free to practice or relax. In the evening, there are faculty concerts. The week ends on Saturday with five and a half hours of student performances.

Students stay in standard double rooms in a dorm on the 600-acre campus, which is at the base of the Rocky Mountains. Three meals a day in the dorm's cafeteria are included. You have access to the College of Music's state-of-the-art facilities, which consist of a two-building complex encompassing 84 practice rooms and four performance spaces. Boulder, a short drive from Denver, is a cosmopolitan college town with a number of good restaurants and plenty of cultural activity. The mountains are nearby, and there's lots of hiking, fishing, and other outdoor activities. *Mile High Jazz Camp, c/o Dr. Willie Hill, University of Colorado at Boulder, College of Music, Campus Box 301, Boulder, CO 80309-0301, tel. 303/492–6352, fax 303/492–5619. Mid-July: 6 days, tuition $210, room and board $175. Sign up by May 1.*

IDAHO **Schweitzer Institute of Music.** Part of the Festival of Sandpoint, a summer-long outdoor music festival held in the northern Idaho mountain resort of Sandpoint, this three-week July and August program is designed for advanced students and young professionals, 18 to mid-30s, who come to study musical masterpieces in an environment emphasizing art over commerce. The Schweitzer Institute includes intensive seminars, critiques, rehearsals, and performances. Although the four courses—conducting, composition, chamber music, and jazz—are not interactive, a few group performances and many social occasions enable you to meet students in other programs and expose yourself to a variety of musical disciplines.

The institute was founded in 1985 by composer and conductor Gunther Schuller, the former director of the Berkshire Music Institute at Tanglewood. Winner of the 1994 Pulitzer Prize for Music Literature, he has some 50 years' experience as conductor, composer, performer, educator, and music journalist. The instructors are experienced teachers and professional musicians who have received numerous awards for their work. Recently they included Donald Erb, composition; Young-Nam Kim, chamber music and violin; Allan Vogel, woodwinds; George Garzone, jazz and tenor sax; Kenny Werner, jazz and piano; Edwin Schuller, jazz and bass.

You are typically in class six hours a day, from 9 to noon and 2 to 5 for all but jazz students, who, because of late-night performances, attend from 2 to 5 and 7 to 10 PM. Class time may be used for rehearsals.

The conducting program, which is limited to 20 participants ages 18 to mid-30s, is taught by Schuller himself. There are intensive seminars plus critiques of conductors' work, rehearsals, and performances. At the end of the program, up to five students share the baton in a concert.

The jazz program, which is limited to 25 students with four instructors, concentrates on techniques of jazz performance but also exposes you to jazz history and criticism. You practice improvising during performances and play both established works and new material by institute students and faculty.

The Resident Contemporary Chamber Music Ensemble accepts eight musicians, one each in piano, flute, clarinet, and horn and takes a string quartet as a group. Instructors provide intensive coaching sessions and master classes; there's also plenty of rehearsal time.

Students in the composition program—only seven are accepted—study in private lessons and seminars. Each participant will have a chamber music composition performed in a public concert. Pianos are provided for each student in composition.

There isn't much leisure time, because even when you aren't in class or rehearsing, you may be playing at a local restaurant for an hour or two or attending a mandatory concert. Part of the program involves observing performances of the Spokane Symphony Orchestra, as well as of leading jazz, blues, country, pop, and rock musicians. Weekends are a bit less busy, and you may want to take advantage of hiking trails; bike rentals; and Lake Pend Oreille, the second-largest freshwater lake west of the Mississippi.

Each year about 50 to 75 students attend the Schweitzer Institute's programs, which run concurrently. You're expected to submit a résumé and an audition tape with your

application as well as letters of reference; applicants to the conducting program must furnish a videotape, and composers must submit a written score. You are encouraged to send letters of recommendation.

The program venue is beautiful Schweitzer Mountain Ski Resort, which overlooks Lake Pend Oreille at 6,000 feet in the Rocky Mountains. Along with a cluster of condos, the complex has a hotel, where you stay in double rooms, though some singles are available (at an extra cost) to the first who request them. Three cafeteria-style meals are served daily, and plans for restaurant-catered meals are under way. Pianos and other large instruments are provided, but smaller instruments should be brought with you. *Festival at Sandpoint, Schweitzer Institute of Music, Box 695, Sandpoint, ID 83864, tel. 208/265–4554, fax 208/263–6858. Late July–mid-Aug.: 21 days, tuition, room, and board $1,600–$1,800. The Festival at Sandpoint has limited scholarship support available for students in the jazz and chamber programs. Application deadline April 30.*

WYOMING **Yellowstone Jazz Camps.** This July camp in the Absaroka Range of the Rockies, not far from Yellowstone National Park, consists of two separate six-day workshops, one devoted to vocal jazz and the other to instrumental, including bass, drums, saxophone, trumpet, piano, guitar, and trombone. Both are open to adults as well as high school and college students at all skill levels. Up to 55 students and 11 or so faculty members attend the instrumental jazz week, 40 students and eight instructors at the vocal week. Teachers have university-teaching or performance experience.

Both the instrumental and vocal weeks fill your time from 8:30 to 5 every day. The instrumental week starts with an audition and theory test, after which you're placed in a big band of 15 to 17 musicians and a combo of five to seven. Most mornings begin with sessions on music theory and improvisation and rehearsals of the various big bands and combos. Afternoons, faculty members give master classes and private lessons ($10 extra per 30 minutes). You're expected to bring your own instrument.

During the vocal week, you spend private time working with an instructor on an arrangement that you will perform solo, with a professional rhythm section, at the student concert. You also practice with a large group of 8 to 12 and a smaller group of 5 to 8 singers; you perform with both at a final concert in Cody. There are also listening classes that train your ear to hear different jazz styles and teach you about the important singers in various jazz traditions.

Evenings find students and instructors taking part in concerts, jam sessions, and clinics, which consist of impromptu discussions about influences, theory, styles, and personal experiences. Both weeks prepare you to perform at a Friday afternoon concert at the Yellowstone Jazz Festival, held in nearby Cody.

The venue, Northwest College's remote mountain retreat, is at an elevation of 8,000 feet and is surrounded by woods and meadows. A short walk yields a great view of Yellowstone. The main lodge has large rehearsal rooms, the camp dining room, a main room with a fireplace, and communal bathing facilities. Adjoining this building are 12 modern cabins, each of which sleeps six (in one room) and is heated by a wood stove. If you'd prefer more privacy, you can pitch your tent or park your RV on-site. Meals are prepared by a family who live in a nearby cottage and have been cooking at the camp ever since the program began back in 1987. The family-style meals typically include pancakes or waffles and sausage for breakfast, soup and sandwiches for lunch, and hamburgers or chicken and baked potatoes for dinner.

In their brief free time, most students focus on outdoor recreation: fishing, riding, hiking, Ping-Pong, volleyball, horseshoes, softball, and the like. *Yellowstone Jazz Camp, c/o Neil Hansen, Northwest College, 231 W. 6th St., Powell, WY 82435, tel. 307/754–6307, fax 307/754–6700. Mid-July: 6 days, tuition $270, room and board $95. Sign up 3 months in advance.*

THE WEST COAST

WASHINGTON **Centrum Music Workshops.** Centrum, a nonprofit center for the arts and creative education, sponsors three exceptional weeklong summer music programs on the grounds of 445-acre Fort Worden State Park. The park is at the tip of the Olympic Peninsula, 2 miles from downtown Port Townsend (pop. 7,000), a town full of restored Victorian-style buildings, on the banks of Puget Sound.

The seven-day mid-June Port Townsend Country Blues Workshop is designed for students of traditional acoustic blues. The faculty includes masters of America's blues traditions, several of them recipients of NEA National Heritage Awards given to artists perceived as outstanding contributors to America's cultural endowment. Instructors from past years have included Howard Armstrong, a multi-instrumentalist proficient on 24 stringed instruments and an original member of the Tennessee Chocolate Drops, a 1920s performance troupe; harmonica player Phil Wiggins; and John Jackson, a guitarist specializing in Piedmont rags and reels. You come into close contact with these instructors while working on technical musicianship. Instruction is offered in guitar, harmonica, vocals, fiddle, and mandolin.

In a typical year, slightly more than 150 students are taught by a dozen or so instructors, some of whom are part of groups or combos that teach collaboratively. Classes of varying sizes are open to musicians at all levels; beginning guitarists are expected to have a rudimentary knowledge of the instrument.

During the week, there are 1¼-hour classes in morning and afternoon sessions. In the morning, you usually attend two group classes, where the emphasis is on playing a particular instrument as you learn new techniques and songs. Each day you build upon skills you've learned the day before. Afternoon classes are often more spontaneous. They are taught by two or more faculty members who may not have played together before and may or may not have even decided exactly what to teach. Instead they collaborate on and improvise a lesson as they go. Evenings, there are jam sessions, dances, parties, films, and student concerts. The workshop culminates at the Port Townsend Blues Festival with three faculty concerts.

The eight-day Festival of American Fiddle Tunes Workshop, which had its 20th anniversary in 1996, is also taught by expert musicians from around the United States. Recent instructors have included Melvin Wine, Kenny Baker, and Armin Barnett. The workshop—open not only to fiddlers but also to pianists, accordionists, and banjo and mandolin players at all levels of experience—exposes you to a variety of regional fiddling styles. Nearly 300 students were taught by 25 instructors in a recent year, and, as for the blues workshop, some of these "instructors" are groups or duos. Also as in the blues workshop, classes last an hour and 15 minutes and vary in size. In the morning, you take two group lessons that focus on teaching new tunes and introducing Cajun, bluegrass, old-time country, and French-Canadian fiddling. Afternoons are spent in tutorials in technique for beginners and intermediates and rehearsals of the several faculty-led bands, which perform at a Friday night dance and a Saturday morning concert. On other evenings, you can jam with fellow students and faculty members, attend faculty concerts, and dance to your heart's content.

The intensive eight-day Bud Shank Jazz Workshop, led by alto saxophonist Bud Shank, is one of the nation's premier summer workshops. This is due to the artistic stature of the dozen-odd faculty, which recently included trumpeter Bobby Shew, pianist George Cables, vocalists Jay Clayton and Jessica Williams, baritone saxophonist Bill Ramsay, tenor saxophonist Don Lanphere, drummer Jeff Hamilton, and guitarist John Stowall, as well as performers J. J. Johnson and Marlena Shaw. Equally noteworthy is the caliber of the program's students—about 250 amateur, collegiate, and professional trumpeters, trombonists, vocalists, pianists, bassists, guitarists, drummers, and baritone, tenor, and alto saxophonists between the ages of 15 to 70 from around the world. The program is geared to players with intermediate to advanced skills, and you're expected to have a basic technical command of your instrument as well as improvisation experience or a basic knowledge of music theory. With your application, you're required to submit a résumé detailing your musical education and performance background. Applicants under 18 must also submit an audition tape.

The workshop has you making music all week long. On the Sunday before classes begin, an audition puts you in one of several five- to eight-player combos based on your skill. Then, from Monday through Friday, you start the day with a 90-minute combo rehearsal and an hour-long class in music theory and improvisation. In the afternoon, there are one-hour master classes, in lecture and demonstration format, in which you are instructed on a particular instrument or style of vocals, as well as further 90-minute combo rehearsals and 45-minute faculty lectures and demonstrations followed by informal faculty concerts. Evenings bring hour-long arranging or jazz history classes and big-band rehearsals. The week ends with one of the West Coast's most prominent music festivals, Jazz Port Townsend, which showcases the talents of workshop faculty and visiting artists.

During these and other Centrum music programs, you stay on the Fort Worden park grounds in single or double dormitory rooms, some of which have an ocean view. Rooms are assigned in order of registration, so if you sign up late, you may not get a view or a single (which here costs the same as a double). You can opt for two or three meals a day, mostly typical cafeteria fare, in Fort Worden's cafeteria. There are also motels, hotels, inns and bed-and-breakfasts, and campgrounds in the area.

Fort Worden State Park has views of the San Juan Islands and two mountain ranges as well as saltwater beaches, ponds, wooded hills with trails, and old military fortifications. Nearby there's also hiking, sailing, kayaking, tennis, scuba-diving, and bicycling; 40 miles away is Olympic National Park. In addition, Port Townsend is full of restaurants, galleries, and crafts shops. *Centrum, Box 1158, Port Townsend, WA 98368, tel. 360/385–3102 or 800/733–3608, fax 206/385–2470. Last wk of June, early July, late July: 7–8 days, tuition $225–$395, housing $165–$195 with 2 meals daily, or $200–$225 with 3. Sign up 9–10 wks in advance.*

SOURCES

ORGANIZATIONS The well-established **International Association of Jazz Educators, IAJE,** (Box 724, Manhattan, KS 66502, tel. 913/776–8744) is devoted to career training for both jazz educators and professional performers. At its annual conference, the association offers seminars, clinics, and workshops on such subjects as rhythm or scatting, and it sponsors the presentation of research papers. IAJE is also the publisher of the *Jazz Educators Journal.*

PERIODICALS The bimonthly *Jazz Educators Journal* is a prime source of information on activities sponsored by its parent association and also those of other jazz organizations. Each March the journal publishes a list of summer music camps and programs. The long-established jazz publication *downbeat* (102 Haven Rd., Elmhurst, IL 60126, tel. 708/941–2030) is a good place to look for listings of jazz study programs and news in the field. *The Instrumentalist,* (200 Northfield Rd., Northfield, IL 60093, tel. 847/446–5000), a monthly magazine for school band and school orchestra directors, is another publication to check for announcements of music activities and programs.

The best source of information on folk and ethnic music programs is the magazine *Sing Out!* (512 E. 4th St., Bethlehem, PA 18015, tel. 610/865–5366). *Dirty Linen* (Box 66600, Baltimore, MD 21239, tel. 410/583–7973) is also a fine periodical in the folk and world music field.

For classical music programs, consult *Strings* magazine (Box 767, San Anselmo, CA 94979, tel. 415/485–6946), especially its Summer Study Guide. Although *Strings* concentrates on the violin and viola, it offers informed access to the classical world in general. *Piano & Keyboard,* which has a new publisher, (Sparrow Hawk Press, Box 2626, San Anselmo, CA 94979 tel. 415/458–8672) takes as its subjects piano, organ, and electric keyboards. It publishes information on classical music and jazz camps and programs. Listings of classical music camps and programs are also available in *The Instrumentalist* (*see above*).

ALSO SEE If melodies and harmonies are your passion, only a music camp will do. But there are other ways to express your creativity: See the chapters on Arts and Crafts Workshops, Painting Workshops, Photography Workshops and Tours, and Writing Conferences and Workshops.

Nature Camps

Written and updated by Melanie Sponholz

ature camps take place in some of America's most beautiful and interesting locations: Death Valley, the woods of New England, the Rocky Mountains, and Yellowstone, Yosemite, and Big Bend national parks. They are essentially adult versions of summer camp: You spend a week camping out or sharing a cabin, eating cafeteria fare or campfire cuisine, and turning in early after a full day of outdoor exploration. But no one sends you to make key chains in the arts and crafts tent or to archery classes. Instead you spend your days and nights studying the natural world.

At nature camps you learn by doing fieldwork, firsthand observation and examination of your subject. You come to understand a stream by wading in, taking a water sample, and scrutinizing the plants and wildlife you find. A visit to a mist net, where birds are caught and banded for tracking, provides a lesson on migration. Most camps take an ecological approach to educating you about the area, which means you learn how geology, botany, animals, birds, insects, and weather patterns interact. At some camps you may concentrate on one subject, like wildflowers or grizzly bears, but you'll invariably learn how that subject fits into the bigger ecological picture. For instance, while studying elk you might learn how a mild winter results in a higher elk population in the spring, which in turn causes a decrease in the population of the plants they eat, and moves bears who feed on elk that die in winter to wander far from their normal territory looking for this increased food source. Or the subject might be how people fit into the ecosystem and how we can have a positive effect on the environment. A camp might also address certain local concerns about endangered species or how to petition a government representative to help pass a conservation bill.

At most nature camps you spend the whole day hiking, from eight or nine in the morning until four or five in the afternoon. Other camps have you bicycling, canoeing, diving, or skiing. The hiking isn't usually strenuous; you proceed slowly, observing your surroundings and stopping often as your instructor tells you about what's around you. Some camps have rough terrain or high altitudes that demand a higher level of physical fitness, and others have van or bus transportation.

Itineraries are usually flexible, in part because you can only learn about what you encounter, and wildlife doesn't follow our schedules. You could start out looking for a mole tunnel and spend an hour watching wasps building a nest. On trips that cover a range of subjects, there is always something to slow down to peer at. You learn to identify plants, examine the layers of rock in gorges, watch birds, and search for animal tracks. If the camp is focused on a particu-

Although writer Melanie Sponholz loves Manhattan, urban life has taught her to truly appreciate her escapes to areas of natural beauty.

lar animal, be prepared to spend some time waiting for your subject to appear.

Camp instructors are naturalists, experts in the subject matter and geographical area of the camp. They are often college professors or National Park Service employees. Groups are kept small, usually between 8 and 20 people, to minimize the impact on the environment and to make them manageable by one or two instructors.

In addition to fieldwork, some camps include a little time in a classroom or laboratory. You may hear a background lecture on bird migration before you visit a mist net, or see a slide show that gives examples of bear tracks so you know what to look for in the woods. In the lab, you relearn how to focus a microscope before bearing down on a slide of pond water to look for microscopic organisms or the chlorophyll-containing plant cells that perform photosynthesis.

Accommodations at nature camps range from tent sites with no electricity or water to air-conditioned dorm rooms; shared bathrooms are the norm. What you eat ranges from bring-your-own-food-and-campstove to basic cafeteria fare or family-style meals. Exceptions to such basic offerings, which do exist, cost more. The essential dining and lodging options, coupled with the fact that many of the camp operators—National Audubon Society, National Wildlife Federation, Yellowstone Institute, etc.—are nonprofit organizations, make nature camps a very affordable vacation. If you're willing to camp and bring your own food, you can find a tent site and a week of instruction for under $200!

A few camps have programs for children, but for the most part trips mentioned below are for adults. The slow pace and long periods of observation aren't suited for young attention spans. Participants range in age from 18 to 80. Most operators report that over 50% of participants are between the ages of 35 and 45, and that women outnumber men. There are usually some college students at each program, especially at camps that can be attended for course credit.

CHOOSING THE RIGHT CAMP

The following questions are important to ask when deciding which nature camp is right for you.

What are the instructors' qualifications? Remember that most of what you're paying for is instruction. Without a good teacher, you may as well be camping out and hiking on your own. Most instructors at the programs listed in this chapter are college professors, well-known researchers in a field of nature study, or veteran park guides.

What is the focus of the camp? Some camps address one topic—geology or wildflowers, for example. Others study all of the elements of a particular area's ecosystem.

How tough are the hikes? Find out if the terrain will be rough, how far you'll walk each day, and whether or not high altitudes are involved if thin air and altitude sickness are concerns.

What is the food like? Partial meal plans or no meal plan at all are not uncommon. At the camps that offer meals, the food is usually standard hot and cold cafeteria fare or basics like macaroni and cheese and hamburgers served family style in a dining hall. There are a few camps that provide meals in a hotel restaurant or offer more of a selection at the cafeteria; their prices are proportionally higher. Vegetarian diets can usually be accommodated; ask about any other special needs. At camps without meal plans, there may be kitchen facilities. Find out if these include cooking and eating utensils, storage space, and refrigerator space. Also ask about nearby grocery stores and restaurants.

What are the accommodations like? The types of accommodations included in the cost of nature camps vary greatly, so make sure you find out exactly what you're getting. There are rarely private rooms, and shared rooms may be shared by more than two people. Rustic cabins may have no electricity or running water. If a tent site is provided, find out if you are responsible for all your own camping equipment. Often you must bring your own sleeping bag or linens and your own towels. The bathroom setup also varies. You'll probably share a bathroom; find out how many people you'll share it with. Hot showers, in fact any showers at all, are not a given, especially at park campgrounds. If bathrooms don't have showers, ask where the nearest facilities are.

What's the cost and what's included? The instruction you receive and transportation to sites that you won't hike to are always included in the price of the camp. Not included is transportation to and from the camp itself. The type of accommodations at nature camps ranges from a tent site to a room at a lodge, so make sure you know exactly what you're getting. There may be a partial meal plan or no meal plan at all. If meals are not included, factor in what it will cost you to bring your own food or eat in local restaurants.

Is laundry service available? It's probably not, but if it is it could save you a suitcase.

How long has the company been in business? The longer the operator has been in business, the more smoothly the camp is likely to run.

How far in advance do I need to book? Most groups ask that people reserve three or more months in advance. You may, however, want to book earlier to make sure you are not left out of popular tours. Signing up early for less popular trips can help ensure that they actually run.

Do you have references from past guests? It is often helpful to talk with someone who has already taken a trip with the outfitter you are considering. That person can supply an unbiased view.

MAJOR PLAYERS

CORNELL'S ADULT UNIVERSITY Among the 40-odd courses offered each summer by Cornell's Adult University (CAU) are several five- to seven-day ecology workshops that resemble college courses in miniature. You work with professors, cover a lot of material, live in dormitories, and eat cafeteria food. Tuition, including full room and board, is $765 per week for adults and $300 to $440 for children, depending on age. A second child may accompany parents at a 50% discount. This chapter includes programs at Cornell's main campus in Ithaca, New York, and one in Cape May, New Jersey, but there are often CAU ecology programs in other areas of the country. Lectures and lab work are combined with a lot of time in the field—on hikes, bird walks, and field trips. Leaders are experts in their field of study, most of them Cornell professors. Up to 300 people attend the summer programs at the main campus each week, but there are never more than 15 students in each workshop.

At the 13,000-acre Ithaca campus, you study the ecology of the area's forests, gorges, farm fields, and lakes. Lodging in the Mary Donlon Residence Hall is included in the cost of courses here. You might share a room with a fellow student or room alone, with bathrooms down the hall. For an additional charge, you can choose a dorm with air-conditioned double rooms and private bathrooms, or opt for a nearby hotel that offers a package rate to participants. Meals in Ithaca are served in Robert Purcell Union; you can get basic hot and cold cafeteria food, as well as burgers and grilled cheese sandwiches. There's also a make-your-own sandwich bar.

A terrific youth program for ages 3 to 16 is part of the courses at the main campus. While parents attend classes, a staff of more than 30 instructors leads up to 120 youngsters through workshops and activities, including windsurfing, watercolor painting, and creative cooking. Families meet in a private CAU dining room for breakfast and dinner. Small children sleep in rooms adjacent to their parents, while teens stay in a separate wing of Mary Donlon Hall with live-in counselors. *Cornell's Adult University, 626 Thurston Ave., Ithaca, NY 14850, tel. 607/255–6260, fax 607/254–4482.*

NATIONAL AUDUBON SOCIETY Founded in 1905, the National Audubon Society has been running 6- to 11-day adult summer camps since 1944. The camps combine the exploration of a specific wilderness area with lessons in political activism. The Audubon Society wants you to leave with a deeper appreciation for the environment and the motivation to write your government representatives about conservation issues, from clean air to endangered species protection.

Whether you go to a camp in Maine, Minnesota, Arizona, Wyoming, or one of the many other Audubon destinations, you spend almost all of your time between 8:30 AM and 5 PM outside observing and learning about the local environment—its ecology, geology, marine life, birds, mammals, plants, insects, and weather. Most camps have about 40 students and eight instructors, so several activity choices are offered for each morning and afternoon session. One group may cover half a mile, stopping frequently to dissect wildflowers, while another group hikes 3 miles to the top of a nearby peak. Program leaders are college or university professors or naturalists.

Accommodations at Audubon camps vary from simple cabins to historic lodges and typical motels, mostly with double rooms and shared baths. Camps typically have a central dining hall where meals are served buffet or family style. Pasta, pizza, quiche, meat loaf, vegetable lasagna, and other simple dishes make up the menu, and vegetarian options are usually available. Different programs provide a varying number of meals. Audubon camps are limited to participants 18 years and older and cost from $495 to $1,075. *Audubon Ecology Camps & Workshops, National Audubon Society, 613 Riversville Rd., Greenwich, CT 06831, tel. 203/869-2017, fax 203/869-4437.*

NATIONAL WILDLIFE FEDERATION It's hard to spend a week in one of the most beautiful, unspoiled areas of the United States without being inspired to take part in its conservation. That's what the National Wildlife Federation (NWF) banks on with its Conservation Summits. Two different Summits annually attract an average of 400 people each to such places as Alaska and the Adirondack Mountains of New York. A combination of nature walks, field trips, and classes are led by a staff of expert naturalists, many of them university professors and National Park Service workers. They instruct you about the ecology, natural history, cultural history, and particular conservation issues of each Summit area, touching also on global environmental concerns and the ways that individuals can have a positive impact on the environment.

Each Summit has a daytime youth program with field trips and classes for kids ages three and up. Teen groups might work on service projects, such as clearing trails and building fire rings. Evening activities, from square dances to slide shows, bring everyone at the Summit together.

Accommodations vary with location and may be in bed-and-breakfasts, hotels, resorts, or conference centers. The total cost of attendance, including room, board, tuition, and the $16 NWF annual membership fee, ranges from $500 to over $900 per adult. *National Wildlife Federation, 8925 Leesburg Pike, Vienna, VA 22184, tel. 703/790-4265 or 800/245-5484, fax 703/790-4468.*

SIERRA CLUB Hosting wilderness excursions that stimulate interest in the environment and provide memorable group experiences has been an intent of the Sierra Club since it was founded in 1901. Today, club members can choose from more than 350 trips each year, in places all across the United States and in many foreign countries. There are bicycling, backpacking, canoeing, skiing, kayaking, and volunteering trips, with each type of trip offered for different ability levels.

Like the National Wildlife Federation, the Sierra Club aims to teach wilderness conservation and environmental protection in a setting that demonstrates the need for them and inspires personal action. Because trip fees cover only the direct cost of the excursion and a portion of the administrative cost of trip organization, costs are low. A one-week exploration within the contiguous 48 states ranges from $285 to $785, plus the $23 to $43 it costs to become a Sierra Club member. Prices vary due to the type of lodging, the number of staff members accompanying the trip, and the necessity of wilderness permits and on-trip airfare.

Volunteer leaders are experts in the geographic area of their trip and the trip's central activity—biking or kayaking, for instance. They also have previous experience as guides and have spent time as Sierra Club trainees. On some trips a naturalist accompanies the leader to provide more in-depth lessons on flora and fauna. Average group size is 12, with an overall range from 8 to 36 participants. Accommodations for most trips are in tents, either in the wilderness or at campgrounds. A few programs have lodging in rustic cabins or lodges, usually with dorm-style accommodations and shared bathrooms. Participants pitch in with daily chores, including meal preparation. The Sierra Club boasts that its tasty meals draw park rangers from miles around. Trip leaders have become experts in the preparation of scrumptious trail meals, and some trips are accompanied by cooks. Who ever knew freeze-dried food could taste so good?

There are some programs designed specifically for families, but children under 18 traveling with an adult can sign up for any trip for which they meet physical fitness and experience requirements. *Sierra Club Outings, 85 2nd St., 2nd Floor, San Francisco, CA 94105, tel. 415/977–5630, fax 415/776–4868.*

YELLOWSTONE INSTITUTE The average Yellowstone tourist spends between 7 hours and 1½ days in the park—only enough to scratch the surface. The Yellowstone Institute, a nonprofit organization established in 1976, encourages you to take a closer look. You can do this by participating in one of its 90 or so yearly field courses, which focus on the park's natural and cultural history.

Fieldwork forms the core of most courses, so minimal time is spent in the classroom. Groups of up to 15 to 20 people hike in different areas of the park. You might observe elk, bison, antelope, and other park mammals, as well as geysers, mudpots, and hot springs—evidence of the park's volcanic history. The things you see serve as illustrations for lessons on the interrelationships of the park environment and its inhabitants. Group leaders are experts on the area and their course topic; many are full-time park employees or professors at area universities.

The programs in this chapter take place at the institute's headquarters in the Lamar Valley, in the northeast corner of the park. Food and lodging are not included in the program fee—which is only $40 to $50 per day—but for $10 a night more you can stay in one of the 16 cabins. These sleep two to four and have no plumbing. A central building contains two classrooms, three bathrooms with showers, and a communal kitchen with refrigerators, a microwave, two stoves, cooking and eating utensils, and plenty of storage space for your food. Most of the institute's programs are designed for adults. With children along, it is best to attend one of the family classes. *The Yellowstone Institute, Box 117, Yellowstone National Park, Wyoming 82190, tel. 307/344–2294, fax 307/344–2294.*

YOSEMITE ASSOCIATION FIELD SEMINARS Since its founding in 1924, the Yosemite Association has offered a growing number of one- to eight-day adult environmental education seminars. Some of them cover a single specific topic, such as those on wildflower pollination, giant sequoias, butterflies, and bighorn sheep, while others have a broader scope, as with those on the park's ecology and natural history.

Almost all seminars consist entirely of day hikes through the park. Groups on trail hikes range from 8 to 20 participants; off-trail groups are typically kept to eight, which prevents damage to the environment and keeps the groups manageable by a single leader. Although the hikes are usually only 5 to 8 miles, high altitudes and uneven terrain can make them physically demanding. Depending on the topic you choose, your leader may stop the group along the way to identify plants, examine geological features, or observe wildlife. All of the association's staff members are naturalists and experts in the geographical area and subject matter of their seminars.

The low price of Yosemite seminars—about $200 for five days—includes the cost of a tent site. You have to bring your own camping equipment, including a camp stove, and your own food. The campgrounds have bathrooms with cold running water but no showers; a nearby concessioner offers showers for a minimal fee. If you would rather stay in one of the park's lodges, reserve over a year in advance.

The seminars in this chapter are based at the Tuolumne Meadows campground, where a campground host is on hand to answer questions and give directions to restaurants in the town of Lee Vining, a 30-minute drive away. If you don't want to camp, there is also a range of hotels in Lee Vining. Yosemite programs are open to participants 18 years and over. *Yosemite Association, Box 230, El Portal, CA 95318, tel. 209/379–2646, fax 209/379–2486.*

FAVORITE CAMPS

THE NORTHEAST

CONNECTICUT **Connecticut Ecology Workshop.** The National Audubon Society's 485-acre sanctuary in the southern New England woods of Greenwich, Connecticut, is the setting for this six-day workshop. You learn about forest and meadow habitats as you hike along the sanctuary's 15 miles of trails, and you explore intertidal zones, beaches, and salt marshes on a field trip to Long Island Sound.

Each day your group of up to 30 participants is divided into four field groups for two half-day sessions. A deciduous forest, old field communities, freshwater communities, and a hemlock gorge are each the focus of single sessions. To fill the rest of your time, you choose from a list of electives covering such topics as wildflower identification, entomology, mushrooms, geology, and ornithology. You might spend the morning studying the wildflowers of the meadow and the afternoon observing meadow insects. Or you could spend a whole day walking in the forest, splitting your time between botany studies and watching some of the more than 100 species of birds in the sanctuary. Evening lectures, discussions, and slide shows highlight local and global conservation issues.

Accommodations are in double-occupancy rooms with twin beds and private bathrooms, in a lodge set in the forest. Hearty meals are served buffet style in a main dining hall, and a vegetarian option is always offered. This workshop is run seven times each summer. *Audubon Ecology Camps & Workshops, National Audubon Society, 613 Riversville Rd., Greenwich, CT 06831, tel. 203/869–2017, fax 203/869–4437. Early July–mid-Aug.: 6 days, $525. Sign up 3 months in advance.*

MAINE **Coastal Ecology.** Audubon's Hog Island camp off the coast of central Maine has been a base for summer programs since 1936. The spruce-fir forest, rocky shoreline, and intertidal and mudflat habitats of the 330-acre refuge are excellent places to study the interrelationships of plants, fungi, and animals with the water, soil, rocks, and air of their environment.

Each day at the camp is divided into morning and afternoon fieldwork sessions. Up to 40 people can participate, and they are broken up into four field groups led by instructors specializing in such topics as botany, marine life, and ornithology. Over the course of the six-day camp, you spend time at each of the different island habitats, observing everything from rock formations to harbor seals. You may spend the morning seining water from ponds and streams to study their plant and animal life through magnifying hand lenses. In the afternoon, a boat trip might take you to one of several offshore seabird nesting sites.

There's an environmental and natural history library and a marine lab with tanks, an herbarium, hundreds of study skins, and microscopes. One afternoon is left open for relaxation, hiking, swimming, volleyball, or use of the camp's learning facilities. Evening talks and workshops are given on topics such as environmental activism, colonial seabird research, astronomy, and marine ecosystems. Overall, Audubon aims to instruct you about human impact on the area's ecosystems and educate you on how to protect global life-support systems by living more compatibly with the environment.

Accommodations are in three wood-frame buildings, two for women and one for both couples and single men. Double rooms have either private or shared bath. All meals are included in the price for this camp and are served buffet or family style in a main dining hall. *Audubon Ecology Camps & Workshops, National Audubon Society, 613 Riversville Rd., Greenwich, CT 06831, tel. 203/869–2017, fax 203/869–4437. July: 6 days, $650. Sign up 3 months in advance.*

NEW HAMPSHIRE **Landscape of the Northern Woods.** Founded in 1876, the Appalachian Mountain Club (AMC) works with the University of New Hampshire in presenting three or four annual field seminars in environmental science and conservation, including this six-day study of the Northern Forest. The seminars attract many college students and teachers and are more strictly academic than many ecology camps. Fieldwork fills the bulk of your time, but background lectures and daily reading assignments on ecology, biology, and conservation theory are also part of each seminar.

The forest's 26 million acres stretch through northern Maine, New Hampshire, Vermont, and New York and include a diverse landscape of mountains, woods, and waterways. You spend each day, rain or shine, in the field, studying the interrelationships of the various ecosystems. For example, you may learn about the link between forest and water ecosystems by observing the effect forest management has on aquatic plant and animal populations. You also look at the role people play in the landscape, from the forest management systems we employ to the impact of our settlements.

The group is limited to 12 students and is led by Daniel Smith, AMC's conservation educator. Smith has a Master's of Forest Science from the Yale School of Forestry and Environmental Studies and has been leading AMC trips for two years.

During the seminar, you stay in the lodge at Pinkham Notch Visitor Center. More than 100 people are accommodated in two-, three-, and four-bunk rooms, and there are large shared bathrooms on each hall. Breakfast and dinner are served in the lodge dining room and included in the price of the seminar, and bag lunches can be purchased at the lodge. There are no special facilities or activities for children, but they may attend the seminar if accompanied by a parent or guardian. *Appalachian Mountain Club, White Mountains Workshops, Pinkham Notch Visitor Center, Box 298, Gorham, NH 03581, tel. 603/466–2727, fax 603/466–2720. Late Aug.: 6 days, $450. Price does not include lunches; sign up 3 months in advance.*

NEW YORK **Birding in the Finger Lakes.** For years Cornell University's campus in Ithaca, New York, has attracted researchers interested in the varied bird life of the Finger Lakes region, and the school's Laboratory of Ornithology is world famous. The field observation that you do during this weeklong workshop is part of your study of avian ecology, habitat conservation, and bird population monitoring.

Workshop leader Charles (Charlie) Smith is a senior research associate in the Department of Natural Resources at Cornell, a specialist in field-study techniques and avian conservation, and he has been the leader of CAU's ornithology programs for more than 20 years. The workshop usually includes a trip to Cornell's Library of Natural Sounds, which began as a collection of recorded bird sounds and has grown to include thousands of other sounds, such as those made by whales and elephants.

You can begin your days by joining Charlie on his 6 AM bird walks, or wait for the scheduled activities to begin at 9. Lectures on such topics as the local bird population, migration, and migrating birds as indicator species for the health of the environment are combined with field trips. In addition to the visit to the sound library mentioned above, you explore the campus bird sanctuary and travel to different observation areas throughout the Ithaca area and other parts of New York, including the Montezuma National Wildlife Refuge. On some days a guest presenter may talk to the group about banding birds for tracking or about the ecological factors that affect bird populations. These activities continue until 3:30, with a break for lunch.

Evenings you're free to participate in Cornell's active summer campus life. There are films, concerts, and guest speakers on a diverse selection of topics. Charlie will probably invite you on at least one owl prowl, too. Most participants in Cornell's workshops stay in double dorm rooms and eat in the cafeteria. *Cornell's Adult University, 626 Thurston Ave., Ithaca, NY 14850, tel. 607/255–6260, fax 607/254–4482. Early July: 7 days, $765–$825. Sign up 3 months in advance.*

NEW YORK **Natural Life in the Finger Lakes.** During this seven-day, Cornell Adult University workshop, Richard Fischer, professor emeritus of environmental education at Cornell, teaches you about the many different environments and inhabitants of the Finger Lakes region. You spend most of your time exploring the fields, bogs, forests, creeks, meadows, lakes, and gorges around the Ithaca campus.

Because daily walks and hikes progress slowly, observing your surroundings and stopping while Professor Fischer talks about what you find, they are more like museum tours than aerobic workouts. Fischer points out how the plant life at the top of a gorge differs from what is found near the stream at the bottom. You compare the trees, undergrowth, insects, and birds found in older sections of forest with those in meadows that are converting to forest. In streams, you use dip nets to examine the algae and insects of the water.

Lectures in the field teach you about plant adaptation, for example, that walnut trees have a chemical in their roots that prevents the seeds of other plants around them from germinating. You also learn to identify wildflowers, and you participate in discussions about human impact on the environment. Your fieldwork and occasional background lectures fill the day from 9 AM to 3:30 PM, with a break for lunch.

In the evening you're free to take advantage of the films, lectures, and concerts on and around campus. Accommodations are in one of the campus residence halls, and dining is cafeteria style in the student union. *Cornell's Adult University, 626 Thurston Ave., Ithaca, NY 14850, tel. 607/255–6260, fax 607/254–4482. Early July: 7 days, $765–$825. Sign up 3 months in advance.*

THE MID-ATLANTIC

NEW JERSEY **Ecology in the Migration Season.** Cape May is the setting for this four-day Cornell Adult University workshop. The end of summer may mean the exodus of swimsuit-clad sunseekers, but October finds the beaches, marshes, rivers, and coastal woods of Cape May populated with a bustling new crowd: wildlife. Herons, ibis, and egrets dot the shoreline. The woods become the temporary home of thrushes, thrashers, orioles, and vireos. And migrant butterflies flutter along the dunes.

Four expert instructors lead you in daily explorations and observations of this unique wildlife gathering. Robert Budliger, recently retired as director of education for the New York State Department of Environmental Conservation, is a specialist in dune ecology. Richard Fischer, professor emeritus of environmental education at Cornell, is a walking encyclopedia on the habits of birds, insects, and plants. Anne Galli is a wetlands specialist and director of the Hackensack-Meadowlands Environmental Center. And Richard McNeil is professor of natural resources at Cornell.

Accommodations and meals are at the beachfront Atlas Inn in the village of Cape May. The program fee is based on double occupancy and includes all meals, accommodations, site visits, taxes, and gratuities. *Cornell's Adult University, 626 Thurston Ave., Ithaca, NY 14850, tel. 607/255–6260, fax 607/254–4482. Early Oct.: 4 days, $585–$730. Sign up 3 months in advance.*

PENNSYLVANIA Family Nature Study Workshop. With nature walks, reptile presentations, and plenty of recreational activities, the four-day workshop at the Pocono Environmental Education Center is great for kids and parents alike. Located in the National Park Service's Delaware Water Gap National Recreation Area, the 38-acre campus has access to more than 200,000 acres of public land with a variety of habitats—pine plantations, hemlock gorges, and deciduous forests. You are sure to spot some of the many warblers that live in the area, and you may see an eagle or a hawk.

Days begin with a morning walk at 7:45, followed by breakfast in the dining hall. The rest of the day is filled with four 1½-hour activity sessions with two or three different activities planned for each. The workshops may be attended by as few as 20 guests, but they are more likely to be filled with up to 100. There are canoe trips, wildflower walks, pond and stream studies, fossil hunts, and classes on botany, birds of prey, environmental issues, and constellations. To break up your nature studies,

PEEC offers classes in tie-dyeing, papermaking, candle making, and other crafts. There are 14 instructors on staff, and each has some expertise in a different natural topic.

After dinner you may hear a guest speaker talk about whales, or you can choose to go to a square dance. Each family (up to six people) stays in a one-room cabin with bunk beds and a full private bathroom. You can bring your own sheets and towels or rent them. A main building contains the arts and crafts center, an indoor pool, a dance floor, and the dining room, where meals are served buffet style. PEEC also offers many three-day family weekends. *Pocono Environmental Education Center, R.D. 2, Box 1010, Dingmans Ferry, PA 18328, tel. 717/828–2319, fax 717/828–9695. July and Aug.: 4 days, $164. Sign up 2 months in advance.*

THE SOUTHWEST

NEVADA Death Valley Ecology Workshop. Most people don't realize that Death Valley National Monument is more than a sea of endless sand dunes. In fact, it encompasses an area that ranges from the sub–sea level Badwater Basin to the 11,000-foot peaks of the Panamint Range. During this seven-day Audubon workshop, you study the geological history of the area; how plants and wildlife have adapted to varying altitudes; the complex relationships between the land and wildlife created by the area's limited natural resources; and the region's rich human history, from the life of Native Americans to the business of mining.

Each day you can choose among hikes, walks, and van trips. You may spend a day identifying desert plants and learning how they can be used as indicators of the salinity, texture, and fertility of the soil. A visit to Ubehebe crater is the basis for a lesson on how exposed layers of rock reveal a history of the shaping forces of ancient seas, glaciers, earthquakes, and volcanoes. A field trip to Big and Little Petroglyph Canyons gives you a chance to see one of the densest concentrations of rock art in North America. Ruined mining towns are reminders of the early settlers and the rich borax, gypsum, gold, and silver deposits that lured them to the area. Observing the kangaroo rat, kit fox, and desert bighorn, you discuss conservation issues and learn how these mammals conserve water and food. Nature photography classes are yet another option.

The Furnace Creek Ranch, a modern motel in the center of the monument, is your home for the week. Dinner your first night and picnic lunches are included in the cost of the workshop. Other meals can be purchased at restaurants in the motel and nearby. *Audubon Ecology Camps & Workshops, National Audubon Society, 613 Riversville Rd., Greenwich, CT 06831, tel. 203/869–2017, fax 203/869–4437. Apr.: 7 days, $995. Price does not include breakfast and most dinners; sign up 3 months in advance.*

TEXAS **Ecology of Big Bend National Park.** Inside the boundaries created by the Rio Grande River, Santiago Mountains, and Chihuahuan Desert, the 1,200 square miles of mountains, hills, river canyons, desert, forests, and grasslands of Big Bend National Park are home to amazingly diverse plant and animal populations. At this weeklong National Audubon Society workshop, you take walks, hikes, and van trips to observe the many species in their various habitats. Vans can reach certain areas, but because the park is undeveloped, walking or hiking is required to reach many interesting sites. To get the most from the trip, you should be able to walk 3 to 5 miles.

More than 400 bird species have been recorded in Big Bend, and September is a particularly good time for bird observation, as numerous migrating species stop in the park to refuel. You might spend a day visiting known feeding areas along the Rio Grande, looking for western bluebirds, vermillion flycatchers, golden eagles, ladder-backed woodpeckers, painted buntings,

and many other species. Many animals, including the prong horn antelope, desert mule deer, gray fox, and the small, piglike javelina, can also be observed in the park. You might study the animal populations of the different park habitats and learn how food sources affect species distribution. Plant studies could include species that are unique to the park, such as the lechuguilla, or a general study of tree adaptation to different altitudes. For an additional charge, you can take a full- or half-day raft trip on the Rio Grande.

You spend the first and last nights of the trip at the Gage, a small inn in Marathon, Texas, in the northern section of the park. Rooms here are double occupancy; some have shared bathrooms. The other nights are spent at Chisos Mountain Lodge, near the center of the park, in basic motel rooms with private bathrooms. Dinner the first night, all lunches (some restaurant, some picnic), and one early morning breakfast are included in the cost of the trip. The rest of your meals must be purchased in local restaurants. *Audubon Ecology Camps & Workshops, National Audubon Society, 613 Riversville Rd., Greenwich, CT 06831, tel. 203/869–2017, fax 203/869–4437. Mid-Sept.: 7 days, $995. Price does not include breakfast or most dinners; sign up 3 months in advance.*

UTAH **Canyon Lands Summit.** Southern Utah University, in the southwestern part of the state, is the base for this seven-day National Wildlife Federation (NWF) program, which explores Bryce Canyon, Zion, and Cedar Breaks national parks. You spend a week learning about the area's natural and cultural history with 400 other participants and 70 NWF leaders.

Everyone comes together for meals, and a long list of morning and afternoon activity choices splits the group into many smaller units of 10 to 40 people. You may hear a morning lecture on the reptiles and amphibians found in Bryce Canyon National Park, break for lunch, then spend the afternoon on a guided nature walk, seeing these creatures firsthand. There are classes on local geology, plant studies, astronomy, and photography, as well as environmentally safe cleaning products and setting up a recycling program in your office or community. Field trips cover such topics as the role of erosion in canyon formation and the bird life of the parks. Nature walks and bus tours are offered, which allows you to choose how physically strenuous your day will be.

Smaller versions of the adult programs are offered for various children's age groups, along with arts and crafts activities and team skills workshops. Evenings there are country line dances, cookouts, slide presentations by park rangers, and other activities.

Accommodations on campus include single and double dormitory rooms with large shared bathrooms, and apartment-style housing, where three double rooms share a bathroom and kitchen. Rooms are also available off campus at a nearby inn. Short of opting for the full cafeteria meal plan, you must buy at least a partial plan, which includes five lunches, two cookouts, and a grounds and administrative fee. *National Wildlife Federation, 8925 Leesburg Pike, Vienna, VA 22184, tel. 703/790–4265 or 800/245–5484, fax 703/790–4468. Early Aug.: 7 days, $520–$865. Sign up at least 6 months in advance.*

THE ROCKIES

COLORADO **Rocky Mountain Ecology.** This six-day workshop given by the Rocky Mountain Nature Association is a fine introduction to the many ecosystems of Rocky Mountain National Park, a 417-square-mile area of montane meadows, valleys, forests, alpine tundra, and mountains northwest of Denver. Founded in 1961, the nonprofit organization offers many other one- to seven-day workshops. All are limited to 12 students and are led by an expert naturalist, in this case Dr. John Emerick, associate professor of environmental sci-

ence at the Colorado School of Mines, who specializes in mountain ecology.

Each day, from 9 AM to 5 PM, you hike in one of the park's ecosystems. During a day in the alpine tundra you learn about the small, low-to-the-ground plants that survive in the treeless, windy environment. In the moist, cool montane zone just below the timberline, the subject turns to the large coniferous trees that dominate the area and the elk and deer that populate it. Excursions throughout the park include lessons on how climate, soil composition, fires, and other factors affect the ecosystem. You also make trips to view park wildlife, such as the beavers who make their homes in ponds and streams. Although the frequent stops for discussion give the hikes a leisurely pace, the high altitude and unpredictable weather demand some stamina.

You and your group camp at the drive-in or hike-in sites of the Kawuneeche Campground. Camp fees are included in the cost of the program, but you must bring your own tent, cooking equipment, and food. A central building has bathrooms with showers. *Rocky Mountain Nature Association, Seminar Coordinator, Rocky Mountain National Park, Estes Park, CO 80517, tel. 970/586–1265. Mid-July: 7 days, $175. Price does not include indoor lodging or meals; sign up 2 months in advance.*

MONTANA **Fins, Feathers, and Fur: Glacier's Wildlife.** This six-day seminar, one of 31 offered by the Glacier Institute, is set on the 2.5 million acres of Glacier National Park and the surrounding wilderness. The Institute was founded in 1983 to promote an appreciation of the area's beauty and an understanding of ecosystem management and sustainability issues.

During this seminar you study the park's wildlife—wolves, wolverines, mountain goats, mountain lions, salmon, and salamanders—and learn what part they play in the park's ecosystem. Moderately strenuous hikes fill each day from 9 to 5, so assess your physical fitness before choosing this trip. Wildlife biologist David Shea, who leads the 16-person group, has a master's degree in resource conservation and has been a summer employee of the park for 25 years. While you explore he teaches you about the role of predator-prey relationships in the ecosystem, the importance of endangered and abundant species, and the survival needs of each animal. He also discusses species interrelationships and wildlife management policies.

Accommodations are in rustic wood cabins that sleep four to five at Glacier Park Field Camp near West Glacier. A common building contains a classroom for quick background lectures, bathrooms with hot showers, and a communal kitchen with cooking and eating utensils. You can either bring food and cook your meals, or eat at local restaurants. Participants in the program must be at least 16 years old. *The Glacier Institute, 777 Grandview Dr., Box 7457, Kalispell, MT 59904, tel. 406/755–1211. Mid-Aug.: 6 days, $235. Price does not include lodging ($10 per night) or meals; sign up 2 months in advance.*

MONTANA **Mountains, Valleys, and Glaciers.** During this five-day Glacier Institute field seminar, you learn about the geological forces that shaped the northern Rocky Mountains of Glacier National Park. The group leader is Dr. Lex Blood, who has a degree in geological engineering and has taught at Flathead Community College for 19 years. On day hikes he teaches you to look at the landscape for clues to its geological past. You observe the valleys and moraines created by glaciers, as well as fossilized algae and mud cracks that provide evidence of the erosion caused by ancient seas. You also study the ongoing effects of ice and water on the topography of the park. You hike every day, and the uneven terrain makes for a few strenuous days.

Accommodations are in rustic wood cabins that sleep four to five at Glacier Park Field Camp near West Glacier. Bathrooms with hot showers are in the common building that is also used for quick background lectures. Meals are not provided, but a communal kitchen with cooking and eating utensils is available, and there are several restaurants nearby. *The Glacier Institute, 777 Grandview Dr., Box 7457, Kalispell, MT 59904, tel. 406/756–3911. Early Aug.: 5 days, $235. Price does not include lodging ($10 per night) or meals; sign up 2 months in advance.*

WYOMING **Audubon Camp in the West.** Wyoming's beautiful Wind River Range, one forest and valley east of the Teton Range, is the setting for this weeklong National Audubon Society workshop on mountain ecology at the Whisky Mountain Conservation Camp, near the town of Dubois in the northwestern quadrant of the state. The daily schedule of two half-day activity sessions is the same as that of other Audubon camps, but at the Camp in the West you have as many as six choices for each session, including classes, hikes, and field trips.

Exploring mountain meadows, pine and sagebrush hills, forests, and creek and river bottoms, you can study geology, plant life, wildflowers, petroglyphs, insects, birds, and mammals. Elk, moose, deer, otter, mink, beaver, antelope, and bison are just some of the mammals in the area, and the bird population includes bald eagles, white pelicans, osprey, trumpeter swans, and three-toed woodpeckers. One day is spent on a field trip to Grand Teton National Park, where you take a float trip on the Snake River, discuss geology and ecology, visit the Indian Museum at Colter Bay, hike to Lake Taggert, and maybe hit some birding hot spots.

You can supplement what you learn in the field with classes on invertebrates, botany, nature drawing, environmental education, Native American culture, medicinal plants, and environmental activism. Evenings, there may be stories around a campfire, a square dance, or a lecture on endangered species or wetlands and forest preservation.

Accommodations are in dormitory-style cabins that sleep two to five people. Some cabins have private baths, while others share a central bathhouse. There are a few cabins with private rooms and baths for couples. Meals are served buffet style in a main dining room, and vegetarian diets can be accommodated. The workshop is offered six times each summer. *Audubon Ecology Camps & Workshops, National Audubon Society, 613 Riversville Rd., Greenwich, CT 06831, tel. 203/869–2017, fax 203/869–4437. Late June–early Aug.: 7 days, $695. Price does not include 1 dinner; sign up 3 months in advance.*

WYOMING **The Tetons: Animal Behavior.** Teton Science School (TSS) has been offering a variety of natural-science field seminars since it was founded in 1967. It uses the mountains, aspen forests, and grasslands of Grand Teton National Park and Elk Refuge as its classroom. With antelope, coyote, beaver, moose, red squirrel, digger wasps, wolves, grouse, osprey, bears, dragonflies, eagles, and bison as inhabitants, it is an ideal location for this five-day study of animal behavior.

Each day, from 8 AM to 4 PM, you and a group of up to 11 others take to the field to observe wildlife, where you work on developing your observation skills, one of the main objectives of the course. Your instructor is the well-known ethnologist Dr. Allen Stokes, professor emeritus of the University of Utah. He teaches you to recognize the nuances of animal behavior and adaptation. You learn to use the observations you make of an animal's behavior to make deductions about its species' survival strategies.

When class is over, you can visit the field science lab, natural science library, or Murie Natural History Museum at the TSS campus. Teton Science School seminars do not include accommodations or meals. The closest lodging is Dornan's Spur Ranch Cabins, about 8 miles west of the campus in Moose, Wyoming, at the southern entrance to Grand Teton National Park. There are one- and two-bedroom cabins, laundry facilities, and a restaurant here. Many other hotels and lodges are found in and around

the towns of Jackson and Teton Village. The national park has lodges and campsites, and Gros Ventre and Forest Service campgrounds are also nearby, but have no showers, electricity, or food services. You need to bring a bag lunch each day. Teton Science School courses are open to participants age 18 and older. *Teton Science School, Box 68, Kelly, WY 83011, tel. 307/733–4765, fax 307/739–9388. Late July: 5 days, $250. Price does not include accommodations or meals; sign up 3 months in advance.*

WYOMING **The Tetons: Geology and Human Culture.** You learn two disciplines during this unusual five-day seminar offered by the Teton Science School and taught by Charles Love, a professor of geology and anthropology at Western Wyoming College. You should have a basic understanding of geology before you sign up.

Professor Love has done extensive research on the archaeology of Jackson Hole and teaches you how 10,000 years of prehistoric peoples used the resources of the area and how modern man is using the area today. On daily hikes, he points out houses being built on active landslides and at the bottom of avalanche tracks. You also visit sites where geologists and archaeologists are working together to discover early settlement and cultural patterns.

Accommodations and meals are not provided by the Teton Science School, but there are many hotel and camping options in and around the town of Jackson (*see* the Animal Behavior camp, *above*). *Teton Science School, Box 68, Kelly, WY 83011, tel. 307/733–4765, fax 307/739–9388. Early Aug.: 4 days, $200. Price does not include accommodations or meals; sign up 3 months in advance.*

WYOMING **Yellowstone Bears: Bones, Signs, and Stories.** The team teaching of this five-day Yellowstone Institute course gives you a thorough education on the bears of Yellowstone National Park. You spend time in the classroom learning about the evolution of carnivores with Dr. Elaine

Anderson, a research associate in zoology at the Denver Museum of Natural History. Dr. Jim Halfpenny, author of *A Field Guide to Tracking in North America*, takes you into the park to map bear trees (those marked with scratches) and other evidence of bear activity as part of a research project on bear distribution in the park. Naturalist and folklorist Jim Garry uses observation of the bear and its habitat to explain its place in Native American myth and storytelling.

Early mornings and evenings are spent looking for bears, since this is when they tend to be most active. You observe from a distance, often with binoculars, both to watch them going about their business unnoticed and because close human-ursine interaction isn't good for either species. In the afternoon you might search for bear tracks and trees, or spend time in the classroom studying the muscular structure of bears and comparing different bear skulls and teeth.

Accommodations are available for $8 a night at the institute's headquarters in cabins with no electricity or plumbing. Bathrooms and kitchen facilities, including cooking and eating utensils, are in a common building. You bring your own bedding, towels, and food. With the exception of special family weeks, Yellowstone programs are for adults only. *The Yellowstone Institute, Box 117, Yellowstone National Park, WY 82190, tel. 307/344–2294. Late June: 5 days, $225. Price does not include accommodations or meals; sign up 3 months in advance.*

WYOMING **Yellowstone: Mammals Great and Small.** The elk, bears, bison, ground squirrels, coyote, and other mammals that populate Yellowstone National Park are the subjects of this five-day Yellowstone Institute program led by Don Streubel, a biology professor at Idaho State University. Professor Streubel teaches a group of 15 students about the role of these animals in the ecosystem of the park.

Streubel leads some early morning bear walks, but most daily programs begin around 8:30 with a background lecture in the common building. You may spend from 15 minutes to an hour in the classroom, hearing the plans for the day's fieldwork or seeing a slide show on the history of mammals. You spend the rest of the day in the field, hiking to nearby observation areas or taking a van to other parts of the park. If spotting a grizzly bear is on the agenda, you may have to wait and watch for a couple of hours in the process, but it's a rare day that you come home disappointed.

The lesson plan is determined by the animals that you encounter. If you observe a coyote feeding on elk carrion, you learn about the role that predator-prey relationships play in the natural control of the animal population. Finding a red squirrel's stash of pinecones may prompt a lesson on hibernation or the effect of animals on the plant population.

Accommodations are available in cabins with no electricity or plumbing at the institute's headquarters (*see* the Bears: Bones, Signs, and Stories camp, *above*). Bathrooms and kitchen facilities, including cooking and eating utensils, are in the common building. *The Yellowstone Institute, Box 117, Yellowstone National Park, WY 82190, tel. 307/344–2294. Mid-June: 5 days, $220. Price does not include accommodations or meals; sign up 3 months in advance.*

THE WEST COAST

CALIFORNIA **Spring into Nature.** The Sierra Club's rustic Clair Tappaan Lodge is the base camp for this seven-day trip in the High Sierras. As winter snows thaw and spring flora comes to life, you explore the Pacific Crest Trail, Donner Pass, Castle Peak, and the many streams, lakes, and meadows near the lodge. Leader Sy Gelman, who has been leading Sierra Club trips for more than 20 years, crafts an itinerary to suit the group and the weather. Naturalist and botanist Tim Messick comes along on daily hikes to help identify the plants and birds you encounter along the way.

Mornings begin with breakfast and a group cleanup. The first day is usually spent hiking to a ridge 3½ miles behind the lodge. From here there is a splendid view of Donner Lake and the surrounding area. You spend another day at Donner Memorial State Park, where you learn the devastating history of the Donner Party, a group of 89 westward-bound pioneers who were trapped here in the brutal winter of 1846–47, in 22 feet of snow. You hike through the park, stopping along streams to look at beaver dams. On other days you hike along the Pacific Crest Trail, drive to Tahoe to explore, and climb Donner Summit or another of the nearby peaks.

Professor Messick talks about the flora and geological features found in each area. He explains how plants have adapted to altitude and discusses the role of glaciers in shaping the mountains. As an expert on the local bird population, he can point out Steller's jays, golden eagles, and the rare gray owl.

Typically you return to the lodge by 3:30 and have a few hours to shower and relax before dinner at 8 PM. In the evening, Tim may give a slide presentation on the ecology of the Sierra Nevada or talk about ecological concerns. If you're so inclined, you can drive to nearby Tahoe or Reno. One former guest claims to have won back the cost of his trip on his evening forays.

The dormitory rooms with double- and triple-decker bunk beds (the topmost bunks are rarely used) and the lodge's shared bathrooms are far from posh, but the showers are hot, and there's an indoor hot tub. You bring your own bedding and towels. A professional chef cooks the meals, and vegetarian alternatives are always available. *Sierra Club Outings, 85 2nd St., 2nd Floor, San Francisco, CA 94105, tel. 415/977–5630, fax 415/977–5630. Mid-June: 7 days, $475. Sign up 3 months in advance.*

CALIFORNIA **Yosemite: Designs and Strategies: Flowers and Their Pollinators.** There's more to the study of wildflowers than identification. At this four-day Yosemite Association seminar you discover how each flower's structure is adapted for different pollinators—bees, butterflies, moths, hummingbirds, and the wind.

The course is led by Richard Keator, who has a Ph.D. in botany from the University of California, Berkeley, and is the author of numerous books on the flowers and plants of California. You take day hikes through alpine, meadow, subalpine forest, and scree habitats, examining the diverse flower population, which includes black-eyed Susans, bull thistles, lupine, and other flora. You study flower shape, color, arrangement, pistil and stamen position, and nectar and pollen production.

You are free most evenings, but one night there is a lecture and slide show. A tent site at the Tuolumne Meadows campsite is included in the cost of the seminar, but you have to bring your own camping equipment. There are central bathrooms, but no showers. You can also stay in a motel in Lee Vining, about a half-hour drive away. Meals are not included, so bring a camp stove or be prepared to drive to local restaurants. *Yosemite Association, Box 230, El Portal, CA 95318, tel. 209/379–2646, fax 209/379–2486. Late July: 4 days, $175. Price includes campsite fee but no meals; sign up 3 months in advance.*

CALIFORNIA **Yosemite Geology: Where the Glaciers Roamed.** In this five-day seminar you learn about the evolution of Yosemite National Park—the volcanic activity, glacial movement, erosion, the great Sierra uplift, and the work of ancient seas. Leader Doris Sloan is a lecturer in environmental sciences at the University of California, Berkeley, where she earned her M.S. in geology and Ph.D. in paleontology. She's been leading trips in the Sierras for 20 years.

You spend your days hiking, from 8:30 to 5, mostly in the Tuolumne Meadows area of the park. You cover only about 5 miles a day, at a relatively slow pace, but because the elevation ranges from 8,600 feet to 11,000 feet, you must be in good physical condition. High country scenery is incredibly dramatic as you hike among rounded granite domes, steep cliffs, waterfalls, and deep valleys, identifying rocks and minerals, observing the shapes created by glaciers and volcanoes, hearing about the effects of plate tectonics, and learning about the history of mining in the area.

You camp at the Tuolumne Meadows campsite (see the Yosemite: Designs and Strategies camp, above). Nights are spent cooking over your camp stove before retiring to your tent under the stars. *Yosemite Association, Box 230, El Portal, CA 95318, tel. 209/379–2646, fax 209/379–2486. Mid-Aug.: 5 days, $200. Price does not include accommodations or meals; sign up 3 months in advance.*

CALIFORNIA **Yosemite: Stars and the Night Sky.** This Yosemite Association seminar takes place under the brilliant night sky, leaving you free during the day to explore the park on your own. For five nights, 20 students gather at 7:30 to observe the stars, moon, Saturn, globular clusters, and nebulae and to listen to lectures given by Ron Oriti, director of the Santa Rosa Junior College Planetarium.

Because the course is planned for a time when the sky is particularly dark, you can readily view the stars with your naked eyes and binoculars, as well as with a telescope. You learn about the motion of the stars and planets, how to use the sun and stars to determine direction, and how to identify stars and constellations. Professor Oriti's lectures cover topics from the ancient Greek myths about the constellations to the modern discovery of black holes. Classes are scheduled to end at 10:30, but fascinated groups often stay up looking and talking until after 1 AM.

A tent site at the Tuolumne Meadows campsite is included in the cost of the seminar. You can also stay in a motel in Lee Vining, about a half hour's drive away.

Meals are not included, so bring a camp stove or be prepared to drive to local restaurants. *Yosemite Association, Box 230, El Portal, CA 95318, tel. 209/379–2646, fax 209/379–2486. Early Aug.: 5 nights, $180. Price does not include accommodations or meals; sign up 3 months in advance.*

WASHINGTON **Birds and Butterflies from Sagebrush to Snow.** During this four-day North Cascades Institute field seminar, you study the birds and butterflies of northern Washington's Methow Valley and the surrounding highlands, an area of subalpine, hill, marsh, pine gorge, and riparian habitats.

Spending time in each environment, you learn how to identify butterfly species, such as the two-tailed tiger swallowtail and Lorquin's admiral, and birds, including several species of tanager. You also learn how preserving the various environments results in a more diverse wildlife population. Leaders Libby Mills, a wildlife biologist and illustrator, and Saul Weisberg, executive director of the North Cascades Institute, ecologist, and writer, share their expert knowledge of the local environment and its wildlife. Because you spend entire days out in the field, hiking to different ecosystems and catching butterflies, come prepared for the Northwest's infamous rain.

Accommodations for the seminar are at the 3M Ranch, near the town of Mazama, at the edge of the wilderness area. A full kitchen, bathrooms with showers, and six beds are available inside the ranch house. You can also camp in a meadow adjacent to the house. You must bring your own food and camping equipment. The institute, established in 1983, offers field seminars throughout the Pacific Northwest aiming to raise awareness about the relationships between living things and their environments. *North Cascades Institute, 2105 Hwy. 20, Sedro Woolley, WA 98284, tel. 360/ 856–5700, ext. 209. Mid-June: 4 days, $165. Price does not include meals; sign up 1 month in advance.*

WASHINGTON **Marine Science Camp.** A 45-minute seaplane ride from Seattle or Vancouver takes you to Spieden Island, the base for this weeklong camp sponsored by the Island Institute, founded in 1990 to educate people about the marine life and natural history of the Puget Sound area. On this trip you observe firsthand the whales, otters, porpoises, and marine birds of the island and explore their habitats, from the shoreline to the depths of the sound.

There are different sessions for adults, young people ages 9 to 18, and families, but the staff is consistent: Four core instructors with degrees in natural science fields, an assistant instructor, a boat skipper, and a kitchen staff.

A 556-acre member of the San Juans, Spieden Island is home to herds of European fallow deer, mouflon sheep, and Asian sika deer, as well as bald eagles and at least 68 other species of birds—but there are no human settlements. Your days are spent hiking, sea kayaking, exploring tide-pools, and cruising aboard the institute's 43-foot charter boat looking for otters, seals, whales, and porpoises. You can also don a wet suit and go snorkeling: Urchins, anemones, sea stars, abalone, crabs, fish, and otters populate the shallow waters just offshore. The last two days of the camp are left open for you to spend more time at your favorite activity.

You're free from 3:30 to 6 PM each day, time that you can use to hike, relax in the Jacuzzi, or do research in the nature library. In the evening, the staff gives talks and presents slide shows that relate to the day's activities.

Accommodations for the camp are in 10 safari-style tents with wood floors and cots. Each tent is shared by two to four adults or three to five children. A rustic cedar lodge central to all of the tents contains the shared bathrooms and hot showers, the dining area, the library, and the swimming pool and Jacuzzi. The gourmet food (a rarity at ecology camps) is served buffet style and includes seafood and vegetarian entrées and fresh baked goods. Three two-bedroom cottages with private kitchens and bathrooms are also available for an additional charge. *Island Institute, Box 661, Vashon, WA 98070, tel. 206/463–6722, fax 206/463–3396. Mid-June–mid-Aug.: 7 days, $700–$1,025. Sign up 2 months in advance.*

ALASKA

SEWARD **Alaska Summit.** This seven-day National Wildlife Federation summit focuses on the complex ecosystems and varied wildlife of the area that surrounds the port town of Seward, on Alaska's Kenai Peninsula. The small town at the head of Resurrection Bay, the gateway to Kenai Fjords National Park, is nestled among jagged mountains blanketed by lush green vegetation and alpine wildflowers. As with most NWF summits, the 400 participants are broken up into smaller groups by their selections from a wide variety of morning and afternoon classes and field trips. Top-notch leadership of both adult and children's programs is provided by 70 to 80 staff members.

Daily hikes and boat excursions into the National Park give you the opportunity to learn about and observe the area's abundant wildlife. Sea mammals here include humpback whales, Stallar's sea lions, harbor seals, and sea otters, while along the shore you'll see bald eagles, mountain goats, moose, and bears. The rocky coastline also has excellent birding, with over 20 species of seabirds nesting both in the park and on the Chiswell and Pye islands of the Alaska Maritime National Wildlife Refuge. When you're not exploring, you can choose from classes on the ecology of Alaska, the cultural history of the native Alutiq peoples, glaciology, and environmental issues, such as the Exxon Valdez oil spill and the endangered species of Alaska.

The Summit is based at the Alaska Vocational Technical Center and the Institute of

Marine Science in Seward. Accommodations are available in Seward bed-and-breakfasts and hotels, or at the Seward city campground for participants with tents or RVs. You must purchase at least a partial meal plan, which includes five lunches and two dinners in the AV Tech Center cafeteria, a seafood cookout dinner, and administrative and facility fees. *National Wildlife Federation, 8925 Leesburg Pike, Vienna, VA 22184, tel. 703/790–4265 or 800/245–5484, fax 703/790–4468. Late June: 7 days, $555–$1,085. Sign up at least 6 months in advance.*

SOURCES

ORGANIZATIONS Aside from the Major Players listed near the beginning of this chapter, the **Nature Conservancy** (1815 N. Lynn St., Arlington, VA 22209, tel. 703/841–5300 or 800/628–6860), a land-trust organization, has travel programs for its members listed in its bimonthly magazine. A subscription to the magazine is included in the annual $35 membership.

If you are interested in joining one or more of the national organizations mentioned in this chapter, please use the following membership addresses and phone numbers. Basic membership ranges from $16 to $35 and includes a subscription to an organization's magazine. You can also elect to donate additional money to a group beyond the membership cost, either annually or on a one-time basis. **National Audubon Society** (700 Broadway, New York, NY 10003, tel. 212/979–3117 or 800/274–4201), **National Wildlife Federation** (8925 Leesburg Pike, Vienna, VA 22184, tel. 703/790–4306 or 800/588–1650), **Sierra Club** (85 2nd St., 2nd Floor, San Francisco, CA 94105, tel. 415/977–5500).

ALSO SEE If you enjoy spending your days outdoors observing wildlife you may want to peruse the Birding, Cultural and Natural History Cruises, and Whale-Watching Cruises chapters.

Painting Workshops

Written by Mary King Nash

Updated by Christine Begley

f you have ever held a paintbrush, dipped it in color, and confronted a blank canvas, you've experienced the dream: You're Georgia O'Keeffe painting cow skulls bleached by a New Mexico sun; Winslow Homer chronicling a nor'easter off the coast of Maine; Thomas Cole examining the wonders of a forest glade in the Catskill Mountains. Your undiscovered genius could turn Rembrandt green with envy and send Picasso back to his blue period. But the first brush stroke brings back reality and, with it, some wishful thinking: "If only I had time, a few uninterrupted days, then I could really paint my masterpiece!"

Sign up for a painting workshop and your wish is granted. Obviously you could always register for a continuing education course at a local college or art school, or a summer program at a community art center. But the opportunity to really focus on your art comes in painting workshops—weeklong programs designed for masters-in-the-making and scheduled when the weather is most pleasant, usually between March and November. Here, away from your everyday environment, you'll enjoy professional instruction, inspiring settings, and perhaps even a warm bed and three square meals a day.

No two programs are quite alike. Some are at inns or resorts; others are run by professional artists for three days or longer. Some are operated for profit (these usually provide greater physical comforts), and some are not-for-profit (these are usually less expensive). Some are at centers that offer only fine art classes; other times, painting is just one of several disciplines being taught. Some programs are better for experts; others appeal primarily to novices.

Some workshops are more serious than others, or more leisurely, more instructive, more social, more expensive, more comfortable, or more scenic. Some are longer than others, or larger. Some are indoors and others are on location. You can rough it at a campground and cook your own meals, bed down in basic dorms and subsist on mystery meat and other institutional fare, or live like a king at posh inns with antiques-filled rooms and exquisite meals. Whether you want to learn a new pastime, perfect a technique, study with a respected artist or learned professor, or simply meet and paint with kindred spirits, there's a painting workshop that's right for you.

Your choice in any one of these categories will not be limited by location; you can take a painting workshop almost anywhere in the United States. Not surprisingly, the settings that draw artists—and these workshops—are some of America the Beautiful's most beautiful: Maine's craggy coast,

Mary King Nash, a freelance writer and editor who lives in New York City, looks forward to the day that she can render images as well as Mary Cassatt. Christine Begley is an art historian who works at Antiques Magazine *in New York City.*

cool Wisconsin lakes, the green Hudson River Valley, the immense Colorado Rockies, California's lush wine country, the redwood forests of the Pacific Northwest. An unusually large number of painting workshops flourish in and around Taos, one of the most art-conscious towns in America, where the light is clear and the colors vibrant. Any artist will tell you the only true way to see any of these places is from the painter's perspective.

In general, painting weeks run from Monday through Friday; participants arrive Sunday afternoon, when there's some kind of get-acquainted event, and leave Friday afternoon or, sometimes, Saturday morning. You might start off the week with a demonstration by the instructor, who establishes your goals and explains techniques; a lecture may begin each succeeding day. Some classes are a bit more free-form; instructors start you off painting what you like and then spend their days moving from one easel to another offering help, tips, and advice on the work in progress. Either way, painting days usually run from between 9 and 10 to between 2:30 and 5; most sessions end with a critique of the day's work. After dark, some centers have lectures, informal group discussions, and other get-togethers; others, especially in areas of considerable beauty, encourage you to explore the area on your own. Most centers have studios that are open around the clock, so that you can keep on painting if your muse is a night owl. Prices for five days range from $175 to $825 for tuition only, $475 to $1,100 for a complete package that includes housing and at least some meals.

Studying the landscape of whatever area you visit and noting particulars of season, color, and light there—experiencing the moment in brilliant, living color—will reveal more about it than you could ever learn sightseeing. And the painting you complete will recall more about your stay than any postcard or photograph. It's the perfect souvenir.

CHOOSING THE RIGHT WORKSHOP

The painting workshops below all offer an attractive location, a respected program, knowledgeable teachers, and a variety of choices. Before donning smock and beret and grabbing your portable easel and paints, though, it's wise to do a little investigating to find the program that suits you best.

What subject matter and medium does the instructor teach? Although landscapes are the most popular topic, some instructors touch on figure painting, still life, or portraiture. Most workshops concentrate on a single medium, usually the one that the instructor is most comfortable with; some, however, leave the decision to you. Watercolor, although hard to master, lends itself to the immediacy of outdoor work, since its translucence reproduces some of the qualities of light you see in many landscapes and seascapes. Oils, although messy, slow, and hard to transport, are also lush and forgiving of mistakes; the colors are opulent and infused with light. You can find some classes in acrylics.

What is the class level? A novice needs to learn the basics, and programs that include daily demonstrations and a lot of supervised instruction best meet a beginner's needs. Intermediate and advanced painters usually want to get right to work; they want less structured classes that allow them to paint on their own, with individual critiques to get them over the rough spots.

Some workshops are open to students at all levels. This is not a problem for a good, experienced teacher, but you may find it irksome. If you're a beginner, you must judge whether you will find it stressful or stimulating to be around more advanced painters. An experienced painter might find beginning-level lectures boring—or might want to learn a thing or two by going back to the basics.

What are the instructor's qualifications? The instructor plays a significant role in how much instruction you receive. Investigate both teaching experience and personal style. Don't take it for granted that a talented artist will be a good teacher, or that you have found the painting experience of a lifetime just because a brochure tells you so. This is especially important if you choose to sign on with an independent workshop, put together by the instructor (who do you think writes those brochures?). If possible, try to arrange a short interview to assess your rapport with the instructor before handing over your money and committing your time. Ask questions about anything that concerns you. If the instructor makes you feel uncomfortable or skirts your questions, consider trying someone else.

How large are the classes? The answer to this question will help you determine how much individual attention the program provides: The more students, the less one-on-one instruction. In most workshops, class size is under 20.

How many instructors are there per class? This is another way of finding out how much personal attention you receive in class. There may be one or more teaching assistants if the class is large.

What are days like? Find out how the day is divided between time in the studio and outdoors, lectures, demonstrations, and free time. Some programs are more intense than others: Some are leisurely half-day sessions, others involve seven or more hours of supervised work, and others fall somewhere in between. At the most rigorous programs, you eat and sleep painting, often working late at night in studios that never close. Decide what you want, then make sure that the program can give it to you. Will you find it relaxing to spend every moment painting?

What is the location like? All the programs described in this chapter are in attractive locations, but what catches the imagination of one painter may leave another cold. If your interest is in capturing the mood of gritty city scenes, you definitely don't want

a program staged by the sea. If you want to paint the sea, you don't want one on a Taos ranch.

What's the cost and what's included? Ask about tuition, meals, accommodations, and supplies. The fee structure varies widely from one painting workshop to the next. The cost for many workshops in big cities, at resorts, and at established art schools that offer intensive programs in addition to full semesters is for tuition alone; it can range from under $150 to more than $800. At other workshops, there's a complete package that includes tuition, lodging, and most or all meals. Sometimes the workshop offers separate packages for tuition and housing; the housing price may or may not include meals. Also find out about any application fees (which may be as much as $100).

In the reviews that follow, we give the price of the complete package when such a package is available. When the workshop offers separate prices for tuition and housing, both fees are given; prices we give for housing also get you three meals a day unless otherwise noted. All prices are per person, and all-inclusive packages and lodging rates are based on double occupancy. If you are alone, you will more than likely have to share with someone, unless you are willing to pay an extra charge that is usually assessed for a single.

Note that some schools supply portable easels or field chairs; occasionally they may furnish brushes, paints, and other essentials. However, you may be more comfortable with your own supplies, so instructors usually send out a materials list.

What are the accommodations like? At workshops that provide accommodations, get a sense of the general level of comfort: Ask how large the rooms are, how they're furnished, and whether baths are private or shared. If you prefer a room of your own, make sure that singles are available. Daily maid service is not a given, except at resorts; your quarters may not have a telephone or television, again except at resorts.

Accommodations can be quite spartan at the many nonprofit arts centers that attract excellent teachers yet keep workshop costs down to enable the widest possible group of students to participate. These can be true bargains, but you may be required to have a roommate or two. In such instances, if what's provided is not to your taste, you can make your own arrangements; with the money you save on the program, you can live in the luxury that suits you. In this case, or if there are no on-site accommodations, ask for lodging recommendations; nearby options may offer discounts to workshop participants.

What is the food like? At some of the nonprofit workshops that keep costs down to allow artists of all income levels to participate, food may be simple and choices may be limited. If you prefer something different, don't buy the meal plan. Usually, menus are regionally biased (if you're painting in the Pacific Northwest, marine fare dominates menus), but nearly always include pasta and straightforward American meat and fish dishes.

What facilities and activities are available for your traveling companions who don't paint? Some programs are better than others for this. Best of all are those held at resorts and inns where other activities are available; next best are programs held in vacation areas with a lot of community activities and facilities. Some painting workshops are at centers that also offer classes in ceramics, creative writing, metalworking, papermaking, photography, printmaking, quilting, weaving, woodworking, or other fine or applied arts or crafts disciplines.

If you do decide to travel with nonpainting companions and the program that interests you is residential, ask what arrangements can be made for them; can they share your room and purchase the meal plan without paying for the workshop? There may or may not be a program for your children.

How long has the workshop been running? Longevity in a workshop is a good indica-tion that people are happy with the instruction provided—and a sign that any questions and challenges you present to the sponsors will have been resolved, probably happily, for other students before you. However, don't dismiss newcomers out of hand, particularly if their credentials are good—say, if the principals or sponsoring organizations have been involved with other noteworthy operations.

Do you have references from past students? To clarify any questions you may have about the instruction, accommodations, and food, there's no substitute for a talk with someone who has painted with the teacher, slept in the beds, and eaten the meals. Even if you call none of the names you're given, the organization's willingness to supply you with references is a good indication that the feedback you get should be positive.

How far in advance do I need to book? Schedules for summer programs are usually set by January or February. Making your commitment this early is never a bad idea, and in some cases it's essential—as for really unusual or popular workshops, which are popular in part because their small size means a lot of individual attention. On the other hand, some schools cancel courses if they don't attract enough students. In most cases, it's safe to make your plans between one and six months ahead of the workshop date. If you can't get in one year, try for the next. If you have your heart set on a specific workshop, it's always worth your while to call, even at the last minute, when you might snag a cancellation.

MAJOR PLAYERS

ACADEMY OF REALIST ART Artist-instructor Gary Faigin believes in the basics, and he offers you a solid foundation in the traditional principles of drawing and painting—namely, how to draw and paint what you see. With his wife, Pamela Belyea, he founded the Academy of Realist Art in

1989, and they run painting programs in Seattle and throughout the Northwest from April through September. A variety of six-day painting workshops are offered in oil, watercolor, and pastel, which focus on classical figure, portrait, still life, and landscape painting, both in the studio and outdoors. Also available are special workshop retreats, including boat tours, backpacking trips, and a women's retreat. The Seattle classes are held in the historic University Heights Center, and the studios stay open until 10 PM. Although tuition may seem high, instructors are all nationally known artists and educators, and evening programs and special events are offered. Classes are limited to 24 students. Tuition for six days is $550–$575, with discounts for early registration. Accommodations are not included, but a list of convenient and reasonably priced housing is available. *5004 6th Ave. NW, Seattle, WA 98107, tel. 206/784–4268, fax 206/783–1410.*

ANDERSON RANCH ARTS CENTER This center, which occupies a complex of 10 buildings on 4 acres of a former sheep ranch 10 miles from Aspen, offers nearly 100 one- and two-week arts workshops every summer, and the number is growing. It was founded in 1966. You can study painting, drawing, and sculpture, among other disciplines—whether you are a beginner or a longtime painter; there's even a children's workshop (Young Raiders of the Lost Art of Drawing and Painting). The ranch's 100-year-old log barns and main house have been skillfully renovated for use as classrooms, and there's a new painting and drawing center that's open 24 hours a day. All teachers are working professionals, and include renowned artists such as Don Nice, Bailey Doogan, and Maura Sheehan. For each workshop, two assistants are on hand in addition to the instructor, to make sure that each student gets plenty of attention; typically, there are up to 15 students in each class. The on-site dormitory-style accommodations, available in private as well as shared rooms, are a bargain; the price starts at $300 a week, including all

meals, for a shared room with single beds and shared bath. At each meal, you have a choice of two or three entrées, one of them vegetarian, and there's always a salad bar. If you want something fancier and are willing to pay $350 to $790 per week, you can stay in nearby Snowmass Village in a luxurious two- or three-bedroom apartment with hot tub, sauna, TV, and mountain-view balcony; these digs come with kitchens, so you can cook your own meals or eat out around Aspen. Tuition costs around $420 for a five-day workshop, plus a $30 registration fee. *Box 5598, Snowmass Village, CO 81615, tel. 970/923–3181, fax 970/923–3871.*

ARROWMONT SCHOOL OF ARTS AND CRAFTS This venerable multimedia fine-arts center occupies a complex of 11 gable-roof buildings and wood-framed cottages that opened in 1945 on a wooded, 70-acre Gatlinburg hillside in eastern Tennessee, not far from the Great Smoky Mountains National Park. Its one- and two-week summer workshops include painting, drawing, and sculpture for beginners through advanced students, along with ceramics, jewelry making, wood turning, and other arts. Informative, college-level courses, they meet between 9 and 11:30 in the morning and again from 1 to 4 in the afternoon, but students can work until midnight in the many studios on campus (and most do). There are usually about 15 students in each class, and the instructors, well-known artists and professors, come from all over the world. The campus has everything you could possibly need: a store that carries books and a selection of supplies, an art gallery, an art library with more than 4,000 titles, and, throughout the summer, slide shows, demonstrations, and lectures. You are housed either in simply furnished single, double, or triple rooms in cottagelike buildings (some with porches); dormitory style in a converted barn; or in the new air-conditioned dormitory, which has a few private rooms with baths. The dining room serves three meals a day, which include vegetarian choices and lots of fruit and salads; there's a barbecue picnic every Wednesday for all Arrowmont students. Tuition is $200 for five-day programs, which usually run from Sunday night through breakfast Saturday, plus $180 to $410 for accommodations and meals. There is a one-time application fee of $100. *Box 567, Gatlinburg, TN 37738, tel. 423/436–5860, fax 423/430–4101.*

DILLMAN'S CREATIVE ARTS FOUNDATION This 250-acre old-timer, established in 1935 on a peninsula in northern Wisconsin's White Sand Lake, is a family resort with a difference: Between May and October, it offers more than 100 workshops in drawing, oils, pastels, and watercolor, for beginners through advanced painters, in addition to the fishing, sailing, swimming, canoeing, waterskiing, hiking, biking, scuba diving, tennis, golf, Ping-Pong, bingo, volleyball, shuffleboard, and badminton that you might expect to find. Teachers are all professional artists, almost all of whom have years of experience as university or art school instructors and who make a living from doing the workshop circuit. Classes have a maximum of 20 students and usually run from 9 to 4 with an hour break for lunch. Participants stay in casually furnished lakeside log cabins (six with fireplaces) or in suites or rooms at the lodge, a somewhat rustic new building with three large studios and a lobby full of Queen Anne–style furnishings. Guest rooms are carpeted and have refrigerators and private bath with shower or tubs. The workshop price, which ranges from $575 to $695, includes accommodations. Children under 10 get reduced rates and those under two are free, as are programs for children accompanying their parents—arts and crafts classes, nature hikes, treasure hunts, and other activities. *Box 98F, Lac du Flambeau, WI 54538, tel. 715/588–3143.*

OX-BOW SUMMER SCHOOL OF ART With a serene landscape of sand dunes, rolling hills, forests, and marshes, this artists' retreat on a 110-acre site on Michigan's Ox-Bow lagoon, near the town of Saugatuck, has been attracting artists since about 1910, when Frederick Frary Fursman and Walter

Clute founded it as a bohemian outpost for plein-air painters. Today, the one- and two-week summer classes available between June and August are sponsored by the School of the Art Institute of Chicago, and you will be hard put to find better courses, not only in painting but also in performance, puppetry, printmaking, sculpture, and glassblowing. Courses here are serious, reflecting the presence of first-rate Art Institute faculty and visiting artists; you spend seven hours painting each day, and there are never more than 20 in a class, beginner through advanced students. After hours, there are lectures and slide presentations, and, on Fridays, a bonfire or other social gathering that encourages a spirit of bonhomie. Also on Friday, an exhibit of a staff member's work opens in the Ox-Bow Gallery, which is in a former resort hotel built shortly after the Civil War. The dining hall is also here, along with the lecture room. Guest rooms, on the second floor, are spartan, with twin beds and dressers and bathrooms down the hall. Meals are served buffet style and are quite good, with plenty of healthful and vegetarian entrées. One-week courses cost about $260 unless they are taken for credit, in which case they cost about $500, plus $348 for lodging and meals. *Ox-Bow Summer Program Office, 37 S. Wabash Ave., Room 707, Chicago, IL 60603, tel. 312/899–7455, fax 312/899–1453.*

WOODSTOCK SCHOOL OF ART The site of this institution, founded in 1968, was once the summer home of New York's Art Students League, and the list of artists associated with the school is long and impressive. Its bucolic 38 acres of lawn, woods, and overgrown gardens, at the foothills of the Catskill Mountains, is surrounded by rolling hills, reservoirs, streams, and golf courses—all inspiring to artists. The school's stone-and-timber buildings, commissioned as a National Youth Administration resident crafts center during the Depression, are now designated state and national historic landmarks; the studios have soaring ceilings and an abundance of north windows that flood the spaces with magnificent light. Classes in topics ranging from landscape painting to printmaking, using mediums from pencils to paints and clay, are available year-round for students at all ability levels, and the directors go to some pains to work out a schedule for each individual. Instructors are all professional artists, and include nationally known painters such as Richard Segalman, Albert Handell, Robert Angeloch, Richard McDaniel, and Staats Fasoldt, all featured in *American Artist* magazine. Classes held throughout the year typically meet between one and four days a week, and they run for anywhere from one week to six months, with entry to a class available at any time. You are also allowed to jump from one class to another, sampling oil painting and printmaking, say, or sculpture, or whatever combination you wish. Also available are about a dozen intensive Monday-to-Friday summer workshops, which cost a moderate $230; winter courses, at $90 to $212 for four weeks, are quite inexpensive. Classes tend to be small (around 10 students), to allow instructors to provide students with a great deal of individual attention. A converted barn with two bedrooms, a living area, and a kitchen can house up to four students (at $90 a week per person), but most participants look to the town of Woodstock for their rooms and meals; the school maintains a housing list for its students with information about motels, rooms in private homes, campgrounds, and other accommodations. *Rte. 212, Box 338, Woodstock, NY 12498, tel. 914/679–2388.*

FAVORITE WORKSHOPS

THE NORTHEAST

CONNECTICUT **American Impressionist Inspiration.** The well-respected Silvermine School of Art, founded in 1950, opens its studios for one-week and weekend workshops at the end of each semester throughout the year. One favorite program has been the workshop that offers artists of all levels the opportunity to paint the favorite landscape sites of three celebrated American impressionists—John Twachtman, Childe Hassam, and J. Alden Weir—using oils, watercolors, or pastels. Students, up to 20 per class, paint on location with instruction from 9:30 to 3:30 and there are individual critiques throughout the session. Instructors are professional painters with wide experience in their respective mediums. If the course isn't available at the time you're ready to sign up for it, you are certain to find another of equal interest. In cold months, students meet in the studio to study figure and still-life compositions; warm months find them setting up easels around the lawns and gardens of the four-acre campus or at nearby parks and historic estates.

There are plenty of attractions outside the classroom, including an art gallery with rotating exhibitions. Accommodations and meals are not included, but many painters stay around the corner at the 10-room Silvermine Tavern ($92–$110 double occupancy per night, including Continental breakfast). Meals there include New England clam chowder, broiled sole, and other New England standbys; you can also take your pick of restaurants around New Canaan. *Silvermine Guild Arts Center, 1037 Silvermine Rd., New Canaan, CT 06840-4398, tel. 203/966–6668, fax 203/966–2763. July: 5 days, tuition $340. Sign up 2 months in advance.*

MAINE **Sebasco Art Workshops.** These five-day workshops in oils and watercolor, first given in 1985, are taught by talented, well-respected instructors at the Rock Gardens Inn, a main building and 10 shingle-and-clapboard cottages, housing from two to six guests each, perched on a peninsula on the coast of Maine. Classes number between 10 and 30, and painters at all levels are accepted, from beginning through advanced; the focus in most workshops is on painting landscapes—especially the inn's gardens, lawns, and seacoast, with its breakers and tide pools—although some do some life drawing and still-life work. The good food and comfortable cottages with fireplaces, private bathrooms, and sun-porches keep painters coming back. You check in Sunday afternoon for a get-acquainted cocktail party, and the workshop ends after lunch on Friday. After breakfast on Monday, following a demonstration of technique by the instructor, you're given a picnic and head for a scenic spot on the grounds or nearby, where you paint until 3 or 4 in the afternoon. A critique at the inn rounds off the painting day. You have access to a heated swimming pool as well as an Olympic-size saltwater pool, a nine-hole golf course, and grass tennis courts; you can also take boat trips, try lawn bowling, and go surf fishing. At dinner, there's always a choice of tasty dishes such as fresh salmon with dill butter, grilled lamb chops with mint pesto, and steamed lobster with drawn butter. *Sebasco Art Workshops at the Rock Gardens Inn, Sebasco Estates, ME 04565, tel. 207/389–1339. June, July, Sept.: 5 days, complete package $750–$850. Sign up 3 months in advance.*

MASSACHUSETTS **Capturing Cape Ann's Rocky Coast.** The Rockport Art Association, a group of 230 artists and more than 900 contributors who are hooked on the beauty of this coastal town, organizes five-day landscape workshops in summer and fall and three-day workshops in the winter, for painters at all levels; you either concentrate on simplifying and planning compositions or on the impressionistic use of color, depending on the instructor. The association was founded in 1927 for the purpose of the advancement and preservation of the visual arts and has been offering these courses since 1986. Instructors are professional painters with nationwide workshop experience, and are noted for a wide range of techniques and styles, from the use of abstract watercolor to structured oils. For the summer workshops, the group, which usually includes about 16–18 participants, first gathers on Sunday evening at the association's center, part of which is a 200-year-old former tavern, for a get-acquainted wine and cheese party; you gather there again at 9 each morning to decide on a painting site—a beach, park, historic building, or other location within walking distance. Then you go out and, after a demonstration by the instructor, paint on your own, usually *alla prima* (completing the work in one sitting), with help as required, until about 3:30, when the instructor critiques each participant's work and the group breaks for lunch. Participants are on their own for accommodations and meals; there's a good selection of restaurants in town, an artsy community whose shops draw crowds of weekenders and day-trippers from nearby Boston, and the association can provide a list of lodging options. *Rockport Art Association, 12 Main St., Rockport, MA 01966, tel. 508/546–6604. June–Aug.: 5 days, tuition $250–$275. Sign up 1–2 months in advance.*

MASSACHUSETTS **Oil Painting** *Alla Prima.* At the Museum of Fine Arts in Boston, this intense, college-level workshop for painters of all levels, emphasizes finishing your landscape, figure, or still-life composition *alla prima,* in one session. This approach helps you work faster and use paint more effectively and teaches you to go with your instincts and take risks. Classes include 15 students and run from Monday through Thursday for three weeks. Instructor Ken Beck, a Boston painter, has exhibited primarily in Boston; his work is in the collections of the Boston Public Library and the Museum of Fine Arts, whose school, established in 1876, sponsors the course. Classes meet from 9 to 1 in the painting studio; afternoons and weekends are given over to independent painting at the school. There's no housing, but a limited number of students can stay in dormitories at other schools in the surrounding Back Bay–Fenway neighborhood; other lodgings in the area, one of Boston's priciest, cost considerably more. Alternatively, because the School of the Museum of Fine Arts is affiliated with Tufts University, registering for the workshops through Tufts makes you eligible for dormitory housing at its Medford, Massachusetts, campus just outside

Boston, about 30 to 45 minutes by public transportation from the museum. A snack shop in the museum building sells soup and sandwiches; there are many other restaurants 5 or 10 minutes' walk away along Huntington Avenue. *School of the Museum of Fine Arts, 230 The Fenway, Boston, MA 02115, tel. 617/267–1219, fax 617/424–6271. June: 12 days (Mon.–Thurs. for 3 wks): tuition $480, housing $465. Housing price does not include meals; sign up 2 months in advance.*

NEW YORK **The New Hudson River School.** The Catskill Mountains and the farmland, gardens, and streams of upstate New York are the subjects of student work at a series of five-day workshops held at the Greenville Arms, William Vanderbilt's 1889 Victorian manor house, on 6 acres in a rural village in New York. Every year from spring through fall it hosts about two dozen one-week workshops in watercolor, pastels, drawing, and oil painting, for beginning through advanced painters, up to 20 per class. Landscape is the usual focus, but workshops in floral painting, experimental techniques, and figure are also offered, with a different well-known artist teaching each. Workshops are in session between 9 and 4 daily, but students often paint after class, since the studio is open around the clock. The program was established in 1981.

The instructor of this class is Betty Lou Schlemm, a renowned artist and respected teacher and author. Classes run from 9 to 4 and are held outdoors, where she will help you concentrate on color, space, light, and movement with watercolor, as well as help artists develop a deeper appreciation of nature through the landscape.

Dispelling the myth that art is born of suffering, this package treats you to antiques-filled rooms with bed linens dried in the sun, as they were in simpler times. The inn's chef cooks delicious country fare: At breakfast, for instance, there's homemade banana-bread French toast or blueberry-buttermilk pancakes. Guests arrive in time for a wine and cheese party on Sunday afternoon and depart after breakfast on Saturday. If you register before April 15, your name is entered in a drawing, and if you win, your whole package is free. You'll find a swimming pool, shuffleboard, and croquet, as well as bikes to rent and tennis and golf nearby. *Hudson River Valley Art Workshops, Box 659, Greenville, NY 12083-0659, tel. 518/966–5219, fax 518/966–8754. Sept.: 5 days, complete package $699 (double), $829 (single). Sign up 1 month in advance.*

NEW YORK **Painting the Big Apple.** The New York Studio School in Greenwich Village is a historic spot in the art world: It was the original home of the Whitney Museum of American Art and, before that, the sculpture studio of Gertrude Vanderbilt Whitney and Daniel Chester French. The school was founded in 1964 and relocated to its current address a year later. It has full spring and fall semesters and offers this two-week Painting Outdoors in New York course for experienced painters in all mediums—oils, acrylics, and watercolors—as part of its summer program of intensive two-, three-, and five-week courses in studio and location painting, drawing, and sculpture. Like all the school's offerings, this one is open by application only: To be considered, you must submit examples of your work and you must paint at the intermediate level, or have considerable experience in drawing. If you're among the 15 to 20 selected, you have the run of the large, skylit studios between 8:30 AM and midnight. You meet here in the morning, then go out and paint until evening. The course's emphasis is on developing your pictorial language and familiarizing you with historical and contemporary landscape imagery; you set up your easels all over the city, painting where you please, as a group or individually. Critiques end each day, and evenings bring talks by art critics, historians, and visiting artists; at the end of the workshop, each painter's cumulative work gets an in-depth examination. Instructors are typically acclaimed working painters with diverse attitudes. *New York Studio School of Drawing, Painting and*

Sculpture, 8 W. 8th St., New York, NY 10011, tel. 212/673–6466, fax 212/777–0996. July: 2 wks (weekdays only), tuition $825. Sign up 2–3 months in advance; application deadline late May.

NEW YORK **The Woodstock Landscape.** This intensive five-day course in oil or pastel landscape painting, one of many offered each summer at the Woodstock School of Art, helps you develop successful paintings with guidance in composition and color theory. Class meets between 9 and 4, either on the campus or in the surrounding countryside to paint nearby Catskills landscapes—beautiful rolling hills, with lots of streams and reservoirs. Instructor Richard McDaniel's work has been included in several museum exhibitions, and he is the author of the *Drawing Book*. There are usually 10 students per group, mostly intermediate or advanced painters. There is limited space in a converted barn with a kitchen, for $90; most students stay and eat in nearby Woodstock. *Woodstock School of Art, Rte. 212, Box 338, Woodstock, NY 12498, tel. 914/679–2388. June: 5 days, tuition $230. Sign up 1 month in advance.*

THE SOUTH

LOUISIANA **Deep South Watercolor Encounters.** Having taught over 300 workshops, M. Douglas Walton knows a thing or two about painting. He teaches and directs this summer program of six 12-day courses at Louisiana Tech University, in the north central part of the state. All courses are in watercolor, but each has a different emphasis—composition, creative expression, color, figure, or design. Each includes daily demonstrations, lectures, and critiques; Walton's approach emphasizes the artist's individuality of expression rather than the end product. Students from the beginner through advanced levels are eligible. Every day, class runs for nine hours. You start by making preparatory sketches, sometimes on location and always under the supervision of Walton and his assistant, then

return to paint in the large studio or sketch still lifes in the adjoining composition room, both of which are open around the clock. (An instructor is there until about 5.) You may complete from one to three paintings per day. Each course includes no more than 30 students. The program was first offered in 1977.

Lodging is available off campus as well as in Louisiana Tech University dormitories; rooms have twin beds, built-in dressers, and communal bathrooms. The eclectic campus, which mixes modern and manor-style buildings, is on the outskirts of tiny, southern-rustic Ruston. Although kitchen privileges are available in the dorms, you can also eat at the college food court, which serves pizza, salads, and the like. *Louisiana Tech University, Box 3182, Ruston, LA 71272, tel. 318/251–4130, fax 318/251–5003. May–Aug.: 12 days, tuition $360–$390, housing $12 (double), $17 (single) a night. Housing price does not include meals; sign up 2 months in advance.*

TENNESSEE **Watercolors in the Smokies.** A five-day watercolor workshop is one of many offered at the Arrowmont School on its 70-acre mountain campus in the eastern part of the state, but the specific content varies from year to year, since it is very much a reflection of the interests of the individual instructors. One might have you covering dry-brush–wet-paper techniques, graphite and watercolor combinations, calligraphic applications and brushwork, or paint layering. With another instructor, you might concentrate on drawing, or work on location, or use a live model. Instructors tend to be from universities, experienced at teaching, and classes usually include no more than 15 students, most of them at the beginner to intermediate level but also including some advanced students.

Dormitory housing is available on a first-come, first-served basis, in single, double, triple rooms with private or adjoining baths, or in simple cottage rooms with communal baths. Meals are included with dormitory housing, and a meal plan is also available to participants staying off campus. *Arrowmont School of Arts and Crafts, Box 567, Gatlinburg, TN 37738, tel. 423/436–5860, fax 423/430–4101. June–mid-Aug.: 5 days, tuition $200, housing and meals $180–$410. Sign up 2–3 months in advance.*

THE MIDWEST

MICHIGAN **Painting on the Banks of Lake Michigan.** The shore of Lake Michigan, with its sand dunes, rolling hills, forests, and marshes, constitutes the principal subject matter for the 20 beginning, intermediate, and advanced landscape painters who take the two-week course at this picturesque 110-acre retreat in Saugatuck, Michigan, sponsored by the School of the Art Institute of Chicago. At times a model is brought in to compound the challenge of rendering the landscape. Classes typically meet from 10 until 5. Instructors are first-rate faculty art professors and visiting painters and teach oils, egg tempera, and other mediums.

Lodging and meals are in a former resort hotel built shortly after the Civil War. Rooms are spare, and meals include lots of granola, salads, and vegetables. *Ox-Bow Summer School of Art, 37 S. Wabash Ave., Room 707, Chicago, IL 60603, tel. 312/899–5130, fax 312/899–1453. Mid-June–mid-Aug.: 7 days, tuition $264–$510 (discounts for seniors available), housing and meals $348. Sign up 3 months in advance.*

WISCONSIN **Landscapes in Pastels, Oils, and Acrylics.** This five-day workshop, one of about 100 visual arts programs offered between spring and fall by Dillman's Creative Arts Foundation, concentrates on teaching students to block in and layer color to express atmosphere in natural light. The painting day begins at 9 with a demonstration and discussion in the studio. In the afternoon, the class, made up of up to 25 painters of all levels, moves outdoors to paint on location with the instructor. Teachers include nationally recognized artists such as Tom Lynch and Bob Hoffman, who have years of teaching experience. Studios are open 24 hours a day.

At this 250-acre family resort on White Sand Lake in northern Wisconsin, accommodations are in lakeside log cabins and the main lodge; at meals, six different entrées are available, all served with homemade bread. *Dillman's Creative Arts Foundation, Box 98F, Lac du Flambeau, WI 54538, tel. 715/588–3143. July: 5 days, package $615. Price does not include meals; sign up 3 months in advance.*

WISCONSIN **Watercolor Retreat.** The Clearing, a retreat center that opened in 1935 and sponsors workshops in the arts, is on 128 acres of woods and meadows on the shores of Green Bay in scenic Door County. All the buildings are log or native stone, and the entire site is on the National Register of Historic Places. Founder Jens Jensen, a landscape designer and conservationist, aimed to create "a source of renewal and communion with nature, a place for clearing one's mind." Accordingly, workshops at the Clearing are informal and relaxing (never with more than 18 students), and encourage every participant to be aware of nature.

In this six-day workshop, long-time Clearing instructor Win Jones offers plenty of one-on-one attention to intermediate watercolorists. After lectures, students work at their own pace, and wherever they prefer—in the studio or outdoors. Classes are limited to 17 students.

Other programs at the Clearing include both independent study and organized classes in photography, weaving, wood carving, nature study, stained glass, quilting, dance, writing, philosophy, and pastels. Pressure is at a minimum here—there are no deadlines or painting schedules apart from the demonstrations by the instructor—and since studios are open around the clock, you can keep your own schedule. For dinner, served family-style, you might find a country-style chicken breast served with rice pilaf, an orange and spinach salad, and cherry cheesecake.

Accommodations are either doubles with private bath or dormitory rooms that sleep three or six. *The Clearing, 12183 Garrett Bay Rd., Box 65, Ellison Bay, WI 54210-0065, tel. 414/854–4088, fax 414/854–9751. Late July: 6 days, complete package $495–$535. Sign up 4 months in advance.*

THE SOUTHWEST

NEW MEXICO **Adventures in Watercolor.** Nestled in the peaceful mountain village resort of Cloudcroft, Mountain Majesty Workshops offers a complete learning experience that extends beyond the classroom. In this five-day watercolor workshop, you learn to create more powerful landscapes that capture the dramatic southwestern vistas. Working both in the studio and on-site, instructor Larry Weston, of the weekly television series "Adventures in Watercolor," emphasizes creating moods in your landscapes. The class, open to students of all levels, meets from 9 to 4 and is limited to 16 students.

In addition to the watercolor workshop, there are about 40 different five-day painting classes, ranging from conceptual impressionism in oil to beginning watercolor. Instructors are all nationally known artists who come from all over the country, including Bill Herring, Sheila Parsons, Alan Flattmann, and Barbara Savage. They give lectures and demonstrations, but the emphasis is on individual attention. Workshops are offered in June, July, and October. In addition, there are classes for children, and outside activities such as exploring the Carlsbad Caverns, horseback riding, golfing, hiking, and tennis. Lodging options include cabins, lodges, and bed-and-breakfasts in Cloudcroft, as well as camping. *Mountain Majesty Workshops, Box 66, High Rolls, NM 88325, tel. 800/682–2547. July: 5 days, tuition $260. Sign up 2 months in advance.*

NEW MEXICO **Taos en Plein Air.** Bill Stewart, one of the many talented painters who call Taos home, conducts this five-day landscape watercolor workshop under the aegis of the Taos Institute of Art at some of his favorite painting spots in Taos Valley. The emphasis is on formal painting problems—particularly composition—as they apply to landscape painting in watercolor. The class, limited to 12 beginning and intermediate painters, meets after breakfast and usually works until dusk, to capture the evening light.

Other programs offered by the institute, which was founded in 1989, cover painting in other mediums, creative writing, local history, weaving, pottery, and photography, among other subjects. You're on your own for accommodations, but the center will make recommendations; and Taos is a good restaurant town, especially for southwestern and Spanish food. *Taos Institute of Art, Box 1389, Taos, NM 87571, tel. 505/758–2793, fax 505/758–2793. Aug.: 5 days, tuition $345. Sign up 5 months in advance.*

TEXAS **Wildflowers in Pencil and Watercolor.** During this five-day workshop at the nonprofit Hill Country Arts Foundation, the focus is on capturing the moods and colors of nature, and on making naturalistic interpretations of the land around the center—16 acres of wildflowers bordering the Guadalupe River at Johnson Creek, 6 miles west of Kerrville and 65 miles northwest of San Antonio. Each day begins with an outdoor sketching trip to create color and value studies. Instructors, who are mostly professional artists and exhibiting painters, give a painting demonstration every day. Although you don't have to be an expert to sign up, some experience in water mediums is recommended. There are up to 15 students in the workshop, which meets from 9 until 3, with an hour break for lunch; the painting studios stay open until 5.

The center, founded in 1958, sponsors a number of other affordable painting workshops throughout the year as well as workshops in subjects such as photography, sculpture, printmaking, jewelry making, folk art, ceramics, and drawing. You're on your own for room and board, but the center will make suggestions. Most students bring bag lunches and eat dinners in local restaurants, which serve everything from Continental fare to ethnic and Texas specialties. *Hill Country Arts Foundation, Box 176, Ingram, TX 78025, tel. 210/367–5121, fax 210/367–5725. June: 5 days, tuition $175. Sign up 2 months in advance.*

THE ROCKIES

COLORADO **Painting the Landscape in Oils.** The Anderson Ranch Arts Center buzzes year-round, but summers are chockablock with workshops, including this 12-day landscape class. Working strictly in oil, this workshop focuses on the experience of painting outside, in the tradition of such 19th-century landscape artists as Corot, Courbet, and van Gogh. Instructor Diane Burko introduces easy ways to respond quickly in oil to the changing light of Colorado vistas, and helps students develop their studies into larger works. Students paint on site as well as in the studio, and instruction is enhanced with group critiques and slide lectures. There is always plenty of individual attention, since there are only 16 students in a class. Although this workshop is open to painters at all levels, participants should have some knowledge of painting and color design, as well as basic drawing skills.

Housing is in dorm rooms, which are extremely economical, especially since their price includes meals, or in more comfortable, more spacious, and more expensive apartments at nearby Snowmass Village; these come without meals but have access to kitchens, hot tubs, whirlpools, and a swimming pool. *Anderson Ranch Arts Center, Box 5598, Snowmass Village, CO 81615, tel. 303/923–3181 or 800/595–2722, fax 303/923–3871. Late June–July: 12 days, tuition $630, housing $300–$450 per wk with meals or $350–$790 per week without. Sign up 4 months in advance.*

WYOMING **The Snake River in Watercolors.** The Snake River Institute, founded in 1988 and headquartered at the Hardeman Ranch in Wilson, Wyoming, 7 miles from Jackson and very near Grand Teton National Park, is the setting for this five-day open-air workshop in watercolor and oil for painters at all levels. Instructors vary from year to year, but are chosen for the passion they bring to their subject and for their ability to teach; Judith DeShong Hall and Hollis Williford, who taught not long ago, added a new dimension to the painting experience by encouraging students to chronicle their work and surroundings in an illustrated journal. Each morning you undertake painting assignments that help you hone your drafting skills amid mountain peaks, glacial lakes, and groves of cottonwoods; during the afternoon, you work individually. Classes never have more than 15 students per instructor.

This workshop is one of more than two dozen offered between April and October on topics relating to the arts and humanities, celebrating the cultures and communities of the American West; other topics range from Pueblo Indian life, art in Santa Fe, and photography in Yellowstone to storytelling and dinosaur digs. The institute can recommend accommodations; meals are available in Wilson, where your options include a deli and two American-style restaurants, and in Jackson, where you'll find everything from fancy French cafés to mom-and-pop spots that serve up meat-and-potatoes fare. *Snake River Institute, Box 128, Wilson, WY 83014, tel. 307/733–2214, fax 307/739–1710. June: 4 days, tuition $350. Sign up 3 months in advance.*

THE WEST COAST

CALIFORNIA **Painting the Goldrush Country.** Paint the historic town of Murphys, in the heart of California's Gold Rush country, in this five-day watercolor workshop led by instructor Doris Olsen, an award-winning artist specializing in landscape painting. The focus of the workshop is on learning to capture the different values and contrasts of colors in this unique landscape: Working exclusively on location, students paint picturesque old barns, country churches, ponds, and street scenes. The workshop begins with a wine and cheese reception on Sunday evening, and meets every day from 9 to 4. It is open to students of all levels.

This is one of a number of workshops offered by Olsen. Other workshops include studio painting, where the focus is on still-life arrangements, and plein air painting in the luxurious gardens surrounding the studio. Classes are limited to 10 students to allow plenty of individual instruction, and students are encouraged to work in both the daylight and the night, to observe and learn to capture the different shadows and light values. Painting weeks generally begin with dinner on Sunday evening and end at 4 PM Friday. Lodging and meals are available in the town of Murphys. *California Gold Country Painting Workshops, 17364 Overland Trail, Sonora, CA 95370, tel. 209/586–2472. Mid-June: 5 days, tuition $250. Sign up 3 months in advance.*

CALIFORNIA **Painting Workshop with Roger Armstrong.** This five-day summer workshop, part of the Art Institute of Southern California's community education program, is a good and affordable introduction to outdoor painting. The class meets from 9 until 2, with an hour-long break for lunch, and works either in the studio or at scenic sites on campus, one of them a grove of stately sycamore trees that survived the 1993 fires. You might cover the nature of color, composition, collage, transparent and opaque techniques, and techniques for working with oil, acrylics, and watercolor; you also learn how to work from sketches and how to give paintings atmosphere. There are about 12 students of all levels in every class. Instructor Roger Armstrong, an expert watercolorist, is a past president of the National Watercolor Society.

The campus of the Art Institute of Southern California, which was founded in 1961 and has been offering this program since 1989, is an oasis of lawns and gardens in Laguna Beach, just 2 miles from the Pacific. Lodging is not included, but you have a choice of hotels and motels around Laguna Beach. Meals are in restaurants; you can take your pick of everything from burgers and fries to Continental fare. *Art Institute of Southern California, 2222 Laguna Canyon Rd., Laguna Beach, CA 92651, tel. 714/497–3309 or 800/255–0762, fax 714/497–4399. Mid-July: 5 days, tuition about $200. Sign up 2 months in advance.*

OREGON **Experimenting with Watercolor.** For two weeks during every summer since 1966, the Creative Arts Community at Menucha, a former estate that serves as a retreat and conference center the rest of the year, has offered one- and two-week workshops in such topics as oil painting, watercolor, drawing, furniture painting, soapstone sculpture, ceramics, and poetry at this wooded, 96-acre property overlooking the Columbia River Gorge. The course, for artists at all levels, is one of several that fill up particularly early with repeaters. They come for the outstanding instructors, practicing artists and teachers, many with M.F.A.'s, and appreciate the warmth of the community and the good food, particularly the homemade bread. You meet not only on location but also in the studio, which is open around the clock, and cover such topics as wet-on-wet, dry brush, and mixed-media combinations. Classes are in session between 9 and noon and 1 and 4 Monday through Friday (you arrive on Sunday and leave after breakfast on Saturday); there are slide shows, lectures, and other programs after dark. There are usually about 10 students in a class.

The course fee includes good meals made with local produce and lodging in a dormitory room with three to five beds (limited private and semiprivate rooms are available at an additional charge). Menucha has a jogging trail, tennis court, volleyball court, and swimming pool. *Creative Arts Community, Box 4958, Portland, OR 97208, tel. 503/760–5837 or 503/236–4109. Aug.: 5–10 days, complete package $475–$875 ($607–$1,161 with private room, $546–*

$1,019 with semiprivate). Sign up 5 months in advance.

WASHINGTON **Capturing Color with Watercolor Painting.** This three-day workshop, one of more than 60 classes offered between March and October by an environmental learning center known as the North Cascades Institute, is held at Brown's Farm, in the majestic Methow Valley. The site has beautiful gardens, creeks, and meadows, and rugged mountain vistas. The class stresses the importance of observation in painting nature, and you experiment with the versatility of watercolor, using both wet-on-wet and dry-brush techniques. After discussions at the farm in the morning, you move outdoors to paint on location in the afternoon and evening under the guidance of an instructor. Each class has no more than 10 students, of all levels, and one instructor, who is chosen based on expertise and teaching ability. Although the whole approach is relaxed and non-judgmental, there's no shortage of instruction; there are individual critiques every day after dinner.

Accommodations, at Brown's Farm Bed and Breakfast, are in shared rustic cabins with fully equipped kitchens; there are no private baths. The rest of the year, the center offers classes in nature studies, photography, birding, creative writing, marine ecology, geology, and drum making. *North Cascades Environmental Learning Center, North Cascades Institute, 2105 Hwy. 20, Sedro Woolley, WA 98284, tel. 360/856–5700, fax 360/856–1934. July: 3 days, package $155. Price does not include meals; sign up 4 months in advance.*

WASHINGTON **Paint the San Juan Islands.** Choose a 6- or 11- day watercolor workshop where you will explore the color and light of Washington's Orcas Island. Moving from site to site, to increasingly complex compositions, you will explore and paint the water, boats, fields, forests, and farms of the Pacific Northwest. Instructor Caroline Buchanan has been teaching watercolor workshops in and around the islands since 1984 and offers classes year-round. Class runs from 10 AM to 4 PM; biking, kayaking, fishing, and hiking are available afterward. The program admits up to 16 students of various levels. Accommodations are in cabins and bed-and-breakfasts in the area. *Buchanan Watercolors, Ltd., Box 218, Olga, WA 98279, tel. 360/376–5509, fax 360/376–5509. July and Sept.: 6 days, $180, 11 days, $270. Sign up 4 months in advance.*

SOURCES

ORGANIZATIONS The **Visual Artist Information Hotline** (tel. 800/232–2789, weekdays 2–5 PM EST or leave message), although not a source of workshop recommendations, can help locate books, resources, and local agencies that provide assistance to visual artists.

PERIODICALS The March issues of the *Artist's Magazine* (F&W Publications, Inc., 1507 Dana Ave., Cincinnati, OH 45207, tel. 513/531–2222) and of *American Artist* (BPI Communications, 1515 Broadway, New York, NY 10036, tel. 212/764–7300) include lists of hundreds of workshops.

BOOKS The *Guide to Art & Craft Workshops,* by Shaw Guides, Inc., available in most city libraries, provides detailed notes about workshops and residency programs throughout the United States.

ALSO SEE Want to channel your creativity in other ways? Turn to Arts and Crafts Workshops, Photography Workshops and Tours, or Writing Conferences and Workshops.

Photography Workshops and Tours

Written by Lori P. Greene

Updated by Stacy Abramson

ike insects in amber, images are held suspended within the framework of a photograph, pieces of time captured. But not every image is equal: Some elicit moods, some bring back memories, and some do nothing at all.

What is it that makes a photograph effective? The angle of the shot, the direction of the light source, the brilliance of the color, the intensity of the subject matter, the clearness or smokiness of the print. These are just some of the points that a good photographer must consider. It is not just a matter of point and shoot.

To make strong photographic statements, you must exercise your mind and cultivate your eye, then practice your technique. One of the best ways for both amateurs and experienced photographers to do this is to enroll in a photography workshop or tour.

In a *workshop* situation, you spend your time in a classroom, studio, and darkroom, and sometimes on location. You focus on specific technical skills, aesthetics, or a particular aspect of photography, such as portraiture, photojournalism, and documentary. Critiques of everyone's work are an integral part of the learning process.

On a photography *tour,* you travel to one or more destinations and spend much energy shooting in the field—landscapes, wildlife, architecture, cityscapes, and more—trying to capture the essence of what you see. You may experiment with challenging light conditions or learn how to observe wildlife patiently before snapping your shutter. If there are facilities for developing your film, there may be critiques, but sometimes you don't see your work until the tour is over.

During some workshops, you are immersed in the image-making process from dawn until late evening. If you're not taking a darkroom course, your film is usually developed overnight so that your photos may be critiqued the next day. This feedback is crucial—it can take your work in new directions—but be forewarned: Critical evaluations by instructors and fellow students are sometimes difficult to swallow. Some teachers and peers are honest to the point of insensitivity, so you must be able to stand up to harsh criticism. The feedback, good or bad, is often the most beneficial part of the course. It can teach you what you did wrong and how to fix it or build your confidence in how you shoot. Furthermore, what you learn from evaluations of other students' work can be applied to your own photography.

There are a variety of institutions that offer photography workshops and tours, in both leafy settings and urban centers. Large photography programs with workshops for students at all levels of experience are offered

Freelance writer Lori P. Greene takes her photography classes while on assignment with her husband, a professional photographer. A former photo editor at The New York Observer, *Stacy Abramson is now a wistful recreational photographer.*

by such institutions as the International Center of Photography in New York, the Maine Photographic Workshops, and the Santa Fe Photographic Workshops. These programs cover aesthetics, printing, computer-generated imagery, hand painting, black-and-white developing, and more—all taught by a diverse faculty consisting of leading professionals.

Smaller institutions, schools, and even individual photographers have programs with a narrower scope. These often focus on a single aspect of photography, one in which the instructor has lots of experience, be it nature, landscape, or underwater photography or perhaps black-and-white printing.

Some institutions have a photography program that complements programs in other art forms. The Touchstone Center for Crafts in Pennsylvania and the Anderson Ranch Arts Center in Colorado, for example, are multiart centers where such crafts as painting, drawing, woodworking, sculpture, and furniture design are also taught. These are good places to take a companion who wants to study something other than photography.

Many photography tours are set up by companies that specialize in outdoor adventure. They are often led by professional outdoor photographers who work alongside you while providing advice on how to frame a picture and what exposure to use. Instruction is less formal than that of workshops, but you may be up at dawn, when the low light transforms even the most mundane scenes into visual wonders. You spend the day touring a given area and learning ways to view it, and at dusk you're still behind the camera while the light once again hangs low.

Tours are generally open to shutterbugs of all levels, but most workshops are designed for either beginning, intermediate, or advanced photographers. A beginner usually knows the basics of using a camera; an intermediate student has taken pictures for a few years and may have a portfolio of work; and an advanced photographer has

shot seriously for several years and may have worked professionally.

Workshops and tours also differ in the intensity of the work at hand. You can pick a workshop in which you must spend dawn to midnight in class, in the field, and in the darkroom, with little time to relax; or you can pick one that meets for only part of the day. Photography tours tend to be even more laid-back, with photography an important part of an overall vacation. You travel from place to place, and although you do receive instruction, it is less time-consuming than the amount offered in workshops. Beginners may enjoy a tour more than a workshop, because it allows you to gain experience in a less pressured atmosphere.

Both photography workshops and tours are costly—prices range from about $325 for five days to $3,750 for two weeks—but most participants get their money's worth. These courses help you focus on the visual part of your world and turn single moments into potent works of art.

CHOOSING THE RIGHT PROGRAM

After you decide what you want to learn and whether you want to take a workshop or a tour, you should investigate all your options. Asking the following questions will help you make the right choice.

How long has the institution or operator been in business and how long has the particular workshop or tour been run? Experience is often the key to smooth programming and trouble-free workings.

What aspect of photography does the workshop or tour focus on? Make sure you sign up for a workshop or tour that addresses your needs. Maybe you want to learn more about composition or develop a new technical skill, such as color processing. Perhaps you want to gain experience shooting portraits or learn to take better scenic shots. If you've always wanted to produce the perfect black-and-white print, then a darkroom workshop is probably the answer. If you aren't drawn to a particular topic but wish to improve your overall skills, try a class that explores personal vision. If you're beyond the beginner's stage, a lighting or portraiture workshop may be right for you. Workshops that explore specific areas of photography, such as photojournalism and documentary photography; special printing techniques; or particular formats, such as view cameras, are usually geared to intermediate or advanced photographers. If you have little interest in the great outdoors, you are probably better off learning in a classroom than taking a tour to the Alaskan wilderness.

What skills and level of experience are required? Some workshops and tours are set up to accommodate photographers with varied skills and experience; others are designed particularly for students who are either beginners, experienced amateurs, or professionals. Sometimes a specific technical skill is required, and sometimes you must submit a qualifying portfolio in order to be accepted into a course.

What type of film and camera format are used? For lots of workshops and tours you must use color slide film, but there are some for fans of black-and-white images. A few classes encourage the use of many kinds of film. Almost all workshops and tours have you shooting with a 35mm camera; if you want to use another format, such as a 2¼ or 8x10 view camera, either look for a course or tour specifically designed for that format or make sure the instructor is willing and able to address your needs.

What equipment do I need to bring? You almost always are responsible for bringing a camera, film, and tripod; sometimes you must have filters and different lenses. If you are asked to bring equipment that you don't own, you may want to choose a different workshop rather than buy, borrow, or rent it.

What is the maximum number of participants? What is the student-to-teacher ratio? Most workshops and tours limit the number of participants. A class of eight is small enough to ensure that each student receives an equal amount of attention and large enough for students to learn from one another without getting bored. A maximum student-teacher ratio of 10 to 1 gives all students enough time to ask questions and have their work evaluated.

How much time is devoted to instruction? Is there free time for other activities? You must decide how much time you want to spend learning, taking pictures, or working in the darkroom. Some workshops are so intensive that you must work from early in the morning to late at night; this kind of schedule is designed to push your creativity to the utmost and improve your skills through constant practice. Other workshops and, particularly, photography tours give you more time to relax and enjoy the scenery.

Are instructors available outside of class? Can private conferences and critiques be arranged? You spend a lot of time with your instructors in class and on field trips, so you may not care to interact with them during your free time. On the other hand, you may enjoy their company and want to spend as much time as you can absorbing their knowledge. If that's the case, pick a workshop or tour in which the instructor stays in the same hotels as students and eats in the same dining hall or restaurants. Sometimes instructors will meet with students privately to discuss their work; sometimes this is not an option.

Where can I see the instructor's work? Before you sign up for any course, it's a good idea to look at samples of the instructor's work. If you like it, there's a good chance you can learn something useful from that person; if you don't, it's unlikely that you will respect what he or she has to say about your own work.

What's the cost and what's included? Workshop fees may or may not include lodging and meals, whereas fees for tours usually do. Unless otherwise stated, prices given in this chapter are per person and include lodging and meals. Lodging is either double occupancy or in multibunk rooms, unless specified differently; when single rooms are available, you must pay a supplement to get one. Whether you sign up for a workshop or a tour, you must bring your own equipment and film. Transportation between shooting locations is most often provided, but ask just to be sure.

Is there a lab fee? Many programs charge a lab fee that covers film processing or chemicals if the workshop concentrates on darkroom work. This could add substantially to the cost of your vacation.

What are the accommodations like? Some institutions have their own housing, which may consist of both private and shared rooms. On tours, you often stay in motels, hotels, or campgrounds. Find out if you must share a room with other students or a bathroom down the hall or, if camping, a tent.

What is the food like? Sometimes you eat in dining halls with cafeteria-style food; sometimes a chef is hired to cook up fancier meals. You may have to rely on local restaurants, so make sure there are enough of them that serve food that appeals to you.

Do you have references from past participants? Try to talk with at least two people who have taken the workshop or tour, but take what they say with a grain of salt. Although they can give you details not found in the brochures, keep in mind that the chemistry between a student and an instructor can greatly affect what the student gets out of the course.

How far in advance must I sign up? For some workshops and tours you must sign up months in advance, but if there's an opening, those that don't require portfolio reviews will usually accept you up until the last minute.

FAVORITE WORKSHOPS AND TOURS

THE NORTHEAST

MAINE **Maine Photographic Workshops.** Established in 1973 by David Lyman, this institution has one of the largest photography programs in the country, with 100 one- and two-week courses each year. It is based in the picturesque seaside village of Rockport on Penobscot Bay, 90 miles north of Portland and 2 miles from the lively resort town of Camden, in an isolated environment that's perfect for concentrating on creative work.

Workshops are offered for students with all levels of technical and artistic experience, from the beginner to the career photographer; each class is limited to between 16 and 18 participants. Most courses on the intermediate and advanced levels require you to submit a portfolio or tear sheets with your application.

Whether you're seeking to develop your skills in taking personal, fine art, or commercial images, you should have no trouble finding the right class. The schedule includes workshops in black-and-white and color photography, portraiture, professional development (such as Introduction to Photojournalism, Fine Art Business, and The Motion Picture Still), the studio, and digital imagery, as well as fine art, travel, stock, and documentary photography. "Foundation" workshops teach beginners the basics of techniques and aesthetics. Master classes are designed for advanced photographers and give them the chance to work with leading experts in the field; recent offerings have included Portrait and Figure Class, The Handmade Photograph, Photographing Cultures, and The World Observed.

The faculty is chosen from some of the best fine art and commercial photographers working today. Recent instructors have included Chris Rainier, Arnold Newman, George Tice, Mary Ellen Mark, Eugene Richards, Jill Enfield, and Sarah Lean, as well as other professionals who have worked for *Life, National Geographic, Sports Illustrated,* and other major magazines, such as Jim Blair, Elizabeth Opalenik, and Bill Allard.

You should be prepared for an intensive schedule. Classes begin at 9, and mornings are busy with lectures, critiques and discussions of students' work, and technical demonstrations. Afternoons usually center on field trips and one-on-one meetings with instructors. A good part of your day is devoted to hands-on experience to learn the skills of your particular workshop. Film and slides are processed overnight so they can be critiqued the next morning. Photographers are often found working in the darkrooms until late at night (darkrooms are open from 8 AM until midnight). In the evenings, you can attend screenings and slide shows devoted to photographic subjects.

The extensive facilities include 50 enlargers in group darkrooms, a color film-processing lab, a library, a gallery, a photography supply store, and a 2,200-square-foot Studio Barn with a wide selection of lights, grip equipment, sets, and props, used mainly for the film (motion picture) program. The recently opened Ernst Haas Photographic Center contains five new classrooms, a 14-enlarger darkroom, and eight private darkrooms.

Lodging and dining are available on campus or nearby. The 100 rooms on campus, available on a first-come, first-served basis, are within walking distance of classrooms and dining. They range from basic dorm rooms with shared bath to homier rooms with TV, telephone, and private bath. Other accommodations include single and double motel rooms and rooms in private residences with private or shared baths. You can also stay at recommended inns and bed-and-breakfasts, which tend to be more expensive. Students are encouraged to take three meals a day at the Homestead, a 19th-century farmhouse, where you dine and network with staff and other workshop participants. Meals are served buffet style, and vegetarian and

special diets can be catered to; on Friday night, a complete banquet is held, with lobster, steak, fresh corn, and pies for dessert. *Maine Photographic Workshops, 2 Central St., Rockport, ME 04856, tel. 207/236–8581, fax 207/236–2558. June–Oct.: 7 days, $450, plus $85–$125 lab fee; 14 days, $900, plus lab fee. Price does not include lodging and meals ($355–$625 per week).*

MASSACHUSETTS **Edward Barry Photographic Services.** Since 1988, this company has specialized in travel and scenic photography workshops that provide concentrated time and new opportunities behind the viewfinder. They are designed for aspiring beginners as well as more experienced photographers. The Whale Watch and Lighthouse Excursion, a five-day workshop in Cape Ann (a peninsula on the northeastern tip of Massachusetts), encourages a supportive rather than competitive critiquing of your work as you learn from each member's knowledge and experience. In lectures or in the field, the workshop covers composition, exposure, lighting, and the effects of lenses and filters in travel and scenic photography. It is limited to eight students with one instructor; if more students wish to join the class, an additional instructor is engaged. The instructors are Edward Barry, who is a veteran photographer, a judge of photography competitions, and a professional photography teacher in New Jersey; and Gene Sellers, a published photojournalist.

The workshop is scheduled from Wednesday through Sunday, and provides enough time to cover all the key sights in the area and allowing for relaxation and rescheduling of specific shoots in case of inclement weather. Field trips for photo shoots include a whale-watching expedition and visits to Thatcher Island, Rockport village and harbor, the coves near Gloucester, Eastern Point Lighthouse, and Annesquam Lighthouse. You're encouraged to develop a personal style as you receive instruction on the use of specific lenses and filters under different light conditions.

Same-day processing is available for E-6 slide film and C-41 print film. At least two evening critiques of your work by instructors and peers are scheduled. Students are expected to bring a 35mm single-lens reflex camera with manual settings, a wide angle to short telephoto zoom lens, a medium telephoto zoom, a tripod, a cable release, and a few filters.

Accommodations and the whale-watching trip are included in the workshop fee. Students stay in Gloucester at Cape Ann Marina, a modern hotel with balcony views of the harbor, a heated indoor pool, and the Gull Restaurant, which serves mainly traditional New England seafood dishes, such as lobster, swordfish, haddock, and halibut, as well as pastas, prime rib, and chicken. Except for an orientation luncheon, participants take care of their own meals and are encouraged to eat together as a group at various restaurants around Cape Ann. *Edward Barry Photographic Services, 203 Beekman La., Neshanic Station, NJ 08853, tel. 908/ 359–0288. Late July: 5 days, $585. Price does not include meals; sign up 1 month in advance.*

NEW HAMPSHIRE **Appalachian Mountain Club.** Founded in 1876, the Appalachian Mountain Club (AMC) promotes the conservation and enjoyment of the natural world and teaches skills needed to safely appreciate the outdoors. Besides courses in outdoor recreation (including hiking, backpacking, camping, bicycling, canoeing, kayaking, and rock climbing), the AMC offers several weekend and four-day nature photography workshops in June, September, October, and December, as well as classes in watercolor, music, storytelling, writing, and drawing.

Two four-day photography workshops in September take advantage of the rugged landscape of the White Mountain National Forest in northern New Hampshire. The Fall Foliage Photography workshop allows you to spend your days examining panoramic mountain and forest landscapes during the lustrous season of autumn color. If weather permits, you spend some time above the tree line. In the evening, you discuss aesthetic and technical problems of nature photography with the instructor. The Waterlight Photography workshop keeps the mountain panorama in mind but concentrates on working with natural light and capturing the subtleties of streams, brooks, and waterfalls on film. You spend most of your day in the field. Both these fall classes are taught by a leading Welsh landscape photographer, Philip H. Evans, who has published two volumes of mountain photography.

These courses are open to photographers at all levels of experience on a first-come, first-served basis, with a student-teacher ratio of 18 to 1. Food and accommodations are included in the workshop fee. Your lodging is at Pinkham Notch Visitor Center at the eastern base of Mt. Washington on Route 16, 10 miles north of Jackson, New Hampshire. The lodge accommodates more than 100 guests in two-, three-, and four-bunk rooms. Hearty, full-course American meals are served at breakfast and dinner, and lunch, sometimes in the form of a trail meal, is also included. You can buy snacks at the center's snack bar.

The AMC sponsors photography programs in three other northeastern locations: Acadia National Park in Maine, the Berkshires of Massachusetts, and New York's Catskills. *Appalachian Mountain Club, Pinkham Notch Visitor Center, Rte. 16, Box 298, Gorham, NH 03581, tel. 603/466–2727, fax 603/466–3871. Sept.: 4 days, $350; for members: $315 ($40 membership fee). Sign up 1 month in advance.*

NEW YORK **International Center of Photography.** Started in 1974 by distinguished photographer Cornell Capa, the International Center of Photography (ICP), a nonprofit institution, has a unique workshop program that takes place within a museum environment and stresses the integration of the history, theory, and practice of photography. In a landmark building along the historic Museum Mile of 5th Avenue on the

Upper East Side of Manhattan, the ICP has an extensive collection of photographs—more than 12,000 original prints—and offers a series of exhibitions. It also has a resource library of books, periodicals, slides, and biographical files. Throughout the year, the ICP schedules a wide selection of courses for students at all levels of experience; these classes cover such varied topics as black-and-white and color photography, portraiture, lighting, photo-journalism and documentary photography, professional training, printing techniques, and the use of specific materials, as well as the development of personal vision.

During the summer, the program consists of more than 45 workshops, many of them lasting four to five days. Classes usually meet daily from 9 AM to 4 PM and combine lectures, demonstrations, critiques, field trips, studio work, and hands-on experience. Many workshops beyond the basic level require a portfolio review before acceptance. Most are limited to 14 to 18 participants, with one instructor and one teaching assistant per class; students may request a private conference with the teacher should they need additional instruction.

Because of its highly regarded reputation and its Manhattan location, the ICP attracts many notable and award-winning professionals to its faculty; recent instructors and lecturers have included William Klein, Ellen Von Unwerth, Mark Seliger, Albert Chong, Sally Gall, Maggie Sleber, and Allen Frame. The center has complete state-of-the-art facilities, including two large black-and-white teaching labs, a film development area, three in-lab classrooms, a large color printing lab, a new digital imaging center, and a nonsilver photography process area. The ICP does not provide student housing, and you're expected to take care of your own meals.

In addition to the summer classes in Manhattan, one- and two-week summer travel workshops are available; these include tuition, lodging, and some meals, and cost between $1,000 and $2,600. These special

workshops have taken place in such areas as Cape Cod, Massachusetts; Tuscany and Lake Como, Italy; and Normandy, France. *International Center of Photography, Education Department, 1130 5th Ave., New York, NY 10128, tel. 212/860–1776, ext. 156, fax 212/360–6490. Late June–early Sept.: 4–5 days, $265–$385, plus $50 lab fee. Price does not include lodging and meals; sign up 2 months in advance.*

RHODE ISLAND **International Photography Workshops.** These workshops, first held in 1984, teach the Zone System of exposure and contrast control in black-and-white printing, which was developed by Ansel Adams. The instructors encourage you to define your goals for each workshop ahead of time, so they can help you gain the technical knowledge you need to achieve these goals as you focus your attention on the creative side of photography. Classes are open to amateurs and professionals who work in a variety of camera and film formats; to encourage interaction between participants and teachers, each workshop allows no more than six students to an instructor.

An intensive workshop is held twice a year on Block Island off the Rhode Island coast. The schedule over the four-day period combines morning lectures and demonstrations on the Zone System, early morning and afternoon hands-on field sessions concentrating on landscape photography, and evening sessions devoted to critiquing portfolios of both students and instructors. Block Island allows opportunities to shoot pictures of rugged coastline, tranquil fields and grasslands, small farmhouses, and the well-preserved examples of Victorian architecture of the hotels and cottages of the harbor village.

The instructors are Jack Holowitz and Steve Sherman, two experts in black-and-white photography and printing. Holowitz, a portrait photographer for 25 years, has conducted seminars sponsored by Kodak throughout the United States and Canada. Sherman, who formerly worked in advertising, now devotes most of his energy to teaching and practicing black-and-white fine art photography. Each year, the two also offer a popular portrait, figure, and darkroom workshop (lasting two days or longer) in Springfield, Massachusetts, and a weeklong landscape photography course somewhere in the Southwest; recent classes have been held in Death Valley and the canyons of Arizona and Utah.

Workshop fees include ground transportation between field and studio locations, but they do not include meals, lodging, and film-related costs. The instructors make arrangements with local hotels and motels for discount rates for participants. Students take their meals at nearby restaurants, and again, the instructors arrange for group rates. *International Photography Workshops, Steve Sherman, 319 Pheasant Dr., Rocky Hill, CT 06067, tel. 203/563–9156; or Jack Holowitz, 114 Bellevue Ave., Springfield, MA 01108, tel. 413/739–3480. Apr. and Nov.: 4 days, $395. Price does not include lodging and meals; sign up 2 months in advance.*

THE MID-ATLANTIC

PENNSYLVANIA **Joe McDonald's Wildlife Photography.** For about 30 weeks throughout the year, this company, founded in 1985, provides a variety of wildlife photography workshops and tours for students who have a basic knowledge of 35mm photography using an SLR camera and interchangeable lenses. Many of the workshops are held in rural central Pennsylvania, while the tours take place in different parts of the United States.

In workshops, the emphasis is on instruction, in the field and in the classroom. Daylight hours from sunrise to late in the afternoon are typically devoted to practicing photography, but they also involve demonstrations, occasional quizzes, exercises in composition, and plenty of discussion and field advice from instructors. Evenings are reserved for slide lectures covering photographic techniques and evaluation of students' work. You receive a number of handouts, including specific shooting guides, assignments, and exposure sheets, all designed to help you get the most out of your shoot. The instructors also cover the wildlife to be encountered in the field.

During photography tours, students receive less formal instruction and spend most of their energy taking pictures of indigenous wildlife, though instructors are always available to provide advice and solutions to problems that arise in the field. The first evening is devoted to an orientation covering wildlife subjects you are expected to see on the tour and technical information that will be useful in the field; on subsequent evenings, students' work is discussed.

Workshops are attended by 6 to 10 participants, so you receive plenty of personal attention from the two instructors and their assistant, who strive to maintain a humorous and relaxed atmosphere. Still, they're quite serious in wanting you to learn how to take better photographs. Many classes are attended by past participants who were pleased by their previous experiences. The instructors are Joe McDonald, who has taken pictures of wildlife for more than 25 years and has written three guides to wildlife photography, his wife, Mary, also a professional photographer, and Dane Hockenbrock.

The McDonalds offer an intensive weeklong nature photography course in rural Pennsylvania. Other four- to seven-day workshops and tours travel to south Florida, the Everglades, Yellowstone National Park, Montana, Arizona, Utah's Zion and Bryce national parks, and the Olympic Peninsula in Washington. Along the way, you photograph birds, wildflowers, and such diverse mammals as the cougar, bobcat, lynx, fox, wolf, otter, black bear, and grizzly bear.

During the Pennsylvania workshops, students stay at a nearby rustic farmhouse in single and double rooms. Three meals a day are included, all served family style.

Participants who sign up for workshops and tours at other locations around the United States stay at AAA-approved moderately priced motels. Included in the cost of these programs are breakfasts of cereal and danishes and lunches of cold cuts, salads, fruits, and desserts, eaten in the field. Dinners, which are not included, are taken as a group at moderately priced local restaurants. *Joe McDonald's Wildlife Photography, R.R. 2, 73 Loht Rd., McClure, PA 17841-9340, tel. and fax 717/543–6423. Workshops: 7 days, $800–$900. Tours: 7– 10 days, $1,000–$2,000. Year-round. Price for workshops and tours away from home base do not include dinner; sign up 2 months in advance.*

PENNSYLVANIA **Touchstone Center for Crafts.** Since 1972, Touchstone Center for Crafts has educated and encouraged its students to develop technical skills and innovative expression in arts and crafts. Located 1½ hours south of Pittsburgh by car, it organizes classes, exhibitions, lectures, and demonstrations for people with a wide range of artistic experience. For 10 weeks during the summer, Touchstone usually has three five-day photography workshops in addition to classes in other crafts, such as pottery, glassblowing, monoprinting, jewelry making, paper art, metal crafts, blacksmithing, fiber arts, and painting. The program also has art classes for children ages 6 through 12 should you wish to bring your child with you.

Workshops for the novice and more experienced photographer combine lectures, discussions, and assignments to strengthen each student's skills. Classes are small, usually from 8 to 10 students. In one beginner's course, you explore basic photography techniques and learn how to develop film. Other workshops, open to all levels of expertise, teach you how to add color to black and white pictures using special development techniques or how to photograph artwork using natural and artificial light. Courses are held Monday through Friday from 9 AM to 4 PM, with studios open to students 24 hours a day. The center has

one darkroom with two enlargers. The lab fee for each class covers the cost of all chemicals and photographic paper that is purchased by Touchstone and used by the students.

Courses are taught by professional artists with teaching experience. In addition to the workshops, the center presents a series of performances on Thursday evenings in July and August. Also on Thursday evenings, students and visitors alike participate in Touchstone's Student Art Auction, where arts and crafts created throughout the week are donated and auctioned, with proceeds used for studio improvements. The Touchstone Gallery features artwork by Touchstone faculty members.

A gentle stream flows through Touchstone's 147-acre campus, with tall oak trees, in the mountains of Pennsylvania. A limited number of rustic cabins (two to four people per cabin) are available on a first-come, first-served basis. You can also camp at the center's tent and RV sites, which have no hookups or cooking facilities. The dining plan offers three meals a day prepared by caterers and served family style in the dining hall. *Touchstone Center for Crafts, R.D. 1, Box 60, Farmington, PA 15437, tel. 412/329–1370, fax 412/329– 1371. Late June–Aug.: 5 days, $150–$280. Price does not include lodging ($60 quad; $75 double per wk for cabin, $25 for campsite) and meals ($80 for 15 meals); sign up 1 month in advance.*

THE SOUTH

FLORIDA **Naturethics.** Founded in 1981 by naturalists John Green and Tom Tyning, Naturethics has an annual schedule of events that combines natural history observation with photography. For more than 20 years, Green and Tyning have led tours, taken pictures, and written books and articles relating to natural history. Their main goal is to provide workshop and vacation tour participants with detailed introductions to the various places being viewed. So instead of just teaching you how to photograph animals and natural settings, the two instructors increase your awareness and understanding of the subjects and environments on your trip. You're encouraged to practice patient observation during the workshop or tour to allow exceptional opportunities to see and identify the behavior and interactions of wildlife and their habitats as you encounter them.

One of Naturethics's most popular and most successful tours visits the Florida Everglades, a unique ecosystem that reveals a fascinating interaction between plants and animals. Each day you discover a different ecological environment, such as the enormous, shallow Florida Bay, freshwater sloughs, tropical hardwood hammocks, and cypress domes. Along the way you see such varied wildlife as birds, butterflies, lizards, alligators, and amphibians. Field events take place during the day and evening, both on foot and in the provided van. The daily schedule features sunrise photography shoots, bird-watching walks, a tram tour of Shark Valley, and a canoe trip.

Although there is no formal photography instruction on the trip, Green and Tyning give tips to anyone who asks. The group comprises up to 12 participants, who usually have a range of photographic experience. Most come with 35mm cameras. There are no facilities for developing film in the park, so you don't get to see your work until the tour is over.

You have the option of camping (bring your own tent and equipment) or staying in nearby cottages or motel rooms, which are not included in the price. All accommodations are in the Flamingo section of the park, on Florida Bay. Good home-cooked meals, prepared by the camp chef, are included, except for one dinner when participants eat together in a local restaurant.

Naturethics has other 7- to 12-day photography tours and weekend excursions around the United States and eastern Canada, including trips to such destinations as southeastern Arizona; New Jersey's Edwin B. Forsythe National Wildlife Refuge; the northern coast of Maine; Cape Cod; the Berkshires in Massachusetts; and Okefenokee in southeastern Georgia. *Naturethics, Box 961, Amherst, MA 01004, tel. 413/256–8739. Mar.: 8 days, $725. Price does not include cabin accommodations or 1 dinner; sign up 2 months in advance.*

FLORIDA **Nikon School of Underwater Photography.** Sponsored by Nikon for photographers who use the Nikonos System, this school provides hands-on underwater photography instruction by top professional photographers at dive locales in the Florida Keys and the Caribbean. All courses are six days and combine classroom and underwater instruction, during which you learn the use of various underwater lenses and accessories. Close-up, macro, and wide-angle lenses and TTL (through the lens) strobe exposures are all covered. Both basic and advanced courses are available only to those with Nikonos underwater camera equipment and scuba certification.

Workshops in Key Largo are taught by Stephen Frink, a frequently published underwater photographer who leads many photo tours to dive destinations each year. Because these Key Largo workshops are so popular, they are open to 25 students; however, no more than 12 divers sign up for other courses. All courses include daily lectures, personal critiques, and dive opportunities; generally two to three hours of instruction and two tank dive excursions are provided each day. E-6 film processing is available for immediate evaluation of images, but you pay extra for film and processing.

Packages at Marina Del Mar Resort in Key Largo include seven nights' accommodations, six days of underwater photographic instruction, six days of diving, tanks, and weights, as well as a daily Continental breakfast. Other meals are taken on your own. *Nikon School of Underwater Photography, Waterhouse Photographic Tours, Box 2487, Key Largo, FL 33037, tel. 305/*

451–2228 or 800/272–9122, fax 305/451–5147. Early June and mid-Sept.: 6 days, $631–$987. Price does not include lunch and dinner; sign up 2 months in advance.

THE SOUTHWEST

ARIZONA **Grand Canyon Expeditions Company Photography Expedition.** In 1964, Grand Canyon Expeditions Company began running commercial trips along the Colorado River through the Grand Canyon; it started offering special-interest excursions in 1984. Twice a year, photographers with a varied range of expertise join veteran outfitters for an eight-day photography expedition that starts at Lee's Ferry near Lake Powell, Arizona, and ends at Pearce Ferry, Arizona. Each tour is limited to 28 participants. You cover some 300 river miles and negotiate nearly 200 exciting rapids as you travel in a 37-foot S-Rig river raft that contains 20 separate compartments and enough room to transport all participants' supplies and equipment. These trips are not totally dominated by photography shoots, so a companion who just wants to experience the river journey should have an equally enjoyable trip. Travel is slow enough to allow more than enough time for swimming, fishing, hiking, and composing the perfect shot.

The expedition lends itself easily to capturing a number of beautiful images of nature. Under the guidance of an expert professional photographer, you have the chance to shoot spectacular geological formations, abundant wildlife, cacti, rushing waterfalls, Native American ruins, and wildflowers. Scenic highlights along the way include Navajo Bridge, Phantom Ranch, Red Wall Cavern, Bright Angel Canyon, Lava Falls, and Granite Park. The changing landscape and lighting conditions along with the personalized instruction provide ample challenges for you to improve your camera skills.

You begin your trip by staying one night at a hotel in Las Vegas at your own cost. After an early morning departure from Las Vegas, the company provides all transportation, camping equipment, waterproof river bags, a waterproof box for your camera and personal items, meals, and beverages. In the evening, you have time for photographic instruction. Afterward you sleep in the canyon under the stars. There is no place to have your photos developed along the way.

Meals are prepared by the boatmen. Breakfasts consist of campfire coffee, tea, juice, fruit, cereal, muffins, and either eggs, pancakes, or french toast. For lunch, you're provided with delicatessen meats, cheeses, breads, and cookies. Dinners include a meat course cooked in Dutch ovens and served with fresh vegetables, salad, biscuits, soup, and dessert. *Grand Canyon Expeditions Company, Box O, Kanab, UT 84741, tel. 801/644–2691 or 800/544–2691, fax 801/644–2699. May–late July: 8 days, $1,695. Price does not include 1 night's lodging; sign up 6 months in advance.*

ARIZONA, NEW MEXICO, UTAH **The Ray McSavaney Photographic Workshops.** Since 1990, this program has included several three- to seven-day workshops that focus on the southwestern landscape. Starting with the premise that photography is a continuous creative process, instructors look at their students' past body of work in addition to concentrating on questions and problems that arise on location. Teachers encourage participants to consider why they chose certain subjects, how they view the world, and how their future photographic goals may best be achieved.

The workshops are open to photographers who work in different formats and have a range of experience. The daily schedule involves on-site instruction, critiques, discussions, and presentations on the aesthetic and technical aspects of photography. To ensure that each student receives an equal amount of personal attention, enrollment for each workshop is limited to eight participants per instructor. The distinguished faculty, chosen from award-winning professionals with years of teaching experience, includes Carol Brown, Neil Chapman, Ray McSavaney, John Nichols, John Sexton, and Jack Waltman.

One of the most popular workshops offered is the Southwest Landscape, which takes you to the heart of the Navajo Nation. The workshop begins early Sunday afternoon at Canyon de Chelly in northeastern Arizona, where you have the opportunity to photograph the architectural remnants of ancient Anasazi cliff dwellings. Midway through the workshop week, the group travels north into Utah to Monument Valley's sandstone sculptures. You attend specially arranged tours that allow ample time for photographing well-known sights and less famous areas in both Arizona and Utah. As you aim to gain a personal sense of the landscape, you also explore the relationship between Native Americans and their land.

Another workshop, the Spirit of the Land— Photographing Northern New Mexico, covers the visually diverse areas around Taos, including Ranchos de Taos, Pueblo de Taos, Chimayo, the Ghost Ranch (painted by Georgia O'Keeffe), and the Taos Mesa; students take pictures of rivers, canyons, valleys, mesas, mountains, and regional architecture. This class ends the day before the renowned Indian Market occurs in Santa Fe, so you can spend the weekend visiting the market before returning home. Other workshops include the Land of Standing Rock, which explores the landscape of eastern Utah (Arches National Park, Canyonlands National Park, Fisher Towers, and La Sal Mountains); the Visual Image, which visits Capitol Reef National Park near Torrey, Utah; and Anasazi Viewpoints, which concentrates on landscapes in Colorado associated with the Anasazi culture.

Workshop tuition does not normally include lodging and meals, except for the Southwest Landscape, which covers lunches, refreshment breaks, and a barbecue dinner. Depending on the workshop, the program makes arrangements for you to stay at mo-

tels, reasonably priced condos, bed-and-breakfasts, or campgrounds near each location. Participants provide their own transportation, and usually travel by car caravan. Ray McSavaney, who runs the workshops, will arrange car pools if necessary. *Ray McSavaney Photographic Workshops, 1984 N. Main St., Studio 402, Los Angeles, CA 90031, tel. 213/225-1730. Mar.–Oct.: 5–7 days, $350–$650. Price does not include lodging and meals; sign up 3 months in advance.*

NEW MEXICO Photo Adventure Tours. Since 1986, this company has organized tours to destinations around the United States while providing informal instruction in the basics of photography along the way. Although the trips are open to all photographers, they are probably best suited to those with less experience who wish to improve their skills in nature and travel photography. Tours are run by professional photographers who usually have an in-depth knowledge of the destination and prior experience photographing the place.

Trips are led by two instructors and limited to 20 participants, accepted on a first-come, first-served basis. The daily schedule generally begins at sunrise so that participants can arrive at sights before other tourists. There are no lectures, classroom demonstrations, or critiques of your work (film is not always developed along the way). Although photography instruction is rather informal, you may ask in advance for individual and more intense guidance. Your tour leaders carry a wide variety of lenses that you may borrow at any time.

Two popular tours visit New Mexico in October. The four-day trip to the Albuquerque Balloon Festival allows you to take shots of the ascension of more than 600 hot-air balloons. A five-day trip covers various sights and landscapes around New Mexico, including White Sands National Monument, Lincoln National Forest, the Badlands of New Mexico, the Zuni Pueblo, Gallup and Route 66, El Morro National Monument, Acoma Pueblo and Sky City, and Laguna Pueblo. Among other U.S. destinations explored by Photo Adventure Tours throughout the year are California, the Navajo areas of Arizona, the redrock canyons of Nevada, Mesa Verde in southern Colorado, Utah's Zion and Bryce national parks, Hawaii, and the Upper Peninsula of Michigan.

Tour packages include lodging, breakfast, and dinner at chain hotels such as Best Western, Holiday Inn, and the Grand Canyon Lodge. Participants eat lunch, often consisting of sandwiches, on location. *Photo Adventure Tours, 2035 Park St., Atlantic Beach, NY 11509-1236, tel. 516/ 371–0067 or 800/821–1221, fax 516/371– 1352. Mid-Sept.–mid-Oct.: 4–5 days, $485– $685; 13 days, $1,895. Price does not include lunch; sign up 2 months in advance.*

NEW MEXICO **Santa Fe Photographic Workshops.** Established in 1990 by Reid Callanan, who has been running photography workshop programs since the mid '70s, this program comprises more than 50 weeklong summer workshops over an eight-week period. Fall and winter workshops are offered as well. Many of these workshops involve field trips that enable you to photograph the stunning mountain and desert landscapes of northern New Mexico, a region that also encompasses distinct Native American and Hispanic cultures.

The program is based at the Workshops Center, a mile and a half from the downtown city plaza. The administrative office, three classrooms, a store, the studio, a digital media lab, and dormitory housing are all at the center. There is also an informal gathering place where cold drinks, coffee, and snacks are available all day long.

Although a few workshops are open to beginners (such as Beginning Photography, Introduction to Color Photography, and Fundamentals of Photoshop), many courses are geared for experienced amateurs and professional photographers, who are required to submit samples of work with their

application. The varied selection includes workshops in landscape, documentary, and studio photography, portraiture, figure study, photojournalism, and lighting techniques as well as new digital media workshops. Workshops are limited to 16 to 18 participants and are taught by established professional photographers. Recent instructors have included Nick Nichols, Greg Gorman, Sam Abell, David Michael Kennedy, Arthur Myerson, Rodney Smith, Craig Stevens, and Joyce Tenneson.

The daily schedule for most workshops involves field trips to locations around Santa Fe and northern New Mexico, critiques and discussions of students' work, and one-on-one meetings with instructors. Film and slides are processed overnight at the workshops' lab so that images can be critiqued the next day.

A series of electronic imaging workshops using Adobe Photoshop software gives you intensive exposure to the techniques and technology used to create digital photography. Through lectures, demonstrations, and personal critiques, you learn image manipulation, retouching, color adjustments, and other creative techniques and then apply these skills to individual projects. These workshops have a more limited enrollment and tend to be targeted more for professionals.

Monday and Wednesday evenings throughout the summer are devoted to slide lectures by instructors, who present their work and talk about their careers and lives in photography. Following the Friday night barbecue, students present slides of their work.

You pay extra to stay in the on-campus dorm housing across the street from the Workshops Center and next door to the studio. About 38 students can be accommodated in the simply furnished single and double rooms with shared or private bath, available on a first-come, first-served basis. You can also stay in recommended local inns, motels, and hotels.

The mandatory meal program includes a gourmet buffet orientation dinner on Sunday evening, a Friday evening barbecue dinner at a nearby ranch, and five lunches that can be taken on field trips, in the dining room, or at picnic tables in the garden. Vegetarian meals are available. You can opt to purchase a pass for buffet breakfasts for the week, but you're on your own for other meals. *Santa Fe Photographic Workshops, Box 9916, Santa Fe, NM 87504, tel. 505/983–1400, fax 505/989–8604. Feb.–Oct.; 5 days, $645–$900, plus $85–$130 lab fee. Price does not include lodging ($225–$350 per wk), mandatory meal program (2 dinners and 5 lunches, $110 per wk), and optional breakfasts ($24 per wk); sign up anytime.*

THE ROCKIES

COLORADO **Anderson Ranch Arts Center.** On a historic campus in Snowmass Village, 10 miles west of the mountain resort community of Aspen, Anderson Ranch Arts Center provides professional and personal development workshops in photography, as well as in other art forms, such as ceramics, painting, drawing, woodworking, sculpture, and furniture design. These intensive one- and two-week courses aim to stretch the creativity of students as they learn new artistic techniques.

Photography workshops at Anderson Ranch began in 1973 and are currently sponsored by Eastman Kodak Company. Workshops are offered for beginners, seasoned professionals, and all those in-between, from traditionalists to those interested in experimenting with technique and vision. Topics include portraiture, platinum and palladium printing, landscape, the nude, view camera technique, photojournalism, and beginning, intermediate, and advanced black-and-white printing. In the past, workshops have also been offered on constructing and shooting with a pinhole camera; creating multimedia slide presentations; and shooting with the alpine light of mountain ridges and tundra.

Classes generally meet from 9 to 5 weekdays for the one- and two-week sessions. You spend your days taking photographs in the studio or on location and participating in critiques of students' work. Instructors review portfolios, provide lab and field demonstrations on technique and artistic development, and meet with students individually to address special interests.

Enrollment is limited to 15 students per workshop. After you register, you fill out a questionnaire that gives the instructor information on your level of experience; the course work is sometimes adjusted to suit your group. One or two faculty members along with one or two assistants lead each class; assistants work individually with students and help them prepare chemicals in the darkrooms. Recent instructors have included many renowned photographers, such as Judy Dater, Jerry Uelsmann, John Sexton, Sam Abell, Barbara Crane, and Ralph Gibson.

The center's facilities contain individual and group printing labs, film processing areas, and finishing and print-viewing spaces. Black-and-white enlargers are available for 35mm, 120, and 4x5 formats. In darkroom courses, you usually are assigned your own enlarger. Labs are open 24 hours weekdays. Workshops have lab fees that cover chemicals and darkroom use but not E-6 color slide processing. E-6 color film is processed at a nearby professional lab during the day and overnight at students' own cost.

Anderson Ranch is situated on 4 acres next to a golf course and encompasses renovated log cabins and barns alongside new buildings. Students have the option of staying in the on-campus dormitory or nearby condominiums; in both places, shared and private rooms generally share a bath. Participants can sign up for a meal plan providing three cafeteria-style meals a day at the on-campus dining hall; faculty and students dine together. A children's art program is run concurrently with the adult program.

The center also sponsors a Field Expeditions Program of one- and two-week photography workshops in the Rocky Mountains, Utah Canyonlands, and the Grand Canyon. Most of these trips are designed for intermediate to advanced students with some hiking and camping experience; they are led by guides and instructors familiar with the locales. Some of these workshops involve river rafting through desert country or horse packing. Fees for the program cover tuition, guides and outfitters, lodging, meals, film pickups for processing, and transportation to sites. *Anderson Ranch Arts Center, Box 5598, Snowmass Village, CO 81615, tel. 970/923–3181, fax 970/923–3871. Early June–Oct.: 1–2 wk on-campus workshops, $400–$1,100, plus $50–$200 lab fee. Early May–early Oct.: 8- to 14-day field expedition workshops, $1,100–$3,000. Price of on-campus workshops does not include lodging and meals ($300–$550 per wk), but field expedition workshops include lodging and meals; registration for summer programs begins in Jan.*

MONTANA **Rocky Mountain School of Photography.** Opened in 1987, this Missoula-based photography school has an 11-week summer career training program and more than 20 weeklong and two-week-long workshops year-round in Missoula and other destinations around the United States.

Several of the weeklong workshops involve nature and landscape photography in Montana and elsewhere, primarily in the West, and others concentrate on photographic technique. These workshops are designed for beginning, intermediate, and advanced students who work with a variety of formats. The daily schedule involves field shooting, lectures by instructors, demonstrations of photographic techniques, and critiques of students' work. All classes are limited in enrollment; the maximum number of students for workshops ranges from 8 to 18.

For most workshops, students may have E-6 color film processed locally to allow discussion of photographs taken during the class.

Typical workshops explore the Montana landscape during different seasons. Winter in Yellowstone National Park is white and serene, the waterfalls stand still, and the park is blanketed in snow. Herds of bison, elk, mule deer, and antelope emerge from their alpine hideaways waiting to be photographed. You will sleep in the Old Faithful Snow Lodge, accessible only by snow coach. Autumn in Yellowstone has an entirely different set of colors. If you choose to take this September trip, you will experience the vibrant reds and greens of the landscape as you shoot photos of the bison shrouded in veils of steam escaping from the geysers. In the Wildlife Up-Close workshop, you spend four days, either in winter or summer, photographing predators that are rarely seen, such as timber wolves, mountain lions, and bobcats. Conducted at WildEyes, a game farm, where wildlife models for photography are raised among thousands of acres of open meadows and alpine forests. You will stay in cabins on a lake outside of Glacier National Park.

The Black-and-White Zone System of Exposure concentrates on the technique devised and practiced by master photographer Ansel Adams to produce fine art black-and-white pictures. The workshop provides darkroom experience in film processing and printing and covers such topics as previsualization; exposing for shadow placement; altering film development; using filters to control contrast; and archival processes of mounting and toning images.

Other weeklong workshops are held in such diverse locations as the desert canyonlands of Arizona; the mountains of Ouray, Colorado, known for its canyons, waterfalls, and wildflowers; Yellowstone National Park; the Northern Cascades in Bellingham, Washington; and Martha's Vineyard, off the Massachusetts coast. Instructors are all professional nature photographers and experienced teachers; the school's founders, Neil and Jeanne Chaput de Saintonge, are permanent staff members, and recent instructors have included Galen Rowel, Bruce Barnbaum, Alison Shaw, Dennis Darling, and David Middleton.

In most of the workshops, you're responsible for your own lodging and meals. The school helps students make arrangements for moderately priced lodging at local hotels, motels, and inns. When you register, you receive a form asking about your lodging preferences. *Rocky Mountain School of Photography, 210 N. Higgins, Suite 101, Missoula, MT 59802, tel. 406/543–0171 or 800/394–7677, fax 406/721–9133. Year-round: 6–8 days, $345–$1,300. Some prices do not include meals and lodging; sign up 3 months in advance.*

THE WEST COAST

CALIFORNIA **Ambient Light Workshops.** Started in 1990, Ambient Light Workshops gives both the novice and the more advanced photographer one-on-one instruction and hands-on experience in the field. During the workshop, each student learns about composition, exposure, lighting, Zone System concepts, the uses of various kinds of films, lenses, and selecting the right subject. The instructors are proficient in a number of camera and film formats, so you can bring along 35mm, 4x5, or 8x10 cameras. Each course is limited to 10 students and the student-teacher ratio is five to one, so you receive a lot of personal attention. Workshops are scheduled to avoid high tourist seasons.

During mid-September, Ambient Light has a one-week workshop that covers Yosemite National Park, Mono Lake, and Bodie Ghost Town, with a variety of outdoor subjects along the way. The program provides all ground transportation in a stretch mini-van for the entire week, starting from Oakland International Airport. In Yosemite, you shoot pictures of waterfalls, giant redwoods, and mountainous landscapes; at Mono Lake, the tufa rock formations, standing 15 feet above water, make interesting subjects, especially beautiful at sunrise and sunset. One day of the workshop is devoted to Bodie Ghost Town, with its late 19th-century buildings well preserved on the eastern edge of the Sierras near Nevada. This workshop is taught by John Mariana, the founder of Ambient Light and an experienced, award-winning landscape photographer who specializes in teaching the use of the simplified Zone System for 35mm and medium-format cameras.

Fees include your lodging inside Yosemite in Yosemite Lodge or in private multibed-room mountain homes, with a fireplace, balconies, a kitchen, and laundry facilities. Singles and doubles are available, and all rooms have their own bathroom. You're responsible for your own meals, so stops are made at grocery stores, restaurants, and cafeterias along the way. Students usually have dinner together at local restaurants for around $10 per person.

Ambient Light Workshops offers other workshops in the Southwest; one travels to Monument Valley, Mesa Verde National Park, and Shiprock, while another visits Durango, Chaco Canyon, the Anasazi ruins, Bisti Badlands wilderness landscape, Great Sand Dunes National Monument, Rancho de Taos Church, Santa Fe, Taos, and Taos Pueblo. *Ambient Light Workshops, Box 246, Clarendon Hills, IL 60514, tel. 312/ 901-36550. Mid-Sept.–Oct.: 4–7 days, $950– $1,500. Price does not include meals; sign up 1 month in advance.*

ALASKA

SOUTHEAST **Alaska Up Close.** Since 1984, Alaska Up Close, based in Juneau, has organized customized photography, wilderness, and natural history tours for groups and independent travelers. A Gathering of Eagles goes from Juneau to the 49,000-acre Chilkat Bald Eagle Preserve in Haines. Between late October and January, as many as 3,500 bald eagles congregate along the Chilkat River to feed on the late salmon run. On the tour, you photograph these spe-cial birds from a nearby roadway. The steep-walled Chilkat Valley is also home to moose, wolves, mountain goats, lynx, coy-otes, foxes, and mink; brown bears often use the area for feeding during the night.

Hyde with Eagles, an eight-day guided group trip to the eagles' meeting place, (called the Eagle Council Grounds), takes place in mid-November. You receive hands-on field instruction in wildlife photogra-phy, including advice on how to shoot pictures of the bald eagles in flight and dur-ing feedings. Lectures and informal discus-sions during the week address such topics as wildlife behavior and low-light and win-ter photography. The program leader also provides information on outdoor photogra-phy in the whole state of Alaska during all seasons.

You travel between Juneau and Haines via a half-day cruise on Lynn Canal and have four days for photography in Chilkat Val-ley. Each day in Haines, your group arrives near the Eagle Council Grounds by bus at the crack of dawn to observe the birds' feeding activity and to prepare for photo opportunities as day breaks. Hot lunch is served in the field to take full advantage of the daylight. The trip includes a visit to Mendenhall Glacier near Juneau for addi-tional nature shots.

Limited to 10 participants, the program is open to anyone with a basic knowledge of 35mm photography; a telephoto lens of at least 300mm and sturdy tripod are recom-mended equipment for the trip. John Hyde, a cinematographer and professional wildlife photographer whose work has appeared in such magazines as *National Geographic, Outside,* and *Smithsonian,* leads the tour with the help of a local naturalist guide and briefings by a state biologist.

You stay in local lodges, small hotels, or motels with restaurants on the premises or nearby. The only meals provided as part of the tour are dinner on the night you arrive in Haines and four lunches at the Chilkat Bald Eagle Preserve.

Alaska Up Close arranges several other tours around the state for photographers and wildlife enthusiasts, but none of these is escorted. The nine-day Naturalist's Alaska, held from late May through August, follows in the footsteps of John Muir as it covers Southeast Alaska's In-side Passage, with its jagged snowcapped mountains, massive glaciers, and luxuriant rain forest. The 10-day Rites of Spring tour in May explores Southeast Alaska's nature highlights of spring migration in the Mendenhill Wetlands State Game Refuge as well as an early fish run in the Stikine and Chilkat valleys; the 14-day Alaska's Parklands, conducted from June through August, visits Denali, Glacier Bay, and Kenai Fjords national parks. *Alaska Up Close, Box 32666, Juneau, AK 99803, tel. 907/789–9544, fax 907/789–3205. Mid-Nov. (Hyde with Eagles): 8 days, $1,595. Late-Oct.–mid-Dec. (A Gathering of Eagles): 7 days, $1,299. Price for Hyde with Eagles does not include all breakfasts, 4 lunches, and most dinners; price for a Gathering of Eagles does not include most meals; sign up at least 1 month in advance.*

STATEWIDE **Joseph Van Os Photo Safaris.** With an emphasis on wildlife and nature photography, this company, started in 1980, offers both workshops and photo safaris open to photographers with all lev-els of experience. On photo safaris, you concentrate on shooting while the com-pany handles the travel details. Guides are well acquainted with the specific destina-tion being covered so that they can show you some of the most notable places in the area to take memorable pictures. You shoot alongside some of America's leading out-door photographers, who are always nearby to provide pointers on how to get your best shot.

On many of these tours, limited to 16 par-ticipants, you spend most of your day tak-ing pictures, aside from lunchtime siestas during hot weather. Companions simply interested in the great outdoors might also enjoy these trips.

On most safaris, you stay in pleasant first-class inns and hotels or tented camps. Your meals are included in the package price; you usually dine in restaurants, though sometimes picnics are provided in the field.

Several of the most popular photo safaris travel to various areas of Alaska. You can photograph brown bears at Katmai National Park, seabirds on St. George, Pribilof Islands, and big game, such as bear, moose, and caribou, in Denali National Park. One trip, The Best of Alaska, covers the diverse landscapes of Denali and Kenai Fjords national parks, as well as the Anan Bear Preserve, part of the Panhandle.

Other destinations visited on safaris include Yellowstone National Park and the Grand Tetons, Colorado's San Juan Mountains, and the San Juan Islands in Washington State. Four separate trips concentrate on photographing wildlife—birds of prey in Colorado and predatory mammals in Montana and California.

Safaris are usually led by one or two instructors. Recent faculty members have included such experienced outdoor photographers as director Joseph Van Os, Perry Conway, John Shaw, Renee Lynn, Tim Davis, Rod Planck, Wayne Lynch, David Middleton, and Jim Zuckerman. *Joseph Van Os Photo Safaris, Box 655, Vashon, WA 98070, tel. 206/463–5383, fax 206/463–5484. Year-round: 5–30-day safaris, $1,495–$9,000. Price for safaris includes lodging and meals; sign up several months in advance.*

SOURCES

ORGANIZATIONS **Photographic Society of America** (3000 United Founders Blvd., Suite 103, Oklahoma City, OK 73112, tel. 405/843–1437) is composed of mostly amateurs but has members at all levels of experience; it aids camera clubs and publishes *PSA Journal.*

PERIODICALS *American Photo* (1633 Broadway, New York, NY 10019, tel. 212/767–6000 or 800/274–4514) is a magazine for advanced amateurs and professional photographers. *Outdoor Photographer* (12121 Wilshire Blvd., Suite 1220, Los Angeles, CA 90025-1175, tel. 310/820–1500) covers outdoor, adventure, and travel photography. *Photo District News* (1515 Broadway, New York, NY 10036, tel. 212/536–5222 or 800/669–1002) is a trade magazine designed for professionals and those who wish to learn more about all aspects of the photography industry. *Popular Photography* (1633 Broadway, New York, NY 10019, tel. 212/767–6000 or 800/274–4514) contains the latest information about cameras, film, and other equipment as well as articles about photographic techniques.

BOOKS The *Guide to Photography Workshops and Schools* (Shaw Guides, 10 W. 66th Street, No. 30-H, New York, NY 10023, tel. 212/799–6464) contains listings for workshops, tours, residences and retreats, organizations, and schools in the United States and Canada. *Photographer's Market* (Writer's Digest Books, FW Publications, 1507 Dana Ave., Cincinnati, OH 45207), updated annually, lists photography workshops around the United States and suggests more than 2,000 places for selling and marketing work.

ALSO SEE To learn a different way to look at your world, turn to Painting Workshops or search for sculpture classes in the Arts and Crafts Workshops chapter.

Spas and Wellness Centers

Written and updated by Bernard Burt

f you're looking for a vacation that will teach you healthier ways to live—and, in the process, restore your mind, body, and spirit—a spa may be the answer. The facilities and treatments available at today's resorts go far beyond those of the old European spas, grand hotels cosseting those who came to sip the waters and socialize. American spas reflect current trends in medical thinking, as well as new approaches to wellness based on traditional natural therapies. They take a holistic view of health and promote preventive medicine, and they are devoted to showing you how exercise, a better diet, and better ways of dealing with stress can make you not only look better but also feel better. You can pick up lots of tips: how to cook without salt, sugar, butter, and sometimes other fats as well, or how to make portions seem larger (serve food on small plates) or make mealtimes more enjoyable (slice meat thinly and fan it out). Stress management techniques are often taught. Exercise classes can include yoga, guided imagery, or aerobics. After a week of relaxed spa life, you will know how good it feels to feel good. Wanting more, you may well take the spa's lessons to heart, and, like many spa guests, make some changes in the way you live when you're not on vacation.

There are all kinds of spas, some of them truly deluxe. Many destination spas are self-contained resorts totally focused on health and fitness; bodywork, such as massages, facials, manicures, and pedicures, are often part of a visit. Along with such services, many spas have stop-smoking or stress-control programs. Some also have optional dining plans, offering healthy, light spa cuisine rather than heavier, fattier foods. Other spas have sports programs or are part of top American sports resorts; you may find sport-specific exercise classes, which, say, add boxing and tennis movements to aerobic workouts.

A few spas are New Age retreats or ranches with health and healing programs based on combinations of ancient therapies and the latest self-help concepts. Other establishments show you how you can strengthen your body against illness through good nutrition and by understanding the relationship between mind and body; some centers focus on the message of Dr. Dean Ornish, author of *Dr. Dean Ornish's Program for Reversing Heart Disease,* who argues for a low-fat, high-fiber diet and regular exercise, or on the teachings of Dr. Deepak Chopra, author of the best-seller *Ageless Body, Timeless Mind,* who believes that health is not merely the absence of disease but a state of well-being that infuses the entire body and mind.

Some spas are medically supervised health and fitness centers, where you are monitored by physicians, physiotherapists, and nutritionists. These centers usually give

Bernard Burt is the founding director of the International Spa & Fitness Association. He publishes SpaGoer *newsletter, and is the author of* Fodor's Healthy Escapes.

you a personalized daily exercise schedule, calorie-controlled meals, and regimented programs to help you stop smoking and learn to deal with stress and excess pounds—both at the center and after you go home.

Spas also come in all price ranges, depending on such variables as accommodations, facilities, location, services, and the amount of supervision. For a seven-day package that includes the spa program, meals, and lodging, expect to pay between $800 and $2,000 per person for a double or between $1,000 and $2,000 (up to as much as $4,000 at a really glamorous spot) for a single. If you want to cut costs, look into the seasonal specials available at some spas. (Florida spas, for instance, offer lower rates in summer.)

Different as spa programs are, similarities emerge when you take a close look. Most spas have packages that include lodging, dining, and activities. Basic spa services such as exercise and body treatments are comparable in quality from one spa to the next, and diet is important no matter where you go, although what constitutes healthful eating may vary. Some spas simply offer a low-calorie diet and a balanced selection from the basic food groups, with fish and chicken several times a week. Others cook with organically grown foodstuffs or have you eating gourmet vegetarian fare. Centers that specialize in fitness or weight loss often offer supervised juice regimens and fasting.

For your first spa vacation, try a spa with a structured program of anywhere from five days to two weeks. Typically, at such establishments, each day begins with a walk and stretching session or yoga or meditation. After breakfast, there might be lectures or workouts. In the afternoon, you may go out for a hike or another walk, or have time free to take advantage of spa services such as aromatherapy or hydromassage. At night, you can enjoy lectures by specialists in different health fields. If you don't like regimentation, look for a resort spa with plenty of activities in addition to the fitness and treatment offerings.

Study the spa's schedule in advance of your visit, and don't hesitate to ask the spa director for advice before you arrive. Several establishments offer personal consultations in such areas as fitness testing, biofeedback, and meditation, as well as one-on-one fitness training. Such advance preparation can be the first step in establishing a personal fitness regimen. Consult your physician before leaving home and take along medical records that will help the spa director plan your schedule.

COMMON SPA FEATURES AND PROGRAMS In order to evaluate the range of programs a spa offers, it helps to understand spa-speak. You'll hear many of the following terms frequently.

Acupressure: Finger massage intended to release muscle tension by applying pressure to the body's acupuncture points.

Alpha Hydroxy Peel: Antiaging skin treatment with varying combinations and strengths of glycolic acid derived from sugar cane, lactic acid from fermented milk, and/or citric acid from fruit, and other skin enhancers.

Aromatherapy: Inhalation of the essences of flowers and other plants intended to relax the skin's connective tissues and stimulate the natural flow of lymph, sometimes combined with massage using aromatic oils.

Ayurvedic medicine: A 4,000-year-old system of medicine that originated in India and involves the use of oils, massage, and herbs to purify the body.

Fangotherapy: Therapeutic mud baths, in which you bathe or have your body wrapped in mud.

Herbal wrap: A treatment in which the body is wrapped in hot linens moistened with herbal infusions, plastic sheets, and blankets; the moisture, heat, and herbal essences are said to promote muscle relaxation and the elimination of toxins.

Hydrotherapy: Underwater massage, alternating hot and cold showers, and other water-oriented treatments.

Inhalation therapy: A treatment during which you breathe hot vapors or steam mixed with eucalyptus oil, either using inhalation equipment or in a special steam room. The goal is to decongest the respiratory system.

Juice fast: A juice-only diet.

Lymph drainage: Manual massage of the lymph glands to stimulate removal of liquid accumulation. Effective in stress control and relaxation, inflammation, and pain caused by congestion of substances in connective tissue.

Neuromuscular therapy: Deep-tissue massage concentrating on areas of chronic pain, muscle weakness, or restricted range of motion. Working on nerve points, neuropain transmitters are interrupted, allowing dysfunctional muscles to relax.

Parcourse: A trail, usually outdoors, punctuated periodically by exercise stations, where you may find simple equipment and a sign instructing you how to use it.

Pilates training: A conditioning system that incorporates a set of mat exercises and muscle-strengthening resistance equipment.

Pritikin diet: Once considered austere but now more frequently followed, the Pritikin diet, developed by the late Nathan Pritikin, consists of 10%–15% protein, 80% complex carbohydrates, and 5%–10% fat. It has been shown to contribute to lower cholesterol and blood pressure.

Reflexology: Massage of the pressure points on the feet, hands, and ears; intended to relax and stimulate healing of the body.

Rolfing: A bodywork system developed by Ida Rolf that improves balance and flexibility through manipulation of rigid muscles, bones, and joints. It is intended to improve energy flow and relieve stress (often related to emotional trauma).

Salt glow: A cleansing treatment (also known as a body scrub or salt glo) using coarse salt to remove dead skin, similar to the loofah body scrub.

Shiatsu: A massage technique developed by Tokujiro Namikoshi that uses finger (*shi*) pressure (*atsu*) to stimulate the body's inner powers of balance and healing.

Sprung floor: A safe, impact-absorbing surface for aerobic and dance studios.

Swedish massage: A type of bodywork involving stroking, kneading, friction, vibration, and tapping that aims to relax muscles gently.

Swiss shower: A shower with several strong water jets aimed at thighs, calves, and back and leg muscles.

Thalassotherapy: A treatment first used by the ancient Greeks performed with seaweed-based products; you are wrapped, scrubbed, and soaked in marine algae. The objective is to stimulate circulation and relax your muscles.

Visualization: Guided imagery intended to stimulate creativity or relaxation.

Water aerobics: Aerobics workouts in a swimming pool, also known as aquacise, aqua-aerobics, aquafit, aquatics, and swimnastics, which include stretching, strength, and stamina exercises that combine water resistance and body movements.

CHOOSING THE RIGHT SPA

The spas in the reviews that follow are some of the best of their type. To choose the one where you will be comfortable and will most effectively profit from the experience, it helps to ask a lot of questions.

What is the daily schedule? You need to find out how structured the program is—will you be expected to conform to the schedule of a group or a schedule set for you when you arrive, or will you have some choice from one day to the next? Some programs are tightly monitored. If you want something less regimented, choose a spa that provides several options in its daily schedule or allows for a personalized program.

How much time do participants spend exercising? If you are used to intense workouts, look for a spa with a full range of classes, one-on-one training, and personal consultation. If you want to kick back and relax, go elsewhere.

Is the spa program adaptable to my fitness level? The age group at spas ranges anywhere from mid-twenties to mid-seventies, but many spas are more suitable than others for any given segment of that range. Make sure that the program's activities can be adapted to your fitness level. If you have any questions about whether you are physically up to the program, talk to your doctor.

Are all guests spa guests? You will get the most personal attention at a destination spa where all guests participate in spa programs. Smaller spas provide more camaraderie among guests and staff.

What's the cost and what's included? Spa packages may include lodging, meals, lectures and workshops, personal services, the use of exercise and recreational facilities, taxes, gratuities, and service charges that cover charges for waiters, housekeepers, and the like, and for personal services included in the packages. In order to properly compare the cost of visiting various spas, you need to find out just what a package includes.

Be especially careful to find out about fees for personal services such as massages and facials. Because these can add up, decide which you want to take advantage of and how often, and then ask which are included in your program package. Bear in mind that a massage advertised as free may turn out to be a half-hour rubdown rather than a full-hour treatment.

Ask hard questions about recreational facilities you plan to use, as well. For instance, if you plan to play a lot of golf in your free time, make sure that the greens fees are included—and at the tee times you prefer, not just at off-hours.

Taxes and gratuities represent a particularly hefty expense. Local and state taxes plus service charges for massages and other personal services can add 25% or more to the cost of your program. Ask how gratuities are handled for housekeepers and dining room staff as well as physical therapists.

Usually transportation to the resort is not part of the package, although transfers from the nearest airport sometimes are. If they're not included and you don't plan to arrive by car, be sure to check on the cost as you price out your trip.

Some spas provide exercise outfits and bathrobes; at others, you must bring your own.

Selected program prices in this chapter, unless otherwise noted, include lodging, meals, lectures and workshops, the use of exercise and recreational facilities, service charges, gratuities, and taxes, and are per person based on double occupancy. They are given as guidelines only for comparative purposes and change frequently.

Will laundry service be available? Daily laundry service is available at some spas at varying extra cost. Some provide this service without charge. Others have laundry facilities so that you can do your own washing. Know what you're getting into and pack accordingly.

What are the accommodations like? Spas range from spartan to luxurious. Find out about both the public spaces and the guest rooms. What is the general level of comfort? How are they furnished? If you must have a TV or telephone, make certain that it's available. If you care about having a private bath, make sure that the program price isn't based on your sharing the facilities down the hall. What arrangements will be made if you come to the spa with a nonparticipating friend or spouse? What are the typical arrangements for solo travelers: Are singles available, or are they assigned a roommate?

At some establishments, spa facilities and accommodations are under the same roof—

a useful setup when the weather is bad. If you want more privacy, find out if lodging alternatives are available that are separated by a long walk from the main facilities.

What's the food like? Especially at spas where weight loss is a goal, you want to hear that the food is tasty and appealingly presented despite its being low in everything that has put on the pounds you're visiting the spa to shed.

If it matters to you or your traveling companion, find out whether alcohol is available. It's usually not, although you can sometimes get wine. If you are not familiar with the spa's food program, ask for more information or sample menus.

Does health insurance cover any part of the program cost? At some spas, medical tests and physiotherapy ordered by your doctor may be reimbursable under your health care plan. Check your health plan's policy on chiropractic therapy, acupuncture, and stress-management programs.

What non-spa activities are available? At some, the extracurricular options include lectures and films on fitness and health matters; after dinner, most participants turn in early, totally exhausted by the physical activities earlier in the day. Other establishments are full-blown resorts, and the spa activities are only the alternatives to tennis, golf, hiking, swimming, beach-combing, and the like; after dark, there may be movies, dancing, and so on. After you have a sense of what the spa program involves, consider how you might like to spend your free time, and then find a spa that can accommodate you. A spa that is part of a larger resort, or one in a lively resort town where there are lots of other things to do, is probably a better choice if you plan to visit with a nonparticipating companion.

How far in advance do I need to book? It's usually necessary to reserve between 2 weeks and 6 months ahead. Often, however, you can give a call and have a room within the week.

How long has the spa been in business? A long, positive history tells you that the spa is doing something right.

Do you have references from past guests? To clarify your ideas about what it's like to stay at a given spa, there's no substitute for a talk with someone who has slept in the beds, eaten the meals, and gone through the program.

FAVORITE SPAS

THE NORTHEAST

MAINE Northern Pines Health Resort. During a bout with thyroid cancer Marlee Turner discovered the importance of holistic health practices. In 1980, to share with others the lessons she learned about nourishing the mind, body, and spirit, she opened this informal spot on a wooded, 68-acre lakefront property. Maine's only health spa, this is a safe place to try a spa for the first time, and many visitors return.

Ms. Turner bases her program on the teachings of Paavo Airola, who stressed a regimen of meditation and yoga and a diet of fresh fruits, vegetables, and whole grains. You can pick and choose from the full daily schedule; mornings are devoted to meditation, stretching exercises, guided walks through the woods, breakfast, and health-oriented and workout classes, leading up to noontime reflection and discussion. After lunch you may take a yoga class or go for another hike on the trails on the property. Daily classes cover topics such as nutrition, stress management, cooking, vitamins, herbs, and meditation. Weekends feature two- or three-day workshops on a variety of subjects, among them osteopathy, art, music, and astronomy. In your free time you can go canoeing, swimming, or jogging, or, for an additional fee, sign up for special services including Swedish massage, reflexology, aromatherapy, beauty treatments, and herbal wraps. Facilities include a sauna, a hot tub, an exercise room, and a flotation tank for a sensory deprivation and relaxation session.

Although the resort has space for up to 30 weekly guests, there are usually no more than 15 visitors per week, which means lots of personal attention from the energetic staff. Well-worn lakeside log cabins dating from the 1920s can provide total seclusion for couples. Lodge rooms and cabins with two bedrooms, added in the 1980s, are on a hillside amid towering pines, spruces, and hemlocks. The cook is on hand to explain the ingredients of the vegetarian communal meals, served buffet style; you can also opt for a supervised juice fast. Most guests are highly educated, well-traveled women, a good percentage of them involved in healing and helping professions. *Northern Pines Health Resort, 559 Rte. 85, R.R. 1, Box 279, Raymond, ME 04071, tel. 207/655–7624, fax 207/655–3321. Year-round: 6 days, $504–$1,374. Price does not include 7% lodging tax or gratuities.*

MASSACHUSETTS **Canyon Ranch in the Berkshires.** The Health and Healing Department at this elegant property on 120 acres of woodland in the Massachusetts mountains teaches you how to prevent and soften the effects of aging via programs and consultations on nutrition, exercise physiology, movement therapy, behavior, and medicine. Other departments at the ranch offer some 40 classes in everything from breathing, meditation, and yoga to hiking, biking, canoeing, snowshoeing, and cross-country skiing. There are also programs that help you to deal with overeating, stop smoking, or learn to control stress.

The ranch's architectural centerpiece is the late-19th-century Bellefontaine Mansion, which now houses the dining room, the library, and the health and healing and arts and crafts centers. Inside a separate ultra-modern 100,000-square-foot spa and fitness center there are exercise and weight-training rooms; a 75-foot swimming pool; a jogging track; tennis, racquetball, and squash courts; and separate spas for men and women with saunas, steam rooms, Jacuzzis, and inhalation rooms. Lodging is in a modern two-story inn with 120 guest rooms and fancier suites, furnished in a

functional, New England style. Glass-enclosed walkways connect the mansion, fitness center, and inn; on the grounds, there are also outdoor tennis courts, an outdoor swimming pool, and walking trails. Meals are low-calorie, consisting of New England specialties cooked with a minimum of salt and fat. *Canyon Ranch in the Berkshires, 165 Kemble St. (Rte. 7A), Lenox, MA 01240, tel. 413/637–4100 or 800/742–9000, fax 413/637–0057. Year-round: 7 days, $2,040–$2,980 single, $1,750–$2,980 double. Price includes a selection of personal services but not 9.7% tax or 18% service charge.*

NEW YORK **Living Springs Lifestyle Center.** A revitalized life and control of health problems are the goals at this homelike, budget-priced retreat within easy reach of New York City. Courses, which are under medical supervision, focus on disease prevention, nutrition, weight management, stress control, and quitting smoking. After a consultation with the staff doctor, you can schedule spa treatments, enjoy the saunas, and, in warm weather, swim in the spring-fed lake. You learn how to prepare nutritious, low-fat meals, too. A medical package that involves blood work ($65–$115) and a 2½-hour doctor visit ($150) is not included in the price.

The retreat's kitchen serves vegetarian buffets. The eight guest rooms with private bath are in a modern, two-level lodge. Commuter trains from Manhattan's Grand Central Terminal stop at Peekskill, where Living Springs transportation can pick you up. *Living Springs Lifestyle Center, 136 Bryant Pond Rd., Putnam Valley, NY 10579, tel. 914/526–2800 or 800/729–9355, fax 914/528–9171. Year-round: 7 days, $895 single, $695 double.*

NEW YORK **Mountain Valley Health Resort.** The desire to lose weight and learn to keep it off are the common objectives of guests at this 15-acre Catskills health resort, opened in 1992. When you arrive, you provide a brief medical history, which spa director Natalie Skolnik then uses to determine your diet and exercise program. At extra cost you can obtain a computerized body analysis, which will tell you the percentage of your body made up of lean muscle, body fat, and water. No subsequent medical supervision or consultation is available.

A supportive camaraderie prevails among guests. The days are structured but nothing is mandatory. You may want to start your day with a walk after breakfast, then go on to morning classes in toning and firming, step aerobics, or swimnastics in the indoor or outdoor pool. Each afternoon there is free time to relax in the sauna, swim, or do yoga. In addition, there are lectures—discussions on how to enjoy eating portion-controlled meals, deal with stress, and incorporate exercise into your daily life. Other services, available at extra charge, include massage, reflexology, shiatsu, manicures, pedicures, and body wraps. There are two tennis courts and hiking and cross-country ski trails; downhill skiing is nearby at Hunter Mountain.

In the attractive dining room, you can choose a 650-, 900-, or 1,200-calorie menu, or opt for a juice fast or vegetarian dishes. The chalet-style lodge comfortably houses 50 to 60 guests. Some accommodations are skylit loft rooms that accommodate four people. The resort's several porches and balconies are popular gathering spots after dinner. *Mountain Valley Health Resort, Box 395, Hunter, NY 12442, tel. 518/263–4919 or 800/232–2772, fax 518/263–4994. Year-round: 7 days, $595–$1,150. Price does not include 8% tax or 15% gratuity.*

NEW YORK **New Age Health Spa.** Creative visualization—whereby the mind leads the body naturally toward a positive outcome—is a key tool at this establishment, which was opened in 1975 as the New Age Health Farm and became the New Age Health Spa in 1986. At that time, Werner Mendel and Stephanie Paradise took over the property and expanded its focus to include fitness, holistic health, personal growth, and spa services. Located on 160

acres in the southern Catskills, it's the closest spa of its type to New York City.

You're free to set your own pace as you pick and choose from among classes in meditation, personal awareness, nutrition, yoga, tai chi, weight training, stretching, and aerobics (in the pool and in the classroom); you can fill your time with supervised morning hikes along country roads and swims in indoor or spring-fed outdoor pools, and by watching videos or reading books from the library of health and wellness titles. The Challenge by Choice ropes course involves climbing a 50-foot tower; you learn the power of teamwork and the pleasure of attaining your goals. Weekend hikes into the high Catskills give you panoramic views of the Hudson River valley. Spa services range from reflexology, aromatherapy, loofah scrubs, mud treatments, manicures and pedicures, facials, and hair treatments to Swedish, shiatsu, and sports massage, along with colonics and Ayurvedic botanical detoxification. Personal consultations in cooking, herbology, hypnotherapy, tarot, and astrology are also available (group sessions free, private sessions at $50 an hour).

Because the owners are usually on hand in the big farmhouse that serves as both social center and dining room, the atmosphere is homey. Graduates of the Culinary Institute of America prepare the meals along guidelines set by the American Heart Association (high carbohydrates, no sugar, and low protein, fats, and salt); many dishes are spiced with herbs grown in the greenhouse behind the kitchen. You might also opt for a supervised juice fast, a 700- to 800-calorie vegetarian diet, or a rotation diet with vegetarian, fish, and poultry meals.

There are five separate guest houses. Rooms have a country look and are small but comfortable, with private baths. The two suites have Jacuzzis. No more than 65 guests are on hand during any given week, most of them educated businesspeople and professionals from New York City and suburban Long Island and New Jersey; some return a few times a year. Transportation to and from Manhattan is available on Sunday and Friday by reservation. *New Age Health Spa, Rte. 55, Neversink, NY 12765, tel. 914/985–7601 or 800/682–4348, fax 914/985–2467. Year-round: 5 days, $965–$1,423 single, $665–$1,047 double. Price includes 2 personal services.*

VERMONT **Green Mountain at Fox Run.** Opened in 1973 by MIT-trained nutritional biochemist, Dr. Alan H. Wayler, this establishment on 20 acres in central Vermont is the country's oldest program devoted to helping women (and only women) develop a diet and exercise plan that they can integrate into their lives at home. Weeklong and five-day retreats teach participants how to control weight and emotions; instead of deprivation, moderation becomes the key. Overcoming feelings of failure is the first step in the process, according to Wayler, because so many come here after losing weight and regaining it. The staff, which includes a registered dietician, an exercise physiologist, and a behavioral therapist, helps you develop your own program. Follow-up support, provided through newsletters and a hot line, is very much part of the program. Massage, manicures, and pedicures are available at an extra charge.

The main lodge, where classes are held, has 26 duplex rooms that accommodate two to four persons and have modern baths; some singles are available. Menus allow for 1,200 or 1,400 calories per day; the food here is low in fat, cholesterol, and sodium and higher in complex carbohydrates. The lodge has exercise equipment such as treadmills, stationary bikes, a NordicTrack, a rowing machine, and free weights. Nearby, there's hiking, skiing, and biking, as well as theater, discount shopping, and historical sites. *Green Mountain at Fox Run, Box 164, Ludlow, VT 05149, tel. 802/228–8885 or 800/448–8106, fax 802/228–8887. Year-round: 5–21 days, $1,100–$5,825.*

VERMONT **New Life Fitness Vacations.** Founded in 1978 by nutrition guru James

LeSage, New Life was one of the country's first fitness-oriented vacation programs. Think of it as a luxurious camp for grown-ups; the goal during its six- and seven-day sessions, conducted at the elegant Inn of the Six Mountains, is to change your lifestyle for the better by helping you shed pounds, increase your stamina, and learn new relaxation, nutrition, and exercise skills. Assisted by a youthful and out-going staff, LeSage takes you through active days that start out with a walk before breakfast and include stretching, conditioning, and aerobics classes; aquacise sessions; yoga; and hikes of 5 miles or more through the Vermont countryside. After dark, there are presentations on nutrition, healthy cooking, self-massage, body alignment, and relaxation as well as discussion about how to integrate what you've learned into your daily life. There are never more than 25 guests on hand. Your program is individually tailored to your goals.

The attractively presented meals are high in fiber, low in fat, and full of complex carbohydrates; they provide between 1,000 and 1,200 calories a day. The spacious, tastefully appointed rooms have private baths, televisions, and phones; some have balconies. On the property there are tennis courts, exercise equipment, a whirlpool, sauna and steam rooms, and indoor and heated outdoor pools; nearby are golf, horseback riding, mountain biking, canoeing, and antiquing. *New Life Fitness Vacations, Box 395, Killington, VT 05751, tel. 802/422–4302 or 800/228–4676, fax 802/422–4321. May–Oct.: 6 days, $1,099–$1,125 single, $980–$999 dou-ble. Price includes 2-hr massages but not 7% Vermont sales tax or 15% service charge.*

VERMONT **Topnotch at Stowe.** This classic New England mountain resort caters to sports enthusiasts and weary urbanites seeking a sophisticated escape close to nature. Its full-service spa, opened in 1989, offers a state-of-the-art exercise program as well as seminars covering such topics as bodywork, skin care and nutrition, and relaxation. There is also an extensive selection of face and body treatments—everything from seaweed wraps to salt scrubs, aromatherapy, and hydrotherapy in a special French tub lined with pulsating jets. Sport-specific classes and conditioning consultations get you in shape for tennis and skiing.

You have a choice of one-on-one training or scheduled aerobics classes every hour between 9 and 4. You can also get a personal fitness assessment, during which your body fat is measured, your blood cholesterol determined, and your flexibility, endurance, and strength tested. You are assigned to one of five levels, and your program begins. Instructors are noted for their sense of humor as well as their teaching skills. You can choose one free treatment or professional service (such as a fitness assessment) per day; for others you pay extra.

In the dining room, you can choose between spa cuisine and international fare. Meals are calorie-controlled, based on 1,000 to 1,300 calories a day for women, and 1,300 to 1,700 calories a day for men. Rooms, located in the main lodge, are furnished with antiques and a library stocked with good bedtime reading. Topnotch is a good bet if your traveling companion is not interested in spa activities. There are special rates for nonparticipating companions, for instance, and plenty of other diversions. Topnotch is known for its tennis program and has 14 courts, and it's not far from Mt. Mansfield, one of New England's best ski areas. Also on the grounds are a 60-foot heated indoor swimming pool, a heated outdoor pool with mountain views, and 30 miles of groomed cross-country trails that link up with the Catamount Trail along the ridge of the Green Mountains. *Topnotch at Stowe, Box 1458, Stowe, VT 05672, tel. 802/253–8585 or 800/451–8686, fax 802/253–9263. Year-round: 5–7 days, $1,210–$2,275 single, $990–$1,645 double. Price includes 1 personal or professional service daily but not 7% tax or 17% service charge.*

THE MID-ATLANTIC

PENNSYLVANIA **Deerfield Manor Spa.** At this 12-acre property in the Pocono Mountains, owner-director Frieda Eisenkraft provides moderate exercise, a healthy diet, and lots of country charm. Most of the 33 guests are high-powered working women, many of whom return every year to renew friendships with one another and staff members and maintain their health. Some come for luxury treatments, and others don't miss an aerobics class; some stick to a strict menu plan while others request extra portions and snack freely. Both weekend and six-day programs are offered, with emphasis on walks and outdoor exercise rather than strength-training equipment.

The "Total Fitness" week's program begins on Sunday, with dinner followed by a meeting with Frieda, who started the spa in 1981. She tells you about the facilities, the food, staff members, and the fitness program, which includes aerobics, step aerobics, body toning, circuit training, stretching, yoga, water aerobics, and guided walks. After breakfast on Monday is an optional exercise orientation and weigh-in. The exercise class schedule changes daily. A few days into the week, guests staying a week can sign up for a free exercise consultation to develop a program to take home. Every evening after dinner there is a different activity, whether it's a demonstration of healthful cooking by the chef or a handwriting analysis by a local graphologist. The atmosphere is laid-back—you're allowed to come and go as you please, and all activities are optional. Caloric intake is a main subject for conversation.

One of the spa's buildings is a lovely white clapboard farmhouse dating from the 1930s; guest rooms there are full of rattan furniture and antiques. In an annex structure, rooms are newer, superclean, and airy, with Laura Ashley bedspreads and cathedral ceilings. All rooms have cable TV and private bath. Three lounges, where you can watch movies, read, socialize, and listen to music, are in the main house, as is the dining room, which serves three meals and an afternoon snack each day. You select your own menu a day in advance as part of a behavior modification program—the idea is that if you plan what you're going to eat, you'll eat less. The nonfat, low-salt entrées and side dishes consist of fresh fruit and vegetables, eggs, cottage cheese, yogurt, bran cereals, wheat bread, fish, and chicken; you consume between 800 and 1,100 calories a day. Supervised juice fasting is also available.

Fitness classes take place in a converted barn; water aerobics are in the heated outdoor pool. The main building has a sauna, manicure room, and massage rooms where, for a fee, you can experience Swedish massage, reflexology, shiatsu, or Reiki, a therapy session during which the practitioner's hands are placed for 3 to 5 minutes on each of 12 different areas of your body in a kind of "laying on" of the hands. Other treatments, such as facials, body buffs, and seaweed wraps, also cost extra. Two tennis courts on an adjacent property are open for matches. Or you might go hiking in the Delaware Water Gap National Recreation Area or Worthington State Park, just a short drive away. An outlet shopping center is also nearby. *Deerfield Manor Spa, 650 Resica Falls Rd., East Stroudsburg, PA 18301, tel. 717/223–0160 or 800/852–4494, fax 717/223–8270. Apr.–mid-Nov.: 6 days, $699–$935; weekend, $210–$340 per person, double. Price does not include 6% tax or 15% service charge.*

VIRGINIA **Hartland Wellness Center.** This establishment, on a 730-acre estate in Virginia's Blue Ridge Mountains, provides health education and exercise in a Christian environment; its 10- and 18-day programs include cooking lessons, private and group counseling, and exercise. The dedicated doctors and educators on the staff, all Seventh-Day Adventists, focus on practical nutritional instruction; they believe that good living habits can prevent many simple ailments. Using a computer, they do a nutritional analysis and recommend a diet that

takes into account your physical condition as well as your weight-loss goals. The center was founded in 1983 and now accommodates up to 23 guests at a time, many of them older and suffering from arthritis, diabetes, obesity, or cancer. Facilities include an indoor swimming pool, nature trails, and a mansionlike treatment center.

After a full day of testing, the staff designs a schedule and recommends an exercise program. Activities begin with breakfast at 6:45 on weekdays. At the treatment center, you might have hydrotherapy, which stimulates circulation by using contrasting hot and cold showers, or a relaxing massage. Three low-fat vegetarian meals are provided daily. Guests stay in rooms furnished with antiques. On weekends, the center has a picnic and schedules trips to area historic sites at no extra charge. *Hartland Wellness Center, Box 1, Rapidan, VA 22733, tel. 540/672–3100 or 800/763–9355, fax 540/672–3107. Year-round: 10 days, $1,500, 18 days, $2,500.*

WEST VIRGINIA **Coolfont Resort and Spectrum Spa.** Nestled in a valley in the Appalachian Mountains near historic Berkeley Springs, this informal, camplike 1,300-acre resort and conference center has been identified with health and environmental programs since 1973. Creating the Spectrum Spa here in 1992, in two barnlike structures, was a labor of love for Coolfont Resort owners Martha and Sam Ashelman, who often join morning hikes and yoga classes or dine with program participants in the main lodge. In addition to a fitness center with an indoor springwater swimming pool, the spa has 16 private rooms for bodywork, a full-service beauty salon, a demonstration kitchen, and an aerobics studio with a sprung floor, specially designed to cushion your bouncing and help prevent injuries. Workouts on cardiovascular and strength-training equipment, including a 15-unit Cybex circuit, are free and unsupervised.

You can choose a structured, scheduled group program, scheduled weekly for between two and five days, or go on your own. Coolfont's spa retreats, limited to 20 participants, introduce you to the latest trends in nutrition, weight management, stress control, and quitting smoking; also on the program are classes in aerobics, yoga, and body-strengthening exercises. You can book spa services as a package in conjunction with a spa retreat or à la carte; these services include massage, herbal wraps, loofah body scrubs, facials, and hair, nail, and skin care. For couples, a two-day massage workshop is scheduled weekends ($750 for two persons). Spa-cuisine meals, included in the programs, are served in a private dining room. The pre-breakfast walk is open to all resort guests.

A special program for mature adults is the Elderhostel weeks with the Peabody Institute of Baltimore (December–March). Corporate executives also train here in professional development programs designed to cultivate teamwork by Outward Bound, the preeminent adventure-learning organization based in Maine.

You can stay in the modern three-story Woodland Lodge, whose 22 rooms have fireplaces and whirlpool baths; in 20 mountain chalets with two bedrooms and double whirlpools; in the Manor House, which is listed on the National Register of Historic Buildings; or in log cabins. Tent and trailer sites are also available. There are two dining rooms; one offers bountiful buffets with a different ethnic or other culinary theme each night and no particular nutritional profile, while the other serves a fixed menu of low-fat, high-fiber meals that run 1,200 to 1,400 calories a day.

A nonprofit foundation sponsors cultural and educational evenings at the resort, including chamber music and National Gallery of Art films. During free time, you can play tennis on the resort's eight outdoor courts or, nearby, soak in the mineral water baths at Berkeley Springs State Park or go antiquing. *Coolfont Resort, Cold Run Valley Rd., Rte. 1, Box 710, Berkeley Springs, WV 25411, tel. 304/258–4500 or* *800/888–8768, fax 304/258–5499. Year-round: 6 days, $973–$1,250 double. Price does not include 6% room tax, $3.65 per night service charge, or gratuities.*

THE SOUTH

FLORIDA **Disney Institute.** A kind of updating of the Chautauqua tradition, the Disney Institute campus adjoining the Walt Disney World Resort provides choices of more than 60 programs designed to enhance creativity, fitness, and relaxation for both parents and their children. For golfers, the three-day course designed by Gary Player can be combined with sport-specific workouts with Cybex strength-training equipment. Teenagers participate in producing TV and radio shows and in games in the full-size gym and basketball court. Some activities are for families, but you set your own schedule, each person following his or her own interests.

The spa is an oasis of calm in the midst of your class schedule. In addition to an indoor exercise pool, its 10 treatment rooms provide a wide range of bodywork and beauty services, including aromatherapy and fangotherapy. Located in the Sports and Fitness Center, which has scheduled classes throughout the day in two large aerobics studios, the spa provides locker rooms for men and women, each with whirlpool, steam room, sauna, grooming amenities, robe and slippers, and workout clothing. Appointments for spa services are priced à la carte, and are available to guests at any hotel in the resort area.

The range of golf and tennis training is designed to enhance and refine skills, rather than retool a player's game. Pre-schedule your classes and spa appointments by calling an Institute program coordinator. Groups are kept small to encourage interaction among participants and instructors; plan well ahead of your arrival, or visit the appointments desk as soon as you check in. Among activity choices included in the three-day mini-mum program are a canoe trip to marsh-lands where a naturalist introduces Florida flora and fauna, followed by a cookout; rock climbing on a 30-foot wall equipped with safety lines; a tennis clinic; a guided bird-watching hike; organic gardening with a horticulturist; fitness for mature adults; and a cooking class along with wine and food tastings. Evenings you get free tickets for concerts, lectures, and screenings of fea-ture films.

Fans of Mickey Mouse and friends can take a class in animation art. The Magic King-dom and EPCOT Center are just down the road, and a one-day pass to any one Walt Disney World theme park is included in your basic plan, as well as free shuttle bus service. But the Disney Institute is a world apart, like a small New England village, complete with lake and golf course, where you pursue personal interests and plea-sures with complete security. Accommoda-tions are in a bungalow or 1- or 2-bedroom town house; both have daily maid service. Meals can be included in your program; if you are in a town house, which has a full kitchen, you can do you own cooking. *Dis-ney Institute, 1960 Magnolia Way, Lake Buena Vista, FL 32830, tel. 407/827–1100 or 800/282–9282, fax 407/397–6420; spa appointments 407/827–4455. Year-round: 3-night basic package $499–$678; 3-night deluxe plan with meals and gratuities $652–$831 double.*

FLORIDA **Doral Golf Resort and Spa.** With its red-tile roof, rotunda-topped villa, and statuary-punctuated formal gardens, this posh spa overlooking five manicured golf courses is like a vision of Tuscany in Florida. Completely self-contained with 48 suites and spa restaurant, garden waterfalls inspired by ancient baths at Terme di Sat-urnia, near Rome, and access to champi-onship golf and tennis, the resort mixes European and American ideas about pro-moting health, with take-home tips for wellness, stress management, nutrition, and looking your best.

Programs are innovative, built around biofeedback (for stress management) and boxing-style aerobics (for fitness); upon arrival, you can choose to concentrate on health and fitness or weight management, or just relax and get beautified. Treatments for muscular and skin problems are a spe-cialty; fango warm mud packs from Italy's Saturnia volcanic springs are part of the massage therapy. Above the upper levels of the villa's central atrium are the sundeck, a lounge, 26 private massage rooms offering a selection of treatments, the coed beauty salon and skin-care treatment rooms, the running track, exercise class rooms, and the men's and women's locker rooms, them-selves equipped with whirlpool, saunas, and steam rooms. The gymnasium and weight room are below the lobby level.

Planning a daily regimen is up to you. There are classes in jazz dance, low-impact aero-bics, and aqua-aerobics, clinics on cooking, tennis, golf, and fishing. Staff specialists plan serious regimens only after comparing your health profile with a computerized model based on nationwide health statis-tics. Most of the aging baby boomers who work out here relish the low-fat meals, sports options, shuttle bus to the beach and Bal Harbour shops. Personal service credits and amenities at the spa are included in packages for four to eight days, or you can plan a one-day spa escape without overnight lodging.

Your choice of accommodations includes the resort's spacious golf lodges or the spa suites. The deluxe suites, redecorated in 1996, feature marble-walled bathrooms with his-and-hers toilets, robes, twin baths, and dressing areas. For the ultimate fan-tasy, book one of the five suites themed to regions of Italy. Located close to Miami International Airport, the 650-acre resort wraps around 15 tennis courts, five golf courses (including tournament favorites Blue Monster and Gold), and the Golf Learn-ing Center run by Jim McLean. *Doral Golf Resort and Spa, 8755 N.W. 36th St., Miami, FL 33178, tel. 305/593–6030 or 800/331–*

7768, 800/713–6725, fax 305/591–9266. Year-round: 4 days, $1,299.89–$1,913.92 double. Day spa packages from $99. Price includes tax and service charge.

FLORIDA **Fit for Life Health Resort & Spa.** Based on his book, *Fit for Life,* author Harvey Diamond teamed up with the former Royal Atlantic Spa to create a new holistic health program in 1996. Located directly on the beach, this is a pleasant, no-frills combination of vacation and learning experiences. Structured for group camaraderie, the daily program includes beach walks, lectures, and exercise. There's an outdoor swimming pool, indoor pool and an indoor gym with exercise equipment. Upstairs, the spa salon provides personal services.

Each day begins with a vigorous walk along the beach, followed by low-impact, step, and water aerobics. You can join a yoga or meditation session or attend classes in vegetarian cooking. In addition, a number of treatments are available, among them massages, salt scrubs, and aromatherapy.

Meals, served in the garden-level dining room, are vegetarian. Breakfast consists of fruits and juices, lunch is an extensive salad bar or baked potatoes, and dinner, served by candlelight, may include vegetarian lasagna or peppers stuffed with wild rice. No coffee or dairy products are available. Juice and water fasts can be arranged.

Accommodations for 100 guests are in a motel-like three-story building. Although rooms are tiny, each has a private bath, TV, phone, and terrace or balcony. *Fit for Life Health Resort & Spa, 1460 S. Ocean Blvd., Pompano Beach, FL 33062, tel. 305/941–6688 or 800/583–3500, fax 305/943–1219. Year-round: 7 days, $899–$1,199 single, $699–$999 double. Price does not include tax or service charges.*

FLORIDA **Hippocrates Health Institute.** The one-week Health Encounter at the Hippocrates Health Institute in West Palm Beach aims to make you knowledgeable about food and its relationship to health.

Program director Brian R. Clement began teaching vegetarianism in Boston more than 30 years ago and moved his institute to this estate in 1985. Residential rather than a resort, the Institute provides optional spa services in addition to the educational program.

The program is highly structured. A typical day begins at 8 with light exercise, breakfast, a blood-pressure check, and a discussion of health and diet. Such nutritional education, as well as regular exercise, massage, reflexology, detoxification, and relaxation are all part of the program, along with classes that teach you life-enhancing skills such as deep relaxation techniques. You also learn how to cook with unprocessed organic vegetables, make sprouts, and grow greens. Once a week you have a session with the massage therapist. Certain days are designated as juice fasts. Throughout the program, a psychologist and physician work with health director Anna Maria Gahns to advise you on personal problems and monitor your progress. The spa has various classrooms and therapy rooms including four swimming pools, a cold plunge pool, a whirlpool, and a sauna.

The program's 30 to 40 participants lodge in cottages, garden apartments, and in the main building, a Spanish-style hacienda, with three luxury suites. Vegan fare (no animal foods or dairy products) is served buffet style at meals, with lots of nuts, seeds, sprouts, herbs, algae, and sea plants. Guests have access to an outdoor swimming pool, and excursions, for which there is no extra charge, are taken to the beach, local museums, and shopping malls. *Hippocrates Health Institute, 1443 Palmdale Ct., West Palm Beach, FL 33411, tel. 407/471–8876 or 800/842–2125, fax 407/471–9464. Year-round: 1 wk, $1,500–$1,900 double.*

FLORIDA **PGA National Resort & Spa.** Here, you can sign up for thalassotherapy, Swedish massages, facials, hydrotherapy, reflexology, and salt-glow treatments; you can also soak in pools that contain mineral salts from the Dead Sea and the French Pyrenees. But what makes this resort different from all other spas is that it's all about sports conditioning: Here you learn how to exercise more safely and more effectively and what to do when you overextend yourself on the playing field—lessons crucial to amateur athletes as well as the pros who train in the private fitness center. Facilities for tennis and golf players are equally strong: The resort's 28,500-square-foot health and racquet club has five indoor courts and 19 Har-Tru outdoor tennis courts (12 lighted for night play), and there are five golf courses. Clinics for golfers and tennis players can be coordinated with personal training in the fitness center to develop a sport-specific program.

The spa building, set in lush tropical gardens, has separate wings for men and women, a central core of treatment rooms, and three private pools and whirlpools outdoors. With the opening in 1996 of the Bramham Institute, a new educational component added classes in bodywork for professionals as well as guests interested in self-care.

Resident nutritionist Cheryl Hartsough works with a team of spa chefs to ensure heart-healthy options in the resort's five restaurants—among them the Italian restaurant, Arezzo, and the poolside Citrus Tree, where Florida seafood is the specialty. The resort's 336 rooms are spacious; those in the main hotel have a private terrace or balcony, king-size beds and sofas, dressing rooms, remote-control TV, and built-in wet bars. The 80 two-bedroom, two-bath suites are even roomier. *PGA National Resort & Spa, 400 Ave. of the Champions, Palm Beach Gardens, FL 33418, tel. 407/627–2000 or 800/633–9150, fax 407/622–0261. Year-round: Daily spa plan with meals $395 double, room only $109–$325, day spa packages from $168.*

FLORIDA **Pritikin Longevity Center.** You can get a massage, a facial, or a manicure at this center on Miami Beach—one of those ubiquitous pink palaces of pleasure. But that's peripheral in this place, a destination where healthy people learn how to safeguard their health and those suffering from heart disease, insulin-dependent diabetes, obesity, and uncontrolled high blood pressure learn how to change the quality of their lives. Exercise, diet, stress-management training, and health counseling are the core curriculum; the program is tightly monitored and leaves little time free for more than an ocean swim or walk on the beach promenade. During the two weeks that most participants spend here, their schedule requires checkups by the medical staff, attendance at lectures, and workouts on a battery of Trotter treadmills, StairMasters, and stationary bikes. Daily sessions of aquatics and aerobics alternate with yoga and other activities. But the program's backbone is the Pritikin diet, which is 10% to 15% protein, 80% complex carbohydrates, and 5% to 10% fat; you learn about the diet both in cooking classes and at meals, which are mostly vegetarian, with regular appearances by fresh fish, pasta, and rice. Being part of the supportive group at the center helps newcomers, who range in age from 18 to 85. The staff is very accessible.

The 100 bedrooms are modestly furnished; some have an ocean view, while others face Collins Avenue. Pritikin alumni have a toll-free hot line, are welcome to return for monthly meetings, and can join support groups around the country. Smaller than the original Pritikin Center in California, this is their only East Coast residential program. *Pritikin Longevity Center, 5875 Collins Ave., Miami Beach, FL 33140, tel. 305/866–2237 or 800/327–4914, fax 305/866–1872. Year-round: 1 wk $3,727 single, $2,028 double.*

GEORGIA **The Sea Island Spa at the Cloister.** It was in 1989 that this spa opened at the venerable Cloister, the grande dame of southern seashore resorts, directly on the pristine Atlantic beach of a private 5-mile barrier island. Sports add a special dimension to this well-mannered seaside escape;

the resort has 54 holes of golf, a Golf Learning Center, 18 tennis courts, water sports, three skeet ranges, bike rentals, fishing charters, and a program of nature hikes and boating expeditions into the tidal creeks and marshes around the island, where bird life is abundant. Instruction is available for most of the recreational activities, including horseback riding, fly fishing, skeet and trap, in addition to programs such as bridge, personal financial planning, and wine tasting.

The spa tailors programs to each guest's needs and goals. A regimen created for golf and tennis players stresses flexibility, strength, and pre-game warm-up rituals. You can work out (with an ocean view) in the spa cardiovascular and strength-training room and aerobics studio. A wide variety of treatments is available, among them thalassotherapy; all are performed away from the beach crowd in private rooms, each of which is used for just one guest. Treatments can be booked à la carte or as one-, two-, three-, or five-day packages. Each February the spa hosts a five-day program for women that includes workshops on interior design and fashion, information about ob-gyn and skin care, and a full complement of fitness classes.

Morning beach walks and stretch classes are open to all resort guests at no charge. There are also aquacise classes in the big outdoor swimming pool. Family-oriented, the resort also has extensive programs for teenagers during school holidays.

Lodging is in handsomely decorated rooms in spacious modern lodges overlooking the beach and the Intracoastal Waterway; private cottages are also available. Meals follow the full American plan, and there's a formal dinner and dancing every night but Sunday. Some spa cuisine is available. You can enjoy fresh seafood at the beachside restaurant. *The Cloister, Sea Island, GA 31561, tel. 912/638–3611 or 800/732–4752, fax 912/638–5814. Year round: Daily spa plan $396–$682 single, $309–$452 double. Price does not include 5% tax or 15% gratuity.*

NORTH CAROLINA Duke University Diet and Fitness Center. Since 1969, the center has provided participants with a plan for weight loss they can take home with them. Involving a team of doctors, clinical psychologists, dieticians, exercise physiologists, and massage therapists, the highly regimented course combines exercise classes, cooking demonstrations, a grocery store tour, and (at additional cost) individual psychotherapy. The program gives you one-on-one sessions in each of four components: nutrition, behavior, fitness, and medical management. Participants include men and women from all walks of life; some want to lose 20 pounds while others are seriously obese or are trying to stop smoking. Many return for refresher courses. There are usually between 90 and 120 in residence.

A typical day begins with breakfast at 7:45, followed by an aerobics class in the gym or indoor pool or a walk on the treadmill or around the scenic campus. Next you might attend a stress-management lecture, and after lunch a demonstration of health-wise cooking methods. Then you might take a tai chi class and a small group workshop. After dinner, you can play volleyball, go to a movie, or nurse a cup of coffee and chat with other participants.

Meals, served in the dining room, are all portion-controlled and low in calories, sodium, fat, and cholesterol. Housing is up to you; the center can make recommendations. Most convenient, and newly redecorated, is Duke Towers Residential Suites (919/687–4444). *Duke University Diet and Fitness Center, 804 W. Trinity Ave., Durham, NC 27701, tel. 919/684–6331 or 800/362–8446, fax 919/682–8869. Year-round: 1-wk program fee $2,400, 2 wks $4,295, 4 wks $5,195.*

NORTH CAROLINA Structure House. This center, founded in 1977, is one of the nation's premier residential weight-loss retreats. It attracts people with disabilities, those who are aging, and people who have 20 to 200 pounds to lose. The goal is to teach you how to control your weight over the long term. The program involves mental and physical conditioning as well as a diet. Among the programs are group sessions with a stress therapist, private counseling, classes in how to choose wisely from a restaurant menu, and instruction on the causes of obesity. Stays of two to four weeks are recommended; alumni can return for a week or more of reinforcement at reduced rates.

The Life Extension Center, which is on the grounds, contains the gym, weight room, treadmills, recumbent bikes, massage rooms, and the indoor pool (connected by terrace to an outdoor pool and sundeck). Select from among step, aquacise, and other aerobics classes; schedule a massage with specialists in deep-muscle therapy or a Swedish-style relaxer; or take a walk on a woodland trail through the rolling 22-acre property. Arrival is on Sunday, and there are 85 to 95 participants on hand at any given time, served by a staff of 30 professionals.

Everyone stays in modern one- and two-bedroom apartments in two-story houses on the grounds. These units have weekly maid service, a washer and dryer, a telephone, and color TVs. Food plans are based on a weekly system that allows each person to plan his or her meals, according to a 1,000- (for women) or 1,200-calorie (for men) per day program. The food is home style. *Structure House, 3017 Pickett Rd., Durham, NC 27705, tel. 919/493–4205 or 800/553–0052, fax 919/490–0191. Year-round: 7 days, $1,599 single, $1,445 double (returnees $903 single, $744 double).*

SOUTH CAROLINA **Hilton Head Health Institute.** Living the good life on this celebrated southern resort island may provide a push to make a change in your life. The medically supervised programs are designed to help you modify your lifestyle and work habits, maintain your weight, stop smoking, lower your cholesterol, and boost your stamina and overall well. Groups of 30 to 45 men and women attend the program for a week to 26 days; each program has

a specific starting date. After a medical screening (included in the program cost), you work with a team of psychologists, nutritionists, and physical fitness specialists to learn about the effects of nutrition and exercise on the body's metabolism and to deal with the effects of stress on productivity and health. Mornings usually begin with a moderately paced walk. Lectures, workshops, exercise classes, and meals are all part of the program during the rest of the day. In your free time, you can take advantage of Hilton Head's beaches, golf, tennis, hiking, biking, and other recreational opportunities. Indoors at the center, you'll find a weight-training unit, stationary bikes, and treadmills.

Program activities take place in a campuslike cluster of villas on the island. Participants share well-decorated apartments, fully equipped for laundry and cooking; each person has a private bedroom and bath. You follow a diet of 800 to 1,100 calories daily during the week but can eat more on weekends; meals are varied but are always high in complex carbohydrates, moderate in proteins, and low in fat, with no sugar or salt. *Hilton Head Health Institute, Box 7138, Hilton Head Island, SC 29938, tel. 803/785–7292 or 800/292–2440 (in Canada, 800/348–2039), fax 803/686–5659. Year-round: 7 days, $1,200–$1,600.*

TENNESSEE **Tennessee Fitness Spa.** This fitness center, housed in a complex of new and old buildings on rolling terrain southwest of Nashville, takes an easygoing approach to weight loss. Conditioning takes the form of canoeing and biking trips and hikes to beautiful and historic sites in the area, and trainer John Alexander and his staff of 16 use country music and line-dancing choreography for aerobics classes. Aquacise classes take place in the 60-foot swimming pool, which is enclosed and heated in winter.

You might begin your day with a hill walk, a 2½-mile warmup to a stretch class and step aerobics. Then you could have a soak in the big hot tub, play some volleyball, or sign up for a massage, facial, haircut, manicure, or pedicure. Meals are low in fat, salt, and sugar; you regularly attend nutrition classes in the dining hall, where the spa chef demonstrates how to prepare healthy dishes. Participants range in age from 20 to 70; many come for a month or more.

Accommodations cost less than at almost any other spa in the country, especially when four people share a quad unit. In addition, there are 20 double rooms in six rustic two-story chalets. *Tennessee Fitness Spa, Rte. 3, Box 411, Waynesboro, TN 38485, tel. 615/722–5589 or 800/235–8365, fax 615/ 722–7441. Year-round except Dec. 15–Feb 1: 7 days, $899 single, $579 double, $499 quad. Price does not include gratuities.*

THE MIDWEST

ILLINOIS **Heartland Spa.** The comforts are down-home and the fitness program upbeat at this spa, which is surrounded by farmland near Chicago; it's a comfortable place to cultivate a personal regimen that you can continue at home.

Designed for up to 28 participants, the program begins with an orientation session that helps you select exercise classes and personal services. Once a barn for prize-winning dairy cows, the main three-level structure houses a 15-meter swimming pool, massage rooms, sauna and steam rooms, and weight-training and cardiovascular conditioning equipment. On the top floor is an aerobics studio with a sprung floor.

Days begin with stretches and a brisk walk, followed by your choice of high- or low-intensity aerobics; the rest of the day, you can take step classes, yoga, or tai chi, or, outdoors, a ropes course. In summer you can hike or paddleboat on the estate's lake. Massages, facials, and sea-salt body exfoliation are an option, although at an additional charge. Every day, the spa delivers a sweat suit and workout clothing appropriate to the weather to your room. Weatherproof access to the fitness center via an underground tunnel makes getting to class easy at all times.

Meals, served in a bright, cheerful dining room, are mainly vegetarian, with 1,500 calories daily for men, 1,200 for women. The diet is high in complex carbohydrates and low in fat, sugar, and sodium. You may find waffles, banana pancakes, or egg-white omelets on the breakfast table. Typical dinner entrées are lasagna and grilled salmon.

Guests stay in a 14-room manor house dating from the 1940s, furnished with pine pieces; at night they gather near the living room fireplace. *Heartland Spa, Rte. 1, Box 181, Gilman, IL 60938, tel. 815/683–2182 (Chicago office 312/357–6465) or 800/ 545–4853, fax 815/683–2144. Year-round: 5 days, $1,625 single, $1,260 double; weekend, $800 single, $720 double.*

MINNESOTA **The Marsh.** In a supportive, self-contained environment close to nature, the Marsh encourages the connection of mind and body through a variety of programs that combine relaxation techniques and energy-building exercises. This "Center for Balance and Fitness" is housed in a dramatic wooden structure overlooking marshland; the interior feels residential, and everything is state-of-the-art, from cardiovascular and weight-training gyms to the 75-foot lap pool and therapy pools, one of which is equipped with a hydraulic lift chair. Designed in 1985 as a health center to showcase innovative programs conceived by Ruth Stricker, the Marsh added six guest rooms in 1993 and more than doubled its space for programs. The 27,000-square-foot structure includes a climbing wall, an art gallery, and a silo-shape meditation tower where a "mental gym" challenges you to work out with brain-teasing games. At the center's hub is a cozy, informal café serving fresh-baked bread and muffins and low-fat breakfasts (included in the fee for overnight guests), lunch, and gourmet dinners.

Your program is individualized and includes the core strength-training program, with scheduled classes in the health center.

Bodywork is available in nine private treatment rooms; personal consultation with wellness specialists is also offered. The staff comprises cardiologists, physical therapists, nutrition counselors, psychologists, and personal trainers who span the fitness spectrum.

Study the class schedule in advance; you can choose from among tai chi, yoga, meditation, Flowmotion, somatics (movements to help you manage chronic pain), centering exercises for alignment and stretching, and back therapy with physiogymnastic balls. For solo workouts, there's a fully equipped training center, indoor and outdoor running tracks, and full lines of Cybex, NordicTrack, and Quinton equipment. The full-swing golf studio and short court racket games provide indoor sports practice. Appointments for personal services in the spa are à la carte. For a relaxing treatment, try hydrotherapy in a French Setma tub or a relaxation chamber that supplies dry heat or steam as rollers gently massage your aching muscles. The spa's specialty is a hydrotherapeutic circuit of steam room, body polish, and water-jet massage.

Guests take dinner in the Moon Terrace dining room or a café; typical dishes are fresh grilled salmon, chicken breast with wild mushrooms, and pork medallions with salsa. Dinners, not included in the accommodations charge, cost about $16 per meal. The six guest rooms have either a queen-size bed or two single beds, a private bathroom and robes, a TV, and lovely marshland views. *The Marsh, 15000 Minnetonka Blvd., Minnetonka, MN 55345, tel. 612/935–2202, fax 612/935–9685. Year-round: Daily $115 for 2 persons, double. Price does not include tax, gratuities, dinner, or lunch.*

OHIO **Sans Souci Health Resort.** This quiet Dayton-area estate is on 80 acres crossed by 6 miles of hiking trails and borders a 600-acre wildlife preserve. It's a great location to practice the healthy lifestyle espoused by the strong but loving owner-director, Susanne Kircher, a registered nurse who acquired the place in 1978. Wake-up exercises and stretching and breathing sessions take place outdoors, where you're serenaded by the birds and cooled by gentle breezes. Mornings begin with a walk around the 1.8-mile, 18-station parcourse; meditation walks take you into the local pine forests.

Every week, six to eight guests embark on the highly structured regimen, which reflects both Kircher's European spa training and the latest thinking in stress and weight management and includes lectures, massage, yoga, aerobics, and exercise in the outdoor swimming pool. You won't find high-tech weight training, but instead long, sustained workouts. Cooking classes show you how to cut out polished rice, butter, and animal fats from your diet; you leave with a copy of Kircher's cookbook, *Sans Souci Spa Dining.* While you're here, meals are mostly vegetarian and provide 800 to 1,000 calories daily. An hour a day is set aside for rest and relaxation; some choose to visit the organic garden or the sprouting place, which supply fresh vegetables and sprouts for summer meals.

Lodging is in the manor house's rooms, which are furnished in English country style and have private baths and dressing areas. *Sans Souci Health Resort, 3745 Rte. 725, Bellbrook, OH 45305, tel. 513/848–4851, fax 513/435–4904. May–Oct.: 6 days, $1,480 single, $1,230 double.*

THE SOUTHWEST

ARIZONA **Canyon Ranch.** Few fitness resorts have more programs and facilities than this 70-acre spread in the foothills of Tucson's Santa Catalina Mountains. Founded in 1979 by Mel and Enid Zuckerman, and sold in 1996 (along with sister properties in Massachusetts' Berkshire Mountains, and on Bali) to a new investment group, this high-desert hideaway's grounds are splendid—full of cactus gardens and tropical trees, with streams meandering among the casitas that cluster around the spa complex, the Life Enhancement Center, and the Health and Healing Center. The Zuckermans continue to be involved in the management of the resort.

Unlike some resorts with rigid programs, the ranch lets you choose your own activities. For instance, you might opt for a cross-training program that includes hiking, biking, workouts in the nine gyms, relaxing spa services, and swimming in the indoor and outdoor pools—the mix is up to you. Or sign up for cooking classes that show you how to prepare healthful fare at home.

Taking a serious approach to prevention of illness, the Life Enhancement Program provides a weeklong regimen for people who want to get on a healthy track, and address personal life improvement goals such as weight management, stress reduction, or smoking cessation. Also, there are special health and well programs designed for groups of people who share medical conditions such as asthma, diabetes, arthritis, and heart disease. Specific weeks are devoted to healthy aging and women's health. Participants focus on improving their health profiles by gaining an understanding of the role played by proper nutrition, exercise, and stress-reduction techniques. In this supportive group atmosphere, you work with professionals in lifestyle change, plus some of the country's foremost physicians and researchers in specific health fields.

A team of 40 health professionals closely monitors your exercise and diet. In addition to such spa staples as sports, aerobics, and nutritional consultations, Canyon Ranch provides professional services such as stress-management counseling, homeopathy, hypnotherapy, and medical checkups, as well as such spa services as massage, aromatherapy, and herbal wraps; these services are covered partly by "point credits" based on the length of your stay. The ranch also provides mountain bikes and transportation to trailheads at no charge.

The morning stretch and walk, open to all, is perhaps the best time to get acquainted with other guests, an interesting cross section of people ranging from young executives and television celebrities to grandmothers; up to 40% of those on hand at any one time are men, and some people return several times a year. CME credits are available for physicians participating in the Life Enhancement Program or other special weeks.

Meals, which use organic ingredients, are low in salt and saturated fat but high in fiber, and are prepared without refined flour or sugar. Guests have the option of lodging in single rooms known as casitas or in suites and private cottages; cottages have a kitchen, living room, and laundry. All accommodations are decorated in desert colors with Southwestern furnishings. *Canyon Ranch 22, 8600 E. Rockcliff Rd., Tucson, AZ 85750, tel. 520/749–9000 or 800/742–9000, fax 520/749–1646. Year-round: 7 nights $2,640; 4 nights $1,560.*

ARIZONA **Marriott's Spa at Camelback Inn.** This quintessential Arizona desert resort, established as a celebrity hideaway at the base of Mummy Mountain in 1936, has the most complete spa facilities in the Phoenix-Scottsdale area: an aerobics room, outdoor whirlpool, hot and cold plunge pools, lap pool, sauna, steam room, Swiss shower, indoor and outdoor massage rooms, and a fitness room with treadmills, StairMasters, video monitors, four types of exercise bicycles, weight-training equipment, and even a health food restaurant. The spa, which occupies a spectacular southwestern-style hacienda and was established in 1989, also offers a variety of packages, including seven-day renewal packages, covering a variety of pampering, fitness, and well services. Here's your chance to try an herbal body treatment, an antiaging facial, a Parisian body polish, aromatherapy, or the like.

Typically, you begin your day with a scenic power walk or a tai chi class. Then, if you're on the seven-day renewal package, you can choose from among a dozen services or schedule a fitness evaluation, designed by the Cooper Aerobics Center (*see below*), or a more extensive lifestyle analysis, all of which are included. All spa guests are supplied with workout clothing, a robe, slippers, and other amenities.

You have your choice of two restaurants that serve tasty, low-fat foods. The spa renewal week includes breakfast and lunch daily and a deluxe room in a private casita, with king-size bed or large twins, decorated in pastels and earth tones. There's a special day camp for kids. *Marriott's Spa at Camelback Inn, 5402 E. Lincoln Dr., Scottsdale, AZ 85253, tel. 602/948–1700 or 800/242–2635, fax 602/596–7018. Year-round: 7 days, $1,741 single, $2,875 for 2 persons. 1-night Spa Getaway $274 for 2 persons. Price includes 1 spa service daily, and breakfast or lunch.*

ARIZONA **Miraval.** Part ranch, part self-discovery center, Miraval combines elements of a spa vacation with lifestyle learning. Inaugurated in 1996, the program options provide lessons in how to balance your life, deal with stress, and prevent illness. Among the challenges: jumping from a 30-foot pole while strapped in a safety harness; grooming horses, with whom you interact on an emotional level; a mountain bike group ride in the desert. There's also a dedicated lap pool (six lanes, 35 meters long), air-conditioned aerobics studio, and full-service spa.

If you prefer to relax by one of the five swimming pools, no bossy instructor will bother you. In fact, southwestern-style relaxation comes with all the comforts in 92 casita guest rooms, and 14 suites equipped with whirlpool tub, fireplace, TV with VCR, and a marble-accented bathroom. Included in the daily rate are all meals at your choice of two restaurants, in-room refreshments, and one personal service at the spa. Tipping is discouraged.

Set on 135 acres of high desert near Tucson, the resort offers spectacular views of the Santa Catalina Mountains. Hikes into the Sonoran Desert are a bonus. *Miraval, 5000 E. Via Estancia Miraval, Catalina, AZ 85739, tel. 520/825–4000 or 800/232–3969, fax 520/792–5870. Year-round: 4 days, $950–$1,785.*

TEXAS **Cooper Aerobics Center.** Dr. Kenneth H. Cooper, a pioneer in research on aerobics, established this Dallas-based center of preventive medicine in 1970 in a stately 63-room redbrick lodge on 30 acres. Today, it is also the home of a first-class fitness resort, known as the Cooper Well Program.

Here, the supportive and highly trained staff helps you cultivate new health habits, teaches stress-management techniques, and demonstrates healthy cooking; these sessions are part of your daily schedule, along with three exercise sessions per day and any other activities you can squeeze in. Four-, 7-, and 13-day programs, each with 15 to 20 participants, are available. Closely monitored, you team up with other guests for morning walks and runs on cushioned indoor and outdoor tracks. You also have access to four lighted Laykold tennis courts and two heated outdoor pools, six lanes wide and 75 feet long. The gym also has a pair of racquetball courts, a steam room, a sauna, a whirlpool, and Cybex strength-training equipment. A variety of medical exams are available here, all at extra cost.

The center attracts people from all walks of life, ages 19 to 75, including health-care professionals. Workshops with Dr. Cooper and other health experts help you manage stress or stop smoking, and individual counseling sessions can be scheduled to work on specific issues.

Program meals are calorie-controlled, low in fat and cholesterol, and served from a demonstration kitchen. One night you visit an Italian restaurant and practice ordering a heart-healthy dinner. You have the option of staying in area motels or in the guest lodge, whose 63 rooms and suites have heavy mahogany king- or queen-size beds, wing chairs, and private bathroom. *Cooper Aerobics Center, 12230 Preston Rd., Dallas, TX 75230, tel. 214/386–4777 or 800/444–5192, fax 214/386–0039 (Cooper Aerobics*

Center Guest Lodge, tel. 800/444–5187). Year-round: 4 days, $1,395–$1,895. Price does not include 6% tax, 20% gratuity, medical tests, or lodging (at Guest Lodge, $92–$256 double).

TEXAS **Lake Austin Spa Resort.** Crew and singles sculling are on the roster of activities at this Texas Hill Country spa, close to Austin. The lake on which it's sited is a prime year-round training camp for local and national rowing clubs. A rower in residence schedules classes for beginners; you can join canoe trips that include hikes and a picnic lunch.

However, the spa's weeklong program incorporates several other exercise choices, among them 2- to 3-mile morning walks, a more strenuous 6- to 12-mile weekly trek, or 2-hour bike rides—all group outings—or, on your own, solo explorations via mountain bike along the ranch roads of the Texas Hill Country. There are also aquacise sessions in the outdoor and indoor swimming pools. In the basic package, instructors teach you step aerobics and help you work toward more advanced conditioning.

A spa package (for which the rates are the same or better than the basic package) allows you to choose a variety of services. If you choose, you can start your program with a fitness assessment or hire a personal trainer. Or you might make appointments for bodywork services, including herbal skin care or herbal wraps, facials, clay body masks, thalassotherapy, Ayurvedic or Swedish massage.

Meals appeal to "Lean Star" tastes: Low-fat barbecued meats, enchiladas, and fajitas complement a salad bar featuring ingredients from the organic garden. Overlooking the lakeshore, lodging complements the camplike atmosphere, with 40 woodsy and antiques-accented rooms, all on one level, furnished with sleigh and pencil-post beds, armoires, and Shaker-style pieces; up to 80 guests can be accommodated. *Lake Austin Spa Resort, 1705 Quinlan Park Rd., Austin, TX 78732, tel. 512/266–2444 or 800/847–5637, fax 512/266–1572. Year-round: 1* night/2 days, $307 single, $277 double; 7 days, $2,090 single, $1,940 double.

UTAH **Franklin Quest Institute of Fitness.** The program at this institution, in the red-rock canyon country near Zion National Park, is intensive and no-frills, involving lots of hikes, exercise classes, and personal instruction on state-of-the-art weight-training and cardiovascular-strengthening equipment. The goal is to start reducing elevated serum cholesterol, blood glucose, and hypertension. Founded in 1974, the institute has undergone rapid growth recently, and is expanding programs in stress management as well as in fitness at all levels.

The one-week program begins on Monday. On arrival you're given a fitness evaluation, including a cardiovascular endurance test, and assigned to one of five groups according to your fitness level. Highly structured, the subsequent daily program includes walks of 1 to 10 miles, along trails that wind up razor-edge cliffs and down to hidden Native American ruins, along rust-color ridges and through meadows full of juniper and desert terrain scattered with sagebrush. In addition, there are workouts in the heated indoor swimming pool, low-impact step aerobics, toning classes, and lectures. Guests with serious weight problems stay a month or more, often shedding 50 pounds. Repeaters make up a majority of the participants, who are mostly women. You have access to the spa pool when it's not being used for classes, and there's no charge to book the outdoor tennis court or indoor racquetball court. With the opening of a skylit multipurpose Megahealth Building in 1992, spa treatments and bodywork, which are à la carte, became more comprehensive.

Meals follow a nutritionally balanced, low-fat, weight-loss plan, with controlled portions of food that is high in complex carbohydrates and low in salt, fat, and sugar; vegan diets are popular.

Accommodations are in modern two-story lodges, each room with twin beds and private bathroom, or older dome-shape units with four beds for budget watchers. *Franklin Quest Institute of Fitness, 202 N. Snow Canyon Rd., Box 938, Ivins, UT 84738, tel. 801/673–4905, fax 801/673–1363. Year-round: 7 days, $1,334–$1,519 single, $939–$1,094 double, $695–$895 quad.*

UTAH **Green Valley Spa and Tennis Resort.** The canyon country of the southern part of the state makes an inspiring setting for the learning experience at Green Valley Spa, which begins with an introduction to how the body's weight-regulating mechanism works and includes trips to supermarkets, cooking workshops, discussion groups, bodywork, and more. In the morning, you do yoga and hike right from the resort into the red-rock hills. After an early morning hike, or after lunch, you can go to the fully equipped gym for conditioning exercises, which help you learn correct posture and body movement. Aquacise classes are given in the 75-foot swimming pool. You can do more hiking in the afternoon or play some tennis. In fact, you can play day or night on the resort's courts (a quartet of them indoors, 15 outdoors) or take classes at the Vic Braden Tennis College, which is on the premises. You can also relax in a Jacuzzi or sign up for one of spa director Carole Coombs's skin or body treatments, done with locally made natural products. Among five services included in the seven-day program are full-body massages, acupressure, reflexology (a pedicure and foot massage combined), and a facial. Additional treatments and personal training can be billed to your account.

The 10-year-old spa building is decorated with accents—for instance, candles, flowers, and linens—whose colors change daily to radiate a different mood. A deep spiritual connection to the physical body and the land is part of the spa philosophy. Periodically a Native American shaman visits to present folklore or read fortune cards.

To help you establish specific goals, and plan your hiking and class schedule to meet these goals, a personal fitness consultation is scheduled. The 25–50 participants each week are housed in apartments with spacious contemporary interiors, including living room, kitchen, private bath, and balcony. A private swimming pool and relaxation garden is exclusively for spa guests. Meals also become a learning experience, prepared in a demonstration kitchen that is part of the dining room, featuring nutritious, low-fat fare, without sugar or salt, that you can make at home. *Green Valley Spa and Tennis Resort, 1515 W. Canyon View Dr., St. George, UT 84770, tel. 801/628–8060 or 800/237–1068, fax 801/673–4084. Year-round: 7 days, $2,900 single or double.*

THE ROCKIES

COLORADO **The Peaks at Telluride.** Skiing, hiking, and spa workouts are a high-energy combination at this Rocky Mountain resort in Southern Colorado. Opened in 1992, the 10-story hotel is in Mountain Village, a cluster of luxury homes, an 18-hole golf course, tennis courts, and ski slopes high above historic Telluride. In the valley, reached by complimentary shuttle bus, tourist-oriented Old Telluride preserves its mining town ambience at the base of a box canyon ringed by waterfalls and hiking trails.

Despite a minimalist modern exterior, the spa hotel is rich in decorative details that capture the art and history of the Rockies. Under the direction of Gayle Moeller, a veteran of several southwestern spa resorts, the ancient Native American kiva bathing and cleansing ritual was introduced here as a prelude to bodywork. Soaking in kiva pools and eucalyptus steam rooms in the men's and women's locker rooms is both relaxing après-ski, and cleansing for the body and mind. Specialty treatments employ Native American as well as Indian Ayurvedic practices, using herbal oils and essences of local wildflowers and pines. Try the "Deep Forest Exfoliation" followed by restorative massage. Skin care prescribed by the spa aestheticians emphasizes protection in the mountain environment.

Classes in lifestyle- and stress-management are regularly scheduled options to sports. Start your day with "Waking Up to Oneness," a welcoming of the new day with chanting and dancing inspired by Native American ceremony, or a session of yoga. Then work out with wall-to-wall Cybex cardiovascular and strength-training equipment, try rock climbing on an indoor wall, play squash, or swim laps. Your personal trainer might also work with celebrity guests like Christie Brinkley or Whitney Houston. The Peaks' Next Level sports performance program focuses on your sports of choice, teaming you with an exercise physiologist, nutritionist, and sports psychologist who design your workouts and sport-specific diet.

Seasons define sports at the Peaks: Ski from the hotel to the lifts, go ice climbing, or trek canyons in the San Juan Mountains. Along the scenic highways (don't miss U.S. Rte. 550) are historic mining towns like Silverton, Durango, and Ouray, where you can visit Victorian-era structures and soak in thermal hot spring pools. Exercise your luck at the Ute Mountain Casino south of Cortez, then explore Anasazi cliff dwellings built in the 14th century at Mesa Verde National Park.

With ski-in/ski-out access, hiking-trail maps in your room, and spa cuisine served on the terrace, the Peaks aims to integrate healthy eating and exercise into your vacation, rather than following a rigid program. Day spa packages are available to hotel guests as well as others in the area, and the KidSpa offers half- and full-day programs for children. The Peaks is situated at 9,500 feet, so altitude sickness may be a problem. Drink lots of water, avoid caffeine and alcohol, and don't exercise excessively during your first days here. This may be the perfect spa for people who like indoor luxuries to be as spectacular as the wilderness outdoors. *The Peaks at Telluride, 624 Mountain Village Blvd., Telluride, CO 81435, tel. 970/728–6800 or 800/789–2220, fax 970/728–6567. Daily rate for 2 persons (no minimum stay) $435–$550 winter, $160–*

$680 summer, suites from $235. 5-day/5-night Next Level package with 3 meals daily, $1,733–$3,000 single, $3,000–$4,000 for 2 persons. Add 12% tax, 15% gratuities.

THE WEST COAST

CALIFORNIA **Cal-a-Vie.** Since they established Cal-a-Vie in 1983, Marlin and William F. Power have been combining attributes of European and American spas here, with the goal of teaching their guests how to become fitter and healthier. Terraced into a southern California hillside, the spa's 24 country villas seem lifted from an area of Provence. Yet the outdoor pool, streams, manicured gardens, and wonderful food are pure American.

The weeklong program is limited to 24 participants, and personal attention is facilitated by a ratio of four staff members per guest. There are men-only, women-only, and coed weeks. After an initial fitness evaluation, the staff recommends a diet and exercise regimen. After that, your daily routine varies little: Mornings are devoted to exercise, afternoons to bodywork and salon treatments. Each day begins with a prebreakfast hike into the hills, followed by aerobic, body-contouring, and pool exercises: Boxercise, for instance, releases stress and builds strength and stamina, while yoga, tai chi, and stretch classes provide a calming counterpoint. Later, in the bathhouse you sample a wide range of therapies: aromatherapy massage, clay body masks, thalassotherapy, facials and massages included in the seven-day package, one of several optional plans.

Robes, shorts, T-shirts, and sweat suits are provided, and guests have been known to wear any of them to the very casual dinner. As you go on to another activity, a fresh set of clothes is supplied. Laundry is picked up and returned daily.

One night the kitchen becomes a classroom, as the chefs demonstrate the secrets of low-fat cooking during dinner. You eat between 1,200 and 1,500 calories per day. The menu includes vegetarian fare as well as chicken and fish. Guests stay in private villas with beamed ceilings, hand-carved furniture, and king-size beds with fluffy down comforters. All guest quarters have private baths. *Cal-a-Vie, 2249 Somerset Rd., Vista, CA 92084, tel. 619/945–2055, fax 619/630–0074. Year-round (closed mid-Dec.–early Jan.): 7 days, $3,750–$4,250 single. Price does not include tax.*

CALIFORNIA **Claremont Resort.** When you work out at this 279-room resort on 22 acres of hillside gardens, you have a view of San Francisco Bay. Although the white-turreted Victorian landmark was built in 1915, the spa complex, added in 1989, and the adjoining wing of 40 deluxe spa suites built in 1996, are state-of-the-art.

The Claremont's facilities include a multi-purpose aerobics studio and weight room, 10 tennis courts (lighted for night play), a heated outdoor pool, a separate lap pool, and, in the locker rooms, whirlpools, steam rooms, and saunas. You can sign up for massages and facials, hydrotherapy and aromatherapy, nutrition counseling, and fitness training, in the form of aerobics, yoga, and stretching classes. Some 30 body-work specialists are on call. The four-day spa package includes a choice of several treatments and can be taken with meals or, for a discount, without. The cost of longer stays is based on your particular program. Workout clothing is provided.

The Claremont is also the site of a highly structured weeklong retreat with Dr. Dean Ornish and specialists in stress management, nutrition, and diet from his Preventive Medicine Research Institute. At this retreat, lectures based on the best-selling *Dr. Dean Ornish's Program for Reversing Heart Disease* demonstrate how a low-stress, no-smoking lifestyle involving exercise and a low-fat vegetarian diet can reverse heart disease within a year. There are also workshops, workouts, yoga, meditation, and specially prepared low-fat meals. This program is limited to 100 participants. Scheduled four times a year, registration is $3,600; call 415/332–2525 or 800/775–7674.

Rooms are spacious, beds oversize, and all baths private. The resort menu offers a regular selection of sophisticated low-fat, low-cholesterol, low-calorie fare; menus indicate exactly how many calories you are consuming. *Claremont Resort, Box 23363, Oakland, CA 94623, tel. 510/843–3000 or 800/551–7266, fax 510/549–8582. Year-round: Daily rate $175–$215 single, $199–$239 for 2 persons, suites to $675 for 2 persons. Spa Retreat package (no meals), 1-night: $238–$258 single, $320–$340 for 2 persons; 2-night: $485–$525 single, $638–$678 for 2 persons. Day spa packages $100–$350. Price does not include tax or 17.5% gratuity.*

CALIFORNIA **The Golden Door.** One of southern California's oldest and most glamorous fitness resorts, the Golden Door teaches you about a healthy lifestyle while utterly pampering you. Opened in 1959 a mile from its present location, the resort now encompasses 177 acres of canyon and orchard. Beyond its ornate brass door, it's a cross between a first-class resort and a Japanese country inn, an enchanted realm of Japanese-style gardens and buildings. The four spacious gyms have glass doors that slide open to fresh air. The graceful bathhouse contains a modern sauna, steam room, Swiss shower, and treatment rooms for body wraps and body scrubs.

During the weeklong programs, you get one-on-one training from the fitness and nutrition specialists. Each day begins with stretches outside, followed by a sunrise mountain hike. The day may include weight training, aerobics, tap dancing, tennis, yoga, and massages and beauty treatments. For returning guests, there's the four-day, eight-hour Inner Door course, at which you are secluded in a teahouse to learn visualization and meditation techniques, work on stress-management skills, and practice creative thinking. The food here is low in fat, cholesterol, salt, and sugar, but rich in fiber; you'll find lots of whole grains. Mid-morning juice or broth, vegetable snacks, and nonalcoholic aperitifs are also served.

No more than 39 guests are accepted for the weeklong programs. Participants come from many backgrounds and countries, but most are middle-aged and success-oriented. Five weeks are reserved for men only, one for couples, and four are coed; the rest of the year is for women only. You stay in one-story stucco buildings patterned after old Japanese inns; rooms are done in muted colors with Japanese wood-block prints on the walls, parquet floors with rugs, sliding shoji screens in the bathrooms, and jalousie windows. Each has a private garden. All guests here have the use of sweat suits, workout clothing, bathrobes, slippers, Japanese robes, and daily laundry service, and transportation to and from San Diego International Airport is included in the package price. *The Golden Door, Box 463077, Escondido, CA 92046, tel. 619/744–5777 or 800/424–0777, fax 619/471–2393. Year-round (closed late Dec.): 7 days, $4,375 single or double; gratuities included, add tax.*

CALIFORNIA **The Oaks at Ojai.** Teaching good exercise habits and motivating you to keep them up at home is the focus of this high-energy spa, housed in a dignified two-story 1918 former country inn built of wood and stone, a landmark on sleepy Ojai's main thoroughfare. Although the lobby's dark green walls and wood-burning fireplace evoke a quieter, gentler era, the fitness regimen and spa cuisine are totally modern. Former professional ice skater and physical fitness instructor Sheila Cluff and her husband Donald bought the place in the 1970s, adding cottages in the gardens surrounding the swimming pool.

The no-frills program includes workouts in the large heated pool, intense aerobics classes rated for different fitness levels, and progressive stretches, along with morning hikes in the hills, brisk walks along country roads, and, late in the day, a stretch-and-

relax class. You can also work out on weight machines. At day's end, you can go for a soak in a nearby hot spring or schedule an hour-long massage, one of several spa services and treatments available at additional cost. Sometimes there are cooking demonstrations or lectures after dinner.

Designed to help participants lose weight, the menu is planned to provide only 1,000 calories daily, and the foods are fresh and natural. In the morning, fruit, muffins, and vitamins are set out at the coffee bar in the main building. There is a mid-morning broth break, and vegetable snacks are available in the afternoon. Dinner is casual.

Guests are diverse, ranging from young professionals to grandmothers; film industry folk, actresses, and homemakers all drop in to shape up and relax, and there are usually a few overweight women in residence for a month or more. Rooms are small and simply furnished and have showers or tubs. Cottages accommodate between one and three guests.

Ojai, located south of Santa Barbara, is an arts center and a favorite with practitioners of several healing faiths; in your free time, if you're interested, you can make appointments with psychics, astrologers, members of the Theosophy movement, and the like. *The Oaks at Ojai, 122 E. Ojai Ave., Ojai, CA 93023, tel. 805/646–5573 or 800/753–6257, fax 805/640–1504. Year-round: 5 days, $975–$1,025 single, $675–$795 double. Daily rate $195–$205 single, $135–$175 double. Spa Day package $89. Price does not include 15.25% tax or 14% service charge.*

CALIFORNIA **The Palms at Palm Springs.** The swimming pool at the center of the resort is the focal point of activities at this informal spa, also owned by Oaks proprietor Sheila Cluff, near the heart of Palm Springs. There are four sessions of water exercise daily, along with aerobics classes, which are held in a small aerobics studio and outdoors under the palms; you can choose from among 14 classes daily. The workouts' goals are to increase flexibility, burn calories, strengthen the heart, and increase lung capacity. The desert climate, the low-calorie diet, and the rigorous exercise quickly yield results. If you need more structure, you can plan a weight-management program with a resident nurse or schedule one-on-one weight training. Personal services—massage, aromatherapy, and a facial—are available at extra cost.

The place appeals to women and their devoted spouses. Most participants are in their middle fifties and in good shape but want to shed a few pounds. In the refurbished Spa Hotel, you can soak in thermal waters and choose from a massage-sauna combination or European treatments for hair, skin, and nails.

The menu provides 1,000 calories daily; food is simply prepared and you eat lots of vegetables, pasta, and chicken. Although the resort's layout is compact, as many as 84 people can be accommodated in the 43 guest rooms, which are in a red-roof manor house and private bungalows with a Spanish colonial air. Some rooms have their own patio; others share a bath. *The Palms at Palm Springs, 572 N. Indian Canyon Dr., Palm Springs, CA 92262, tel. 619/325–1111 or 800/753–7256, fax 619/327–0867. Year-round: 5-night midweek package, $995 single, $675–$845 double. Daily rate (2-night minimum) $199–$209 single, $135–$179 double. Spa Day package $89. Price does not include 15.25% tax or 14% service charge.*

CALIFORNIA **Pritikin Longevity Center.** This was the first of the country's institutions dedicated to the diet and exercise regimen developed in the late 1970s by the late Nathan Pritikin. Healthy people sign up for the strictly regimented, medically supervised programs here to preserve their health and learn to control their diet. Others come to lose weight, lower their cholesterol, or manage their blood pressure. The four-week program helps people with heart disease, insulin-dependent diabetes, and other serious health problems.

A full physical examination, with a treadmill stress test and a complete blood-chemistry analysis, marks the beginning of the program, which involves exercise, nutrition and health education, stress-management counseling, and medical services. The daily schedule packs in cooking classes and lectures along with three exercise sessions-workouts in the well-equipped gym or walks along the beach or down the Santa Monica pier. (Swimmers must use a nearby hotel pool or the ocean.) Diet is also a key to Pritikin life; chefs cook without added fat, salt, or sugar, and meals are largely vegetarian, although fish and chicken are served several times a week. The guest services desk makes appointments for massages or acupuncture sessions, which cost extra. The program lasts for 13 or 26 days, and the doctor and physiologist assigned to work with you when you arrive monitor your progress throughout.

Housed in a beachfront hotel, the center has modern rooms with private baths. The larger, more expensive quarters have a Jacuzzi tub and ocean views. Participating companions staying in the room with you get a reduced rate. *Pritikin Longevity Center, 1910 Ocean Front Walk, Santa Monica, CA 90405, tel. 310/450–5433 or 800/421–9911, fax 310/450–3602. Year-round: 13 days, $6,409 with full program, $2,405 for person sharing room. 7 days for returnees, $3,480 with full program, $1,511 2nd person sharing. Price does not include gratuities.*

CALIFORNIA **Skylonda Fitness Retreat.** The goals of the seven-day programs at this establishment on 16 forested acres of coastal hills south of San Francisco is to help people lose weight and recharge physically and spiritually. Opened in 1992, the program was expanded under new management in 1996.

The program involves walks, yoga, meditation, weight training, aerobics, aquatic exercises, and massage. Twice a day you hike through the spectacular redwood forests and golden meadows of the South Bay Peninsula, which separates the Pacific

Ocean from San Francisco Bay, a part of California rarely seen by visitors or residents. The day also includes an hour of silence and reflection. From the 6 AM wake-up call to the 9 PM close of evening programs, you interact closely with the up to 30 other guests during hikes, circuit training with PACE equipment, aquatics classes, yoga and stretch relaxation classes, and other fitness activities. Facilities include an indoor lap pool, a weight-training circuit, a spa facility with sauna and steam rooms, and an open-air whirlpool. Appointments for a massage, facial, manicure, and pedicure come with the program. The imaginative cuisine of head chef Sue Chapman draws on the region's fresh organic produce, game, and fish; she pays close attention to the nutritional needs of the rigorous exercisers here but keeps the fat content of the diet to less than 10% per week.

Accommodations are in a spacious three-story log lodge with a library and stained-glass windows. Each of the 15 bedrooms has double beds with duvets and a private bath. Workout clothing is supplied, and transportation to and from San Francisco International Airport is included in the price. *Skylonda Fitness Retreat, 16350 Skyline Blvd., Woodside, CA 94062, tel. 415/851–4500 or 800/851–2222, fax 415/851–5504. Year-round: 7 days, $2,500 single or double; weekends, $325 single, $275 double. Add tax and gratuities.*

HAWAII

THE BIG ISLAND **Kalani Honua Conference Eco Resort.** Weeklong courses in traditional Hawaiian arts and crafts are the focal point of the activity at this institution, which was founded 15 years ago on the site of an old Hawaiian school and is now the state's largest retreat for intercultural and environmental studies. But there are also classes in gourmet vegetarian cooking, bodywork, and movement practices of the East and West. In addition, you'll find a Japanese-style spa with a communal hot

tub, sauna, massage rooms, classes in yoga, aerobics, and meditation, a fitness center with strength-training equipment, an 85-foot swimming pool, and hiking trails. Therapeutic services, available à la carte, include acupressure, shiatsu, Rolfing, and traditional *lomilomi* massage, the rocking, rhythmical massage of ancient Hawaiian royalty. For relaxing, there are hammocks under the palms, a Jacuzzi, and tennis and volleyball courts.

Meals, served buffet style on an ocean-view terrace, include fresh tropical fruits and real Kona coffee, and there is usually a vegetarian main course and a fish or fowl option at dinner. The lush seaside setting is close to Kilauea, the world's most active volcano. Many guests venture off on their own to explore craters or secluded beaches among the lava flows, one of which has clothing-optional bathing.

Native Hawaiians make up part of the large staff, and many have professional experience in traditional healing arts. With campsites under the stars, little cottages, and private and shared rooms in two-story octagonal cedar *hales* (lodges) ranged around the secluded, manicured grounds, the retreat has space for up to 100 people at a time. Most guests are active, college-educated men and women between the ages of 25 and 55. *Kalani Honua Eco Resort, R.R. 2, Box 4500, Pahoa, HI 96778, tel. 808/965–7828 or 800/800–6886, fax 808/965–9613. Year-round: Daily rate $45–$75 per person without meals, tent site $20. Meal package $35 daily.*

MAUI **Grand Wailea Resort, Hotel and Spa Grande.** The 50,000-square-foot Spa Grande at this posh resort offers the state's most extensive health and fitness facilities. In addition to 10 individual and private Jacuzzi areas, there are Roman-style whirlpools 20 feet in diameter and 42 individual treatment rooms, where you can enjoy five different facials and seven types of massage, including lomilomi. The unique Polynesian sand bath has you wrapped in moist ti plant leaves topped by volcanic sand, which is heated to make you sweat. Stress management, nutrition, and fitness counseling is available, and spa director Darryll Leiman has specialists to work on a personalized program. You can also join classes in the spa's exercise studio.

Except for the classes, all spa services are à la carte. However, a variety of one-day packages is available. The Terme Wailea circuit, which every package guest gets, involves treatments designed to exfoliate and cleanse the skin: a loofah scrub or Japanese *goshi-goshi* (an exfoliating washcloth) scrub; a Swiss shower; and skin treatments with Maui mud, seaweed, papaya enzyme, or other herbs, applied as you rest in enormous marble tubs inlaid with gold mosaic.

The resort's 787 rooms, located in an eight-story complex, all have an ocean view, private terrace, and modern bath. There are 14 tennis courts, two 18-hole golf courses, Maui's only indoor racquetball and squash courts, and a children's camp. Catamaran cruises and water sports on the beach are other diversions. The resort has Italian and Polynesian restaurants and a Japanese-style eatery with a sushi bar and tatami rooms. *Grand Wailea Resort, Hotel and Spa Grande, 3850 Wailea Alanui Dr., Wailea, HI 96753, tel. 808/875–1234 or 800/888–6100, fax 808/874–2424. Year-round: Daily $380–$580, suites $1,000–$10,000 for 2 people. Day Spa packages $209–$349.*

OAHU **Ihilani Resort and Spa.** The spa programs at this 387-room luxury hotel on Oahu's leeward coast, 25 minutes from Honolulu International Airport, are inspired by the seaside location and by ancient Hawaiian healing therapies, among them special Hawaiian thalasso treatments that involve seaweed, salt scrubs, and facial masks with marine algae. Opened in 1994, the spa offers one-day packages as well as four- to seven-day programs that include personal services, meals, gratuities, and tax.

Terraced into a hillside facing Pearl Harbor, the spa has separate sections for men and

women, a coed aerobics studio and weight room, and private patios for alfresco massage. Each treatment room has a high-tech tub that circulates fresh seawater through a special water massage unit imported from France. The resort has an outdoor lap pool, as well as beaches on a protected lagoon.

The kitchen here uses locally grown produce, fresh fish, and lots of herbs. Meals are low in sodium, sugar, and fat. Guests stay in spacious oceanfront rooms, some with private terraces; seven suites come with a whirlpool. Each room has a marble bathroom. *Ihilani Resort and Spa, 92-10001 Olani St., West Oahu, HI 96707, tel. 808/679–0079 or 800/626–4446, fax 808/ 679–3387. Year-round: 4 days, $2,098 single, $1,618–$2,834 double. Day Spa packages $140–$295.*

SOURCES

ORGANIZATIONS **International Spa & Fitness Association** (informally known as I/SPA; 113 S. West St., Alexandria, VA 22314, tel. 703/838–2930, fax 703/838–2950) is dedicated to enhancing the spa experience and provides consumer updates on member resorts, among other information. Association members include resort owners and managers, affiliated day spas, consultants, travel agents, educators, and suppliers of spa products.

PERIODICALS Three quarterly newsletters provide information about spas. "Custom Spas" (Custom Spa Vacations, 1318 Beacon St., Brookline, MA 02146, tel. 617/566–5144, fax 617/731–0599) lists, evaluates, and gives prices for spa vacation packages. "Bernard Burt's SpaGoer" (2400 Virginia Ave., C715, Washington, DC 20037, fax 202/331–0036) reviews new resorts and gives special attention to spas in California, Florida, Europe, and Asia. The quarterly publication and annual directory of spa vacations, *Spa-Finder* (Spa-Finders, 91 5th Ave., Suite 301, New York, NY 10003, tel. 212/924–6800 or 800/255–7727, fax 212/924–7240), lists package prices and has a regional index and a glossary of spa terms. *Spa* magazine, published quarterly, has features on international travel, well-being, and renewal (5305 Shilshoe Ave. NW, Seattle, WA 98107, tel. 206/789–6506, fax 206/789–9193.

BOOKS *Adventure Learning in a Spa Environment,* by Gregory D. Hagin (from I/SPA; *see above*), is a case study of the ropes course program at the New Age Health Spa. *The Bath,* by Diane von Furstenberg, documents historic and contemporary bathing styles, including European and American spas. *Bodywork,* by Thomas Claire, is a consumer's guide to massage and how to make the most of it, published by Morrow. *California Spas,* by Laurel Olson Cook, offers a detailed survey of spas and hot springs throughout the state. *Fodor's Healthy Escapes,* by Bernard Burt, reviews, in depth, 240 spas, health resorts, retreats, and cruises in the United States, Canada, Mexico, and the Caribbean; an updated fifth edition was published in 1996 by Fodor's/Random House. *Hawaii Eco-T Directory,* by Shelly Addix (Leeward Community College, Community Services, 96-045 Ala Ike, AD-121, Pearl City, HI 96782), describes hikes, trip outfitters, spiritual retreats, and environmental program resources throughout the Hawaiian Islands. *Taking the Waters,* by Alev Lytle Croutier, is an illustrated book about European and American spas.

ALSO SEE If mastering the discipline of a healthy lifestyle intrigues you, check out the Holistic Centers chapter.

Volunteer Research Vacations

Written and updated by Sean Elder

n the hit film *Jurassic Park,* the mathematician played by Jeff Goldblum declares to irresponsible scientist Richard Attenborough that a real scientist doesn't build on or borrow knowledge gathered by others, something the bad doctor clearly has done to reconstruct dinosaur DNA. Goldblum asserts that a real scientist plunges into the dark alone, boldly going where no man has gone before.

This is nonsense, of course. Outside of the movies—where stars clad in lab coats are forever turning away from their microscopes or computers to cry "Eureka!"—scientists very rarely tackle problems by themselves. Discovery arises from research, and scientific research is plodding, methodical, and usually builds on the fieldwork of others.

For any armchair scientist who has aspired to the role of scientific researcher, a volunteer research project is just the thing. These projects generally teach new skills and allow participants to employ them in the context of a disciplined research effort. All these projects have a stated goal or premise, and while your part in achieving the goal or proving the premise may be small, it is as essential as that of the group leader.

Though there is no average volunteer vacation, the ones included here typically last from two to three weeks; cost anywhere from $300 to $3,000; require no special education, background, or level of physical fitness; and are open to anyone over 18 (some programs will admit younger people with a parent's permission).

Most organizations will send a briefing that gives all kinds of information about the trip and its objectives. It tells about the weather, how hard the trip will be, and how to prepare, and it includes a checklist of things you're going to need.

CHOOSING THE RIGHT PROJECT

Obviously, you first need to know what type of work the project involves, whether it's dolphin monitoring or photo cataloging. Then ask the following questions before you sign up.

How long has the project been using volunteers? Chances are that a project on which volunteers have been working for two or more years will be better equipped to handle your needs than one that has just begun to use volunteers.

Who (or what) benefits from the volunteers' labor? Many of the organizations listed are affiliated with various academic institutions and international research groups and are happy to tell you what use is made of the work you do. Sometimes the information you gather is donated to one school or research center; other times it is shared by all interested parties.

Sean Elder writes a Web-site review column for the New Yorker, *as well as articles for many other publications.*

Is any special background or training required? Although most trips do not demand special abilities, some do: The dolphin trips need strong swimmers, while the search for moose bones on Isle Royale calls for greater-than-average physical stamina.

What will I learn by working on this project? Many outfitters promise that you will come away with a sense of accomplishment, an appreciation for the subject matter of your research, and maybe even a greater understanding of a particular ecosystem. But some projects are more like courses in which you learn specific skills: how to identify humpback whales for example, or what the various cries of the loon mean.

What special qualifications does the project director and/or instructor have? Many volunteer vacations are headed by researchers and scientists noted in their field. Ask about their credentials, number of years of experience, and their familiarity with the subject that's covered.

How much hands-on experience do participants get? On some projects, the researcher does most of the interesting work and you watch from the sidelines. On others, you are encouraged, even expected, to participate.

Is there a doctor in the house? Some of the trips described in this chapter take place in wilderness conditions, miles from any hospitals or medical stations. Check to see that the leader or someone on the trip knows first aid and CPR.

What's the cost and what's included? Prices of volunteer vacations vary substantially from the generally inexpensive Wildlands Studies trips ($385) to some of the more blue-chip Earthwatch trips ($3,935). Some projects may appear inexpensive until you realize the cost does not include airfare, accommodations, and meals. Unless otherwise stated, prices for the trips listed here include three meals daily, double-occupancy lodging, and local transportation but not airfare. Although as a rule prices include tents and cooking gear, they usually do not include sleeping bags and other personal camping gear; be sure to ask.

How are the fees used? It can be satisfying to know where your hard-earned vacation dollars are going. Earthwatch, for instance, gives you an estimate of the entire cost of the project showing a breakdown of your share.

Are fees and other expenses tax-deductible? If the parent organization is nonprofit, the chances are good that you can deduct some part of your vacation cost, including your airfare, as a charitable contribution. Also ask your accountant.

What sort of food and accommodations are provided? Since lodging varies from a comfortable bed in a mountain lodge to a patch of ground beneath a pup tent, it's best to know where you can expect to lay your head. Some trips supply their own cook, but on other projects it's catch-as-catch-can, and you can only eat so much macaroni and cheese.

Will laundry service be available? If it is, you can certainly pack lighter.

Is there free time? And what is there to do with it? Although a long day of bear-trapping may leave you too tired to consider doing much of anything come evening, whale-watching in Hawaii could well be complemented by a little night music.

Do you have recommendations from past participants? Some organizations have notes from former volunteers in their briefings, but it is even better to speak with former volunteers yourself.

How far in advance do I need to book? You must sign up for the most popular projects many months in advance, but some projects don't fill up and you can join them at the last minute.

MAJOR PLAYERS

EARTHWATCH This organization has been providing scientists with the funding and volunteers they need to address ecological problems around the world since 1972. In that time, Earthwatch has raised $26 million in capital and human resources and mobilized over 40,000 volunteers. In one year it sponsored 160 projects around the world, 37 of them in the United States. To get funding from Earthwatch, a scientist submits a proposal, then undergoes a peer-review process in which the worth and necessity of the project is evaluated. Money is raised largely through volunteers who pay for the opportunity to participate in the project. No special skills are required for any Earthwatch volunteer, just curiosity and a willingness to learn. Volunteers range in age from 16 to 85, but most are 25 to 60 years old. Group size varies greatly, from 2 to 22. Although Earthwatch is associated with the protection of endangered species, the list of disciplines its research trips cover includes art history, cultural anthropology, and paleontology. The average trip is two weeks, and your contribution—$700 to $3,935—covers food, lodging, and a portion of the project's expense. Ask for an EarthCorps Briefing, which tells you everything you need to know about any particular project. *680 Mt. Auburn St., Box 9104, Watertown, MA 02272-9104, tel. 617/926–8200 or 800/776–0188, fax 617/926–8532.*

WILDLANDS STUDIES Since 1980, this organization has been providing volunteers with hands-on experience on wild-land field projects in the United States and Canada. Wolf habitat projects, in which you can run with the wolves or at least in their wake, have been a Wildlands Studies staple since 1982; trips of this nature are now available in Idaho, Montana, and Washington. The organization also sponsors research trips focusing on bighorn sheep, spotted owls, and grizzly bears. Volunteers are generally 19 to 35 years old, although there is no upper age limit. You can get college credits through San Francisco State University for participating in these projects, but enrollment is not limited to students. Course costs are manageable at $300 to $400, which includes

lodging but not food. *3 Mosswood Circle, Cazadero, CA 95421, tel. and fax 707/632–5665.*

FAVORITE PROJECTS

At press time, few sponsors knew with any certainty what projects would be available in the coming years. All the trips listed here are *likely* to be continued, but you should double-check with the organization to make sure that the trip is in fact being offered and all the information given—price, date, destination—is current.

THE MID-ATLANTIC

PENNSYLVANIA **A Woman of the Streets.** For anyone living in an urban environment, the idea of spending your vacation among the homeless must sound like a busman's holiday. But for anyone concerned with the plight of homeless women in particular, especially those interested in developing or honing basic field social work skills, this research vacation is a natural.

Like most towns their size, Allentown, Bethlehem, and Easton, Pennsylvania have homeless shelters and kitchens just for women. The circumstances of these shelters' patrons differ in some respects from those of homeless women in other parts of the country (this part of the state is still recovering from the demise of the steel industry), but many story elements remain constant: job loss, pregnancy, spousal abuse, divorce, drug and alcohol abuse, jail, hunger, despair.

University of California epidemiologist Erika Lehmann wants to know more about the predicament of homeless women in this area, and the work you do with her—interviewing women in homeless shelters and recording the results of your conversations—will benefit not only her research but the local shelters and kitchens who will use the information to better understand those they serve. Your trip starts with a crash course in basic interview techniques as well as the overall objectives and philosophy of Lehmann's research. After some initial supervision, you will soon find yourself interviewing not only homeless women but those at-risk women in SRO (Single Resident Occupancy) hotels, one step above the street.

Lehmann is fascinated by what forces render some people homeless and others merely poor, and she tempers her curiosity with compassion. You will be able to explore the meaning of your work with other volunteers, all of whom are housed in a comfortable hostel. It may be the nicest home you see for two weeks. *Earthwatch, 680 Mt. Auburn St., Box 9104, Watertown, MA 02272-9924, tel. 617/926-8200 or 800/776-0188, fax 617/ 926-8532. Feb.–June: 2 wks, $1,095. Sign up 2–3 months in advance.*

VIRGINIA **Get Crabby.** The charms of the Chesapeake Bay are many, especially in the summer: swimming, sailing, eating blue crabs. Here's a trip that combines all those things, though with considerably less lolling about than that scenario might imply. And on this expedition you won't just be eating the renowned blue crabs; you'll be *meeting* them as well.

Half the nation's blue crabs come from the Chesapeake Bay, but little is known about the crustacean's early life. Hatched in the bay, the newly postlarval blue crab makes its perilous way to the continental shelf to mature before returning to the bay to reproduce, starting the whole cycle all over again. Dr. John McConaugha of Old Dominion University wants to know more about the crab's cycle, and the South's appetite for the adult makes this inquiry a culinary as well as economic and scientific one.

Volunteers stay in the Barrier Island Field Station. Days begin at 7:30 AM, and a good portion of them are spent in a small boat on the lagoons of the Virginia Coast Reserve. There you will place and collect small traps that attract the postlarval blue crabs at the stage when they are ready to make the continental shelf trip. Your observations of them, and their possible predators, are key to the crab research.

Humidity is the word for the bay in the summer; dress accordingly. Days end at a civilized 4:30 PM, leaving you with plenty of time to engage in those more traditional activities associated with the Chesapeake. The research should not adversely affect your appetite. *Earthwatch, 680 Mt. Auburn St., Box 9104, Watertown, MA 02272-9924, tel. 617/ 926-8200 or 800/776-0188, fax 617/926– 8532. July–Sept.: 1 wk, $995; 2 wks, $1,695. Sign up 2–3 months in advance.*

THE SOUTH

FLORIDA **Searching for Dolphins in the Sea.** Human fascination with dolphins began long before the days of Flipper: A fresco depicting a few of the sea mammals mid-frolic adorned the queen's chamber at the Palace of Knossos in 1600 BC. For anyone who has envied those Homo sapiens who swim with—and sometimes even touch—bottle-nosed dolphins, this Earthwatch project is a must.

In one of the outfitter's most popular programs, up to five volunteers primarily observe, photograph, and survey dolphins that have been tagged. You gather information on the animals' social skills, sexual habits, and signature whistling.

Once a year, in June, a team of 14 to 22 volunteers assists in capturing dolphins for tagging, and then releasing them. The animals are captured with large nets dropped from motorboats, and occasionally handlers are called upon to jump from the fast-moving boats to disentangle a dolphin that's endangered. Consequently, your swimming skills should be strong. For that matter, *you* should be strong: Bottle-nosed dolphins weigh up to 600 pounds and can be troublesome during capture operations ("One female we captured in 1975 was named Killer for good reason," Earthwatch ominously notes).

The project is executed along the central west coast of Florida, near Sarasota, in the shallow bays of the Gulf of Mexico; these mild waters are well protected and abundant in sea life. Volunteers stay in a large house with a pool and dock, and you share the responsibilities of shopping and cooking.

You spend from eight to nine hours each day in the Florida sun, so sunscreen and other protection are a must. There's also a lot of bouncing about in small boats, so those prone to seasickness should be prepared or stay away. *Earthwatch, 680 Mt. Auburn St., Box 9104, Watertown, MA 02272-9924, tel. 617/926-8200 or 800/776-0188, fax 617/926-8532. Year-round: 15 days, $1,695 (observation). June: 15 days, $2,495 (capture/release). Sign up 2-3 months in advance.*

GEORGIA **The Slow Study of Turtles.** Consider the lot of the loggerhead sea turtle. Every two to six years, the nesting female comes ashore on Georgia beaches, digs a nest cavity, lays about 120 golf ball-size eggs, buries them in the sand, and returns to the sea, leaving the hatchlings to fend for themselves. Those that aren't eaten in their shells—by raccoons, ghost crabs, and other predators—scramble into the brine, often to be consumed by sharks, killed by motorboats, or drowned by fishing nets. The nursery years of those that survive are spent, it is believed, floating in the Gulf Stream on mats of seaweed, unattended by adults. Small wonder that they look so tough.

Since 1973, the Caretta Research Project has been monitoring and protecting the hatchlings in a cooperative agreement with the U.S. Fish and Wildlife Service, which oversees the Wassaw Island National Wildlife Refuge. The long-term goals of the project are to learn more about the giant turtles and their nesting habits, to protect the eggs and hatchlings, and to involve the public in the fate of these animals, which has been on the threatened-species list since 1978.

This is a vacation for people who like the beach and who like to work at night. Volunteers are needed weekly throughout the summer for two separate seasons. In the egg-laying season, which runs from early May through mid-August, you spend most of the night patrolling Wassaw Island's 6 miles of beaches with a team of up to nine people, searching for female sea turtles. When you find the 250- to 400-pound creatures, you tag and measure them after they have completed their nesting activities. In the hatching season—August to mid-September—your nightly job is to monitor the nests made earlier in the summer, trying to protect the eggs from predators, and then to escort the hatchlings in their triumphant scramble to the sea. During the early August weeks, participants may see both adults and hatchlings.

Island leaders and assistants school you in all necessary research techniques and acquaint you with sea turtle fact and lore. The teams of nine stay in two small cabins in the center of the island (coed arrangements depend on the male-female makeup of each group) and eat together. Meals may consist of such dishes as grilled chicken, stir-fries, and spaghetti. You are expected to help out with the housekeeping. Since almost all work is done at night, there's plenty of free time to read, relax, swim, birdwatch, and, in general, enjoy the land. However, volunteers are cautioned to marshal their energies; turtle maintenance can run through the night. Remember: The Georgia coast in summertime is subtropical, and there is no air-conditioning. You may want to bring a fan. *Caretta Research Project, Savannah Science Museum, 4405 Paulsen St., Savannah, GA 31405, tel. 912/355-6705, fax 912/355-0182. Mid-May-mid-Aug. (egg-laying season): 7 days, $425. Late July-mid-Sept. (hatching season): 7 days, $425. Sign up 2-3 months in advance.*

KENTUCKY **Going Underground.** Few who have survived the mines of Kentucky could ever imagine that someone would volunteer to spend two weeks underground on their vacation—-let alone pay for the experience. But Kentucky's Mammoth Cave is more than just a former mine; the largest cave system in the world, with a history that dates from more than 4,000 years ago, the Mammoth is a subterranean walk through history. As a volunteer in this ongoing experiment in cave archaeology, you become a piece of that history.

Under the direction of George Crothers, a doctoral candidate in archaeology at Washington University, photographer Charles Sedlund, and U.S. Park Service Cultural Resource Specialist Bob Ward, you and a small team of volunteers will explore the cave for artifacts in the largest study of the cave's remains ever attempted. There's a lot to discover here. Mammoth Cave was first mined by Native Americans for gypsum, and has since been operated as a saltpeter mine (the substance was used for gunpowder during the War of 1812), a tuberculosis hospital, a mushroom farm, a wedding chapel, and now a tourist attraction. This is the fourth season of chronicling the remains of this World Heritage Site.

Clad in overalls and hiking boots, you will spend each eight-hour day rotating between three separate crews: discovery, mapping, and photography. Whereas morning in the discovery crew might mean picking up and preserving some vintage trash, afternoon in the mapping crew may have you learning to navigate underground.

The Green River ferry takes you back to the Maple Springs Research Center, near Nashville, at the end of each day. Food is provided by a local restaurant and is described as "hearty country cuisine," which includes fried catfish and spaghetti. *Earthwatch, 680 Mt. Auburn St., Box 9104, Watertown, MA 02272-9924, tel. 617/926–8200 or 800/776–0188, fax 617/926–8532. July–Nov.: 10 days, $695. Sign up at least 2 months in advance.*

THE MIDWEST

MICHIGAN **Moose, Meet Wolf.** In 1949, wolves from Canada crossed an ice floe and moved to moose-infested Isle Royale National Park. Rather than decimating the moose population, the wolves stabilized it and allowed the island's overgrazed vegetation to recover. A famous U.S. National Park Service study of the animals' symbiotic relationship began in 1958; this Earthwatch project is a continuation of that study. It yields evidence of the essential nature of wolf predation, at a time when wolves are once again being hunted from the air.

Those who come hoping to run with the wolves, be forewarned: Volunteers spend their days doing one thing—hiking the island looking for moose bones. About 2,400 dead moose have been recovered in this fashion in the past 35 years. Teams of up to five search for the bones and bring them back to home base. Most data recording (bones are analyzed for disease and decay) is done by a staff assistant.

Dr. Rolf Peterson, a Michigan Technological University professor of wildlife ecology who heads the program, takes great pains to warn all comers of the strenuous, demanding nature of moose-bone hunting. This is not a routine backpacking trip; in your search for bones you go over and under fallen trees, march through wetlands, traipse over beaver dams, and, in general, get wet and cold, all the while carrying 40 pounds on your back. There is no electricity or hot showers at the campsite, and toilets are of the pit type. This trip defines roughing it. Because you have to carry the food, meals are comprised of lightweight grains and powdered drinks. An oatmeal or granola breakfast is usually accompanied by coffee, cocoa, or Tang; lunch may be a hearty gorp mix, and dinner is warm and instant.

What has kept volunteers coming back for more than 30 years is the natural beauty of the island. The nation's least-visited national park outside of Alaska, Isle Royale is surrounded by the cold waters of Lake Superior. It is a haven for birds, beavers, wolves, and, of course, moose—a little piece of Eden in the Great Lakes region. If long days in primal nature appeal to you, and you don't mind getting wet and dirty, this is the week for you. Think of how good that first hot shower will feel. *Earthwatch, 680 Mt. Auburn St., Box 9104, Watertown, MA 02272-9924, tel. 617/926–8200 or 800/ 776–0188, fax 617/926–8532. July–Aug.: 7 days, $750. Sign up 2–3 months in advance.*

WISCONSIN **Loons of the Great Lakes.** The modern loon has inhabited the earth for 10 million years, and its relatives date from 50 million years ago, but today the loons of the Great Lakes region are in trouble. Their number has been dwindling, and, more distressing, dead loons have been found to have high levels of mercury in their blood.

This is bad enough for the poor loon, but it may be bad news for its neighbors as well. Loons are an indicator species, meaning that their welfare is a barometer for the health of the entire ecosystem. In order to better read that barometer, scientists need more information about the noble bird, its demographics, and its tolerance for mercury.

Toward that end, project director James Paruk is looking for bird-watchers—serious bird-watchers—to join him at the Whitefish Point Bird Observatory in the Seney National Wildlife Refuge in a swamp south of Lake Superior. Volunteers will be comparing the breeding success and survival of six pairs of loons that have exhibited differing levels of mercury in their blood. After a day of field training, your team of four to six will while away the remaining nine full days at observation stations in the brush, where you can sit comfortably and watch the loons through binoculars and spot scopes. Strenuous activity is not involved. "Extreme patience and alertness are required," Paruk says, and he means it. The expected work week is 40 hours. You're given a list of 20 normal behaviors, such as courtship, nest building, foraging, locomotion, resting, preening, and chick rearing, and you check off the behavior each time the loon you're observing does it.

Teams working in June and July set out in motorboats with nets to assist in capturing the birds. Captured birds are banded and weighed, and blood samples are drawn.

Your job is largely to assist the researchers by holding the spotlights and the birds themselves, once they're in the boat.

A furnished cabin is your home for the 12 days. Usually just two people share each bedroom. Volunteers and staff share the responsibility of preparing meals, which might consist of spaghetti, a barbecue, or a local specialty such as whitefish. Paruk plays the guitar and encourages other pickers and strummers to bring their instruments. The loons supply the harmony.

The song of the loon is loud enough to carry over 200 acres and varied enough to carry a best-selling album (*Voices of the Loon* sold over 80,000 copies). "When in June 1987 the last dusky seaside sparrow died, the extinction merited a news story here and there," wrote nature writer Sue Hubbell. "But when bad things happen to loons, and they do, we raise a ruckus." Long live the loon. *Earthwatch, 680 Mt. Auburn St., Box 9104, Watertown, MA 02272-9924, tel. 617/ 926–8200 or 800/776–0188, fax 617/926– 8532. May–Aug.: 12 days, $1,195. Sign up at least 2 months in advance.*

THE SOUTHWEST

ARIZONA **On the Edge of the Cliff.** Archaeologists have long been fascinated by the cliff dwellings found in the remote area of Arizona's Sierra Ancha mountains. Dating from the 13th century, these remains show masterful craftsmanship, defying gravity on the precipitous cliffs. You may ask yourself how they made such long-lasting habitations, why the entrance ways are so small, or the $64,000 question: What were those Native Americans doing up there, anyway?

Anasazi, Hohokam, Mogollan—ancestors of the Hopi—lived within the confines of what is now the Tonto National Forest. But until the 13th century, they lived at low altitudes in small communities. What caused the upward mobility that followed, and how did the drought of 1276–99 affect that move? Was the shift purely agrarian (different crops for different climates) or did aggression from roaming enemies cause the farmers of the time to band together in these beautiful, fortresslike communities?

Dr. Richard Lange of the Arizona State Museum has been asking these questions for the last 15 years; along with Dr. Richard Ciolek-Torrello of Statistical Research he is looking for answers among the 21 cliff dwellings in the middle Cherry Creek area. This is where you come in. After a 1- to 4-mile hike each morning, you will assist the research team as they measure and photograph each room. You will become intimately familiar with the building techniques and materials of these ancient peoples, and in the dry silence of these 1,500-meter-high structures you can imagine what it must have been like to live here. A fortunate few have even enjoyed overnight stays in the dwellings. The rest of the time you'll be with a sleeping bag in a two-person tent, or under a sky full of stars. *Earthwatch, 680 Mt. Auburn St., Box 9104, Watertown, MA 02272-9924, tel. 617/926–8200 or 800/776–0188, fax 617/926–8532. Oct.: 2 wks, $995. Sign up 2–3 months in advance.*

TEXAS **Lord of the Flies.** The nation's wetlands are vanishing. Land has been preserved and, in some cases, even created for new wetlands, to offset that which has been destroyed or developed. In an attempt to tell working wetlands from mere wet land, Dr. Ralph Garano, a research associate at Oregon State University, has been studying wetland insects, especially caddis flies, since 1980. Caddis flies are one barometer of a wetlands ecosystem, and through a sampling of them Dr. Garano can predict the health and longevity of the area. He first, however, needs to know the particulars of a healthy wetlands caddis fly. The landscape of Big Bend National Park provides a convenient laboratory, because nestled among the rocks and gorges are springs with their own ecosystems and, yes, caddis flies.

The Big Bend area, though located within the United States, is more reminiscent of central Mexico, or the moon. It has a desert climate, with mostly clear, sunny days. Daytime shade temperatures are usually in the 50s in winter; in May, the mercury could climb above 100°F. You work at elevations of 4,000 to 5,000 feet in rough, barren terrain.

As a volunteer researcher in Garono's team, you will spend one to four hours of each morning hiking over this magnificent region (bordered by Mexico, Texas, and New Mexico) to retrieve fluorescent-light fly traps laid the night before; in the evening the process is reversed. Back at your tent camp you will remove and categorize caddis flies (Garono has already discovered new species) as well as take water samples.

Be forewarned: The work is meticulous and the desert landscape is treacherous. Trips are run in the early spring to beat the ungodly heat; even so, dehydration and loss of electrolytes are a real concern. You should be in good physical condition. Persons with respiratory and/or heart problems would be at risk. But the rewards are great: Day Six, the halfway point, you are free to explore Big Bend National Park. The six-hour hike up the Southern Rim trail affords you an unsurpassed view of the Rio Grande canyon and the mountains of Mexico beyond. *Earthwatch, 680 Mt. Auburn St., Box 9104, Watertown, MA 02272-9924, tel. 617/926–8200 or 800/776–0188, fax 617/926–8532. Mar.–Apr.: 2 wks, $895. Sign up 2–3 months in advance.*

THE ROCKIES

IDAHO **Meet the Mountain Lion.** Is it actually possible for mountain lions and people to get along? Human intrusion on what was once mountain lion turf has resulted in habitat fragmentation, a term used to describe a situation in which a species' habitat range is divided by human development. This has had some dire consequences: Mountain lions feed on cattle and horses, causing ranchers to hunt the lions down; and within the mountain-lion community, rates of inbreeding and infanticide increase. That's right—mountain lions sometimes eat their young.

By tagging and monitoring these animals, scientists seek to determine how the mountain lion survives when its habitat is noncontinuous. They hope to gain a better understanding of the effects and consequences of habitat fragmentation on the mountain lion and, by extrapolation, on other large predators.

Working in winter, in rugged country near Pocatello, Idaho and the Utah border, teams of six to eight researchers and volunteers capture and radio-collar mountain lions. In summer, other groups of six to eight researchers and volunteers monitor those lions, keeping track of where they go and what they eat. (Data from this project indicates a preference for deer, even when cattle are present.)

Teams working from January to February have a tougher go of it. They search the area for fresh kills—usually young deer—and then, with the help of local trackers and their hounds, follow, capture, and tag the lions responsible. To participate, you must be in good shape and able to hike up and down mountain slopes in the snow; it helps to have experience reading maps.

The summer teams work from July through September, radio-monitoring tagged lions. This means lots of time standing on hillsides, watching a monitor to see where the lions go (you get to know your teammates *very* well), and recording compass bearings of the lions. You are taught the necessary compass- and map-reading skills during orientation. You also learn to use a field guide to identify plants on predation sites, information that is recorded on a computer and used to determine the relationship between the size of a patch of vegetation and its usefulness as a hiding spot for mountain lions on the prowl.

The work day in winter is long, starting at 5 AM and running until 9 PM. In summer, volunteers begin working the eight-hour shift at 9 AM. The winter crew stays in a ranch house owned by one of the hound men, and meals tend to be heartier than those offered in summer, with lots of stews for dinner. Summer volunteers camp out in several two- and three-person tents and cook over an open campfire—pancakes for breakfast and meat and potatoes for dinner. In both seasons, cold sandwiches, vegetables, and fruit are eaten in the field. Earthwatch staff will lead volunteers on hikes for fun when time permits.

Esprit de corps is an important part of this project; principal investigators Dr. John Laundre, research associate and visiting assistant professor at Purdue University and Idaho State University, and Dr. Donald Streubel, professor of biology at Idaho State University, have a great love of mountain lions, and by the end of the week, so will you. *Earthwatch, 680 Mt. Auburn St., Box 9104, Watertown, MA 02272-9924, tel. 617/926–8200 or 800/776–0188, fax 617/926–8532. Jan.–Feb.: 7 days, $1,395. July–Oct.: 10 days, $1,395. Sign up as far in advance as possible for winter sessions, 2–3 months for summer sessions.*

MONTANA **The Study of Streams.** Tamer than rivers and less majestic than lakes, small streams are nonetheless important in western ecosystems. For this Yellowstone Ecosystem Studies (YES) project, you are encouraged to get your feet wet while helping researchers to understand how disturbances in the landscape, such as fires, erosion, and pollution, affect streams and the neighboring habitats.

You join research directors Andrew Marcus and Wayne Minshall as they explore the stream ecology of either Cache Creek or Soda Butte Creek (locations alternate yearly), two streams that enter the Lamar Valley in Yellowstone National Park. The scenery here is spectacular, and the fish are usually biting, so bring your rod and be sure to get a fishing license. You rub antlers with bison, elk, moose, and antelope, and the Lamar Valley is no stranger to bears and coyotes.

Each group of up to eight volunteers begins with basic training, when you collect sediment samples from flowing streams, measure the depth of pools, and estimate the fish population. You use a variety of research equipment, including traditional nets and sieves as well as handheld computers that show a map of the area and indicate your location as you hike. This is done by transmitting a signal via satellite. You would probably never expect to see yourself vacuuming algae off river rocks, and neither would the buffalo beside you. You're in the field between 7:30 AM and 3 PM most days, and you must be able to walk up to 4 miles in that time.

You're in good hands with the research directors. Marcus has been involved in wilderness expeditions since he was two; he accompanied his father, a geographer, on research trips in high alpine settings from New Zealand to Nepal. Minshall is recognized as an international authority in the field of stream ecology; he was collecting data from the water while the Yellowstone fires raged in 1988.

The two leaders expect you to have fun. On each creek trip you are treated to two cabins with bunk beds, shower, kitchenette, and refrigerator in Cooke City. All meals are prepared by a staff cook using a propane stove. It's basic meat and potatoes with some vegetarian options.

You're going to get wet while working on this project, and you have to be prepared for both hot and cold weather; even in the summer, snow is not unheard of.

YES, formerly the Yellowstone Project, is the brainchild of Montana State University professor Robert Crabtree. The organization, which also tracks coyotes, birds, and grizzlies and conducts alpine lake surveys in the national park, is famous for disseminating its research. *Yellowstone Ecosystem Studies, Box 6640, Bozeman, MT 59771, tel. 406/587–7758, fax 406/587–7590. Aug.: 11 days, $1,245; sign up at least 2 wks in advance.*

MONTANA **Tracking the Coyote with Computers.** While many animal-tracking vacations make use of such time-tested tools of the trade as compass, binoculars, and field notebook, the Yellowstone Ecosystem Studies (YES) nine-day Wild Dogs expedition gives you hands-on experience with equipment of the 90s: palmtop computers. Used in conjunction with traditional tracking devices, such as radio equipment and spotting scopes, these handheld PCs allow researchers to record the pack size, litter size, and den behavior of the wily coyote and transmit the information from the field directly to orbiting satellites so that the data can be shared by land management agencies, academic institutions, and nature writers.

The project's main objective is to figure out if coyotes have filled the niche in Yellowstone National Park that was vacated by the gray wolf. You and a group of up to nine other volunteers work with seasoned research biologists in locating den sites and then recording the social and feeding behavior of coyotes. You leave for the field at 7 AM and return at 4:30 PM, and you must be able to hike in moderate terrain. (In winter trips you do your tracking on cross-country skis.) At least one full day is left open for you to enjoy the park however you see fit—hiking, biking, fishing, and more.

Accommodations are in Cooke City, Montana, in either a house or cabin (it varies from year to year). Usually two or three volunteers are assigned to a single bedroom, and bathrooms are shared. There is a staff cook, but volunteers are encouraged to help prepare meals. You might eat pizza, pasta salad, or barbecue chicken. You're shuttled in a Suburban to Yellowstone, a ride that could take 15 minutes or an hour, depending on where the coyotes are expected to be. *Yellowstone Ecosystem Studies, Box 6640, Bozeman, MT 59771, tel. 406/587–7758, fax 406/587–7590. Mid-May–mid-June: 9 days, $1,295. Sign up 2 wks in advance.*

THE WEST COAST

CALIFORNIA **Bobcats and Foxes near the Big City.** San Francisco comedian Bob "Bobcat" Goldthwaite was probably unaware when he took that sobriquet that there were other bobcats in the vicinity. However, right across the bay, where Marin County meets the Golden Gate Bridge, there are lots of them—along with gray foxes, deer, seals, even mountain lions.

The idyllic preserve known as the Golden Gate National Recreation Area (GGNRA), 76,000 acres of unsullied nature, wraps around San Francisco's northern and western shoreline and is just minutes from downtown. The extraordinary natural diversity of the place sets it apart from other wilderness areas and makes it an ideal place to study wildlife. This Earthwatch project, called California Carnivores, concentrates on the area's bobcat and gray fox populations. Its purpose is to learn more about how these two animals interact with each other and how the local human population affects them.

As a volunteer, you spend 13 days assisting project directors Dr. Judd Howell and Geographic Information System expert Marcia Seminoff-Irving as they radio-track the cat and the fox, watching the animals as they rest during the day and as they hunt and roam at night. Carnivore research is demanding and time-consuming: Your work day begins at 8 AM, when you're given your field assignment for the day, and ends after dusk. Up to 10 volunteers can sign up for each session, and they are divided into teams of two. You do a lot of hiking up and down rocky slopes, so a little aerobic preparation wouldn't hurt. You learn how and where to place cameras to film the animals and how to collect and examine the film. Some volunteers are chosen to assist in capturing and radio-collaring additional bobcats and foxes. The information you gather is used to plot the movements and habits of each species.

The housing for this project is primo: the Headlands Institute, in the GGNRA's Ft. Mason, a former military installation at the Marin Headlands. It contains classrooms, two dormitories with rooms that accommodate four to six people, and a dining hall. The views of the bay and the bridge are unsurpassed. Earthwatch is just one group that uses the institute, so you can expect to meet other boarders from all over the world, from kids to senior citizens.

Breakfasts and such basic dinners as spaghetti and broiled chicken are prepared by the Headlands Institute's experienced chef, and the staff makes bag lunches—cold cuts, peanut butter, and cheese, as well as fruit and yogurt for the field. At least two evenings are set aside for enjoying the pleasures of San Francisco, which, for lovers of good food and music, remain legion. *Earthwatch, 680 Mt. Auburn St., Box 9104, Watertown, MA 02272-9924, tel. 617/926–8200 or 800/776–0188, fax 617/926–8532. Feb.–May: 13 days, $995. June–Sept.: 13 days, $1,295. Sign up 2 months in advance.*

CALIFORNIA **Who Will Pay the Bill?** To anyone visiting the northern coast of California, they seem ubiquitous, but in fact the American white pelican has only two breeding colonies in the state. One, in the Klamath Basin along the California-Oregon border, is in a protected wildlife refuge. However, nearby farms use pesticides and fertilizers, and these combined with drought conditions in the basin have affected the bird's nesting and foraging grounds. A census of pelicans in 1990 and 1991 measured heavy losses, while breeding success rates have fluctuated wildly in the years since. What is killing the pelican?

Counting crows may be easy work but surveying pelicans requires a bit more diligence. Under the instruction of Dr. Daniel Anderson and graduate researcher Polo Moreno, both of UC Davis' Wildlife, Fish and Conservation Biology Department, volunteers will spend two weeks capturing and radio-banding the birds as well as monitoring their behavior (by sight and radio), collecting samples from foraging areas, and building bird-watching blinds.

The redwood forest of the Pacific Northwest is justly celebrated as one of the natural wonders of the world; your work on this trip will bring you into daily contact with the "Redwood Cathedral" as well as the more pristine high-altitude, sagebrush-juniper woodland (and the views that altitude affords). Temperatures vary there, even in the summer; shorts and a rain poncho will serve you equally well. A comfortable motel is your base camp, and free time is provided to take in the local attractions, including the Lava Beds National Monument and Mt. Shasta. *University Research Expeditions Project, University of California, Berkeley, CA 94720-7050, tel. 510/ 642–6586, fax 510/642–6791. Late June– early Aug.: 2 wks, $1,095. Sign up 2–3 months in advance.*

WASHINGTON **Don't Call Them Killer Whales.** They're orcas, as any kid who saw *Free Willy* can tell you. In fact, Kenneth Balcomb, vice president of the Center for Whale Research, was involved in the campaign to free the whale that played Willy, but that's another story. When not working for the liberation of movie whales, Balcomb spends at least part of his year in Puget Sound, counting orcas. Seems there used to be more of them than there are now.

Between 1966 and 1976, 50 orcas in Puget Sound were either killed or removed to provide specimens for marine parks around the world. In 1976, Balcomb was asked to take an orca census, and his findings revealed that there were only 68 of the noble mammals left. Since then, Balcomb's Orca Survey has tallied the population on an annual basis, and since 1988 this census project has been run in conjunction with Earthwatch. Although the population of orcas has grown to 91, Balcomb still needs volunteers to help count dorsal fins and work toward gaining an understanding of the factors that affect orca numbers.

Your team of 5 to 10 volunteers and 4 staff members begins work off the shore of San Juan Island at 9 AM and ends about 5 PM. Weather permitting, half of you cruise the sound aboard a trimaran and a small motorboat, photographing whales and recording your sightings in logbooks. You also assist in recording the animals' underwater mewlings. The other half of your group stays at the house and either assists with developing the photos or enters the data into a field computer. Teams rotate from day to day. The results of the survey are published in scientific papers as well as in lay texts such as *Life* and *Newsweek.*

Your base is a waterfront house on San Juan Island, a popular summer vacation retreat. There are shared rooms and baths in the house, but many people prefer to sleep in sleeping bags on the porch, which overlooks the water and can accommodate everyone. Meals are prepared by the staff with one volunteer each evening; expect fresh fish, crab, and shellfish, according to the season, as well as vegetables from the house garden. You eat in the house's dining room or outside at picnic tables behind the house.

This is a trip for the amateur naturalist; you can spend your free time admiring the sea life of Puget Sound and the other wildlife surrounding it, including eagles, hawks, deer, raccoons, and rabbits. For those with a less rural leaning, there's an artsy movie theater in Friday Harbor, 12 miles away, and live music at a nearby tavern.

Balcomb says you should be prepared for boring, rainy days when you don't see any whales; those clear, sunny days when the whales appear then become all the more rewarding. Those prone to seasickness should think twice about this trip. *Earthwatch, 680 Mt. Auburn St., Box 9104, Watertown, MA 02272-9924, tel. 617/926–8200 or 800/776–0188, fax 617/926–8532. June– Sept.: 10 days, $1,795. Sign up 2–3 months in advance.*

WASHINGTON **The Grizzly Bear Truth.** The much-maligned and mythologized grizzly bear once roamed over much of the western United States, but hunting, trapping, and loss of habitat have resulted in its virtual decimation. The grizzly now survives in less than 2% of its former range, and the North Cascades are part of that territory. A critically important grizzly population has been discovered here, and Wildlands Studies needs your help in determining its exact size and researching its habits.

Your group of 12 volunteers assembles in Seattle, and then carpools to central Washington, where you begin hiking across the North Cascades. You spend the first few days in backcountry field workshops, learning about bear ecology, research techniques, and backcountry survival, and also familiarizing yourself with the forested landscapes and wildlife populations in the Wildlands study area. Project leader is Bill Gaines, a specialist in the conservation of endangered species.

For the next 10 days, you assist Gaines and his wildlife specialists while backpacking through the Cascades, one of the nation's greatest mountain ranges, with jagged peaks, glaciated canyons, hanging valleys, and mountain lakes. You collect evidence of bear habitation, such as hair and scat, and document track and den locations. You also observe bear activity patterns and behavior. All findings and observations are recorded in field journals and provided to wildlife biologists involved in the preservation of the grizzly.

This trip is not for the faint of heart. Summer mountain weather runs the gamut from 90°F to the occasional snow squall. You spend 6 to 10 hours in the field, and although on most days you hike only a mile or less, every few days you must hike 5 miles to a new site. Prior research experience is not required, but you must bring binoculars and field notebooks as well as your own camping (you sleep in the backcountry) and hiking gear. A good pair of broken-in hiking boots is essential. Food is purchased locally during scheduled group shopping trips, and cooking duties are shared.

The last two days, still in the backcountry, are devoted to workshops summing up and evaluating what has been learned. The outing ends on a festive note, with a guest speaker and a barbecue. San Francisco State University will give you credit for participating. *Wildlands Studies, 3 Mosswood Circle, Cazadero, CA 95421, tel. and fax 707/632–5665. Mid-July: 14 days, $385. Price does not include $50 application fee or $175 for food, gas, and miscellaneous expenses; project fee due by May 25. Sign up 2–4 months in advance.*

WASHINGTON **Will the Wolf Survive?** The timber wolf (*Canis lupus*) once had the greatest range of any living terrestrial animal—with the exception of human beings. While the latter has done more than any other creature to eliminate the former, it is heartening to know that some of us are now cheering the wolf's ultimate survival. Because of the pressures of development and habitat loss, these animals have been driven to near extinction in the lower 48, and hunters have been recruited to decimate their numbers in Alaska. But field reports indicate that wolves are making a tenuous return in the mountains of Montana, Idaho, and Washington, venturing into their former habitats through narrow wildland corridors between mountains that border the United States and Canada.

Since 1982, Wildlands Studies has been monitoring the wolf's return in Idaho and Montana; in 1990, the organization launched a similar study in Washington. Headed up by Paul Joslin, president of the Conservation Society for Wolves and Whales and a pioneer of wolf howling survey methods, this study is being conducted in the Cascade Mountain Wildlands. It is one of the most popular programs Wildlands offers, and small wonder: Not only do volunteers get to hike through the spectacular Cascades, but they also spend a good deal of time conducting a howling survey after the sun goes down. This means that you and the other volunteers hike and drive up backcountry service roads while howling like wolves to see what responds.

Your days are spent in more traditional pursuits: searching for tracks, scat, and other physical evidence of wolves. You collect samples and record your findings in field journals. The group of 12 generally sticks together, but for the wolf howling surveys you break up into pairs. During the typical wolf program, research is done from tented base camps near roads and on short backpacking trips. Free time may find you fishing or simply communing with nature.

Most volunteers are 18 to 35 years old. No previous research experience is required to participate, but curiosity and a sense of humor come in handy. All necessary skills, including howling, are taught on site under the direction of wildlife specialists and the U.S. Forest Service. Compass and map reading are also covered.

Camping and cooking responsibilities are shared, with meals prepared at base camp on portable stoves or over campfires. You may eat freeze-dried food, pasta, fresh vegetables, dried fruits, soups, nuts, and granola. Participants bring their own tents or share with others. The temperature in summer is usually in the 70s or 80s, with occasional showers; be sure to bring rain gear and clothing that can be layered. Many of the locations surveyed are accessible only by car, and cars are supplied by the volunteers, so getting accepted to work on the Wolf Habitat project is like getting a date in high school: Your chances are a whole lot better if you've got wheels. San Francisco State University gives you credit for joining this one. *Wildlands Studies, 3 Mosswood Circle, Cazadero, CA 95421, tel. and fax 707/632–5665. Mid-Aug.: 14 days, $385. Price does not include $50 application fee or $100–$250 for food, gas, miscellaneous expenses, and some special research equipment; project fee due by May 25. Sign up 2–4 months in advance.*

ALASKA

SOUTHEAST **Words to Match My Mountains.** Like Alaska itself, the Wrangell Mountains Project is outsize and overblown compared to the other projects in this chapter. It pushes the envelope in terms of time (seven weeks) and expense ($2,550, plus airfare), but it is well worth it, especially for those interested in science and writing.

Anyone who's ever been subjected to a first-year writing class has had to begin with the fundamentals: Describe a paper clip, a classroom, the person sitting beside you. Those enrolled in the Wrangell Mountains Project are faced with a more formidable challenge: Describe the Wrangell–St. Elias National Park and Preserve. Twelve times the size of Yosemite, surrounded by peaks that reach 16,390 feet and the continent's most active glaciers, this park is on the outer edge of Alaska's tourist future.

While most of the land within the park boundaries is federally owned, some lands around the gold rush–era town of McCarthy, where the project is based, are privately owned. Local landowners retain their subsistence-hunting and access rights; feelings about tourism are, let us say, mixed. Part of the project's goal is to educate tourists and perhaps even a few locals about their surroundings. The project also aims to explore the complex geological, ecological, and cultural factors that have shaped this landscape, and it touches on the critical management issues that will determine the region's future.

Fourteen volunteers interested in ecology, botany, geology, and land management hone their research skills by observing and investigating nature in the field, and writing reports, including a required term paper. Volunteers write descriptive material and guidelines suggested for the future management of the park. All of this work is donated to the park and the project library.

The project includes two extensive (and sometimes rigorous) journeys into the backcountry. The first takes you along the 25-mile-long Kennicott Glacier, upon which you travel and camp. Studying the glacier, you and the other volunteers reconstruct ecological and geological history. You learn to recognize signs of ecological change in the rock, ice, and streams, and record your findings in logbooks.

The second trip takes you high into the alpine regions of the mountain landscapes, where you travel off-trail through meadows and tundra, in the playing fields of the golden eagle and the grizzly bear. During this time, you work on backcountry projects of your own devising—your report is also given to the park and the project library.

In the program's headquarters is the Old Hardware Store, a National Historic Site. It houses the library and is home to a small number of graduate students, who are not working with you. Here, too, is the big kitchen where meals are cooked and eaten in communal fashion. Expect fresh vegetables, hearty pastas, and soups.

You sleep in tents (provided by some volunteers) along McCarthy Creek and have plenty of time for introspection.

Benjamin Shaine, the program's founder, has been leading research groups into the Wrangell Mountains for 20 years; he wrote a novel, *Alaska Dragon,* which is about the region and its inhabitants. Edward LaChappelle, also a project leader, is a McCarthy resident claimed to be "one of the world's experts on snow and ice," and a writer as well. San Francisco State University gives you college credit for participating in this project. *Wildlands Studies, 3 Mosswood Circle, Cazadero, CA 95421, tel. and fax 707/ 632–5665. June–Aug., 7 wks, $1,650. Price does not include $900 group expenses; sign up 2–3 months in advance (program fees due May 25, group expenses due June 1.*

HAWAII

THE BIG ISLAND **How to Identify a Humpback.** Like Shriners returning to Vegas, humpback whales return to the Hawaiian waters every winter, creating the largest concentration of humpbacks in the North Pacific. The whales come back to the Islands with but a single impulse: procreation. Adult males come a-courting, singing long, complex songs to prospective females. And since 1982 Earthwatch volunteers have joined staff researchers from the Kewalo Basin Marine Laboratory to document their annual return.

Some of the objectives of this project, called Humpbacks of Hawaii, vary from year to year, but two goals remain constant: the identification of the whale population by age and sex, and a better understanding of the dynamics of the interisland whale migration.

One of the project scientists videotapes the whales as they cavort and compete for females underwater, and this footage is reviewed by the team each evening. You and three to six other volunteers assist in sighting and locating whales and recording data in a log. You spend a good portion of your two-week stay aboard a 17-foot Boston Whaler equipped with an 88-horsepower outboard engine, taking still photographs of whales when they surface. These photos help to identify whales by such characteristic features as their tails, known as flukes, which are as distinctive as human fingerprints, if somewhat larger. Some team members are in contact with the boat by radiotelephone from an elevated sighting station on land.

Back at the rented house that serves as base for the project, you learn how to analyze the photos by matching them with data from previously identified whales. All volunteers take turns working with the boat team, the shore team, and the photographic analysis team.

Days are long: You awake at 6 AM, arrive back at base at 5:30, and then begin cleaning equipment, developing photos, and logging data. The communally cooked dinners—generally consisting of pasta dishes and salads—are followed by briefings and educational lectures. Staff members are knowledgeable about the area. There is at least one full day off, and you are encouraged to take in the Big Island's sights, including Hawaii Volcanoes National Park. Although this trip doesn't require volunteers to be especially fit, those prone to seasickness or sensitive to extensive exposure to heat or sunlight should think twice about joining. *Earthwatch, 680 Mt. Auburn St., Box 9104, Watertown, MA 02272-9924, tel. 617/926–8200 or 800/776–0188, fax 617/926–8532. Late Jan.–Mar.: 13 days, $2,095. Sign up 2–3 months in advance.*

MAUI **Maui's Humpback Service Trip.** Despite practically prohibitive prices, this trip may very well be an experience of a lifetime. The small town of Lahaina, known by many as the whale capital of the world, is tucked between the base of the West Maui Mountains and the Pacific Ocean. Many locals, however, refer to Lahaina as the "birthing room." It is here, along the town's tranquil blue shores, where many humpback whales give birth. On this outing you become part of the long-term whale-monitoring project. The mornings are spent observing and recording behavioral data. In the afternoons, you are free to snorkel, hike, and explore. While the work itself is not strenuous, be prepared to hike some steep rocky roads to get to the sites. The second part of the week is spent in eastern Maui, exploring the 10,000-foot Haleakala volcano, the town of Hana, and other spectacular scenery. *Sierra Club Outing Dept., 85 2nd St., 2nd Floor, San Francisco, CA 94109, tel. 415/977–5522. Late Mar.–early Apr.: 1 wk, $1,070. Cost does not include airfare.*

SOURCES

ORGANIZATIONS **Volunteer in Technical Assistance** (1600 Wilson Blvd., Suite 500, Arlington, VA 22209, tel. 703/276–1800) matches your skills with projects in need of volunteers. The **Points of Light Foundation** (1737 H St. NW, Washington, DC 20006, tel. 800/879–5400) can put you in touch with a volunteer center that has community-based projects near you.

PERIODICALS *Earthwatch* magazine is the house organ of Earthwatch (Earthwatch Membership Service, Box 8037, Syracuse, NY 13217, tel. 617/926–8200) and the way to find out about its projects. Published bimonthly, it's slick and (generally) well written. Its "Field Notes" section gives you a sense of the variety of projects.

BOOKS *Shaw Guide to Academic Travel* (Shaw Guides) contains everything from bear treks on the Maine coast to Faulkner seminars in Oxford, Mississippi. *Volunteer Vacations* (Chicago Review Press), by Bill McMillon, is as thorough a guide to all types of volunteer trips as you will find. Its profiles of sponsoring organizations are interspersed with short, lively narratives about the experiences of individual volunteers on specific programs.

ALSO SEE If you want to volunteer, but you would rather build trails or homes than count fins, turn to the chapter on Volunteer Vacations in Public and Community Service. If you're interested in science, but you'd rather not work so hard, look into Cultural and Natural History Cruises, Nature Camps, or Whale-Watching Cruises.

Volunteer Vacations in Public and Community Service

Written by M. T. Schwartzman

Updated by Stacy Abramson

ould you like to help build a hiking trail that stretches from New York to North Dakota? Or preserve pictographs in Arizona's Redrock Country? And would you be willing to pay a small fee for the opportunity? If so, maybe a volunteer vacation is for you.

Spending your vacation as a volunteer enables you to give as well as to get, turning hard work into good works and getting a relatively low-cost vacation at the same time. In these days of budget cuts and belt tightening, the need for volunteers is felt in all sorts of places by all sorts of organizations that serve small communities and the public at large. Where and how you contribute depend on what you hope to accomplish. If you want to leave your office routine behind and get outdoors, you can sign on to work as a campground host in a park or to crew on a sailing ship. If you're looking for something a little more "charitable," helping the homeless and rebuilding inner-city housing are among your choices. Public service can also entail working on a model farm, helping run the museum at a state historic site, or donating time at a wildlife sanctuary.

Volunteer positions generally take the form of either construction and maintenance or education, and of the two, the former is by far the more common. Also, because park services are typically short staffed, there are lots of volunteer projects in parks, offered both by nonprofit groups and by the parks themselves. As a result, one of the most plentiful jobs open to volunteers is trail building and maintenance in national and state parks across the country and along the length of the original volunteer-built trail—the Appalachian Trail.

A typical trail-maintenance crew consists of 10 to 20 people, who work out of a back-country field camp to which they often must hike the first day. Led by one, sometimes two, experienced leaders, crews make camp near the work site for a week or so at a time. The next few days might be spent clearing debris, improving and rerouting an existing trail, or building new trails, followed by a day for rest and relaxation. You might take advantage of the recreational opportunities of the wilderness, such as hiking, fishing, or climbing, or, if you're in a more developed setting, do a little sightseeing. (Though some volunteer projects are very work intensive, the ones listed in this chapter offer a good balance between labor and leisure; this is, after all, your vacation.) Then the cycle repeats—a few more days of work, followed by another day or two off, and finally a return to "civilization."

In return for your time and effort, you generally pay very little. Some volunteer programs charge no fee, while others cost

---

M. T. Schwartzman has written about the Appalachian Trail—one of the most popular destinations for volunteers—for the Appalachian Mountain Club's magazine, AMC Outdoors, *and* Fodor's National Parks and Seashores of the East.

---

significantly less than a similar nonworking trip. The cost of mounting the project is subsidized by charitable contributions or by park budgets. However, the same budget cuts that reduce the number of paid staff also reduce the money available for volunteer programs, and individual projects come and go with funding.

Luckily, there is usually a similar project in a similar or even the same location. For example, in 1996, both Volunteers for Peace and Appalachian Mountain Club offered similar programs in Maine's Baxter State Park. Sometimes groups act as cosponsors; Volunteers for Peace shares projects with both the Appalachian Mountain Club and Habitat for Humanity. In fact, checking around may save you money, since cosponsoring agencies often don't charge the same amount for the same trip (*see* Choosing the Right Project, *below*).

A little-known benefit of volunteering is the chance to meet people from many different backgrounds and cultures. Volunteer vacations are often international in character. On some programs, particularly those offered by Volunteers for Peace, as many as 80% of the volunteers may be from other countries. Many of these foreign visitors want to experience U.S. culture in a more profound way than they could as tourists; others, like their American counterparts, might just be looking for a way to travel cheaply, to get involved in a particular type of work, or to receive school credit.

The organizations and projects listed below are happy to accommodate all ages, ability levels, interests, and time commitments. So if you're interested in a vacation not just to feel good but to do good, you can do very well indeed by joining the nationwide corps of volunteers. It may just be the hardest vacation you'll ever love.

CHOOSING THE RIGHT PROJECT

It's important to match the right person to the right project, for both the volunteer's and the project's sakes, so the first order of business, before you apply for anything, is to take stock of your skills and interests. Because many volunteer crews have limited space and are often filled on a first-come, first-served basis, sponsoring agencies usually ask applicants to list several choices; you may very well not get your first or even second pick, so be sure to list only those projects you would truly like to work on. To know that, be ready to ask some questions:

What are my responsibilities? Like any job, you're required to perform certain tasks on a daily or weekly schedule. In addition to the project work, these may include housekeeping or cooking duties at a base camp or communal living quarters.

What are the working conditions like? Locations range from inner cities to wilderness, and work sites can be in offices or museums, dense woods or open fields. If projects are conducted outdoors, make sure you know what the climate is like, and be aware that work usually continues rain or shine.

Is physical work involved? Some, but not all, volunteer work involves manual labor. Find out how strenuous it is, and make sure that your physical fitness is up to the challenge. Keep in mind that trail maintenance is usually very physically demanding and is even harder at high altitudes. For clearing really heavy debris, though, pack animals are often employed.

What's the cost and what's included? Most volunteer programs require that you pay to join. Sometimes, this is a nominal fee to cover the sponsoring organization's administrative costs. Other projects charge up to several hundred dollars to offset the expense of meals or housing. Registration fees are payable in advance, but additional charges may be payable upon arrival at the work site. When there's a fee for the trips listed below, it covers accommodations and all your meals. When there's no fee, such as for government jobs, be sure to find out what's provided and what's not—it varies greatly. Sometimes the same organization even provides different benefits for different jobs. Transportation between your home and the project is never included. You probably need to bring your own work clothes, such as work gloves and boots, and you may be asked to buy and wear a uniform on the job; however, hard hats, safety goggles, and other tools and equipment are generally provided when needed. One of the most important "safety items" to check on is accident insurance. Some projects, usually government-run programs, provide workers' compensation insurance, while others offer no coverage and may require that you carry your own and sign a liability waiver.

One more note about cost: Different organizations that offer similar or even the same projects don't necessarily charge the same amounts. A little shopping around can be worth your while, but make sure you know what's included in each so you're not comparing apples and oranges.

What are the accommodations like? Housing is as varied as the projects and locations where they take place. Primitive cabins or campsites are typical accommodations for backcountry work; there may be no showers or other plumbing, and the work site may be a good hike away. On other trips, home is a tent at a drive-up campground or perhaps a lodge, while in more populated settings, you often find community-style living in a dormitory. Some projects, however, make no provisions for housing, and you must find your own, although often the sponsor can offer advice on finding a nearby campground or other inexpensive place to stay.

What is the food like? In projects where meals are provided, they differ according to setting. In the backcountry, food is usually packed in and cooked out. Often, it's vegetarian, as much for practical as for philosophical reasons. Cuisine is generally prepackaged but not freeze-dried, and there's usually fresh fruit and vegetables at least for the first few days. Closer to electricity, you may find more meat, but meals still run the gamut from home-cooked dinners in a private home to college cafeteria

fare. On some projects, you may occasionally find yourself as chief cook and bottle washer, literally, so you and your fellow volunteers might be what determines how good the chow really is. On other trips, such as the Sierra Club's, a cook often accompanies each work crew.

What are the medical facilities like? Accidents happen, especially if you're doing manual labor. If the project is at a remote wilderness site, there needs to be, at a minimum, adequate first-aid materials and a group leader trained in first aid.

What kind of training or instruction is there? Most volunteer work requires no previous experience, and you are trained on the job in the skill or task to be performed. In some cases, previous experience in the use of certain equipment, such as chain saws, may be preferred.

How much leisure time is there and what are the recreational opportunities? Most programs provide for personal time, but what there is to do depends on the locale. In rural and wilderness settings, you can take advantage of the opportunities for outdoor recreation. In urban jobs, entertainment is more likely to be indoors.

Can I take part if I have a medical condition or dietary restriction? If there are any special circumstances that might put you at risk or be difficult for the organizers to accommodate, be sure to ask ahead of time. For example, in trail building or maintenance, you may anger some bees along the way—not good if you're allergic to bee stings. If you follow a special diet, the food provided may not fit the bill. In both cases, you could bring along what you need (a bee-sting kit and dietary supplements), but if you're going to a remote wilderness site, you may be too limited in what you can carry or too far from medical facilities for it to be practical. A medical examination may be required for participation; if so, find out who pays for it.

Is there a minimum or maximum age? In most programs, participants have ranged from teenagers to septuagenarians; but because of the physically demanding nature of much of the work, most tend to be in their 20s and 30s. Though organizations do not generally exclude an older prospective volunteer because of a set maximum age, they need to be sure all participants can handle a project's rigors. As for minimums, you must generally be at least 18, but in some cases, younger volunteers are accepted if they are accompanied by an adult or have the signed permission of a parent or legal guardian. The Appalachian Mountain Club offers trips for specific age groups in summer. For example, a 50+ Crew Trip is devoted to volunteers 50 years and older; there's also a trail crew program for teens between the ages of 16 and 19.

Is there a minimum time commitment? Some volunteer positions, particularly at national or state parks, require that you spend at least two to four weeks in a position. This is especially true for summer volunteers or where extensive training is involved. Most of those listed below, however, require just a week or 10 days.

Is there any religious affiliation? Some volunteer work, especially housing construction and other inner-city projects, is church sponsored, and the day may begin or end with a prayer meeting or other devotion. If you are not particularly devout, this may not be for you.

Do you have references from past volunteers? It's always helpful to ask for references. Talking to people who've worked on a project can help you understand how strenuous the work is, how well run the organization is, how good the food or housing is, or whatever else is important to you. You may not feel like following up on many, or even any, but if a sponsoring organization refuses to give you names, it should put up a red flag. It may also be a good idea to speak to whomever is leading the trip or to someone who led it in the past. Talking to the cook might help, too, if you follow a particular diet.

How long has the project been running? It probably doesn't matter how long a particular project has been running, but it might very well matter how long the organization has been running similar projects. Often, training and logistics are complicated enough that experience is necessary to put on a well-managed project. Talking to current or former trip leaders can give you a sense of how well organized projects are.

How far in advance do I need to book? This varies by organization and, since many trips are filled on a first-come, first-served basis, by the popularity of the particular project. Where Volunteers for Peace advises you to sign up six weeks in advance, the Sierra Club recommends at least six months. On the other hand, there are many projects with plenty of room for volunteers, and not much advance notice is generally needed.

MAJOR PLAYERS

AMERICAN HIKING SOCIETY This Washington-based national organization, which lobbies Congress and acts as an environmental advocate on behalf of 100 affiliated clubs, runs one- to two-week volunteer vacations. Having recently celebrated its 20th anniversary, the American Hiking Society's mission is to establish, maintain, and protect the nation's footpaths. One of its largest and most ambitious accomplishments has been the construction of the American Discovery Trail, the country's first coast-to-coast trail, extending from the Pacific Ocean at Point Reyes National Seashore in California and ending at the Atlantic Ocean at Cape Henlopen State Park in Delaware. This brainchild of the American Hiking Society has become such a successful project that it's evolving into its own nonprofit organization, the American Discovery Trail Society, whose sole purpose is coordinating and maintaining the coast-to-coast trails. Volunteers on other trips do construction and maintenance on a large number of trails, mainly in national forests. The tasks involved include building bridges, dams, and trails, installing fences, planting vegetation, constructing outhouses, and drilling holes for dynamite placement. One group disassembled an abandoned airplane that had been left in a wilderness area.

Rustic settings are a constant, usually in heavily wooded areas in the mountains—some as high as 10,000 feet—and often near a stream or lake. Most trips have base camps with water pumps or wells and outhouses. Volunteers bring their own tents, but food is provided; group meals are cooked over a campfire.

Crew size is 10 to 12 people, with a $50 registration fee for all trips, which are one or two weeks in length. Volunteers should be in good physical condition, able to hike at least 5 miles a day, and ready to supply a tent and sleeping bag. Insurance is provided by the federal agency supervising the work. In addition to sponsoring its own projects, the society provides information on those offered by other organizations in its directory, *Helping Out in the Outdoors* (*see* Sources, *below*). *AHS Box 20160, Washington, DC 20041, tel. 301/565–6713, fax 301/565–6714.*

APPALACHIAN MOUNTAIN CLUB Founded in 1876, the AMC was a charter member of the Appalachian Trail Conference (*see below*) and is now its biggest member. Since 1919, the club has enlisted volunteers for trail-maintenance programs throughout the Northeast and today keeps up 1,400 miles of trail, including a 350-mile stretch of the Appalachian Trail. Historically, the club's main focus has been on its birthplace, the White Mountains of New Hampshire, but its projects now extend throughout the United States.

Volunteer Trail Crew projects run for a week or longer out of five base camps: Camp Dodge in the White Mountains, New Hampshire; Bascom Lodge in the Berkshire Mountains of Massachusetts; Echo Lake Camp in Acadia National Park, Maine; a camp in New York's Catskill Mountains;

and the club's newest outdoor center at the Delaware Water Gap National Recreation Area, in New Jersey. Lodging at the base camps includes electricity and running water, and menus are varied, with fresh fruits and vegetables. Members of the trail crews tend to come from the Northeast, since that's where the camps are. Weeklong trail crew programs typically cost $35. Tools, training, room and board, and most necessary equipment are provided. Insurance is not provided, and volunteers, who must be over 16, must sign a waiver of liability. *5 Joy St., Boston, MA 02108, tel. 617/523–0636, fax 617/523–0722.*

APPALACHIAN TRAIL CONFERENCE Constructed in the 1920s and '30s, the 2,159-mile Appalachian Trail, which passes through 14 eastern states from Maine to Georgia, was the nation's first national scenic trail and is still the world's longest continuously marked footpath. Founded in 1925 to help build the AT, as it's known, the Appalachian Trail Conference (ATC) currently acts as a coordinator for 32 organizations that help maintain and improve the trail, including moving sections of the original route to newly acquired land. Workers are dispatched to help with local projects in conjunction with the National Park Service, U.S. Forest Service, state agencies, and member clubs.

The ATC divides its volunteer work force into four crews: Southern, Mid-Atlantic, Maine, and Vermont. You can work a one- to six-week stint, and no previous trail-building experience is necessary. However, you should be familiar with rustic outdoor living, since accommodations consist of tent camps set up near the work site. The conference provides training, safety gear, tools, and meals. Each seven- or eight-person work crew is led by a staff of one or two, who act as camp coordinator and crew leader. You must be 18 or older and in good physical condition—the manual labor required can be considerable. Over the years, volunteers have come from across the country and around the world, from all sorts of backgrounds and occupations. No fees are charged to sign up or to participate, and insurance is provided by the supervising federal agency—either the park or forest service, depending on the location of the particular trail segment. *Box 807, Harpers Ferry, WV 25425, tel. 304/535–6331, fax 304/535–2667.*

HABITAT FOR HUMANITY INTERNATIONAL

Founded in 1976, Habitat for Humanity (HFHI) became better known when Jimmy Carter's involvement brought the organization national exposure in the early '80s. The group's goal is simple: to eliminate poverty-level housing worldwide using volunteer labor and donated money and materials. Today, HFHI conducts projects in all 50 states and 48 foreign countries and has built over 40,000 houses around the world. Though secular in its mission, HFHI's local partners are often church groups, and the workday may begin or end with prayer.

Volunteering with HFHI stretches the definition of a vacation, but the hard work you put in brings immediate and visible results—the construction of a new home for someone who needs it. No carpentry skills are needed; the house leader for each team is either a professional or a very skilled amateur, and a job can be found for people of all ages and abilities. Project cost varies depending on how far away you work and lodging can mean a home or dorm. Volunteers are covered by accident insurance but must sign a liability waiver anyway.

One of the most popular Habitat trips is the Jimmy Carter Work Project, in which the former president and first lady take part. Although the goals and work remain the same, the project moves to a different location each year—a South Dakota Sioux Indian reservation in 1994, south-central Los Angeles in 1995, and Hungary in 1996. In June 1997, Habitat's 13th annual Jimmy Carter Work Project, in association with the Federation of Appalachian Housing Enterprises, Inc. (22 community-based nonprofit housing organizations in Central Appalachia), is organizing "Hammering in the Hills," where volunteers build houses for families with low incomes in rural parts of Kentucky, Tennessee, Virginia, and West Virginia. If you volunteer during this annual building blitz, you may get a chance to rub elbows, or share nails, with Carter himself. *HFHI Volunteer Services Dept., 121 Habitat St., Americus, GA 31709, tel. 912/924–6935 or 800/HABITAT, ext. 549, fax 912/924–6541. Information is also available about HFHI's Global Village 1–3 week programs.*

NATIONAL PARK SERVICE

The park service's Volunteers in Parks (VIP) program provides opportunities to work and live in any of the 350 units under the service's jurisdiction. Each park runs its own program. From Maine to Hawaii and Alaska to Florida, in big cities, small towns, and remote wilderness areas, positions are available that are as diverse as their locations. In addition to trail-maintenance worker, you can choose to be a public information officer, living-history actor, brochure writer or designer, campground host, shuttle-bus driver, cabinetmaker, librarian, photographer, computer programmer, or teacher. Living and working conditions vary according to your job, and housing is only available at some of the large parks. Some parks reimburse volunteers for out-of-pocket expenses to cover local travel, meals, and uniforms. A medical examination, paid for by the federal government, is required, and you're covered by workers' compensation. You must be 18 or older; younger participants may become VIPs at parks in their own communities or at other sites as part of a family or organized and supervised group. *U.S. Dept. of the Interior, 1849 C Street NW, Box 37127, Washington, DC 20240, tel. 202/208–6843.*

SIERRA CLUB

The Sierra Club was founded in 1892 for the purposes of wilderness preservation and restoration and has been running volunteer vacations since 1957. The club's original focus was Yosemite, but today it organizes more than 80 service trips every year to destinations nationwide. Perennial favorites include Denali National Park in

Alaska, Chaco Canyon in New Mexico, and Acadia National Park in Maine. Other projects are geographically mobile, such as the North Country Scenic Trail, a planned route that will stretch 2,000 miles from New York to North Dakota by the year 2000, or airplane wreckage removal trips, which rid remote locations of debris as needed.

Most projects are 7- to 10-day outings to secluded sites, where you do trail maintenance, revegetation, cleanup, or campsite restoration. Half of the days are for work, the other half for play. Since training is provided on the job, no special skills are required, but you must be physically fit and supply your own camping equipment. The club provides all other tools and equipment, as well as meals. In fact, the club emphasizes good food perhaps more than any of the other organizations listed. On many outings, the staff includes a cook, who must first attend a wilderness-cooking training seminar and assist on one outing as a trainee. A number of trips cater to vegetarians, and other special diets can sometimes be accommodated if requested in advance. Living quarters are primitive campsites near the work site with few facilities.

Work crews, ranging in size from 8 to 20 volunteers, are led by a staff of 2 to 4 Sierra Club representatives. The trip leader has attended a Red Cross Advanced First Aid course or the equivalent. About half of the volunteers come from California, and many return year after year to complete the work they started, especially on trail-maintenance projects. The club's service trips typically range from $200 to $480. They're among the most expensive volunteer vacations, though cheaper than the club's guided outings. (This is largely the result of the club's high profile and overhead; it incurs a lot of expenses in promoting itself and its goals.) Insurance is not included. *85 2nd St., 2nd Floor, San Francisco, CA 94105, tel. 415/977–5522, fax 415/977–5797.*

STATE PARKS DEPARTMENTS Many states have volunteer programs similar to that of the federal government. The most common

opportunities are as campground hosts, but volunteers are also needed to produce park newsletters, serve as information officers, do trail maintenance and construction, help develop interpretive programs, and perform general office work. On-site housing is often provided, especially for campground hosts, and food and utilities may be included as well, depending upon the program and your position. Training, tools, and other equipment are usually furnished, and some expenses for local travel may be reimbursed. There is generally no sign-up fee, and you're usually covered by workers' compensation. The only states that don't have campground host programs are Arkansas, Hawaii, Kentucky, Louisiana, Mississippi, and Rhode Island. Many of the states that do have such programs are also happy to work out a special project with you that matches your interests with a park's needs. For more information, call the parks department of the state you're interested in.

VOLUNTEERS FOR PEACE The aim of VFP is to promote volunteer work camps in the United States and 60 other countries. Its *International Workcamp Directory* (see Sources, *below*) lists 50 or so domestic projects each year, such as helping the homeless, building houses, urban gardening, conservation, and working with underprivileged children. About half of these projects repeat annually. On many projects, especially those in inner cities on the East Coast, you may work with more than one local organization. Teams range from 6 to 12 individuals, and a leader, sometimes two, oversees each group. On 95% of the projects the work is indoors, and more than 80% of volunteers are foreigners. Those under age 18 are not accepted.

A registration fee of $175 covers room and board; a few projects, usually those in more expensive locations, such as Alaska, also require an additional fee, ranging from $50 to $100. Some camps serve only vegetarian meals. Accommodations vary according to location, but the most common setting is a dorm with bunk beds or mattresses on the floor. Men and women are often housed in the same room, and a cooperative living arrangement prevails. In other words, you are responsible for housekeeping chores as well as your volunteer work. Accident insurance is not provided. *43 Tiffany Rd., Belmont, VT 05730, tel. 802/259–2759, fax 802/259–2922.*

MAINE **Baxter State Park.** This 200,000-acre wilderness preserve two hours north of Bangor is home to Mt. Katahdin, the northern terminus of the Appalachian Trail. Here you and 10 other Volunteers for Peace can take part in lakeshore restoration, grounds keeping, landscaping, and carpentry projects at Katahdin Stream, Kidney Pond, and Daicey Pond. Free time can be spent swimming, canoeing (canoes provided), hiking, and watching the resident wildlife, which includes moose, bear, and loons. Lodgings are primitive log cabins with neither electricity nor running water. Volunteers must bring a sleeping bag, backpack, boots, and rain gear. *Volunteers for Peace, 43 Tiffany Rd., Belmont, VT 05730, tel. 802/259–2759. Mid-July: 14 days, $175. Sign up 6 wks in advance.*

MASSACHUSETTS **Berkshire Volunteer Crew.** The Berkshire Volunteer Trail Crew, in conjunction with Massachusetts' Department of Environmental Management, is responsible for the maintenance of 50 miles of trail on the 12,000-acre Mt. Greylock reservation. Each week a group of six to eight volunteers tackles trail construction and maintenance on the highest peak in the state. Projects include constructing rock staircases, cutting new trail, building water bars, clipping brush, and clearing drainage. You and the rest of the crew will overnight at the rustic Bascom Lodge, a wood-and-stone edifice built in the 1930s on the summit of Mt. Greylock. From here you can enjoy spectacular sunsets, read a book by the fireplace, indulge in the family-style meals, or explore some of the Berkshire's

cultural activities. *AMC Trails Program, Mt. Greylock Visitor Center, Box 1800, Lanesboro, MA 01237, tel. 413/443–0011, fax 413/442–9010. June–Aug.: 1 wk, $50.*

MASSACHUSETTS **Cape Cod Seashore.** Want to spend a week at the beach? On this Sierra Club service trip, you and 15 others maintain trails and boardwalks, help stabilize sand dunes, and rehabilitate cranberry bogs in the Cape Cod National Seashore. Free-time activities include a tour, led by a guide from Massachusetts Audubon, of North Monomoy Island, a national wildlife refuge that is flooded with birds on their autumn migration. Other possibilities include a whale-watching trip out of Provincetown or excursions to Nantucket and Martha's Vineyard. You can also hike or bike and simply enjoy the beach, wildflowers, sand dunes, and pine forests. Housing is at Paine's Campground, a private facility with hot showers in a wooded area within walking distance of the Atlantic beach. At least once during the trip you help prepare the day's meals and clean up afterward. *Sierra Club Outing Dept., 85 2nd St., 2nd Floor, San Francisco, CA 94105, tel. 415/977–5522, fax 415/977–5797. Mid-Sept.: 7 days, $315. Sign up 6–8 months in advance.*

NEW YORK **Hudson River Sloop *Clearwater.*** Whether you take the helm of this 106-foot replica of a 19th-century sailing ship or guide elementary school children through a series of water tests, you can help spread the word about why the Hudson River needs to be protected, what dangers it faces, and how to keep it clean. No previous sailing experience is necessary. Just sign on to crew for a week at a time, and you get training in sailing techniques, such as hoisting the sails, and other shipboard operations, like swabbing the decks. Most important, you act as a representative of the *Clearwater* in its mission of environmental advocacy.

Crews of six volunteers eat and sleep aboard ship, assisting a sailing staff of seven—the captain, mates, engineer, and cook—plus an educator and perhaps a sailing apprentice.

In spring, a second boat hosts four more volunteers. Though you should be 18 or older if you're on your own, students 16 to 18 can apply through an internship program and children 10 to 15 may crew if accompanied by a parent. Team members are selected for diversity; a mix of teenagers and senior citizens is typical.

Family-style, mostly vegetarian, meals are served in a galley three times a day. At night you retire below decks to a dorm-style main cabin that accommodates 12 in twin beds or a secondary cabin that sleeps three. There is no electricity aboard ship and no shower. Water is carried aboard for bathing, and at certain docks, you can shower at the homes of members who live nearby. *Hudson River Sloop Clearwater, 112 Market St., Poughkeepsie, NY 12601, tel. 914/454–7673. Mid-Apr.–mid-Nov.: 7 days, $70. Price includes membership as well as meals; sign up 8–10 wks in advance. Summer trips are in high demand so sign up early. Fall trips are suggested.*

THE MID-ATLANTIC

PENNSYLVANIA **House Building in Philadelphia.** In a project sponsored locally with the Philadelphia Yearly Friends meeting, Volunteers for Peace sends 10 volunteers to build houses for low-income families in the City of Brotherly Love. Carpentry, electrical, and other construction skills are helpful but not required. During your stay in the city, you live with a Quaker family and attend church along with the other volunteers. *Volunteers for Peace, 43 Tiffany Rd., Belmont, VT 05730, tel. 802/259–2759. July–Aug.: 14 days, $175. Sign up 6 wks in advance.*

VIRGINIA **Appalachian Trail.** "Perhaps the hardest work you have ever performed," the Appalachian Trail Conference warns about this ongoing project in southwest Virginia. You might find yourself doing trail design and construction or rough carpentry, building shelters and bridges, rehabilitating an eroded trail, or clearing and managing open areas, but be warned: Along the way you could be breaking and moving rocks, digging holes, and splitting logs.

Each trip has a base camp, where there are showers and laundry facilities, plus cabins that house two or three people in bunks. From there, you are transported by van to a field camp, which may be a primitive site or a cabin compound with a water source nearby. Here you sleep in a tent or cabin and, in addition to trail work, pitch in with such chores as cleaning, cooking, washing dishes, and sharpening tools. Meals, prepared in a tent kitchen, consist of fresh meat and vegetables; menus feature the likes of chili, chops, fish, or pasta, with side dishes of salad and rice. Plenty of fruit, candy bars, and cookies are on hand for a quick energy boost between meals. Insurance is included.

One-week schedules start with orientation and instruction on Wednesday, followed by work from Thursday to Monday. Tuesday, the day off, is spent at base camp. Free time is set aside for sightseeing, swimming, fishing, rock climbing, hiking, caving, or just loafing. *Appalachian Trail Conference Southern Volunteer Crew, Box 10, Newport, VA 24128. Late May–late Aug.: 7 days, no charge. Sign up 3 months in advance.*

WEST VIRGINIA **Holistic Holiday.** Each year, Volunteers for Peace sends 10 to 15 volunteers to the Gesundheit Institute, an ongoing work camp dedicated to building a holistic community. Located in Pocahontas County in southwestern West Virginia, the institute is set on 314 rural acres. The ultimate goal is to build a hospital where fun and art are major parts of the healing process. However, major funding is still lacking, so most of the tasks for volunteers are on the grounds—landscaping, gardening, and small construction projects. A full schedule of group activities, such as swimming outings, hiking excursions, and parties, keeps you busy even when you're not working. Home during your stay is a yurt—a round, tentlike structure. While at the institute, you're expected to pitch in with cooking and cleaning. *Volunteers for Peace, 43 Tiffany Rd., Belmont, VT 05730, tel. 802/259–2759. Late Aug.: 14 days, $175. Sign up 6 wks in advance.*

THE SOUTH

ARKANSAS **International Learning and Livestock Center.** The Heifer Project, founded in 1944, is dedicated to easing global hunger by promoting sound livestock management practices. At the group's 200-acre livestock center, in the hills of rural Arkansas, you can help the eight full-time staff members teach the public, especially visiting schoolchildren, about the issues of world hunger. Among the displays are the Education Trail, which features the Global Village: a re-creation of the Barrio, an Appalachian House, an African House, and a Guatemalan House. At the Guatemalan Hillside Farm, 2½ acres of steep, eroded hillside, you learn how small-scale farmers can use limited resources to become self-sufficient. Other sites demonstrate livestock management techniques.

Depending on your abilities and the center's needs, you can assist with farm chores, such as milking the goats, cleaning the barns, or cultivating the new organic garden; help in the community kitchen or office; assist in the Center's new teamwork course; guide schoolchildren on tours along the Education Trail; or work on construction projects, such as fence building or painting, that expand the facilities or keep up existing structures. Because farm work is hard and potentially dangerous, no minors are accepted. Volunteers should be healthy and strong; those who are less physically fit can work indoors. The center accommodates up to 30 volunteers, from all over the country and the world, in furnished houses, one set up for couples and the other for individuals. Another option accommodation is the "Heifer Hilton," an open-air bunk barn with canvas curtains instead of outside walls or screens, and mattresses on wood platforms. Meals are served in the Cookshack, a screened-in kitchen with all the essentials. *Heifer Project International, International Learning and Livestock Center, Rte. 2, Box 33, Perryville, AR 72126, tel. 501/483–6623. Year-round: 1 wk–1 year, $75 a week. Sign up 2–3 months in advance.*

THE MIDWEST

MICHIGAN **Emerging Leaders Program.** If you are interested in combining work with at-risk kids with some spirituality and minimalist living, this program in Ann Arbor is for you. You will facilitate an adventure-based camping program together with young people from a variety of communities. The program focuses on community building; outdoor skills such as backpacking and ecological camping; and folk arts, and Native American spirituality. Operating under the "Freedom Model," all decisions here are made by the entire community, including the campers. You and four others will live in tents just outside of Ann Arbor. *Volunteers for Peace, 43 Tiffany Rd., Belmont, VT 06730, tel. 802/259–2759. Late July, $175. Sign up 6–8 wks in advance.*

MISSOURI **Campground Host.** Want free lodging just 7 miles from Branson, the new country-music center of the South? Many do, which is why Table Rock State Park is the most popular park in Missouri's VIP program. The 356-acre park is in the Lakes Region of southwest Missouri, amid the Ozark Mountains' White River Hills, and it borders the northeast shore of 53,000-acre Table Rock Lake. As a campground host, you greet incoming campers, collect fees, act as a public information officer, perform light maintenance, and help run campground activities. Recreational opportunities within the park include hiking, boating, fishing, and swimming.

Table Rock was the pilot park in Missouri's volunteer program, which now includes 35 parks across the state. Other popular units, all with trout hatcheries, are Lebanon's Bennett Spring State Park and Cassville's

Roaring River State Park, both 3,000-acre units in the Lakes Region, and Salem's Montauk State Park, 1,300 acres in the southeast. Insurance is provided. *Missouri Dept. of Natural Resources, Division of State Parks, Volunteer Program Coordinator, Box 176, Jefferson City, MO 65102, tel. 800/334–6946. Mar.–Oct.: 4-wk minimum, no charge. Sign up 12 months in advance.*

THE SOUTHWEST

ARIZONA Redrock Archaeology, Coconino National Forest. Rising 2,000 feet above the Verde Valley, on the southern edge of the Colorado Plateau between Flagstaff and Sedona, is Redrock Country, which is known for its deep-red sandstone formations and immense canyons. If you're a hiker, photographer, bird-watcher, or wildflower lover, you've found your trip.

Working closely with the Forest Service, an archaeologist, and 14 other volunteers, your task is to record the largest known pictograph site in the Redrock Canyon country. Thus far, about 150 panels have been found that date back as far as the Archaic Period (8000 BC to 1000 BC). You preserve pictographs through documentation—photography, photo tracing, scale drawing—as well as through graffiti removal. Camping at elevations of over 4,000 feet, you'll have plenty of free time to hike, take pictures, and enjoy the surrounding hues. *Sierra Club Outing Dept., 85 2nd St., 2nd Floor, San Francisco, CA 94109, tel. 415/977–5522, fax 415/977–5797. Late Apr.: 1 wk, $285. Sign up 6 months in advance.*

NEVADA Living History Interpreter. Visitors to Spring Valley State Park come to hike, participate in water sports on 65-acre Eagle Valley Reservoir, and explore the pioneer ranch lands nearby. You can help bring the area's ranching past to life for them by reenacting some facet of history. Working as an interpretive assistant, you research, design, and present a living-history program, including dressing up in period costume.

There are other volunteer positions at Spring Valley, including campground host and trail maintenance worker, and there are interpretive assistant positions at other Nevada parks as well, though duties are likely to vary, from posting signs and leading hikes to developing lectures, slide shows, and self-guiding nature trails. Nevada's Volunteer in Parks program is extensive, accepting volunteers for more than 50 positions at 16 park units plus state and district headquarters. Camping space, sometimes including utilities, is provided for some positions. *Spring Valley State Park, Star Rte., Box 201, Pioche, NV 89043, tel. 702/962–5102, or for all state parks, Administrator, Nevada Division of State Parks, Capitol Complex, Carson City, NV 89710, tel. 702/687–4370. Year-round: no minimum commitment, no charge. Sign up 4 wks in advance.*

THE ROCKIES

WYOMING Museum Volunteer. Want to be a prospector, blacksmith, or mountain man? As a museum volunteer at one of Wyoming's historic sights, you get to dress in period costume and act in living-history demonstrations. The two most popular sites for volunteers are South Pass City State Historic Site and Fort Bridger State Historic Site.

South Pass, outside Lander, is a collection of 11 buildings that remain from the original capital of the Dakota Territory. Now open to the public, the whole town re-creates a gold mining town of the 1860s. In addition to historical reenactment, you can help set up and maintain exhibits, work in the museum shop, answer visitors' questions, and assist with administrative duties.

Ft. Bridger, in the town of the same name, was the original outpost of Jim Bridger, a fur trader, trapper, and pioneer who was one of the first settlers in this area. Here work involves teaching visitors what life was like in the wild, wild West by dressing in period costume and acting as a tour guide through eight historical buildings.

Volunteer opportunities in museums are also available at four other locations: Fort Phil Kearny State Historic Site in Story, Guernsey State Park in Guernsey, Trail End State Historic Site in Sheridan, and Fort Fetterman State Historic Site in Douglas. You'll have to find your own accommodations, and meals are not included. *Wyoming Dept. of Commerce, Division of State Parks & Historic Sites, 6101 Yellowstone Rd., Cheyenne, WY 82002, tel. 307/777–6323. Late May–mid-Sept.: 2-wk minimum, no charge. Sign up at least 2 wks in advance.*

THE WEST COAST

CALIFORNIA **Santa Cruz Island.** This Sierra Club vacation, cosponsored with the Nature Conservancy, is extremely popular, and volunteers have been turned away in the past. The island, the largest of the eight Channel Islands, is so biologically diverse that it has been compared to the Galápagos. It's located 25 miles off the coast of Santa Barbara, and 90% of the land is owned and managed by the Nature Conservancy. While on the island, you and nine other volunteers mostly perform trail upkeep, but there may also be general chores—painting, fence repair, and hay pitching—at the historic central ranch facility. Housing is in nearby cabins. In your free time, you can explore the ranch, the mountains, and the beaches. *Sierra Club, Dept. 05618, San Francisco, CA 94139, tel. 415/776–2211, fax 415/776–4868. Mid-Apr. and late Oct.: 7 days, $400. Sign up 6–8 months in advance.*

CALIFORNIA **Tahoe Rim Trail.** Just as the Appalachian Trail was built more than half a century ago, today a 150-mile hiking and equestrian trail along the ridge tops surrounding Lake Tahoe is being constructed, thanks to a group based in South Lake Tahoe. The goal is to enhance the lake's recreational opportunities while preserving its scenic beauty. Construction began in 1984, and three-fourths of the trail loop, including 50 miles that follow the existing

Pacific Crest Trail, has been completed. The final leg is scheduled for completion by the year 2000.

Work entails typical trail-building tasks: clearing debris, raking, clipping brush, and using rock bars to extract rocks. Training, safety equipment (hard hats), and trail-building tools are the only items provided. The rest—including work gloves and boots, insurance (a liability waiver is required), food, and lodging—is your responsibility. You can live in a nearby campground or motel or pitch a tent close to the work site.

Volunteers of all ages and abilities are welcome; there's plenty of work to go around and never enough hands. Those under 17 can take part with signed parental permission. In fact, families often volunteer together. Crews of 1 to 50 are led by at least one crew leader, and though many volunteers come from the local community, they also have traveled from as far away as England to participate. *Tahoe Rim Trail, 4647 Stateline, NV 89449, tel. 702/588–0686, fax 702/588–8737. Mid-June–mid-Oct.: 1 day–4 months, no charge. No advance registration necessary.*

CALIFORNIA **Tuolomne Meadows, Yosemite National Park.** Here you'll be drinking in the beauty of the quiet lakes and starry skies, but working, too, as you join 13 other volunteers to revegetate abandoned trails tucked away in the park's sierras. When naturalist John Muir passed through the area in the late 19th century, it was serene and peaceful. It still is, but now, over 100 years later, the meadows ·with the glacially carved peaks towering above, have been overused and need attention. This is one of Sierra Club's more rigorous and rewarding trips—you'll work five- or six-day stints with a two-day break in between. Because you'll be working and lifting heavy materials at elevations of over 8,600 feet, you must be in good shape before you go. Your work site is a 2-mile hike from the base camp, but the Park Service supplies pack animals to carry project materials. All food and equipment is provided, but come ready to camp. Don't forget your moleskin. *Sierra Club Outing Dept., 85 2nd St., 2nd Floor, San Francisco, CA 94109, tel. 415/977–5797, fax 415/977–5522. Mid-Aug: 5–6 days, $325. Sign up 6 months in advance.*

ALASKA

SOUTHEAST **Glacier Bay.** Here's a relatively inexpensive way to spend 10 days in Alaska's famous Glacier Bay National Park, renowned for its 16 tidewater glaciers. Part of this Sierra Club trip is spent doing trail maintenance and other varied tasks in the immediate vicinity of Bartlett Cove, at the entrance to the park and 11 miles from the town of Gustavus. During this time, you stay at the Bartlett Cove Campground. The rest of the trip you work on more remote trails; after hiking 4 to 5 miles, you set up camp near the new site. All work is done with hand tools, which must be carried to the camp along with all food and cooking gear, since there is no pack support. You and the nine other trip members help prepare all meals, which are vegetarian. In your free time, you can sea kayak, hike, fish, or take a small-boat excursion to see the calving glaciers. *Sierra Club, Dept. 05618, San Francisco, CA 94139, tel. 415/776–2211, fax 415/776–4868. Mid-June: 10 days, $575. Sign up 6–8 months in advance.*

SOURCES

BOOKS *Helping Out in the Outdoors* (American Hiking Society, Box 20160, Washington, DC 20041, tel. 301/565–6704, fax 301/565–6714) is an annual 968-page directory of more than 2,000 volunteer jobs and internships in parks and forests nationwide. The *International Workcamp Directory* (Volunteers for Peace, 43 Tiffany Rd., Belmont, VT 05730, tel. 802/259–2759, fax 802/259–2922) is put out every April for summer and fall volunteer placement. *National Volunteers in Parks Directory* (Solutions) is a listing of campground-host positions available throughout the United States. *AMC Outdoors,* (5 Joy St., Boston, MA 02108, tel. 617/523–0636, fax 617/523–0722) is published 10 times a year and offers a detailed calendar of events: workshops, day trips, weekend trips, family programs, and longer volunteer trips.

ALSO SEE If you're interested in volunteering but would prefer to make a more intellectual and less physical contribution, check out the chapter on Volunteer Research Vacations.

Whale-Watching Cruises

Written by Melissa Rivers

Updated by Heidi Sarna

 close encounter with whales in their natural habitat is a thrilling experience. Hearing the resonant whoosh of a cetacean exhaling and witnessing such acrobatics as spy-hopping (a whale poking its head straight up out of the water for a look around), breaching (leaping almost entirely out of the water and coming down with a thunderous splash), and skimming (feeding at the surface), you can't help feeling these magnificent animals' awesome size and beauty. You can see whales from many spots along the California and New England coastlines, but the best way to get up close and personal with these creatures is to take a whale-watching cruise.

Whale-watching cruises generally last from 4 to 15 days. Some of them travel to feeding, breeding, or calving grounds, while others cruise along a portion of a whale migration route. Some boats dock in a different port each evening, some anchor in secluded natural harbors and coves, and others keep moving through the night.

The biggest difference among these cruises, however, is the boats, which range from small sail-powered vessels to full-size cruise liners. Sailboats are quiet and have less impact on the environment than motorized boats. They also tend to be small and have limited passenger space, tight sleeping quarters, shared bathrooms, and tiny galleys in which simple, family-style meals are prepared. The range of motorized vessels runs from smallish cabin cruisers originally built for sportfishing to converted fishing trawlers and pleasure yachts to the largest floating hotels. The larger boats provide more space and privacy and have kitchens that can cook more elaborate meals. The size of the boat also determines the entertainment facilities, which may include a bar (even the smallest sailboats usually have at least a liquor cabinet from which you can buy drinks), a lounge equipped with a high-tech entertainment system, a hot tub, and a pool. Small boats can go places that cruise liners can't, and when you cruise on a small boat, you are close to the water and, thus, close to the whales. On a cruise liner, you watch the whales from high above the water, but the ship is more stable than a small boat, and this can be easier on the stomach in rough seas.

Because whales migrate, whale-watching is a seasonal activity, and the season varies from place to place. These huge mammals spend summer in cooler-climate feeding grounds and winter in warmer-water breeding and calving grounds. February through April is the best time for watching whales in Hawaii, California, and Baja California,

Melissa Rivers has written about Mexico, Canada, and the Orient. In summer she travels from her inland Oregon home up the West Coast to Alaska in search of memorable whale encounters. Heidi Sarna, a contributor to many Fodor's guides, has marveled at the grace and beauty of whales off the coast of southern Alaska, the Hawaiian islands, and New England.

and June through August is best in southeastern Alaska, New England, and on both coasts of Canada.

Different cetaceans frequent different waters. Humpbacks that live in the North Pacific migrate between summer feeding grounds off Alaska to winter breeding and calving grounds off Hawaii or the coast of Baja. Humpbacks in the North Atlantic winter in the Caribbean and, in summer, move to the Gulf of Maine and the Bays of Massachusetts and Fundy, where they mingle with sperm whales, minkes, finbacks, and the rare right whale.

Pilot and false killer whales are also seen in Hawaiian waters during the winter. Orcas (killer whales) are most prevalent in Washington's Puget Sound and along the coast of British Columbia, with resident pods in those waters year-round; however, transient orca pods have been spotted from Glacier Bay in Alaska to Monterey Bay in California.

Gray whales are easily spotted along the West Coast during their annual migrations from calving grounds in Mexican lagoons and Hawaiian bays to summer feeding grounds in Alaskan waters. The warm waters of Baja lagoons such as San Ignacio are now famous for encounters with gray cows and calves. A winter trip around the Baja Peninsula with stops in San Ignacio Lagoon, Magdalena Bay, and the Sea of Cortez affords your best chance for seeing the widest variety of whales (up to 10 different species, including the famous blue whale, the largest creature on earth) on one trip.

This is not the average spectator sport. It's more like a seagoing game of hide-and-seek. Whales are unpredictable, so be prepared to wait and watch patiently, scanning the water for signs. You may see what looks like rain spattering on the water; this is a sign that herring are surfacing—and whales are sure to follow. Sometimes it seems the whales don't want to be watched; other times they might rub up against the boat. Also unpredictable are the weather and sea conditions. You can get wet and chilled (it's often 20 degrees colder on the water than onshore), and some people get seasick.

On most whale-watching cruises, you focus on observing aquatic mammals and, sometimes, other wildlife, but you don't spend every waking hour in pursuit of them. Your day is usually divided between active whale-watching or whale-seeking and shore excursions, snorkeling, swimming, and just lolling about. On some cruises, talks are given covering the history and culture of the ports of call along the route.

Whales are warm-blooded, air-breathing mammals that, along with dolphins and porpoises, belong to the order Cetacea, which is divided into two suborders, Mysticeti (baleen) and Odontoceti (toothed). Baleen whales, including blue, gray, humpback, minke, and right whales, are grazers, seining krill through the fringed, comblike plates that hang from their upper jaw. Toothed whales, including beaked, beluga, orca, and sperm whales, are predatory, catching fish, squid, and other marine creatures in their teeth.

Whale-watching cruises grew out of concern for the whales' welfare. By the early 20th century, many species had been hunted nearly to extinction, and by mid-century, pollution was seen as a threat to all whales. In the 1960s, people concerned with humankind's effect on the environment used the plight of whales as a symbol of their cause, and the condition of whales became a bellwether for the condition of the planet. The interest in whales quickly grew, and by the late 1970s, whale-watching had become a booming tourist industry. Today people pay from $100 to $500 a day to cruise the waters looking for whales.

CHOOSING THE RIGHT CRUISE

Each whale-watching cruise is different. The following questions will help to determine if a given cruise is right for you.

Which or how many species are seen on this trip? Most cruises travel in or through waters that attract several species, although some focus on a particular whale, with any other species you come across considered a bonus.

When is the best time to take this trip? What is the record for spotting whales on this trip? Some trips are run several times over a period of months, but if you ask, you may find out that the sighting record is better in one or two of those months.

What are the conditions of the sea? Some waters are nearly always calm and others are always choppy; some waters change from season to season. If you tend to get seasick, the condition of the sea is a major point to consider when deciding which cruise to take.

What kind of boat is used and how many passengers does it carry? You have to weigh the pros and cons of traveling on small sailboats versus large or giant motor-powered vessels, but make sure you know what kind of boat is used for the trip you are considering. It's commonplace for outfitters to charter different boats for various trips, so even if you know the outfitter, be sure to ask about the boat. Also, the size of the boat alone doesn't mean much until you know how many passengers it carries. Because each boat is arranged and outfitted uniquely, it is difficult to give an ideal ratio of passengers to boat length, but a trip with 15 people is certain to be quite different from one with 150.

Is the cruise round-trip? Some cruises start and end at the same port, but just as many are one-way only, leaving you to get home from the final stop. This can add substantially to the cost of your trip, because you may have to fly out of a different airport or travel long distances to return to the one at which you originally arrived.

What ports of call are visited? Some trips make many stops, while others hardly stop at all. If you are interested in touring Alaskan towns, for instance, pick a cruise that makes a few stops. If you prefer cruising to walking, choose a trip that stays at sea.

How long has the company been in business and how long has it been offering this particular trip? Companies learn from experience. One that has been running trips for a few years probably knows how to handle problems and make a trip run smoothly better than a new enterprise would.

What are the trip leaders' qualifications? Try to find a trip led by a marine biologist or natural historian with an expertise in cetaceans. On the better trips, this person also has knowledge of the area's other wildlife as well as its vegetation and geology and will pass it on to you.

What sort of commentary is provided? Some trips are intense short courses in all things cetacean. Virtually everything that happens is narrated, and much of your time is spent being educated about what you will see or have just seen. Other trips are less formal, and you receive information only on whale behavior that you see.

What shore excursions are available and is there an additional fee for these? You may find that the shore excursions are an equally interesting part of the cruise you pick, but the added cost can put the cruise out of your price bracket.

What's the cost and what's included? Prices of whale-watching cruises vary considerably, depending on the type of ship, the number of days, and the destination. The best way to compare prices of cruises is to figure out the cost per day. Unless otherwise stated, prices quoted in this chapter are per person and include lodging on board (in shared bunk rooms on smaller ships and in double cabins on cruise liners) as well as three meals a day while at sea. Transportation to the boat, port charges, and shore excursions are not included, unless stated otherwise.

What are the accommodations like? On smaller ships you must sleep in bunk rooms with other participants and share a bathroom. On cruise liners you may pay for a single cabin with a private bath. Between these two extremes, there is a variety of sleeping arrangements.

Is laundry service available? Generally, only the largest ships have laundry facilities, but always ask. Also find out if there's a laundromat at one of the ports and whether or not you'll have the time to use it. If you can wash your clothes, you can bring far fewer of them. Except for the full-size cruise ships, no boat in this chapter has laundry service. Get the lowdown on likely weather conditions and pack accordingly.

What is the food like? This will depend upon the individual boat—and its cook. Some outfitters have established reputations for serving good to excellent meals on board. Also find out if meals are served at preset seatings with tables assigned or if you can sit where you choose. Assigned seating is great for making friends (you eat with the same people every day) but can be difficult to deal with if you and your tablemates aren't a good match.

How far in advance do I need to book? Most cruise operators ask that you sign up at least a couple of months in advance—some advise even earlier—but all sell passage until the departure date if space remains available.

Do you have references from past guests? It always helps to talk with someone who has taken the trip.

MAJOR PLAYERS

AMERICAN CETACEAN SOCIETY Created in 1967, this nonprofit group is the oldest whale protection organization in the world. Through whale-watching trips, which are usually led by someone with an advanced marine science degree, the society hopes to foster interest in cetacean conservation and research. Its whale-watching cruises were started in 1973 and now travel to Alaska, British Columbia, Baja, and the Canadian High Arctic. Different vessels are chartered in each area, so accommodations vary. Cooks make use of the best local produce to serve meals of many cuisines. Fresh fruits are available, and the homemade desserts always gain high praise on trip evaluations. Cruises last from 7 to 11 days and cost between $1,575 and $2,425 for ACS members; nonmembers either add 10% of the trip price or join ACS at $35 for a single membership, $45 per family. All ages are welcome, but there are no special programs for children. *Box 1391, San Pedro, CA 90733-1391, tel. 310/548–6279, fax 310/ 548–6950.*

NATURAL HABITAT ADVENTURES Created in 1983, this travel company merged with Biological Journeys in 1995, a well-established nature tour operator that offered whale-watching trips in Baja California as well as other international destinations for 15 years. As part of its expansion program, in late 1996 Natural Habitats opened a sister company, Planet Expeditions (tel. 800/ 233–2433), which offers camping trips on the shore of the San Ignacio Lagoon for close-up whale encounters. Planet Expeditions trips are more active, less expensive, and a bit less luxurious than those of Natural Habitats. They also tend to attract younger travelers and employ local guides, as opposed to academic professionals and experts.

Leaders of Natural Habitats tours may be scientists, teachers, or another type of professional, but all are experts in particular subjects or the places visited. Natural Habitats Baja cruise expeditions are aboard the 95-foot *Searcher,* a trawler refitted for natural history cruises. In other regions, different ships are chartered. *Searcher* sleeps about 30 passengers in 16 cabins, all of which have small bunks, reading lights, and limited storage space. There are four shared bathrooms and two hot showers; a comfortable, windowed lounge equipped with a library, VCR, and slide projector; and a pilothouse. Meals are a mix of California and Continental cuisines and include homemade breads, soups, and plenty of fresh fruit and fish. Sightings are announced over the public-address system, and video cameras and a hydrophone capture the sights and sounds of the day. The Baja cruise is 10 days and costs $2,895. Children are welcome. *2945 Center Green Ct. S, Unit H, Boulder, CO 80301, tel. 303/449–3711 or 800/543–8917, fax 303/449–3712.*

FAVORITE CRUISES

THE NORTHEAST

CANADA, MAINE, AND MASSACHUSETTS **From Prince Edward Island to Boston.** This 15-day late-summer cruise in the Canadian Maritimes and along the coast of Maine is reliable for sighting minke, finback, and humpback whales. The 207-foot motor yacht *Nantucket Clipper,* which carries 100 passengers, spends several days in the Bay of Fundy and cruises along the forested coastlines of New Brunswick, Nova Scotia, and Maine. It also allows a full day at Jeffreys Ledge, off the coast of Massachusetts, where sightings this time of year are virtually guaranteed.

Whales are the primary focus of this Clipper Cruise Line itinerary, but the trip takes in the culture and history of the region, too. A historian briefs you on the ports of call, which include Charlottetown, Prince Edward Island (port of embarkation), Halifax, Nova Scotia, and Boston (port of disembarkation). Optional city tours are available in each port. You can also choose to hike with the ship's naturalist through the bogs of Campobello Island, in New Brunswick, and on Mount Desert Island, part of Maine's Acadia National Park.

The *Nantucket Clipper* has staterooms of various sizes (priced accordingly), but all are narrow and have low beds and private bathrooms. Passengers gather for socializing and evening lectures in the spacious forward lounges. Meals, prepared by chefs trained at the Culinary Institute of America, are served in single open seatings. Regional specialties are highlighted, and most entrée selections are cooked to order. *Clipper Cruise Line, 7711 Bonhomme Ave.,*

St. Louis, MO 63105, tel. 314/727–2929 or 800/325–0010. Late Aug.–early Sept.: 15 days, $3,800–$5,600. Sign up 6 months in advance.

MASSACHUSETTS **Sailing a Tall Ship.** Dirigo Cruises is the only New England operator that offers multiple-day whale-watching cruises out of Boston. Aboard the two-masted 95-foot schooner *Harvey Gamage,* the six-day trips with up to 26 passengers combine whale-watching, New England history, and the opportunity to sail on a tall ship and pick up such seaman's skills as rigging, hoisting, knot tying, and splicing.

Although the itinerary may change with the wind, the tide, and the most recent sightings, the typical cruise spends up to three days at Stellwagen Bank observing groups of feeding humpback, finback, and minke whales, as well as other marine life and seabirds. Your other days are filled with cruising between historic coastal towns such as Salem, Provincetown, and Gloucester. On most trips, you're in port every night but one, so there is time to go ashore and explore. A marine biologist presents daily lectures, videos, and slide shows on the wildlife found around Massachusetts Bay. The ship returns to port in Boston.

The mainmast of the *Harvey Gamage* towers 91 feet above the water. This beautiful wooden schooner, built in 1973, is equipped with a main saloon, a galley, shared heads, and tight bunk rooms (doubles, triples, and one quad) with washbasins. You can sleep under the stars above deck if you like (bring your own sleeping bag), and the leaders try to arrange one night out at Stellwagen Bank so that, weather and moon permitting, you can see whales at night. The showers on board are cold freshwater, but hot showers are available at the marinas of most ports. Hearty meals consisting of a variety of meats, seafood, and fresh produce are served family style in the main saloon. On fair weather days, you might have buffet-style meals on deck or even a shoreside picnic. Children of all ages are permitted, but small tots don't always fare well on a six-day cruise. *Dirigo Cruises, 39 Waterside La., Clinton, CT 06413, tel. and fax 860/ 669–7068. Aug.: 6 days, $795. Sign up 3–4 months in advance.*

THE WEST COAST

CALIFORNIA **Monterey Bay's Marine World.** This trip differs from the others in this chapter in that most of your time is spent on land. Shearwater Journeys, founded in 1978 by Debra Shearwater, offers a weeklong, land-based trip for up to 14 participants. From sunrise to sunset, you learn about the rich ecosystem of Monterey Bay, especially about the whales.

The week begins with a tour of the Monterey Bay Aquarium's various exhibits—Debra used to be a tour guide there. You spend five or six days looking for whales and other marine life from the Monterey Peninsula's Point Lobos State Park, Point Piños, and Año Nuevo (a breeding ground for elephant seals). For the last two days, you ply the waters on a 60-foot motor-powered vessel during the day. You travel past Cannery Row to Point Piños, at the southern edge of the bay. Because it juts out into the migration track of the gray whale, this point is a top spot for viewing, both from land and sea. During the whales' peak traveling time in January, it's not unusual to scan the horizon and count 50 to 100 passing whales each day. You may also see shoals of dolphins that frequently escort the migrating whales.

It is easy to get caught up in Debra's enthusiasm, not only for cetaceans but for all of the marine and avian life inhabiting the bay. Bring along a camera and take plenty of shots—your photos can help researchers track and identify the migrating grays and various orcas, northern right whales, Dall porpoises, and Risso's dolphins that come into Monterey Bay. You might even get the chance to assist in hydrophone recordings of dolphin communication.

Evenings are dedicated to learning from local experts, who present slide shows and videos. Afterward you retire to your room at a small motel in Pacific Grove, within easy walking distance of the rocky shoreline of Point Piños. Family-style breakfasts are eaten at the motel; sack lunches, in the field; and dinner, in local restaurants. Van transportation between sites is provided. Children over 12 are welcome. *Shearwater Journeys, Box 190, Hollister, CA 95024, tel. 408/637–8527. Jan.–Feb. and Aug.–Oct.: 8 or 9 days, $1,600–$1,800. Sign up at least 3 months in advance.*

CALIFORNIA TO BAJA **Baja and the Sea of Cortez.** The first portion of this 11-day American Cetacean Society cruise is much like any other trip along Baja's Pacific coast, with stops on several islands and a few days at San Ignacio Lagoon, where curious mother whales and their calves often approach boats. But rather than double back to San Diego from there, this cruise continues 150 miles south to Magdalena Bay, where gray whales calve. It then takes you another 150 miles to the southern tip of Baja, rounds it, and heads north into the Sea of Cortez (also known as the Gulf of California), where warmer, calmer waters offer refuge to whales, dolphins, manta rays, whale sharks, and hundreds of species of tropical fish.

This trip has been run in various forms since 1973, and past participants have spotted as many as 10 different cetacean species, including several of the larger whales (finback, blue, sperm, gray, Byrde's, pilot, and humpback).

Each morning you have free time to snorkel among brilliantly colored parrot fish, damselfish, and rainbow wrasses, or to hike throughout the numerous island sanctuaries for a look at frigate birds, blue-footed boobies, royal terns, and other tropical seabirds. Afternoons are usually spent whale-watching as you sail toward the evening's anchorage.

The trip is aboard the 95-foot cabin cruiser *Searcher.* Thirty-odd passengers stay in 16 cabins, each with two to four bunks and a sink. There are also four shared heads, two hot freshwater showers, a library, and a galley where meals are served family style. Slide lectures about whales and other wildlife and a preview of the next day's activities are presented each evening. Children as young as eight have been on this trip, but there are no special activities or facilities for them. This is a one-way trip, and you must arrange your own return from the final stop in La Paz, a small city on Baja's gulf coast. *American Cetacean Society, Box 2639, San Pedro, CA 90731-0943, tel. 310/548-6279, fax 310/548-6950. Mid-Mar.: 11 days, $2,425. Sign up 3 months in advance.*

CALIFORNIA TO BAJA Baja Whale Camp. A spin-off of Natural Habitat Adventures, sister-company Planet Expeditions was created in late 1996 to offer active, affordable adventure trips. The tours, less luxurious than those of Natural Habitats, attract younger travelers and the adventurous who are interested in experiencing a place in depth and are unconcerned about fancy amenities.

Planet Expeditions offers five-day camping trips (which Natural Habitats had offered since 1990) on the shore of the San Ignacio Lagoon. Early morning on the first day, you take a bus from San Diego to the Tijuana Airport and fly to San Ignacio, where you board another bus to the camp. On day five you are back in San Diego by late afternoon. In between, you spend three full days in pursuit of the Pacific gray whale, thousands of which annually migrate from the rich feeding grounds of Alaska's Bering Sea to the lagoons of the Baja Peninsula to breed in the warm, calm waters. Skiffs (small six- to eight-passenger motorized boats) take guests searching for whales and afford close-up views of the 50-foot mammals—sometimes close enough to touch! Local guides, skiff drivers and cooks are employed; naturalist leaders may be professionals or students who are knowledgeable about gray whales. Besides skiff trips, other activities include slide shows and guides' natural history presentations, bird-watching, and exploring the surrounding mangrove estuaries by skiff or sea kayak. There is also a library of natural history guidebooks to read through.

The semipermanent camp accommodates 20 guests in walk-in, double-occupancy tents with cots, linens, and pillows. Toilets and freshwater showers are available on-site. Meals are cooked in the kitchen tent and feature fresh fish dishes and stews. *Planet Expeditions, 2945 Center Green Ct., Suite H, Boulder, CO 80301, tel. 800/233-2433, fax 303/349-3712. Late Jan.–late Mar.: 5 days, $1,495. Sign up 4–6 months in advance.*

CALIFORNIA TO BAJA To Baja with the Best. Nearly every whale-watching outfit runs a tour down Baja California's Pacific coast, but no one has been doing it longer than the *Pacific Queen*. Its 10-day whale-watching trip has been led by the same biologist on the same boat with the same captain since 1971. The San Diego Natural History Museum, in conjunction with Palomar College, sponsored the first whale-watching trips to Baja California's San Ignacio Lagoon. It was on these early trips that encounters were first made with the famous "friendly" gray whales, which allow humans to touch them.

Museum marine biologist and second skipper Margie Stinson and another biologist or geologist now lead the trip independently, taking up to 30 passengers aboard the 88-foot *Pacific Queen* on round-trip expeditions out of San Diego to the lagoon, where gray whales come to mate and deliver their young. On the way, you stop to see Baja's desert canyons and the seal rookeries, wildflowers, ospreys, herons, and other wildlife of Todos Santos, West San Benito, Cedors, and San Martin islands. At the lagoon, you board skiffs to get close to the gray whales.

The *Pacific Queen* is a sportfishing motorboat, outfitted with five double and five quad bunk rooms, two hot-water showers, and three heads. The ship's cook whips up amazingly bountiful meals in a postage-stamp galley. The cuisine is a mix of American and Mexican fare, with plenty of fresh seafood. Evenings are filled with slide shows and talks presented by the naturalists. Children are allowed on a case-by-case basis. *Pacific Queen, Fisherman's Landing, 2838 Garrison St., San Diego, CA 92106, tel. 619/726–2228, 619/224–4965, or 619/221–8500, fax 619/222–0799. Jan.–Apr.: 10 days, $1,500. Sign up 3–6 months in advance.*

ALASKA

SOUTHEAST **Killer Whales in Prince William Sound.** Traveling farther north than other trips, along the Alaskan coast to Prince William Sound, Alaska Wilderness Sailing Safaris makes a seven-day run in search of killer and humpback whales. You couldn't hope for more qualified leaders than the company's owners, Drs. Jim and Nancy Lethcoe, two naturalists who have written volumes about the glaciers, geology, and natural history of the sound and have more than two decades of experience guiding trips in Alaskan waters.

You begin your journey either in Valdez, taking the 9:30 AM tour boat ($94 round-trip), or in Whittier, taking the 2:15 PM boat ($108 round-trip), traveling to the Growler Island Wilderness Camp. The four-hour boat rides are narrated, and on arrival you are treated to an all-you-can-eat cookout with salmon, chicken, ribs, and vegetarian preparations. From the camp, the Lethcoes lead groups of three or four in search of the killer whales that reside in the sound and the humpbacks that feed here each summer. Finback and minke whales are also spotted in the area from time to time, and you can usually count on seeing porpoises, sea lions, harbor seals, sea otters, puffins, and bald eagles.

To locate the best sighting areas each day, the Lethcoes keep in contact with a network of other scientists studying this virtually undisturbed 10,000-square-mile wilderness area. Besides watching the whales and other wildlife, you visit Columbia and Meare's glaciers, go kayaking for a closer look at the shoreline, and hike in the Chugach National Forest.

The Lethcoes operate the 40-foot *Arctic Tern III*, a Nordic 40 sailboat. The boat has compact but comfortable quarters and carries four to six passengers. Bunk rooms are tiny and heads are shared, but the boat has a full galley. Healthy menus emphasize fresh fruits and vegetables, and special menus are available on request. There is a small library of books on the history, ecology, and geology of Prince William Sound, as well as a dinghy and inflatable kayaks for guest use. Families are welcome. *Alaska Wilderness Sailing Safaris, Box 1313, Valdez, AK 99686, tel. 907/835–5175, fax 907/835–3765. Late Apr.–mid-Sept.: 6 days, $1,560. Sign up at least 1–2 months in advance.*

SOUTHEAST **Sailing with Humpbacks into Frederick Sound.** Famous for its glaciers, its spectacular scenery, its abundant wildlife, and, of course, its whales, southeast Alaska's waterways are prime feeding grounds for humpbacks. Enter the *Island Roamer*, a 68-foot sailing yacht that carries a dozen people on 11-day cruises along the coastal waterways.

You gather in Prince Rupert, British Columbia, for orientation and take a floatplane (about $225) to the boat's anchorage in Petersburg (the trip is also done in reverse, where you sail from Prince Rupert and take the floatplane back from Petersburg). The itinerary is flexible, but you are sure to spend at least five days in Frederick Sound, the stomping ground of minke whales and Dall porpoises and the summer home of several hundred humpbacks. Although cetaceans are the focus on this trip, other wildlife is discussed in detail when it's encountered, as are the glaciers along the route. Small inflatable boats are used to take you ashore for hiking.

The crew of four has several years of practical field experience, along with backgrounds in marine biology, ecology, ornithology, and anthropology. Accommodations are in cabins with two berths each. You share the three heads, which have hot showers. Meals are prepared using local seafood and produce, and wine is served with dinner. Evening discussions and slide shows focus on marine mammals of the North Pacific, and there is an extensive library on board. The trip also includes a stop in Ketchikan, where, depending on the time available, you can explore the town and the area's totem poles. This tour is quite popular and often sells out far in advance. Children are permitted. *Bluewater Adventures, 3-252 E. 1st St., N. Vancouver, BC V7L 1B3, Canada, tel. 604/980–3800, fax 604/980–1800. Mid-June–July: 11 days, $2,400. Sign up at least 3–6 months in advance.*

HAWAII

OAHU, KAUAI, MAUI, AND THE BIG ISLAND

Saving the Humpbacks. American Hawaii Cruises' seven-day whale-watching sail is about as far from roughing it as you can get on any whale-watching trip. But who says learning is synonymous with deprivation! Marine researchers and naturalists from the Pacific Whale Foundation, the oldest and largest marine research and conservation group on Maui, accompany the whale-watching cruises aboard the luxury liner SS *Independence.* The naturalists—at least one and sometimes two—guide the week's whale-watching and offer several onboard programs: a two-hour slide presentation on the marine mammals of Hawaii's waters; a lecture exploring conservation issues, specifically looking at the humpback (on the endangered species list) and the monk seal; and a mini onboard museum displaying samples of whale baleen, lice, and barnacles, as well as informational brochures. Passengers are encouraged to ask questions about Hawaii's unique marine environment. If time permits while in port, you can also book one of six Eco-adventure shore excursions offered by the Founda-

tion, such as guided snorkeling and sailing trips.

Humpbacks are the stars of this trip. However, unlike past cruises, this itinerary no longer includes a full day at sea off the shores of Maui, the best whale breaching area in the Hawaiian islands. Whale viewing opportunities are limited to a full day at sea en route to Kauai and late afternoons at sea when leaving the ports of Kauai and Maui. From deck, you can often see the humpbacks near Kauai and the Big Island, although they are usually far from the ship. Ports of call are Kona and Hilo on the Big Island, Kahului on Maui, and Nawiliwili on Kauai.

Fine dining is part of any luxury cruise experience, and this trip is no exception. In 1993 the cruise line began offering traditional Hawaiian specialties made with fresh local ingredients from each island. At the beginning of the week, you are assigned to a table at one of two evening seatings, and you continue to dine with the same people all week. As the ship spends the rest of the year doing traditional cruises, it is equipped with an abundance of facilities: lounges and bars, saunas, massage rooms, and a movie theater, fitness center, shopping arcade, sports deck, pool, and game room. Kids under age 18 sail free year-round.

Cabins come in a variety of sizes—with prices to match. The *Independence* has a crew of more than 300 and can carry nearly 800 passengers, but even when full it doesn't seem crowded. *American Hawaii Cruises, 2 North Riverside Plaza, Chicago, IL 60606, tel. 312/466–6000, fax 312/466–6001. Jan.–Mar.: 7 days, $1,145–$3,195. Sign up 6–12 months in advance.*

SOURCES

ORGANIZATIONS All of the following are involved in cetacean research and education and can be contacted for more information on whale-watching (including day trips) in North America: **Allied Whale** (College of the Atlantic, 105 Eden St., Bar Harbor, ME 04609, tel. 207/288–5644, fax 207/288–4126); **American Cetacean Society** (Box 1391, San Pedro, CA 90733-1391, tel. 310/548–6279, fax 310/548–6950); **Center for Oceanic Research and Education (CORE)** (75 Essex Ave., Gloucester, MA 01930, tel. 508/283–0313 or 800/942–5464, fax 508/283–6089); **Center for Whale Research** (Box 1577, Friday Harbor, WA 98250, tel. 360/378–5835); **West Coast Whale Research Foundation** (1200–925 W. Georgia St., Vancouver, BC V6C 3L2, Canada, tel. 604/731–2166).

PERIODICALS "Spirit of the Sound" (Box 945, Friday Harbor, WA 98250, tel. 360/378–4710), a quarterly newsletter published by the Whale Museum, covers issues affecting marine mammals.

BOOKS The *Oceanic Society Field Guide to the Gray Whale* (Sasquatch Books) profiles the migration cycles and behavior of gray whales and lists prime viewing areas from Alaska to Baja California. The *Sierra Club Handbook of Whales and Dolphins,* by Stephen Leatherwood, Randall Reeves, and Larry Foster, is a useful reference to what you'll see in the wild, with photos, illustrations, and descriptions of various cetaceans. *Where the Whales Are,* by Patricia Corrigan, describes several species and lists North American whale-watch tour operators.

ALSO SEE If you enjoy studying nature from the decks of a boat, turn to the Cultural and Natural History Cruises chapter, or if you'd prefer seeing wildlife on its own turf, look at the Birding and Nature Camps chapters.

Writing Conferences and Workshops

Written and updated by David Low

hether you're an aspiring poet, a published novelist, or a born raconteur who wants to get your stories down on paper, you may find a writers' conference or workshop a good way to learn more about the process of writing or to make contacts in the publishing world. Conferences and workshops also provide writers with the chance to meet others with similar concerns, anxieties, and struggles. And if you've started to wonder if writing is worth pursuing as a profession, as an avocation, or even at all, attending a conference may help clarify what role it will play in your future.

Most of the conferences contained in this chapter offer daily workshops in a few areas of writing, along with lectures on the writing craft and readings by faculty and participants. Some also feature panels or talks with editors, literary agents, publishers, and other professionals from the business side of publishing. Frequently, when a program concentrates more on the technical and creative aspects of writing rather than on the business side of publishing, the term *workshop,* rather than *conference,* is used in the name of the program.

Workshops usually engage instructors and students in discussions of participants' work, although some also provide writing exercises or talks relating to technique. At many conferences, you bring works in progress, in hopes of getting feedback and suggestions for revisions from instructors and peers. Panel discussions often address such practical matters as how to write a book proposal or how to get a literary agent. And there are programs that welcome beginners and offer classes on the basics of writing.

Most writing conferences focus on poetry and general fiction, but several also include courses in nonfiction, essay writing, or particular genres of fiction, such as mysteries, science fiction, and romance novels. Other gatherings concentrate on particular topics, such as women's issues, or on types of writing, such as children's books and nature writing.

Workshops and conferences attract a diverse group in terms of age, race, profession, and level of experience. Some accept you on the basis of a writing sample, while others are simply first come, first served. There are workshops for everyone from beginners looking for guidance to those looking to turn pro to pros who want to refine or expand their repertoire. Nearly every program in this chapter has faculty who are published writers with teaching credentials; occasionally, instructors also include editors, literary agents, or journalists.

Although conferences can provide useful feedback and encouragement about your writing, there may be negative aspects to these gatherings as well. Like many artists,

---

David Low, a published fiction writer and book editor, has attended several writing conferences.

writers can be an eccentric, unpredictable, competitive, and even fairly insensitive bunch. Along with the objective commentary and helpful advice, you may well hear criticism that is not constructive and seems off-the-wall or even hurtful. There is no way to predict people's reactions, and that is part of exposing your work to the public. Many of the teachers at these conferences are adept at clearly pointing out the strengths and weaknesses of a manuscript while remaining supportive. Published writers, especially those who have achieved some fame, don't always make the best teachers of writing because they're so used to having their own egos massaged. There are even some who believe—mistakenly—that giving tough, mean-spirited evaluations of student work means that they're being honest. That old rule applies here: Being good at doing something doesn't necessarily translate into being good at teaching it. Most program directors, however, make a point of hiring writers with good reputations as teachers. You may even get lucky and get one who understands your work in a way that no one ever has before.

If you choose a program that focuses on the business of being a writer, don't expect to get your manuscript read and published then and there. Generally, guest speakers from the publishing world don't spend much time with individual participants; that's not what they've been paid to do. It is generally bad form to force a manuscript on an editor or agent in this context. Concentrate instead on making business contacts that could prove valuable later on.

Many conferences and workshops meet on college campuses, where participants stay in dormitories and eat at central dining halls. That may mean merely adequate accommodations and unexciting cafeteria food, but in general the college settings provide pleasant, tranquil environments. Most college towns do tend to have a variety of good—or at least interesting—restaurants, and some lodgings include kitchen facilities, allowing you to prepare your own meals.

A number of conferences take place in more dramatic or festive surroundings—a mountain retreat, a remote wilderness, a seaside resort, or the heart of a big city. Accommodations may be in hotels near the ocean or ski lodges amid spectacular scenery. Some of these conferences also pay special attention to food, hiring their own cooks to prepare sophisticated meals.

This chapter's programs vary in cost from less than $500 to more than $2,000, depending largely upon whether lodging and meals are part of the package, but taking into account the reputation and location of the program as well. Conferences at colleges tend to be less expensive, unless you wish to receive undergraduate or graduate credit. The cost of those held elsewhere tends to increase when you consider accommodations and meals that are not included in the price.

CHOOSING THE RIGHT PROGRAM

First decide what type of instruction would most benefit your work—a workshop that concentrates on the craft of writing and will help you improve a manuscript, or a conference that emphasizes the nuts and bolts of getting published—then ask the organizers the following questions.

What are the requirements for acceptance? Conference requirements vary. Some programs accept all applicants; these are usually open to anyone interested in writing. Others require that you submit a writing sample with the application; these tend to attract writers who have passed the beginner's stage.

How many students attend and how big are the classes? The number of participants at a program, and the number in any given seminar or workshop within it, varies wildly. Generally speaking, the lower the student-to-teacher ratio the better, especially if you want your writing to get personal attention. On the other hand, an inspiring lecture is no less so if given before a large crowd.

How much time is spent in workshops versus lectures? If you're attending a conference to get a response to your work and advice on revisions, choose a program that allows more time for discussions of students' writing than for lectures.

How much of the day is spent in class and is there time to write and relax? Most workshop sessions last 2½ to 3 hours (some go on longer) and are given in either the morning or afternoon. That leaves the other part of the day alternately free, filled with lectures and panel discussions, or open for taking another workshop on a different topic. If your chosen workshop spends classroom time on critiquing and editing, find out if you'll have time to write during the conference or if you're meant to arrive at the program with material to revise.

Are there organized nonworkshop activities? Most conferences schedule after-class activities of some sort, including readings by instructors and panel discussions, but these events are often optional. If you're attending a conference to improve your writing, it's wise to choose one that allows time to absorb what you've learned in class, and has less socializing.

How long has the workshop or conference been operating? Although newer programs may be perfectly fine, one that's been around for a few years will probably have dealt with and even be able to anticipate just about any situation or questions that may arise.

Who will be on staff when you want to go? Staff members should be described in the conference brochure, but don't count on past instructors being there when you go. When you know exactly who will be teaching, try to read some of their work. If you like a writer's work, chances are he or she will have something valuable to pass on to you about writing.

Are private conferences with faculty scheduled and can you choose which faculty member you'd like to meet with? Many programs include one private conference with a faculty member as part of the fee, some charge extra for private consultations, and only a very few allow for additional private meetings. You generally have your private meeting with your workshop leader.

Are faculty accessible to students at all times or only in classes? Although some teachers are open to meeting outside of class, don't assume that this is part of the program. It's rare that a faculty member is available to students every minute during the conference.

Are there workstations available? If you're planning to write while at a conference, find out if there is space available to do so. Some conferences provide rooms with a writing desk, and a few even have typewriters and computers available. For the most part, however, you should expect to supply your own writing equipment.

What's the cost and what's included? Many conferences include tuition, meals, and lodging in one price, others offer a meal and/or lodging package at additional cost, and some expect you to take care of your own lodging and meals. Unless otherwise noted, prices in this chapter include tuition, double occupancy lodging, and meals. Some programs also charge a $30 to $50 application fee or a reading fee, ranging from $10 to $60, for manuscript evaluations or personal conferences.

Are scholarships available? Some programs offer financial aid or fellowships based on the quality of your work. Applicants for aid must usually apply far in advance of the regular deadline, and some scholarships require recommendations.

What are the accommodations like? Many conferences are at colleges, where you stay in dormitories; others are at hotels or resorts with fancier digs. Most college dorm lodgings have both single and double rooms, with single rooms usually costing a bit more. At hotels and resorts you most often share accommodations with another workshop participant, but if you are determined to have a room of your own and are willing to pay the extra money for it, chances are no one will stop you.

What is the food like? You might be served standard cafeteria fare, but sometimes a chef is hired to prepare superior meals. The workshop's setting—college campus or resort hotel—will be your first clue as to the caliber of the cuisine.

How far in advance do I need to book? Generally speaking, the sooner the better. Some workshops accept students by the quality of a submitted piece of writing, and that takes some time. Others are on a first-come, first-served basis, and can fill up fast. In either case, however, if there's still room at the last minute, you may get in.

Do you have references from past participants? It's often helpful to talk with people who have attended the conference in the past. They may be able to tell you how much or how little they got out of it. It's best, however, to talk with more than one person, since personality and talent could have a big effect on the writer's experience.

FAVORITE PROGRAMS

THE NORTHEAST

CONNECTICUT **Wesleyan Writers Conference.** Nonfiction workshops distinguish this six-day conference from those that concentrate only on poetry and fiction. The annual event has been held at the Wesleyan campus since 1956. Seminars, readings, and manuscript consultations give you the opportunity to work closely with the conference's distinguished faculty and participants as you gain new perspectives on your own work.

You can choose among daily seminars in fiction, poetry, and nonfiction; most people attend one to two seminars in a particular genre regularly and sample the others. Typical morning and early afternoon meetings deal with the novel, the short story, fiction techniques, poetry, screen writing, literary journalism, and the memoir. A faculty of nationally known writers lead the seminars. You may also register for a manuscript consultation with a staff member.

During the late afternoon and evening, you may attend workshops, student and faculty readings, guest lectures and talks by writers, and sessions with editors, agents, and publishers. The keynote lecture features a writer of national reputation; Joyce Carol Oates, David Halberstam, Donald Justice, and Robert Stone have spoken in the past.

Writers of all levels of experience, ages, and backgrounds are welcome, and about 100 people attend each year. Scholarships and teaching fellowships are awarded on the basis of work submitted; otherwise acceptance is on a first-come, first-served basis.

You stay in campus dormitories in single rooms with shared bath, and meals are provided. You also have access to the university's athletic center with tennis courts and a swimming pool, and Olin Library, with its outstanding poetry collection. Wesleyan University is in Middletown, Connecticut, 30 minutes from Hartford and New Haven and two hours from either Boston or New York City. *Wesleyan Writers Conference, Anne Greene, Director, Wesleyan University, Middletown, CT 06459, tel. 860/685–3604, fax 860/685–2441. Late June: 6 days, $740. Price includes single room; sign up anytime, but scholarship and fellowship application deadline is 3rd Fri. in Apr.*

MAINE **The International Film & Television Workshops.** Established in 1973, this program comprises more than 200 workshops in all aspects of filmmaking and photography, including a half dozen 7- and 14-day writing courses for first-time screenwriters as well as published writers who want to refine their work in the company of their peers and under the guidance of a professional writer. Workshop leaders are respected Hollywood screenwriters, and recent classes have included Script and Story Structure, Creating the Film Character, Writing for Television, Screenwriter's Master Class, and Writing Television Documentaries.

Each workshop is limited to 15 writers, but enrollment is generally around 10. To be admitted to most classes you must submit a writing sample and résumé and have the specified amount of professional experience. The workshops begin at 9 AM and you stay busy with lectures, critiques, discussions, and screenings all morning. Afternoons are devoted to writing and one-on-one consultations with instructors. You spend evenings in screenings or writing your assignment for the following day.

This program is based on a 20-acre campus in the small, tranquil New England village of Rockport, on Penobscot Bay, 90 miles north of Portland and 2 miles from the lively resort town of Camden. If you opt for the lodging plan, you have a choice of accommodations in Rockport, from standard motel rooms to lodging in period houses; singles, doubles, and dorms are available. You can also arrange lodging for yourself at local motels, bed-and-breakfasts, and inns. Most students take their meals at the Homestead, a 19th-century farmhouse; food is served buffet style and includes lobster on Friday nights. At mealtimes students are able to share ideas with the film, television, and writing professionals attending and teaching classes. *The Workshops, 2 Central St., Rockport, ME 04856, tel. 207/236–8581 or 800/227–1541, fax 207/236–2558. May–Oct.: 7–14 days, $495–$795. Price does not include lodging and meals ($375–$650 per wk); sign up as early as possible.*

MASSACHUSETTS **Cape Cod Writers' Conference.** Run by the Cape Cod Writers' Center, this six-day conference, established in 1963, includes courses and lectures on the craft of writing and the path to publication. Five courses are offered, meeting for 90 minutes a day, Monday through Friday. The lecture courses, which allow for some group discussion, deal with fiction, nonfiction, juvenile writing, poetry, and writing for television and film. Evening lectures cover the writing process and the publishing business. You can schedule conferences and manuscript evaluations with instructors, as well as with the book editor and literary agent who are in residence for the entire program (each personal conference and manuscript evaluation costs extra). Class leaders are published writers and writing teachers.

Attendees number about 150 and have different levels of writing experience; manuscripts may be submitted in advance for evaluation, but this is not required. The program is held at the Craigville Conference Center, near Hyannis. You can choose to stay at the conference center, which has a dining room that serves three meals a day (included in the daily rate), or at one of the numerous local bed-and-breakfasts. *Cape Literary Workshops/Cape Cod Writers' Center, Arlene Joffe Pollack, Executive Director, c/o Cape Cod Conservatory of Music and Arts, Rte. 132, West Barnstable, MA 02668, tel. 508/375–0516, fax 508/362–7459. Mid-Aug.: 6 days, $85 per course. Price does not include lodging (about $70 per night at nearby inns) or meals; sign up anytime.*

MASSACHUSETTS **Cape Literary Workshops.** This six-day program provides practical discussion on how manuscripts may be revised for publication. It is composed of four-hour morning workshops on the novel, poetry, children's book writing, biography, nonfiction, and screenplay writing. The event has been offered since 1986 by the Cape Cod Writers' Center, which also sponsors the Cape Cod Writers' Conference (*see above*).

A Sunday evening orientation session begins the program. Workshops meet mornings Monday through Friday; in the afternoon you are free to write or explore the area. Enrollment for each workshop is limited to 10 participants. Faculty members are published writers with experience in conducting workshops. You are encouraged, but not required, to send some of your current work in advance.

Workshops meet at Our Lady of the Cape Catholic Church Parish Center in West Brewster. You arrange for your accommodations at nearby bed-and-breakfasts or motels and dine in area restaurants. *Cape Literary Workshops/Cape Cod Writers' Center, Arlene Joffe Pollack, Executive Director, c/o Cape Cod Conservatory of Music and Arts, Rte. 132, West Barnstable, MA 02668, tel. 508/375–0516, fax 508/362–7459. Mid-Aug.: 6 days, $325. Price does not include lodging or meals; sign up anytime.*

MASSACHUSETTS **New England Writers' Workshop.** Both the writing craft and the business of publishing are covered in this intensive five-day program geared to novelists and short-story writers. Each workshop leader meets with up to 15 participants to discuss and evaluate student writing in the morning. During the afternoon, guest authors, editors, and agents speak about their professions and answer questions. You schedule one manuscript consultation with your instructor.

The faculty are established authors and college-level writing teachers. Recent staff members have included C. Michael Curtis, conference director and senior editor at the *Atlantic,* and the novelists and short-story writers Jill McCorkle, Elinor Lipman, and Elizabeth Cox. Guest speakers have included novelists John Updike, Stephen King, and Tim O'Brien; Faith Sale, senior editor at Putnam; Charles Everitt, publisher, Globe Pequot Press; and literary agents from New York. Approximately 40 students attend, most of whom have been writing for a few years. The conference is small enough to allow all questions at lectures to be answered and for staff members to get to know the participants personally.

The workshop takes place at Simmons College in Boston, in the Fenway neighborhood, near the Museum of Fine Arts, Symphony Hall, and the Isabella Stewart Gardner Museum. You can choose to stay in a room at the college residence hall or opt to arrange your own lodging elsewhere. Meals are available at the campus cafeteria or at the Longwood Galleria, a restaurant complex only a five-minute walk from campus. There are no scheduled evening activities. *New England Writers' Workshop,*

Simmons College, Jean Chaput Welch, Assistant Director, 300 The Fenway, Boston, MA 02115, tel. 617/521–2090, fax 617/521–3199. Mid-June: 5 days, $675 with lodging ($525 without lodging). Price does not include meals; sign up at least a wk in advance.

NEW HAMPSHIRE **The Frost Place Annual Festival of Poetry.** This weeklong gathering of poets, established in 1979, takes place at Robert Frost's old farmhouse on a ridge overlooking the White Mountains of northern New Hampshire. The guest faculty consists of six nationally known poets, and each of them presides over one day of the festival. In the past, Maxine Kumin, Brad Leithauser, Charles Simic, and the late Amy Clampitt have participated. Mornings are devoted to lectures. You may attend two guest faculty afternoon workshops; during one of these, you receive a critique of your work. On other afternoons, you take part in critique workshops with each of the four resident faculty, all of whom work closely with students during the week.

The festival creates an informal, friendly environment with small workshops of six to eight participants; guest faculty classes have an additional six to eight auditors, who do not have their work critiqued. Readings by faculty and students are scheduled in the evenings.

You must submit three pages of poetry to be considered for admission; about 120 people apply each year and about 45 are accepted. Attendees are usually in their thirties and have often been writing for several years.

The Frost Place can offer suggestions about where to stay in the area, including guest houses and inns that cost from $20 to $45 a night. Keep in mind that this area is a popular vacation spot in summer, so you must book far in advance. Also in the vicinity are bed-and-breakfasts and accommodations with kitchens. The festival arranges six catered lunches at a special rate. *The Frost Place Annual Festival of Poetry, Donald Sheehan, Executive Director, Ridge Rd., Franconia, NH 03580, tel. 603/823–5510.*

Late July–early Aug.: 7 days, $385–$400. Price does not include lodging or meals; sign up between early Jan. and mid-June.

NEW YORK **Feminist Women's Writing Workshops.** Since 1974 these weeklong workshops have provided a supportive environment for beginning and experienced women writers of all ages and backgrounds. The weekday schedule consists of small group critiques and writing sessions, workshops, evening readings, and talks. You may work in one or more genres, including poetry, fiction, personal essay, autobiography, drama, and journal writing.

The faculty here is made up of workshop alumnae who have become published writers, performance artists, and university teachers. The program invites a visiting professional writer to conduct seminars and give a reading. New applicants are asked to submit a writing sample, and the conference encourages writers with all levels of experience to apply. About 40 to 45 women attend each year.

The workshops are held on the pleasant 170-acre campus of William Smith and Hobart Colleges in Geneva, on the shore of Seneca Lake, the largest of central New York's Finger Lakes. The town is equidistant from Syracuse, Rochester, and Ithaca, each about an hour away. You have a private room in campus housing. Lunch and dinner are served at the campus dining hall, and Continental breakfast is delivered to the residences.

Attendees have access to campus facilities, including a pool, a weight room, and tennis courts. Nearby are such sites as the Harriet Tubman House, the Women's Hall of Fame in Seneca Falls, and the Montezuma Wildlife Refuge, known for its great blue herons. *Feminist Women's Writing Workshops, Margo Gumosky and Kit Wainer, Codirectors, Box 6583, Ithaca, NY 14851, no phone. Mid-July: 7 days, $500. Sign up anytime.*

NEW YORK **Hofstra University Summer Writers' Conference.** At this intensive 10-day program, first held in 1972, five to six 2½-hour workshops are scheduled daily; these are conducted by distinguished writers in poetry, nonfiction, fiction, writing for children, playwriting, screenwriting, and such genres as mysteries and science fiction. Students usually attend one or two workshops.

Workshop size varies from 5 to 18 participants. Leaders are established authors who often teach professionally. A half-hour conference for manuscript discussion is scheduled with a faculty member. Free time is given over to writing and readings by guest writers, presentations by faculty, and visits from a publisher, editor, or literary agent. The conference begins with a reception to welcome students and ends with a special banquet featuring a speech by a respected writer; Oscar Hijuelos, Hilda Wolitzer, and Jeffrey Sweet are among past speakers.

Applicants who want to take the program for credit must submit a writing sample no longer than five pages to demonstrate competence in written English, but acceptance is basically first come, first served. Applicants who don't want credit need not submit a writing sample. There are about 30 to 60 participants each year, ranging in age from 19 to 70; some are beginners, while others may have been published in newspapers and literary magazines.

The conference meets at Hofstra University in Hempstead, Long Island, about 25 miles from New York City. Many participants live nearby and commute to the conference. If you come from out of town, you can stay in the residence halls, which are furnished simply and have shared bathrooms. No meal plan is offered, although you may choose to dine at the college cafeteria. *Hofstra University Summer Writers' Conference, Lewis Shena, Codirector, UCCE, 375 Hofstra University, Hempstead, NY 11550-1009, tel. 516/463–4016, fax 516/564–0061. Mid-July: 10 days, $375–$2,200. Price includes only 1 meal; sign up anytime.*

NEW YORK **Manhattanville College Summer Writers' Workshops.** This five-day, noncredit conference offers morning workshops of 15 students in fiction writing, journal writing, children's literature, poetry, creative nonfiction, and the writer's craft, which is designed for beginners. Afternoons feature a special methods class for writing teachers, a tour of *Reader's Digest,* a session with an editor and literary agent, a workshop on magazine writing, a class with a noted author, and readings by faculty members.

The program has workshop leaders who are well-known writers with previous teaching experience; recent faculty members have included Maureen Howard, Philip Lopate, Lore Segal, Robert Cormier, and Phyllis Theroux. Applicants submit a two-page letter indicating their goals and accomplishments. The approximately 80 participants average in their late 20s and early 30s, though people from all ages, professions, and backgrounds are encouraged to apply.

The workshops take place at Manhattanville College, whose suburban campus in Purchase, Westchester County, is located 45 minutes from New York City and five minutes from White Plains and the Connecticut border. Participants reside in single and double rooms in campus dormitories. Meals may be purchased at the campus dining hall and the college food court. Several good restaurants are within walking distance of the campus or a short drive away. *Office of Adult and Special Programs, Ruth Dowd, Dean, Manhattanville College, 2900 Purchase St., Purchase, NY 10577, tel. 914/694–3425, fax 914/694–3488. End of June: 5 days, $560 tuition and 2 lunches; $25–$27.50 per night, lodging. Prices do not include other meals. Application deadline: early June.*

NEW YORK **New York State Summer Writers Institute at Skidmore College.** First offered in 1987, this monthlong program, sponsored by Skidmore College and the State University of New York at Albany, is divided into two 14-day sessions with courses in fiction, nonfiction, and poetry.

Each three-hour course meets three times a week and is attended by 16 students.

If you're working on a novel, you can register at no extra cost for tutorial sessions with senior fiction fellow, novelist Douglas Glover. Tuesday and Thursday afternoons are devoted to roundtable discussions with visiting faculty, who in the past have included Joyce Carol Oates, Russell Banks, Susan Sontag, and Ann Beattie. The faculty consists of prominent writers and teachers; recent instructors were Bharati Mukherjee, Marilynne Robinson, Francine Prose, and Richard Howard.

You must submit a brief letter describing relevant information (previous workshop experience, degrees, special interests) and a writing sample. The program attracts about 100 students from across the country. The range of participants is between 19 and 68, with most being in their twenties and thirties.

The institute is held at Skidmore College in Saratoga Springs, New York, a historic resort about 175 miles north of New York City. Students who stay on campus are housed in air-conditioned single rooms, unless a double is requested, and eat in the college dining hall or at nearby restaurants. All students can use the college swimming pool, tennis courts, and gym; the college also has an active series of summer arts events, and the New York City Ballet and the Philadelphia Orchestra are in residence at the Saratoga Performing Arts Center. If you attend the second of the two sessions, in late July, you will be around for the start of Saratoga Springs's Thoroughbred racing season. *New York State Summer Writers Institute, Office of the Dean of Special Programs, Maria McColl, Program Assistant, Skidmore College, Saratoga Springs, NY 12866-1632, tel. 518/584–5000, ext. 2264, fax 518/581–7400, ext. 2179. July: 14–28 days, $1,100–$2,200 with lodging and meals ($640–1,280 without). Sign up anytime.*

NEW YORK **Remember the Magic: the International Women's Writing Guild Summer Conference.** This seven-day writing conference for women emphasizes the joy of creativity and personal and professional empowerment. Started in 1977, it combines writing with other art forms. Each day there are 60 workshops, which are 75 minutes long and fall into four major categories: Writing: Nuts and Bolts of It; Transformation of Self; Storytelling and Non-Linear Knowledge; and The Arts and the Body. You may take up to six workshops a day. Readings and special events are scheduled during the evening.

The conference is open to 450 women regardless of professional portfolio, age, or background. The week attracts a diverse group, many participants being in a transitional period of their life—having recently experienced such major events as a divorce or the departure of children from home. The 60-member faculty have a variety of interests, accomplishments, and teaching backgrounds.

The program takes place at Skidmore College in Saratoga Springs, about 175 miles north of New York City. You stay in modern dorms in air-conditioned or non-air-conditioned double rooms (or a single for a higher price) and eat in the campus dining hall, which has a wide choice of dishes, including fruits, vegetables, and salads. *International Women's Writing Guild Summer Conference, Hannelore Hahn, Executive Director, Box 810, Gracie Station, New York, NY 10028, tel. 212/737–7536, fax 212/737–9469. Mid-Aug.: 7 days, $600–$700. Sign up anytime.*

NEW YORK **Robert Quackenbush's Children's Book Writing and Illustrating Workshops.** This unique five-day workshop, held annually since 1982, provides the opportunity to work with Robert Quackenbush, a prolific author and illustrator of children's books with more than 160 fiction and nonfiction books for young readers to his credit, including mysteries, biographies, and songbooks.

The goal here is to learn how to create books for children—from start to finish—and to help free you from creative blocks.

The workshop focuses on picture books and is limited to 10 participants.

Class meets daily from 9 to 4 with one hour for lunch. The week begins with a discussion of each individual's plan or idea for a book, and by the end of the week, participants have a project ready in manuscript and/or dummy form to submit to a publisher. Lectures and readings cover such topics as how to develop projects for today's children and today's market or how to work with a publisher in the production of a book. You may work individually or in groups, and Quackenbush provides daily feedback to each student or group. Depending on the needs of the class, the workshop may include a talk with a visiting editor and trips to a publisher's offices or a relevant local exhibition.

The class attracts both professional and beginning writers and artists of different ages from all over the world; admission occurs after a phone interview or a staff review of your writing samples. Many workshop alumni have had their class projects published. You're responsible for arranging your own hotel and meals, although Quackenbush can suggest places to stay and dine in the area. His studio, where workshops take place, is situated on Manhattan's Upper East Side, within walking distance of several major museums and galleries. *Robert Quackenbush's Children's Book Writing and Illustrating Workshops, 460 E. 79th St., New York, NY 10021, tel. and fax 212/744–3822. Mid-July: 5 days, $650. Price does not include lodging or meals; sign up by June 15.*

NEW YORK **Vassar College Institute of Publishing and Writing: Children's Books in the Marketplace.** This annual six-day conference, started in 1982, concentrates on how the children's book industry works. Leading authors, artists, editors, designers, and agents in the field meet with those who want to learn about publishing and become part of the industry.

Monday to Friday, you spend mornings with writers and editors of children's literature, who review and discuss your writing proposals (although submitting a proposal is not required). During the afternoon and evening, workshops and lectures deal with various aspects of the industry: The Editorial Process, Creating the Picture Book, Deciphering a Contract, and The Production Process are just a few examples. Artists' portfolios are reviewed on the last day, and there is a festive luncheon.

Past instructors and speakers have included writers Nancy Willard and Mary Jane Auch, artists Barry Moser and Ed Young, literary agent Ethan Ellenberg, Scholastic executive editor Dianne Hess, and artists' representative Dilys Evans. The limited enrollment of 25 allows for serious consideration of individual projects. Applicants aren't screened—"I want a good mix of experience and innocence," says director Barbara Lucas. "They tend to reinforce each other."

The conference is held at Vassar College, located in Poughkeepsie in the heart of the Hudson River valley, 75 miles north of New York City. Participants are housed in dormitories and take their meals at the central dining hall. The tranquil 1,000-acre campus encompasses fields, walking paths, gardens, two lakes, and 200 species of trees. You can use Vassar's athletic facilities for swimming, squash, tennis, jogging, and golf. *Vassar College, Maryann Bruno, Coordinator, Institute of Publishing and Writing, 124 Raymond Ave., Poughkeepsie, NY 12601, tel. 914/437–5903. Mid-June: 6 days, $800 with lodging and meals ($525 without). Sign up by May 1.*

VERMONT **Bennington Writing Workshops.** The peaceful, 500-acre campus of Bennington College in southwestern Vermont provides a fine environment in which to write new work and revise manuscripts. The two separate two-week sessions each offer six hours of workshops in fiction, poetry, and nonfiction per week, as well as evening readings by students and prominent authors, hour-long tutorial meetings with faculty, and panel discussions on magazine and book publishing with profes-

sionals from the industry. The rest of the time is reserved for writing.

Publishers and editors are in residence for three days, offering advice on how to submit manuscripts. Faculty are selected for the quality of both their writing and teaching experience. Past staff members have included fiction writers George Garrett and Rick Moody, poets Lynn Emanuel and Jonathan Holden, and nonfiction writers Thomas M. Disch and Lucy Grealy.

Approximately 90 writers, both beginning and published, attend each session, and some stay for both (or four weeks); individual workshops are limited to 12 students. You must submit a brief writing sample and a summary of your related experience. Students stay in modest single dormitory rooms, with meals served in the Commons dining hall. The on-campus Carriage Barn Café is open at night after readings for receptions for students and teachers. Good restaurants, charming country stores, and a spring-fed lake for swimming are all within walking distance of the campus. *Bennington Writing Workshops, Liam Rector, Director, Box BR, Bennington College, Bennington, VT 05201, tel. 802/442–5401, ext. 160, fax 802/442–6164. July: 14 days, $1,380 with lodging and meals ($885 without). Price includes single room; sign up as far in advance as possible. Financial aid applications are due Apr. 15.*

VERMONT **Bread Loaf Writers' Conference.** One of the oldest (established in 1926) and best-known writers' conferences in the country, the 11-day Bread Loaf Writer's Conference offers an opportunity for sustained dialogue between established and aspiring writers, as well as teachers of writing.

Authors come here to discuss writing as a craft and a profession. Lectures, craft classes, and panel discussions are offered. The conference focuses on workshops, which each meet five times. Poetry, fiction, and literary nonfiction workshops are limited to 10 people. Faculty and staff fellows read from their own work during the afternoon and evening. Editors, agents, and publishers make brief visits to the conference and provide panels and lectures.

The faculty is made up of professional writers. Recent faculty members have included Francine Prose, Mark Doty, Patricia Hampl, Jorie Graham, Scott Spencer, Joanna Scott, and Richard Bausch. You can attend as a contributor or an auditor. Contributors each have one private conference with a faculty member and must submit writing samples ahead of time. Auditors may attend all conference events but don't have private conferences with the faculty. About 230 writers, from a wide range of ages and backgrounds, attend each year.

The conference is held at Middlebury College's summer campus in the Green Mountain National Forest in Ripton, Vermont. You stay in campus houses in double rooms with shared baths. Meals are served in the Bread Loaf Inn's dining room, with food prepared by the college dining service.

Middlebury's summer campus has tennis and volleyball courts. Swimming, excellent fishing, hiking, riding, golf, and antiquing are all available nearby. *Bread Loaf Writers' Conference, Carol Knauss, Administrative Coordinator, Middlebury College, Middlebury, VT 05753-6125, tel. 802/388–3711, ext. 5286, fax 802/443–2087. Late Aug.: 11 days, $1,600 ($1,535 for auditors). Financial aid applicants must contact the Writers' Conference by mid-Feb. for guidelines and apply by Apr. 1.*

VERMONT **Wildbranch Workshop in Outdoor, Natural History, and Environmental Writing.** First offered in 1988, this weeklong workshop is aimed squarely at writers who want to improve and learn how to market their outdoor, natural history, or environmental writing. Some 25 to 30 fiction writers, journalists, and essayists of all levels attend. Because the resident faculty are on campus during the entire session, you have ample opportunity to get feedback on your manuscript.

Three courses involving writing, reading, and discussions of student work are given

daily—Getting Personal, The Natural History of the Familiar, and Outdoor Writing as Literature—as well as a works-in-progress course open to intermediate and advanced writers; each course is limited to 10 students. You attend one of these daily, along with lectures and workshops offered by visiting faculty, who are usually editors and professional writers or journalists; one of these sessions generally deals with the business side of nature writing. You're not required to submit a writing sample unless you plan to take the works-in-progress course.

The three resident faculty members have recently included Steve Bodio, contributing editor and book reviewer for *Fly, Rod & Reel* magazine; Gale Lawrence, naturalist and teacher; and Joel Vance, a former writer for the Missouri Conservation Department. There are usually four visiting faculty.

The workshop convenes on the Sterling College campus in north central Vermont, 1½ hours from Burlington, 4½ hours from Boston, and 3 hours from Montreal. You stay in the school's dormitories, and singles are usually available; three meals a day are provided at an informal dining hall. Appropriately, there is wonderful canoeing, hiking, bicycling, swimming, and fishing at nearby lakes and streams. *Wildbranch Workshop in Outdoor, Natural History, and Environmental Writing, David Brown, Director, Sterling College, Craftsbury Common, VT 05827, tel. 802/586–7711 or 800/648–3591, fax 802/586–2596. Late June: 7 days, $775. Price includes single or double room; sign up by May 15.*

THE MID-ATLANTIC

MARYLAND **Writers' Workshops at St. Mary's.** You must submit a writing sample with your application to participate in one of the three workshops offered at St. Mary's College of Maryland, in the south-central part of the state. The two-week Intensive Poetry Writing Workshop, the two-week

Fiction Writing Workshop, and the 10-day Writer's Community Retreat, all concentrate on the art and craft of writing in classes of fewer than 16, with supportive instructors who are published writers as well as teachers.

The Intensive Poetry Writing Workshop consists of five hours of morning and afternoon classes in which you write and discuss your work with instructors and classmates. On weekends, some 14 guest poets give readings and run 90-minute workshops and seminars; they are also available for individual consultation. Past guest poets have included Grace Cavalieri, Lucille Clifton, and James Haba.

The Fiction Writing Workshop involves five hours daily of morning and afternoon classes devoted to various aspects and techniques of fiction writing, such as plotting, point of view, and character development. You study published works of fiction (usually short stories), do writing exercises, and participate in critiques of students' work. During one of the weekends of the session, there are readings, workshops, and seminars by guest authors.

The 10-day Writer's Community Retreat has an unstructured format designed to allow you to work according to a schedule that you design on your own. Based on the wishes of retreat participants—and with their help—the three guest instructors organize three 90-minute workshops. The rest of the time is left for participants to enjoy the surroundings and write.

You stay on campus in single air-conditioned dormitory rooms with kitchens. You can either cook your own meals or eat in nearby restaurants. St. Mary's is in historic St. Mary's City, 10 miles from the Chesapeake Bay in the heart of Tidewater Maryland. *Writers' Workshops at St. Mary's, Dr. Michael Glaser, Director, St. Mary's College of Maryland, St. Mary's City, MD 20686, tel. 301/862–0239. Late May: 10–14 days, $425–$825. Price includes single room and kitchen facilities but not meals; sign up before May 1.*

PENNSYLVANIA **Cumberland Valley Fiction Writers Workshop.** Devoted exclusively to fiction writing, this six-day conference offers aspiring writers the opportunity to work closely with an established author and provides an intensive yet informal experience. It consists of four workshops, limited to 10 participants each, that meet five times a week from 4:30 to 6:30. Class time is spent discussing and critiquing the students' work. Each faculty member gives an evening reading, and a two-hour afternoon writers roundtable allows a question-and-answer session with the teachers. You have at least one private conference with your workshop leader. One day during the week, you all take a hike on the Appalachian Trail and visit nearby Fuller Lake for a picnic and swimming.

The faculty includes award-winning short story writers and novelists who also teach at the university level; recent instructors have included Lorrie Moore, Madison Smartt Bell, and Robert Olmstead. You must submit a 10-page writing sample with your application, and places are awarded on a first-accepted, first-reserved basis.

The 30 to 40 participants are diverse in age, experience, and occupation. Most of them come from Pennsylvania and nearby states, and many students commute from home. Although most write serious mainstream fiction, writers of historical fiction, fantasy, or other genre fiction are also welcome. The atmosphere is congenial and supportive.

Workshops meet at Dickinson College, a small liberal arts college in Carlisle, Pennsylvania, just 20 miles west of Harrisburg, the state capital, and two hours by car from Philadelphia or Washington, D.C. You stay in the college residence hall, two to a suite with private bedrooms, a common living area, and bath. You can take meals at the school's dining hall on a pay-as-you-go basis; several restaurants and food shops are within walking distance.

You have access to the college athletic facilities, including a pool, tennis courts, and a gymnasium. The surrounding area has many historic sites of interest, and Pennsylvania Dutch Country is nearby. *Cumberland Valley Fiction Writers Workshop, Judy Gill, Program Director, Department of English, Dickinson College, Box 1773, Carlisle, PA 17013-2896, tel. 717/245-1291. Late June: 6 days, $455 with lodging and no meals. Price includes single room in suite; sign up by May 15.*

THE SOUTH

GEORGIA **Southeastern Writers Association Workshop.** This weeklong conference has workshops in poetry, the novel, playwriting, the short story, mass-market fiction, nonfiction, writing for children, and inspirational writing. The goal is to help the 100 participants along the path to getting published and offer the opportunity to network with fellow writers.

Although applicants aren't screened and a manuscript is not required for acceptance, you have the option of submitting one for evaluation in each of three categories. You receive a written critique and a personal consultation during the program. The faculty consists of publishing professionals who are willing to share time with students both in and out of class. Other activities include a poetry reading, a writing contest, an awards banquet, and evening lectures by guest editors and writers.

The conference takes place at Epworth-by-the-Sea, a large hotel and conference center on St. Simons Island, 60 miles south of Savannah. You have your choice of singles, doubles, and triples at the hotel, and all meals are provided. Faculty and students eat together. The conference encourages participants to bring their families. The island has six golf courses, a pool, beaches, walking paths, historic buildings, fishing, and the restaurants and shops in St. Simons village. *Southeastern Writers Association Workshop, Nancy Knight, Director, 4021 Gladesworth La., Decatur, GA 30035, tel. 404/288-2064. Late Aug.: 7 days, $380-$595 with lodging and meals ($200 with-*out). *Sign up anytime; manuscript submission by June 1.*

KENTUCKY **Green River Writers Novel in Progress Workshop.** This weeklong conference is designed for the beginning novelist who has a work either in progress or completed and who wants a professional critique and peer support. Monday through Friday is spent in groups of five to seven participants, with each group led by a faculty member. Each workshop has a different focus—horror/fantasy, romance, mystery, other genres, and mainstream writing—and you schedule an hour-long private conference with your workshop leader. You choose one workshop as your main focus, and your work is scrutinized during this course; you may also sit in on any or even all of the other classes. On Saturday morning there are lectures on such topics as publishing short story collections, writing for children, and collaborating on a novel. A panel discussion by editors and literary agents fills Saturday afternoon, after which you have a 15-minute private meeting with them. The program ends with a Saturday night buffet at which you mingle with the 30 or so other participants, instructors, and visiting panelists.

All instructors are published novelists, and most also have teaching experience. The faculty changes from year to year, although there are usually many familiar faces among both the teachers and students who have returned. You must submit a synopsis or outline of your novel, along with three chapters or 60 manuscript pages. Several participants have already completed novels and are attending the program for feedback and advice on how to publish their work.

The conference is held at the University of Louisville's Shelby campus in a suburban area of East Louisville. You stay in small, graduate student dorms in private or shared rooms, with shared baths. The dorms have TVs, kitchens, and dining areas. You take care of your own meals, which you can cook yourself; some participants opt to dine in local restaurants. *Green River Writers Novel in Progress Workshop,*

Sandra Daugherty, Program Director, 11906 Locust Rd., Middletown, KY 40243, tel. 502/245–4902. Early Jan.: 7 days, $275. Price does not include lodging ($14–$19 per night) or meals; sign up by Dec. 1.

KENTUCKY **Writers Retreat Workshop.** This 10-day workshop welcomes approximately 30 participants (half of whom are usually returning students) who have a novel in progress or ideas for a novel. To be accepted, you must submit an application along with a description of the novel you plan to work on while at the workshop. Founded in 1987 by the late Gary Provost and his wife Gail, the Writers Retreat Workshop has been attended by writers of every level, beginners to already published authors, from age 25 to 85—all firmly committed to improving their writing skills.

Workshop instructor Alice Orr, a nationally known author and agent, conducts classes daily after breakfast and provides writing assignments; in the afternoons, students return to their rooms to write. For the first few days, classes focus on story sense and dramatic structure. After these classes, an editor-in-residence consults with each student on his or her plot. Evenings there are often informal gatherings, talks, and readings.

During the week, sessions are held to help participants develop their editing skills. Returning students take part in mock publishing house editorial conferences. Throughout the 10 days, you meet with several of the staff members for individual feedback. Recent faculty has included workshop director Gail Provost, mystery writer Frank Strunk, Australian children's author Margaret McAlister, New York agent and editor Peter Rubie of L. Perkins Associates, and Michael Palmer, who writes best-selling medical thrillers.

The program takes place at Marydale Retreat Center in northern Kentucky, about 5 miles from the Greater Cincinnati Airport. The center is situated in a quiet setting of rolling hills near a pond. Hearty meals are served buffet style. Each student has a private bedroom with a bed, desk, and sink; rooms with private commodes are assigned to the first fully registered students. *Writers Retreat Workshop. Mailing address: Write It/Sell It, Box 139, South Lancaster, MA 01561-0139, tel. 800/642– 2494 for brochure, fax 508/368–0287. May: 10 days, $1,595 (new students), $1,435 (returning students). Sign up several months in advance.*

NORTH CAROLINA **Duke University Writers' Workshop.** With the aim of creating an atmosphere of generosity and support rather than competition, this program includes seven workshops, limited to 10 to 15 writers each, covering fiction, poetry, playwriting, the memoir, and writing fundamentals. Each workshop meets for three hours, Monday through Friday mornings, and includes one 30-minute conference with the workshop leader. Two afternoons are given over to readings by faculty and participants, and another two are free for writing or relaxation and guest lectures. The program, first held in 1979, ends with a group luncheon and a talk by a guest speaker, usually a local professional writer.

The faculty are all published authors and experienced teachers. Workshop sessions balance criticism and instruction—you discuss manuscripts' strengths and weaknesses, and explore possible revisions. Participants are all serious about writing but vary in experience; most workshops require a writing sample and/or a letter describing your goals for the class.

The program meets on the campus of Duke University in Durham. Participants stay in local hotels rather than on campus, and there is no meal plan. You can swim, golf, and play tennis on the university grounds. *Duke University Writers' Workshop, Georgann Eubanks, Director, Box 90703, Durham, NC 27708-0703, tel. 919/684–5375, fax 919/681–8235. June: 6 days, $350. Price does not include lodging and includes only 1 meal; sign up anytime.*

TENNESSEE **Sewanee Writers' Conference.** This 12-day program of workshops, readings, and lectures on the craft of writing, first held in 1990, takes place at the University of the South in Sewanee, Tennessee. The *Sewanee Review,* a distinguished literary publication, makes its home at the school, and such celebrated authors as Robert Penn Warren, Katherine Anne Porter, Ford Madox Ford, Peter Taylor, and Jean Stafford have lived and worked in the town. The program is supported by a fund established through the estate of the late playwright Tennessee Williams.

On the daily schedule, craft lectures alternate with workshops in fiction, poetry, and playwriting. You choose one workshop to attend when you sign up and attend its five sessions; in your free time, you may also audit other workshops. There are two instructors per workshop; you meet once privately with one of them to discuss your work in progress. Critics, agents, directors, and editors sit on panels or hold Q&A sessions in the mornings; afternoons and evenings are devoted to readings by workshop faculty and guest writers.

The faculty is made up of highly respected writers: Recent faculty members have been fiction writers John Casey, Tim O'Brien, Susan Minot, and Francine Prose; poets Maxine Kumin and Derek Walcott; and playwrights Tina Howe and Horton Foote. Guest speakers have included editors Robert Giroux and David Godine and writers Arthur Miller, William Styron, and the late Peter Taylor.

Applicants are selected on the strength and promise of their work. You must send in 10 to 15 pages of poetry, 20 to 40 pages of fiction, or a one-act play with your application. There are 105 participants in the program, and 15 students in each workshop.

The University of the South's rural campus, distinguished by ivy-covered Gothic buildings, is in south-central Tennessee, 45 miles southeast of Chattanooga and 90 miles northwest of Nashville. You stay in single or double dormitory rooms with shared bathrooms. The full meal plan,

served on campus, includes a salad bar, low-calorie items, and vegetarian selections. The university summer session and the Sewanee Summer Music Center sponsor films, lectures, and concerts, and you're within walking distance of tennis courts, lakes, and a golf course. Biking, jogging, hiking, rock climbing, and horseback riding are also available. *Sewanee Writers' Conference, Cheri Peters, Administrator, 310 St. Luke's Hall, University of the South, Sewanee, TN 37383-1000, tel. 615/598– 1141. Late July: 12 days, $1,200. Sign up between Jan. and late spring.*

THE MIDWEST

ILLINOIS **Mark Twain Writers Conference.** This relaxed event, established in 1985, consists of four five-day gatherings held during four separate weeks in June, July, August, and October. Each five-day period concentrates on different aspects of writing, reflected in workshop titles such as Magazines and Short Story, Fiction, and Nonfiction; Writing for Children and Storytelling; Travel Writing, Adventure Writing, and Writing Your Autobiography; and Books and Humor. You attend morning lectures and afternoon workshops on the writing craft and may also arrange a private conference with a faculty member. The goal for each participant is to take home a polished version of a work-in-progress or the beginning of a new work.

Instructors are published writers and editors. Recent faculty members have included award-winning travel writer Sharon Lloyd Spence, premier midwestern storyteller Gladys Coggswell, nationally acclaimed humorist Karyn Buxman, and James C. Hefley, the director of the conference. Only 25 participants, accepted on a first-come, first-served basis, attend each of the four sessions. They are a diverse group from all levels of writing experience and education.

The four gatherings take place at the peaceful Heartland Lodge, a first-rate resort nestled between the Mississippi and Illinois rivers in Pike County, Illinois. Conference attendees stay in comfortable, air-conditioned double rooms at the lodge, where they also have all their meals and snacks, including two festive dinners prepared by the resort's resident cook, Grandma Blanche. Horseback riding is available at additional cost. The lodge is a 45-minute drive east of the northeastern Missouri town of Hannibal, Mark Twain's boyhood home, where you may visit several sites associated with the 19th-century author and take a riverboat ride and tours of the town's historic district. *Mark Twain Writers Conference, Cyndi Allison, Coordinator, 921 Center St., Hannibal, MO 63401, tel. 800/747–0738, fax 314/221–2462. June, July, Aug., Oct: 5 days, $465. Sign up by Feb.*

ILLINOIS **Mississippi Valley Writers Conference.** This six-day conference, established in 1974, provides professional guidance to writers at all levels of experience. There are nine hour-long writing workshops daily—led by professional authors—in poetry, writing for children, nonfiction, the short story, and romantic fiction; two workshops cover the novel, and there's also a class for beginners on basics and a course in photography. Each workshop has 15 to 20 participants, and each student gets a private conference with the workshop leader, who will critique a 10-page manuscript if it's submitted in advance. You may submit a manuscript for each and every workshop you take. Evenings are devoted to readings by faculty and students, and on the last night there's a banquet, during which students receive awards for their writing.

The conference is held at Augustana College, a liberal arts institution on the banks of the Mississippi River that serves as the area's major arts center. You stay in a campus dormitory, and although meals are served in the cafeteria, it's all home cooking. *Mississippi Valley Writers Conference, David Collins, Director, or Bess Pierce, Secretary, Student Center, Augustana College, Rock Island, IL 61201, tel. 309/764–5540.*

Early June: 6 days, $50 (1 workshop), $80 (2 workshops), $40 for the 3rd or additional workshops. Price does not include lodging ($100 for 6 nights) or meals ($100 for 15); sign up by May 15.

INDIANA **RopeWalk Writers Retreat.** New Harmony, Indiana, now a typical midwestern small town, was the site of two experiments in communal and utopian living in the 19th century; the restored buildings built and used by their creative thinkers are the backdrop for this intellectual retreat. The aim is to provide writers with expert instruction and advice in a small workshop setting where there's plenty of opportunity for interaction among the 50 or so attendees—usually about a dozen per workshop.

The conference offers fiction, poetry, and sometimes nonfiction workshops, and you get one individual conference with your leader. Workshops meet three times a week, and lectures on technique and discussion groups are held twice weekly. Evenings are usually reserved for readings by faculty and guests.

The faculty consists of four to five published authors who often also work as teachers. Recent faculty members have included Ann Beattie, Stephen Dobyns, Heather McHugh, and Andrew Hudgins. Only scholarship applicants' work is screened and evaluated beforehand. Full-paying applicants submit manuscripts with their applications; materials are then forwarded to workshop leaders to be read before the workshop begins. Participants are usually college educated and range in age from 22 to 65.

You can stay at the New Harmony Inn and Conference Center, the retreat's Shaker-simple headquarters, or choose the less expensive lodgings of the Barn Abbey, a rustic dormitory with double rooms. The area also has many bed-and-breakfasts. You take breakfast and lunch at the Barn Abbey dining room, and two dinners are provided; other nights you dine on your own in town. *RopeWalk Writers Retreat, Linda Cleek, Program Coordinator, c/o Extended*

Services, University of Southern Indiana, 8600 University Blvd., Evansville, IN 47712, tel. 812/464–1989 or 800/467–8600, fax 812/465–7061. Mid-June: 6 days, $395. Price does not include lodging ($15–$75 per night) and most dinners; sign up by mid-May (late Apr. for scholarship applications).

IOWA **Iowa Summer Writing Festival.** Home to the famed Iowa Writers' Workshop, a two-year graduate program, the University of Iowa has also sponsored this Summer Writing Festival since 1987. Perhaps the largest writing conference in the country, this noncredit program offers more than 125 workshops lasting one week, as well as some weekend options. Choose from a variety of topics and genres—from writing of novels, short stories, poetry, essays, and plays to creative nonfiction, women's writing, writing with ethnic variety, children's books, romance novels, science fiction, and the memoir.

Workshops start with Sunday supper, orientation, and a class meeting. For the rest of the week, classes convene for three hours each afternoon. Although workshop instructors may also suggest writing exercises and readings of published work, the primary text for classes is student writing; the group discusses each writer's work, and leaders encourage and critique you both in class and in private conferences.

Monday through Friday at 11 AM is the Elevenses, a series of presentations, lectures, and panels. In the evening there are readings by guest authors, often followed by question-and-answer sessions. Mornings and some evenings, you're free to write, read, research, and meet with other writers. An open-mike night gives everyone a chance to share his work.

The faculty consists mostly of published writers, many of them University of Iowa graduates or teachers. Workshops are open to any adult—first come, first served—who wants to participate; there are classes for beginning, intermediate, and advanced writers, and all are limited to 12 students.

The University of Iowa is in Iowa City, in the southeastern part of the state. You are responsible for arranging your own accommodations, but there are several options: a campus residence hall, an on-campus hotel, and the downtown Holiday Inn, within walking distance of the school. Meals are also up to you (except for the welcome supper and the banquet at the end of the week), and again, there are many options—residence hall kitchens and cafeterias, campus dining rooms, and nearby restaurants. The university sponsors several summer cultural programs, including theater and musical performances. *Iowa Summer Writing Festival, Peggy Houston or Amy Margolis, Division of Continuing Education, 116 International Center, University of Iowa, Iowa City, IA 52242, tel. 319/335–2534, fax 319/335–2740. June–July: 4–7 days, $150–$375. Price does not include lodging or meals; sign up by early Mar.*

MINNESOTA **Mississippi River Creative Writing Workshop in Poetry and Fiction.** This gathering at St. Cloud State University, established in 1974, is Minnesota's longest-running and best-known creative writing conference. The program lasts two weeks and involves eight formal meetings, Monday through Thursday afternoons. It is especially recommended for beginners or those who want to brush up on their creative writing skills.

Poet and short-story writer Bill Meissner, who teaches at St. Cloud State University, leads the first week of workshops; he gives daily writing exercises and conducts group discussions about fiction, poetry, and nonfiction.

During the second week, you can meet and talk with four or five visiting published authors, who read from and lecture about their own work, and answer questions. Guest speakers are selected for both their writing skills and their abilities and reputations as entertaining and personable teachers; past visitors have included poet Robert Bly and novelists Jon Hassler and Kate Green.

No writing sample is required, and each year about 35 to 40 people attend, representing many ages, backgrounds, and professions; many come from the surrounding area. The group stays together as a unit throughout the program, but may be split up occasionally for discussions or class exercises. The program may be taken for undergraduate or graduate credit.

You can stay in university student housing or opt for the reasonably priced area accommodations. You're responsible for your own meals, but there are several restaurants near the campus. *Mississippi River Creative Writing Workshop in Poetry and Fiction, Dept. of English, Riverview 106, St. Cloud State University, St. Cloud, MN 56301-4498, tel. 612/255–3061. Mid-June: 8 days over a 2-wk period, $297–$320. Price does not include lodging or meals; sign up anytime.*

MINNESOTA **Split Rock Arts Program.** This program consists of 45 intensive weeklong workshops in both the literary and visual arts—some 16 of them devoted to writing, with topics ranging from creative nonfiction, the short story, essay writing, and journals and diaries to children's picture books, poetry, and the nature of creativity. Most of these require about 60 hours in and out of class, including some work done before you arrive. There are about 16 students in each group.

Participants are typically highly motivated, ranging in age from 18 to 80; they're usually not earning a living from their art but are committed avocational artists who come here for the opportunity to work with renowned practicing writers and artists. The faculty are all also accomplished teachers with the experience to direct and challenge their students at different levels.

The Split Rock program, which was founded in 1983, takes place at the University of Minnesota's campus in Duluth, on the hills overlooking the western tip of Lake Superior and the city's harbor. Some workshops are conducted as retreats at the university's Cloquet Forestry Center, southwest of Duluth, amid 160-year-old red pine trees.

Lodging is not included in your fee, but residences and two-bedroom apartments on campus are available. You may fix your own meals in your apartment's kitchen; eat out around Duluth; or buy a meal ticket good for any 10 meals—breakfast, lunch, or dinner—at the dining center. If you attend workshops at the Cloquet Forestry Center, your fee includes lodging at the center and meals in its dining hall. *Split Rock Arts Program, University of Minnesota, 306 Wesbrook Hall, 77 Pleasant St. SE, Minneapolis, MN 55455, tel. 612/624–6800, fax 612/625–2568. July–Aug.: 6 days, $330–$350 ($584 with lodging and meals at Cloquet Forestry Center). Price of Duluth workshop does not include lodging or meals; sign up in Mar.*

OHIO **Antioch Writers' Workshop of Yellow Springs.** This seven-day program at Antioch College, a central Ohio cultural center, creates a supportive environment for writers at all levels of experience. The conference was established in 1986.

Classes and lectures run from morning to midafternoon daily and cover the novel, the short story, poetry, nonfiction, playwriting, writing for children, and other topics. During the afternoon, agents, editors, and other publishing professionals make presentations. In the evening, there are readings by faculty and visiting writers, followed by sharing and critique sessions, in various genres, that can run until midnight.

The 20-member faculty consists of professional writers, many of them with several years of teaching experience. Of the conference's 80 participants, 30 at the more advanced level participate in intensive seminars in the short story, poetry, and memoir. Because the student-to-faculty ratio is a low four-to-one, you have ready access to instructors. Manuscripts submitted in advance will be read and discussed with you privately.

Single and double dorm rooms are available at Antioch; you can get a special rate at the 8-mile-distant Xenia Holiday Inn; or you can pitch a tent at the 2,000-acre John Bryant State Park, 4 miles from Antioch. You can take your meals in the campus cafeteria on a meal plan or on a pay-as-you-go basis, or eat at restaurants in town. Dorm rooms have refrigerators and microwaves. The conference begins with a special banquet that features a keynote speech by a prominent writer.

Antioch College is 30 minutes from Dayton and an hour from Columbus and Cincinnati. The area has a number of pleasant shops, and there's a 1,000-acre nature preserve with hiking trails and a 9½-mile bike path open to cyclists, walkers, joggers, and skaters. Tuition discounts are available for repeat attendees and residents of neighboring counties. *Antioch Writers' Workshop of Yellow Springs, Judy DaPolito, Director, Antioch University, Box 494, Yellow Springs, OH 45387, tel. 513/767–7068, fax 513/767–6470. Mid-July: 7 days, $425–$475. Price does not include lodging or meals; sign up in advance.*

THE SOUTHWEST

NEW MEXICO **Santa Fe Writers' Conference.** Recursos de Santa Fe, a nonprofit educational organization, sponsors this intensive five-day conference, which gives emerging poets and fiction writers the chance to meet well-known authors and benefit from their instruction. At the core of the conference are small, morning and afternoon workshops in fiction and poetry, which are limited to 12 participants each. During these meetings, you concentrate on manuscript editing and the creative process. You attend lectures by agents and editors in the afternoon, and readings by faculty of their works in the evening. Nearby Native American ruins provide the striking setting for a special evening reading given by an author familiar with the Southwest.

Six poets and fiction writers with considerable teaching experience lead workshops. Recent faculty have included poets Robert Creely and Arthur Sze and fiction writers Madison Smartt Bell, Robert Boswell, Antonya Nelson, and David Morrell. Participants are chosen by the quality of their work; you submit 10 pages of your writing in order to be accepted. You may schedule one private conference with a workshop leader for evaluation of your manuscript.

Workshops meet at Plaza Resolana, a small conference center facility near Santa Fe's historic plaza. You stay in single or double rooms right at the center, where you are provided with breakfast and lunch, as well as with dinner the first evening of the conference. The neighborhood is brimming (over-brimming, perhaps) with shops, restaurants, and galleries, and you're only a short walk from art and history museums, Native American vendors selling their wares, and the landmark La Fonda Hotel.

Recursos de Santa Fe also sponsors a seven-day playwriting workshop and a five-day workshop concentrating on the personal essay. *Santa Fe Writers' Conference, Peter Eichstaedt, Program Director, Recursos de Santa Fe, 826 Camino de Monte Rey, Suite A-3, Santa Fe, NM 87505, tel. 505/982–9301, fax 505/989–8608. Late July–early Aug.: 5 days, $730 ($930 for singles). Sign up anytime.*

NEW MEXICO **Taos School of Writing.** This weeklong conference takes place in the dramatic mountains of the Kit Carson National Forest, 9,000 feet above sea level (you may want to prepare yourself for altitude sickness if you aren't accustomed to such heights). First held in 1993, it is made up of small workshops concentrating on fiction and nonfiction writing (the number of classes varies according to the number of attendees). You spend mornings in groups of no more than 12, critiquing student manuscripts and discussing the writing process; faculty rotate through all classes to keep the instruction lively and varied. Authors, editors, and agents speak in the afternoons and then stay on for two-hour group discussions. You have several hours of free time right after lunch for reading, hiking, writing, or napping. Evenings are open for writing, readings by students and faculty, and informal meetings.

Instructors include prize-winning writers, as well as a visiting agent and editor who provide valuable perspectives on the marketplace. The program also invites visiting lecturers, among them, in the past, Tony Hillerman and Roger Zelazny. When you apply, you must submit a manuscript of no more than 20 pages; although there are no restrictions on subject matter or style, poetry and screenplays are not allowed. The faculty determines admissions based on the quality of the writing. Many of the students here have been writing for several years; some have published their work or come from journalism, teaching, and writing-related professions.

The school is in the Taos Ski Valley, 23 miles north of the town of Taos and about three hours from Albuquerque. Workshops convene at Thunderbird Lodge, a wood-frame ski resort where everyone stays and takes their meals—its dining room offers some of the best eating in the area. There is hiking all around, and you can visit Taos Pueblo, the Millicent Rogers Museum, Kit Carson's home, the D. H. Lawrence Ranch, or the awesome Rio Grande Gorge. *Taos School of Writing, Suzanne Spletzer, Administrator, Box 20496, Albuquerque, NM 87154, tel. 505/293–0303, fax 505/237–2665. Mid-July: 7 days, $1,050. Manuscript submission deadline: May 15.*

THE ROCKIES

COLORADO **Aspen Writers' Conference.** The craft of writing and the work of participants are the focal points of this conference first held in 1976. Mornings are devoted to workshops in fiction, poetry, and literary nonfiction (each limited to 15 writers). Afternoons, staff members give craft lectures. A business program features presentations by agents, editors, and publishers, who are available for questions. There are usually special guest speakers, often from the international literary scene. Past guests have included novelist Michael Ondaatje and poet Miroslav Holub.

The faculty is made up of accomplished writers, most of whom have taught at the university level; recently you might have studied with Gerald Stern, Ron Carlson, Jane Smiley, and Shelby Hearon. You're asked to submit a poetry or prose manuscript with your application, and you should have some knowledge of contemporary literature. There are usually about 60 participants per session.

The weeklong program takes place at the Aspen Institute–Aspen Meadows, a conference center complex. You stay in guest rooms at the Meadows, which all have floor-to-ceiling windows or balconies with views of the nearby mountains and the Roaring Fork River. Writers take care of their own meals. Aspen has a number of good restaurants, as well as lovely Victorian-style buildings. Attendees may enjoy local music, art, dance, and theater, as well as outdoor activities such as hiking, rafting, biking, camping, horseback riding, fishing, and ballooning. The conference organizer, the Aspen Writers' Foundation, also sponsors other literary educational programs for adults and children. *Aspen Writers' Conference, Box 7726, Aspen, CO 81612, tel. 970/925–3122, fax 970/920–5700. Early–mid-June: 7 days, $495. Price does not include lodging ($85 per night private room, $58 shared) or meals; sign up at least 2 months in advance.*

MONTANA **Environmental Writing Institute.** First held in 1990, this five-day workshop is devoted exclusively to nature and environmental writing. It's sponsored by the University of Montana in conjunction with the Teller Wildlife Refuge, the private 1,300-acre preserve 45 miles south of Missoula that is the program's venue. From Sunday through Thursday, you spend mornings in workshops discussing and critiquing each other's work. Afterwards, you have free time to write, read, contemplate the scenery, or soak in a hot spring. You may also go hiking, rafting, fishing, bird- or wildlife watching in the refuge; the nearby Bitterroot Range has some of the country's finest alpine and subalpine landscape.

You meet, lodge, and dine in remodeled rustic farm buildings. Most rooms are doubles, but there are a few singles available at the same rate; all meals are homemade. Guests, including local writers and wildlife biologists, often stay for dinner and talk informally with participants. One evening, the workshop leader gives a public reading of his or her work.

To be among the 14 participants, you must apply with a résumé and a nonfiction manuscript on an environment-related or nature topic. Past leaders have included Peter Matthiessen, Wendell Berry, Gretel Ehrlich, and Richard Nelson. *Environmental Writing Institute, Henry Harrington, Director, Environmental Studies Program, University of Montana, Missoula, MT 59812, tel. 406/243–2904, fax 406/243–6090. Late May: 6 days, $550. Sign up by March 31.*

MONTANA **Yellow Bay Writers' Workshop.** This informal weeklong conference sponsored by the University of Montana encompasses workshops in poetry, fiction, and creative nonfiction. It's held in northwestern Montana, at the Flathead Lake Biological Research Station at Yellow Bay, 55 miles south of Glacier National Park. Flathead is the largest natural freshwater lake in the United States west of the Mississippi.

Four instructors, all professional writers, lead workshops of up to 15 students. Past faculty have included Ian Frazier, Marilynne Robinson, Thomas McGuane, James Tate, Poet Laureate Robert Hass, Carolyn Kizer, and Joy Williams. You attend daily workshops, along with lectures on the writing craft and readings by other students; evenings are devoted to faculty readings. Each year a guest editor or publisher leads a discussion or panel on publishing. In-

structors also stay at the conference site, so you have many opportunities to converse with them. To apply, you must submit a brief manuscript and one-page biography. The average participant is 35 to 40 years old and has been writing independently for several years.

You sleep in rustic one-room cabins with shared bath. Meals are served in a cafeteria on the grounds. In your free time you may go swimming, fishing, and boating or canoeing in Yellow Bay; bookstores, restaurants, galleries, and theaters are in Big Fork (15 miles away) or Polson (18 miles distant). *Yellow Bay Writers' Workshop, Center for Continuing Education, University of Montana, Missoula, MT 59812, tel. 406/243–2094, fax 406/243–2047. Mid-Aug.: 7 days, $735 with lodging and meals ($435 without). Sign up by 1st wk of July.*

THE WEST COAST

CALIFORNIA **Annual Book Passage Travel Writers' Conference.** Sponsored by a lively Marin County bookstore noted for its nearly encyclopedic travel section, this four-day conference covers travel writing in all its manifestations. Donald George, editor-in-chief of Global Network Navigator and a former *San Francisco Examiner* travel editor, has chaired the Thursday-through-Sunday event since its beginnings in 1992. The conference deals with writing for guidebooks, magazines, and newspapers, and writing travel literature; you learn everything from how to market yourself and break into new publications to how to develop a guidebook proposal and whether or not to hold out for electronic rights. George and two other veteran travel scribes teach daily, three-hour morning workshops that deal with a variety of topics, such as how to prepare a manuscript (as in "Where do you put your name?"), how to write a query that sells, and how to get published on the Internet. In the afternoon, students choose two 90-minute panels each day from eight offerings. These panels vary from year to year but always showcase representatives from the major travel information providers, including Fodor's publisher Bonnie Ammer, Lonely Planet Publications U.S. publisher Eric Kettunen, *Condé Nast Traveler* Asia Pacific editor Simon Wincester, *Travel & Leisure* senior editor Barbara Peck, and *Los Angeles Times* travel editor Leslie Ward, among others. Every participant has ample opportunity to ask questions. In 1996 the keynote speakers were Jan Morris and Isabel Allende.

Most participants who don't live in the area lodge at the Corte Madera Inn, where many of the workshop meetings are held. The inn, a modern Best Western property, has a certain California ambience (weathered-shingle siding, a landscaped courtyard, and a swimming pool complete with hot tub). Area restaurants offer a varied choice of sophisticated California and Italian fare. Good shopping is just across the street, and the Wine Country and the pleasures of the city are a short drive away. *Book Passage, 51 Tamal Vista Blvd., Corte Madera, CA 94925, tel. 415/927–0960. Mid-Aug.: 4 days, about $450. Price does not include lodging (about $85 per night including Continental breakfast); sign up any time.*

CALIFORNIA **Idyllwild Arts Summer Program.** Readings, critiques, and some writing exercises fill the mornings of the weeklong adult writing courses at this renowned school's summer program, established in 1950; assignments and individual conferences take place in the afternoons and evenings. Courses are intensive, limited to 15 participants; they may include workshops in the writer's journal and creative writing in all genres. Published professional writers attend these courses alongside near novices, and classes are small enough for everyone to get individual attention.

The school is in Southern California's San Jacinto Mountains, near the town of Idyllwild, a 2½-hour drive from Los Angeles or San Diego, on 205 acres surrounded by the San Bernardino National Forest. There's plenty of hiking, swimming, rock climbing, and other outdoor recreational activities nearby. Because this program covers arts other than writing, there are also music concerts, artist lectures, theatrical performances, and gallery openings.

You can stay on campus in singles or doubles in the motel-like residence halls, which have private baths, or pitch your tent or park your trailer in a nearby public campground. Meals are available at a special weekly rate at the school cafeteria but may also be purchased individually. Many writers' workshop participants eat off campus in local coffee shops and restaurants. Arts programs for children aged 5 to 18 are also available. *Idyllwild Arts Summer Program, Box 38, Idyllwild, CA 92549, tel. 909/659–2171, ext. 365, fax 909/659–5463. July: 6 days, $690 with lodging and meals ($790 for singles; $415 without lodging and meals). Sign up anytime.*

CALIFORNIA **Napa Valley Writers' Conference.** This weeklong conference focuses not on getting published but on the writing craft. Four poetry and four fiction workshops run concurrently, with 12 students in each workshop; you attend one of them for two to three hours each day. Participants in the New Poetry workshop remain with the same teacher all week as they create new poems. Fiction writers attend workshops with each of the four fiction faculty members. Fiction writers get to discuss their own manuscripts in a private meeting with the instructor of their choice. The schedule also includes talks by the staff on the writing craft and panels of visiting editors and agents.

This conference is held on the lovely Napa Valley College campus, which is surrounded by the hills and vineyards of the famous wine-growing region. With only eight teachers and about 100 participants, the conference is small enough that a faculty-student rapport develops that you won't find at larger conferences. Evening readings by faculty members are scheduled at local wineries, with some of the host's vintages served at the reception.

Faculty members are chosen for the quality of their teaching as well as their writing; past teachers have included Ron Hansen, Christopher Tilghman, Pam Houston, Jorie Graham, and Robert Pinsky. Applicants submit a manuscript and a letter describing their writing background. Most participants have attended other workshops or university writing programs, although talented beginners are also accepted.

Participants generally stay in area motels, and except for the opening night reception where dinner is served and the final night's picnic, you're on your own for meals. Wonderful restaurants line both sides of the highway through the valley; the school cafeteria serves breakfast and lunch, and several delis and fast-food restaurants are within walking distance. *Napa Valley Writers' Conference, Anne Matlack Evans, Managing Director, Napa Valley College, 2277 Napa–Vallejo Hwy., Napa, CA 94558, tel. 707/253–3070, fax 707/253–3015. Late July or early Aug.: 6 days, $450. Price does not include lodging and most meals; sign up by June 1 (by May 15 for scholarships).*

CALIFORNIA **Santa Barbara Writers Conference.** This eight-day conference stands out for the variety of genres its workshops cover—from poetry, fiction, juvenile writing, and biography and autobiography, to playwriting, screen writing, nonfiction, mystery, science fiction, and humor. Each year some 360 beginning and more experienced writers come to the conference, held at the Miramar Hotel in the seaside Montecito, just outside Santa Barbara, to hone their craft and work toward getting published.

Workshops run Saturday through Thursday. From morning until mid-afternoon, you're in class; after that, you may attend lectures by well-known writers on technique and the publishing business. Personal conferences with the faculty of 29 established writers may be arranged each day. In the evening, you attend talks by such successful writers as Ray Bradbury and William Styron; in the late evening, you can pick up further pointers on manuscripts at still other workshops.

Participants are accepted on a first-come, first-served basis. The seaside hotel at which you also stay has swimming, tennis, and hiking. The conference provides two barbecues and a wine and cheese party; you're responsible for your other meals, which may be taken in the hotel dining room or at nearby restaurants. *Santa Barbara Writers Conference, Barnaby and Mary Conrad, Codirectors, Box 304, Carpinteria, CA 93014, tel. and fax 805/684–7003. Late June: 8 days, $800–$1,200 with lodging ($350 without). Price does not include most meals; sign up by May 15.*

CALIFORNIA **Squaw Valley Community of Writers.** In July and August, the Squaw Valley Community of Writers, established in 1969, sponsors four separate weeklong programs devoted to poetry, screen writing, fiction, and nonfiction. It also presents—in conjunction with the University of California, Davis—a program called the "Art of the Wild," which is devoted to writing of all forms inspired by wilderness, nature, and the environment.

Each of these programs offers small group workshops of up to 12 participants who meet in the morning to discuss and critique one another's work. You spend afternoons at craft sessions; panels on editing, publishing, and literary agents; or discussions on scripts and films. Staff and participants eat dinner together, and staff members read from their works in the evening.

The faculty are all published writers or professional screenwriters, and most of them have been teaching for years. For the fiction and nonfiction programs, the staff also includes working editors and literary agents. Recent instructors have been writers Richard Ford, Robert Stone, and Pam Houston; poets Rita Dove, Galway Kinnell, Sharon Olds, and Gary Snyder; and screenwriter Frank Pierson. Amy Tan is among the alumnae; she frequently gives talks and reads. Admission to each program is based on submitted manuscripts. The Squaw Valley Community of Writers strives to attract people of varying age, geographical origin, and experience in writing and wilderness travel, so that you may meet writers from many of the United States as well as from Australia and Canada, ranging in age from 20 to 74. Financial aid is available.

The workshops are conducted off-season at the Squaw Valley ski resort, 5 miles north of Lake Tahoe at 6,200 feet in the Sierra Nevada. You stay in single or double rooms in houses and apartments with kitchens; camping is also available. Dinners, which are included, are served buffet style in a large restaurant; you take care of your own breakfast and lunch. There are numerous local cafés and restaurants. Sunrise nature walks in the Sierras are part of the Art of the Wild program.

The Squaw Valley Community of Writers also sponsors a four-day workshop in October called "Travel Writing for Poets and Writers," which focuses on the art and craft of literary travel writing. *Squaw Valley Community of Writers, Brett Hall Jones, Executive Director, Box 2352, Olympic Valley, CA 96146, tel. 916/583–5200 June–Aug. or 916/274–8551 Sept.–May.; for the Art of the Wild, c/o Jack Hicks, Dept. of English, UC Davis, Davis, CA 95616, tel. 916/752–1658. July–Aug.: 7–8 days, $725–$900 with lodging ($560 without). Price does not include breakfast or lunch; apply by May 10.*

OREGON **The Flight of the Mind.** Nurturing literary writing by women in a noncompetitive, feminist environment is the aim of this program started in 1984. Classes focus on the work of women writers. At two separate weeklong sessions, workshops are available in poetry, fiction, novel writing, and nonfiction; some courses address specific topics such as From Autobiography to Short Story, Investigating the Mystery, and Fantasy and Science Fiction.

For three hours each day, either in the morning or afternoon, each participant meets with her class of up to 14 students and her workshop leader. Although students do not have private conferences about their work with the faculty, leaders make an attempt to give everyone the same amount of attention; the arrangement does push you to work hard. Evenings, leaders and students read from their work, and there are occasional staff lectures.

Leaders select participants based on a writing sample and an autobiographical statement of up to two pages; they attempt to assemble a group whose cultural background and experience are as diverse as that of the nine published women authors who act as the instructors; recent faculty have included Ursula K. LeGuin, Grace Paley, Naomi Shihab Nye, and Elizabeth Woody. About 70 women attend each session.

Workshops are held at the Dominican Order's retreat center, St. Benedict's, in the pine-forested foothills of the Cascade Mountains some 50 miles east of Eugene. In your free time, you can go hiking, swimming, or river rafting, or have a soak in an area hot spring.

Lodging options include single or double dorm rooms or a large dorm room for eight with shared baths, and a few private cabins; camping is nearby. The workshop organizers' own kitchen staff use lots of fresh produce and bake their own breads; desserts are low in sugar. *The Flight of the Mind, Judith Barrington and Ruth Gundle, Coordinators, 622 S.E. 29th Ave., Portland, OR 97214, tel. 503/236–9862, fax 503/233–0774. Late June: 7 days, $590–$785. Sign up by mid-Apr.*

WASHINGTON **Port Townsend Writers' Conference.** This 10-day program aims to help aspiring writers polish their work, to develop wider audiences for good writing, and to make authors feel part of a community where writing is a vocation rather than a business. The conference was founded in 1974.

You have two workshop options. If you have some writing experience and want an intensive program, go for full enrollment; it gives you a daily two-hour manuscript workshop in fiction, poetry, writing for children, or nonfiction prose as well as one scheduled conference with your teacher. If you have less experience or if you don't want to work as hard, plan for open enrollment; you don't attend manuscript workshops, but you may attend the daily classes in writing technique, journal writing, and other topics. Some classes and the manuscript workshop run concurrently, but full-enrollment students are welcome to attend other classes as their schedules permit. Readings by faculty and lectures on the writing craft are open to all as are the receptions that follow two of the readings and a salmon bake on the beach on the first Sunday evening.

The faculty represents some of the country's finest writers, including Pulitzer, Guggenheim, and MacArthur award winners. Of the some 150 participants who attend annually, most range in age from 35 to 50 and have college degrees in writing or have been writing seriously for at least a couple of years; open-enrollment students are usually less experienced. There are no more than 16 students in any workshop. Admission with full-enrollment status is based on the quality of the writing samples you submit with your application; open enrollment is first come, first served.

The setting is Fort Worden, a 445-acre state park 2 miles from Port Townsend at the tip of the Olympic Peninsula, on Puget Sound; there are fine views of its islands and the distant mountains. You stay in single dormitory rooms at the park, or, if they're full, in the motels, hotels, bed-and-breakfasts, and campsites nearby. You may sign up for two or three meals a day at the dining hall. In your free time, you can hike the wooded hills and explore the area's ponds, saltwater beaches, and old military fortifications. Port Townsend, a historic seaport community, is full of restored Victorian buildings, restaurants, galleries, and crafts shops. *Port Townsend Writers' Conference, Carol J. Bangs, Program Director, Box 1158, Port Townsend, WA 98368, tel. 206/385–3102, fax 206/385–2470. July: 10 days, $570–*

$755 with lodging and meals ($300–$425 without). Price includes single room; sign up by early June; financial aid deadline is May 1.

SOURCES

ORGANIZATIONS Poets & Writers, Inc. (72 Spring St., 3rd Floor, New York, NY 10012, tel. 212/226–3586, fax 212/226–3963) is the central source of practical information for the literary community in the United States, offering current news about conferences, grants, award competitions, and readings, as well as expert advice on resources and the process of publishing creative work. Several other organizations around the country provide useful information to U.S. writers on literary conferences, events, and competitions, in addition to counseling on the publishing business; some sponsor research libraries and local workshops, readings, and other activities to promote literature in their area. The larger regional organizations include **Arizona Authors' Association** (3509 E. Shea Blvd., Suite 117, Phoenix, AZ 85028, tel. 602/867–9001); **Austin Writers' League** (1501 W. 5th St., Suite E-2, Austin, TX 78703, tel. 512/499–8914, fax 512/499–0441); **Beyond Baroque Literary Arts Center** (681 Venice Blvd., Venice, CA 90291, tel. 310/822–3006, fax 310/827–7432); **Just Buffalo Literary Center** (2495 Main St., Suite 436, Buffalo, NY 14214, tel. 716/832–5400, fax 716/832–5710); **The Loft** (Pratt Community Center, 66 Malcolm Ave. SE, Minneapolis, MN 55414, tel. 612/379–8999); **National Writers Association** (1450 S. Havana, Suite 424, Aurora, CO 80012, tel. 303/751–7844, fax 303/751–8593); **New Hampshire Writers and Publishers Project** (Box 2693, Concord, NH 03302, tel. 603/226–6649, fax 603/226–0035); **Poetry Society of America** (15 Gramercy Park, New York, NY 10003, tel. 212/254–9628, fax 212/673–2352); **The Writer's Center** (4508 Walsh St., Bethesda, MD 20815, tel. 301/654–8664, fax 301/654–8667); **Writers Connection** (Box 24770, San Jose, CA

95154, tel. 408/445–3600, fax 408/445–3609); **The Writer's Voice** (West Side YMCA, 5 W. 63rd St., New York, NY 10023, tel. 212/875–4124, fax 212/875–4176); and **The Writers' Workshop** (212 Flatiron Building, 20 Battery Park Ave., Asheville, NC 28801, tel. 704/254–8111).

PERIODICALS *Poets & Writers Magazine* (72 Spring St., New York, NY 10012, tel. 212/226–3586, fax 212/226–3963), an essential news journal for writers, features author interviews, articles on writing and the publishing industry, and information on grants, contests, workshops, and calls for manuscripts. *Poetry Flash* (1450 4th St., No. 4, Berkeley, CA 94710, tel. 510/525–5476, fax 510/525–6752) contains author interviews, book reviews, and an extensive calendar of literary events, mainly, but not exclusively, in the western part of the United States. *The Writer* (120 Boylston St., Boston, MA 02116-4615, tel. 617/423–3157, fax 617/423–2168), *Writer's Digest* (1507 Dana Ave., Cincinnati, OH 45207, tel. 513/531–2222; subscriptions tel. 800/333–0133), and *Writers' Journal* (Box 25376, St. Paul, MN 55125, tel. 612/730–4280, fax 612/730–4356) all offer essays on the writing process and the publishing business.

BOOKS The *Guide to Writers Conferences* (Shaw Guides) and *Novel and Short Story Writer's Market* (Writer's Digest Books) both provide extensive listings of U.S. writers' conferences and workshops. Poets & Writers, Inc. (*see* Organizations, *above*) also publishes an annual listing of writers' conferences.

ALSO SEE If your creative spirit yearns for other outlets, see the chapters on Arts and Crafts Workshops, Painting Workshops, and Photography Workshops and Tours.

Appendix: Where the Programs Are

ALASKA

Birding, *50–51*

Cultural and Natural History Cruises, *86, 88–90*

Cultural Tours, *106*

Nature Camps, *186–187*

Photography Workshops and Tours, *218–220*

Volunteer Research Vacations, *263–264*

Volunteer Vacations in Public and Community Service, *278*

Whale-Watching Cruises, *286–287*

ARIZONA

Archaeology, *9–10*

Arts and Crafts Workshops, *31–32*

Birding, *46, 48–49*

Cultural Tours, *103–104*

Garden Tours (garden), *135*

Holistic Centers, *147*

Photography Workshops and Tours, *213–214*

Spas and Wellness Centers, *238–240*

Volunteer Research Vacations, *256–257*

Volunteer Vacations in Public and Community Service, *276*

ARKANSAS

Archaeology, *7*

Volunteer Vacations in Public and Community Service, *275*

BAJA CALIFORNIA, MEXICO

Cultural and Natural History Cruises, *85*

Whale-Watching Cruises, *284–286*

BRITISH COLUMBIA, CANADA

Birding, *49–50*

Cultural and Natural History Cruises, *85–86, 87*

CALIFORNIA

Arts and Crafts Workshops, *36–37*

Birding, *48–49*

Cooking Schools, *71–72*

Cultural and Natural History Cruises, *84–85*

Cultural Tours, *102–103*

Foreign-Language Immersion Programs, *117–120*

Garden Tours, (gardens), *135–136*

Garden Tours (tour), *129*

Holistic Centers, *149–153*

Nature Camps, *183–185*

Painting Workshops, *200–201*

Photography Workshops and Tours, *218*

Spas and Wellness Centers, *243–247*

Volunteer Research Vacations, *260–261*

Volunteer Vacations in Public and
Community Service, *277–278*

Whale-Watching Cruises, *284–286*

Writing Conferences and Workshops, *309–312*

COLORADO

Arts and Crafts Workshops, *35*

Birding, *47–48*

Cooking Schools, *70–71*

Cultural Tours, *104–105*

Holistic Centers, *147–148*

Music Programs, *165*

Nature Camps, *180*

Painting Workshops, *200*

Photography Workshops and Tours, *216–217*

Spas and Wellness Centers, *242–243*

Writing Conferences and Workshops, *308*

CONNECTICUT

Garden Tours (tour), *126*

Nature Camps, *175*

Painting Workshops, *194*

Writing Conferences and Workshops, *292*

DELAWARE

Garden Tours (garden), *132*

FLORIDA

Arts and Crafts Workshops, *23*

Birding, *44–45*

Cultural and Natural History Cruises, *83–84*

Photography Workshops and Tours, *211–213*

Spas and Wellness Centers, *231–234*

Volunteer Research Vacations, *253–254*

GEORGIA

Arts and Crafts Workshops, *23–24*

Campus Vacations, *59*

Cooking Schools, *68–69*

Garden Tours (tour), *127–128*

Spas and Wellness Centers, *234–235*

Volunteer Research Vacations, *254*

Writing Conferences and Workshops, *301*

HAWAII

Birding, *51*

Cultural Tours, *106–107*

Garden Tours (tour), *129*

Holistic Centers, *154*

Spas and Wellness Centers, *247–248*

Volunteer Research Vacations, *264–265*

Whale-Watching Cruises, *287*

IDAHO

Cultural Tours, *105–106*

Music Programs, *165–166*

Volunteer Research Vacations, *257–258*

ILLINOIS

Cooking Schools, *69*

Cultural Tours, *102*

Garden Tours (gardens), *134*

Spas and Wellness Centers, *237*

Writing Conferences and Workshops, *303–304*

INDIANA

Campus Vacations, *60–61*

Cultural Tours, *102*

Music Programs, *161–162*

Writing Conferences and Workshops, *304–305*

IOWA

Holistic Centers, *146–147*

Writing Conferences and Workshops, *305*

KANSAS

Archaeology, *8–9*

Music Programs, *162–163*

KENTUCKY

Cultural Tours, *102, 103*

Volunteer Research Vacations, *254–255*

Writing Conferences and Workshops, *301–302*

LOUISIANA

Arts and Crafts Workshops, *24–25*

Cultural and Natural History Cruises, *83*

Garden Tours (tour), *128*

Painting Workshops, *197*

MAINE

Arts and Crafts Workshops, *14–15*

Birding, *43*

Campus Vacations, *55–56*

Cultural Tours, *100*

Garden Tours (tour), *126*

Holistic Centers, *142–143*

Nature Camps, *175–176*

Painting Workshops, *194–195*

Photography Workshops and Tours, *206–207*

Spas and Wellness Centers, *225–226*

Volunteer Vacations in Public and Community Service, *273*

Whale-Watching Cruises, *283*

Writing Conferences and Workshops, *292–293*

MARYLAND

Cooking Schools, *67–68*

Writing Conferences and Workshops, *299–300*

MASSACHUSETTS

Arts and Crafts Workshops, *15–16*

Cooking Schools, *64*

Cultural Tours, *100–101*

Garden Tours (garden), *129–130*

Garden Tours (tour), *126*

Holistic Centers, *143–144*

Painting Workshops, *195–196*

Photography Workshops and Tours, *207–208*

Spas and Wellness Centers, *226*

Volunteer Vacations in Public and Community Service, *273*

Whale-Watching Cruises, *283–284*

Writing Conferences and Workshops, *293–294*

MICHIGAN

Painting Workshops, *198*

Volunteer Research Vacations, *255–256*

Volunteer Vacations in Public and Community Service, *275*

MINNESOTA

Birding, *45*

Spas and Wellness Centers, *237–238*

Writing Conferences and Workshops, *305–306*

MISSISSIPPI

Garden Tours (garden), *133–134*

MISSOURI

Cultural Tours, *102–103*

Garden Tours (garden) *134–135*

Music Programs, *163*

Volunteer Vacations in Public and Community Service, *275–276*

MONTANA

Cultural Tours, *106*

Garden Tours (tour), *128*

Holistic Centers, *148*

Nature Camps, *180–181*

Photography Workshops and Tours, *217–218*

Volunteer Research Vacations, *258–259*

Writing Conferences and Workshops, *308–309*

NEBRASKA

Birding, *45–46*

NEVADA

Arts and Crafts Workshops, *32–33*

Nature Camps, *178–179*

Volunteer Vacations in Public and Community Service, *276*

NEW BRUNSWICK, CANADA

Whale-Watching Cruises, *283*

NEW HAMPSHIRE

Campus Vacations, *56*

Foreign-Language Immersion Programs, *111–113*

Garden Tours (tour), *126*

Nature Camps, *176*

Photography Workshops and Tours, *208*

Writing Conferences and Workshops, *294–295*

NEW JERSEY

Arts and Crafts Workshops, *20–21*

Birding, *43*

Nature Camps, *177–178*

NEW MEXICO

Arts and Crafts Workshops, *33–34*

Cooking Schools, *69–70*

Cultural Tours, *103–104*

Painting Workshops, *199*

Photography Workshops and Tours, *213–216*

Writing Conferences and Workshops, *307–308*

NEW YORK

Arts and Crafts Workshops, *16–18*

Campus Vacations, *56–57*

Cooking Schools, *64–66*

Cultural Tours, *101*

Foreign-Language Immersion Programs, *113–114*

Garden Tours (gardens), *130–132*

Garden Tours (tours), *126–127*

Holistic Centers, *144–145*

Nature Camps, *176–177*

Painting Workshops, *196–197*

Photography Workshops and Tours, *208–209*

Spas and Wellness Centers, *226–228*

Volunteer Vacations in Public and Community Service, *273–274*

Writing Conferences and Workshops, *295–298*

NORTH CAROLINA

Arts and Crafts Workshops, *25–27*

Campus Vacations, *59–60*

Garden Tours (tour), *128*

Music Programs, *160–161*

Spas and Wellness Centers, *235–236*

Writing Conferences and Workshops, *302*

NORTH DAKOTA

Birding, *45*

Music Programs, *163–164*

NOVA SCOTIA, CANADA

Whale-Watching Cruises, *283*

OHIO

Arts and Crafts Workshops, *29*

Campus Vacations, *61*

Cultural and Natural History Cruises, *84*

Cultural Tours, *103*

Music Programs, *164–165*

Spas and Wellness Centers, *238*

Writing Conferences and Workshops, *306–307*

OKLAHOMA

Cultural Tours, *102, 103*

OREGON

Arts and Crafts Workshops, *37–38*

Birding, *49*

Cultural and Natural History Cruises, *86–87*

Cultural Tours, *105–106*

Garden Tours (garden), *136–137*

Holistic Centers, *153–154*

Painting Workshops, *201–202*

Writing Conferences and Workshops, *312*

PENNSYLVANIA

Arts and Crafts Workshops, *21–22*

Birding, *43*

Campus Vacations, *58*

Garden Tours (garden), *132–133*

Garden Tours (tours), *127*

Holistic Centers, *145–146*

Nature Camps, *178*

Photography Workshops and Tours, *210–211*

Spas and Wellness Centers, *229–230*

Volunteer Research Vacations, *252–253*

Volunteer Vacations in Public and Community Service, *274*

Writing Conferences and Workshops, *300–301*

PRINCE EDWARD ISLAND, CANADA

Whale-Watching Cruises, *283*

RHODE ISLAND

Campus Vacations, *57–58*

Cultural and Natural History Cruises, *82–83*

Cultural Tours, *100–101*

Foreign-Language Immersion Programs, *114–115*

Photography Workshops and Tours, *209–210*

SOUTH CAROLINA

Archaeology, *7–8*

Cultural and Natural History Cruises, *83–84*

Garden Tours (tours), *127–128*

Spas and Wellness Centers, *236*

SOUTH DAKOTA

Archaeology, *9*

TENNESSEE

Archaeology, *8*

Arts and Crafts Workshops, *27–29*

Cultural and Natural History Cruises, *83*

Painting Workshops, *197–198*

Spas and Wellness Centers, *236–237*

Writing Conferences and Workshops, *302–303*

TEXAS

Arts and Crafts Workshops, *34*

Birding, *46–47*

Nature Camps, *179*

Painting Workshops, *199–200*

Spas and Wellness Centers, *240–241*

Volunteer Research Vacations, *257*

UTAH

Arts and Crafts Workshops, *35–36*

Birding, *46*

Cultural Tours, *104*

Nature Camps, *179–180*

Photography Workshops and Tours, *213–214*

Spas and Wellness Centers, *241–242*

VERMONT

Arts and Crafts Workshops, *18–20*

Cooking Schools, *66–67*

Foreign-Language Immersion Programs, *115–117*

Garden Tours (tour), *126*

Spas and Wellness Centers, *228–229*

Writing Conferences and Workshops, *298–299*

VIRGINIA

Archaeology, *6*

Birding, *43–44*

Cultural Tours, *101*

Garden Tours (garden), *133*

Holistic Centers, *146*

Spas and Wellness Centers, *230*

Volunteer Research Vacations, *253*

Volunteer Vacations in Public and Community Service, *274*

VIRGIN ISLANDS (BRITISH AND U.S.)

Cultural and Natural History Cruises, *91*

WASHINGTON

Arts and Crafts Workshops, *38*

Birding, *49–50*

Cultural and Natural History Cruises, *85–88*

Garden Tours (garden), *137*

Music Programs, *167–169*

Nature Camps, *185–186*

Painting Workshops, *202*

Volunteer Research Vacations, *261–263*

Writing Conferences and Workshops, *312–313*

WEST VIRGINIA

Archaeology, *6–7*

Arts and Crafts Workshops, *22–23*

Birding, *43–44*

Cooking Schools, *68*

Music Programs, *159–160*

Spas and Wellness Centers, *230–231*

Volunteer Vacations in Public and Community Service, *274–275*

WISCONSIN

Arts and Crafts Workshops, *29–31*

Painting Workshops, *198–199*

Volunteer Research Vacations, *256*

WYOMING

Birding, *48*

Holistic Centers, *148–149*

Music Programs, *166–167*

Nature Camps, *181–183*

Painting Workshops, *200*

Volunteer Vacations in Public and Community Service, *276–277*

Notes

Notes

Notes

Notes

Notes

Notes

Notes